Applications and Development of Underwater Robotics and Underwater Vision Technology

Applications and Development of Underwater Robotics and Underwater Vision Technology

Topic Editors

Jingchun Zhou
Wenqi Ren
Qiuping Jiang
Yan-Tsung Peng

MDPI

Basel • Beijing • Wuhan • Barcelona • Belgrade • Novi Sad • Cluj • Manchester

Topic Editors

Jingchun Zhou
College of Information Science and Technology
Dalian Maritime University
Dalian
China

Wenqi Ren
School of Cyber Science and Technology
Sun Yat-Sen University
Guangzhou
China

Qiuping Jiang
School of Information Science and Engineering
Ningbo University
Ningbo
China

Yan-Tsung Peng
Department of Computer Science
National Chengchi University
Taipei
Taiwan

Editorial Office
MDPI AG
Grosspeteranlage 5
4052 Basel, Switzerland

This is a reprint of the Topic, published open access by the journals *Journal of Marine Science and Engineering* (ISSN 2077-1312), *Machines* (ISSN 2075-1702), *Remote Sensing* (ISSN 2072-4292) and *Sensors* (ISSN 1424-8220), freely accessible at: https://www.mdpi.com/topics/R3U6PHZ69X.

For citation purposes, cite each article independently as indicated on the article page online and as indicated below:

Lastname, A.A.; Lastname, B.B. Article Title. *Journal Name* **Year**, *Volume Number*, Page Range.

ISBN 978-3-7258-4121-9 (Hbk)
ISBN 978-3-7258-4122-6 (PDF)
https://doi.org/10.3390/books978-3-7258-4122-6

Contents

Xiaotian Wang, Xinnan Fan, Pengfei Shi, Jianjun Ni and Zhongkai Zhou
An Overview of Key SLAM Technologies for Underwater Scenes
Reprinted from: *Remote Sens.* **2023**, *15*, 2496, https://doi.org/10.3390/rs15102496 . . . . **1**

Chenglong Hou, Zhiguang Guan, Ziyi Guo, Siqi Zhou and Mingxing Lin
An Improved YOLOv5s-Based Scheme for Target Detection in a Complex Underwater Environment
Reprinted from: *J. Mar. Sci. Eng.* **2023**, *11*, 1041, https://doi.org/10.3390/jmse11051041 . . . . . **29**

Fei Wang, Yujie Yang, Jingchun Zhou and Weishi Zhang
An Onboard Point Cloud Semantic Segmentation System for Robotic Platforms
Reprinted from: *Machines* **2023**, *11*, 571, https://doi.org/10.3390/machines11050571 . . . . **46**

Dehuan Zhang, Wei Cao, Jingchun Zhou, Yan-Tsung Peng, Weishi Zhang and Zifan Lin
Two-Branch Underwater Image Enhancement and Original Resolution Information Optimization Strategy in Ocean Observation
Reprinted from: *J. Mar. Sci. Eng.* **2023**, *11*, 1285, https://doi.org/10.3390/jmse11071285 . . . . . **59**

Bin Hu, Yiqiang Zhao, Guoqing Zhou, Jiaji He, Changlong Liu, Qiang Liu, et al.
Coupling Dilated Encoder–Decoder Network for Multi-Channel Airborne LiDAR Bathymetry Full-Waveform Denoising
Reprinted from: *Remote Sens.* **2023**, *15*, 3293, https://doi.org/10.3390/rs15133293 . . . . **80**

Huapeng Yu, Ziyuan Li, Wentie Yang, Tongsheng Shen, Dalei Liang and Qinyuan He
Underwater Geomagnetic Localization Based on Adaptive Fission Particle-Matching Technology
Reprinted from: *J. Mar. Sci. Eng.* **2023**, *11*, 1739, https://doi.org/10.3390/jmse11091739 . . . . . **99**

Dongmei Yang, Tianzi Zhang, Boquan Li, Menghao Li, Weijing Chen, Xiaoqing Li and Xingmei Wang
Underwater Image Translation via Multi-Scale Generative Adversarial Network
Reprinted from: *J. Mar. Sci. Eng.* **2023**, *11*, 1929, https://doi.org/10.3390/jmse11101929 . . . . . **114**

Nick van der Geest, Lorenzo Garcia, Roy Nates and Fraser Borrett
New Insights into Sea Turtle Propulsion and Their Cost of Transport Point to a Potential New Generation of High-Efficient Underwater Drones for Ocean Exploration
Reprinted from: *J. Mar. Sci. Eng.* **2023**, *11*, 1944, https://doi.org/10.3390/jmse11101944 . . . . . **131**

Rong Jia, Bin Lv, Jie Chen, Hailin Liu, Lin Cao and Min Liu
Underwater Object Detection in Marine Ranching Based on Improved YOLOv8
Reprinted from: *J. Mar. Sci. Eng.* **2024**, *12*, 55, https://doi.org/10.3390/jmse12010055 . . . . **145**

Xiaoyang Zhao, Zhuo Wang, Zhongchao Deng and Hongde Qin
G-Net: An Efficient Convolutional Network for Underwater Object Detection
Reprinted from: *J. Mar. Sci. Eng.* **2024**, *12*, 116, https://doi.org/10.3390/jmse12010116 . . . . . . **163**

Rebeca Chinicz and Roee Diamant
A Statistical Evaluation of the Connection between Underwater Optical and Acoustic Images
Reprinted from: *Remote Sens.* **2024**, *16*, 689, https://doi.org/10.3390/rs16040689 . . . . **178**

Zonglin Liu, Meng Wang, Hanwen Hu, Tong Ge and Rui Miao
An Underwater Localization Method Based on Visual SLAM for the Near-Bottom Environment
Reprinted from: *J. Mar. Sci. Eng.* **2024**, *12*, 716, https://doi.org/10.3390/jmse12050716 . . . . . . **197**

Charles Sutherland, Alan D. Henderson, Dean R. Giosio, Andrew J. Trotter and Greg G. Smith
Sensing Pre- and Post-Ecdysis of Tropical Rock Lobsters, *Panulirus ornatus*, Using a Low-Cost Novel Spectral Camera
Reprinted from: *J. Mar. Sci. Eng.* **2024**, *12*, 987, https://doi.org/10.3390/jmse12060987 . . . . . . **216**

Jungwoo Lee, Ji-Hyun Park, Jeong-Hwan Hwang, Kyoungseok Noh, Youngho Choi and Jinho Suh
Artificial Neural Network for Glider Detection in a Marine Environment by Improving a CNN Vision Encoder
Reprinted from: *J. Mar. Sci. Eng.* **2024**, *12*, 1106, https://doi.org/10.3390/jmse12071106 . . . . . **234**

Daohua Lu, Junxin Yi and Jia Wang
Enhanced YOLOv7 for Improved Underwater Target Detection
Reprinted from: *J. Mar. Sci. Eng.* **2024**, *12*, 1127, https://doi.org/10.3390/jmse12071127 . . . . . **245**

Chunlu Cui, Penglei Ma, Qianli Zhang, Guijie Liu and Yingchun Xie
Grabbing Path Extraction of Deep-Sea Manganese Nodules Based on Improved YOLOv5
Reprinted from: *J. Mar. Sci. Eng.* **2024**, *12*, 1433, https://doi.org/10.3390/jmse12081433 . . . . . **263**

Zhe Chen, Guohao Xie, Xiaofang Deng, Jie Peng and Hongbing Qiu
DA-YOLOv7: A Deep Learning-Driven High-Performance Underwater Sonar Image Target Recognition Model
Reprinted from: *J. Mar. Sci. Eng.* **2024**, *12*, 1606, https://doi.org/10.3390/jmse12091606 . . . . . **281**

Lin Zhang, Lianwu Guan, Jianhui Zeng and Yanbin Gao
Autonomous Underwater Vehicle Navigation Enhancement by Optimized Side-Scan Sonar Registration and Improved Post-Processing Model Based on Factor Graph Optimization
Reprinted from: *J. Mar. Sci. Eng.* **2024**, *12*, 1769, https://doi.org/10.3390/jmse12101769 . . . . . **308**

Xuanye Hu, Yi Yang, Zhiyu Liao, Xinghua Zhu, Renxin Wang, Peng Zhang and Zhiqiang Hu
Wake Detection and Positioning for Autonomous Underwater Vehicles Based on Cilium-Inspired Wake Sensor
Reprinted from: *Sensors* **2025**, *25*, 41, https://doi.org/10.3390/s25010041 . . . . **331**

Hua Zhao, Chao Xu, Jiaxing Chen, Zhexian Zhang and Xiang Wang
BGLE-YOLO: A Lightweight Model for Underwater Bio-Detection
Reprinted from: *Sensors* **2025**, *25*, 1595, https://doi.org/10.3390/s25051595 . . . . **352**

remote sensing

Review

An Overview of Key SLAM Technologies for Underwater Scenes

Xiaotian Wang [1,*], Xinnan Fan [2], Pengfei Shi [2], Jianjun Ni [2] and Zhongkai Zhou [2]

1 School of Computer and Information, Hohai University, Nanjing 210000, China
2 School of Information Science and Engineering, Hohai University, Changzhou 213002, China; fanxn@hhuc.edu.cn (X.F.)
* Correspondence: wxthhu@hhu.edu.cn

Abstract: Autonomous localization and navigation, as an essential research area in robotics, has a broad scope of applications in various scenarios. To widen the utilization environment and augment domain expertise, simultaneous localization and mapping (SLAM) in underwater environments has recently become a popular topic for researchers. This paper examines the key SLAM technologies for underwater vehicles and provides an in-depth discussion on the research background, existing methods, challenges, application domains, and future trends of underwater SLAM. It is not only a comprehensive literature review on underwater SLAM, but also a systematic introduction to the theoretical framework of underwater SLAM. The aim of this paper is to assist researchers in gaining a better understanding of the system structure and development status of underwater SLAM, and to provide a feasible approach to tackle the underwater SLAM problem.

Keywords: underwater vehicles; SLAM; vision sensors; acoustic sensors; deep learning

1. Introduction

Since the beginning of the 21st century, the importance of applied research on autonomous positioning technology for mobile robots has grown. A global navigation satellite system (GNSS) is an effective and accurate solution for the robots' own positioning and movement trajectory [1]. However, in some environments where GPS is not available or when a priori information is insufficient, other solutions must be found. Simultaneous localization and mapping was introduced to the field of robotics, which entails the robot obtaining environmental information through sensors carried by itself in an unknown environment. During the process of navigation and localization, a structural consistency map of the surrounding environment is built. Compared to traditional localization methods, SLAM is a small-sized and cost-efficient instrumentation method [2,3]. Through the efforts of researchers, SLAM has been implemented in drones, sweeping robots, unmanned vehicles, smart wearable devices, and other devices [4]. Figure 1 below shows the application of SLAM in some scenarios.

Figure 1. The application of SLAM technology in different scenarios.

Unmanned underwater vehicles (UUVs) have become a popular option for underwater exploration due to their safety, portability, and cost-effectiveness. UUVs can be divided

Citation: Wang, X.; Fan, X.; Shi, P.; Ni, J.; Zhou, Z. An Overview of Key SLAM Technologies for Underwater Scenes. *Remote Sens.* **2023**, *15*, 2496. https://doi.org/10.3390/rs15102496

Academic Editors: Yan-Tsung Peng, Wenqi Ren, Jingchun Zhou and Qiuping Jiang

Received: 28 March 2023
Revised: 2 May 2023
Accepted: 4 May 2023
Published: 9 May 2023

into two categories: remotely operated vehicles (ROVs) and autonomous underwater vehicles (AUVs) [5–7]. UUVs are mainly used for marine resource investigation, undersea biology research, underwater structure detection, and marine data collection. The precise positioning and navigation tasks of underwater vehicles are difficult because the underwater environment blocks radio signals such as GPS, and the inertial navigation approach is prone to accumulate errors underwater [8]. Conventional underwater positioning methods such as short baseline (SBL) and ultrashort baseline (USBL) require the installation of a base array with a receiver device in the target area or require a periodic position correction by the AUV [9]. Although these methods are useful, they are costly, and the range of exploration is limited by the beacons. In addition, the vehicles need to surface frequently and often face more exertion. To address these challenges, many researchers have started to investigate how SLAM techniques can be applied to the underwater domain [10,11], thus bringing new possibilities for autonomous positioning and navigation of underwater vehicles.

In 1986, SLAM was first introduced at the IEEE Robotics and Automation Conference to address the spatial uncertainty description and transformation representation. Cheeseman [12] pioneered the use of probabilistic estimation methods for robot localization and mapping, and subsequently, this field of research has been pursued by numerous researchers. SLAM technology has likely gone through three stages of development. From 1986 to 2004, the classical era of SLAM development was mainly focused on the proposal of probabilistic estimation methods, such as the extended Kalman filter (EKF) [13], the particle filter (PF) [14], and the maximum likelihood estimation (MLE) [15]. From 2004 to 2015, SLAM entered the era of algorithm analysis, which included the study of algorithm observability, convergence, sparsity, and consistency. Since 2016, the field has shifted to address the robustness of SLAM [16]. This research includes algorithm robustness, scalability, efficient algorithms under resource constraints, high-level perception, and algorithm adaptiveness. More recently, with the emergence of computer vision and deep learning methods, there has been a shift towards SLAM methods based on deep learning [17–19].

In recent years, the widespread deployment of vision sensors and the rapid advancement of computer vision have led to the emergence of visual SLAM as an alternative to traditional SLAM approaches [20]. Compared to sonar, laser, and infrared range sensors, visual sensors have several advantages in terms of cost, use, and information acquisition capability, and have demonstrated a high accuracy in scenarios with adequate lighting and texture. Depending on the camera type, visual SLAM can be classified into monocular SLAM [21,22], stereo SLAM [23,24], and RGB-D SLAM [25,26]. Additionally, depending on the implementation scheme, visual-based SLAM methods can be divided into feature-based methods (e.g., ORB-SLAM [27–29]), direct methods (e.g., large-scale direct monocular SLAM (LSD-SLAM) [30]), and semidirect methods (e.g., semidirect visual ranging (SVO)) [31,32]. Of the existing systems, ORB-SLAM is a popular visual SLAM solution which utilizes Oriented FAST and rotation BRIEF [33] key-point detectors to match features across successive images. This key-frame-based approach was derived from prior SLAM variants (PTAM [34], DT-SLAM [35]). ORB-SLAM has been tested with mobile robots in various scenarios and has achieved promising results.

In 2000, Williams et al. [36] presented the results of applying a simultaneous localization and map building (SLAM) algorithm to estimate the motion of a submersible vehicle. Scans obtained from an on-board sonar were processed to extract stable point features in the environment, thus constructing a map of the environment and estimating the vehicle's location. This work was the first instance of a deployable underwater implementation of the SLAM algorithm. However, underwater scenes are typically unstructured and difficult to navigate due to the presence of illumination, texture, turbidity, and hydrodynamics. This makes it difficult for camera sensors to accurately extract features, and many land-based algorithms cannot be applied to underwater scenes. To obtain reliable estimates, SLAM for underwater scenes typically requires the use of specialized sensors such as inertial measurement units (IMU), Doppler velocity log (DVL), and depth sensors [37]. Acoustic and laser sensors are also widely used for sensing the underwater environment [38,39]. The fusion of different sensors has become an important approach in solving underwater SLAM. Despite its relative maturity in traditional scenarios, its application in underwater robot localization and navigation is still in its development stage and is a complex research area. Figure 2 illustrates some SLAM algorithms that can be used in underwater environments.

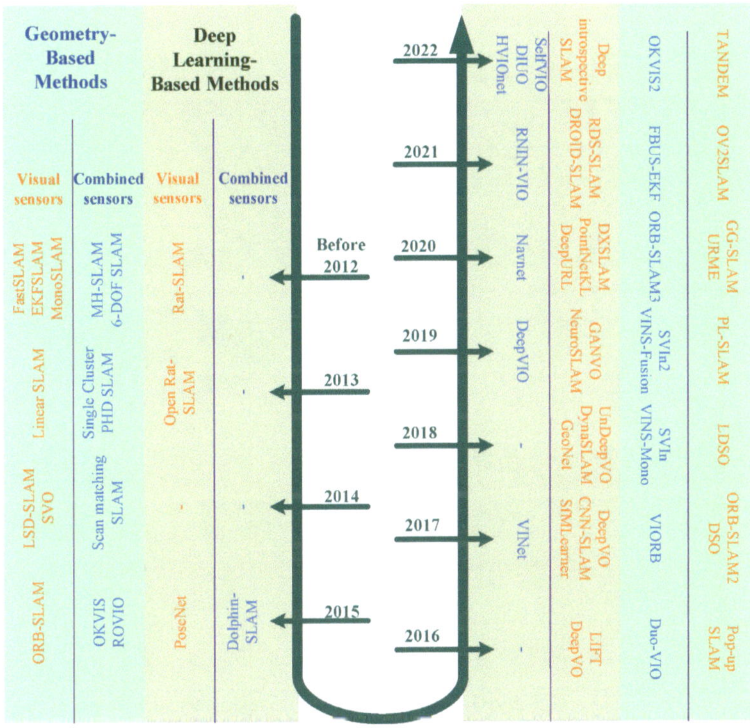

Figure 2. Partial list of SLAM algorithms that have been used in underwater environments in the last decade.

In recent years, underwater SLAM technology has developed rapidly, playing an important role in underwater positioning and surveying. However, it still lacks a systematic evaluation. Therefore, after carefully reviewing the relevant literature of underwater SLAM, this paper summarizes the development of this field. We chose recent related research papers in the underwater environment according to the basic framework, research focus, and development direction of underwater SLAM. The main contributions of this paper are as follows: 1. the development of underwater SLAM is introduced systematically; 2. from the framework of SLAM, the following parts of underwater visual SLAM are mainly introduced: sensors, front-end visual odometry, back-end state optimization, loop closure detection and mapping; 3. we collect the key points and difficult points that need to be solved in the development of underwater SLAM; 4. from the perspective of the application environment and technology development of underwater SLAM, the future development direction of this field is studied. This paper provides a comprehensive review of the key SLAM technologies for underwater robots. It is organized as shown in Figure 3. In Section 1, the research background about underwater robots, SLAM, and underwater SLAM is introduced. Section 2 compares recent underwater SLAM methods based on the theoretical framework of SLAM systems. Section 3 analyzes the main problems of current underwater SLAM. Section 4 makes an estimation of the future development trend and applications of underwater SLAM, in addition to which relevant datasets are presented and relevant experiments are conducted. Finally, the conclusion is summarized in Section 5. This paper provides a comprehensive review of the key technologies of underwater SLAM in terms of research background, field applications, theoretical framework, existing methods, problems, and future trends. It is hoped that this work can provide guidance and help to researchers in related fields.

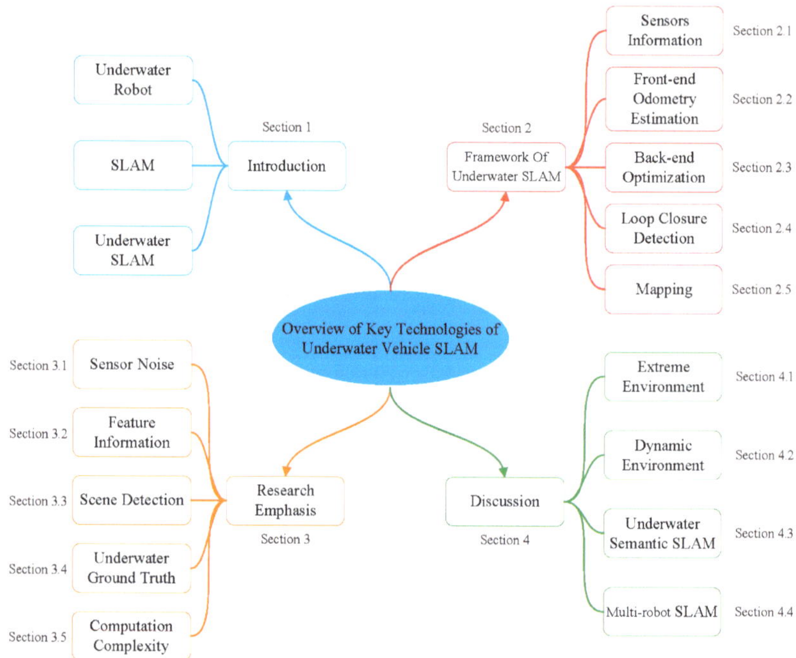

Figure 3. Structure diagram for underwater simultaneous localization and mapping of this paper.

2. Framework of Underwater SLAM

A simultaneous localization and mapping system consists of three processes: perception, localization, and mapping. Proprioception sensors and exteroception sensors are used to obtain information about the environment, thus allowing the robot to estimate and locate its own position and pose. Following this, a map of the environment is generated. The SLAM problem is essentially a state estimation problem, which is mathematically expressed in terms of equations of motion and equations of observation.

$$\begin{cases} x_k = f(x_{k-1}, u_k, w_k) \\ z_{k,j} = h\left(y_j, x_k, v_{k,j}\right) \end{cases} \tag{1}$$

where x_k denotes the robot position at time k, u_k denotes the robot input at time k, w_k denotes the noise at time k, $z_{k,j}$ is the observation data at time k for the jth waypoint, y_j denotes the jth waypoint, and $v_{k,j}$ is the noise at time k for the jth waypoint. Figure 4 is a schematic of the visual slam process.

Visual SLAM is a commonly used sensing method for underwater robots and is one of the main topics of this paper [40]. Figure 5 presents the basic theoretical framework of visual SLAM, which consists of sensor data, front-end, back-end, loop-closure detection, and mapping. Sensor data are collected and sent to the front end, which uses a visual odometer for interframe motion estimation. Loop closure is used to reduce the cumulative error and drift caused by the accumulation of sensor noise and model errors. The back end processes the camera positional and loop-closure detection information measured by the visual odometer at different moments and optimizes it to obtain globally consistent trajectories and maps.

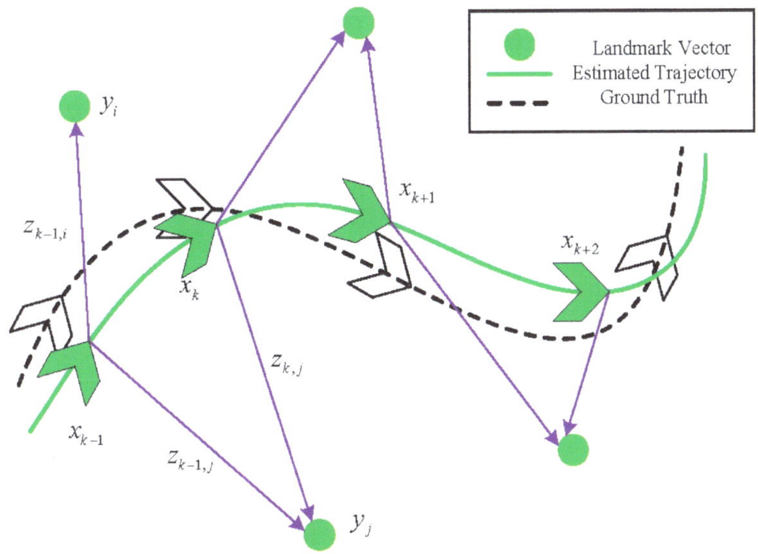

Figure 4. Schematic diagram of the SLAM process. The dashed line is the real trajectory. The solid line is the estimated trajectory. The related description of individual variables are listed under Formula (1).

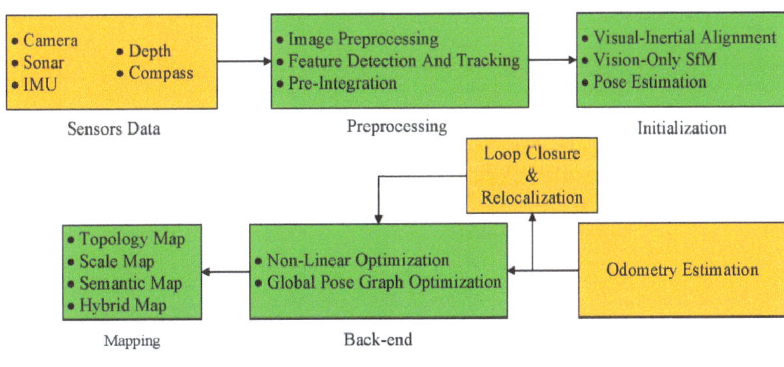

Figure 5. Process of underwater SLAM system.

However, due to the unstructured characteristics and complexity of the underwater environment, conventional SLAM methods can cause various problems when directly used in this domain. To address this problem, this section presents a schematic analysis of the various aspects of underwater SLAM systems based on the framework process of SLAM systems (Figure 5). Moreover, this section summarizes the existing approaches of researchers. Specifically, Section 3.1 describes the improved underwater SLAM from the sensor perspective for the specificity of the underwater environment; Section 3.2 analyzes the front-end odometry estimation with a vision focus; Section 3.3 presents the back-end optimization algorithm for underwater SLAM; Section 3.4 describes the principles and related methods for loop-closure detection in underwater SLAM systems. Finally, Section 3.5 summarizes the mapping approach of underwater SLAM.

2.1. Sensor Information

SLAM systems are capable of deriving the current position, estimating the trajectory, and constructing a map of the environment from the information acquired by their sensors. In comparison to traditional GPS satellite navigation and landmark navigation, a SLAM system relies solely on its sensor information for calculation. The accuracy of mapping is contingent upon the abundance of sensor information regarding the sensed underwater environment. Since GPS and inertial measurement units are not viable options for underwater navigation due to the environment's rejection of them, research has shifted to the use of underwater visual SLAM. Cameras can capture a vast amount of texture information in the underwater environment and are less expensive than the alternatives, making vision-based underwater SLAM a popular research topic [41].

However, underwater scenes are highly unstructured and uncertain. This presents a challenge to underwater robots due to their own structure and the underwater environment, which can lead to blurred imaging, shadowing, and distortion. Consequently, this results in a low signal-to-noise ratio of images, leading to a difficulty in accurately extracting underwater features, errors in matching accuracy, and even a potential tracking failure. Thus, research into underwater SLAM is always challenging, and the selection of sensors and the processing of information are of utmost importance [42].

2.1.1. Proprioceptive Sensors

Proprioceptive sensors are crucial components of underwater robots, enabling them to obtain their own state and position information without external assistance. Commonly used proprioceptive sensors include the depth sensor, Doppler velocity log (DVL), inertial measurement unit (IMU), and compass. The DVL works by transmitting acoustic pulses and receiving Doppler displacement echoes to calculate the vehicle's velocity. The compass provides a directional reference, while the IMU, composed of an accelerometer and a gyroscope, is responsible for measuring acceleration and angular acceleration. The depth sensor, meanwhile, calculates the depth of the vehicle based on the water pressure. With the velocity, orientation, acceleration, and depth information provided by these proprioceptive sensors, underwater robots can estimate their position and pose without external assistance, thereby allowing for the realization of underwater SLAM.

2.1.2. Exteroceptive Sensors

(1) Vision Sensors

SLAM based on vision sensors is an important class of SLAM algorithms, which can be classified into monocular, stereo, and RGB-D SLAM depending on the type of camera used. Additionally, algorithms such as ORB-SLAM3 can also be employed for pinhole and fisheye cameras.

- Monocular Camera

  Monocular cameras use a single lens to generate images, offering advantages such as a low cost, a simple structure, and usability. Mono SLAM was the first implementation of real-time monocular vision SLAM. In underwater scenarios, Hidalgo et al. conducted controlled experiments using ORB-SLAM under different setup conditions, as reported in their paper [43]. The results demonstrated that ORB-SLAM could be used effectively under the conditions of a sufficient illumination, low flicker, and rich scene features. On the other hand, they also indicated that monocular cameras were susceptible to light variations, object motion, and texture blurring when used in underwater scenarios.

  Ferrera et al. [44] presented a new monocular visual odometry method that was robust to turbid and dynamic underwater environments. Results showed that the optical flow method had better tracking performance than the classical descriptor-based methods. The optical flow tracking was further enhanced by adding a retracking mechanism, making it robust to short occlusions caused by environmental dynamics. The algorithm was evaluated on both simulated and real underwater datasets and could be used in applications such as underwater archaeology. Roznere et al. [45] proposed a real-time depth estimation method for underwater monocular camera images by fusing measurements from a single-beam echosounder. The proposed method matched the echosounder measurements with the detected feature points of the monocular SLAM system and then integrated them into the monocular SLAM system to adjust the visible map points and scale. They implemented the proposed method in ORB-SLAM2 and evaluated its performance in a swimming pool and the ocean to verify the improved effect of image depth estimation, which proved that the method had a certain application value in underwater exploration and mapping.

- Stereo Camera
  In monocular camera SLAM, the scale problem cannot be determined due to the lack of depth information. In contrast, a stereo camera can acquire the distance between the camera and the object using the parallax principle. Mei et al. [46] presented a relative SLAM for the constant-time estimation of structure and motion with a stereo camera system as the only sensor. This approach employed a topological metric representation of relative position sequences based on a heuristic quadtree approach, which allowed for real-time processing while not strictly limiting the size of the maps that could be constructed. Moreover, Pi et al. [47] proposed a visual SLAM method based on a stereo camera as a sensor, leveraging the SURF algorithm for feature detection and matching and the EKF to fuse the feature coordinates and AUV pose to enable motion estimation in real time and feature map construction. Furthermore, Zhang et al. [48] suggested an underwater stereo visual–inertial localization method (FBUS-EKF) based on an open-source benchmark in the EKF framework. This method fused inertial and visual information and eliminated severe noise in order to implement a SLAM system. Experimental results indicated that the typical localization error of the FBUS-EKF method was less than 3%. Thus, stereo cameras hold great promise for the accurate proximity operation and localization of underwater robots.
- RGB-D Camera
  RGB-D cameras can obtain RGB maps and depth maps directly by physical ranging. According to their principles, they can be divided into structured light methods (e.g., Kinect v1) and time of flight methods (e.g., Kinect v2). However, existing RGB-D cameras typically use infrared light, which is severely attenuated in underwater environments and has high measurement limitations. As a result, it is difficult to use RGB-D cameras as vision sensors for underwater vision SLAM. Therefore, monocular and stereo cameras remain the most popularly used underwater vision sensors.

(2) Sonar Sensors
The lack of illumination in the underwater environment can significantly impact the quality of the final images. To overcome this issue, sonar can be used to detect and locate objects in the absence of light by exploiting their property of reflecting sound waves. Compared to vision, sound waves demonstrate a smaller attenuation rate and longer propagation distance than light in marine scenes and are not affected by light and geomagnetic interference. Sonar sensors can be categorized into forward-looking sonar (FLS), side-scan sonar (SSS), and acoustic lens sonar (ALS) according to the scanning mode. FLS can be further divided into single-beam sonar and multibeam sonar. The basic principles of sonar SLAM are shown in Figure 6.

- Single-beam Sonar
  Sonar is an essential external detection sensor for simultaneous localization and mapping in underwater vehicles. To this end, a variational Bayesian-based simultaneous localization and mapping method for autonomous underwater vehicle navigation (VB-AUFastSLAM) was proposed based on the Unscented-FastSLAM (UFastSLAM) and the variational Bayesian (VB) approaches [49]. The

proposed algorithm was validated in an open-source simulation environment, and its effectiveness in the marine environment was subsequently verified by constructing an underwater vehicle SLAM system based on an inertial navigation system, a Doppler velocity log (DVL), and a single-beam mechanical scanning imaging sonar (MSIS).

- Multibeam Sonar
  Multibeam sonar (MBS), as sonar for underwater sounding, has become one of the most dominant survey instruments employed in marine activities. The multibeam echosounder (MBES) typically consists of a projector and a hydrophone, which are responsible for transmitting and receiving echo soundings to measure topography. An MBE can have several hundred beams, making it the most suitable sonar sensor for deep water-terrain applications [50]. In [51], a filter-based multibeam forward-looking sonar (MFLS) algorithm for underwater SLAM was presented. Environmental features were extracted using an MFLS and the acquired sonar images were converted to a sparse point-cloud format by threshold segmentation and distance-constrained filtering to avoid a computational explosion problem. Furthermore, the method also fused DVL, IMU, and sonar data of the underwater vehicle to estimate the position of the vehicle and generate an occupancy grid map using a SLAM method based on a Rao–Blackwellized particle filter (RBPF) [52].
- Side-scan Sonar.
  Although MBS has a high resolution, it is a bathymetric tool rather than an imaging system. Side-scan sonar (SSS), with a wider range of applications, is now a commonly used tool for detecting submarine targets such as wrecks, mines, and pipelines. SSS can visually provide acoustic imaging of the seafloor morphology with a relatively high resolution. MBS and SSS have good complementarity in detecting seafloor targets and can improve the accuracy of underwater SLAM. Side et al. [53] described a side-scan sonar SLAM system for online drift compensation for underwater robots. The processing chain consisted of an automatic landmark detector, an automatic data association module, and the SLAM filter. In order to improve the robustness of the whole system while satisfying real-time performance, a batch processing method based on joint compatibility branch and bound (JCBB) was used for data association [54]. The effectiveness of the system was verified in sea trials. Furthermore, there are other sonar systems such as synthetic aperture sonar (SAS) [55] and dual-frequency identification sonar (DIDSON) [56]. A comprehensive survey of sonar SLAM can be found in [57–59].

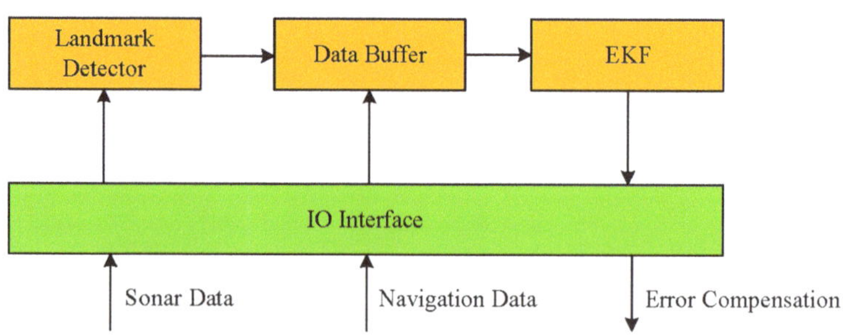

Figure 6. System structure of SLAM based on sonar.

(3) LiDAR Sensors
LiDAR sensors are capable of providing high-frequency range measurements that can operate consistently in complex lighting conditions and optically featureless scenarios [60]. Compared to camera or sonar imaging, laser-scanning imaging can provide higher-resolution 3D measurements of the seafloor in scenes lacking texture underwater. These point cloud data, generated by LiDAR, can provide easy access to

the SLAM system. Moreover, the data generated by LiDAR can be used to accurately map the seafloor and create detailed 3D models. Additionally, LiDAR sensors can be used to detect objects in the environment, allowing for the creation of more accurate navigational maps. Therefore, LiDAR has become a popular choice for seafloor mapping and navigation.

Collings et al. [61] deployed an underwater LiDAR system in parallel with an MBES to survey Kingston Reef of Rottnest Island, Western Australia. In that paper, the relative accuracy and characteristics of underwater LiDAR and multibeam sonar were compared and summarized to map the habitat. Massot et al. [62] proposed a bathymetric SLAM solution for underwater vehicles. The alignment problem of point clouds collected from a single-line-laser structured-light system was solved. In that work, the relative uncertainty in the vehicle localization was reduced by using time-constrained subgraphs. Three translational degrees of freedom and one localization degree of freedom were also used for positional estimation. However, the system could not utilize traditional SLAM image features. Palomer et al. [63] used a 3D underwater laser-scanning system to achieve underwater pipeline structure mapping on a Girona 500 AUV, which can be used for SLAM framework construction.

However, the data quality of LiDAR measurements is susceptible to extreme environments and the point cloud alignment errors caused by the smoothness of the motion. Therefore, the use of single-laser sensors in underwater SLAM environments is more restrictive. Debeunne et al. [64] provides a comprehensive survey on visual–LiDAR SLAM. Solutions using vision, LiDAR, and sensor fusion of both modalities are highlighted.

2.1.3. Multiple Sensors

Single types of sensors often have certain drawbacks when used in underwater SLAM systems. To improve the accuracy and robustness of underwater SLAM, some scholars have integrated multiple sensors into the system. The resulting sensor fusion enables underwater SLAM with a higher accuracy and robustness [39]. Common fusion methods include vision–inertial SLAM (composed of vision and IMU), laser–vision SLAM (composed of laser and vision), and multisensor SLAM (combining sonar, IMU, vision, etc.). Multisensor fusion can be further divided into data layer fusion, feature layer fusion, and decision layer fusion, according to the level of fusion. Coupling complexity can be categorized into loosely coupled, tightly coupled, and ultratightly coupled. Additionally, fusion methods can further be divided into weighted average method, Kalman filter, Bayesian estimation, D-S evidence theory, fuzzy logic, neural network, and so on (as shown in Figure 7).

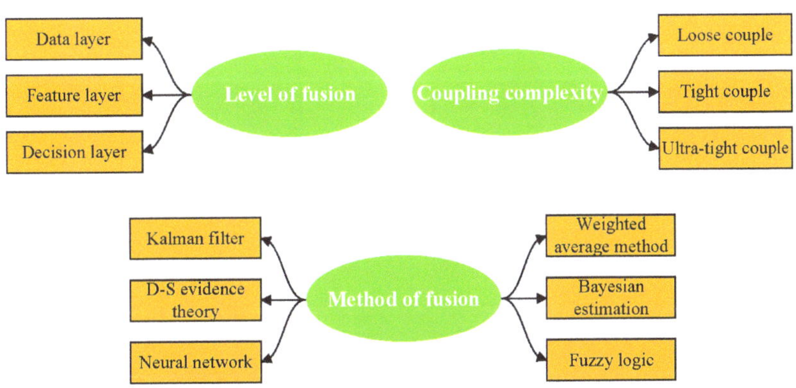

Figure 7. Multiple sensors fusion methods classification.

The two sensing modalities, visual and inertial measurement, provide complementary characteristics that can effectively improve the accuracy of visual–inertial odometry or SLAM. Generally, the main visual–inertial localization methods can be divided into two categories: a class of Kalman filter based methods, such as MSCKF [65] and ROVIO [66]; and a class of graph-based optimization methods, for instance, OKVIS [67] and VINS-Mono [68].

OKVIS was the first relatively complete visual–inertial fusion scheme and has become the basis for many multisensor SLAM algorithms. This method was built with a tightly coupled fusion to best utilize all measurements. Cost functions (combining visual and inertial terms in a fully probabilistic manner) were used for the nonlinear optimization. At the algorithmic level, that paper provided a rigorous probabilistic derivation of the IMU error terms and the respective information matrix, as well as the association of contiguous image frames. At the system level, hardware and algorithms were developed for accurate real-time SLAM. Compared to the filter-based method, a higher accuracy was achieved, although the computational effort was increased. In 2022, Leutenegger proposed OKVIS2 [69], which featured the creation of pose-graph edges through the marginalization of common observations, which could be fluidly turned back into landmarks and observations upon loop closure.

VINS-Mono is a visual–inertial system consisting of a monocular camera and a low-cost inertial measurement unit. In that paper, a robust and versatile monocular visual–inertial state estimator was proposed. A tightly coupled, nonlinear optimization method was used to fuse pre-integrated the IMU measurements and feature observations to obtain a highly accurate visual inertial odometer. The global consistency was enhanced by a four-degree-of-freedom pose map optimization. In addition, the system could save and load maps efficiently for map reuse and map combination.

SVIn2 [70] presented a tightly coupled key-frame-based simultaneous localization and mapping system. The method fused visual sensors, IMU, depth meters, and sonar to address the problem of localization drift and tracking loss, which is particularly relevant for underwater environments. Moreover, a loop-closure detection and relocalization function based on the bag-of-words (BoW) library was implemented to further improve the performance of the system. The structure of SVIn2 is shown in Figure 8.

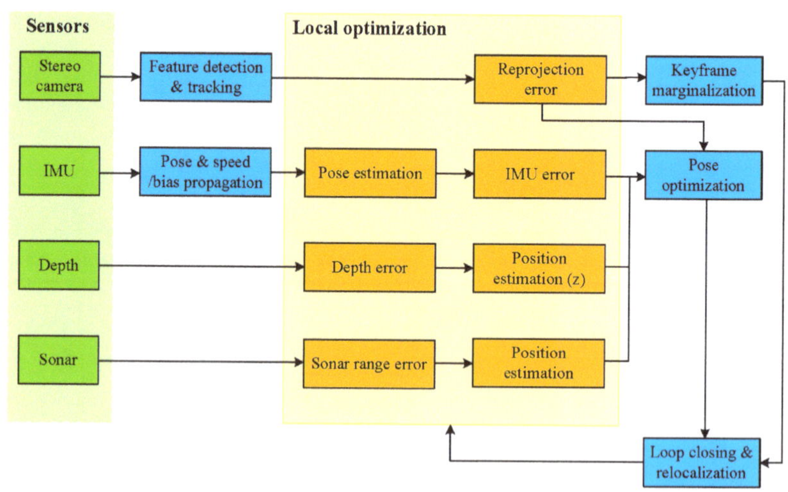

Figure 8. System structure of SVIn2: an underwater SLAM system using sonar, visual, inertial, and depth sensors.

Remark: In addition to improving the accuracy of sensor-acquired information, preprocessing the acquired information (e.g., underwater image enhancement) is another way to improve the effectiveness of SLAM. Commonly used underwater image enhancement algorithms include adaptive histogram equalization (AHE [71]), median filtering (MF [72]), and dark channel prior (DCP [73,74]) algorithms. An extensive review of underwater image enhancement can be found in [75,76].

2.2. Front-End Odometry Estimation

As the front end of the system, the odometer estimate calculates the relative poses by continuously tracking the egomotion of the camera and provides better initial values for the back end. Global trajectories are reconstructed by integrating relative poses for a given initial state. This paper aims to investigate the use of visual data for odometry estimation as they are a common way of perceiving underwater. By exploring this phenomenon, we aim to provide insights into the development of more effective odometry estimation methods for underwater applications.

Visual odometry is a method of camera motion estimation that utilizes the adjacent image information acquired from the camera to determine the relative displacement of static feature points on consecutive frames, thereby calculating relative translation and rotation increments. Furthermore, the final camera motion can be determined by connecting them to a trajectory on a global reference coordinate system. In terms of implementation methods, visual odometry can be divided into two distinct categories: geometry-based methods and deep-learning-based methods.

The geometry-based methods can be further divided into feature-based method and direct method. Among them, the feature method extracts feature points (FAST, SIFT, SURF, ORB etc.) in the image by an algorithm that computes matching feature points in adjacent frames and uses geometric relationships to obtain the rotation matrix and translation matrix of the camera. The goal of the feature point method is to minimize the reprojection error, which is typically achieved by computing the difference between the coordinate values of the pixels. The structure diagram of feature-based visual odometry is shown in Figure 9.

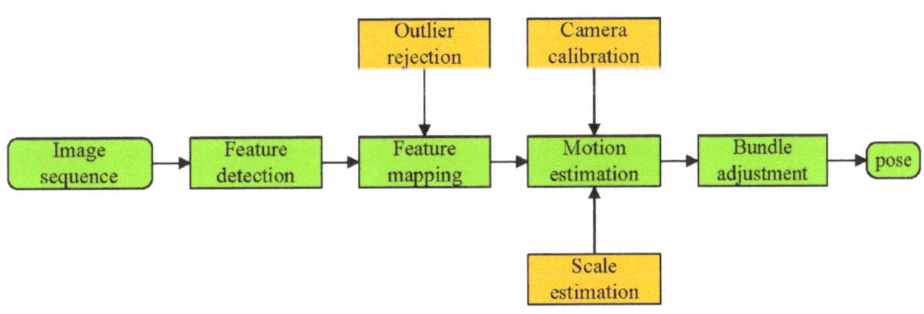

Figure 9. Structure diagram of feature-based visual odometry.

In contrast to the feature-based method, direct methods [77] such as SVO [32] and DSO [78] minimize the photometric error, and the function takes the form of subtracting the grayscale values of the pixels. Direct methods usually match two consecutive images based on the assumption of constant grayscale. The feature point method relies on a more repetitive feature extractor, and correct feature matching. The direct method is more applicable compared to the feature method when there are many repetitive textures in the environment and there is a lack of corner points. However, the direct method is relatively more computationally intensive and usually requires GPU-based computational acceleration. The comparison results between the feature-based method and the direct method are shown in the Table 1.

Unlike geometry-based methods, deep learning methods extract high-level feature representations from images without traditional feature extractors. In underwater scenarios, deep learning methods are often an excellent underwater visual odometry solution.

Early deep learning visual odometry generally consisted in a method of replacing some of the work in the system with deep learning, and such methods were generally referred to as hybrid visual odometry [79]. Subsequently, some end-to-end visual odometry based purely on neural networks were gradually proposed by scholars [80,81]. Based on the availability of ground-truth labels in the training phase, end-to-end visual odometry systems can be further classified into supervised visual odometry and unsupervised visual odometry [82,83]. The visual odometry structure diagram based on deep learning methods is shown in Figure 10.

Table 1. Comparison of feature-based method and direct method of visual odometry.

Classification	Feature-Based Method	Direct Method
Concept	Based on feature point matching; minimize the reprojection error	Based on gray invariant; minimize the luminosity error
Advantage	Strong robustness and high precision	Can be used in scenes with repetitive textures and missing corners
Disadvantage	Both quantity and quality of feature points are required	Sensitive to illumination changes; difficult to realize loop-closure detection and relocation
Characteristic	Data association and pose estimation are decoupled; builds sparse maps; loop-closure detection and relocation are required	Data association and pose estimation are coupled; builds semidense or dense maps; suitable for multisensor fusion

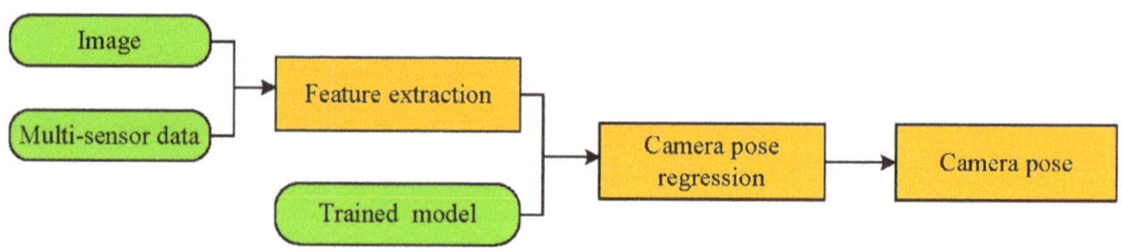

Figure 10. Visual odometry structure diagram based on deep learning methods.

Remark: for a more detailed overview of the VO section, please refer to [84–86].

2.3. Back-End Optimization

SLAM is essentially an estimation of the uncertainty in the robot itself and the surrounding space. As time accumulates, front-end odometry estimates accumulate errors in the estimation of camera poses. Based on the front-end odometry, the back end can perform the state optimization of the entire system at a larger scale and over a longer period of time. For underwater vision SLAM, the mainstream state optimization algorithms include the extended Kalman filter, based on filtering theory, and graph optimization, based on nonlinear optimization theory. To date, the research into the application of these algorithms to the underwater environment has been limited, and further study is needed to determine their effectiveness.

In the SLAM solution process, the linear optimization utilizes a filter model, which is based on Bayesian probability theory. This filter model allows for the conversion of the SLAM problem into the determination of the joint probability of the camera subject pose and the spatial features of the surrounding environment.

The goal of graph-optimization SLAM is to estimate the maximum a posteriori (MAP) of the pose of the mobile robot based on the environmental observations, namely,

$$X^* = argmax(P(X|U)) \tag{2}$$

where X represents the pose of the robot, and U represents the constraint condition. Through the Bayes theorem, we can get:

$$P(X|U) \propto \prod_{i} P(x_{i+1}|x_i, u_i) * \prod_{ij} P(x_j|x_i, u_{ij}) \tag{3}$$

The key to graph-optimization SLAM is to compute the maximum posterior optimization result when the probability distribution is maximized. That is, solving for the maximum posterior probability of the variable to be estimated is transformed into solving for the maximum likelihood estimate.

Loop-closure detection is the commonly used back-end optimization approach (refer to Section 2.4 for details), in addition to BA [87] (minimizing the reprojection error of the map by jointly optimizing the map and the poses) or pose–map optimization (representing the pose–map relationship as a computational map to be optimized) strategies to obtain a more global composition map and pose estimation.

2.4. Loop-Closure Detection

Loop-closure detection is a method for the global optimization of maps, which is used to suppress the error accumulation between the estimated and real values of the camera poses. During the camera movement, the algorithm calculates the similarity between maps to determine whether the camera has reached a visited scene. Upon detection, the information is transmitted to the back end for optimization, ensuring that the estimated trajectory is geometrically consistent and the accumulated error is eliminated. The flow chart of the loop-closure detection is shown in Figure 11.

The underwater scene is highly dynamic and lacks texture and structural features, making feature information from underwater sensors problematic when applied to loop-closure detection compared to structured ground environment information. These factors increase the difficulty of loop-closure detection, likely leading to false or missed detection events. The cumulative error resulting from missed detection events significantly affects the accuracy of positioning and framing. Moreover, the wrong loop-closure results inputted to the back end for optimization can even cause a failure of the entire SLAM system.

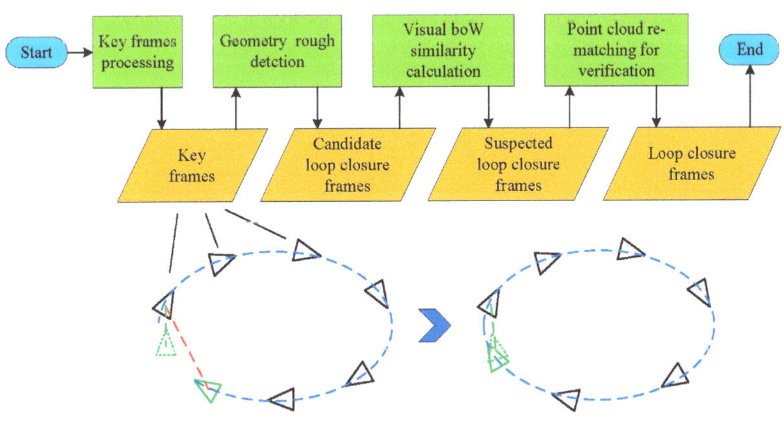

Figure 11. Flow chart of the loop-closure detection.

Traditional loop-closure detection is based on a bag-of-words (BoW) model to store and use the visual features of the detector. Scene recognition is achieved by matching manually designed sparse features or pixel-level dense features [88]. Common methods include DBoW2 [89], FBoW [90], and iBoW-LCD [91].

Bonin et al. [92] presented an experimental evaluation of a hash-based loop-closure detection method for underwater autonomous vehicles utilizing a new global image descriptor called network-hash-based loop closure (NetHALOC). The conversion from images to hashes resulted in significantly fewer data to process, share, compare, and transfer in global navigation, localization, or mapping tasks. To demonstrate the performance of the proposed closed-loop detection method, a comprehensive test was conducted using many real underwater images, which were compared by three different high-quality global image descriptors. The results showed that the proposed method was suitable for underwater visual SLAM applications.

However, the problem was complicated by light, visual range, distortion, and the motion of camera in underwater scenes. Because deep neural networks extract high-level features, these methods are more robust to viewpoint and scene changes. Memon et al. [93] proposed a new hyperdictionary deep learning method. Unlike the traditional BoW dictionary, it made use of more advanced and abstract features. The proposed method did not require the generation of a vocabulary list, which made it memory efficient. Instead, it stored the exact features, which were few and had a small memory usage.

Loop-closure detection based on deep learning has been demonstrated to provide more robust and effective visual features, with better results for position recognition. In the context of underwater scenes, deep learning methods have been shown to exhibit a higher accuracy and stronger robustness than traditional methods. As such, loop-closure detection based on deep learning is an important future research direction for underwater SLAM, offering the potential to achieve an improved accuracy and robustness [94–97].

Remark: Robots are subject to rapid motion or other factors that may lead to image matching and trajectory tracking failure. Consequently, loop-closure detection may not be suitable for such applications [98,99]. As an alternative, relocalization recalculates the camera pose by leveraging the map or repositioning based on map stitching, which provides a more versatile and robust system.

2.5. Mapping

Mapping is an essential component of mobile robotics, as it allows the robot to build a model that accurately reflects the environment. Underwater maps, in particular, have become increasingly important for marine scientific research. These maps typically serve several functions, such as localization, navigation, obstacle avoidance, reconstruction, and interaction. The representation of the final map generated by an underwater SLAM system can vary depending on the method and the implemented functionalities. Generally, these maps can be divided into several categories.

(1) Topology Map

Topological maps possess a high degree of abstraction and are well-suited to environments with large areas and simple structures. This approach represents the environment as a graph in a topological sense, with nodes in the graph corresponding to a feature state or location in the environment. Key frames are utilized as nodes of the map, and common data associations between them are used as edges of the map. By abstracting the map into nodes and edges in line with graph theory, the maps' compatibility with human thinking is improved [100]. Choset et al. proposed a novel approach to simultaneous localization and mapping (SLAM) that utilized the topology of free space to localize the robot on a partially constructed map [101].

Topological maps can be used for path planning, due to their relatively small storage and search space, making them computationally efficient. Furthermore, they enable the utilization of numerous sophisticated and efficient search and inference algorithms [102]. However, topological maps typically lack metric information and are therefore unsuitable for navigation. The use of such maps relies on the identification and matching of topological nodes. If the environment is too similar, topological map methods may have difficulty distinguishing between two points.

(2) Scale Map

- Raster Map
  The raster map divides the 3D environment space into cubes of equal size, each representing an area of 3D space in the real environment. The value of each cube reflects the probability of an obstacle existing in the corresponding 3D space. The raster map preserves as much information as possible about the entire environment, enabling self-positioning, path planning, localization, navigation, and obstacle avoidance. Furthermore, it has great advantages for fusing multisensor information, such as weighted average methods and D-S evidence inference methods. However, as the size of the environment increases, more computation and storage space are required. When the number of rasters increases, for instance in large-scale environments or when the environment is divided in greater detail, the maintenance behavior of the map becomes more difficult. The search space in the localization process is large and, without a better simplification algorithm, real-time performance is poor [103].
- Landmark Map
  Geometric features of the environment are represented using parametric features (e.g., points, lines, and planes). Based on the feature point density, these can be further classified into sparse, semidense, and dense maps. Notably, sparse road maps can only be used for localization, whereas dense maps can be used for navigation and obstacle avoidance functions [104].
- Point Cloud Map
  The environment is described by a large number of three-dimensional spatial points, discretizing all objects in the environment into a dense point cloud [105]. Such point cloud maps are suitable for localization, navigation, obstacle avoidance, and 3D reconstruction. Meanwhile, large-scale environments necessitate a greater amount of computation and more storage space.

(3) Semantic Map
Semantic maps are composed of several distinguishable semantic elements, which can be either scene types or object types. The emphasis is placed on associating semantic concepts with objects in the map, giving them a more abstract meaning. Furthermore, these maps enable mobile robots to act more intelligently and perform more complex interaction tasks [106]. However, the types of objects in different environments often differ. On the one hand, it is not possible to assign semantic concepts to all objects when constructing semantic classes. On the other hand, objects of the same type may differ significantly, while objects of different classes may be more similar, making it difficult to create cognitive maps for complex environments. Furthermore, the complex cognitive map creation algorithm also necessitates a greater computational effort.

(4) Hybrid Map
Currently, no single map representation is capable of adequately meeting all task requirements (localization, navigation, obstacle avoidance, path planning, 3D reconstruction, interaction, etc.) and performance criteria (high accuracy, speed, low computational effort, small storage space, etc.). Consequently, it would be more advantageous to describe the underwater environment using multiple different map representations, thereby harnessing the advantages of each and ultimately achieving different objectives.

3. Research Emphasis and Difficulties

According to the above, we have summarized some selected works on underwater SLAM in Table 2. However, considering the special characteristics of the underwater environment, traditional SLAM algorithms have encountered many problems when expanding to this domain. Thus, there are still many unsolved issues concerning underwater SLAM that require attention.

Table 2. Summary of selected works on underwater SLAM.

	Sensors	Method	Optimization	Loop Closure	Scenario
LSD-SLAM [30]	Mono	Direct	Pose graph	Yes	Large-scale, consistent maps
DSO [78]	Camera	Direct and sparse	Nonlinear joint	No	-
SVO [31]	Mono	Semidirect	Minimize reprojection error	No	-
ORB-SLAM2 [28]	Mono, stereo, RGB-D	Indirect	BA	Yes	Textured environment
ORB-SLAM3 [29]	Mono, stereo, RGB-D, pinhole, fisheye, IMU	Indirect	BA	Yes	Textured environment
ROVIO [66]	IMU, camera	Direct	EKF	No	Employed in UAV
OKVIS [67]	Camera, IMU	Indirect	Marginalization of key frames	No	Hand-held indoor motion, bicycle riding
OKVIS2 [69]	Stereo, IMU	Indirect	Marginalization of common observations	Yes	-
SVIn2 [70]	Stereo, IMU, Depth, Sonar	Indirect	Tightly coupled	Yes	Underwater environments
VINS-Mono [68]	Mono, IMU	Indirect	Tightly coupled and pose graph	Yes	Employed in UAV
MSCKF [65]	Mono, stereo, IMU	Indirect	EKF	No	Real-World environment trajectory
DeepVIO [107]	Stereo, IMU	Self-supervised learning method	-	No	-
SelfVIO [108]	Mono, IMU	Self-supervised learning method	-	No	-
Dolphin SLAM [109]	Sonar, camera, DVL, IMU	Indirect	Bioinspired	Yes	Underwater environments
AEKF-SLAM [110]	Sonar (mainly)	Indirect	AEKF	Yes	Underwater environments
[63]	Laser, AHRS, DVL, pressure sensor	Indirect	EKF	No	Underwater pipe structure
[111]	Mono	Indirect	BA	Yes	Autonomous underwater ship hull inspection

3.1. Sensor Noise

Sensors usually have a limited operating depth, making applications costlier. The working depth and cost of underwater sensors vary depending on the type of sensor and the application scenario [112]. For instance, the operational depth of an underwater IMU is typically limited to a few hundred meters and comes at a low cost. Conversely, sonar systems can operate at depths reaching several thousand meters but are comparatively expensive. Cameras and laser radars generally have shallow operational depths in the tens of meters range, yet their costs remain high. In general, underwater sensors such as visualization sonar (imaging sonar), profiling sonar, DVL, IMU, camera, and depth gauge have distinct characteristics that make it difficult to obtain the same high quality of environmental sensing data as that of land-based LIDAR/cameras. Moreover, the accuracy of sensor data from cameras and other sensors is limited underwater, particularly in environments affected by low light, turbidity, and currents [113,114]. Consequently, the positional estimation and mapping tasks often result in a significant bias due to sensor noise, which varies depending on the situation, especially in large-scale environments where a new calibration is required to achieve better system estimates. Therefore, the modeling of sensor noise is a challenging yet critical task.

3.2. Feature Limitation

Landmark recognition is essential for maintaining the estimated position of a robot, reducing uncertainty in the system, and identifying the position prior to movement. The unstructured nature of underwater environments, however, presents a challenge for feature extraction and matching, as there are few obvious objects or features in most scenes [115]. Additionally, optical sensors, such as cameras, are prone to interference from light and turbidity, while also experiencing decreased imaging results due to the limited field of view in deep-water environments [116,117]. While sonar sensors may provide a larger field of view and improved feature extraction compared to optical sensors, they are still subject to interference from a variety of external factors during actual measurements, including an uneven distribution of the seawater medium, fluctuations generated by the robot's own motion underwater, and noise from marine animals and reverberation interference.

3.3. Scene Detection

Loop-closure detection refers to the ability of a mobile robot to determine when it has reached a location for which a map has been previously constructed, and then to update and correct the originally constructed map, with the main purpose of eliminating the long-term accumulated error of the SLAM system. As previously stated, the underwater environment does not have many structural features, and it undergoes large dynamic changes, making it difficult to perform closed-loop detection, and likely leading to false or missed detection events [118]. Moreover, compared to structured ground environment information, the feature information of underwater vision and acoustics presents additional challenges when used for closed-loop detection [119,120]. These false or missed detection events can lead to cumulative errors, which significantly affect the accuracy of positioning and composition.

3.4. Underwater Ground Truth

Given the GPS-denied nature of underwater scenarios, obtaining the true value of a robot's position and trajectory is a difficult task due to the errors of underwater sensors. Acoustic positioning systems such as LBL [121], SBL, and USBL require extensive base-array installation work and tend to have a greater position uncertainty than the modern resolution of multibeam or interferometric side scan sonar, making them costly. Furthermore, true underwater values are especially difficult to obtain in deep-sea and cave scenarios, resulting in a relatively small number of reliable datasets specific to underwater SLAM. (We have collected some publicly available underwater datasets for use [122–127], as detailed in Appendix A).

3.5. Computational Complexity

The computational complexity of SLAM systems is influenced by the size of the exploration environment and is closely related to the methods used for feature extraction, tracking, data association [128], and filtering. The location landmarks, map elements, and other such features generated by the robot as it moves through the underwater environment are identified and monitored, increasing the uncertainty of the associated computation [129]. Compared to surface environments, underwater environments such as oceans, lakes, and reservoirs have a huge space and complex underwater robot activities, making it difficult to achieve a balance between accuracy and speed for SLAM systems. To date, improving the accuracy in large-scale environments has remained a challenge for underwater SLAM applications.

4. Discussion

In the previous section, we discussed the system framework of underwater SLAM and the current research difficulties. In this section, we study the future development direction of underwater SLAM from the perspective of application environment and technological development, so as to open up new ideas for the research of underwater SLAM.

4.1. Underwater SLAM in Extreme Environments

In complex or confined underwater environments, such as underwater energy storage facilities, docks, flooded tunnels, and sewers, human inspection is often dangerous or impractical, necessitating remote inspection using unmanned underwater vehicles. Implementing such systems, however, becomes more difficult when the size and motion of the robot must be considered [130]. Furthermore, underwater SLAM systems are hindered by the low illumination, turbidity, and lack of features in these environments, severely limiting the capabilities of underwater inspection robots to manually controlled, low-quality visual inspections. This is a key research direction for scholars to explore [131,132].

4.2. Underwater SLAM in Dynamic Environments

Considering the pose calculation principle of SLAM systems, dynamic objects in a SLAM process will seriously affect feature matching and calculation results. On land, SLAM in dynamic environments is a hot research topic [133–135]. However, underwater dynamic phenomena are very common, such as sea creatures, water flow caused by robot motion, bubbles, etc. Maps generated in dynamic environments are more flawed than those generated in static environments. Aiming at underwater SLAM problems in dynamic environments is also more difficult. As an end-to-end feature learning method, deep learning technology provides a new idea for dynamic feature extraction and processing. Unlike direct and feature-based methods that use physical models or geometric theory, deep learning methods provide an alternative to solve problems in a data-driven way. Benefiting from the ever-increasing quantity of data and computational power, these methods can generate accurate and robust systems for tracking motion and estimating the structure of real-world scenes. They are rapidly evolving into a new field of research [136]. However, considering that an underwater dataset is not enough, and the algorithm is facing the problem of scene applicability, the work of underwater dynamic SLAM based on deep learning is slow yet still destined to be an important method to solve dynamic problems in the future (as shown in Figure 12).

Figure 12. Effect of dynamic, weakly textured objects on underwater SLAM (green squares with crosses inside mean feature points).

4.3. Underwater Semantic SLAM

Most current SLAM systems are based on geometric features and ignore the semantic information of objects in the environment, resulting in a relatively homogeneous system function. With the continuous development of deep learning in the field of computer imaging, researchers have started to incorporate target recognition and semantic segmentation into SLAM to achieve more complex functions. Semantic SLAM refers to a SLAM system that obtains semantic information while acquiring the geometric structure information in the environment during the mapping process, and at the same time recognizing the independent individuals in the environment [137]. This semantic information includes information about the position, pose, and functional attributes of the individuals. With this semantic information, robots can more effectively cope with complex scenarios and refine and improve service tasks. Semantic extraction is currently a deep learning approach that uses deep neural networks to process images, such as segmentation and recognition, and add labels, and the training results determine the final effect of semantic SLAM. In specific underwater environment tasks, such as underwater salvage, underwater defect detection, marine biological analysis, and other underwater tasks, the semantic recognition of captured objects during SLAM is required [138]. However, the accurate generation of image-based obstacle maps in cluttered underwater environments is extremely demanding for the robustness of underwater robotic SLAM systems. Moreover, such recognition can be affected by lighting conditions and moving objects (e.g., schools of fish), which can lead to misjudgments. The presence of a large number of dynamic objects is also detrimental to the final composition. Therefore, there are still many challenges for the application of semantic SLAM in underwater environments [139]. The schematic diagram of underwater semantic segmentation is shown in Figure 13.

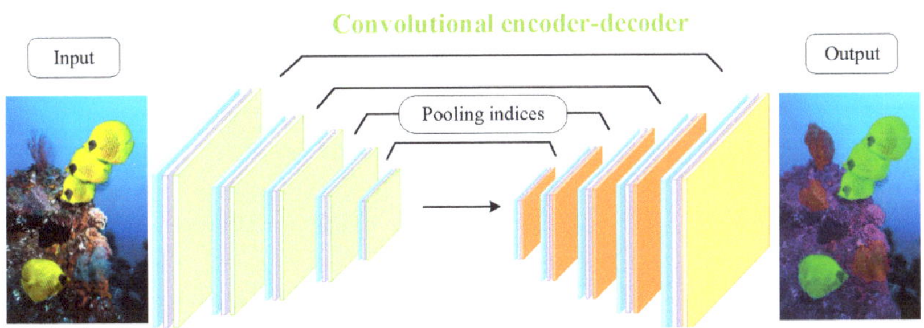

Figure 13. Schematic diagram of underwater semantic segmentation.

4.4. Multirobot Underwater SLAM

Different from SLAM in indoor scenes, underwater scenes have a large area and a single structure, thus relying on a single robot will result in low efficiency [140]. To address this, multirobot SLAM requires technical elements such as a system to build multiple SLAM systems and to collect information from each robot. Moreover, map fusion, an important process in multirobot SLAM, combines multiple local maps estimated by the robot team into a global map [141].

The fusion of multiple local maps is usually done using a loopback detection method that identifies whether multiple robots have visited the same scene. Additionally, a robot federation approach can be employed, allowing another member of a robot team to be observed in the images of that member. However, when multiple robots operate in environments with multiple similar scenes, they are likely to identify different points with similar scenes as the same location, leading to erroneous results from the loopback detection. Furthermore, the viewpoint positions of the cameras mounted on each robot are not guaranteed to be identical, making it difficult to observe the same place. Moreover, the descriptors of each scene differ, thus making it impossible to detect loopback even when the same place is observed. Establishing an effective fusion process of multiple maps is the focus of multirobot underwater SLAM research [142,143].

5. Conclusions

This paper systematically discussed the key technologies of SLAM in underwater scenes, including theoretical background, system framework, existing methods, problems, applications and development trends.

In this paper, the methods of sensor information, front-end odometry estimation, back-end optimization, loop-closure detection, and mapping in the underwater SLAM system framework were summarized. The sensor information part involved proprioceptive sensors, exteroceptive sensors (visual, acoustic, and LiDAR), and multiple sensors; the front-end odometry estimation part involved geometry-based methods (feature methods and direct methods) and deep-learning-based methods. The back-end optimization part involved the extended Kalman Filter based on filtering theory and graph optimization based on nonlinear optimization theory. The loop-closure detection part involved bag-of-words methods and deep-learning-based methods. The mapping part analyzed different types and characteristics of maps. Furthermore, this paper also outlined the specific research difficulties of underwater SLAM, including sensor noise, feature information, scene detection, ground truth, and computational complexity. From the perspectives of extreme environment, dynamic environment, underwater semantic SLAM, and underwater multirobot SLAM, the future research directions and focuses of underwater SLAM were presented.

Our research results link the latest research results in the fields of underwater robotics, computer vision, and machine learning, and provide guidance to future researchers for understanding feasible approaches to apply emerging technologies to solve underwater robot localization and composition problems.

Author Contributions: Conceptualization, X.W. and X.F.; methodology, X.W.; validation, X.F., P.S. and J.N.; formal analysis, X.W. and Z.Z.; resources, X.F. and P.S.; writing—original draft preparation, X.W.; writing—review and editing, X.W., X.F., P.S., J.N. and Z.Z. All authors have read and agreed to the published version of the manuscript.

Funding: This research was funded by the National Key R&D Program of China, Grant/Award Number: 2022YFB4703405; the Fundamental Research Fund for the Central Universities, Grant/Award Number: B220202020; the Fundamental Research Funds for the Central Universities, Grant/Award Number: B220203032.

Data Availability Statement: Datasets relevant to our paper are available online.

Conflicts of Interest: The authors declare no conflict of interest.

Abbreviations

The explanations of some abbreviations in the text are shown as follows:

SLAM	Simultaneous localization and mapping	SSS	Side-scan sonar
GNSS	Global navigation satellite system	ALS	Acoustic lens sonar
GPS	Global Positioning System	VB	Variational Bayesian
UUV	Unmanned underwater vehicles	UFast	Unscented-fast
ROV	Remotely operated vehicles	MSIS	Mechanical scanning imaging sonar
AUV	Autonomous underwater vehicles	MBS	Multibeam sonar
SBL	Short baseline	MBES	Multibeam echosounder
USBL	Ultrashort baseline	MFLS	Multibeam forward looking sonar
EKF	Extended Kalman filter	RBPF	Rao–Blackwellized particle filter
PF	Particle filter	JCBB	Joint compatibility branch and bound
MLE	Maximum likelihood estimation	SAS	Synthetic aperture sonar
ORB	Oriented FAST and Rotation BRIEF	DIDSON	Dual-frequency identification sonar
LSD	Large-scale direct	MSCKF	Multistate constraint Kalman filter
SVO	Semidirect visual odometry	FBUS	Fiducial-based, underwater stereo
PTAM	Parallel tracking and mapping	BoW	Bag-of-words
DT	Deferred triangulation	AHE	Adaptive histogram equalization
IMU	Inertial measurement units	MF	Median filtering
DVL	Doppler velocity log	DCP	Dark channel prior
6-DOF	Six-degree-of-freedom	SIFT	Scale-invariant feature transform
LBL	Lone baseline	SURF	Speed up robust feature
ROVIO	Robust visual inertial odometry	SVO	Semidirect visual odometry
VIO	Visual inertial odometry	DSO	Direct sparse odometry
SVIn	Sonar, visual, inertial	MAP	Maximum a posteriori
VINS	Visual–inertial state	BA	Bundle adjustment
CNN	Convolutional neural networks	NetHALOC	Network hash-based loop closure
SfM	Structure from motion	AHRS	Attitude and heading reference system

Appendix A

One of the difficulties of underwater SLAM is the acquisition of underwater truth values, which indirectly leads to a scarcity of datasets dedicated to underwater localization and composition. In this paper, we present several publicly available underwater SLAM datasets that can be used by researchers for experimental comparisons. Refer to Table A1 for details.

The Aqualoc dataset is dedicated to the development of simultaneous positioning and map construction methods for underwater vehicles navigating near the seafloor. Data sequences were recorded in three different environments: a harbor at a few meters depth, and two sites at depths of 270 and 380 m. The data acquisition was performed by ROVs equipped with a monocular monochrome camera, a low-cost inertial measurement unit, a pressure sensor, and a computational unit. The collected data consisted of 17 sequences, provided as ROS packages and used as raw data. The sequence images of the dataset are shown in Figures A1 and A2.

Table A1. Description of underwater SLAM datasets in recent years.

Simulated datasets produced using UWSim (2016) [122]	This paper provides an open collection of seven different simulated datasets produced using an underwater simulation. Those datasets present three trajectories and two simulated seafloor visual data based on real coral reef mosaics.
Underwater caves sonar and vision dataset (2017) [123]	The dataset was collected with an autonomous underwater vehicle test bed in the unstructured environment of an underwater cave. The vehicle was equipped with two mechanically scanned imaging sonar sensors to simultaneously map the cave's horizontal and vertical surfaces, a Doppler velocity log, two inertial measurement units, a depth sensor, and a vertically mounted camera imaging the sea floor for ground-truth validation at specific points.
Datasets collected by an underwater sensor suite (2018) [124]	The proposed sensor suite was used to collect sonar, visual, inertial, and depth data in a variety of environments. More specifically, shipwreck and coral reef data were collected during field trials in Barbados. More data were collected at Fantasy Lake, NC, and at different locales near High Springs, FL.
Aqualoc (2019) [125]	The data sequences composing this dataset were recorded at three different depths: a few meters, 270 m, and 380 m. Seventeen sequences were made available in the form of ROS bags and as raw data. For each sequence, a trajectory was also computed offline using a structure-from-motion library in order to allow the comparison with real-time localization methods.
VAROS synthetic underwater dataset (2021) [126]	Pose sequences were created by first defining waypoints for the simulated underwater vehicle. The scenes were rendered using the ray-tracing method, which generates realistic images by integrating direct light and indirect volumetric scattering. The VAROS dataset version 1 provides images, inertial measurement unit (IMU), and depth gauge data, as well as ground-truth poses, depth images, and surface normal images.
A bathymetric mapping and SLAM dataset with high-precision ground truth for marine robotics (2022) [127]	This paper presents a dataset with four separate surveys designed to test bathymetric SLAM algorithms using two modern sonar sensors, typical underwater vehicle navigation sensors, and a high-precision (2 cm horizontal, 10 cm vertical) real-time kinematic (RTK) GPS ground truth.

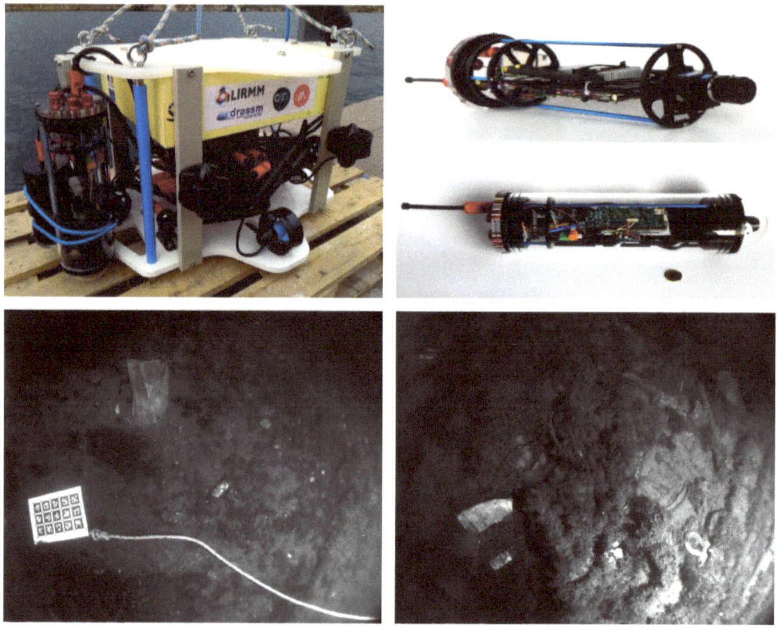

Figure A1. Port sequence of the Aqualoc dataset.

Figure A2. Archaeological sequence of the Aqualoc dataset.

References

1. Zhu, N.; Marais, J.; Bétaille, D.; Berbineau, M. GNSS position integrity in urban environments: A review of literature. *IEEE Trans. Intell. Transp. Syst.* **2018**, *19*, 2762–2778. [CrossRef]
2. Durrant-Whyte, H.; Bailey, T. Simultaneous localization and mapping: Part I. *IEEE Robot. Autom. Mag.* **2006**, *13*, 99–110. [CrossRef]
3. Bailey, T.; Durrant-Whyte, H. Simultaneous localization and mapping (SLAM): Part II. *IEEE Robot. Autom. Mag.* **2006**, *13*, 108–117. [CrossRef]
4. Van Nam, D.; Gon-Woo, K. Solid-state LiDAR based-SLAM: A concise review and application. In Proceedings of the 2021 IEEE International Conference on Big Data and Smart Computing (BigComp), Jeju Island, Republic of Korea, 17–20 January 2021; pp. 302–305.
5. Cho, H.; Jeong, S.K.; Ji, D.H.; Tran, N.H.; Vu, M.T.; Choi, H.S. Study on control system of integrated unmanned surface vehicle and underwater vehicle. *Sensors* **2020**, *20*, 2633. [CrossRef]
6. Petillot, Y.R.; Antonelli, G.; Casalino, G.; Ferreira, F. Underwater robots: From remotely operated vehicles to intervention-autonomous underwater vehicles. *IEEE Robot. Autom. Mag.* **2019**, *26*, 94–101. [CrossRef]
7. Blidberg, D.R. The development of autonomous underwater vehicles (AUV); a brief summary. *Proc. IEEE Icra* **2001**, *4*, 1–12.
8. Zhao, W.; He, T.; Sani, A.Y.M.; Yao, T. Review of slam techniques for autonomous underwater vehicles. In Proceedings of the 2019 International Conference on Robotics, Intelligent Control and Artificial Intelligence, New York, NY, USA, 20 September 2019; pp. 384–389.
9. Paull, L.; Saeedi, S.; Seto, M.; Li, H. AUV navigation and localization: A review. *IEEE J. Ocean. Eng.* **2013**, *39*, 131–149. [CrossRef]
10. Burguera, A.; Bonin-Font, F.; Font, E.G.; Torres, A.M. Combining Deep Learning and Robust Estimation for Outlier-Resilient Underwater Visual Graph SLAM. *J. Mar. Sci. Eng.* **2022**, *10*, 511. [CrossRef]
11. Burguera, A.; Bonin-Font, F. *Localization, Mapping and SLAM in Marine and Underwater Environments*; MDPI: Basel, Switzerland, 2022.
12. Smith, R.; Self, M.; Cheeseman, P. Estimating uncertain spatial relationships in robotics. In *Autonomous Robot Vehicles*; Springer: Berlin/Heidelberg, Germany, 1990; pp. 167–193. [CrossRef]
13. Bailey, T.; Nieto, J.; Guivant, J.; Stevens, M.; Nebot, E. Consistency of the EKF-SLAM algorithm. In Proceedings of the 2006 IEEE/RSJ International Conference on Intelligent Robots and Systems, Beijing, China, 9–15 October 2006; pp. 3562–3568.
14. Van Der Merwe, R.; Doucet, A.; De Freitas, N.; Wan, E. The unscented particle filter. In Proceedings of the Advances in Neural Information Processing Systems, Cambridge, MA, USA, 1 January 2000; Volume 13.
15. Dutilleul, P. The MLE algorithm for the matrix normal distribution. *J. Stat. Comput. Simul.* **1999**, *64*, 105–123. [CrossRef]
16. Cadena, C.; Carlone, L.; Carrillo, H.; Latif, Y.; Scaramuzza, D.; Neira, J.; Reid, I.; Leonard, J.J. Past, present, and future of simultaneous localization and mapping: Toward the robust-perception age. *IEEE Trans. Robot.* **2016**, *32*, 1309–1332. [CrossRef]
17. Chen, W.; Shang, G.; Ji, A.; Zhou, C.; Wang, X.; Xu, C.; Li, Z.; Hu, K. An overview on visual slam: From tradition to semantic. *Remote Sens.* **2022**, *14*, 3010. [CrossRef]
18. Lai, T. A Review on Visual-SLAM: Advancements from Geometric Modelling to Learning-Based Semantic Scene Understanding Using Multi-Modal Sensor Fusion. *Sensors* **2022**, *22*, 7265. [CrossRef]
19. Teed, Z.; Deng, J. Droid-slam: Deep visual slam for monocular, stereo, and rgb-d cameras. *Adv. Neural Inf. Process. Syst.* **2021**, *34*, 16558–16569.
20. Macario Barros, A.; Michel, M.; Moline, Y.; Corre, G.; Carrel, F. A comprehensive survey of visual slam algorithms. *Robotics* **2022**, *11*, 24. [CrossRef]
21. Davison, A.J.; Reid, I.D.; Molton, N.D.; Stasse, O. MonoSLAM: Real-time single camera SLAM. *IEEE Trans. Pattern Anal. Mach. Intell.* **2007**, *29*, 1052–1067. [CrossRef]
22. Tateno, K.; Tombari, F.; Laina, I.; Navab, N. Cnn-slam: Real-time dense monocular slam with learned depth prediction. In Proceedings of the IEEE Conference on Computer Vision and Pattern Recognition, Honolulu, HI, USA, 21–26 July 2017; pp. 6243–6252.
23. Gomez-Ojeda, R.; Moreno, F.A.; Zuniga-Noël, D.; Scaramuzza, D.; Gonzalez-Jimenez, J. PL-SLAM: A stereo SLAM system through the combination of points and line segments. *IEEE Trans. Robot.* **2019**, *35*, 734–746. [CrossRef]
24. Engel, J.; Stückler, J.; Cremers, D. Large-scale direct SLAM with stereo cameras. In Proceedings of the 2015 IEEE/RSJ International Conference on Intelligent Robots and Systems (IROS), Hamburg, Germany, 28 September–2 October 2015; pp. 1935–1942.
25. Kerl, C.; Sturm, J.; Cremers, D. Dense visual SLAM for RGB-D cameras. In Proceedings of the 2013 IEEE/RSJ International Conference on Intelligent Robots and Systems, Tokyo, Japan, 3–7 November 2013; pp. 2100–2106.
26. Sturm, J.; Engelhard, N.; Endres, F.; Burgard, W.; Cremers, D. A benchmark for the evaluation of RGB-D SLAM systems. In Proceedings of the 2012 IEEE/RSJ International Conference on Intelligent Robots and Systems, Vilamoura-Algarve, Portugal, 7–12 October 2012; pp. 573–580.
27. Mur-Artal, R.; Montiel, J.M.M.; Tardos, J.D. ORB-SLAM: A versatile and accurate monocular SLAM system. *IEEE Trans. Robot.* **2015**, *31*, 1147–1163. [CrossRef]
28. Mur-Artal, R.; Tardós, J.D. Orb-slam2: An open-source slam system for monocular, stereo, and rgb-d cameras. *IEEE Trans. Robot.* **2017**, *33*, 1255–1262. [CrossRef]
29. Campos, C.; Elvira, R.; Rodríguez, J.J.G.; Montiel, J.M.; Tardós, J.D. Orb-slam3: An accurate open-source library for visual, visual–inertial, and multimap slam. *IEEE Trans. Robot.* **2021**, *37*, 1874–1890. [CrossRef]

30. Engel, J.; Schöps, T.; Cremers, D. LSD-SLAM: Large-scale direct monocular SLAM. In Proceedings of the Computer Vision–ECCV 2014: 13th European Conference, Zurich, Switzerland, 6–12 September 2014; Proceedings, Part II 13; Springer: Berlin/Heidelberg, Germany, 2014; pp. 834–849.
31. Forster, C.; Pizzoli, M.; Scaramuzza, D. SVO: Fast semi-direct monocular visual odometry. In Proceedings of the 2014 IEEE International Conference on Robotics and Automation (ICRA), Hong Kong, China, 31 May–7 June 2014; pp. 15–22.
32. Forster, C.; Zhang, Z.; Gassner, M.; Werlberger, M.; Scaramuzza, D. SVO: Semidirect visual odometry for monocular and multicamera systems. *IEEE Trans. Robot.* **2016**, *33*, 249–265. [CrossRef]
33. Rublee, E.; Rabaud, V.; Konolige, K.; Bradski, G. ORB: An efficient alternative to SIFT or SURF. In Proceedings of the 2011 International Conference on Computer Vision, Barcelona, Spain, 6–13 November 2011; pp. 2564–2571.
34. Klein, G.; Murray, D. Parallel tracking and mapping for small AR workspaces. In Proceedings of the 2007 6th IEEE and ACM International Symposium on Mixed and Augmented Reality, Nara, Japan, 13–16 November 2007; pp. 225–234.
35. Herrera, D.C.; Kim, K.; Kannala, J.; Pulli, K.; Heikkilä, J. Dt-slam: Deferred triangulation for robust slam. In Proceedings of the 2014 2nd International Conference on 3D Vision, Tokyo, Japan, 8–11 December 2014; Volume 1, pp. 609–616.
36. Williams, S.B.; Newman, P.; Dissanayake, G.; Durrant-Whyte, H. Autonomous underwater simultaneous localisation and map building. In Proceedings of the Proceedings 2000 ICRA. Millennium Conference. IEEE International Conference on Robotics and Automation. Symposia Proceedings (Cat. No. 00CH37065), San Francisco, CA, USA, 24–28 April 2000; Volume 2, pp. 1793–1798.
37. Hashemi, M.; Karmozdi, A.; Naderi, A.; Salarieh, H. Development of an integrated navigation algorithm based on IMU, depth, DVL sensors and earth magnetic field map. *Modares Mech. Eng.* **2017**, *16*, 235–243.
38. Menaka, D.; Gauni, S.; Manimegalai, C.T.; Kalimuthu, K. Challenges and vision of wireless optical and acoustic communication in underwater environment. *Int. J. Commun. Syst.* **2022**, *35*, e5227. [CrossRef]
39. Vargas, E.; Scona, R.; Willners, J.S.; Luczynski, T.; Cao, Y.; Wang, S.; Petillot, Y.R. Robust underwater visual SLAM fusing acoustic sensing. In Proceedings of the 2021 IEEE International Conference on Robotics and Automation (ICRA), Xi'an, China, 30 May–5 June 2021; pp. 2140–2146.
40. Fuentes-Pacheco, J.; Ruiz-Ascencio, J.; Rendón-Mancha, J.M. Visual simultaneous localization and mapping: A survey. *Artif. Intell. Rev.* **2015**, *43*, 55–81. [CrossRef]
41. Hodne, L.M.; Leikvoll, E.; Yip, M.; Teigen, A.L.; Stahl, A.; Mester, R. Detecting and suppressing marine snow for underwater visual slam. In Proceedings of the 2022 IEEE/CVF Conference on Computer Vision and Pattern Recognition Workshops (CVPRW), New Orleans, LA, USA, 19–20 June 2022; pp. 5101–5109.
42. Zhang, S.; Zhao, S.; An, D.; Liu, J.; Wang, H.; Feng, Y.; Li, D.; Zhao, R. Visual SLAM for underwater vehicles: A survey. *Comput. Sci. Rev.* **2022**, *46*, 100510. [CrossRef]
43. Hidalgo, F.; Kahlefendt, C.; Bräunl, T. Monocular ORB-SLAM application in underwater scenarios. In Proceedings of the 2018 OCEANS-MTS/IEEE Kobe Techno-Oceans (OTO), Kobe, Japan, 28–31 May 2018; pp. 1–4.
44. Ferrera, M.; Moras, J.; Trouvé-Peloux, P.; Creuze, V. Real-time monocular visual odometry for turbid and dynamic underwater environments. *Sensors* **2019**, *19*, 687. [CrossRef]
45. Roznere, M.; Li, A.Q. Underwater monocular image depth estimation using single-beam echosounder. In Proceedings of the 2020 IEEE/RSJ International Conference on Intelligent Robots and Systems (IROS), Las Vegas, NV, USA, 24 October 2020–24 January 2021; pp. 1785–1790.
46. Mei, C.; Sibley, G.; Cummins, M.; Newman, P.; Reid, I. RSLAM: A system for large-scale mapping in constant-time using stereo. *Int. J. Comput. Vis.* **2011**, *94*, 198–214. [CrossRef]
47. Pi, S.; He, B.; Zhang, S.; Nian, R.; Shen, Y.; Yan, T. Stereo visual SLAM system in underwater environment. In Proceedings of the OCEANS 2014-TAIPEI, Taipei, Taiwan, 7–10 April 2014; pp. 1–5.
48. Zhang, P.; Wu, Z.; Wang, J.; Kong, S.; Tan, M.; Yu, J. An Open-Source, Fiducial-Based, Underwater Stereo Visual-Inertial Localization Method with Refraction Correction. In Proceedings of the 2021 IEEE/RSJ International Conference on Intelligent Robots and Systems (IROS), Prague, Czech Republic, 27 September–1 October 2021; pp. 4331–4336.
49. Mu, P.; Zhang, X.; Qin, P.; He, B. A Variational Bayesian-Based Simultaneous Localization and Mapping Method for Autonomous Underwater Vehicle Navigation. *J. Mar. Sci. Eng.* **2022**, *10*, 1563. [CrossRef]
50. Melo, J.; Matos, A. Survey on advances on terrain based navigation for autonomous underwater vehicles. *Ocean. Eng.* **2017**, *139*, 250–264. [CrossRef]
51. Cheng, C.; Wang, C.; Yang, D.; Liu, W.; Zhang, F. Underwater localization and mapping based on multi-beam forward looking sonar. *Front. Neurorobot.* **2022**, *15*, 189. [CrossRef]
52. Grisetti, G.; Stachniss, C.; Burgard, W. Improved techniques for grid mapping with rao-blackwellized particle filters. *IEEE Trans. Robot.* **2007**, *23*, 34–46. [CrossRef]
53. Siantidis, K. Side scan sonar based onboard SLAM system for autonomous underwater vehicles. In Proceedings of the 2016 IEEE/OES Autonomous Underwater Vehicles (AUV), Tokyo, Japan, 6–9 November 2016; pp. 195–200.
54. Neira, J.; Tardós, J.D. Data association in stochastic mapping using the joint compatibility test. *IEEE Trans. Robot. Autom.* **2001**, *17*, 890–897. [CrossRef]
55. Gerg, I.D.; Monga, V. Deep Multi-Look Sequence Processing for Synthetic Aperture Sonar Image Segmentation. *IEEE Trans. Geosci. Remote. Sens.* **2023**, *61*, 4200915. [CrossRef]

56. Belcher, E.; Hanot, W.; Burch, J. Dual-frequency identification sonar (DIDSON). In Proceedings of the 2002 Interntional Symposium on Underwater Technology (Cat. No. 02EX556), Tokyo, Japan, 19 April 2002; pp. 187–192.
57. Jiang, M.; Song, S.; Li, Y.; Jin, W.; Liu, J.; Feng, X. A survey of underwater acoustic SLAM system. In Proceedings of the Intelligent Robotics and Applications: 12th International Conference, ICIRA 2019, Shenyang, China, 8–11 August 2019; Proceedings, Part II 12; Springer: Berlin/Heidelberg, Germany, 2019; pp. 159–170.
58. Fallon, M.F.; Folkesson, J.; McClelland, H.; Leonard, J.J. Relocating underwater features autonomously using sonar-based SLAM. *IEEE J. Ocean. Eng.* **2013**, *38*, 500–513. [CrossRef]
59. Evers, C.; Naylor, P.A. Acoustic slam. *IEEE/ACM Trans. Audio Speech Lang. Process.* **2018**, *26*, 1484–1498. [CrossRef]
60. Maksymova, I.; Steger, C.; Druml, N. Review of LiDAR sensor data acquisition and compression for automotive applications. *Proceedings* **2018**, *2*, 852.
61. Collings, S.; Martin, T.J.; Hernandez, E.; Edwards, S.; Filisetti, A.; Catt, G.; Marouchos, A.; Boyd, M.; Embry, C. Findings from a combined subsea LiDAR and multibeam survey at Kingston reef, Western Australia. *Remote Sens.* **2020**, *12*, 2443. [CrossRef]
62. Massot-Campos, M.; Oliver, G.; Bodenmann, A.; Thornton, B. Submap bathymetric SLAM using structured light in underwater environments. In Proceedings of the 2016 IEEE/OES Autonomous Underwater Vehicles (AUV), Tokyo, Japan, 6–9 November 2016; pp. 181–188.
63. Palomer, A.; Ridao, P.; Ribas, D. Inspection of an underwater structure using point-cloud SLAM with an AUV and a laser scanner. *J. Field Robot.* **2019**, *36*, 1333–1344. [CrossRef]
64. Debeunne, C.; Vivet, D. A review of visual-LiDAR fusion based simultaneous localization and mapping. *Sensors* **2020**, *20*, 2068. [CrossRef]
65. Mourikis, A.I.; Roumeliotis, S.I. A multi-state constraint Kalman filter for vision-aided inertial navigation. In Proceedings of the 2007 IEEE International Conference on Robotics and Automation, Rome, Italy, 10–14 April 2007; pp. 3565–3572.
66. Bloesch, M.; Omari, S.; Hutter, M.; Siegwart, R. Robust visual inertial odometry using a direct EKF-based approach. In Proceedings of the 2015 IEEE/RSJ International Conference on Intelligent Robots and Systems (IROS), Hamburg, Germany, 28 September–2 October 2015; pp. 298–304.
67. Leutenegger, S.; Furgale, P.; Rabaud, V.; Chli, M.; Konolige, K.; Siegwart, R. Keyframe-based visual-inertial slam using nonlinear optimization. In Proceedings of the Robotis Science and Systems (RSS), Berlin, Germany, 24–28 June 2013.
68. Qin, T.; Li, P.; Shen, S. Vins-mono: A robust and versatile monocular visual-inertial state estimator. *IEEE Trans. Robot.* **2018**, *34*, 1004–1020. [CrossRef]
69. Leutenegger, S. Okvis2: Realtime scalable visual-inertial slam with loop closure. *arXiv* **2022**, arXiv:2202.09199.
70. Rahman, S.; Li, A.Q.; Rekleitis, I. Svin2: An underwater slam system using sonar, visual, inertial, and depth sensor. In Proceedings of the 2019 IEEE/RSJ International Conference on Intelligent Robots and Systems (IROS), Macau, China, 3–8 November 2019; pp. 1861–1868.
71. Hitam, M.S.; Awalludin, E.A.; Yussof, W.N.J.H.W.; Bachok, Z. Mixture contrast limited adaptive histogram equalization for underwater image enhancement. In Proceedings of the 2013 International Conference on Computer Applications Technology (ICCAT), Sousse, Tunisia, 20–22 January 2013; pp. 1–5.
72. Lu, H.; Serikawa, S. Underwater scene enhancement using weighted guided median filter. In Proceedings of the 2014 IEEE International Conference on Multimedia and Expo (ICME), Chengdu, China, 14–18 July 2014; pp. 1–6.
73. Yang, H.Y.; Chen, P.Y.; Huang, C.C.; Zhuang, Y.Z.; Shiau, Y.H. Low complexity underwater image enhancement based on dark channel prior. In Proceedings of the 2011 Second International Conference on Innovations in Bio-Inspired Computing and Applications, Shenzhen, China, 16–18 December 2011; pp. 17–20.
74. Hou, G.; Li, J.; Wang, G.; Yang, H.; Huang, B.; Pan, Z. A novel dark channel prior guided variational framework for underwater image restoration. *J. Vis. Commun. Image Represent.* **2020**, *66*, 102732. [CrossRef]
75. Sahu, P.; Gupta, N.; Sharma, N. A survey on underwater image enhancement techniques. *Int. J. Comput. Appl.* **2014**, *87*, 19–23. [CrossRef]
76. Zhou, J.; Yang, T.; Zhang, W. Underwater vision enhancement technologies: A comprehensive review, challenges, and recent trends. *Appl. Intell.* **2023**, *53*, 3594–3621. [CrossRef]
77. Newcombe, R.A.; Lovegrove, S.J.; Davison, A.J. DTAM: Dense tracking and mapping in real-time. In Proceedings of the 2011 International Conference on Computer Vision, Barcelona, Spain, 6–13 November 2011; pp. 2320–2327.
78. Engel, J.; Koltun, V.; Cremers, D. Direct sparse odometry. *IEEE Trans. Pattern Anal. Mach. Intell.* **2017**, *40*, 611–625. [CrossRef]
79. Bruno, H.M.S.; Colombini, E.L. LIFT-SLAM: A deep-learning feature-based monocular visual SLAM method. *Neurocomputing* **2021**, *455*, 97–110. [CrossRef]
80. Zhou, Z.; Fan, X.; Shi, P.; Xin, Y. R-MSFM: Recurrent multi-scale feature modulation for monocular depth estimating. In Proceedings of the IEEE/CVF International Conference on Computer Vision, Montreal, QC, Canada, 10–17 October 2021; pp. 12777–12786.
81. Fan, X.; Zhou, Z.; Shi, P.; Xin, Y.; Zhou, X. RAFM: Recurrent atrous feature modulation for accurate monocular depth estimating. *IEEE Signal Process. Lett.* **2022**, *29*, 1609–1613. [CrossRef]
82. Wang, R.; Pizer, S.M.; Frahm, J.M. Recurrent neural network for (un-) supervised learning of monocular video visual odometry and depth. In Proceedings of the IEEE/CVF Conference on Computer Vision and Pattern Recognition, Long Beach, CA, USA, 15 April 2019; pp. 5555–5564.

83. Wagstaff, B.; Peretroukhin, V.; Kelly, J. Self-supervised deep pose corrections for robust visual odometry. In Proceedings of the 2020 IEEE International Conference on Robotics and Automation (ICRA), Paris, France, 31 May–31 August 2020; pp. 2331–2337.
84. Teixeira, B.; Silva, H.; Matos, A.; Silva, E. Deep learning for underwater visual odometry estimation. *IEEE Access* **2020**, *8*, 44687–44701. [CrossRef]
85. Wang, K.; Ma, S.; Chen, J.; Ren, F.; Lu, J. Approaches, challenges, and applications for deep visual odometry: Toward complicated and emerging areas. *IEEE Trans. Cogn. Dev. Syst.* **2020**, *14*, 35–49. [CrossRef]
86. Wirth, S.; Carrasco, P.L.N.; Codina, G.O. Visual odometry for autonomous underwater vehicles. In Proceedings of the 2013 MTS/IEEE OCEANS-Bergen, Bergen, Norway, 10–14 June 2013; pp. 1–6.
87. Triggs, B.; McLauchlan, P.F.; Hartley, R.I.; Fitzgibbon, A.W. Bundle adjustment—A modern synthesis. In Proceedings of the Vision Algorithms: Theory and Practice: International Workshop on Vision Algorithms, Corfu, Greece, 21–22 September 1999; Springer: Berlin/Heidelberg, Germany, 2000; pp. 298–372.
88. Qader, W.A.; Ameen, M.M.; Ahmed, B.I. An overview of bag of words; importance, implementation, applications, and challenges. In Proceedings of the 2019 International Engineering Conference (IEC), Erbil, Iraq, 23–25 June 2019; pp. 200–204.
89. Gálvez-López, D.; Tardos, J.D. Bags of binary words for fast place recognition in image sequences. *IEEE Trans. Robot.* **2012**, *28*, 1188–1197. [CrossRef]
90. Uijlings, J.R.; Smeulders, A.W.; Scha, R.J. Real-time bag of words, approximately. In Proceedings of the ACM International Conference on Image and Video Retrieval, New York, NY, USA, 8 July 2009; pp. 1–8.
91. Garcia-Fidalgo, E.; Ortiz, A. ibow-lcd: An appearance-based loop-closure detection approach using incremental bags of binary words. *IEEE Robot. Autom. Lett.* **2018**, *3*, 3051–3057. [CrossRef]
92. Bonin-Font, F.; Burguera Burguera, A. NetHALOC: A learned global image descriptor for loop closing in underwater visual SLAM. *Expert Syst.* **2021**, *38*, e12635. [CrossRef]
93. Memon, A.R.; Wang, H.; Hussain, A. Loop closure detection using supervised and unsupervised deep neural networks for monocular SLAM systems. *Robot. Auton. Syst.* **2020**, *126*, 103470. [CrossRef]
94. Hong, S.; Kim, J.; Pyo, J.; Yu, S.C. A robust loop-closure method for visual SLAM in unstructured seafloor environments. *Auton. Robot.* **2016**, *40*, 1095–1109. [CrossRef]
95. Cattaneo, D.; Vaghi, M.; Valada, A. Lcdnet: Deep loop closure detection and point cloud registration for lidar slam. *IEEE Trans. Robot.* **2022**, *38*, 2074–2093. [CrossRef]
96. Gao, X.; Zhang, T. Unsupervised learning to detect loops using deep neural networks for visual SLAM system. *Auton. Robot.* **2017**, *41*, 1–18. [CrossRef]
97. Merrill, N.; Huang, G. Lightweight unsupervised deep loop closure. *arXiv* **2018**, arXiv:1805.07703.
98. Williams, B.; Klein, G.; Reid, I. Automatic relocalization and loop closing for real-time monocular SLAM. *IEEE Trans. Pattern Anal. Mach. Intell.* **2011**, *33*, 1699–1712. [CrossRef]
99. Qin, T.; Li, P.; Shen, S. Relocalization, global optimization and map merging for monocular visual-inertial SLAM. In Proceedings of the 2018 IEEE International Conference on Robotics and Automation (ICRA), Brisbane, QLD, Australia, 21–25 May 2018; pp. 1197–1204.
100. Blochliger, F.; Fehr, M.; Dymczyk, M.; Schneider, T.; Siegwart, R. Topomap: Topological mapping and navigation based on visual slam maps. In Proceedings of the 2018 IEEE International Conference on Robotics and Automation (ICRA), Brisbane, QLD, Australia, 21–25 May 2018; pp. 3818–3825.
101. Choset, H.; Nagatani, K. Topological simultaneous localization and mapping (SLAM): Toward exact localization without explicit localization. *IEEE Trans. Robot. Autom.* **2001**, *17*, 125–137. [CrossRef]
102. Chen, Q.; Lu, Y.; Wang, Y.; Zhu, B. From topological map to local cognitive map: A new opportunity of local path planning. *Intell. Serv. Robot.* **2021**, *14*, 285–301. [CrossRef]
103. Thoma, J.; Paudel, D.P.; Chhatkuli, A.; Probst, T.; Gool, L.V. Mapping, localization and path planning for image-based navigation using visual features and map. In Proceedings of the IEEE/CVF Conference on Computer Vision and Pattern Recognition, Long Beach, CA, USA, 15–20 June 2019; pp. 7383–7391.
104. Cheng, W.; Yang, S.; Zhou, M.; Liu, Z.; Chen, Y.; Li, M. Road mapping and localization using sparse semantic visual features. *IEEE Robot. Autom. Lett.* **2021**, *6*, 8118–8125. [CrossRef]
105. Li, J.; Zhan, J.; Zhou, T.; Bento, V.A.; Wang, Q. Point cloud registration and localization based on voxel plane features. *ISPRS J. Photogramm. Remote. Sens.* **2022**, *188*, 363–379. [CrossRef]
106. Nüchter, A.; Hertzberg, J. Towards semantic maps for mobile robots. *Robot. Auton. Syst.* **2008**, *56*, 915–926. [CrossRef]
107. Han, L.; Lin, Y.; Du, G.; Lian, S. Deepvio: Self-supervised deep learning of monocular visual inertial odometry using 3d geometric constraints. In Proceedings of the 2019 IEEE/RSJ International Conference on Intelligent Robots and Systems (IROS), Macau, China, 3–8 November 2019; pp. 6906–6913.
108. Almalioglu, Y.; Turan, M.; Saputra, M.R.U.; de Gusmão, P.P.; Markham, A.; Trigoni, N. SelfVIO: Self-supervised deep monocular Visual–Inertial Odometry and depth estimation. *Neural Netw.* **2022**, *150*, 119–136. [CrossRef]
109. Silveira, L.; Guth, F.; Drews, P., Jr.; Ballester, P.; Machado, M.; Codevilla, F.; Duarte-Filho, N.; Botelho, S. An open-source bio-inspired solution to underwater SLAM. *IFAC-PapersOnLine* **2015**, *48*, 212–217. [CrossRef]
110. Yuan, X.; Martínez-Ortega, J.F.; Fernández, J.A.S.; Eckert, M. AEKF-SLAM: A new algorithm for robotic underwater navigation. *Sensors* **2017**, *17*, 1174. [CrossRef]

111. Kim, A.; Eustice, R.M. Real-time visual SLAM for autonomous underwater hull inspection using visual saliency. *IEEE Trans. Robot.* **2013**, *29*, 719–733. [CrossRef]
112. Felemban, E.; Shaikh, F.K.; Qureshi, U.M.; Sheikh, A.A.; Qaisar, S.B. Underwater sensor network applications: A comprehensive survey. *Int. J. Distrib. Sens. Netw.* **2015**, *11*, 896832. [CrossRef]
113. Köser, K.; Frese, U. Challenges in underwater visual navigation and SLAM. *AI Technol. Underw. Robot.* **2020**, *96*, 125–135.
114. Amarasinghe, C.; Ratnaweera, A.; Maitripala, S. Monocular visual slam for underwater navigation in turbid and dynamic environments. *Am. J. Mech. Eng.* **2020**, *8*, 76–87. [CrossRef]
115. Guth, F.; Silveira, L.; Botelho, S.; Drews, P.; Ballester, P. Underwater SLAM: Challenges, state of the art, algorithms and a new biologically-inspired approach. In Proceedings of the 5th IEEE RAS/EMBS International Conference on Biomedical Robotics and Biomechatronics, Sao Paulo, Brazil, 12–15 August 2014; pp. 981–986.
116. Muhammad, N.; Strokina, N.; Toming, G.; Tuhtan, J.; Kämäräinen, J.K.; Kruusmaa, M. Flow feature extraction for underwater robot localization: Preliminary results. In Proceedings of the 2015 IEEE International Conference on Robotics and Automation (ICRA), Seattle, WA, USA, 26–30 May 2015; pp. 1125–1130.
117. Cong, Y.; Gu, C.; Zhang, T.; Gao, Y. Underwater robot sensing technology: A survey. *Fundam. Res.* **2021**, *1*, 337–345. [CrossRef]
118. Negre, P.L.; Bonin-Font, F.; Oliver, G. Cluster-based loop closing detection for underwater slam in feature-poor regions. In Proceedings of the 2016 IEEE International Conference on Robotics and Automation (ICRA), Stockholm, Sweden, 16–21 May 2016; pp. 2589–2595.
119. Hu, M.; Li, S.; Wu, J.; Guo, J.; Li, H.; Kang, X. Loop closure detection for visual SLAM fusing semantic information. In Proceedings of the 2019 Chinese Control Conference (CCC), Guangzhou, China, 27–30 July 2019; pp. 4136–4141.
120. Mukherjee, A.; Chakraborty, S.; Saha, S.K. Detection of loop closure in SLAM: A DeconvNet based approach. *Appl. Soft Comput.* **2019**, *80*, 650–656. [CrossRef]
121. Techy, L.; Morganseny, K.A.; Woolseyz, C.A. Long-baseline acoustic localization of the Seaglider underwater glider. In Proceedings of the 2011 American Control Conference, San Francisco, CA, USA, 29 June–1 July 2011; pp. 3990–3995.
122. Duarte, A.C.; Zaffari, G.B.; da Rosa, R.T.S.; Longaray, L.M.; Drews, P.; Botelho, S.S. Towards comparison of underwater SLAM methods: An open dataset collection. In Proceedings of the OCEANS 2016 MTS/IEEE Monterey, Monterey, CA, USA, 19–23 September 2016; pp. 1–5.
123. Mallios, A.; Vidal, E.; Campos, R.; Carreras, M. Underwater caves sonar data set. *Int. J. Robot. Res.* **2017**, *36*, 1247–1251. [CrossRef]
124. Rahman, S.; Karapetyan, N.; Li, A.Q.; Rekleitis, I. A modular sensor suite for underwater reconstruction. In Proceedings of the OCEANS 2018 MTS/IEEE Charleston, Charleston, SC, USA, 22–25 October 2018; pp. 1–6.
125. Ferrera, M.; Creuze, V.; Moras, J.; Trouvé-Peloux, P. AQUALOC: An underwater dataset for visual–inertial–pressure localization. *Int. J. Robot. Res.* **2019**, *38*, 1549–1559. [CrossRef]
126. Zwilgmeyer, P.G.O.; Yip, M.; Teigen, A.L.; Mester, R.; Stahl, A. The varos synthetic underwater data set: Towards realistic multi-sensor underwater data with ground truth. In Proceedings of the IEEE/CVF International Conference on Computer Vision, Montreal, BC, Canada, 11–17 October 2021; pp. 3722–3730.
127. Krasnosky, K.; Roman, C.; Casagrande, D. A bathymetric mapping and SLAM dataset with high-precision ground truth for marine robotics. *Int. J. Robot. Res.* **2022**, *41*, 12–19. [CrossRef]
128. Song, C.; Zeng, B.; Su, T.; Zhang, K.; Cheng, J. Data association and loop closure in semantic dynamic SLAM using the table retrieval method. *Appl. Intell.* **2022**, *52*, 11472–11488. [CrossRef]
129. Cieslewski, T.; Choudhary, S.; Scaramuzza, D. Data-efficient decentralized visual SLAM. In Proceedings of the 2018 IEEE International Conference on Robotics and Automation (ICRA), Brisbane, QLD, Australia, 21–25 May 2018; pp. 2466–2473.
130. Carreno, Y.; Willners, J.S.; Petillot, Y.; Petrick, R.P. Situation-Aware Task Planning for Robust AUV Exploration in Extreme Environments. In Proceedings of the IJCAI Workshop on Robust and Reliable Autonomy in the Wild, Montreal, QC, Canada, 19 August 2021.
131. Watson, S.; Duecker, D.A.; Groves, K. Localisation of unmanned underwater vehicles (UUVs) in complex and confined environments: A review. *Sensors* **2020**, *20*, 6203. [CrossRef]
132. Aitken, J.M.; Evans, M.H.; Worley, R.; Edwards, S.; Zhang, R.; Dodd, T.; Mihaylova, L.; Anderson, S.R. Simultaneous localization and mapping for inspection robots in water and sewer pipe networks: A review. *IEEE Access* **2021**, *9*, 140173–140198. [CrossRef]
133. Xiao, L.; Wang, J.; Qiu, X.; Rong, Z.; Zou, X. Dynamic-SLAM: Semantic monocular visual localization and mapping based on deep learning in dynamic environment. *Robot. Auton. Syst.* **2019**, *117*, 1–16. [CrossRef]
134. Sun, Y.; Liu, M.; Meng, M.Q.H. Improving RGB-D SLAM in dynamic environments: A motion removal approach. *Robot. Auton. Syst.* **2017**, *89*, 110–122. [CrossRef]
135. Ni, J.; Wang, X.; Gong, T.; Xie, Y. An improved adaptive ORB-SLAM method for monocular vision robot under dynamic environments. *Int. J. Mach. Learn. Cybern.* **2022**, *13*, 3821–3836. [CrossRef]
136. Chen, C.; Wang, B.; Lu, C.X.; Trigoni, N.; Markham, A. A survey on deep learning for localization and mapping: Towards the age of spatial machine intelligence. *arXiv* **2020**, arXiv:2006.12567.
137. Yu, C.; Liu, Z.; Liu, X.J.; Xie, F.; Yang, Y.; Wei, Q.; Fei, Q. DS-SLAM: A semantic visual SLAM towards dynamic environments. In Proceedings of the 2018 IEEE/RSJ International Conference on Intelligent Robots and Systems (IROS), Madrid, Spain, 1–5 October 2018; pp. 1168–1174.

138. Himri, K.; Ridao, P.; Gracias, N.; Palomer, A.; Palomeras, N.; Pi, R. Semantic SLAM for an AUV using object recognition from point clouds. *IFAC-PapersOnLine* **2018**, *51*, 360–365. [CrossRef]
139. Wen, S.; Li, P.; Zhao, Y.; Zhang, H.; Sun, F.; Wang, Z. Semantic visual SLAM in dynamic environment. *Auton. Robot.* **2021**, *45*, 493–504. [CrossRef]
140. Chang, Y.; Ebadi, K.; Denniston, C.E.; Ginting, M.F.; Rosinol, A.; Reinke, A.; Palieri, M.; Shi, J.; Chatterjee, A.; Morrell, B.; et al. LAMP 2.0: A robust multi-robot SLAM system for operation in challenging large-scale underground environments. *IEEE Robot. Autom. Lett.* **2022**, *7*, 9175–9182. [CrossRef]
141. Pire, T.; Baravalle, R.; D'alessandro, A.; Civera, J. Real-time dense map fusion for stereo SLAM. *Robotica* **2018**, *36*, 1510–1526. [CrossRef]
142. Paull, L.; Huang, G.; Seto, M.; Leonard, J.J. Communication-constrained multi-AUV cooperative SLAM. In Proceedings of the 2015 IEEE international conference on robotics and automation (ICRA), Seattle, WA, USA, 26–30 May 2015; pp. 509–516.
143. Ji, P.; Li, X.; Gao, W.; Li, M. A Vision Based Multi-robot Cooperative Semantic SLAM Algorithm. In Proceedings of the 2022 34th Chinese Control and Decision Conference (CCDC), Hefei, China, 15–17 August 2022; pp. 5663–5668.

Journal of
Marine Science and Engineering

MDPI

Article

An Improved YOLOv5s-Based Scheme for Target Detection in a Complex Underwater Environment

Chenglong Hou [1], Zhiguang Guan [1,*], Ziyi Guo [1], Siqi Zhou [1] and Mingxing Lin [2]

[1] Shandong Provincial Engineering Lab of Traffic Construction Equipment and Intelligent Control, Shandong Jiaotong University, Jinan 250357, China; 21106009@stu.sdjtu.edu.cn (C.H.); zyg_sddy@163.com (Z.G.); 21106011@stu.sdjtu.edu.cn (S.Z.)
[2] School of Mechanical Engineering, Shandong University, Jinan 250061, China; mxlin@sdu.edu.cn
* Correspondence: guanzhiguang@sdjtu.edu.cn

Abstract: At present, sea cucumbers, sea urchins, and other seafood products have become increasingly significant in the seafood aquaculture industry. In traditional fishing operations, divers go underwater for fishing, and the complex underwater environment can cause harm to the divers' bodies. Therefore, the use of underwater robots for seafood fishing has become a current trend. During the fishing process, underwater fishing robots rely on vision to accurately detect sea cucumbers and sea urchins. In this paper, an algorithm for the target detection of sea cucumbers and sea urchins in complex underwater environments is proposed based on the improved YOLOv5s. The following improvements are mainly carried out in YOLOv5s: (1) To enhance the feature extraction ability of the model, the g^nConv-based self-attentive sublayer HorBlock module is proposed to be added to the backbone network. (2) To obtain the optimal hyperparameters of the model for underwater datasets, hyperparameter evolution based on the genetic algorithm is proposed. (3) The underwater dataset is extended using offline data augmentation. The dataset used in the experiment is created in a real underwater environment. The total number of created datasets is 1536, and the training, validation, and test sets are randomly divided according to the ratio of 7:2:1. The divided dataset is input to the improved YOLOv5s network for training. The experiment shows that the mean average precision (mAP) of the algorithm is 94%, and the mAP of the improved YOLOv5s model rises by 4.5% compared to the original YOLOv5s. The detection speed increases by 4.09 ms, which is in the acceptable range compared to the accuracy improvement. Therefore, the improved YOLOv5s has better detection accuracy and speed in complex underwater environments, and can provide theoretical support for the underwater operations of underwater fishing robots.

Keywords: underwater target detection; improved YOLOv5; g^nConv; HorBlock; hyperparameter evolution; data augmentation

Citation: Hou, C.; Guan, Z.; Guo, Z.; Zhou, S.; Lin, M. An Improved YOLOv5s-Based Scheme for Target Detection in a Complex Underwater Environment. *J. Mar. Sci. Eng.* **2023**, *11*, 1041. https://doi.org/10.3390/jmse11051041

Academic Editor: Sergei Chernyi

Received: 14 April 2023
Revised: 1 May 2023
Accepted: 11 May 2023
Published: 13 May 2023

1. Introduction

In traditional aquaculture, high nutritional seafood, such as sea cucumbers and sea urchins, has been loved by fishers. Unlike land plants, sea cucumbers and sea urchins live on underwater reefs at depths of 12 13 m. The traditional fishing method mainly relies on two methods, netting and underwater fishing by divers [1]. Although netting can greatly reduce the cost of fishing, it will cause serious damage to the ecological environment of the seafloor in the long term. Manual fishing can avoid damage to the seafloor ecological environment, but the cost of manual fishing is relatively high. Therefore, the research on underwater fishing robots has greatly promoted the development of underwater aquaculture industry [2,3]. In order to realize the automation of underwater robots for sea cucumber and sea urchin fishing operations, the target detection of sea cucumber and sea urchin is especially important.

Underwater imaging quality is poor due to the complex underwater environment that are susceptible to light and other factors [4]. The current detection for sea cucumbers and sea urchins is mainly optimized in two aspects: on the one hand, the target detection network is optimized to enhance the extraction of underwater image features; on the other hand, image enhancement algorithms are used to improve the quality of underwater images and make the features of underwater images more obvious [5]. In this paper, the target detection network is optimized by enhancing the model's ability to extract features from underwater images, so as to achieve the accurate detection of sea cucumber and sea urchin in complex underwater environments. Currently, some researchers are applying the target detection framework based on convolutional neural networks (CNNs) to the underwater aquaculture industry, which plays an important role in the identification, monitoring, and fishing of underwater seafood [6]. Algorithms on underwater target detection have also been developed; Chen et al. [7] proposed a RetinaNet-based target detection algorithm for underwater robot, which uses Dense Net instead of ResNet to build a backbone network, and uses convolutional layer stacking instead of the original single convolutional operation to reduce the weight of the network. Qiang et al. [8] proposed an improved single shot multibox detector (SSD) target detection algorithm using ResNet instead of the VGG convolutional neural network of SSD, which led to a large improvement in the accuracy of the algorithm. Deng et al. [9] proposed a marine organism detection algorithm based on the improved SSD algorithm, in which a feature fusion module and a feature augmentation module were designed. The algorithm improves the overall detection accuracy of the algorithm for marine organism targets with only a small increase in computation and number of parameters. Wang et al. [10] proposed an underwater target image edge detection algorithm based on ant colony optimization and reinforcement learning, which can effectively extract underwater contour information, better maintain image texture, and has ideal anti-interference performance. Guo et al. [11] proposed an underwater target detection and localization method using feature maps and CNN-based classification, which is superior in underwater signal classification and target localization. Zeng et al. [12] proposed an underwater target detection based on Faster R-CNN and adversarial occlusion network, which can obtain better robustness for underwater seafood.

Currently, deep learning-based targets detection algorithms are mainly divided into one-stage algorithm and two-stage algorithm. The representative algorithms of one-stage are: OverFeat, YOLO series algorithm, SSD and RetinaNet, etc. The images inputting to the network enters directly into the convolutional neural network, and the features can be extracted to predict the classification and location of objects. Two-stage algorithms include: R-CNN, SPP-Net, Fast R-CNN, Faster R-CNN and R-FCN, etc. Two-stage algorithms are characterized by taking the input image and performing candidate region proposal (RP) before classifying it by convolutional neural network. This feature can make the accuracy of the network improve, but due to the feature extraction of the candidate region, it will make the detection speed of the network drop greatly and cannot meet the real-time detection requirements. In underwater target detection, one-stage algorithms are widely used mainly because of its fast detection speed and relatively high detection accuracy. In the YOLO series algorithm, Li et al. [13] proposed an improved YOLOv3ST model, embedded two attention mechanisms, and proposed a K-means clustering algorithm to adapt to multi-scale feature prediction to improve underwater small target detection accuracy. Guo et al. [14] proposed a fast detection scheme for marine organisms based on an improved MSRCP image augmentation algorithm. Zhang et al. [15] proposed a lightweight underwater target detection method based on MobileNetV2, YOLOv4 [16] algorithm and attentional feature fusion. Chen et al. [17] proposed an improved YOLOv4 for detecting underwater targets by replacing the up-sampling module with a deconvolution module and incorporating depth-separable convolution into the network. Li et al. [18] proposed an improved YOLOv5s underwater scallop recognition algorithm, mainly using the group convolution and inverse residual modules instead of the backbone network. The mAP was able to reach 88.2%. Li et al. [19] proposed an improved YOLOv5 based on adding triplet attention and multi-scale detection to meet the shortcomings existing for small target detection. Li et al. [20]

proposed an improved CME-YOLOv5 network to detect fish and small targets in dense groups, and the algorithm showed good detection performance when applied to densely distributed fish and small targets. Currently, the YOLO series algorithms have been applied to the detection of underwater targets. YOLOv5 has smaller trained weight files, faster detection, and higher mAP compared to YOLOv3, YOLOv4 and other models [21]. However, due to the poor imaging quality of the underwater dataset, the original YOLOv5 model did not achieve the ideal results in the target detection process [22].

Therefore, in order to accurately and quickly identify sea cucumbers and sea urchins in the complex environment underwater, an improved YOLOv5s underwater target detection algorithm is proposed to complete underwater fishing operations more effectively. The research content and innovation are mainly in the following aspects: (1) For the underwater dataset with inconspicuous image features, the backbone network of YOLOv5s is improved so that its ability to extract image features is enhanced, thus improving the recall of sea cucumbers and sea urchins. (2) For the accuracy problem of model training, the hyperparameters controlling the model training are optimized by using genetic algorithm, so as to improve the accuracy of model training. (3) For the overfitting phenomenon of model training caused by the lack of underwater datasets, offline data augmentation is performed on the datasets, which can effectively improve the generalization ability of the model.

2. Materials and Methods

2.1. Dataset Creation

The dataset used in the experiment is from the Zhanjiang Underwater Robotics Competition URPC2021 Underwater Optics Competition dataset. The dataset uses two of the categories: sea cucumbers and sea urchins. The images of the dataset are obtained from videos taken by underwater robots in real underwater environments. The image resolutions are 720 × 405 and 400 × 300 pixels. The selected dataset includes 1536 images in total, and the training set, validation set and test set are randomly divided at the ratio of 7:2:1. After the division is completed, the annotation information, category ratio and size distribution are counted again to ensure that the distributions of training set, validation set and test set are similar. In the process of dataset labelling, the Labelimg software with version number 1.8.6 was used to manually label sea cucumbers and sea urchins with rectangular boxes, and finally the labelling file in YOLO format was obtained. The labeling process of the Labelimg software is shown in Figure 1.

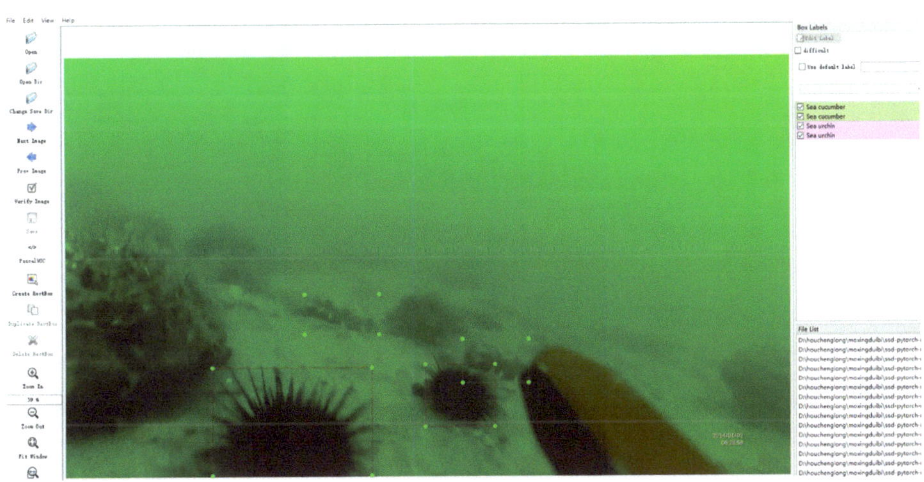

Figure 1. The Labelimg software labeling process.

There are two types of data augmentation: one is offline data augmentation and the other is online data augmentation. In order to improve the generalization ability of the model, online data augmentation and offline data augmentation are used in the dataset. The online data augmentation used in this paper is Mosaic data augmentation, which is mainly used to generate a new image by stitching four randomly selected images into one image with a random size ratio. The advantage of this operation is not only to increase the richness of the image itself, but also to increase the number of samples. Mosaic data augmentation is shown in Figure 2.

Figure 2. Mosaic data augmentation.

The offline data augmentation is performed by randomly translating, flipping, cropping and rotating each image in several ways at random combinations. An image generated after offline augmentation is shown in Figure 3. After the offline data augmentation, the training set, the validation set and test set are respectively increased by 4196, 1245 and 623 images. Meanwhile, the number of datasets samples before and after offline data augmentation and the number of category labels are shown in Table 1. After the dataset augmentation is completed, the dataset needs to be manually labelled.

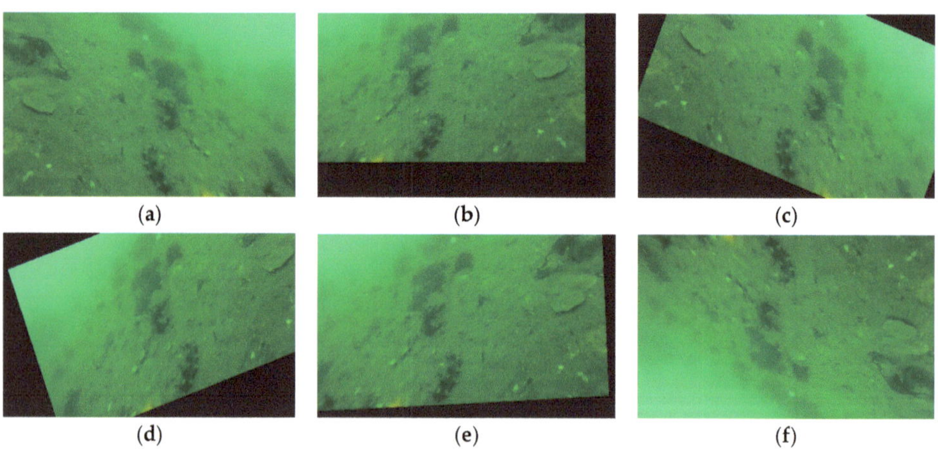

Figure 3. Image offline data augmentation: (**a**) Original image; (**b**) Translate + horizontal flip; (**c**) Translate + rotate; (**d**) Horizontal flip + rotate + translate; (**e**) Rotate (**f**) Vertical flip.

Table 1. Number of data set labels.

Category	Dataset		
	Training set (Original/Augmentation)	Validation set (Original/Augmentation)	Test set (Original/Augmentation)
Sea Cucumber	2771/15774	801/4482	446/2276
Sea Urchin	4403/22374	1339/6918	644/3016

2.2. *YOLOv5 Target Detection Algorithm*

YOLOv5 target detection is a regression-based algorithm in the one-stage algorithm. When the image is input into the network, it goes directly into the convolutional neural network for feature extraction, and in the output layer, the object classification and location regression prediction is carried out. In this paper, the newer version 6.1 of YOLOv5 is used. For ensuring the detection accuracy, the lightweight version of the model is also fully considered; YOLOv5s is selected for training in the experiment. The YOLOv5s network structure is shown in Figure 4.

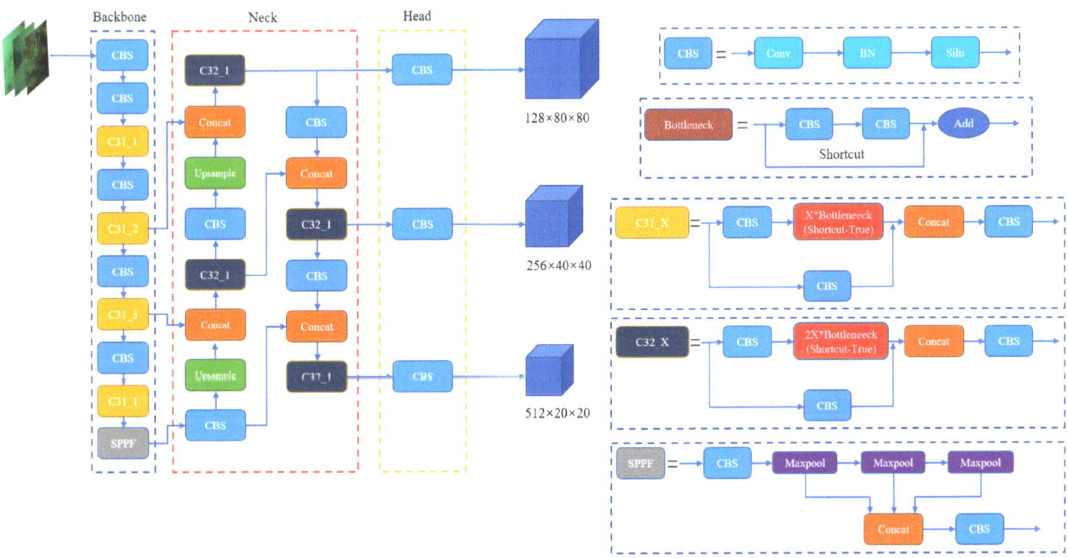

Figure 4. YOLOv5s network structure.

The network structure of YOLOv5s is mainly composed of the backbone, neck, head and detect, whose structural components and features are as follows:

(1) The backbone is the feature extraction network of YOLOv5s, which is mainly composed of the convolutional module, C3 module and SPPF module [23]. When the image enters the network, it goes through these modules for feature extraction, respectively, and the extracted features can be called the effective feature layer, which contains the feature information of the image.

(2) The neck is an enhanced feature extraction network composed of FPN, which mainly fuses features from three effective feature layers of different scales in the backbone part. The fusion process is mainly upward and downward fusion in the form of feature pyramids. At the same time, YOLOv5s uses down-sampling for large-scale effective feature layers, and fuses the features with other scale effective feature layers, which greatly preserves the semantic features of the images.

(3) The head performs the classification and regression of network prediction. CIoU loss [24] is applied to compute the loss in training process. At the same time, the generated multiple prediction bounding boxes are suppressed away by non-maximal suppression to obtain a most accurate prediction bounding box.

The YOLOv5 target detection algorithm can achieve a relatively high mAP for target detection of land-based clear datasets. However, target detection of underwater datasets still needs to be optimized to recognize sea cucumbers and sea urchins easily. When optimizing the target detection algorithm, the main focus is to improve the accuracy of the algorithm in the underwater environment. Moreover, the detection speed of the algorithm should be ensured.

2.3. Improved YOLOv5s Network Design

The backbone is mainly improved in the YOLOv5s network, which is used to extract features from the images of sea cucumbers and sea urchins. In this paper, the HorBlock module is added after each C3 module. The HorBlock module is a self-attentive sub-layer based on g^nConv to achieve an arbitrary order of priority complexity exchanges. The improved YOLOv5s backbone improves the feature extraction ability for sea cucumbers and sea urchins. The structure diagram of the improved YOLOv5s network is shown in Figure 5. Meanwhile, the hyperparameters are optimized using a genetic algorithm, and the original hyperparameters of YOLOv5s are evolutionary transferred based on the COCO dataset. The experiment uses the evolved hyperparameters based on the improved network model to obtain the optimal hyperparameters, which can effectively improve the recognition accuracy of the network. In YOLOv5s version 6.1, three scales feature maps are output in the head: 20 × 20, 40 × 40 and 80 × 80. Sea cucumbers and sea urchins appear larger in the image when they are closer to the lens. In this case, the 20 × 20 scale is used to predict the larger objects in the image. However, sea cucumbers and sea urchins appear smaller in the image when they are further from the lens; 40 × 40 and 80 × 80 scales are used to predict medium and small-sized objects in the image. The parameters of the improved YOLOv5s network are shown in Table 2.

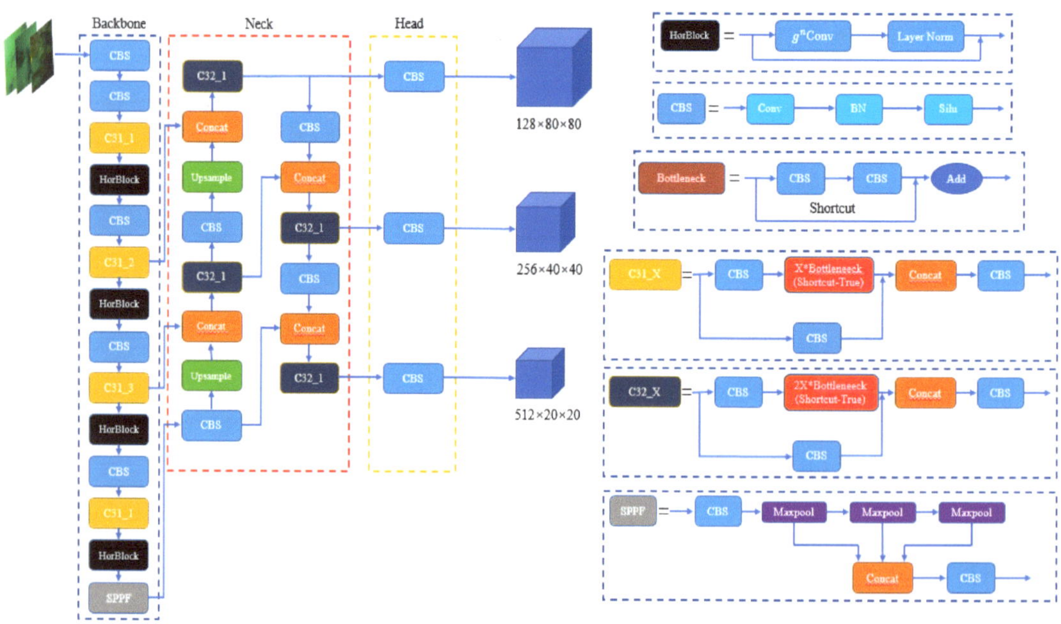

Figure 5. Improved YOLOv5s network structure.

Table 2. Improved YOLOv5s network parameters.

Layer Number	Network Layer	Input Dimension	Stride
0	Conv 6 × 6	3 × 640 × 640	2
1	Conv 3 × 3	32 × 320 × 320	2
2	C3	64 × 160 × 160	-
3	HorBlock	64 × 160 × 160	-
4	Conv 3 × 3	64 × 160 × 160	2
5	C3	128 × 80 × 80	-
6	HorBlock	128 × 80 × 80	-
7	Conv 3 × 3	128 × 80 × 80	2
8	C3	256 × 40 × 40	-
9	HorBlock	256 × 40 × 40	-
10	Conv 3 × 3	256 × 40 × 40	2
11	C3	512 × 20 × 20	-
12	HorBlock	512 × 20 × 20	-
13	SPPF	512 × 20 × 20	-
14	Conv 1 × 1	512 × 20 × 20	1
15	nn.Upsample	256 × 20 × 20	-
16	Concat	256 × 40 × 40	-
17	C3	512 × 40 × 40	-
18	Conv 1 × 1	512 × 40 × 40	1
19	nn.Upsample	128 × 40 × 40	-
20	Concat	128 × 80 × 80	-
21	C3	256 × 80 × 80	-
22	Conv 3 × 3	128 × 80 × 80	2
23	Concat	128 × 40 × 40	-
24	C3	256 × 40 × 40	-
25	Conv 3 × 3	256 × 40 × 40	2
26	Concat	256 × 20 × 20	-
27	C3	512 × 20 × 20	-
28	Detect	128 × 80 × 80 256 × 40 × 40 512 × 20 × 20	-

2.3.1. Self-Attentive Sub-Layer HorBlock Based on g^nConv

Due to the complex environment underwater, some sea cucumbers and sea urchins cannot be recognized effectively, and there are problems of missed detection and low accuracy. Therefore, in order to solve this problem, the HorBlock module, which is a self-attention sub-layer based on g^nConv, is added to the YOLOv5s model. Its main purpose is to improve the recognition accuracy of sea cucumbers and sea urchins, and reduce the influence of the surrounding environment. The g^nConv used in the HorBlock module is designed to perform higher-order spatial interactions through gated convolution and recursion. It is highly flexible, customizable and compatible, and able to extend second-order interactions in self-attentiveness to arbitrary orders without much additional computation. The g^nConv can be used as a plug-and-play module to form an independent module or embedded in various convolution-based models. The g^nConv is built using standard convolution, linear projection, and element multiplication, whose basic operation is gated convolution ($gConv$). Let $t \in I^{H\times W\times C}$ be the input feature and the output of the gated convolution $y = gConv(t)$ can be written as [25]:

$$\left[b_0^{H\times W\times C},\ d_0^{H\times W\times C}\right] = \theta_{in}(t) \in I^{H\times W\times 2C} \tag{1}$$

$$y = \theta_{out}(f(d_0) \odot b_0) \in I^{H\times W\times C} \tag{2}$$

where, θ_{in}, θ_{out} are linear projection layers and f is the depth convolution. Note that $(f(d_0) \odot b_0)^{(i,c)} = \Sigma_{j\in\Omega}\, w^c_{i\to j} {d_0}^{(j,c)} {b_0}^{(i,c)}$, where, Ω_i is the local window centered on i and w

is the convolution weight of *f*. Thus, the above equation introduces the interaction between adjacent features $b_0^{(i)}$ and $d_0^{(i)}$ via element-wise multiplication. Since each $b_0^{(i)}$ interacts with its neighboring feature $d_0^{(i)}$ only once, the interaction in *gConv* is considered as a *1-order* interaction.

After implementing *1*-order spatial interactions with *gConv*, $g^n Conv$ is constructed by introducing higher-order interactions. First, a set of projection features b_0 and $\{d_m\}_{m=0}^{n-1}$ are obtained using θ_{in} [25]:

$$\left[b_0^{H\times W\times C_0}, d_0^{H\times W\times C_0}, \ldots, d_{n-1}^{H\times W\times C_{n-1}}\right] = \theta_{in}(t) \in I^{H\times W\times (C_0+\Sigma_{0\le m\le n-1} C_m)} \tag{3}$$

Then, perform the gated convolution recursively using [25]:

$$b_{\mathrm{m}+1} = f_m(d_m) \odot g_m(b_m)/\delta, \qquad m = 0,1\ldots,n-1 \tag{4}$$

where, they scale the output by *1/δ* to stabilize the training. $\{f_m\}$ are a set of depth-wise convolution layers, and $\{g_m\}$ are used to match the dimension in different orders [25]:

$$g_m = \begin{cases} Identity, & m = 0 \\ Linear(C_{m-1}, C_m), & 1 \le m \le n-1 \end{cases} \tag{5}$$

$$C_m = \frac{C}{2^{n-m-1}}, \qquad 0 \le m \le n-1 \tag{6}$$

C_m is the channel dimension, and finally, the last recursive output d_n is fed into the projection layer θ_{out} to obtain the result of $g^n Conv$.

In this paper, spatial modeling operations that are representative and perform different interaction sequences are compared, as shown in Figure 6, where the blue structure is a feature and the gray structure is the feature's adjacent region. Each spatial model individually shows the spatial interactions between the feature and the neighboring regions. (a) Standard convolutional operations do not explicitly consider spatial interactions. (b) Dynamic convolution introduces the SE module, which makes the weights dynamic and improves the modeling ability of convolution by adding channel interactions [26–28]. (c) The self-attentive operation performs second-order spatial interactions through two consecutive matrix multiplications [29]. (d) The $g^n Conv$ uses gated convolution and a recursive design to implement arbitrary-order spatial interactions [25].

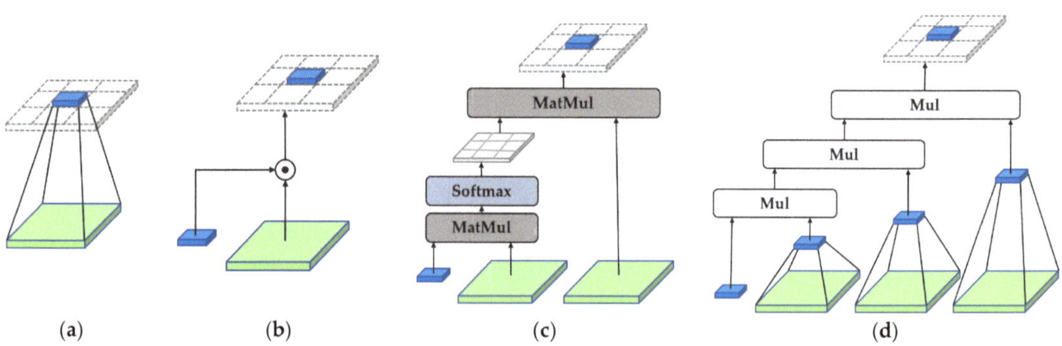

Figure 6. Representative spatial modeling operations performing different interaction sequences: (**a**) Standard convolutional operations; (**b**) Dynamic convolution operations; (**c**) Second-order spatial interaction operations; (**d**) Arbitrary-order space interaction operations.

The HorBlock constructed by combining the g^nConv module with Layer Norm is incorporated into the backbone network, which can enhance the network's performance by further extracting the input images features.

2.3.2. Hyperparametric Evolution Based on a Genetic Algorithm

Hyperparameter evolution uses a genetic algorithm for optimization [30]. During model training, hyperparameters control all aspects of model training. Having the best hyperparameters is important to the training outcome, but it is also a greater challenge. Due to the unknown correction between high-dimensional search space and the fitness of each point, traditional hyperparameter evolution methods such as grid searches are difficult to meet the requirements. Therefore, hyperparameter evolution based on a genetic algorithm is a better selection for hyperparameter optimization methods [31,32], which can obtain desired results.

There are 29 hyperparameters in YOLOv5s that regulate the training process. With such a large number of hyperparameters, the optimal solution for each parameter can be obtained using a genetic algorithm, and then can get the optimal hyperparameter results. For each hyperparameter in the training process, it can be considered as an independent variable x. The result obtained by performing network training is y. In YOLOv5s, seven results for representation are used. They are: "metrics/precision", "metrics/recall", "metrics/mAP 0.5", "metrics/mAP 0.5:0.95", "val/box loss", "val/obj loss" and "val/cls loss". At the same time, a fitness function needs to be defined to judge the effect of the input x. Fitness is the precision (P), recall (R), and the fraction-weighted sum of mAP 0.5 and mAP 0.5:0.95, independent of the loss part. For the variant x, after training, the result y is returned. If the calculated fitness is higher than the current one, the variant can be considered effective, and the parameters of the variant will be saved at this time. This experiment is set to mutate once every 50 epochs, 300 times in total. The one with the best mutation effect is selected as the final result of mutation. A comparison of the hyperparameter evolution results is shown in Table 3.

Table 3. Comparison of hyperparameter evolutionary results.

Parameter	lr0	lrf	Momentum	Weight Decay	Warmup Epochs	Warmup Momentum	Warmup Bias lr	Box	cls	cls pw
Original	0.001	0.01	0.937	0.0005	3.0	0.8	0.1	0.05	0.5	1.0
After Evolution	0.00886	0.01	0.85395	0.0004	3.0549	0.84169	0.06114	0.10873	0.2	1.0017
Parameter	**obj**	**obj pw**	**iou t**	**anchor t**	**fl gamma**	**hsv h**	**hsv s**	**hsv v**		**degrees**
Original	1.0	1.0	0.20	4.0	0.0	0.015	0.7	0.4		0.0
After Evolution	1.0651	0.75344	0.2	3.2016	0.0	0.01024	0.36303	0.18256		0.0
Parameter	**translate**	**scale**	**shear**	**perspective**	**flipud**	**fliplr**	**mosaic**	**mixup**	**copy paste**	**anchors**
Original	0.1	0.5	0.0	0.0	0.0	0.5	1.0	0.0	0.0	3
After Evolution	0.14064	0.39425	0.0	0.0	0.0	0.5	1.0	0.0	0.0	3.9496

The main genetic operator for hyperparametric evolution uses crossover and mutation. During the training process, it is the offspring created with 80% probability and 0.04 variance based on the best combination of parents from all previous generations. The results are saved separately for each time and for the highest fitness. Each hyperparameter is visualized in the evolutionary process, as shown in Figure 7. Each figure corresponds to a hyperparameter, where the x-axis represents the value of the hyperparameter and the y-axis represents fitness. The concentration of data points gradually decreases as the color changes from yellow to gray. The yellow color indicates a higher concentration of data points, while the vertical line indicates that a parameter has been fixed and will no longer be subject to further mutation.

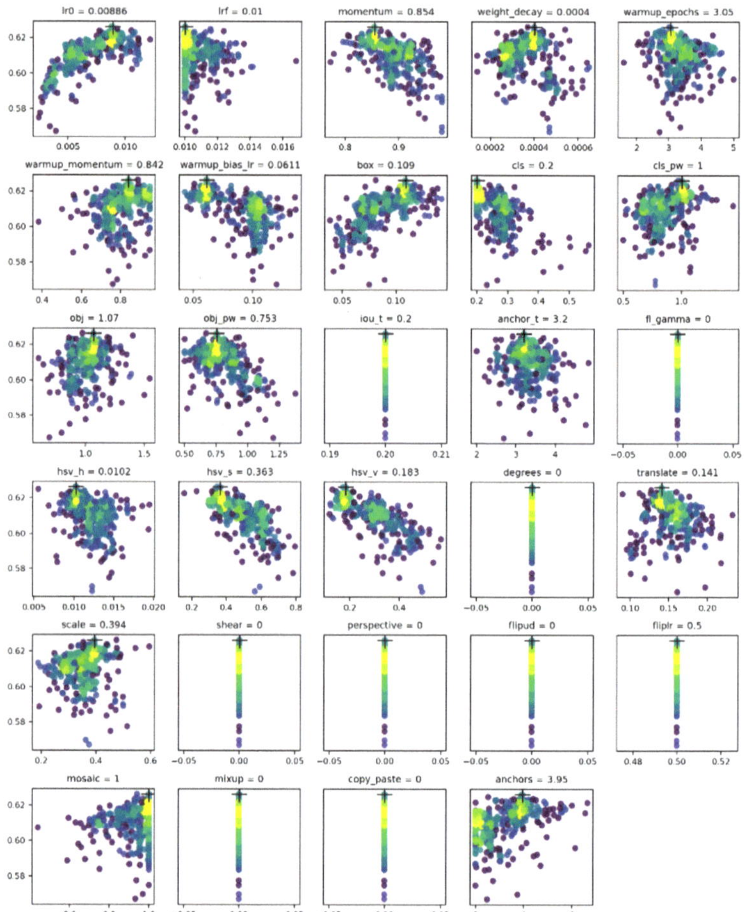

Figure 7. Visualization of the hyperparametric evolutionary process.

2.4. Evaluation Indicators

The loss function of YOLOv5s mainly consists of three components: bounding box regression loss, classification loss and objectness loss. The loss function is calculated as follows [33]:

$$L = L_{box} + L_{cls} + L_{obj} \tag{7}$$

where, L_{obj} is obtained by the CIoU loss function, and the CIoU calculation formula is as follows [33]:

$$L_{CIoU} = 1 - IoU + \frac{\rho^2(b,\ b^{gt})}{c^2} + av \tag{8}$$

$$a = \frac{v}{1 - IoU + v} \tag{9}$$

$$v = \frac{4}{\pi^2}(\arctan\frac{w^{gt}}{h^{gt}} - \arctan\frac{w}{h})^2 \tag{10}$$

where, $\rho^2(b, b^{gt})$ is the Euclidean distance between the real bounding box and the prediction bounding box. c is the length of the diagonal of the smallest outer rectangle of the real bounding box and the prediction bounding box. v is the distance between the aspect ratio of the real bounding box and the prediction bounding box. a is the weight coefficient. w is the width of the prediction bounding box. h is the height of the prediction bounding box. w^{gt} is the width of the real bounding box. h^{gt} is the height of the real bounding box.

In the classification loss, the loss is calculated via binary cross entropy, which is characterized by the fact that it is calculated only when the detected target is a positive sample. The bounding box regression loss is divided into two parts: loss with the target and loss without the target, which is different from the other two loss functions in that it is calculated regardless of positive or negative samples.

3. Results and Discussion

3.1. Model Training

The model training platform is achieved based on the Python 3.8 PyTorch 1.10 deep learning framework. The system environment is Windows 10, and training is performed using a GPU configured with CUDA version 11.1 and the neural network acceleration library cuDNN. The overall configuration of the training environment is shown in Table 4.

Table 4. Training environment configuration table.

Item	Parameter
Operating System	Windows 10
Central Processing Unit	Intel(R) Core(TM) i5-11400F
GPU	GeForce RTX 3090
Graphics Card Driver	CUDA 11.1
Software Environment	OpenCV-Python 4.5.5.62
Deep Learning Framework	PyTorch 1.10.2

All models are not loaded with pre-training weights during the training process. As the hyperparameter evolution based on the genetic algorithm is adopted, the default hyperparameters are no longer used in model training. The initial learning rate is 0.00886. At this learning rate, the model converges faster. As mAP continues to increase and the loss continues to decrease, the model reaches its optimal state finally. The weight decay coefficient is 0.0004, and the momentum factor is 0.85395. In the training, the batch size is 32, the optimizer uses Adam optimizer [34] and epochs are 200. The image sizes in the input network are resized to the default size of 640 $\times$ 640 pixels. The loss variation curves and mAP variation curves of the improved YOLOv5s model and the original YOLOv5s model are shown in Figure 8.

From the curve changes in the figure, it can be seen that the two models start to converge rapidly after 20 epochs, when the loss values start to decrease rapidly and the mAP rises rapidly. After 50 epochs, the loss and the mAP changes start to become smaller and tend to stabilize. From Figure 8a, the bounding box regression loss of the improved YOLOv5s model is higher than that before the improvement, but the convergence speed is better than that of the original model. Because the initial learning rate of the improved model is larger when using hyperparameter evolution, bounding box regression loss of the model becomes larger. From Figure 8b,c, the curves for classification loss and objectness loss are smoother and less volatile. In terms of the objectness loss, overfitting occurred for the original model during training, whereas the improved model can solve the overfitting. From Figure 8d, the improved YOLOv5s model has a higher mAP in the training process, and the convergence speed is also faster.

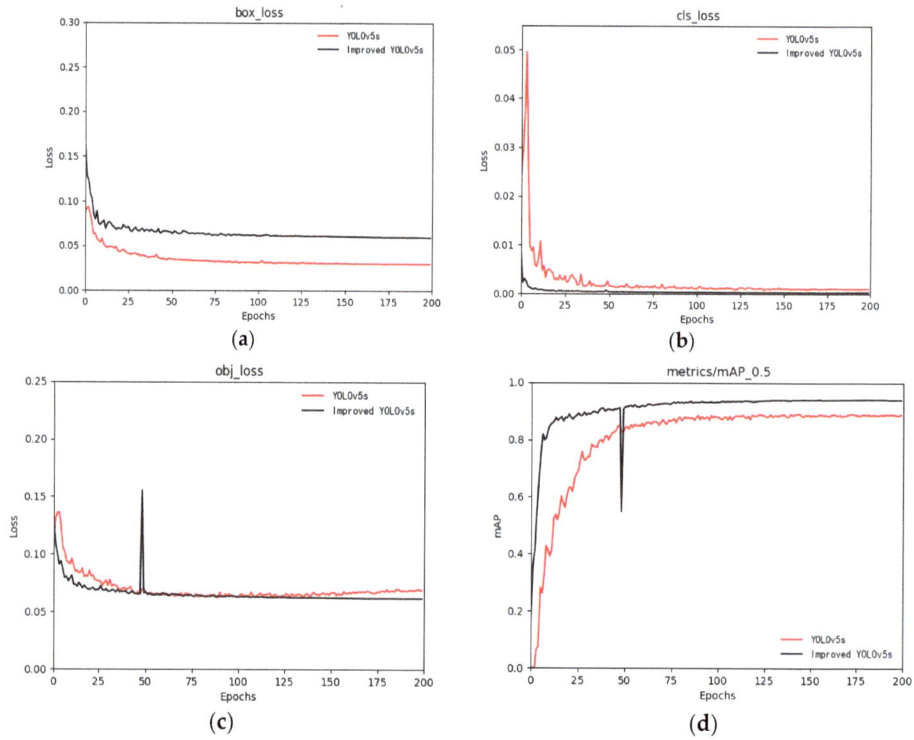

Figure 8. Loss and mAP variation curve: (**a**) Bounding box regression loss; (**b**) Classification loss; (**c**) Objectness loss; (**d**) mAP.

3.2. *Analysis of Results*

In this experiment, the average precision (AP), mAP and mean detection time will be used to evaluate the performance of the model. Their calculation equations are as follows [33]:

$$AP = \int_0^1 \frac{TP}{TP+FP} d\frac{TP}{TP+FN} \quad (11)$$

$$mAP = \frac{1}{N}\sum_{i=1}^{N} AP_i \quad (12)$$

where, TP is the number of cases where the true case is positive and the predicted outcome is positive. FP is the number of cases where the true case is negative and the predicted outcome is positive. FN is the number of cases where the true outcome is positive and the predicted outcome is negative.

3.2.1. Analysis of Ablation Experiments

Ablation experiments are carried out for different improvements of the improved YOLOv5s of the same dataset, which can get the impact of the fusion of self-attentive sub-layer HorBlock, hyperparameter evolution and offline data augmentation on the accuracy of the model. The comparison results are shown in Table 5.

Table 5. Comparison results of ablation experiments.

HorBlock	Hyperparametric Evolution	Offline Data Augmentation	mAP/%	Parameters/M	Average Detection Time/ms
			89.5	7.02	7.09
√			90.4	11.19	14.09
√	√		91.5	11.20	11.54
√	√	√	94.0	11.20	11.18

According to the data in Table 5, after adding the HorBlock module, the mAP of the improved YOLOv5s increases by 0.9% compared with the original YOLOv5s, which indicates that the network pays more attention to sea cucumbers and sea urchins and reduces the influence of useless features. While using the hyperparameter evolution, the mAP increases by 1.1%, which indicates that the adjustment of hyperparameters can help the network obtain a better result in the training process. The mAP increases by 2.5% with offline data augmentation, which indicates that the original samples are relatively not rich enough. The use of data augmentation can greatly enrich the samples and improve the generalization ability of the model. The final detection accuracy of the model increases by 4.5% compared with the original YOLOv5s. Therefore, the model is able to meet the experimental requirements in terms of the detection accuracy. The experimental result also shows that parameters in the improved YOLOv5s increases by 4.18 M compared with them in the original YOLOv5s and increases by 4.09 ms considering the average detection time. The comparison effect of the original model and the improved model is shown in Figure 9.

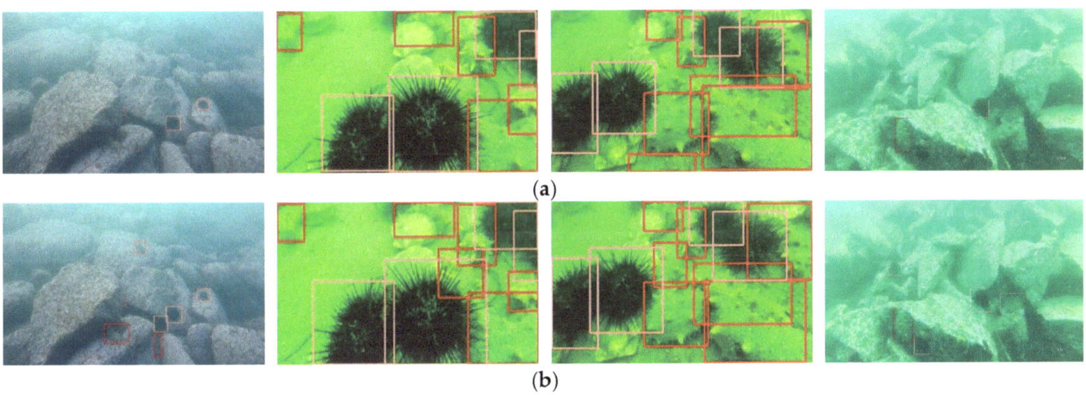

Figure 9. Comparison effect between the original model and the improved model: (**a**) Original model; (**b**) Improved model.

From Figure 8, it can be seen that both the detection accuracy and the recall rate are low, and the objectness loss of the prediction bounding box is high in the original model. The detection accuracy and recall rate are improved in the improved model. In addition, as shown by the comparison of the middle images, the objectness loss of the prediction bounding box of the improved model is lower and the bounding box selection of the detected sea cucumbers and sea urchins is more accurate.

3.2.2. Comparative Analysis of Model Detection Effects

To further validate the performance of the improved YOLOv5s model, a comparison experiment is conducted with RetinaNet, SSD, YOLOv4, YOLOv5m, YOLOV5l and YOLOv5x. In the experiment, all other models use default parameters and all models are not loaded with pre-training weights during the training process. The ratio of the training set, validation set and test set for all models during training is 7:2:1. The experimental results are shown in Table 6. where the mAP of the improved YOLOv5s is 11.75%, 10.31%, 8.08%, 3.2%, 3.1% and 3% higher than that of RetinaNet, SSD, YOLOv4, YOLOv5m, YOLOV5l and YOLOV5x, respectively. The parameters of the improved YOLOv5s are 4.18 M larger than those of the original YOLOv5s, but smaller than those of the other models. The improved YOLOv5s has an average detection time that is 6.29 ms slower than that of SSD, but it is 93.84 ms, 6.46 ms, 6.63 ms, 6.18 ms and 2.63 ms faster than those of RetinaNet, YOLOv4, YOLOv5m, YOLOv5l and YOLOv5x, respectively. The AP of sea cucumber and sea urchin detected using the improved YOLOv5s are both better than those detected with the other models. The detection effect of the models is shown in Figure 10. The improved YOLOv5s, in terms of both missed and false detections, significantly improved, and the regression accuracy is improved compared to the other models.

Table 6. Comparison data between different models.

Models	Sea Cucumber AP/%	Sea Urchin AP/%	mAP/%	Parameters/M	Average Detection Time/ms
RetinaNet	72.23	92.27	82.25	36.1	105.02
SSD	78	90	83.69	24.5	4.89
YOLOv4	77	95	85.92	64.36	17.64
YOLOv5s	83.9	95.1	89.5	7.02	7.09
YOLOv5m	87.0	94.6	90.8	20.88	17.81
YOLOv5l	86.5	95.2	90.9	46.14	17.36
YOLOv5x	87.3	94.8	91.0	86.18	13.81
Improved YOLOv5s	91.2	96.7	94.0	11.20	11.18

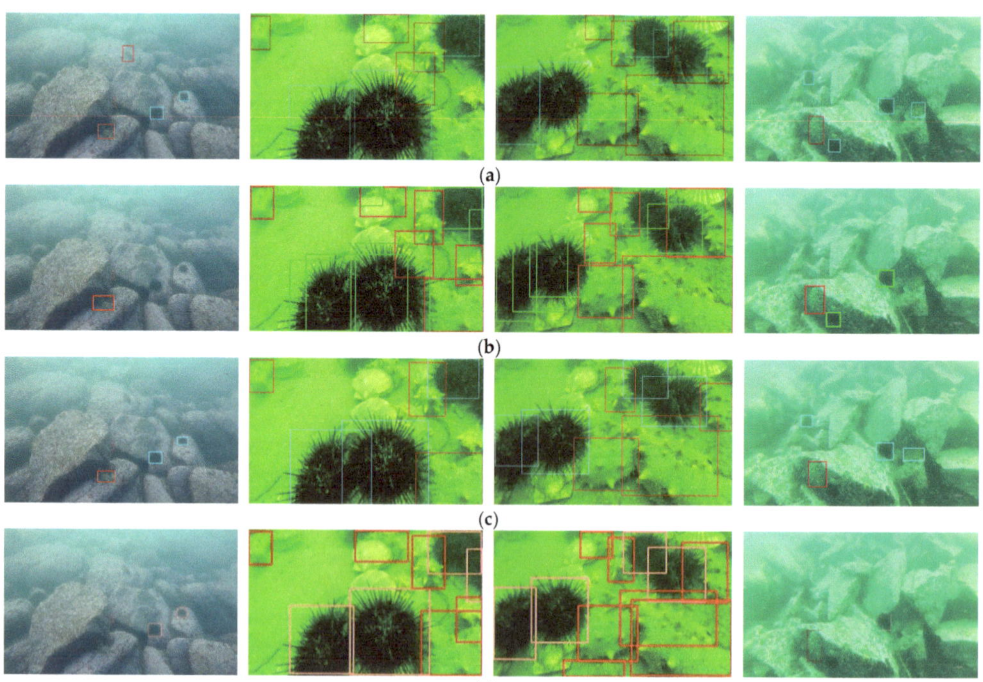

(a)
(b)
(c)
(d)

Figure 10. *Cont.*

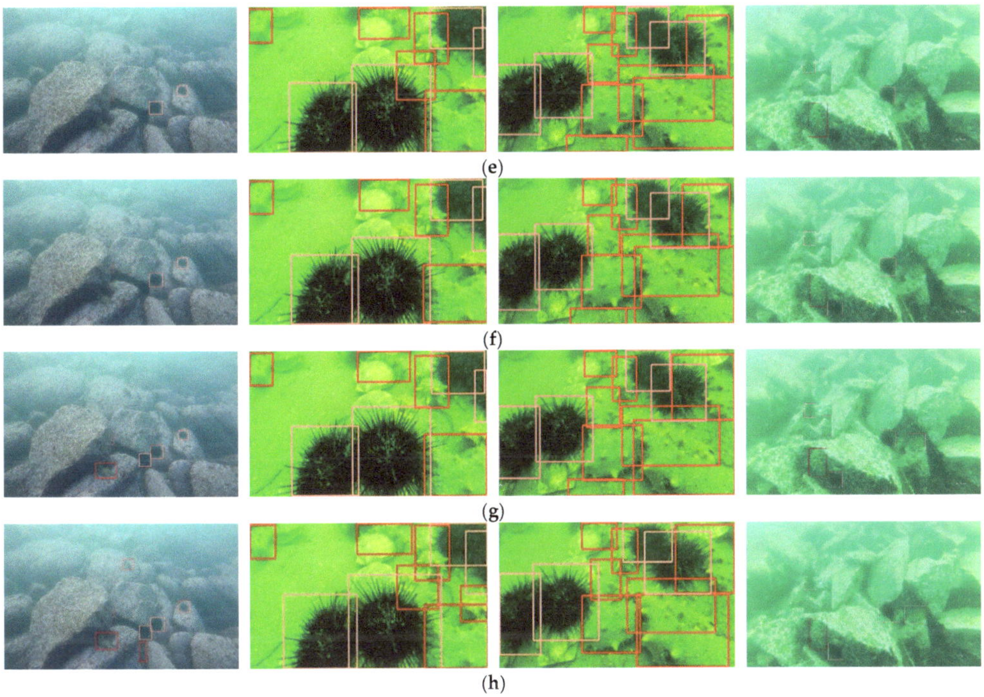

Figure 10. Inter-model detection results graph: (**a**) RetinaNet (**b**) SSD; (**c**) YOLOv4; (**d**) YOLOv5s; (**e**) YOLOv5m; (**f**) YOLOv5l; (**g**) YOLOv5x; (**h**) Improved YOLOV5s.

4. Conclusions

In this paper, a target detection algorithm based on improved YOLOv5s is proposed that can adapt to accurately recognize and detect sea cucumbers and sea urchins in complex underwater environments. The main improvement of YOLOv5s is to integrate the HorBlock module into the backbone network to enhance the feature extraction ability of the backbone network. The original hyperparameters of the improved YOLOv5s are adjusted using a hyperparameter evolution method based on a genetic algorithm to obtain hyperparameters suitable for complex underwater environments, which enables the model to obtain the optimal recognition accuracy during the training process. In this experiment, online and offline data augmentation methods are used to process the dataset. Mosaic data augmentation is used for online data augmentation, while offline data augmentation is achieved by expanding the dataset. During the experimental process, the ablation experiment and the comparison experiment of each model are conducted, respectively. In the ablation experiment, the methods of the HorBlock module, genetic algorithm hyperparameter evolution and offline data augmentation are experimentally verified. The final experimental results show that although the improved YOLOv5s has a slight decrease in detection speed, mAP increases by 4.5% compared to the original model. In the model comparison experiments, the improved YOLOv5s model has a higher mAP than the RetinaNet, SSD, YOLOv4, YOLOv5m, YOLOV5l and YOLOV5x models.

Due to the complex underwater environment, the underwater datasets have certain difficulties in the acquisition process. The underwater environment is affected by light and plankton in the water. This greatly affects the clarity of underwater images, which brings some difficulties in making the dataset and training the network model. Therefore, the image enhancement algorithms to improve the clarity of underwater images is a crucial task in the underwater data processing process. In future research, more kinds of datasets should be collected and image enhancement algorithms should be added to the datasets during training and detection. Moreover, the network model should continue to be optimized and the detection speed should also be improved while continuing to improve the accuracy of the model, which will be a direction of continued research in the future.

Author Contributions: Conceptualization, C.H. and Z.G. (Zhiguang Guan); methodology, C.H., Z.G. (Zhiguang Guan) and M.L.; software, C.H.; validation, C.H.; data curation, S.Z.; writing—original draft preparation, C.H. and Z.G (Ziyi Guo); writing—review and editing, Z.G. (Zhiguang Guan) and M.L.; supervision, M.L.; funding acquisition, Z.G. (Zhiguang Guan) All authors have read and agreed to the published version of the manuscript.

Funding: This work is supported by Natural Science Foundation of Shandong Province (ZR2020ME267), Major Science and Technology Innovation Project of Shandong Province (2019JZZY020703), Science and Technology Support Plan for Youth Innovation in Universities of Shandong Province Colleges and Universities (2019KJB014).

Institutional Review Board Statement: Not applicable.

Informed Consent Statement: Not applicable.

Data Availability Statement: The raw data cannot be shared at this time as the data also form part of an ongoing study.

Conflicts of Interest: The authors declare no conflict of interest.

References

1. Guan, Z.G.; Hou, C.L.; Zhou, S.Q.; Guo, Z.Y. Research on Underwater Target Recognition Technology Based on Neural Network. *Wirel. Commun. Mob. Comput.* **2022**, *2022*, 4197178. [CrossRef]
2. Kang, S.; Yu, J.C.; Zhang, J. Research Status of Micro Autonomous Underwater Vehicle. *Robot* **2023**, *2*, 218–237.
3. Li, L.; Yang, X.; Qin, X.J.; Wang, Y.Q. Research Status and Development Trend of Wall-climbing Cleaning Robots. *Mach. Build. Autom.* **2023**, *52*, 1–6.
4. Zhou, J.C.; Pang, L.; Zhang, W.S. Underwater image enhancement method by multi-interval histogram equalization. *IEEE J. Ocean. Eng.* **2023**, *48*, 474–488. [CrossRef]
5. Zhou, J.C.; Zhang, D.H.; Zhang, W.S. Cross-view enhancement network for underwater images. *Eng. Appl. Artif. Intell.* **2023**, *121*, 105952. [CrossRef]
6. Yuan, X.; Guo, L.X.; Luo, C.T.; Zhou, X.; Yu, C. A survey of target detection and recognition methods in underwater turbid areas. *Appl. Sci.* **2022**, *12*, 4898. [CrossRef]
7. Chen, W.; Wei, Q.Y.; Zhang, J.F.; Guo, B.Y. Target detection of underwater vehicle based on RetinaNet. *Comput. Eng. Des.* **2022**, *43*, 2959–2967.
8. Qiang, W.; He, Y.Y.; Guo, Y.J.; Li, B.Q.; Hi, L.J. Exploring Underwater Target Detection Algorithm Based on Improved SSD. *J. Northwestern Polytech. Univ.* **2020**, *38*, 747–754. [CrossRef]
9. Deng, Q.; Lin, M.X. Marine Organism Detection Algorithm Based on Improved SSD. *Comput. Technol. Dev.* **2022**, *32*, 51–56.
10. Wang, X.H.; Zhu, Y.G.; Li, D.Y.; Zhang, G. Underwater Target Detection Based on Reinforcement Learning and Ant Colony Optimization. *J. Ocean Univ. China* **2022**, *21*, 323–330. [CrossRef]
11. Guo, T.T.; Song, Y.Z.; Kong, Z.J.; Lim, E.; López-Benítez, M.; Ma, F.; Yu, L.M. Underwater Target Detection and Localization with Feature Map and CNN-Based Classification. In Proceedings of the 2022 4th IEEE International Conference on Advances in Computer Technology, Information Science and Communications (CTISC), Suzhou, China, 22–24 April 2022; pp. 1–8.
12. Zeng, L.C.; Sun, B.; Zhu, D.Q. Underwater target detection based on Faster R-CNN and adversarial occlusion network. *Eng. Appl. Artif. Intell.* **2021**, *100*, 104190. [CrossRef]
13. Li, J.F.; Zhu, Y.W.; Chen, M.X.; Wang, Y.L.; Zhou, Z.Q. Research on Underwater Small Target Detection Algorithm Based on Improved YOLOv3. In Proceedings of the 2022 16th IEEE International Conference on Signal Processing (ICSP), Beijing, China, 21–24 October 2022; pp. 76–80.
14. Guo, T.X.; Wei, Y.H.; Shao, H.; Ma, B.Y. Research on Underwater Target Detection Method Based on Improved MSRCP and YOLOv3. In Proceedings of the 2021 IEEE International Conference on Mechatronics and Automation (ICMA), Takamatsu, Japan, 8–11 August 2021; pp. 1158–1163.
15. Zhang, M.H.; Xu, S.B.; Song, W.; He, Q.; Wei, Q.M. Lightweight Underwater Object Detection Based on YOLOv4 and Multi-Scale Attentional Feature Fusion. *Remote Sens.* **2021**, *13*, 4706. [CrossRef]
16. Bochkovskiy, A.; Wang, C.-Y.; Liao, H.-Y.M. Yolov4: Optimal speed and accuracy of object detection. *arXiv* **2020**, arXiv:2004.10934.
17. Chen, L.Y.; Zheng, M.C.; Duan, S.Q.; Luo, W.L.; Yao, L.G. Underwater Target Recognition Based on Improved YOLOv4 Neural Network. *Electronics* **2021**, *10*, 1634. [CrossRef]

18. Li, S.S.; Li, C.; Yang, Y.; Zhang, Q.; Wang, Y.H.; Guo, Z.Y. Underwater scallop recognition algorithm using improved YOLOv5. *Aquac. Eng.* **2022**, *98*, 102273. [CrossRef]
19. Li, Y.; Bai, X.Y.; Xia, C.L. An Improved YOLOV5 Based on Triplet Attention and Prediction Head Optimization for Marine Organism Detection on Underwater Mobile Platforms. *J. Mar. Sci. Eng.* **2022**, *10*, 1230. [CrossRef]
20. Li, J.Y.; Liu, C.N.; Lu, X.C.; Wu, B.L. CME-YOLOv5: An Efficient Object Detection Network for Densely Spaced Fish and Small Targets. *Water* **2022**, *14*, 2412. [CrossRef]
21. Cao, J.R.; Zhuang, Y.; Wang, M.; Han, F.T.; Zheng, X.H.; Gao, H. ECA-based YOLOv5 Underwater Fish Target Detection. *Comput. Syst. Appl.* **2023**, *32*, 1–8.
22. Lei, F.; Tang, F.F.; Li, S.H. Underwater Target Detection Algorithm Based on Improved YOLOv5. *J. Mar. Sci. Eng.* **2022**, *10*, 310. [CrossRef]
23. He, K.M.; Zhang, X.Y.; Ren, S.Q.; Sun, J. Spatial Pyramid Pooling in Deep Convolutional Networks for Visual Recognition. *Pattern Anal. Mach. Intell. IEEE Trans.* **2015**, *37*, 1904–1916. [CrossRef]
24. Gevorgyan, Z. SIoU loss: More powerful learning for bounding box regression. *arXiv* **2022**, arXiv:2205.12740.
25. Rao, Y.M.; Zhao, W.L.; Tang, Y.S.; Zhou, J.; Lim, S.-N.; Lu, J.W. Hornet: Efficient high-order spatial interactions with recursive gated convolutions. *arXiv* **2022**, arXiv:2207.14284.
26. Bert, D.B.; Xu, J.; Tinne, T.; Luc, V.G. Dynamic fifilter networks. *Adv. Neural Inf. Process. Syst.* **2016**, *29*, 1–14.
27. Chen, Y.P.; Dai, X.Y.; Liu, M.C.; Chen, D.D.; Yuan, L.; Liu, Z.C. Dynamic convolution: Attention over convolution kernels. In Proceedings of the IEEE/CVF Conference on Computer Vision and Pattern Recognition, Seattle, WA, USA, 13–19 June 2020; pp. 11030–11039.
28. Hu, J.; Shen, L.; Sun, G. Squeeze-and-excitation networks. In Proceedings of the IEEE Conference on Computer Vision and Pattern Recognition, Salt Lake City, UT, USA, 18–23 June 2018; pp. 7132–7141.
29. Vaswani, A.; Shazeer, N.; Parmar, N.; Uszkoreit, J.; Jones, L.; Gomez, A.N.; Kaiser, Ł.; Polosukhin, P. Attention is all you need. *Adv. Neural Inf. Process. Syst.* **2017**, *30*, 5998–6008.
30. Katoch, S.; Chauhan, S.S.; Kumar, V. A review on genetic algorithm: Past, present, and future. *Multimed. Tools Appl.* **2020**, *80*, 8091–8126. [CrossRef]
31. Aszemi, N.M.; Dominic, P.D.D. Hyperparameter optimization in convolutional neural network using genetic algorithms. *Int. J. Adv. Comput. Sci. Appl.* **2019**, *10*, 269–278. [CrossRef]
32. Bochinski, E.; Senst, T.; Sikora, T. Hyper-parameter optimization for convolutional neural network committees based on evolutionary algorithms. In Proceedings of the 2017 IEEE international conference on image processing (ICIP), Beijing, China, 17–20 September 2017; pp. 3924–3928.
33. Du, W.S.; Zhu, Y.J.; Li, S.S.; Liu, P. Spikelets detection of table grape before thinning based on improved YOLOV5s and Kmeans under the complex environment. *Comput. Electron. Agric.* **2022**, *203*, 107432. [CrossRef]
34. Kingma, D.P.; Ba, J. Adam: A method for stochastic optimization. *arXiv* **2014**, arXiv:1412.6980.

machines

MDPI

Article

An Onboard Point Cloud Semantic Segmentation System for Robotic Platforms

Fei Wang, Yujie Yang, Jingchun Zhou * and Weishi Zhang

College of Information Science and Technology, Dalian Maritime University, Dalian 116000, China; feiwang@dlmu.edu.cn (F.W.)

* Correspondence: zhoujingchun@dlmu.edu.cn

Abstract: Point clouds represent an important way for robots to perceive their environments, and can be acquired by mobile robots with LiDAR sensors or underwater robots with sonar sensors. Hence, real-time semantic segmentation of point clouds with onboard edge devices is essential for robots to apprehend their surroundings. In this paper, we propose an onboard point cloud semantic segmentation system for robotic platforms to overcome the conflict between attaining high accuracy of segmentation results and the limited available computational resources of onboard devices. Our system takes raw a sequence of point clouds as inputs, and outputs semantic segmentation results for each frame as well as a reconstructed semantic map of the environment. At the core of our system is the transformer-based hierarchical feature extraction module and fusion module. The two modules are implemented with sparse tensor technologies to speed up inference. The predictions are accumulated according to Bayes rules to generate a global semantic map. Experimental results on the SemanticKITTI dataset show that our system achieves +2.2% mIoU and 18× speed improvements compared with SOTA methods. Our system is able to process 2.2 M points per second on Jetson AGX Xavier (NVIDIA, Santa Clara, USA), demonstrating its applicability to various robotic platforms.

Keywords: semantic segmentation; point cloud; transformer; sparse tensor; robot

Citation: Wang, F.; Yang, Y.; Zhou, J.; Zhang, W. An Onboard Point Cloud Semantic Segmentation System for Robotic Platforms. *Machines* **2023**, *11*, 571. https://doi.org/10.3390/machines11050571

Academic Editor: Dan Zhang

Received: 18 April 2023
Revised: 17 May 2023
Accepted: 20 May 2023
Published: 22 May 2023

1. Introduction

A point cloud is a set of 2D or 3D points, describing the geometric characteristics of objects in a scene. With the development of sensor technology, it has become more and more convenient for robots to collect point clouds from the environment [1]. For example, ground mobile robots can collect a 3D point cloud through LiDAR (light detection and ranging) devices; and underwater robots can use sonar devices to acquire a 2D point cloud of the sea environment. Hence, from both an academic and industrial perspective, point-cloud-based scene perception has attracted great attention [2,3].

Despite the tremendous potential of point cloud semantic segmentation, it faces significant challenges that must be addressed to make it practical for real-world applications. One of the primary issues is the high computational cost required to process and analyze large volumes of point cloud data. This limitation makes it hard to deploy point cloud segmentation systems on resource-constrained devices, especially for robotic platforms with edge devices.

Existing methods for semantic segmentation of point clouds consist of three categories: point-based methods, multi-view-based methods, and voxel-based methods. Each of the three semantic segmentation methods has its own set of advantages and disadvantages. The original point-based methods [4,5] are effective for segmenting large outdoor scenes but are computationally inefficient. On the other hand, the multi-view-based methods [6,7] are computationally efficient but can result in information loss and reduced segmentation accuracy when projecting 3D structures into 2D. Meanwhile, the voxel-based methods [8,9] perform better in 3D data, but dense convolutional neural networks are less efficient due to sparsity. While combining this method with sparse operations can improve efficiency, existing methods still cannot meet both efficiency and accuracy requirements simultaneously.

To realize real-time prediction for devices such as robots, we propose a real-time semantic segmentation system for point clouds based on use of a transformer and sparse convolution (TSR-Net). Firstly, we pre-process the data collected by LiDAR to obtain 3D data based on the sparse tensor. Next, we propose a sparse convolutional neural network involving two parts: feature extraction and fusion. To improve the ability of the network to learn global semantic features, we present a global feature extraction module (GFEM) in the feature extraction section. The GFEM helps to capture global semantic information from the point cloud data to improve the precision and accuracy of the segmentation results. Additionally, we introduce a channel attention module (CAM) in the feature fusion section to fuse different levels of semantic features, further enhancing the accuracy of the segmentation results. Finally, we obtain local segmentation maps by post-processing the data and further construct a global semantic map. Our main contributions are:

(1) We propose a real-time semantic segmentation system of point clouds for robotic platforms to achieve both high accuracy and high efficiency with limited computational onboard devices. Our system outputs predictions for each point cloud and a reconstructed global semantic map.
(2) We present a global feature extraction module and a channel attention module based on a transformer for hierarchical feature extraction and fusion. The two modules are lightweight in design and implemented with spare representations to speed up the inference time.
(3) Experimental results show that our system outperforms existing state-of-the-art methods on the SemanticKITTI dataset by 2.2% mIoU (mean intersection over union) and 18× speedup. It can process 2.2 million points per second on NVIDIA Jetson AGX Xavier, demonstrating its applicability to a variety of robotic platforms.

2. Related Work

Existing semantic segmentation of point cloud methods fall into the following three main categories:

Raw point-based methods usually learn features directly from unordered point cloud data, such as STPC [4], and PAConv [5]. In particular, PAConv's convolution kernel is a combination of multiple weight matrices. During the process, the coefficients of these weights are obtained by adaptive learning of the location relationships of the points. This data-driven approach to constructing convolutional kernels gives PAConv great flexibility to deal better directly with the point cloud data.

Multi-view-based methods typically involve projecting 3D data onto 2D images [10] and processing them using convolutional operations, as seen in PolarNet [6] and SqueezeSegV3 [7]. To address the problem of different feature distributions at different locations in the LIDAR images, SqueezeSegV3 proposes a spatially adaptive convolutional technique that adjusts the weights based on the input and location within the image.

Voxelization-based methods convert point cloud data into a dense grid and use 3D convolution for processing. Several methods have been developed to improve the computational efficiency of dense convolution, such as SPVNAS [8], Minkowski-Net [9], and MVASPP [11]. Minkowski-Net handles high-dimensional data by employing generalized sparse convolution and 4D spatio-temporal convolution. On the other hand, MV-ASPP extends PolarNet by using a pyramidal structured network to combine feature information at multiple scales and an ASPP module to expand the perception field.

The above is a division based on different representations of the data. In order to decrease the computational effort of the rasterization method, we introduce a sparse tensor into the system. Sparse convolution is a powerful technique utilized in some deep learning models to reduce the computational effort of point cloud data processing by performing convolutions only on non-empty regions. This technique reduces the computation quantity by computing convolutions only on the effective raster. Models such as Latticenet [12] and Cylinder3d [13] have successfully implemented sparse convolution. In particular, Cylinder3d is a 3D object detection model that uses sparse convolution and a columnar segmentation network to improve the prediction accuracy for objects such as vehicles and pedestrians, by leveraging an asymmetric residual module.

To increase the segmentation accuracy, we introduced the transformer module into the system. The transformer architecture, based on the self-attentive mechanism, has yielded great results in language processing (NLP). By abandoning convolutional operations and capturing global dependencies in the input sequence through attention only, this architecture is highly scalable. Building upon the success of the transformer model in NLP, many researchers have introduced it into the field of image recognition [14]. For example, models such as Segmenter [15] and TransUNet [16] have been proposed. TransUNet combines the advantages of the UNet model and the transformer structure, adding local accuracy to the extraction of global information.

In addition, transformers have also been introduced in the field of point cloud data processing, such as PST2 [17] and P4Transformer [18]. P4Transformer captures dynamic information in point cloud data by uses the transformer to self-attention on local features, while PST2 adopts a two-module approach consisting of STSA and RE to effectively capture both temporal and spatial information in of point cloud sequences.

The point-based method is able to segment large outdoor scenes, but is computationally inefficient. The multi-view-based method is computationally efficient, but the dimensionality reduction projection process causes information loss and accuracy degradation. The voxel-based method is less efficient for dense convolutional neural networks. In addition, the time and space complexity of computing the self-attentive mechanism in the transformer structure is high, and it is difficult to apply the transformer structure directly to the original data. Therefore, in order to achieve real-time prediction for devices such as robots, we propose a real-time semantic segmentation system for point clouds based on a transformer and using sparse convolution.

3. Method

This section provides an introduction to our proposed TSR-Net system. The system comprises several modules, including point cloud data pre-processing, feature extraction, feature fusion, post-processing, and semantic map construction.

3.1. Overview

The framework of the TSR-Net system is shown in Figure 1. Firstly, the system preprocesses LiDAR data to obtain a sparse tensor-based representation.

Secondly, we propose a network that uses a transformer module for feature extraction and fusion. In this regard, the feature extraction network learns semantic features of point clouds at different scales by expanding the receptive field of the network through multiple 3×3 convolutions, ReLU functions, and down-sampling convolutions with a stride of 2. The feature fusion network combines the results of deconvolution with the corresponding features in the feature extraction layer through concatenation operations. The global feature extraction block (GFEB) and channel attention module (CAM) are designed on this basis. We use the GFEB to learn the importance of different regions of the higher-order semantic features and adjust the corresponding weights to perform feature enhancement. The CAM is used to fuse the different levels of semantic features.

After prediction, the TSR-Net system transforms the sparse tensor-based raster representation into a point cloud and generates a semantic segmentation map of the local scene. After point cloud registration, the TSR-Net system updates semantic labels using Bayes' rule and eventually obtains a global semantic map.

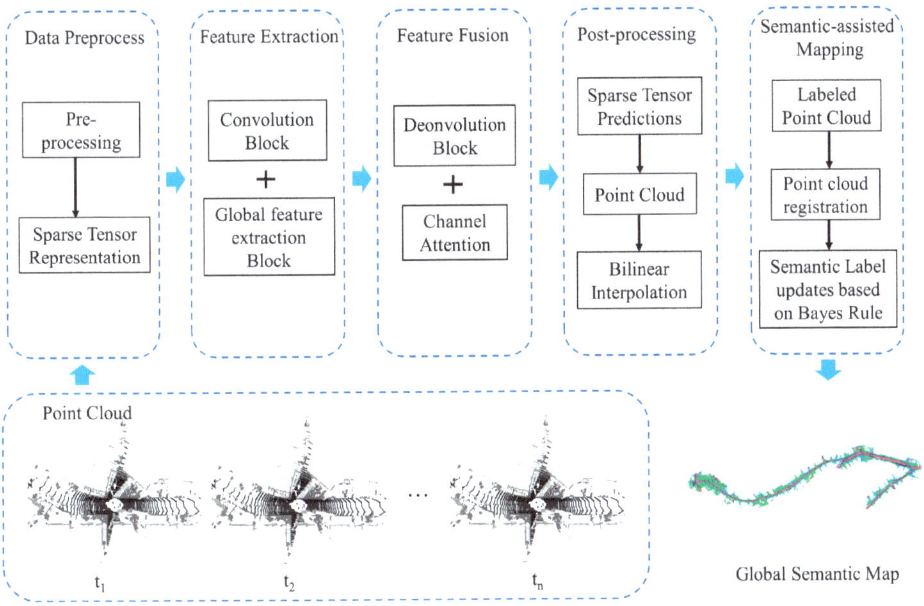

Figure 1. Architecture of our onboard point cloud semantic segmentation system.

3.2. Feature Extraction Module

In this module, we expand the perceptual field of the network by multiple 3 × 3 convolutions, ReLU functions, and subsampling convolutions with a stride of 2 to learn the semantic features of point clouds at different scales.

To obtain remote information from the data, we added the transformer encoder module to the deeper layers of the feature extraction network. This module creates an association for each element in the higher-order feature map and distinguishes the importance of features in different regions. It is structured as described below, starting with a given input feature $X \in R^{N \times C}$. Positional encoding of the input feature X is achieved by a sparse convolutional operation conv with kernel size equal to stride. Thus, the feature $X_P \in R^{N' \times C'}$ is obtained. The formula is as follows:

$$X_P = \text{conv}(X) \tag{1}$$

The feature X_L is obtained by adding the normalization function LayerNorm after the feature X_P, where $X_L \in R^{N' \times C'}$:

$$X_L = \text{LayerNorm}(X_P) \tag{2}$$

The attention layer then receives the feature X_L. The attention function computes the query and the dot product of all keys and then divides each dot product by $\sqrt{d_k}$. We combine these queries to form a matrix $Q \in R^{N' \times h \times d_k}$, $C' = h \times d_k$. The keys and values are also combined to form a matrix $K \in R^{N' \times h \times d_k}$ and $V \in R^{N' \times h \times d_v}$, $C' = h \times d_v$. The formula of the attention function is as follows:

$$Q = X_L \cdot W_q \tag{3}$$

$$K = X_L \cdot W_k \tag{4}$$

$$V = X_L \cdot W_v \tag{5}$$

$$\text{Atten} = \text{Softmax}\left(\frac{\text{Q}\cdot\text{K}^{\text{T}}}{\sqrt{\text{d}_\text{k}}}\right)\cdot\text{V} \tag{6}$$

where W_q, W_k and W_v are shared parameter matrices, d_k denotes the dimension of query and key, d_k denotes the dimension of value, and the output dimension of the attention function is $R^{N' \times h \times d_v}$.

To enhance the computational speed of the self-attentive layer, we use a multi-head attention structure with the number of heads set as 8. Firstly, h different linear mappings of queries, keys, and values are performed. Then the new queries, keys, and values obtained after each mapping are subjected to the parallel operation of the atten function, respectively, to generate the d_v dimensional output. The formula is as follows:

$$X_M = \text{Concat}(\text{head}_1, \ldots, \text{head}_h)W^O \tag{7}$$

$$\text{head}_i = \text{Atten}\left(Q\cdot W_i^Q,\ K\cdot W_i^K,\ V\cdot W_i^V\right) \tag{8}$$

where the linear transformation parameters are $W_i^Q \in R^{C' \times d_k}$, $W_i^K \in R^{C' \times d_k}$, $W_i^V \in R^{C' \times d_v}$ and $W^O \in R^{h \times d_v \times C'}$.

$X_M \in R^{(N' \times C')}$ is a multi-headed attention layer output. The final output feature $X_{out} \in R^{(N \times C)}$ is obtained by summing X_M with the input feature X through the Layer Norm and ReLU functions, and then recovering the position-encoded deconvolution $conv_T$. The formula is as follows:

$$X' = \text{ReLU}(\text{LayerNorm}(X_M + X)) \tag{9}$$

$$X_{out} = \text{conv}_T(\text{output}) \tag{10}$$

3.3. Feature Fusion Module

To enhance the fusion of semantic features at various levels, a channel attention module has been introduced into the feature fusion network. This module creates attention masks in the channel dimension to select critical channels. The input features are compressed to improve computational efficiency. The structure is as follows: firstly, the input features $X \in R^{N \times C}$ are aggregated using global average and maximum pooling, resulting in $X_a \in R^{(1 \times C)}$ and $X_m \in R^{(1 \times C)}$:

$$X_a = \text{avg\_Pool}(X) \tag{11}$$

$$X_m = \text{max\_Pool}(X) \tag{12}$$

The multilayer perceptron (MLP) then accepts these two features, where C is the number of channels and r is the reduction rate. The output features of the MLP are summed element-wise and then passed through a sigmoid function to generate the attentional feature M_c.:

$$M_c = \sigma(\text{MLP}(X_a) + \text{MLP}(X_m)) \tag{13}$$

Finally, we obtain the output feature X_{out} of the module by multiplying M_c and X using the following formula:

$$X_{out} = M_c \cdot X \tag{14}$$

3.4. Semantic Map Building

In the process of constructing the semantic map, we transform each frame of the data under the global coordinate system based on LOAM [19] and correlate the before and after frames of the data. Then, the labels of the multi-frame data sequences are updated by Bayes' rule to generate a global semantic predictive map for the current scene.

We use point-to-edge and point-to-plane mapping calculations to associate the current frame with the previous frame's point cloud. In the computation, we combine semantic labeling and mapping calculations to weight the labeled similarity and the distance of the corresponding points. First, we denote the edge point as e and the plane point as p. The distances from the point to the edge and plane, respectively, are:

$$d_i^e = \frac{\left|\left(x^e_{(t+1,i)} - x^e_{(t+1,j)}\right) \times \left(x^e_{(t+1,i)} - x^e_{(t,j)}\right)\right|}{\left|x^e_{(t,j)} - x^e_{(t,l)}\right|} \tag{15}$$

$$d_i^p = \frac{\left|\begin{array}{c}\left(x^p_{(t+1,i)} - x^p_{(t,j)}\right)\\ \left(\left(x^p_{(t,j)} - x^p_{(t,l)}\right) \times \left(x^p_{(t,j)} - x^p_{(t,m)}\right)\right)\end{array}\right|}{\left|\left(x^p_{(t,j)} - x^p_{(t,l)}\right) \times \left(x^p_{(t,j)} - x^p_{(t,m)}\right)\right|} \tag{16}$$

The similarity of labels between corresponding points is calculated as follows:

$$S_i = \exp\left(-\frac{1}{2}\left(D_{(t+1,i)} - D_{(t,j)}\right)\theta^{-1}\left(D_{(t+1,i)} - D_{(t,j)}\right)\right) \tag{17}$$

where $D_{(t+1,i)}$ is defined as the predicted label distribution for the point $x_{(t+1,i)}$. The closest point to $x_{(t+1,i)}$ is $x_{(k,j)}$. The association formula is then calculated as follows:

$$f(T_{t+1}) = \sum\nolimits_{i\in e_{t+1}} S_i d_i^e + \sum\nolimits_{j\in p_{t+1}} S_j d_j^p = Sd \tag{18}$$

Then, the nonlinear formula is optimized using the Levenberg–Marquardt algorithm. The final result is an optimal inter-frame transformation matrix T_{k+1}.

At moment t + 1, we define the label distribution in the semantic map as the conditional probability $P\left(z_{t+1}\middle|x_0^{t+1}\right)$. According to Bayes' rule, the point cloud labels in the global map are updated as:

$$P\left(z_{t+1}\middle|x_0^{t+1}\right) \leftarrow \frac{1}{K'_{t+1}}\frac{\hat{P}(z_{t+1}|x_{t+1})}{P(z_t)}P\left(z_t\middle|x_0^t\right) \tag{19}$$

where $K_{t+1} = P\left(z_{t+1}\middle|x_0^{t+1}\right)$.

4. Experiment

4.1. Settings

We chose SemanticKITTI as the experimental data for the TSR-Net system. This dataset is semantically labeled with 20 objects, such as fences, motorcyclists, and sidewalks. The dataset consists of 22 sequences scanned by LiDAR in different scenes. Each sequence contains LiDAR point clouds ranging from 200 to 4500 frames. We used sequences 00–10 with semantic annotation for our experiments. A frame was selected from every 5 frames for use in the experiments. The ratio of the experimental data used for training, validation, and testing was 6:2:2.

The evaluation metrics for the TSR-Net system are accuracy (acc) and mIoU. The accuracy is the percentage of all correct predictions made by the system over the total experimental data. The mIoU is an average for each category of the intersection ratio in the dataset. The calculation formula is as follows:

$$acc = \frac{TP + TN}{TP + TN + FT + FN} \tag{20}$$

$$mIoU = \frac{1}{k+1}\sum\nolimits_{i=0}^{k}\frac{P_{ii}}{\sum_{j=0}^{k} P_{ij} + \sum_{j=0}^{k} P_{ji} - P_{ii}} \tag{21}$$

Our system was implemented using the Minkowski Engine on hardware with an Intel Core i9-10980XE (3.0 GHz) and 32 GB RAM memory. The system was parameter optimized using Adam, with a learning rate of 0.0001, momentum of 0.9, batch size of 16, and maximum number of iterations set to 300.

4.2. Semantic Segmentation Results

The feature extraction and fusion module of the TSR-Net system uses 3D-Unet as a baseline model. Figure 2 depicts the system and 3D-Unet's visualization results on SemanticKITTI.

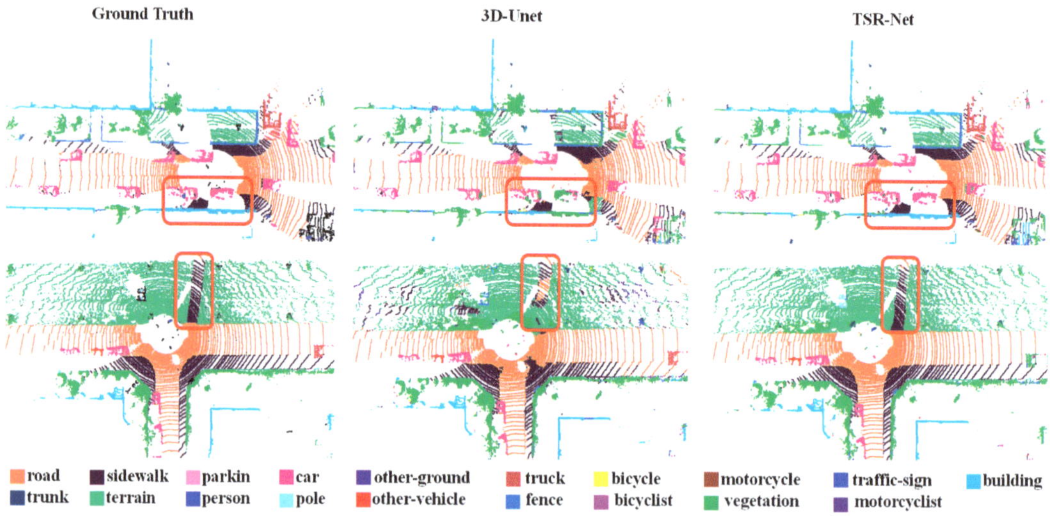

Figure 2. Visualization of typical segmentation results on the SemanticKITTI dataset. The red boxes highlight the differences in the segmentation results.

As can be seen from the figure, 3D-Unet is able to broadly identify predictive targets. For example, the model can identify pavement information such as cars, roads, and vegetation. However, the segmentation results of 3D-Unet are not accurate enough to delineate effectively the boundaries of large-scale objects. For example, in the first scenario, with multiple cars on the road, the 3D-Unet model was unable to fully recognize the outline information of some of the cars and confused the cars with the vegetation. In addition, the 3D-Unet model also confused buildings at the edge of the road with vegetation and did not fully recognize them. In the second scene, the model was unable to identify accurately the location of the sidewalk in the terrain. In addition, the model is not sufficiently accurate to identify other vehicles and confuses them with cars. Our system is able to effectively address these issues. We have focused our segmentation efforts on the recognition of boundaries of large-scale objects, and the model is also able to identify effectively the contour information of objects such as cars, sidewalks, and parking.

From the above analysis, it is clear that the TSR-Net system improves the real-time semantic segmentation of the system by focusing the segmentation on the boundary recognition of large-scale objects through the global feature extraction and channel attention modules.

In addition, we conducted a comparative analysis of the TSR-Net system and existing models on the large-scale public outdoor dataset SemanticKITTI. Table 1 shows the specific statistical results.

Table 1. Evaluations of our TSR-Net and existing methods on the SemanticKITTI dataset.

Method	Real-Time	Acc/%	mIoU/%	Car	Bicycle	Motorcycle	Truck	Other-Vehicle	Person	Bicyclist	Motorcyclist	Road	Parking	Sidewalk	Other-Ground	Building	Fence	Vegetation	Trunk	Terrain	Pole	Traffic-Sign
RPVNet [20]	no	-	70.3	**97.6** *	**68.4** *	68.7	44.2	61.1	75.9	74.4	73.4	93.4	70.3	80.7	33.3	**93.5** *	72.1	86.5	**75.1** *	71.8	**64.8** *	61.4
FusionNet [21]	no	91.8	61.3	95.3	47.5	37.7	41.8	34.5	59.5	56.8	11.9	91.8	68.8	77.1	30.8	92.5	69.4	84.5	69.8	68.5	60.4	66.5
STPC [4]	no	-	54.6	94.7	31.1	39.7	34.4	24.5	51.1	48.9	15.3	90.8	63.6	74.1	5.3	90.7	61.5	82.7	62.1	67.5	51.4	47.9
(AF)2-S3Net [22]	**yes** *	-	69.7	94.5	65.4	**86.8** *	39.2	41.1	**80.7** *	**80.4** *	**74.3** *	91.3	68.8	72.5	53.5	87.9	63.2	70.2	68.5	53.7	61.5	**71.0** *
SPVNAS [8]	**yes** *	-	66.4	97.3	51.5	50.8	59.8	58.8	65.7	65.2	43.7	90.2	67.6	75.2	16.9	91.3	65.9	86.1	73.4	70.0	64.2	66.9
AMVNet [23]	**yes** *	-	65.3	96.2	59.9	54.2	48.8	45.7	71.0	65.7	11.0	90.1	71.0	75.8	32.4	92.4	69.1	85.6	71.7	69.6	62.7	67.2
SqueezeSegV3 [7]	**yes** *	88.6	55.9	92.5	38.7	36.5	29.6	33.0	45.6	46.2	20.1	91.7	63.4	74.8	26.4	89.0	59.4	82.0	58.7	65.4	49.6	58.9
TSR-Net (ours)	**yes** *	**92.4** *	**72.5** *	92.3	36.6	59.1	**85.4** *	**68.8** *	45.8	79.1	63.8	**94.9** *	**73.8** *	**84.5** *	**74.0** *	90.5	**78.5** *	**89.2** *	58.6	**82.7** *	60.7	60.9

* The value in bold is the best result for each column.

Our system outperformed existing models in the mIoU metric and was 2.2% better than the sub-optimal model based on multiple inputs [20]. Compared with the existing voxelization method [22], which has the best segmentation performance and can be applied in real-time, our results were 2.8% better in the mIoU metric. In terms of segmentation accuracy, our system demonstrated and improvement of 0.6% over the voxelization-based model [21]. Compared to a multi-view-based approach [23], our system performed 7.2% better in terms of mIoU.

The results confirm that the system showed a significant performance improvement in semantic segmentation. Compared with other existing models, our TSR-Net demonstrated a significant advantage in segmenting nine classes of objects such as trucks, roads, parking, and sidewalk.

4.3. Hyperparameters

To test the effectiveness of different modules and the effect of different raster sizes on the system, two comparison experiments were conducted on the SemanticKITTI dataset.

Firstly, to test our proposed GFEB and CAM modules, we added them separately to the 3D-Unet, thus constituting four systems: the baseline model, the baseline model with GFEB added, the baseline model with CAM added, and our TSR-Net. Table 2 shows the comparison results in terms of accuracy, mIoU metrics, and prediction time per frame. Compared to the baseline model, the system showed improvements of 1.6% in the mIoU metric and 16.6 ms in the per-frame prediction time with the addition of GFEB. With the addition of CAM, the system improvements were 3.3% in the mIoU metric and 14.4 ms in the per-frame prediction time. With the addition of both modules, the system improved by 7.6% and 0.9% in the mIoU metric and accuracy, respectively. The prediction time increased by 22.2 ms.

Table 2. Performance comparison under different model settings.

Method	Acc/%	mIoU	Time/ms
3D Unet	91.5	64.9	70.8
3D Unet + GFEB	92.1	66.5	87.4
3D Unet + CAM	91.7	68.2	85.2
3D Unet + GFEB + CAM (TSR-Net)	92.4	72.5	93.0

The results show that both of our proposed modules can enhance the system's segmentation performance with a small increase in prediction time, and that adding both modules at the same time improves the system most significantly.

Secondly, to test the impact of different raster sizes on the segmentation results, we conducted experiments based on raster sizes of 6, 10, and 20 cm. Table 3 shows the results of our comparison in terms of accuracy, mIoU metrics, and prediction time per frame for different raster sizes.

Table 3. Segmentation performances of our system using different voxel sizes.

Voxel Size/cm	Acc/%	mIoU/%	Time/ms
6	92.6	71.9	115.0
10	91.8	70.3	75.7
20	89.5	65.4	42.1

The results show that the larger the raster, the shorter the prediction time for a single frame, and the shortest time for a single frame was 42.1 ms when the raster is 20 cm. However, in terms of the mIoU metric, the smaller the raster the better was the segmentation performance of the system. The best results were obtained at a raster size of 6 cm, with 1.4% higher performance than at 10 cm.

4.4. Efficiency Comparisons

Table 4 represents the results of the efficiency comparison between TSR-Net and the existing model on the GTX 3090 server. Since our system uses sparse convolution for operations, its FLOPs (floating-point operations per second) are calculated as follows:

$$\text{FLOPs} = 2 \times (C_{in} \times K - 1) \times N \times C_{out} \tag{22}$$

where C_{in} and C_{out} are the numbers of input and output channels, N is the number of effective rasters in the convolutional layer, and K denotes the average convolutional kernel size.

Table 4. Comparison of the efficiency of our TSR-Net with existing methods.

Methods	Params/M	FLOPs/G	Device	Time/ms
RPVNet [20]	24.8	239	Tesla V100	1687
FusionNet [21]	-	-	GTX 1080	900
SPVNAS [8]	12.5	147.6	GTX 1080Ti	259
SqueezeSegV3 [7]	26.2	1030.4	-	142
TSR-Net (our)	91.9	≈65.3	GTX 3090	93

As can be seen from Table 4, the TSR-Net system has a high number of parameters but only about 65 G of computation, which is more than half the current low [8]. Although we increased the segmentation accuracy by adding global feature extraction and channel attention modules, thus increasing the number of parameters, the value of the FLOPs did not improve significantly. This is due to the fact that our system is based on a sparse tensor. The size of the computation in the system is related to the number of effective rasters in the convolutional layers. The computational effort of the system can be significantly reduced depending on the sparsity of the data.

In addition, we tested the efficiency of the TSR-Net system on the NVIDIA Jetson AGX Xavier platform. We tested the prediction times of the TSR-Net system in eight different power modes for four sequences 00, 02, 04, and 06. Figure 3 shows the statistical average prediction times for the different power modes.

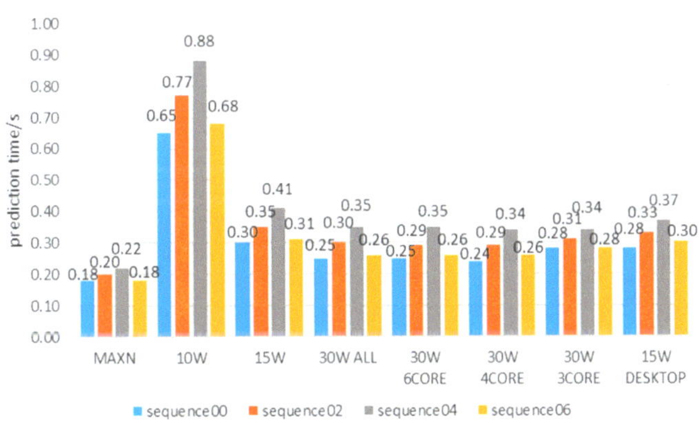

Figure 3. Inference time of our system on the NVIDIA Jetson AGX Xavier with different device modes.

Our system is able to achieve a prediction speed of 0.19 s per frame in MAXN mode. The system has a prediction speed of 0.75 s per frame in 15 W DESKTOP mode. In addition, the difference in prediction speed is not significant, at about 0.28 s per frame for different CPU cores with 30 W power. As existing LiDAR data is acquired at a frequency of 10 Hz, it takes an average of 0.1 s to acquire one frame of point cloud data. When the time to predict each frame of the point cloud is less than or equal to the acquisition time, it can be concluded that the system can make predictions in real-time. In practice, we sample the point cloud data by sampling one frame of the point cloud sequence for every two frames of data, to achieve a frame rate of 5 FPS. Therefore, it can be considered that a prediction rate of 5 FPS (0.2 s per frame) meets the requirements for real-time applications.

4.5. Semantic Map Building

To visualize the real-time segmentation effect of the TSR-Net system, we constructed a global semantic map on the GTX 3090 server. Figure 4 shows the semantic map of our system for the SemanticKITTI dataset 05 sequence scenes. The left-hand side of the image shows a top view of the 05 sequence scene, and the right-hand side shows a zoomed-in view of each of the two partial scenes. During the construction of the semantic map, we censored the data of sequence 05 and updated the semantic labels by taking one frame from every three consecutive frames.

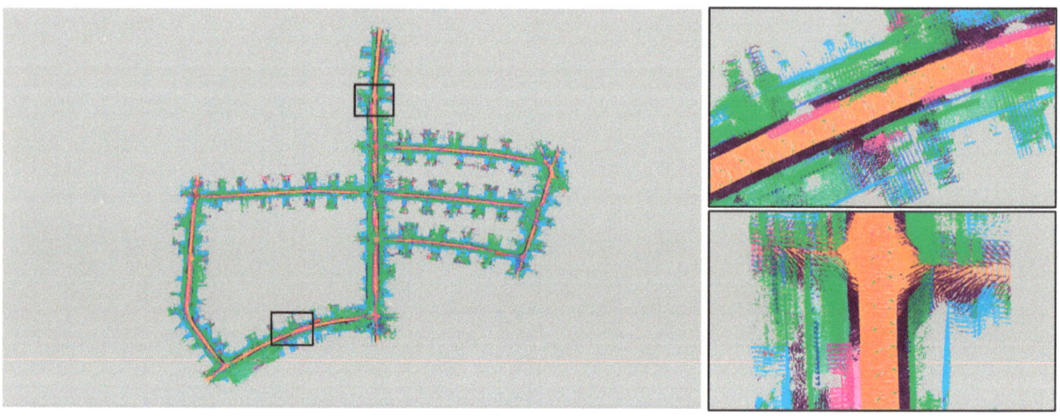

Figure 4. Visualization of the global semantic map reconstructed by our system. The staining scheme of Figure 4 is the same as that of Figure 2.

5. Discussion

Our system consists of five parts: data preprocessing, feature extraction, feature fusion, data post-processing, and semantic map construction. The system takes point cloud data as input and outputs a global semantic map. From an efficiency perspective, the data preprocessing and post-processing modules take 5 ms and 1 ms per frame, respectively. The feature extraction and feature fusion modules take 93 ms per frame. The time consumed by the semantic map construction can be neglected. Therefore, our TSR-Net system takes 99 ms per frame for point cloud processing, and outputs semantic segmentation results at a rate of 5 frames per second. The global semantic map module reconstructs the semantic map by taking one frame every two frames of data. Our system uses a grid-based method for processing. Compared with voxel-based models, our system reduces the FLOPs metric by more than half. Compared with fusion models based on multiple data representation forms, our system reduces the FLOPs metric by 174 G.

From a performance perspective, compared with multi-view-based models, our system improved by 7.2% in terms of mIoU indicator. Compared with voxel-based models, our system improved by 6.1% in terms of the mIoU indicator. Compared with fusion models based on multiple data representation forms, our system improved by 2.2% in terms of the mIoU indicator. In addition, our system performs real-time segmentation of point cloud data. Compared with non-real-time models such as RPVNet, our system's feature extraction and feature fusion modules improved by 2.2% in terms of the mIoU indicator.

Compared with real-time models such as (AF)2-S3Net, our system improved by 2.8% in terms of the mIoU indicator.

Finally, from a system perspective, the existing semantic segmentation system Semantic SLAM [24] projects laser point clouds into depth images for semantic segmentation, and then performs point cloud registration and map reconstruction. The focus of the Semantic SLAM system is on pose estimation and semantic map construction. This system utilizes only the RangeNet++ model for semantic segmentation, and our work can replace this. The TSR-Net system focuses on real-time semantic segmentation to solve the problem of real-time system accuracy.

6. Conclusions

We propose a method to solve the problem of onboard semantic segmentation of point clouds for robotic platforms with limited computational resources. The proposed system includes two plug-and-play modules, GFEB and CAM, which are used for learning global contextual information and fusing semantic information at different scales, respectively. After segmenting each single frame, the system uses semantic information to enhance global map building and update labels in the global map with predictions for each frame. To improve the computational efficiency of the system, all net operations are implemented based on a sparse tensor, and pre-processing and post-processing are involved for data transformation between raw 3D points and a sparse tensor.

A series of experiments with SemanticKITTI to test the performance of our system and evaluations against state-of-the-art methods are presented. From the results, we conclude that: (1) the two presented plug-and-play and lightweight modules, GFEB and CAM, can significantly improve the accuracy of semantic segmentation models (+7.6% mIoU) with a limited increase of inference time (16.2 ms per frame). (2) Our system outperforms state-of-the-art methods by 2.2% mIoU and about 18× speedup, resulting in a better balance between accuracy and efficiency for real-time applications. (3) Our system can classify 2.2 million points per second on NVIDIA Jetson AGX Xavier, which demonstrates its ability for use with a variety of robotic platforms with limited computational resources.

Author Contributions: Conceptualization, W.Z.; methodology, F.W.; software, Y.Y.; validation, F.W. and J.Z.; resources, J.Z.; writing—original draft preparation, F.W. and Y.Y.; writing—review and editing, Y.Y. and W.Z.; funding acquisition, F.W. All authors have read and agreed to the published version of the manuscript.

Funding: This research was funded by the National Natural Science Foundation of China, grant number 62103072, Dalian Excellent Youth Talent Fund Project, grant number 2022RY23, and the Fundamental Research Funds for the Central Universities No. 3132023256.

Data Availability Statement: Not applicable.

Conflicts of Interest: The authors declare no conflict of interest.

References

1. Teixeira, M.A.S.; Nogueira, R.d.C.M.; Dalmedico, N.; Santos, H.B.; Arruda, L.V.R.d.; Neves, F., Jr.; Pipa, D.R.; Ramos, J.E.; Oliveira, A.S.d. Intelligent 3D Perception System for Semantic Description and Dynamic Interaction. *Sensors* **2019**, *19*, 3764. [CrossRef]
2. Limeira, M.; Piardi, L.; Kalempa, V.C.; Leitao, P.; Oliveira, A.S.d. DepthLiDAR: Active Segmentation of Environment Depth Map Into Mobile Sensors. *IEEE Sens. J.* **2021**, *21*, 19047–19057. [CrossRef]
3. Teixeira, M.A.S.; Neves, F., Jr.; Koubaa, A.; Arruda, L.V.R.d.; Oliveira, A.S.d. DeepSpatial: Intelligent Spatial Sensor to Perception of Things. *IEEE Sens. J.* **2020**, *21*, 3966–3976. [CrossRef]
4. Fang, Y.; Xu, C.; Cui, Z. Spatial transformer point convolution. *arXiv* **2020**, arXiv:2009.01427.
5. Xu, M.; Ding, R.; Zhao, H. Paconv: Position adaptive convolution with dynamic kernel assembling on point clouds. In Proceedings of the 2021 IEEE/CVF Conference on Computer Vision and Pattern Recognition, Nashville, TX, USA, 19–25 June 2021.
6. Zhang, Y.; Zhou, Z.; David, P. Polarnet: An improved grid representation for online lidar point clouds semantic segmentation. In Proceedings of the 2020 IEEE/CVF Conference on Computer Vision and Pattern Recognition, Seattle, DC, USA, 14–19 June 2020.
7. Xu, C.; Wu, B.; Wang, Z. Squeezesegv3: Spatially-adaptive convolution for efficient point-cloud segmentation. In Proceedings of the 2020 European Conference on Computer Vision, Glasgow, UK, 23–28 August 2020.

8. Tang, H.; Liu, Z.; Zhao, S. Searching efficient 3d architectures with sparse point-voxel convolution. In Proceedings of the 2020 European Conference on Computer Vision, Glasgow, UK, 23–28 August 2020.
9. Choy, C.; Gwak, J.Y.; Savarese, S. 4d spatio-temporal convnets: Minkowski convolutional neural networks. In Proceedings of the 2019 IEEE/CVF Conference on Computer Vision and Pattern Recognition, Long Beach, CA, USA, 15–21 June 2019.
10. Zhou, J.C.; Zhang, D.H.; Ren, W.Q. Auto Color Correction of Underwater Images Utilizing Depth Information. *IEEE Geosci. Remote. Sens. Lett.* **2022**, *19*, 1–5. [CrossRef]
11. Chidanand, K.S.; Al-Stouhi, S. Multi-scale voxel class balanced ASPP for LIDAR pointcloud semantic segmentation. In Proceedings of the IEEE/CVF Winter Conference on Applications of Computer Vision, Waikoloa, HI, USA, 5–9 January 2021.
12. Rosu, R.A.; Schütt, P.; Quenzel, J. Latticenet: Fast point cloud segmentation using permutohedral lattices. *arXiv* **2019**, arXiv:1912.05905.
13. Zhu, X.; Zhou, H.; Wang, T. Cylindrical and asymmetrical 3d convolution networks for lidar segmentation. In Proceedings of the 2021 IEEE/CVF Conference on Computer Vision and Pattern Recognition, Nashville, TX, USA, 19–25 June 2021.
14. Zhou, J.C.; Zhang, D.H.; Zhang, W.S. Underwater image enhancement method via multi-feature prior fusion. *Appl. Intell.* **2022**, *52*, 16435–16457. [CrossRef]
15. Strudel, R.; Garcia, R.; Laptev, I.; Schmid, C. Segmenter: Transformer for Semantic Segmentation. In Proceedings of the 2021 IEEE/CVF International Conference on Computer Vision (ICCV), Montreal, QC, Canada, 10–17 October 2021.
16. Chen, J.; Lu, Y.; Yu, Q. TransUNet: Transformers Make Strong Encoders for Medical Image Segmentation. *arXiv* **2021**, arXiv:2102.04306.
17. Wei, Y.; Liu, H.; Xie, T.; Ke, Q.; Guo, Y. Spatial-Temporal Transformer for 3D Point Cloud Sequences. In Proceedings of the 2022 IEEE/CVF Winter Conference on Applications of Computer Vision (WACV), Waikoloa, HI, USA, 3–8 January 2022.
18. Fan, H.; Yang, Y.; Kankanhalli, M. Point 4D Transformer Networks for Spatio-Temporal Modeling in Point Cloud Videos. In Proceedings of the 2021 IEEE/CVF Conference on Computer Vision and Pattern Recognition (CVPR), Nashville, TN, USA, 19–25 June 2021.
19. Zhang, J.; Singh, S. LOAM: Lidar Odometry and Mapping in Realtime. In Proceedings of the Robotics: Science and Systems 2014, Berkeley, CA, USA, 12–16 July 2014.
20. Xu, J.; Zhang, R.; Dou, J. Rpvnet: A deep and efficient range-point-voxel fusion network for lidar point cloud segmentation. In Proceedings of the 2021 IEEE International Conference on Computer Vision, Montreal, QC, Canada, 11–18 October 2021.
21. Zhang, F.; Fang, J.; Wah, B. Deep FusionNet for Point Cloud Semantic Segmentation. In Proceedings of the 2020 European Conference on Computer Vision, Glasgow, UK, 23–28 August 2020.
22. Cheng, R.; Razani, R.; Taghavi, E. (AF)2-S3Net: Attentive Feature Fusion with Adaptive Feature Selection for Sparse Semantic Segmentation Network. In Proceedings of the 2021 IEEE/CVF Conference on Computer Vision and Pattern Recognition, Nashville, TN, USA, 20–25 June 2021.
23. Liong, V.E.; Nguyen, T.; Widjaja, S. AMVNet: Assertion-based Multi-View Fusion Network for LiDAR Semantic Segmentation. *arXiv* **2020**, arXiv:2012.04934.
24. Chen, X.; Milioto, A.; Palazzolo, E.; Giguère, P.; Behley, J.; Stachniss, C. SuMa++: Efficient LiDAR-based Semantic SLAM. In Proceedings of the 2019 IEEE/RSJ International Conference on Intelligent Robots and Systems (IROS), Macau, China, 3–8 November 2019.

Journal of
*Marine Science
and Engineering*

MDPI

Article

Two-Branch Underwater Image Enhancement and Original Resolution Information Optimization Strategy in Ocean Observation

Dehuan Zhang [1,†], Wei Cao [1], Jingchun Zhou [1,*,†], Yan-Tsung Peng [2,*,†], Weishi Zhang [1,*] and Zifan Lin [3]

1 School of Information Science and Technology, Dalian Maritime University, Dalian 116026, China
2 Department of Computer Science, National Chengchi University, Taipei 116011, China
3 Department of Electrical and Electronic Engineering, University of Western Australia, Perth, WA 6009, Australia
* Correspondence: zhoujingchun@dlmu.edu.cn (J.Z.); ytpeng@cs.nccu.edu.tw (Y.-T.P.); teesiv@dlmu.edu.cn (W.Z.)
† These authors contributed equally to this work.

Abstract: In complex marine environments, underwater images often suffer from color distortion, blur, and poor visibility. Existing underwater image enhancement methods predominantly rely on the U-net structure, which assigns the same weight to different resolution information. However, this approach lacks the ability to extract sufficient detailed information, resulting in problems such as blurred details and color distortion. We propose a two-branch underwater image enhancement method with an optimized original resolution information strategy to address this limitation. Our method comprises a feature enhancement subnetwork (FEnet) and an original resolution subnetwork (ORSnet). FEnet extracts multi-resolution information and utilizes an adaptive feature selection module to enhance global features in different dimensions. The enhanced features are then fed into ORSnet as complementary features, which extract local enhancement features at the original image scale to achieve semantically consistent and visually superior enhancement effects. Experimental results on the UIEB dataset demonstrate that our method achieves the best performance compared to the state-of-the-art methods. Furthermore, through comprehensive application testing, we have validated the superiority of our proposed method in feature extraction and enhancement compared to other end-to-end underwater image enhancement methods.

Keywords: underwater image enhancement; adaptive feature selection; two-branch network; original resolution information enhancement

Citation: Zhang, D.; Cao, W.; Zhou, J.; Peng, Y.-T.; Zhang, W.; Li, Z. Two-Branch Underwater Image Enhancement and Original Resolution Information Optimization Strategy in Ocean Observation. *J. Mar. Sci. Eng.* **2023**, *11*, 1285. https://doi.org/10.3390/jmse11071285

Academic Editor: Fabio Bruno

Received: 10 May 2023
Revised: 21 June 2023
Accepted: 22 June 2023
Published: 25 June 2023

1. Introduction

The quality of underwater images is significantly diminished by light absorption, and scattering [1], such as color distortion and contrast decrease. For ocean engineering [2], and underwater archaeology, acquiring high-vision underwater images is crucial [3].

Many techniques based on image enhancement, image restoration, and deep learning have been thoroughly investigated to enhance the visual effects of single underwater images. Image pixel values are directly processed using enhancement approaches [4,5] to improve particular image qualities, such as color, contrast, and brightness. Image quality enhancement is treated as an inverse problem using physical imaging models and prior restrictions in image restoration-based approaches [6,7]. Deep learning has recently achieved exceptional performance [8–10] and image processing [11–14] benefits from the robust modeling capabilities of neural networks and the rich feature information extracted from enormous amounts of training images. Many deep learning-based techniques [15–17] are designed to draw vital information for improving the visual performance of underwater images.

At present, the underwater image enhancement methods with better performance mostly use the U-net structure as the main framework, and the U-net structure gives the same weight to the multi-resolution information, ignoring the importance of the original resolution, but the image enhancement largely relies on the representation of original resolution pixels, which prompts us to propose a multi-resolution information enhancement network (MIEN), which contains a feature enhancement subnetwork (based on Unet) and an original resolution subnetwork. The feature enhancement subnetwork branch comprehensively uses the characteristics of the Unet structure to focus the network on multi-resolution features and extract the features of different objects in different scenes. FEnet facilitates subsequent image recovery. The original resolution subnetwork does not have any downsampling operations and pays more attention to the dependencies between pixels to promote detail enhancement. Compared with other enhancement methods, we not only consider the global information of different scales when performing feature enhancement but also pay attention to the detailed information of the original size, which makes the enhanced image better visual effects and provides better help for subsequent work such as object recognition. The main contributions are as follows:

(1) To enhance the extraction ability of detailed information, we design an original resolution subnetwork (ORSnet) to extract scene detail information at the original resolution without any up-sampling and down-sampling, to retain the scene detail feature information at the original resolution to the greatest extent.

(2) Our proposed adaptive feature selection module (AFSM) can extract the global information of underwater images from different scales and allow the network to process different information. We introduced adaptive coefficients to promote AFSM effectively fuse remote context information.

(3) To better solve the problem of image blurring, we developed the Semantic Feature Reconstruction Module (SFRM), which uses different convolutions to obtain semantic feature information, and then reconstructs the semantic features of the image through the fusion mechanism to make the visual effect of the image closer to the ground reality.

The remainder of the paper is structured as follows: Section II thoroughly analyzes learning-based and conventional UIE techniques. The proposed MIEN is then thoroughly introduced in Section III. In Section IV, we examined several novel methods on various datasets and ran ablation experiments, and application tests to test the capability of the MIEN. Section V is where we wrap up our discussion and make recommendations for further work.

We will demonstrate how our method outperforms existing techniques in terms of enhancing underwater images. We will provide quantitative metrics such as image quality assessment scores and subjective evaluations to support our claims. By showcasing the superior performance of our method, we will illustrate the need for an improved approach.

2. Related works

Many UIE techniques, which can be generally separated into traditional methods [18–35] and deep learning techniques [2,36–46], have recently been presented to address blurring and color cast.

2.1. Traditional Underwater Image Enhancement Methods

At that time, visual enhancement of underwater images was mostly achieved by modifying the RGB space pixel values. The blue channel, which predominates in underwater images, was stretched toward the lower level following the Rayleigh distribution by Ghani and Isa [18], whereas the inferior red channel was stretched toward the higher level. These techniques provide results that look brilliant, but they are prone to overexposure issues. Additionally, it is unable to effectively resolve the precise content and suspended materials [18]. As we all know, refraction and absorption lead to deteriorated underwater image quality. Underwater restoration techniques frequently employ the Jaffe-McGlamery model [19]. Numerous researchers developed several transmission estimating techniques based on Jaffe-McGlamery and inversely achieved the reconstructed findings. To optimize the visual contrast, Liu and Chau [20], developed a loss function based on quadtree subdivision and found the ideal transmission map. A technique for underwater dehazing was suggested by Li et al. [21], which included a global underwater light estimating algorithm and a regression model-based medium transmission estimate algorithm. An adaptive attenuation-curve prior, created by Wang et al. [22] and based on the statistical distribution of pixel values, is a non-local prior. To lessen the effects of water interference, Xie et al. [23] included a forward scattering component in the formulation model together with the normalized total variation and sparse previous information.

But there is a crucial distinction between the scattering model and the deteriorated undersea appearance that cannot be overlooked. The complexity of underwater imaging is increased by its optical characteristics. Other widely used conventional techniques take advantage of the statistical patterns in the unique look of underwater images. In [24] it is initially suggested to use a dark channel before disclosing the statistics of outside images. To accomplish visual enhancement, Chiang and Chen [25] enhanced the dark channel and coupled the wavelength-dependent compensatory techniques. After that, by examining the applicability of the absorption in underwater images, Drews et al. [26] created the underwater dark channel. Before anticipating a more reliable transmission, Liang et al. [27] introduced the underwater dark channel. Before underwater image restoration, Peng et al. [28] proposed the generalized dark channel and included an adaptive color correction in the construction.

Moreover, Carlevaris-Bianco et al. [29] suggested a straightforward prior that estimates the transmission using the stark differences in attenuation across the RGB color channels in water. Ref. [29] discovered that the red wavelength attenuates more quickly than the green and blue ones. A red channel technique that restores the color connected to the short wavelength was created by Galdran et al. [30]. Li et al. [31,47] developed a unique histogram distribution prior based on the minimal information loss assumption. To rectify the image color, Akkaynak and Treibitz [32] included the depth information and altered the underwater image creation.

Although the usual model-based approaches mentioned above have some influence on solving the color cast problem, traditional underwater image enhancement methods are only helpful for a particular kind of underwater image because of the influence of lighting. Additionally, because of the fixed formations and models, image restoration approaches are challenged by the exact assessment of the degradation concerns.

2.2. Learning-Based Underwater Image Enhancement Methods

Deep learning has advanced significantly in a lot of low-level vision missions. A growing number of researchers are beginning to apply it to the enhancement of underwater images [36]. Researchers have put much effort into developing novel sample generation techniques, more efficient learning techniques, and network topologies in recent years.

Because image transfer techniques have succeeded, Fabbri et al. [37] suggested using CycleGAN [38] to create synthetic underwater images. Then, GAN-based deep models are extensively investigated, including FGAN [39], DenseGAN [40], MLFcGAN [41], and FUnIE-GAN [42]. A real-world underwater image enhancement benchmark (UIEB), made up of 890 paired real-world underwater images, was later created by Li et al. [45]. According to the subject's preferred visual style, the associated enhancement references are manually chosen among enhancement candidates. The reference-based performance evaluation [48] and the investigation of deep learning-based techniques for UIE [2,43] both benefited considerably from the work of UIEB.

Researchers also looked at novel learning techniques and network topologies to make the most of the few highly visual underwater images available. Li et al. [45] proposed the WaterNet gated fusion network with the UIEB dataset, which fuses the inputs with three projected confidence maps to provide an improved result. When Qi et al. [44] introduced correlation feature matching units to transmit the mutual correlation of the two input branches, [44] suggested the Underwater Image Co-Enhancement Network (UICoE-Net). Li et al. [43] proposed learning rich feature information from various color spaces and attention weights through transmission maps. As a result, [43] designed the Ucolor encoder-decoder enhancement network.

Combined with the characteristics of underwater imaging, Wu et al. [49] proposed a novel two-stage underwater image convolutional neural network (CNN) based on structure decomposition (UWCNN-SD), the first stage is designed to design a preliminary enhancement network containing high-frequency and low-frequency enhancement networks to achieve the initial enhancement of underwater images, and the second stage proposes a refined network to further optimize the color of underwater images to obtain underwater images with higher visual quality. Ding et al. [50] proposed an efficient dual-stream method to improve the quality of underwater images, in which a significant area refinement algorithm is designed to solve the problem of chromatic aberration of the image, and a global appearance adjustment algorithm is designed to improve the clarity of the image and obtain a clearer enhanced image. Yan et al. [51] proposed an attention-guided dynamic multi-branching neural network (ADMNNet) to acquire high-quality underwater images, in which attention-guided dynamic multi-branching blocks are used to combine attributes under different RF into a single-stream structure to improve the diversity of feature representations. Fu et al. [52] proposed a two-branch network to compensate for global distortion and local contrast reduction, respectively. The use of a global-local network greatly simplifies the learning problem, allowing a lightweight network architecture to be used to process underwater images. Lin et al. [53] proposed a new two-stage network for underwater images, which divides the recovery process into two stages, horizontal and vertical distortion recovery, so that the network can effectively solve the scattering and absorption problems. In the first phase, they propose a model-based network that embeds underwater physical models directly into the network to deal with horizontal distortion. In the second stage, they propose a new Attenuation Coefficient Priority Attention Block (AC-PAB) to adaptively recalibrate the RGB channel feature map of images affected by vertical distortion. Yu et al. [54] proposed a new multi-attention path aggregation network (APAN), which uses a path aggregation network structure with a backbone network and bottom-up path extension features to enhance semantic features, enhance feature extraction capabilities, and improve the visual effect of underwater images. As the existing underwater image enhancement methods primarily rely on the U-net structure, which emphasizes the extraction of global information, it often results in the loss of image details. To address this limitation, we propose a multi-resolution information enhancement network that enhances features at various resolutions, with particular emphasis on the original resolution. This approach aims to mitigate the loss of image detail information.

3. Proposed Method

The proposed MIEN is divided into two branches: the feature enhancement subnetwork and the original resolution subnetwork. The feature enhancement subnetwork focuses on the drawing of global information, AFSM is used to enhance the extraction of global features of underwater images to solve the problem of color casting. To emphasize the preservation of detailed information, we devised the original resolution subnetwork, which focuses on retaining the feature details of the original resolution layer in underwater images. As a result, our MIEN can produce excellent results for image recovery. The MIEN frame is shown in Figure 1.

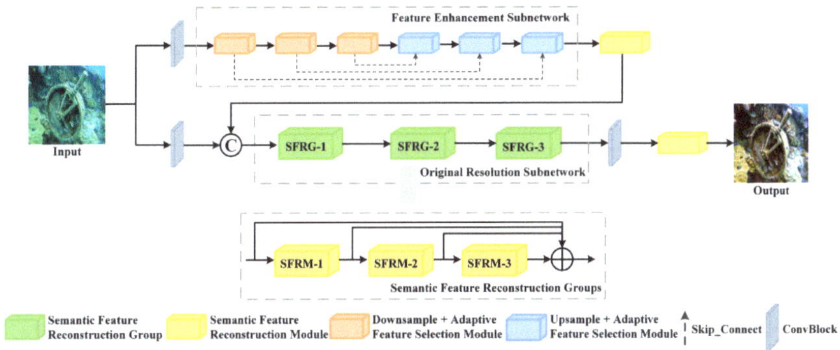

Figure 1. The structure of MIEN. MIEN contains two branches, the upper branch is the feature enhancement subnetwork for extracting features of different resolutions, and the lower branch is the original resolution subnetwork for extracting local information.

3.1. Feature Enhancement Subnetwork

We develop a feature enhancement subnetwork (FEnet) based on the Unet structure, which focuses on multi-resolution features. In FEnet, we propose the adaptive feature selection module to extract the various scenes in the underwater image and extract the global features in the low-resolution. As a result, FEnet can obtain better feature representation for high-quality image reproduction.

Adaptive Feature Selection Module

The enhancing feature selection module, the adaptive channel selection module, and the adaptive spatial selection module make up the adaptive feature selection module(AFSM). These three branches work together to extract global information and provide our network the capacity to handle various information kinds in various ways. Additionally, we can tackle the issue of information overload and enhance the effectiveness and precision of task processing by incorporating an adjustable coefficient to force AFSM to concentrate on the essential information of the present task among the various input information. Thus, for high-quality image restoration, our AFSN obtains improved feature representations. The module framework is shown in Figure 2.

(1) ASSM

The UIE task relies heavily on context relationships in space, so to further enhance the spatial information of features, we introduce ASSM. Additionally, we incorporate an adaptive parameter (α) in the ASSM to dynamically adjust the weighting of the entire ASSM branch. The initial value of α is set to 0, and its optimal value is gradually learned during the training process. By incorporating this adaptive parameter, our AFSN effectively integrates long-range spatial contextual information, thus enhancing its learning capacity.

First, we compress channel features with convolutional layers and use Softmax to obtain spatial attention weights:

$$\omega_j^s = \frac{\exp\left(A_j^{s'}\right)}{\sum_{m=1}^{N} \exp(A_m^s)}, \tag{1}$$

where $N = H \times W$ is the number of pixels. A_j^s represented squeeze channel-wise, j represents the j-th pixel. The input features are reshaped into $R^{HW \times 1 \times 1}$ after a convolution, and then softmax to generate spatial attention weights $\omega_j^S \in R^{HW \times 1 \times 1}$. The ω_j^S is then multiplied by the input features to generate spatial long-range contextual features $D^S \in R^{C \times 1 \times 1}$.

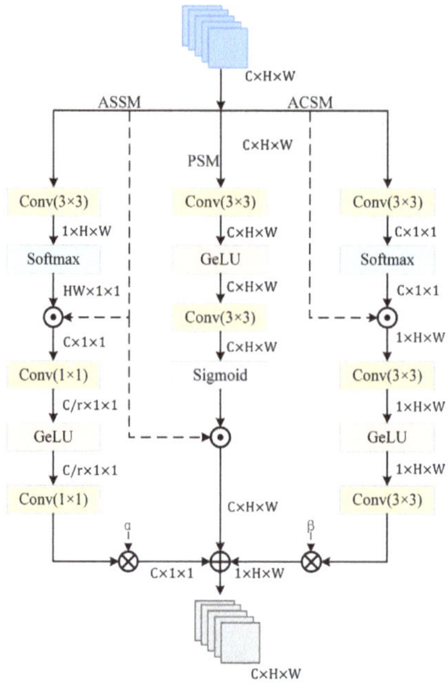

Figure 2. The overall architecture of AFSM. The AFSM is divided into three branches: ASSM, ACSM, and EFSM.

Attention weights and raw characteristics are multiplied in a matrix to acquire information about the distant spatial context:

$$D^s = \sum_{j=1}^{N} \omega_j^s B_j^s, \tag{2}$$

where we reshape an input $X \in R^{C\times H\times W}$ to obtain $B^s \in R^{C\times HW}$, $D^s \in R^{C\times 1\times 1}$ represents spatial features.

Finally, α is used for feature transformation and feature fusion. As in Formula (3):

$$\begin{aligned} Out_{ASSM} = &\left(\alpha W_{s2}(W_{s1} \sum_{j=1}^{N} \frac{\exp(W_k X_j)}{\sum_{m=1}^{N} \exp(W_k X_m)} X_j) \right. \\ &\left. \times \frac{1}{2}[1 + erf(W_{s1} \sum_{j=1}^{N} \frac{\exp(W_k X_j)}{\sum_{m=1}^{N} \exp(W_k X_m)} X_j \Big/ \sqrt{2})] \right), \end{aligned} \tag{3}$$

where W_{s1} stands for a 1×1 convolutional layer, W_{s2} represents a GeLU activation layer, and a 1×1 convolutional layer, α for an adaptive learning weight, W_k represents a convolutional layer to squeeze channel-wise features: $A^s = W_k X$, $A^s \in R^{1\times H\times W}$, and $Out_{ASSM} \in R^{C\times 1\times 1}$ represents the output of ASSM.

(2) ACSM

The underwater image color recovery task relies heavily on the context relationship in the channel, so to further enhance the channel information of the feature, we introduce ACSM. Besides, We also have introduced an adaptive parameter(β) in ACSM to adjust the result weighting of the entire branch of ACSM, the initial value of β is set to 0, and the optimal value is gradually learned. AFSM efficiently fuses long-range channel-wise contextual data owing to its adaptive learning weight.

First, the spatial features are compressed with average pooling, and the channel attention weights are obtained using Softmax. As in Equation (4):

$$\omega_j^c = \frac{\exp\left(A_j^c\right)}{\sum_{m=1}^{c} \exp(A_m^c)}, \tag{4}$$

where C is the number of channels, A_j^c indicates squeeze spatial-wise, j represents the j-th pixel, c represents the channel dimension, ω^c represents the channel-wise attention weights.

Attention weights and raw characteristics are multiplied in a matrix to generate remote channel context data. similar to Formula (5):

$$D^c = \sum_{j=1}^{c} \omega_j^c B_j^c, \tag{5}$$

where we reshape an input $X \in R^{C\times H\times W}$ to obtain $B^c \in R^{C\times HW}$, $D^s \in R^{C\times 1\times 1}$ indicates channel features.

Finally, we introduce an adaptive weight for feature transformation and feature fusion. As in Formula (6):

$$\begin{gathered} Out_{ACSM} = \left(\beta W_{c2}(W_{c1} \sum_{j=1}^{N} \frac{\exp(Pool_{avg}X_j)}{\sum_{m=1}^{c} \exp(Pool_{avg}X_m)} X_j) \right. \\ \left. \times \frac{1}{2}[1 + erf(W_{c1} \sum_{j=1}^{N} \frac{\exp(Pool_{avg}X_j)}{\sum_{m=1}^{c} \exp(Pool_{avg}X_m)} X_j \Big/ \sqrt{2})]\right), \end{gathered} \tag{6}$$

where W_{c1} represents a 3×3 convolutional layer, W_{c2} represents one GeLU activation layer and one 3×3 convolutional layer, β represents an adaptive learning weight, $Out_{ACSM} \in R^{1\times H\times W}$ represents the output of ACSM.

(3) EFSM

To enhance the global information of the image, we introduce EFSM to aggregate them with the other two branches to ensure that the main information of the input image is retained while obtaining the context features of space and channel.

The main features are first extracted using convolutional layers, and the weights of the extracted features are obtained using Sigmoid. As in Formula (7):

$$\omega_j^P = \sum_{j=1}^{P} \sigma W_{p2}(W_{p1}(X_j \times \frac{1}{2}[1 + erf(X_j \big/ \sqrt{2})]), \tag{7}$$

where $X \in R^{C\times H\times W}$ indicates the input, $P = C\times H\times W$ is the number of pixels. W_{p1} represents one GeLU activation layer and one 3×3 convolutional layer, W_{p2} represents a 3×3 convolutional layer, σ represents a Sigmoid activation layer, ω_j^P represents the detailed features weights.

Finally, the corresponding element point multiplication operation is performed between the weight and original feature to get the global feature. As in Formula (8):

$$Out_{EFSM} = \sum_{j=1}^{P} \omega_j^p B_j^p, \tag{8}$$

where $B \in R^{C\times H\times W}$, $Out_{PSM} \in R^{C\times H\times W}$ represents the output of EFSM.

By combining the three branches of the ASSM, ACSM, and EFSM, our proposed method achieves a more comprehensive enhancement of both global and local information. This enables the FEnet to effectively process different types of features, ensuring that the network prioritizes the extraction of global information while addressing the color bias issue in images. AFSM can be formulated as follows:

$$Out_{AFSM} = Out_{ASSM} + Out_{ACSM} + Out_{EFSM}. \quad (9)$$

3.2. Original Resolution Subnetwork

Most of the existing methods [40,41,43] adopted the Unet architecture to extract image information of different resolutions of images through downsampling, but underwater enhanced images strongly rely on the features of the original resolution space, and Unet-based methods process the original resolution image features and low-resolution features to the same extent. According to the characteristics of image enhancement, we have added an original resolution branch based on the Unet-based method, which can directly process the original resolution image, and better preserve the details and features, avoiding the loss of detail features resulting in reducing the resolution. To keep the feature resolution fixed, ORSnet does not use any upsampling or downsampling operations, so that the network can retain spatial details to the greatest extent. It is composed of Semantic Feature Reconstruction Groups (SFRG).

Semantic Feature Reconstruction Module

The SFRG comprises a Semantic Feature Reconstruction Module (SFRM) and AFSM, under the premise of unchanged original resolution, retaining the global feature information from the input map to the output map to generate high-resolution underwater images. We introduce the multi-scale structure, which can solve the problem of loss of detail features caused by a single convolution. The module frame structure is shown in Figure 3.

Firstly, 3×3 and 5×5 convolution kernels are used to extract essential features, respectively. Such as formula (10), where $k \in \{3, 5\}$.

$$F_c = \sum_{j=1}^{N} W_k(X_j \times \frac{1}{2}[1 + erf(X_j / \sqrt{2})]), \quad (10)$$

where $X \in R^{C \times H \times W}$ indicates the input, W_k represents one GeLU activation layer, and one $k \times k$ convolutional layer.

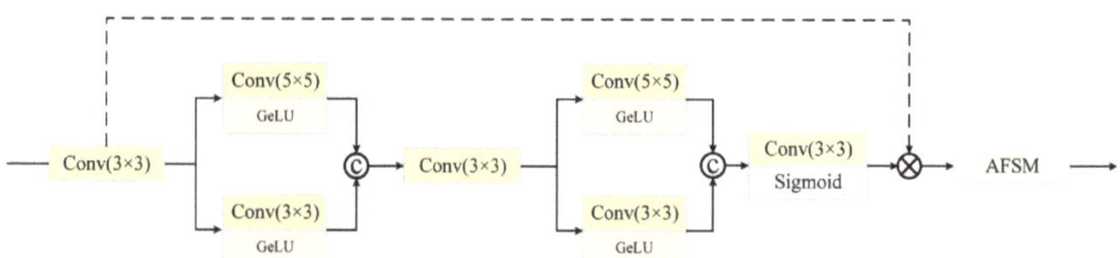

Figure 3. The overall architecture of the Semantic Feature Reconstruction Module. We use 3×3 and 5×5 to obtain different ranges of sensory fields, and then enhance the features by obtaining weights.

The generated feature map is convoluted to achieve fusing features:

$$G_f = W_3(cat(F_3, F_5)), \quad (11)$$

where W_3 represents one GeLU activation layer and one 3×3 convolutional layer, F_3, F_5 represent the characteristic map convolved by a convolution kernel of 3×3 and 5×5, respectively. The cat denotes a concatenate operation.

Extract features from the fused feature and utilize Sigmoid to obtain the weights of important features:

$$\omega_f = \sigma(W_3(G_f \times \frac{1}{2}[1 + erf(G_f / \sqrt{2})])), \quad (12)$$

where σ indicates the Sigmoid, ω_f represents the weight of extracted features.

Finally, the point multiplication operation is performed between the weights and the original features to preserve the global feature information:

$$Out_{SFRM} = \sum_{j=1}^{N} \omega_j^N B_j^N, \tag{13}$$

where N is the number of pixels, and Out_{SFRM} represents the output of SFRM. Input the feature map generated by SFRM into the AFSM module and output the feature map.

3.3. Loss Function

Underwater images suffer from limitations such as low brightness, image blurring, and color deviation. Previous approaches to underwater image enhancement that rely solely on a single loss function may not yield satisfactory results in image restoration. We comprehensively consider the absolute error loss L_1 and the minimization of the perceived loss L_p, and the loss function suitable for underwater images is designed. L_2 loss is often used in previous image recovery tasks, but its flaws can overly penalize more significant errors and reduce the quality of image recovery. We use the minimization of total error losses. It is defined as follows:

$$L_{l1} = \|I_{out} - I_{label}\|_1, \tag{14}$$

where I_{out} and I_{label} represent enhanced images and labeled images from UIEB, respectively. L_1 loss calculates absolute values by comparing them pixel by pixel.

Another loss is perception loss, which compares the features obtained from the enhanced image with those obtained from the original image, bringing high-level information closer. Referential perceived loss helps improve the performance of our network, resulting in images with better visual effects. The perceived loss defined on a pre-trained VGG-19 network on ImageNet can be expressed as:

$$L_P = \frac{1}{H^*W} \sum_{i=1}^{H} \sum_{j=1}^{W} \left[\varphi(I_{out})_{i,j} - \varphi(I_{label})_{i,j} \right]^2, \tag{15}$$

where the feature map of the pool-3 layers of a VGG-19 network trained on ImageNet is represented by $\varphi()$. The height and width of the feature map are denoted by H and W.

The total loss function is as follows:

$$L_t = \lambda_1 L_{l1} + \lambda_2 L_P, \tag{16}$$

where λ_1 and λ_2 are hyperparameters set empirically to 1 and 0.2, respectively.

4. Experiments and Analysis

4.1. Preparation

4.1.1. Data

In contrast to other computer vision applications, obtaining clear underwater images is complicated since the small amount of publically available data. The training data set was only just suggested in UIEB [45]. It includes 890 image pairings that include both distorted and ground-truth underwater images. The remaining 90 images are utilized for validation after we randomly choose 800 image pairings to use as the training set.

4.1.2. Training Settings

Our method trains 500 epochs using batch learning techniques during training. There are 8 batches in each. The network is optimized using AdamW, and the learning rate is set at 0.0001. The training images have a resolution of 256 × 256 × 3. The UIEB validation [45], UIEB_test60, MABLs [55], UFO120 [56], EUVP [42] and the U45 [57] were chosen for testing throughout the testing phase.

4.1.3. Methods for Comparison

We investigated seven comparison techniques on UIEB, including IBLA [58], SMBL [55], GDCP [28], HLRP [59], Ucolor [43], and WaterNet [45], to confirm the improvements and outcomes obtained by our method. For the deep learning-based comparison method, we retrained using a partitioned dataset.

4.2. *Evaluation of Underwater Images*

4.2.1. Objective Evaluation Metrics

We use the non-reference underwater image quality measure (UIQM) [60], CCF [61], naturalness image quality evaluator (NIQE) [62], contrast enhancement image quality (CEIQ) [63], Shannon (SH), mean-square error (MSE), feature similarity index measure (FSIM) [64], peak signal-to-noise-ratio (PSNR) [65], and structural similarity (SSIM) [66] to evaluate the underwater image quality quantitatively. This CCF is a feature-weighted combination of the colorfulness index, contrast index, and fog density index, which are used to predict the color loss caused by absorption, the blurring caused by forward scattering, and the foggy caused by backward scattering. In addition, for CCF we also removed the color component. The MSE is a measure that reflects the degree of difference between an estimator and an estimated amount. The FSIM uses feature similarity for quality evaluation. The PSNR calculates the average error between the input and output based on error-sensitive image quality evaluation. The three components of an image—illumination, contrast, and structure—are often assessed using the SSIM. The underwater image colorfulness measure (UICM) [60], underwater image sharpness measure (UISM) [60], and underwater image contrast measure (UIConM) [60] are the three underwater image attribute measures that make up the UIQM. The UIQM formula is as follows:

$$UIQM = c_1 \times UICM + c_2 \times UISM + c_3 \times UIConM, \tag{17}$$

where c_1, c_2 and c_3 are the coefficients. We set their values to: c_1 = 0.0282, c_2 =0.2953, and c_3 = 3.5753.

4.2.2. Underwater Image Evaluation of Different Scenarios

The proposed method is tested using actual underwater images with three color deviations. Figure 4 displays a few subjective sample outcomes from various techniques. In Figure 4b, the IBLA enhances contrast but is unable to enhance the yellow- and green-toned underwater images. GDCP introduces reddish or greenish hues based on the findings in Figure 4c. In Figure 4d, the improvement produced by WaterNet was darker than the outcomes of other techniques, indicating poor visual contrast. This may also result in color bias as the WaterNet approach creates a white balance channel, which is sometimes inaccurate for enhancing images. The estimated transmission map is dependent on the information from the red channel, thus while SMBL considerably improves the yellow-toned images, it fails to work with images that have high red channel attenuation, as seen in Figure 4e. Ucolor employs a multi-color spatial encoder to enable enhanced image colors to be more authentic, however, as the subjective results image shows, Ucolor does not solve the problem of blurred edges. From a color-correction standpoint, Ucolor's enhancing outcomes produce greater visual quality. The enhanced image is closer to GT and has outstanding aesthetic effects when using the HLRP approach in blue-green situations, but in green scenarios, the improved image's color darkens and makes it difficult to detect finer details, as illustrated in Figure 4g. The explanation might be that these physical model-based methods require a precise prior model, which is very challenging to get. In contrast, our approach efficiently eliminates the greenish, blue, and bluish-green tones without adding any artificial colors. This result demonstrates the effectiveness of the proposed approach in generalizing across various underwater scenarios. Additionally, the technique suggested in this paper may eliminate the majority of the haze-like effects and raise the clarity of the features in the image.

Haze-like underwater images are more impacted by effects, which are brought on by different wavelength attenuation, than underwater images with distinct color deviations. As seen in Figure 5, these contrast methods are not very effective in dehazing, and some methods can even cause overexposure problems. Contrarily, our technique successfully enhances the visibility of underwater images by removing haze while restoring true color.

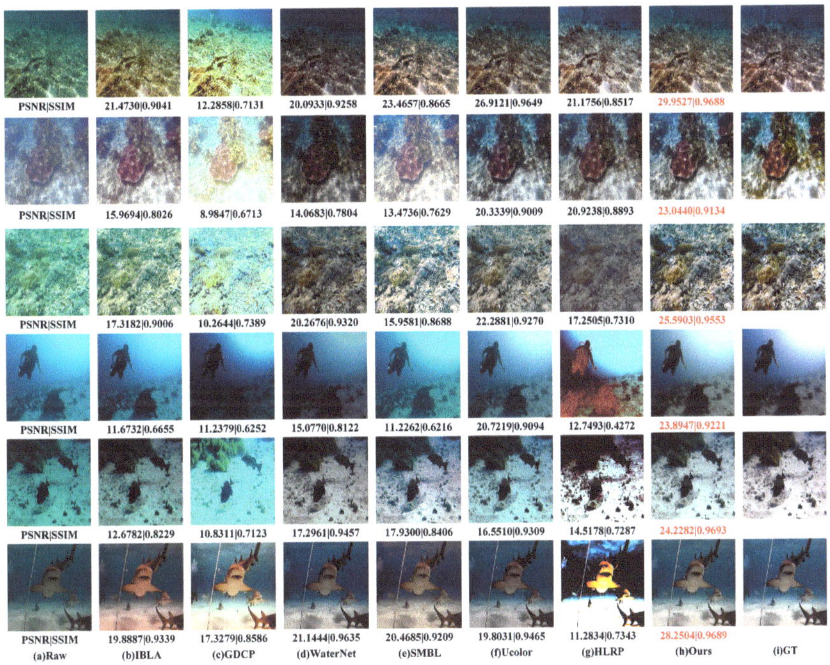

Figure 4. Results of qualitative comparison of 90 random images in UIEB. The contrast methods are (**a**) Raw, (**b**) IBLA [58], (**c**) GDCP [28], (**d**) WaterNet [45], (**e**) SMBL [55], (**f**) Ucolor [43], (**g**) HLRP [59], (**h**) Ours, (**i**) Ground-Truth.

Figure 5. Comparisons of results on the haze-like dataset. At the bottom of this image are the scores for PSNR and SSIM.

In Figure 6, we can see that GDCP and HLRP still exhibit color casts and water retention when processing images, and GDCP methods are overexposed. The enhanced image of the IBLA method will have a reddish cast, which will affect the visual effect. The image enhanced by the SMBL method appears overly shadowed, resulting in some blurred details. The WaterNet and Ucolor methods enhance the visual effect of the image, and our method can achieve this effect.

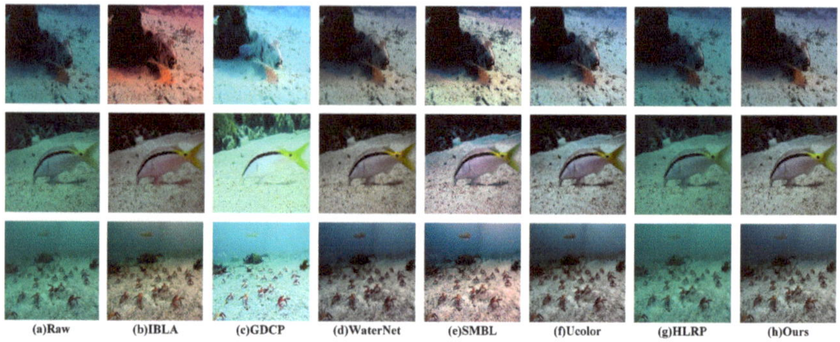

Figure 6. Visual comparisons on images. (**a**) represents the original image from UIEB_test, (**b**–**h**) showcases the results obtained by IBLA [58], GDCP [28], WaterNet [45], SMBL [55], Ucolor [43], HLRP [59], and our proposed method, respectively.

Figure 7 shows a subjective comparison of our method with the comparative method on the UFO120 dataset. In Figure 7, IBLA, GDCP, and HLRP all over-enhance during image enhancement, making the image shadow too heavy, resulting in unclear image edges. The image enhancement results of the WaterNet method in the third row of Figure 7 still retain some water effects. Ucolor visualizes better than other methods but still causes some fog effects, resulting in blurry images that are not sharp enough. Our method, both in terms of eliminating the effects of water and color recovery, is superior to other methods, and our method does not cause other post-enhancement effects.

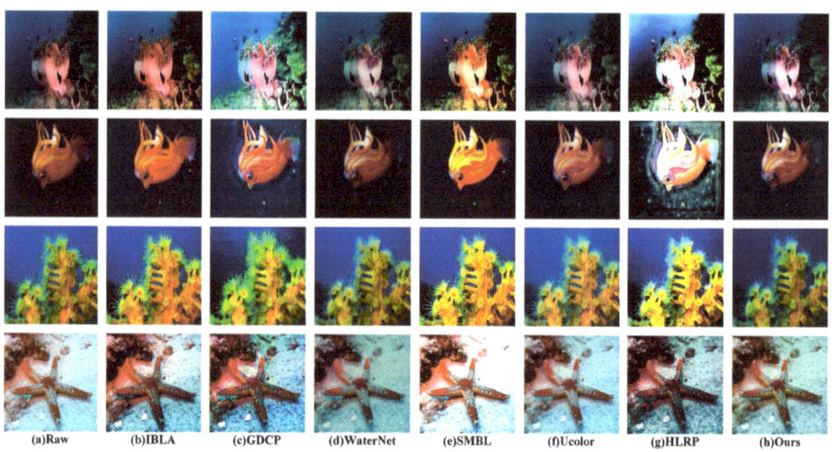

Figure 7. Visual comparisons on images. (**a**) represents the original image from UFO120, (**b**–**h**) showcases the results obtained by IBLA [58], GDCP [28], WaterNet [45], SMBL [55], Ucolor [43], HLRP [59], and our proposed method, respectively.

In Figure 8, we compared it in the MABLS dataset, and compared to other methods, we eliminated the water effect when processing, making the image closer to the GT effect and sharper than other methods.

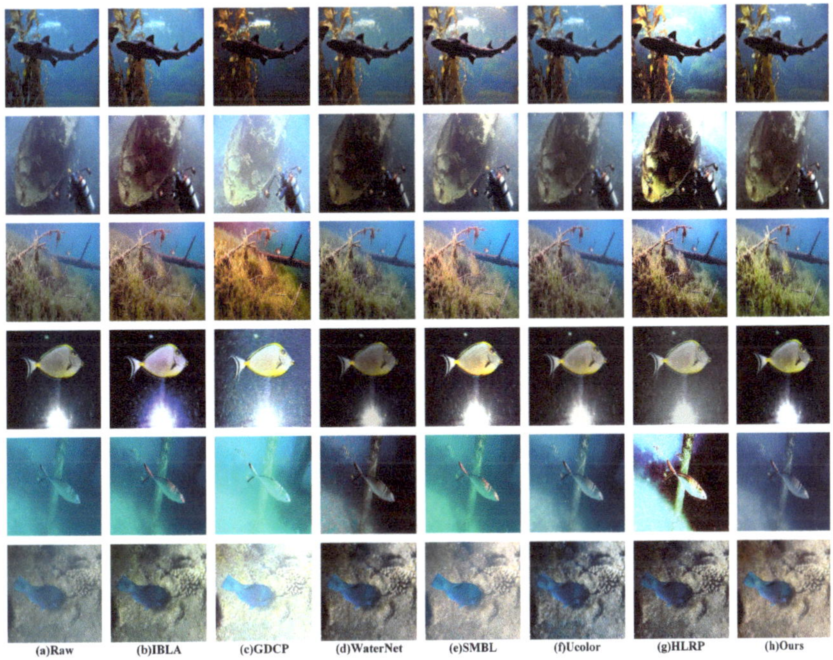

Figure 8. Visual comparisons on images. (**a**) represents the original image from MABLs, (**b–h**) showcases the results obtained by IBLA [58], GDCP [28], WaterNet [45], SMBL [55], Ucolor [43], HLRP [59], and our proposed method, respectively.

In Figure 9, the IBLA and Ucolor methods are better preserved during the enhancement process but do not eliminate the influence of water, which directly affects the visual effect. The GDCP method causes a blue-green color cast during the enhancement process, and excessive enhancement leads to the loss of some detailed information. The SMBL method enhances images with overexposure and loss of detail, while WaterNet and our method solve these problems very well and have good visual effects.

We assessed the proposed strategy using both full-reference and non-reference objective metrics in our objective tests. As shown in Table 1, our technique performed well in terms of PSNR and SSIM measures, but the UIQM indicators showed only moderate performance. As discussed in Table 1, the objective indicators currently being developed for underwater images sometimes conflict with visual perception. This is because human vision has not evolved to match the conditions of aquatic environments. Using human visual perception as the sole method for color-correction of underwater images can be entirely unreliable since when people view an underwater image, humans tend to focus on the center of the scene or anything that appears vivid or interesting. Although this approach may work well for images with good aesthetic appeal, it does not consider attenuation and backscattering. Furthermore, Table 1 demonstrates that our strategy is more advantageous than the alternatives. In previous studies on underwater image enhancement, our proposed approach, which enhances contrast and corrects color casts in underwater images, showed competitive performance.

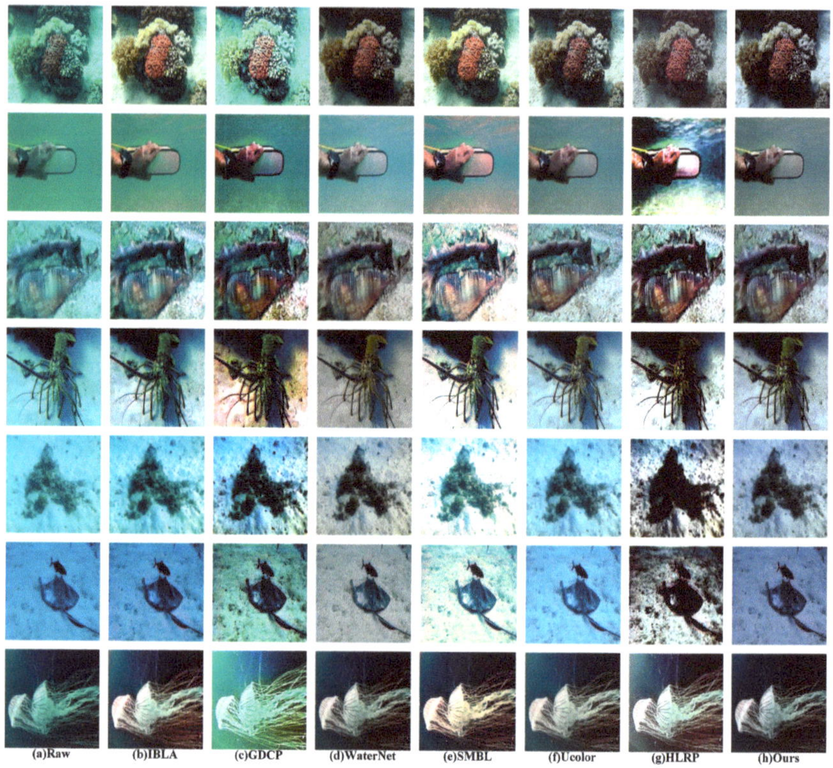

Figure 9. Visual comparisons on images. (**a**) represents the original image from U45 and EUVP, (**b–h**) showcases the results obtained by IBLA [58], GDCP [28], WaterNet [45], SMBL [55], Ucolor [43], HLRP [59], and our proposed method, respectively.

Table 1. Objective comparison of different enhancement techniques. Red in the table denotes best performance, blue denotes inferior performance.

Dataset	Method	IBLA	GDCP	WaterNet	SMBL	Ucolor	HLRP	Ours
UIEB_val	PSNR	17.9884	13.3856	17.3488	16.5970	20.9615	16.4516	23.1424
	SSIM	0.8048	0.7474	0.8132	0.7950	0.8635	0.6720	0.9119
	MSE	0.0891	0.2281	0.1445	0.1601	0.0972	0.1650	0.0729
	FSIM	0.9326	0.8988	0.9185	0.9229	0.9395	0.8464	0.9556
	CEIQ	3.2835	3.2076	3.1008	3.3067	3.2090	3.2763	3.3734
	UIQM	2.4900	2.6697	2.9165	2.5430	3.0495	2.1772	2.9566
	Average	4.2350	3.4468	4.1589	4.0008	4.8210	3.8764	5.2112
UIEB_test	CEIQ	3.1802	3.1207	2.9826	3.1425	3.0533	2.7885	3.1624
	UIQM	1.8344	2.1100	2.3986	1.9039	2.4813	1.9850	2.5254
	Average	2.5073	2.6154	2.6906	2.5232	2.7673	2.3868	2.8439
U45	CEIQ	3.2491	3.1914	3.1863	3.2491	3.2826	3.2986	3.3178
	UIQM	2.3877	2.2750	2.9570	2.3877	3.1481	2.7960	2.9153
	Average	2.8184	2.7332	3.0717	2.8184	3.2154	3.0473	3.1166

In addition, we chose Ucolor, the method with the highest UIQM among the comparison methods, and subjectively compared it with our method. It can be seen in Figure 10, although our method is inferior to Ucolor in terms of UIQM indicators, our visuals are superior to the Ucolor method.

Figure 10. In the UIEB dataset, Ucolor is subjectively compared with our method.

4.3. Ablation Experiments

In Table 2, we perform ablation research using the following experiments to better manifest the function of enhancement models in the MIEN architecture:

1. MIEN removes AFSM operation (w/o AFSM);
2. MIEN removes SFRM operation (w/o SFRM);
3. MIEN deleted FEnet operation (w/o FEnet);
4. MIEN deleted ORSnet operation (w/o ORSnet).

The scores of PSNR, SSIM, MSE, FEIM, CEIQ, and UIQM when removing different modules are given in Table 2. It can be found that the quantitative results are significantly reduced by removing different components, while MIEN has the best performance and quantitative results.

Table 2. Qualitative comparison of the different components of the proposed method. The bold font indicates the best.

Metric	w/o FEnet	w/o ORSnet	w/o AFSM	w/o SFRM	Ours
PSNR	20.7856	21.2991	22.8955	23.0597	**23.1424**
SSIM	0.8582	0.8711	0.9066	0.9037	**0.9119**
MSE	0.1025	0.0963	0.1141	0.1138	**0.0729**
FSIM	0.8912	0.8943	0.9465	0.9480	**0.9556**
CEIQ	3.2510	3.3271	3.3097	3.3540	**3.3734**
UIQM	2.8512	2.9375	2.9009	2.9148	**2.9566**
Average	4.7558	4.8721	5.1409	5.1777	**5.2112**

Inside AFSM, we did w/o ASSM, w/o ACSM, w/o EFSM, and w/o α, β corresponding ablation experiments to prove the effectiveness of the AFSM module. Table 3 demonstrates how we configured w/o ASSM to exclusively remove ASSM and the associated option α. Similarly, we create w/o ACSM, which solely removes ACSM and the associated option β. We created the w/o EFSM option, which eliminates EFSM. As evidence of the efficacy of the ACSM, ASSM, and EFSM, the relevant indicators of AFSM, w/o ASSM, w/o ACSM, and w/o EFSM all decreased. The adaptive learning weights α and β are then removed using the proposal w/o α, β. The correlation of indicators for adaptive learning weights w/o α, β is also reduced when compared to AFSM, demonstrating their efficiency. As a result of a few more settings, our AFSM significantly improves image restoration.

Inside SFRM, we set w/o 3×3, w/o 5×5, w/o one layer multiscale, w/o two layers multiscale, and w/o AFSM corresponding ablation experiments to prove the effectiveness of the AFSM module. We configured w/o 3×3, which removes the 3×3 convolution in the multiscale part, as shown in Table 4. Similar to this, we created the w/o 5×5 algorithm. We came up with w/o two layers of multiscale, which removes the multiscale part. The relevant indicators of w/o 3 × 3, w/o 5 × 5, w/o one layer multiscale, and w/o two layers multiscale all decreased when compared to the SFRM, demonstrating the efficiency of the multiscale section. In addition, we suggest the deletion of the Adaptive Feature Selection Module, abbreviated as w/o AFSM. The fact that w/o AFSM has fewer than the corresponding indicators of SFRM shows how effective the Adaptive Feature Selection Module is. In conclusion, our SFRM significantly improves image color restoration.

Table 3. Ablation study in AFSM. The bold font indicates the best.

Metric	w/o ASSM	w/o ACSM	w/o EFSM	w/o SAM	w/o CAM	w/o α	w/o β	w/o α, β	Ours
PSNR	22.4899	22.5163	22.6754	23.0010	21.9513	22.0468	22.8911	22.8080	**23.0597**
SSIM	0.8794	0.8990	0.8987	0.8115	0.9010	0.8905	0.8872	0.9024	**0.9037**
MSE	0.1257	0.1191	0.1209	0.1300	0.1257	0.1180	0.1140	0.1148	**0.1138**
FSIM	0.9169	0.9254	0.9447	0.9351	0.9194	0.9267	0.9099	0.9418	**0.9480**
CEIQ	2.9867	2.9987	3.1182	3.0081	2.9971	3.1007	3.2016	3.2004	**3.3540**
UIQM	2.8927	2.9001	2.8871	2.8775	2.9068	2.9111	2.9081	2.9051	**2.9148**
Average	5.0067	5.0201	5.0672	5.0839	4.9250	4.6411	5.1140	5.1072	**5.1777**

Table 4. Ablation study in SFRM. The bold font indicates the best.

Metric	w/o 3 × 3	w/o 5 × 5	w/o OLMS	w/o TLMS	w/o AFSM	Ours
PSNR	22.8857	22.6449	21.9864	22.3551	22.0011	**22.8955**
SSIM	0.9030	0.9022	0.8816	0.8927	0.8993	**0.9066**
MSE	0.1187	0.1253	0.1307	0.1220	0.1146	**0.1141**
FSIM	0.9305	0.9129	0.9317	0.9188	0.9092	**0.9465**
CEIQ	3.2774	3.2835	3.0943	3.1742	3.1904	**3.3097**
UIQM	2.6421	2.3569	2.9004	2.8928	2.8803	**2.9009**
Average	5.0867	4.9959	4.9440	5.0186	4.9610	**5.1409**

We contrasted the suggested enhancement framework and the two enhancement modules using actual underwater images. Figure 11 displays the outcomes of the comparison. The underwater image improved by the Adaptive Feature Selection Module retains some detailed information when the original resolution subnetwork is removed, and only Unet containing the Adaptive Feature Selection Module is used, as shown in Figure 11.

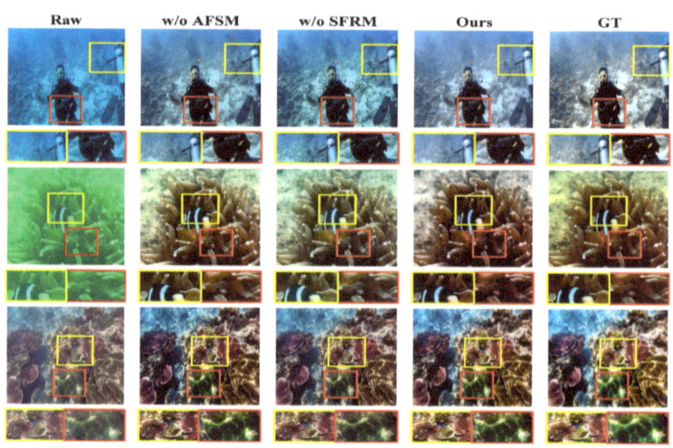

Figure 11. Comparison of ablation experimental results of different components. The yellow and red boxes in the figure correspond to the enlarged image below the image, respectively.

The image has normal colors, but the image background still has some underwater color styles. Underwater images enhanced by the Semantic Feature Reconstruction Module showed greater contrast and clarity when the Adaptive Feature Selection Module was disabled, and just the Original Resolution subnetwork was employed.

Nonetheless, as seen in Figure 11, the image still has some hazy effects in addition to a distinct underwater color pattern. Our technique makes use of the Adaptive Feature Selection Module for image color correction and the original resolution subnetwork for texture detail restoration. This significantly raises the caliber of underwater images.

4.4. Application Test

The edge of the image is the essential feature of the image, and the so-called edge refers to the discontinuity of the local characteristics of the image. Mutations in information, such as grayscale or structure are called edges. For example, mutations in grayscale, color mutations, texture structures, etc. An edge is the end of one area, and the beginning of another, and the feature can be used to extract features and segment the image. To show that our method works well in feature extraction, we compare edge detection with different technologies, as shown in Figure 12. In Figure 12, it is clear that our method can depict the outline and details of the objects in the figure in greater detail than other comparison methods and is closer to the ground truth. MIEN-enhanced images can recognize the contour and feature information of the target, which manifests that MIEN has demonstrated superior performance in feature extraction.

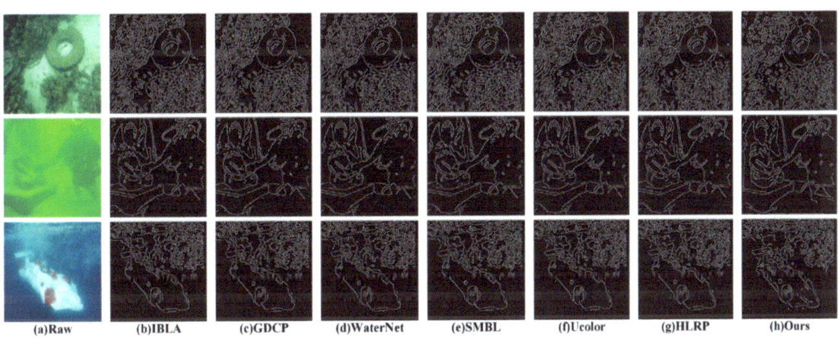

Figure 12. Plot of results of edge detection on UIEB. From left to right are (**a**) Raw, (**b**) IBLA [58], (**c**) GDCP [28], (**d**) WaterNet [45], (**e**) SMBL [55], (**f**) Ucolor [43], (**g**) HLRP [59], (**h**) Ours.

We measured the number of essential feature matches from the underwater image and the output image by MIEN. The algorithm we use is Scale Invariant Feature Transform (SIFT), that is, the description vector of the same local features is the same under different-size images. In Figure 13, we can see that the enhanced image group has significantly more critical feature-matching points than the original image group, which can prove that MIEN can make the enhanced image acquire more detailed information.

Figure 13. Significance detection of the result of feature matching. The first line is the feature-matching result of the original image group, and the second line is the feature-matching result of the enhanced image group.

5. Conclusions

In this paper, we present the multi-resolution information enhancement network (MIEN) for UIE. Our proposed MIEN uses two-branch to enhance the global and local information of underwater images, especially the design of the original resolution subnetwork, which specifically solves the problem of insufficient attention to original resolution information in the Unet structure. Compared to the current network architectures, MIEN extracts more scale-specific information, and global and low-level data are combined on each scale. Many tests are carried out, and quantitative and qualitative comparisons with cutting-edge methods are undertaken, demonstrating that our design delivers considerable gains. At the same time, how to effectively solve the trade-off problem in intensity value and detail, enhance image details while eliminating the overexposure problem of enhanced images, optimize our methods more accurately, and produce clearer images is the direction of our future development. Our approach might also be investigated for other computer vision subjects like segmentation and salient object recognition, as feature aggregation is crucial for solving computer vision problems using deep learning.

Future research should focus on addressing the limitations of paired datasets and the scarcity of reliable ground truth in underwater image enhancement. Innovative methods need to be developed to generate realistic and effective ground truth data specifically tailored for the underwater domain. This will improve the training and evaluation of models, leading to more accurate and reliable performance in underwater imaging applications.

6. Discussion

We evaluated the performance of our proposed MIEN in classical underwater image datasets, using both referenced and unreferenced metrics to verify that our approach outperforms other advanced methods. In future work, we will focus on optimizing the run time of our approach and improving the accuracy of the enhancement effect.

Author Contributions: Conceptualization, D.Z.; methodology, D.Z.; software, W.C. and J.Z.; validation, J.Z. and Y.-T.P.; formal analysis, J.Z. and Z.L.; investigation, W.C. and J.Z.; resources, J.Z. and W.Z.; data curation, J.Z., Z.L. and W.C.; writing-original draft preparation, J.Z.; writing-review and editing, W.C., J.Z. and Y.-T.P.; visualization, J.Z. and W.Z.; supervision, J.Z. and W.Z.; project administration, J.Z. and W.Z.; funding acquisition, W.Z. All authors have read and agreed to the published version of the manuscript.

Funding: This research was funded by the National Natural Science Foundation of China (No. 61702074), the Liaoning Provincial Natural Science Foundation of China (No. 20170520196), the Fundamental Research Funds for the Central Universities (Nos. 3132019205 and 3132019354), and the Cultivation Program for the Excellent Doctoral Dissertation of Dalian Maritime University.

Institutional Review Board Statement: Not applicable.

Informed Consent Statement: Written informed consent has been obtained from the patients to publish this paper.

Data Availability Statement: The references [42,45,57] provide open access to the data used in this research.

Acknowledgments: We would like to express our sincere appreciation to the anonymous reviewers and the editor for their valuable comments and constructive suggestions.

Conflicts of Interest: The authors declare no conflict of interest.

Abbreviations

The following abbreviations are used in this manuscript:

UIE	Underwater Image Enhancement
FEnet	Feature Enhancement Subnetwork
ORSnet	Original Restoration Subnetwork
MIEN	Multi-resolution Information Enhancement Network
AFSM	Adaptive Feature Selection Module
ASSM	Adaptive Spatial Selection Module
ACSM	Adaptive Channel Selection Module
EFSM	Enhancing Feature Selection Module
SFRG	Semantic Feature Reconstruction Group
SFRM	Semantic Feature Reconstruction Module
UIQM	Underwater Image Quality Measure
NIQE	Naturalness Image Quality Evaluator
CEIQ	Contrast Enhancement Image Quality
MSE	Mean-square Error
FSIM	Feature Similarity Index Measure
PSNR	Peak Signal-to-noise-ratio
SSIM	Structural Similarity
UICM	Underwater Image Colorfulness Measure
UISM	Underwater Image Sharpness Measure
UIConM	Underwater Image Contrast Measure

References

1. Zhou, J.; Zhuang, J.; Zheng, Y.; Li, J. Area Contrast Distribution Loss for Underwater Image Enhancement. *J. Mar. Sci. Eng.* **2023**, *11*, 909. [CrossRef]
2. Jiang, Q.; Gu, Y.; Li, C.; Cong, R.; Shao, F. Underwater image enhancement quality evaluation: Benchmark dataset and objective metric. *IEEE Trans. Circuits Syst. Video Technol.* **2022**, *32*, 5959–5974. [CrossRef]
3. Johnson-Roberson, M.; Bryson, M.; Friedman, A.; Pizarro, O.; Troni, G.; Ozog, P.; Henderson, J.C. High-resolution underwater robotic vision-based mapping and three-dimensional reconstruction for archaeology. *J. Field Robot.* **2017**, *34*, 625–643. [CrossRef]
4. Li, T.; Rong, S.; He, B.; Chen, L. Underwater image deblurring framework using a generative adversarial network. In Proceedings of the OCEANS 2022-Chennai, Chennai, India, 21–24 February 2022; pp. 1–4.
5. Fan, G.D.; Fan, B.; Gan, M.; Chen, G.Y.; Chen, C.P. Multiscale low-light image enhancement network with illumination constraint. *IEEE Trans. Circuits Syst. Video Technol.* **2022**, *32*, 7403–7417. [CrossRef]
6. Peng, Y.T.; Lu, Z.; Cheng, F.C.; Zheng, Y.; Huang, S.C. Image haze removal using airlight white correction, local light filter, and aerial perspective prior. *IEEE Trans. Circuits Syst. Video Technol.* **2019**, *30*, 1385–1395. [CrossRef]
7. Berman, D.; Treibitz, T.; Avidan, S. Diving into haze-lines: Color restoration of underwater images. In Proceedings of the British Machine Vision Conference (BMVC), London, UK, 4–7 September 2017; Volume 1.
8. Li, K.; Wu, L.; Qi, Q.; Liu, W.; Gao, X.; Zhou, L.; Song, D. Beyond single reference for training: underwater image enhancement via comparative learning. *IEEE Trans. Circuits Syst. Video Technol.* **2022**, *33*, 2561–2576. [CrossRef]
9. Gao, R.; Li, R.; Hu, M.; Suganthan, P.N.; Yuen, K.F. Dynamic ensemble deep echo state network for significant wave height forecasting. *Appl. Energy* **2023**, *329*, 120261. [CrossRef]
10. Gao, R.; Cheng, W.X.; Suganthan, P.; Yuen, K.F. Inpatient discharges forecasting for singapore hospitals by machine learning. *IEEE J. Biomed. Health Inform.* **2022**, *26*, 4966–4975. [CrossRef]
11. Ren, W.; Liu, S.; Ma, L.; Xu, Q.; Xu, X.; Cao, X.; Du, J.; Yang, M.H. Low-light image enhancement via a deep hybrid network. *IEEE Trans. Image Process.* **2019**, *28*, 4364–4375. [CrossRef]
12. Ren, W.; Pan, J.; Zhang, H.; Cao, X.; Yang, M.H. Single image dehazing via multi-scale convolutional neural networks with holistic edges. *Int. J. Comput. Vis.* **2020**, *128*, 240–259. [CrossRef]

13. Liu, J.; Shang, J.; Liu, R.; Fan, X. Attention-guided global-local adversarial learning for detail-preserving multi-exposure image fusion. *IEEE Trans. Circuits Syst. Video Technol.* **2022**, *32*, 5026–5040. [CrossRef]
14. Liu, J.; Fan, X.; Jiang, J.; Liu, R.; Luo, Z. Learning a deep multi-scale feature ensemble and an edge-attention guidance for image fusion. *IEEE Trans. Circuits Syst. Video Technol.* **2021**, *32*, 105–119. [CrossRef]
15. Zhou, J.; Sun, J.; Zhang, W.; Lin, Z. Multi-view underwater image enhancement method via embedded fusion mechanism. *Eng. Appl. Artif. Intell.* **2023**, *121*, 105946. [CrossRef]
16. Wang, Y.; Zhang, J.; Cao, Y.; Wang, Z. A deep CNN method for underwater image enhancement. In Proceedings of the 2017 IEEE international conference on image processing (ICIP), Beijing, China, 17–20 September 2017; pp. 1382–1386.
17. Zhang, Y.; Chen, D.; Zhang, Y.; Shen, M.; Zhao, W. A Two-Stage Network Based on Transformer and Physical Model for Single Underwater Image Enhancement. *J. Mar. Sci. Eng.* **2023**, *11*, 787. [CrossRef]
18. Ghani, A.S.A.; Isa, N.A.M. Underwater image quality enhancement through integrated color model with Rayleigh distribution. *Appl. Soft Comput.* **2015**, *27*, 219–230. [CrossRef]
19. Jaffe, J.S. Computer modeling and the design of optimal underwater imaging systems. *IEEE J. Ocean. Eng.* **1990**, *15*, 101–111. [CrossRef]
20. Liu, H.; Chau, L.P. Underwater image restoration based on contrast enhancement. In Proceedings of the 2016 IEEE International Conference on Digital Signal Processing (DSP), Beijing, China, 16–18 October 2016; pp. 584–588.
21. Li, C.; Guo, J.; Guo, C.; Cong, R.; Gong, J. A hybrid method for underwater image correction. *Pattern Recognit. Lett.* **2017**, *94*, 62–67. [CrossRef]
22. Wang, Y.; Liu, H.; Chau, L.P. Single underwater image restoration using adaptive attenuation-curve prior. *IEEE Trans. Circuits Syst. I Regul. Pap.* **2017**, *65*, 992–1002. [CrossRef]
23. Xie, J.; Hou, G.; Wang, G.; Pan, Z. A variational framework for underwater image dehazing and deblurring. *IEEE Trans. Circuits Syst. Video Technol.* **2021**, *32*, 3514–3526. [CrossRef]
24. He, K.; Sun, J.; Tang, X. Single image haze removal using dark channel prior. *IEEE Trans. Pattern Anal. Mach. Intell.* **2010**, *33*, 2341–2353.
25. Chiang, J.Y.; Chen, Y.C. Underwater image enhancement by wavelength compensation and dehazing. *IEEE Trans. Image Process.* **2011**, *21*, 1756–1769. [CrossRef] [PubMed]
26. Drews, P.L.; Nascimento, E.R.; Botelho, S.S.; Campos, M.F.M. Underwater depth estimation and image restoration based on single images. *IEEE Comput. Graph. Appl.* **2016**, *36*, 24–35. [CrossRef] [PubMed]
27. Liang, Z.; Ding, X.; Wang, Y.; Yan, X.; Fu, X. GUDCP: Generalization of underwater dark channel prior for underwater image restoration. *IEEE Trans. Circuits Syst. Video Technol.* **2021**, *32*, 4879–4884. [CrossRef]
28. Peng, Y.T.; Cao, K.; Cosman, P.C. Generalization of the dark channel prior for single image restoration. *IEEE Trans. Image Process.* **2018**, *27*, 2856–2868. [CrossRef]
29. Carlevaris-Bianco, N.; Mohan, A.; Eustice, R.M. Initial results in underwater single image dehazing. In Proceedings of the Oceans 2010 Mts/IEEE Seattle, Washington, DC, USA, 20–23 September 2010; pp. 1–8.
30. Galdran, A.; Pardo, D.; Picón, A.; Alvarez-Gila, A. Automatic red-channel underwater image restoration. *J. Vis. Commun. Image Represent.* **2015**, *26*, 132–145. [CrossRef]
31. Li, C.; Guo, J.; Chen, S.; Tang, Y.; Pang, Y.; Wang, J. Underwater image restoration based on minimum information loss principle and optical properties of underwater imaging. In Proceedings of the 2016 IEEE International Conference on Image Processing (ICIP), Phoenix, AZ, USA, 25–28 September 2016; pp. 1993–1997.
32. Akkaynak, D.; Treibitz, T. Sea-thru: A method for removing water from underwater images. In Proceedings of the IEEE/CVF Conference on Computer Vision and Pattern Recognition, Long Beach, CA, USA, 15–20 June 2019; pp. 1682–1691.
33. Zhou, J.; Pang, L.; Zhang, D.; Zhang, W. Underwater Image Enhancement Method via Multi-Interval Subhistogram Perspective Equalization. *IEEE J. Ocean. Eng.* **2023**, *48*, 474–488. [CrossRef]
34. Zhuang, P.; Ding, X. Underwater image enhancement using an edge-preserving filtering retinex algorithm. *Multimed. Tools Appl.* **2020**, *79*, 17257–17277. [CrossRef]
35. Yuan, J.; Cao, W.; Cai, Z.; Su, B. An underwater image vision enhancement algorithm based on contour bougie morphology. *IEEE Trans. Geosci. Remote Sens.* **2020**, *59*, 8117–8128. [CrossRef]
36. Anwar, S.; Li, C. Diving deeper into underwater image enhancement: A survey. *Signal Process. Image Commun.* **2020**, *89*, 115978. [CrossRef]
37. Fabbri, C.; Islam, M.J.; Sattar, J. Enhancing underwater imagery using generative adversarial networks. In Proceedings of the 2018 IEEE International Conference on Robotics and Automation (ICRA), Brisbane, Australia, 21–25 May 2018; pp. 7159–7165.
38. Zhu, J.Y.; Park, T.; Isola, P.; Efros, A.A. Unpaired image-to-image translation using cycle-consistent adversarial networks. In Proceedings of the IEEE International Conference on Computer Vision, Venice, Italy, 22–29 October 2017; pp. 2223–2232.
39. Li, H.; Zhuang, P. DewaterNet: A fusion adversarial real underwater image enhancement network. *Signal Process. Image Commun.* **2021**, *95*, 116248. [CrossRef]
40. Guo, Y.; Li, H.; Zhuang, P. Underwater image enhancement using a multiscale dense generative adversarial network. *IEEE J. Ocean. Eng.* **2019**, *45*, 862–870. [CrossRef]
41. Liu, X.; Gao, Z.; Chen, B.M. MLFcGAN: Multilevel feature fusion-based conditional GAN for underwater image color correction. *IEEE Geosci. Remote. Sens. Lett.* **2019**, *17*, 1488–1492. [CrossRef]

42. Islam, M.J.; Xia, Y.; Sattar, J. Fast underwater image enhancement for improved visual perception. *IEEE Robot. Autom. Lett.* **2020**, *5*, 3227–3234. [CrossRef]
43. Li, C.; Anwar, S.; Hou, J.; Cong, R.; Guo, C.; Ren, W. Underwater image enhancement via medium transmission-guided multi-color space embedding. *IEEE Trans. Image Process.* **2021**, *30*, 4985–5000. [CrossRef] [PubMed]
44. Qi, Q.; Zhang, Y.; Tian, F.; Wu, Q.J.; Li, K.; Luan, X.; Song, D. Underwater image co-enhancement with correlation feature matching and joint learning. *IEEE Trans. Circuits Syst. Video Technol.* **2021**, *32*, 1133–1147. [CrossRef]
45. Li, C.; Guo, C.; Ren, W.; Cong, R.; Hou, J.; Kwong, S.; Tao, D. An underwater image enhancement benchmark dataset and beyond. *IEEE Trans. Image Process.* **2019**, *29*, 4376–4389. [CrossRef]
46. Zhou, J.; Zhang, D.; Zhang, W. Cross-view enhancement network for underwater images. *Eng. Appl. Artif. Intell.* **2023**, *121*, 105952. [CrossRef]
47. Li, C.Y.; Guo, J.C.; Cong, R.M.; Pang, Y.W.; Wang, B. Underwater image enhancement by dehazing with minimum information loss and histogram distribution prior. *IEEE Trans. Image Process.* **2016**, *25*, 5664–5677. [CrossRef]
48. Hou, G.; Li, Y.; Yang, H.; Li, K.; Pan, Z. UID2021: An underwater image dataset for evaluation of no-reference quality assessment metrics. *ACM Trans. Multimed. Comput. Commun. Appl.* **2023**, *19*, 1–24. [CrossRef]
49. Wu, S.; Luo, T.; Jiang, G.; Yu, M.; Xu, H.; Zhu, Z.; Song, Y. A two-stage underwater enhancement network based on structure decomposition and characteristics of underwater imaging. *IEEE J. Ocean. Eng.* **2021**, *46*, 1213–1227. [CrossRef]
50. Ding, D.; Gan, S.; Chen, L.; Wang, B. Learning-based underwater image enhancement: An efficient two-stream approach. *Displays* **2023**, *76*, 102337. [CrossRef]
51. Yan, X.; Qin, W.; Wang, Y.; Wang, G.; Fu, X. Attention-guided dynamic multi-branch neural network for underwater image enhancement. *Knowl.-Based Syst.* **2022**, *258*, 110041. [CrossRef]
52. Fu, X.; Cao, X. Underwater image enhancement with global–local networks and compressed-histogram equalization. *Signal Process. Image Commun.* **2020**, *86*, 115892. [CrossRef]
53. Lin, Y.; Shen, L.; Wang, Z.; Wang, K.; Zhang, X. Attenuation coefficient guided two-stage network for underwater image restoration. *IEEE Signal Process. Lett.* **2020**, *28*, 199–203. [CrossRef]
54. Yu, H.; Li, X.; Feng, Y.; Han, S. Multiple attentional path aggregation network for marine object detection. *Appl. Intell.* **2023**, *53*, 2434–2451. [CrossRef]
55. Song, W.; Wang, Y.; Huang, D.; Liotta, A.; Perra, C. Enhancement of underwater images with statistical model of background light and optimization of transmission map. *IEEE Trans. Broadcast.* **2020**, *66*, 153–169. [CrossRef]
56. Islam, M.J.; Luo, P.; Sattar, J. Simultaneous enhancement and super-resolution of underwater imagery for improved visual perception. *arXiv* **2020**, arXiv:2002.01155.
57. Li, H.; Li, J.; Wang, W. A fusion adversarial underwater image enhancement network with a public test dataset. *arXiv* **2019**, arXiv:1906.06819.
58. Peng, Y.T.; Cosman, P.C. Underwater image restoration based on image blurriness and light absorption. *IEEE Trans. Image Process.* **2017**, *26*, 1579–1594. [CrossRef] [PubMed]
59. Zhuang, P., Wu, J.; Porikli, F.; Li, C. Underwater image enhancement with hyper-laplacian reflectance priors. *IEEE Trans. Image Process.* **2022**, *31*, 5442–5455. [CrossRef]
60. Panetta, K.; Gao, C.; Agaian, S. Human-visual-system-inspired underwater image quality measures. *IEEE J. Ocean. Eng.* **2015**, *41*, 541–551. [CrossRef]
61. Wang, Y.; Li, N.; Li, Z.; Gu, Z.; Zheng, H.; Zheng, B.; Sun, M. An imaging-inspired no-reference underwater color image quality assessment metric. *Comput. Electr. Eng.* **2018**, *70*, 904–913. [CrossRef]
62. Mittal, A.; Soundararajan, R.; Bovik, A.C. Making a "completely blind" image quality analyzer. *IEEE Signal Process. Lett.* **2012**, *20*, 209–212. [CrossRef]
63. Yan, J.; Li, J.; Fu, X. No-reference quality assessment of contrast-distorted images using contrast enhancement. *arXiv* **2019**, arXiv:1904.08879.
64. Zhang, L.; Zhang, L.; Mou, X.; Zhang, D. FSIM: A feature similarity index for image quality assessment. *IEEE Trans. Image Process.* **2011**, *20*, 2378–2386. [CrossRef] [PubMed]
65. Jagalingam, P.; Hegde, A.V. A review of quality metrics for fused image. *Aquat. Procedia* **2015**, *4*, 133–142. [CrossRef]
66. Wang, Z.; Bovik, A.C.; Sheikh, H.R.; Simoncelli, E.P. Image quality assessment: from error visibility to structural similarity. *IEEE Trans. Image Process.* **2004**, *13*, 600–612. [CrossRef]

remote sensing

MDPI

Article

Coupling Dilated Encoder–Decoder Network for Multi-Channel Airborne LiDAR Bathymetry Full-Waveform Denoising

Bin Hu [1,2], Yiqiang Zhao [1,*], Guoqing Zhou [3], Jiaji He [1], Changlong Liu [4], Qiang Liu [1], Mao Ye [1] and Yao Li [1]

1 School of Microelectronics, Tianjin University, Tianjin 300072, China; hubin@email.tjut.edu.cn (B.H.); dochejj@tju.edu.cn (J.H.); qiangliu@tju.edu.cn (Q.L.); mao_ye@tju.edu.cn (M.Y.); liyao@tju.edu.cn (Y.L.)
2 Technical College for the Deaf, Tianjin University of Technology, Tianjin 300382, China
3 College of Geomatics and Geoinformation, Guilin University of Technology, Guilin 541004, China; gzhou@glut.edu.cn
4 Fifty-Fourth Research Institute of China Electronics Technology Group Corporation, Shijiazhuang 050081, China; liuclcti@163.com
* Correspondence: yq_zhao@tju.edu.cn

Abstract: Multi-channel airborne full-waveform LiDAR is widely used for high-precision underwater depth measurement. However, the signal quality of full-waveform data is unstable due to the influence of background light, dark current noise, and the complex transmission process. Therefore, we propose a nonlocal encoder block (NLEB) based on spatial dilated convolution to optimize the feature extraction of adjacent frames. On this basis, a coupled denoising encoder–decoder network is proposed that takes advantage of the echo correlation in deep-water and shallow-water channels. Firstly, full waveforms from different channels are stacked together to form a two-dimensional tensor and input into the proposed network. Then, NLEB is used to extract local and nonlocal features from the 2D tensor. After fusing the features of the two channels, the reconstructed denoised data can be obtained by upsampling with a fully connected layer and deconvolution layer. Based on the measured data set, we constructed a noise–noisier data set, on which several denoising algorithms were compared. The results show that the proposed method improves the stability of denoising by using the inter-channel and multi-frame data correlation.

Keywords: full-waveform denoising; deep learning; airborne LiDAR; bathymetry

Citation: Hu, B.; Zhao, Y.; Zhou, G.; He, J.; Liu, C.; Liu, Q.; Ye, M.; Li, Y. Coupling Dilated Encoder–Decoder Network for Multi-Channel Airborne LiDAR Bathymetry Full-Waveform Denoising. *Remote Sens.* **2023**, *15*, 3293. https://doi.org/10.3390/rs15133293

Academic Editors: Jingchun Zhou, Wenqi Ren, Qiuping Jiang and Yan-Tsung Peng

Received: 30 May 2023
Revised: 25 June 2023
Accepted: 26 June 2023
Published: 27 June 2023

1. Introduction

Airborne full-waveform LiDAR is a type of laser ranging system that can store and record the complete reflected echo signal of the target in a very short sampling interval and with a large capacity, so it can obtain a high-range resolution [1]. The scanning modes of airborne LiDAR detection systems mainly include linear scanning and oval scanning. The advantage of linear scanning is that the system can maximize the acquisition of the light energy of the normal incident and nearby angles of the target, but the disadvantage is that the structure is complex and requires high synchronization accuracy. The Airborne LiDAR Bathymetry (ALB) system described in this paper adopts an ovoid scanning mode with a light structure; the incidence angle of the scanning mode is relatively stable, which is conducive to avoiding the direct reflection of the surface mirror and reducing differences in echo energy [2,3].

Airborne LiDAR is widely used in land cover classification [4], marine resource detection [5,6], and vegetation detection [7] because of its high measuring efficiency, wide working range, high measuring accuracy, and ability to obtain the physical characteristics of the target. Because 532 nm blue-green light has good water permeability, laser radar at this wavelength is used to measure the depth of the seafloor. Since the laser beam from the atmosphere enters through the sea surface and travels through the water, the energy returned to the detector will be reduced, which will reduce the peak signal-to-noise ratio of the seafloor signal and increase the uncertainty of the distance measurement [8]. The full waveform collected by the ALB system can be regarded as composed of the sea-surface, water scattering, and seabed signals. Sea-surface signals are easily lost due to the influence of waves, the scattered part of the water scattering signal is relatively stable, and weak seafloor echoes are affected by the terrain, water quality, and other factors, so the integrity of the signal needs to be repaired through multi-frame correlation.

The maximum measured depth and accuracy are also affected by the water quality, target reflectance, background noise, and flight altitude [9]. As shown in Figure 1, the multi-field-of-view detection structure is widely used in airborne full-waveform sounding systems, and the multi-channel data in the field of view can be used to improve the dynamic range and accuracy of detection [5]. The small field in the middle is used as a shallow-water channel to obtain the energy-concentrated shallow-water echo, while the remaining external field of view is used as a deep channel to receive weak submarine echo signals in deep water owing to a stronger gain and a larger field of view.

Different field-of-view echoes have similar structures, so the target characteristics reflected by multi-channel signals can be used to optimize the target peak signal-to-noise ratio.

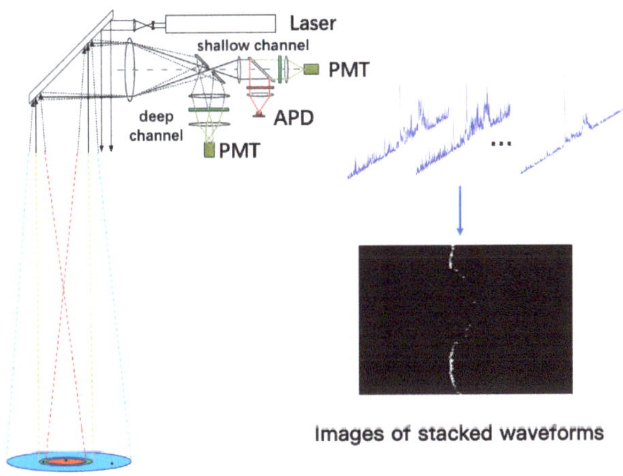

Figure 1. Introduction of multi-channel full-waveform airborne LiDAR.

Although the hardware architecture of airborne LiDAR has been improved, the process of the laser light returning to the detector after traveling through the atmosphere, the air–sea interface, and the water is extremely complex.

Random background light can produce Gaussian noise, and sudden changes in the seafloor topography or the scattering of water can produce sparse noise. Therefore, the mixed noise contained in the full waveform of ALB has a great influence on the seabed signal. Traditional algorithms, such as wavelet filtering [10], EMD filtering [11], waveform decomposition [12], and deconvolution [13], are widely used in this field. However, the effect of such algorithms is often limited by manually adjusted parameters. Full-waveform data can be regarded as a one-dimensional time series, so deep learning is widely used in LiDAR data processing [14,15]. Super-resolution technology can restore the echo with a higher sampling rate without upgrading the hardware [16,17]. Although multi-channel information has been proven to be effective for echo classification, denoising and signal enhancement have not been used [5,6]. Due to the structural similarity between consecutive waveforms and the physical correlation between different channels of the same frame [18], they can be used to further improve the signal sampling rate and reduce noise [19]. However, with the increase in the detection distance, the intensity of the LiDAR echo signal steadily decreases. To solve the above problems, this paper will further explore the influence of the signal correlation between channels on full-waveform denoising. The main contributions of this paper are as follows:

- Based on a multi-task deep learning architecture and a centroid alignment algorithm, we propose a novel LiDAR denoising technique for multi-channel ALB systems that can improve the stability of denoising.
- The NLEB module is proposed, and the loss function is optimized to explore the impact of intra-channel autocorrelation and inter-channel structural similarity on LiDAR signal enhancement.
- We analyzed the characteristics of multi-channel ALB data and the limitations of the denoising algorithm by using measured data.

2. Related Work

In order to improve the accuracy of the ALB system, traditional algorithms and methods based on deep learning are proposed for filtering, echo classification, and resolution enhancement.

2.1. Model-Based Methods

The detection accuracy depends on the position error when the full waveform is decomposed into sub-echo components, and the transmitted waveform is generally considered to be Gaussian-like [20]. Due to the influence of cross-medium transmission, the echo may be affected by trailing, ringing, and other phenomena, resulting in a reduction in ranging accuracy in the subsequent waveform decomposition [21]. Researchers often use the trigonometric function, quadrilateral function, and exponential function to decompose the echo into water surface, water backscatter, and underwater signals [22,23]. For a seabed signal with certain distortion, a model with a generalized Gaussian distribution or lognormal distribution can be used to fit the signal. The multi-Gaussian decomposition method based on initial parameters is not suitable for the peak detection of distorted pulses in extremely shallow water with high overlap [24]. The combination of dynamic threshold and wavelet filtering [8,10] can improve the ability to recognize weak signals, but the selection of the wavelet basis function and decomposition scale need to be adjusted for different water depths. The Richardson–Lucy deconvolution [13,25] algorithm can be used to extract the interface response function to separate multiple targets with a short distance, but the algorithm relies on multiple iterations, which tend to produce noise and sound effects. Therefore, superimposing structurally similar subsequences in multiple frames [19] can significantly improve the peak signal-to-noise ratio of submarine signals. B-spline [26] and Wiener deconvolution algorithms [27] require no prior knowledge and avoid short-distance stacking losses, but they are too sensitive to noise. Neighborhood and multidimensional space–time information [28] can be used to improve the peak signal-to-noise ratio of seafloor signals, and waveform superposition can improve the detection rate of weak seafloor signals. However, parameter debugging in traditional algorithms still limits the processing performance of ALB echoes [29]. The existing waveform processing methods do not make full use of the correlation between multi-frame data, and stacking the average results of adjacent frames lacks stability in the ALB system [30].

2.2. Learning-Based Methods

With the development of deep learning in the field of time-series data processing, researchers have become inclined to use deep learning to automatically extract full-waveform features [15,17] from data. Unsupervised denoising based on an encoder–decoder has achieved good results [14,31]. The deconvolution layer is used for upsampling, and high-quality echo signals can be obtained at a low sampling rate [16,32]. By combining the prior knowledge provided by echo classification with the denoising algorithm [33], the parameter selection strategy can be optimized for different scenes, which can optimize the peak signal-to-noise ratio of the target. Artificial features such as the echo width, skewness, and kurtosis, combined with machine learning methods such as support vector machines [7] and random forest models [34], can be used to distinguish between deep-water, shallow-water, and land echoes. However, hand-extracted features require specialized knowledge and extensive preprocessing. The feature weights of key positions can be optimized by converting the airborne waveform into a time-series diagram and extracting the high-dimensional temporal and spatial features of the Gramian angular field time-series diagram using the mature network architecture in the image field [35,36]. Based on the LSTM module and one-dimensional convolution module, the time sequence dependence and local spatial features of signals can be extracted [37,38]. Since sea-surface and seabed signals are not fixed in each frame signal, the denoising effect of ALB signals is limited. The seabed topography is complicated and easily affected by impulse noise, so it is necessary to introduce a nonlocal [39] processing module or use multi-frame features to alleviate the problem of the model falling into the local optimal solution.

3. Materials

3.1. Analysis of ALB Data

ALB data mainly include the sea-surface echo, water backscatter, and seabed echo. With the increase in the laser transmission distance in the sea, the backscatter will be broadened, which will affect the shape and position of the sea-bottom echo. Multi-channel airborne LiDAR uses a high-sensitivity photomultiplier tube to improve the detection of weak sea-bottom signals, but this also leads to greater echo noise. The received power of a sea-surface echo can generally be expressed as follows:

$$P_s = \frac{P_0 \cdot \rho \cdot exp[-2\sigma H] \cdot A \cdot E}{2\pi H^2} \tag{1}$$

where P_s is the sea-surface-reflected power, P_0 is laser emission peak power, ρ is the air attenuation coefficient, A is the receiving optical aperture, E is the receiving system efficiency, H is the aircraft flight altitude, and σ is the sea-surface reflectivity. The received power of the seabed can generally be expressed as follows:

$$P_b = \frac{P_0 \cdot R \cdot (1-\rho)^2 \cdot exp[-2(\sigma H + \tau D)] \cdot A \cdot E}{2\pi (H + D/n)^2} \tag{2}$$

where P_b is the seabed-reflected power, R is the bottom reflectivity, τ is the effective attenuation coefficient, and n is the refractive index of seawater.

In order to further analyze the correlation between multi-channel echoes, we used Monte Carlo models to simulate deep- and shallow-water echoes in different states. We monitored a million photons at once that move randomly through the water and disperse using the Henyey–Greenstein function. By varying the scattering attenuation coefficient of seawater to simulate various water conditions, we changed the longest distance of photon propagation as well as the forward distance of photons at each step.

As shown in Figure 2, the x- and y-axes are the time and normalized amplitude, respectively. The red curve is the waveform of the shallow-water channel, and the blue curve is the waveform of the deep-water channel. The main differences between the deep- and shallow-water channels are the field angle and gain. As shown in Figure 2a,b, when the water depth is relatively shallow, obvious sea-surface echoes can be observed in both channels, but shallow-water channels are more sensitive to underwater signals. As shown in Figure 2c,d, the seabed signals of deep channels become more obvious with the increase in water depth, and the data between channels also show a stronger correlation. The echos of deep and shallow channels can be decomposed into the surface, seabed, and backscatter, and the seabed signal gradually weakens and slides to the right until it disappears.

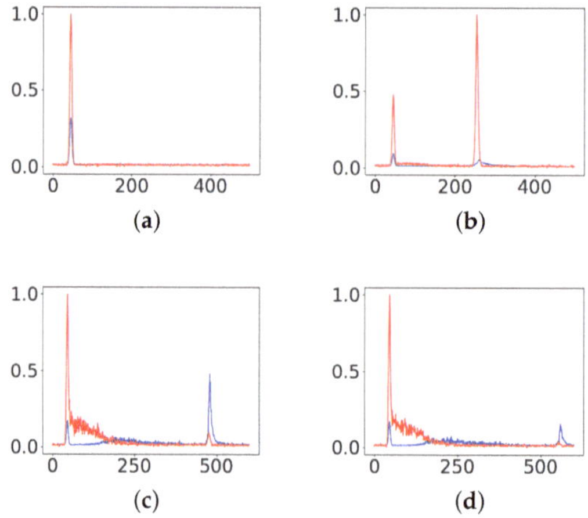

Figure 2. Visual comparison of simulation data in deep-water channel and shallow-water channel denoising. (**a**) Extreme shallow-water waveform; (**b**) shallow-water waveform with a strong bottom return; (**c**) deep-water waveform; (**d**) shallow-water waveform with a weak bottom return.

3.2. Measured Data Set

As shown in Figure 3, the data in this flight experiment were collected near the west side of Weizhou Island at a flight altitude of 500 m. The echoes of a LiDAR sea survey performed in the evening with good weather were used as the original data set. The flight area was bounded by a longitude of 109°00′ to 109°05′ east and a latitude of 21°01′ to 21°03′ north. The total area of the test area was about 41 km^2, and the flight width corresponding to the route was 350 m. At the junction of the sea area and the land area, the aircraft flew along 12 north–south navigation belts, each of which was 1.5 km long, and the side overlap rate of the navigation belt was higher than 0.3. In the figure, the navigation belt in red (east–west) was used for system parameter checking and calibration, and the belt in green was used for accuracy checking. To avoid inertial measurement unit (IMU) error accumulation, a figure-of-eight flight was performed before entering the test area. The LiDAR device was mounted on a single-engine turboprop lightweight general-purpose aircraft and is equipped with a positioning and orientation system. The pitch angle and roll angle of the route were generally not more than 2°. The slope of the aircraft did not exceed 22° when turning.

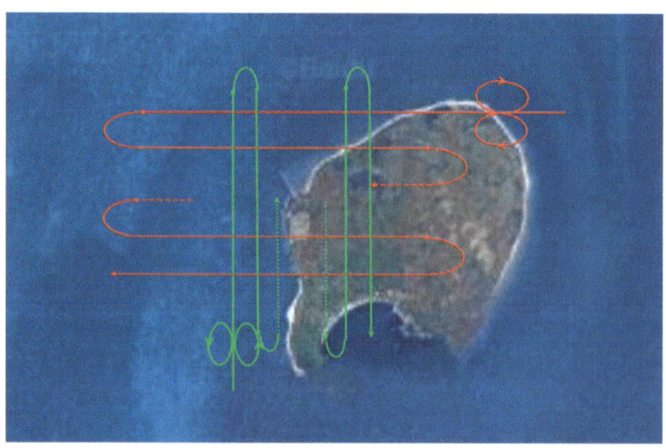

Figure 3. Measured scene.

The measured signal cannot provide a pure echo for testing, so we extracted the first 200 points and the last 200 points of the echo to estimate the noise and added them to the original echoes according to different scales to obtain noise and noisier pairs of echoes. We selected continuous echoes to generate a 2D tensor and ensured that the maximum depth change of the echo in each 2D tensor did not exceed 2 m. Considering the speed and angle of view of the aircraft, we stacked 100 frames as a tensor. Therefore, redundant information in multiple frames could be used to eliminate noise. The system parameters of full-waveform LiDAR are shown in Table 1. The water depth in the tested sea area is between 0.3 m and 25 m. The beam divergence angle of the prototype is 0.2 mrad, the scanning angle is 10°, the measurement accuracy of the scanning angle is better than 0.003, the repetition rate is 5.5 kHz, the laser linewidth is 0.05 nm, and the pulse width is 3.3 ns; the aircraft speed was 200 km/h.

Table 1. The system parameters of full-waveform LiDAR.

Parameters	Parameter Indexes
Beam divergence angle	0.2 mrad
Laser emission frequency	5.5 kHz
Laser emission power	17.4 W/532 nm,18 W/1064 nm
Pulse energy	3.05 mJ/532 nm, 3.5 mJ/1064 nm
Pulse width	3.3 ns
Detection range	500–1000 m
Scanning mode	Constant-angle conical scan
Scanning angle	±10°
Scanning speed	10 revolutions per second
Receiving aperture	0.2 m
Detection minimum energy	8×10^{-9} W
Maximum receiving frequency	2 GHz

4. Proposed Method

In this section, we provide the details of preprocessing, the nonlocal encoder block (NLEB), and the architecture of proposed model.

4.1. Preprocessing of Full Waveform

Laser transmission on the sea surface and in the water results in random noise in the full waveform, but the position of the seabed echo is relatively stable in adjacent frames. As shown in Figure 4, by aligning and stacking multiple frames, the similarity of adjacent frames can be highlighted without modifying key information, such as the sea surface, backscatter, and underwater.

To alleviate the impact of abnormal echoes on multi-frame denoising, the echo of the lost sea surface is filtered through the hard threshold of the pulse width and amplitude. Then, the amplitude of the signal is normalized according to the maximum and minimum values of the echoes in each channel. Although the transmitted waveform is a Gaussian pulse with concentrated energy, the sea-surface echo will deform due to the random jitter of the sea surface. The idea of eliminating the echo noise from the ALB system by stacking signals and using related information from multiple echoes has long been proposed to improve the accuracy of seawater depth calculations. Because the water depth does not change much between adjacent frames, echoes in the same field of view have structural similarity [9,40]. Before stacking multi-frame data, we highlight the relative position of the sea surface and seabed through the centroid alignment of the sea surface. The centroid calculation formula is as follows:

$$t_c = \frac{u_1t_1 + u_2t_2 + \cdots + u_nt_n}{u_1 + u_2 + \cdots + u_n} = \frac{\sum_{i=1}^{n} u_it_i}{\sum_{i=1}^{n} u_i} \quad (3)$$

where t_c represents the corrected centroid time, t_i represents the corresponding time of each sampling point of the pulse, and u_i corresponds to the amplitude of each sampling point. Then, we convert 100 waveforms to the same position according to the centroid position of the sea surface to form a two-dimensional tensor.

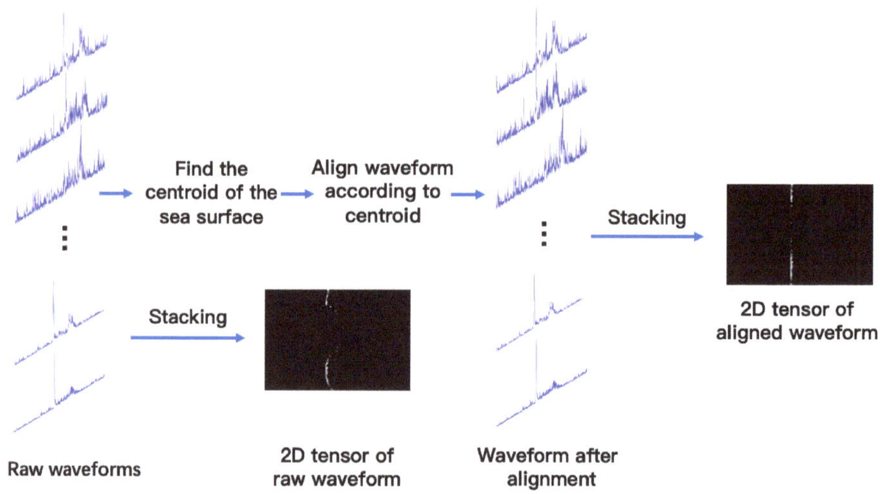

Figure 4. The basic principle of full-waveform stacking.

4.2. Nonlocal Encoder Block

Due to the impact of background noise, sea-surface jitter, underwater transmission, and other factors on ALB, the received full-waveform signal-to-noise ratio is unstable. However, the sampling rate of the receiving circuit is very high, and the submarine signals covered by the laser in the same field of view are very close, so there is also a correlation between non-adjacent echoes. Using the traditional nonlocal module to extract the distance dependence of non-adjacent echoes will greatly increase the calculation cost [41]. To reduce the consumption of resources and make full use of the spatial correlation between features, we propose an NLEB module with a wide acceptance domain in the spatial domain.

Due to the strong correlation with the close position of the echo in the field of view, context feature extraction can be improved by multi-layer stacked convolution. Including LSTM or using a large-scale convolution kernel will not only enhance the long-distance dependence extraction effect but also add more parameters and decrease computational efficiency. Multiple small-scale dilated convolution stacks are widely used in image denoising, which depends on fewer parameters and increases the nonlinear extraction ability of the model. So, we rely on a convolution kernel size of 3 for stacking, focusing on expanding the spatial-scale sensitivity field. The details of NLEB are shown in Figure 5. It consists of three two-dimensional convolution layers with the kernel size (3,3), and the dilation rate is set to (1,1), (2,1), and (4,1). The kernels are not dilated in the input's time-domain direction. By expanding the convolution of the spatial direction, the receptive field of NLEB can extract features from similar positions between frames without increasing the amount of computation. A batch normalization layer is introduced to accelerate convergence and prevent over-fitting.

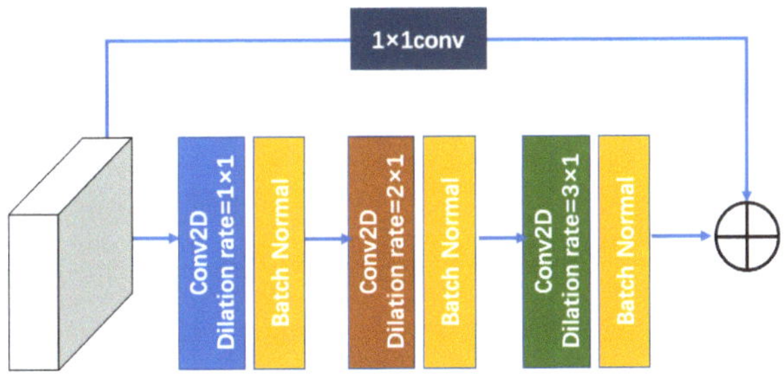

Figure 5. The details of nonlocal encoder block.

4.3. CNLD-Net Architecture

As previously stated, structural similarity exists between echoes collected in the same area with different gains and fields of view. The idea of eliminating ALB system echo noise by stacking signals and using related information from multiple echoes has long been proposed. To improve the denoising effect, we built a multi-branch network to improve its robustness to weak signals. As shown in Figure 6, our proposed architecture combines NLEB and the idea of multi-task learning. Following the preprocessing process described above, adjacent frames are roughly aligned and stacked according to the sea-surface position before being input into the network.

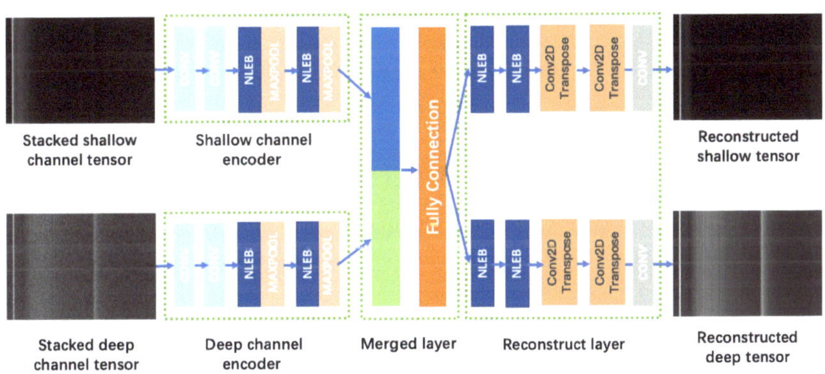

Figure 6. The architecture of CNLD-Net.

CNLD-Net first extracts multi-frame features through two identical branches comprising a convolution module, two NLEB modules, and two max-pooling layers. The two encoders are used to extract local and nonlocal information from deep- and shallow-water channels, respectively. The two branches' features are then flattened and concatenated as the input of two fully connected layers. We use the reconstruction layer to restore the denoised two-dimensional tensor for each channel from the shared representation. After obtaining the denoised tenors, we can obtain the denoised waveforms by detaching them. The decoding part of the CNLD network also includes two identical branches, which are composed of two NLEB modules, two deconvolution operations, and one convolutional layer. The deconvolution layer is the inverse operation of descending sampling, also known as transposed convolution, which can be used to improve the time resolution of the full waveform and restore stacked signals from the upsampling of compressed features. The dimension values after each layer in CNLD are presented in Table 2.

Table 2. Details for each CNLD layer.

Module	Layer	Kernel (Size, Stride)	Dimension or Neurons (Bs, C, L) [α]
Stacked image input	\	\	(64,1,2000 × 100)
shallow encoder /deep encoder	Conv-2d	(3 × 3,2)	(64,16,1000 × 50)
	Conv-2d	(3 × 3,2)	(64,32,500 × 25)
	NLEB		(64,64,500 × 25)
	NLEB		(64,128,500 × 25)
	Dense		1000
Merged layer	Concatenated		2000
Reconstruction layer	Dense		1,600,000
	NLEB		(64,64,500 × 25)
	NLEB		(64,32,500 × 25)
	Conv-2d-Transpose	(3 × 3,2)	(64,32,1000 × 50)
	Conv-2d-Transpose	(3 × 3,2)	(64,16,2000 × 100)
	Conv2d	(1 × 1,1)	(64,1,2000 × 100)
Stacked image output	\	\	(64,1,2000 × 100)

[α] *Bs*, batch size; L, data length of the waveform; C, number of channels.

The training optimization's loss function is set as follows:

$$loss = \frac{1}{K}\Sigma_{i=1}^{K}(||\hat{S}_i - S_i||^2 + ||\hat{D}_i - D_i||^2) \quad (4)$$

where S_i is the original data from the shallow channel, D_i is the original data from the deep channel, $\hat{S}_i$ is the reconstructed tensors from the shallow channel, $\hat{D}_i$ is the reconstructed tensors from the deep channel, and K is the number of training samples of each channel. The reconstruction layer improves the time resolution by introducing a deconvolution kernel, which is also called transposed convolution. Transposed convolution fills the input features with $s-1$ zeros between every two elements. The strides s here can be understood as the magnification of the resolution, and the convolution operation with a stride of 1 is performed on the input features after filling. The width of the output features of the transposed convolution layer can be expressed as:

$$o = (w-1) \times s - 2p + k \quad (5)$$

where w represents the size of the input feature, s represents the stride, p represents the padding size, and k represents the size of the transposed convolution kernel.

4.4. Performance Metrics

To evaluate the denoising ability of the proposed method, we added specified noise to measured data sets at different water depths. Then, the signals that contained noise were processed by using the proposed method, AWT [42], EMD-STRP [10], CAENN [14], 1D-Nonlocal [43], and MS-CNN [6]. Finally, the effects of the six methods were compared; the methods were evaluated by determining the following two parameters:

Root mean square error (RMSE):

$$RMSE = \sqrt{\sum_{i=1}^{N}(x_i - \tilde{x}_i)^2/N} \quad (6)$$

Signal-to-noise ratio (SNR):

$$SNR = 10log(\frac{\sum_{i=1}^{N} x_i^2}{\sum_{i=1}^{N} (x_i - \tilde{x}_i)^2}) \quad (7)$$

Since the input and output of the network are stacked images, the parameters are calculated based on the detached waveform, where x_i represents an original waveform, $\tilde{x}_i$ is an output, N is the number of waveforms, and $\bar{x}$ represents the mean signal amplitude.

5. Experiments

5.1. Comparison of Signal Denoising Method

As mentioned above, the measured data were collected by the ALB system on a evening flight and at an altitude of 500 m. A total of 50,000 pieces of data with different water depths were selected, and the noise–noisier data set was constructed. We adopted the strategy of five-fold cross-validation to carry out the experiment, in which four units were selected for training and the remaining one unit was used for testing.

We chose the first 200 and the last 200 points of the signal to calculate the average power. Then, we generated random noise based on the noise coefficient and added it to the original signal to build a noise data set.

The rightmost column in the table shows the time taken to process a single signal. There is no difference in signal denoising time between the deep-water channel and shallow-water channel. The denoising time of the traditional algorithm is significantly higher than that of the deep-learning-based method. Although we extracted multi-channel and non-neighborhood features, our proposed method can still achieve high performance. With the increase in the noise coefficient, the signal-to-noise ratio decreases. Tables 3 and 4 present the RMSE and SNR of shallow-water channels and deep-water channels, respectively, with different noise coefficients. The signal-to-noise ratio of the deep-water channel after denoising is slightly higher, mainly due to the significant improvement in the seabed signal caused by high gain. The denoising algorithm based on the adaptive wavelet or soft threshold can preserve the details of the signal when processing shallow-water channel data. However, with the decrease in the signal-to-noise ratio, the problem of noise misjudgment is difficult to alleviate. Combining correlation analysis and empirical mode decomposition methods can preserve IMF components with high correlations; thus, reconstructing signals can improve the ability to retain weak signals. The signal-to-noise ratios of the CAENN and non-neighborhood architectures are significantly improved, but their RMSE values are also higher than that of the EMD-STRP algorithm due to the low stability of seabed signals in shallow-water channels and the single-frame-based network architecture. Although it is better at removing Gaussian noise, its ability to retain the target signal is not strong. The MS-CNN architecture introduces a channel attention mechanism, resulting in a significant decrease in RMSE. The proposed CNLD structure further improves the signal-to-noise ratio by considering the structural similarity of multi-frame data and the data correlation between channels.

Table 3. MSE and SNR values of different Gaussian noise variances in shallow channel.

Methods	5		10		15		20		Time
	RMSE	SNR	RMSE	SNR	RMSE	SNR	RMSE	SNR	
AWT [10]	0.012	20.55	0.015	18.62	0.023	14.95	0.039	11.51	0.007 s
EMD-STRP [42]	0.012	21.03	0.016	18.55	0.023	14.96	0.042	10.59	0.019 s
CAENN [14]	0.036	24.08	0.042	20.76	0.062	18.37	0.087	16.61	0.003 s
1D-Nonlocal [43]	0.057	23.94	0.064	19.84	0.054	18.42	0.063	16.91	0.008 s
MS-CNN [6]	0.028	30.54	0.034	26.17	0.048	22.41	0.036	18.17	0.006 s
CNLD	0.019	38.58	0.026	33.48	0.031	26.92	0.036	22.94	0.005 s

Table 4. MSE and SNR values of different Gaussian noise variances in deep channel.

Methods	5		10		15		20		Time
	RMSE	SNR	RMSE	SNR	RMSE	SNR	RMSE	SNR	
AWT [10]	0.025	20.91	0.028	19.88	0.032	18.62	0.046	15.49	0.007 s
EMD-STRP [42]	0.024	21.28	0.027	20.12	0.033	18.47	0.047	15.14	0.019 s
CAENN [14]	0.052	32.81	0.054	30.53	0.057	28.04	0.064	22.62	0.003 s
1D-Nonlocal [43]	0.059	33.91	0.065	31.66	0.064	28.81	0.073	23.03	0.008 s
MS-CNN [6]	0.049	36.82	0.057	33.48	0.055	31.62	0.068	28.18	0.006 s
CNLD	0.027	40.16	0.045	37.25	0.052	33.48	0.062	29.25	0.005 s

The SNR and RMSE after denoising in deep-water channels are higher than those in shallow-water channels, because a high gain simultaneously improves the signal-to-noise ratio of the target signal and noise, resulting in a decrease in denoising stability. The wavelet denoising effect of the soft threshold gradually outperforms the EMD algorithm as the noise coefficient increases, indicating that the extraction of correlation feature components in single-frame data is susceptible to Gaussian noise. The method based on deep learning is also superior to traditional algorithms in deep-water channel data denoising, with CAENN having a signal-to-noise ratio lower than 1D-nonlocal, indicating that optimizing the non-neighborhood feature extraction of time-domain signals can improve the signal-to-noise ratio of weak echoes submerged in noise. As the noise coefficient increases, the RMSE of 1D nonlocal gradually decreases compared to CAENN, indicating that non-neighborhood features exhibit high stability at low signal-to-noise ratios. The MS-CNN architecture combines multi-channel correlations to optimize the signal-to-noise ratio for denoising. Although the attention mechanism is introduced, the lack of adjacent frame features makes it unstable in preserving weak signals. Our proposed CNLD architecture not only considers the local similarity characteristics of similar positions in multiple frames of data within the channel but also considers the high-dimensional correlation of data between channels. Therefore, it can display a better denoising level with a lower root mean square error and the lowest signal-to-noise ratio. Below, we further compare the denoising effects by visualizing stacked echoes and single-frame echoes, with the shallow-water channel results at the top and deep-water channel results at the bottom of each grouping.

Figure 7a,b show the stacked noise echoes and pure echoes, respectively. The two white vertical lines, representing the sea-surface and sea-bottom signals, indicate that the preprocessed stacked echo has relevance. The darker the color in the stacked image, the lower the noise, and it is obvious that the superimposed noise echoes are generally gray. Compared to Figure 7b,c, it can be seen that the color of EMD-STRP after denoising is darker, indicating a more significant effect on Gaussian noise. By comparison with Figure 7e,f, it can be seen that the convolutional neural network based on the encoder–decoder can remove Gaussian noise by relying on multi-layer convolution to extract the high-dimensional features of echoes, but the white part of CAENN presents obvious distortion. However, 1D nonlocal networks retain more noise while preserving the target signal without deformation. MS-CNN in Figure 7g significantly improves the ability to remove Gaussian noise and retains effective signals by introducing attention modules for deep- and shallow-water channels. However, due to the high randomness of laser sea survey data, the channel correlation characteristics will also lead to denoising distortion. As shown in Figure 7h, the denoising result of the proposed method is most similar to the ground truth. By extending the receptive field in the spatial direction, the correlation of stacked signals of the deep-water channel and shallow-water channel can be fully exploited. Therefore, our proposed method can distinguish low-reflectivity targets from noise, reduce noise near the right white line, and preserve the seafloor signal.

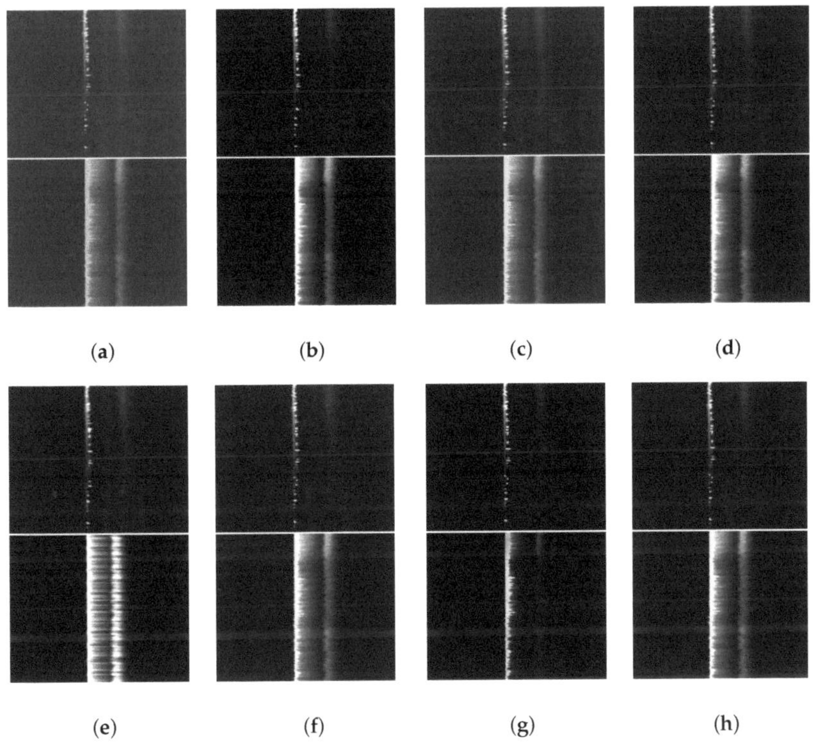

Figure 7. Visual comparison of measured stacked images. (**a**) Noise signal; (**b**) ground truth; (**c**) AWT; (**d**) EMD-STRP; (**e**) CAENN; (**f**) 1D-Nonlocal; (**g**) Ms-CNN; (**h**) CNLD.

We selected a frame of signals with obvious sea-surface and sea-bottom echoes in deep- and shallow-water channels for visual comparison to verify the ability of the proposed algorithm to retain the sea-bottom signal. As shown in Figure 8, the interference noise of LiDAR echo signals mainly includes system noise generated by internal hardware, as well as non-system noise generated by external environmental factors, such as the atmosphere and water. We selected one frame of echoes for visualization; the backscatter between the sea-surface and seabed signals was received by deep-water channels with a larger field of view. Figure 8a,b are, respectively, the original signal after adding a noise factor of 25 and the pure signal. Figure 8c,d demonstrate the denoising result of dynamic frequency-domain filtering and EMD-STRP. Although Gaussian noise can be removed by local refinement, the weak signal on the seabed is still confused with noise. As shown in Figure 8e,f, data-driven denoising methods can learn high-dimensional temporal features in echoes and thus can better remove Gaussian noise. However, the scattering of seawater and the low reflectivity of the seafloor will lead to the distortion of the weak seafloor signal during denoising. By introducing one-dimensional nonlocal features, the aliasing of Gaussian noise and of the target signal can be further alleviated. Figure 8g has a lower noise signal-to-noise ratio, mainly reflected in the smoother bottom noise of the signal and the better fit to the ground truth after denoising near the peak of the dual-channel seabed signals. It can improve the ability to retain weak echoes but also retains more jitter. As shown in Figure 8h, our proposed method makes use of the multi-frame correlation to improve the signal-to-noise ratio of seafloor signals. By taking into account the characteristics of multi-channel signals, CNLD retains more details and improves the stability of denoising. In general, the proposed method has a higher signal-to-noise ratio and a lower MSE than other methods, achieving the best denoising effect.

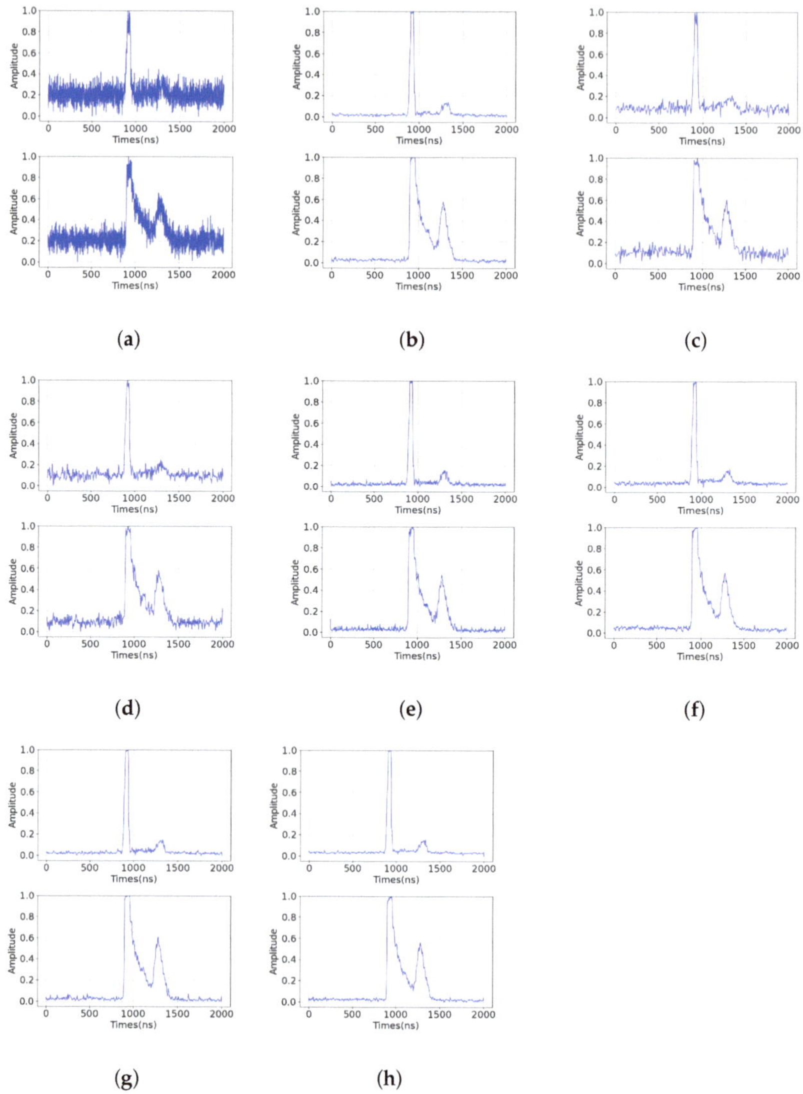

Figure 8. Visual comparison of measured waveforms. (**a**) Noise signal; (**b**) ground truth; (**c**) AWT; (**d**) EMD-STRP; (**e**) CAENN; (**f**) 1D-NONLOCAL; (**g**) Ms-CNN; (**h**) CNLD.

5.2. Comparison of Different Dilation Rates

The deep-water channel and shallow-water channel of multi-channel airborne LiDAR share the same optical system, but the field-of-view angle and detector gain are different. Therefore, there is a correlation between echoes from different channels and between adjacent frames. We designed various parameters to compare the effects of perceptual spatial fields. When multiple layers of dilated convolution are introduced, local information may be lost due to the gridding effect. Therefore, an HDC (hybrid dilated convolution) architecture [44] is referred to in the design of dilation rates for multi-layer dilated convolution. The expansion rate of stack unwrapping convolution cannot have a common divisor greater than 1, so the characteristics of local and nonlocal echoes can be comprehensively considered. We adopted three-layer stacked convolution as the basic architecture of the NLEB module. As shown in Figure 9a, the receptive fields of three conventional convolution stacks with a dilation rate of 1 can be regarded as traditional convolution stacks. As shown in Figure 9b,c, dilation rates of 1,2,3 and 1,2,5, respectively, in the spatial direction can expand the receptive field. In order to explore the ability of the proposed network to extract spatial features, we used dilated convolution in both spatiotemporal directions and only in the spatial direction.

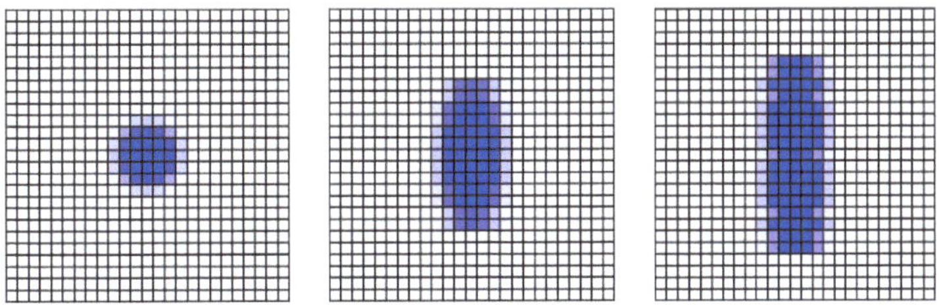

(a) (b) (c)

Figure 9. Comparison of different dilation rates in spatial direction. (**a**) Dilation rates = (1,1,1); (**b**) dilation rates = (1,2,3); (**c**) dilation rates = (1,2,5).

As shown in Table 5, with the increase in the dilation rate in the convolution layer, the signal-to-noise ratio of (1,2,2) is significantly higher than that of (1,1,1). Using dilated convolution can enlarge the local receptive field, so the signal-to-noise ratio is more reliable. When dilated convolution is used in both directions, the signal-to-noise ratio does not improve significantly and even becomes lower. This is because introducing dilated convolution in the time dimension can increase the receptive field, but it will destroy the dependency of the time series. More adjacent echoes can be covered by setting the dilation rates of the three stacked convolution layers to 1, 2, and 5. However, the improvement effect is not obvious when compared with setting the dilation rates to 1, 2, and 3. This is because the correlation or similarity of full-waveform data also decreases with the increase in the spatial distance. Using a large-scale convolution kernel to extract time-series features can improve the extraction ability of local features, but it will reduce the efficiency of network convergence. Therefore, the NLEB module proposed in this paper can enhance the efficiency of extracting the similarity of multi-frame echoes by using stacked small-kernel dilated convolution.

Table 5. Denoising effect of different dilation rates in measured experiment.

SNR	Evaluation	Non	Dilation Rates in Spatial Direction			Dilation Rates in Both Directions		
		(1,1,1)	(1,2,2)	(1,2,3)	(1,2,5)	(1,2,2)	(1,2,3)	(1,2,5)
5	RMSE	0.041	0.035	0.023	0.022	0.033	0.029	0.031
	SNR	37.22	38.68	39.37	39.32	38.74	39.28	39.33
10	RMSE	0.047	0.042	0.036	0.035	0.043	0.047	0.049
	SNR	33.66	34.51	35.36	35.33	34.92	35.27	35.32
15	RMSE	0.038	0.040	0.041	0.043	0.041	0.046	0.044
	SNR	28.81	29.76	30.18	29.86	29.95	30.19	30.20
20	RMSE	0.043	0.045	0.048	0.050	0.046	0.051	0.049
	SNR	25.47	25.63	26.09	25.87	25.94	26.01	26.02

5.3. Ablation Experiment

To verify the contribution of the multi-channel correlation and the proposed NLEB module to noise reduction, we designed Baseline-Net. As shown in Figure 10, this architecture uses our proposed NLEB module to extract features and uses a deconvolution module to recover signals.

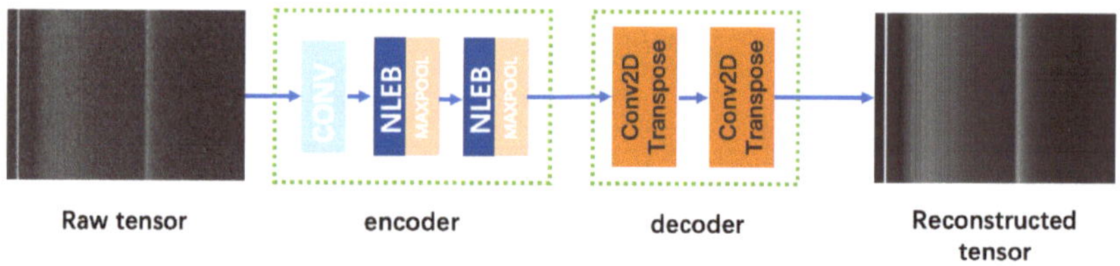

Figure 10. The architecture of Baseline-Net.

As shown in Table 6, under the condition of the same noise coefficient, the multi-frame deep-water echo after stacking has a stronger detector gain and a higher signal-to-noise ratio, but the RMSE of the shallow-water channel is lower and the denoising stability is better. Due to the adjustment of the gain and field-of-view angles in deep- and shallow-water channels, there are some blind spots in seabed exploration. Therefore, the signal-to-noise ratio of CNLD-Local is significantly higher than the baseline single-channel denoising effect. After the introduction of the proposed NLEB module, the RMSE of the CNLD model is significantly lower than that of the CNLD-Local model, indicating that the enhancement of the receptive field makes the denoising model more robust.

Table 6. Ablation experiment using measured data.

Signal	SNR_Noise	Baseline		Baseline		CNLD-Local		CNLD	
		RMSE	SNR	RMSE	SNR	RMSE	SNR	RMSE	SNR
Shallow channel	5	0.038	34.91	-	-	0.031	36.25	0.021	38.58
	10	0.029	28.29	-	-	0.041	31.63	0.026	33.48
	15	0.051	22.71	-	-	0.038	24.65	0.031	26.92
	20	0.069	20.29	-	-	0.043	22.27	0.036	22.94
Deep channel	5	-	-	0.053	37.65	0.049	38.19	0.027	40.16
	10	-	-	0.075	34.69	0.054	35.69	0.045	37.25
	15	-	-	0.082	30.32	0.057	32.95	0.052	33.48
	20	-	-	0.088	28.37	0.072	28.56	0.062	29.25

5.4. Analysis of Limitations

Because of rapid changes in the environment, not all data between scene channels have a strong correlation. By further analyzing the limitations of the laser sea denoising algorithm through stacked echo diagrams, it can be seen that sea-surface and seabed signals have strong randomness. As shown in Figure 11a, the positions of the sea surface and seafloor change between multiple frames, but their relative positions remain unchanged, showing a good correlation. As shown in Figure 11b, due to the fast flight of the aircraft or sea-surface jitter, the fast transformation of the target signal will cause the correlation to weaken after multi-frame stacking. Although the method proposed in this paper uses the centroid of the sea surface to detect the signal, no alignment method can optimize the denoising effect by using the echo similarity after the sea surface is lost. As shown in Figure 11c, the sea-surface signal has strong randomness, and the field-of-view angle of the deep-water channel is larger, resulting in a higher probability of receiving the target signal. However, shallow-water channels are limited by the field-of-view angle scale and gain, which reduces the probability of receiving effective signals. As shown in Figure 11d, when the laser hits trees, multiple targets will be generated. However, the gain and sensitivity of deep- and shallow-water channels to targets are different, so when the echoes appear saturated or there are multiple targets, the correlation of data between channels will also decrease.

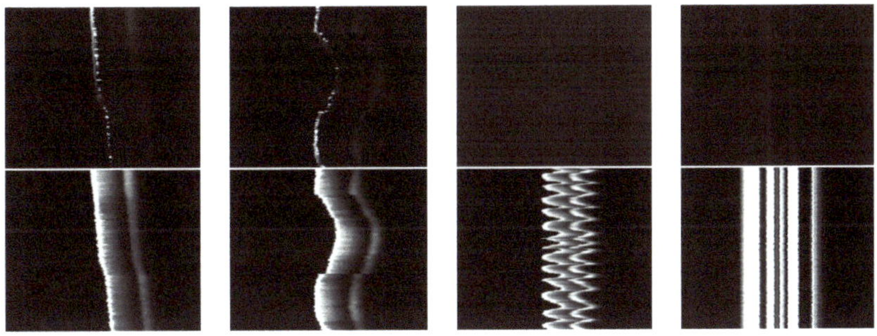

(a) (b) (c) (d)

Figure 11. Visual comparison of stacked images. (**a**) Strong correlation; (**b**) weak correlation; (**c**) channel anomaly; (**d**) multiple echoes.

As shown in Figure 12, limiting denoising factors are analyzed through the visualization of a single waveform. As shown in Figure 12a, the correlation of echoes is mainly reflected in sea-surface and seabed signals. After normalization, seabed signals are significantly different due to the different gains of deep- and shallow-water channels. The field of view of the deep-water channel is large, so more water body backscattering can be received, resulting in the deformation of seabed signals. As shown in Figure 12b, hardware circuit overheating, random background light, and other factors may lead to the availability of data in a single channel in some cases, so the data correlation between channels may fail in some cases. As shown in Figure 12c, due to the difference in gains of deep- and shallow-water channels, the target signal of the shallow-water channel is normal when the deep-water channel is saturated, and the deep-water channel will receive more target signals due to a stronger gain.

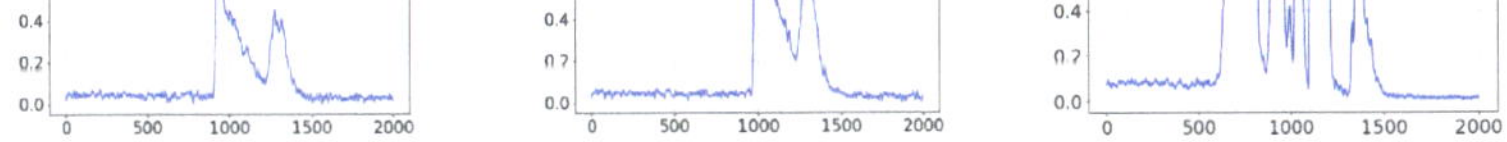

(a) (b) (c)

Figure 12. Visual comparison of single waveform. (**a**) Weak correlation; (**b**) channel anomaly; (**c**) multiple echoes.

6. Conclusions

In this paper, a denoising method for a multi-channel ALB full waveform is proposed. Firstly, an alignment method based on surface centroids was used to highlight the structural similarity between consecutive frames. Then, we introduced the NLEB module to enhance the spatial receptive field, and the correlation extraction efficiency of the sea-surface and seabed echoes was optimized. Finally, we designed a CNLD network based on a multitasking learning architecture to mine signal correlations between channels and simultaneously reconstruct denoised deep and shallow channel echoes in an end-to-end manner.

Through ablation experiments, we found that the correlation between multiple waveforms in the same channel exhibits high stability, and the correlation between channels is constrained by channel gain differences, field-of-view angle differences, and the signal's dynamic range. However, the signal correlation between channels can still improve the retention of weak seafloor signals. The proposed method can obtain the highest SNR with the lowest RMSE under different noise variances. In the future, we will further optimize the method of extracting channel correlations and improve the robustness of the model through data enhancement and the introduction of prior physical knowledge.

Author Contributions: Conceptualization, Y.Z.; Methodology, B.H.; Validation, J.H. and Q.L.; Investigation, C.L.; Resources, M.Y. and Y.L.; Funding acquisition, G.Z. All authors have read and agreed to the published version of the manuscript.

Funding: This work is supported by the Guangxi Innovative Development Grand Grant (No. 2018AA13005).

Data Availability Statement: The data presented in this study are available on request from the corresponding author. The data are not publicly available due to project confidentiality agreement.

Conflicts of Interest: The authors declare no conflict of interest.

References

1. Ke, J.; Lam, E.Y. Temporal Super-resolution Full Waveform LiDAR. In Proceedings of the Imaging and Applied Optics 2018 (3D, AO, AIO, COSI, DH, IS, LACSEA, LS&C, MATH, pcAOP), Orlando, FL, USA, 25–28 June 2018; Optica Publishing Group: Washington, DC, USA, 2018; p. CTh3C.1. [CrossRef]
2. Balsa-Barreiro, J.; Avariento, J.; Lerma, J. Airborne light detection and ranging (LiDAR) point density analysis. *Sci. Res. Essays* **2012**, *7*, 3010–3019. [CrossRef]
3. Baltsavias, E. Airborne laser scanning: Basic relations and formulas. *ISPRS J. Photogramm. Remote Sens.* **1999**, *54*, 199–214. [CrossRef]
4. Hermosilla, T.; Ruiz, L.A.; Recio, J.A.; Balsa-Barreiro, J. Land-use Mapping of Valencia City Area from Aerial Images and LiDAR Data. In Proceedings of the GEOProcessing 2012: The Fourth International Conference in Advanced Geographic Information Systems, Applications and Services, Valencia, Spain, 30 January–4 February 2012.
5. Huang, T.; Tao, B.; He, Y.; Hu, S.; Xu, G.; Yu, J.; Wang, C.; Chen, P. Utilization of multi-channel ocean LiDAR data to classify the types of waveform. In Proceedings of the SPIE Remote Sensing 2017, Warsaw, Poland, 11–14 September 2017; p. 61. [CrossRef]
6. Zhao, Y.; Yu, X.; Hu, B.; Chen, R. A Multi-Source Convolutional Neural Network for Lidar Bathymetry Data Classification. *Mar. Geod.* **2022**, *45*, 232–250. [CrossRef]
7. Chen, D.; Peethambaran, J.; Zhang, Z. A supervoxel-based vegetation classification via decomposition and modelling of full-waveform airborne laser scanning data. *Int. J. Remote Sens.* **2018**, *39*, 2937–2968. [CrossRef]
8. Zhao, X.; Xia, H.; Zhao, J.; Zhou, F. Adaptive Wavelet Threshold Denoising for Bathymetric Laser Full-Waveforms With Weak Bottom Returns. *IEEE Geosci. Remote Sens. Lett.* **2022**, *19*, 1503505. [CrossRef]
9. Mader, D.; Richter, K.; Westfeld, P.; Maas, H.G. Correction to: Potential of a Non-linear Full-Waveform Stacking Technique in Airborne LiDAR Bathymetry. *PFG—J. Photogramm. Remote Sens. Geoinf. Sci.* **2022**, *90*, 495–496. [CrossRef]
10. Long, S.; Zhou, G.; Wang, H.; Zhou, X.; Chen, J.; Gao, J. Denoising of Lidar Echo Signal Based on Wavelet Adaptive Threshold Method. *ISPRS—Int. Arch. Photogramm. Remote Sens. Spat. Inf. Sci.* **2020**, *XLII-3/W10*, 215–220. [CrossRef]
11. Cheng, X.; Mao, J.; Li, J.; Zhao, H.; Zhou, C.; Gong, X.; Rao, Z. An EEMD-SVD-LWT algorithm for denoising a lidar signal. *Measurement* **2021**, *168*, 108405. [CrossRef]
12. Zhou, G.; Long, S.; Xu, J.; Zhou, X.; Wang, C. Comparison analysis of five waveform decomposition algorithms for the airborne LiDAR echo signal. *IEEE J. Sel. Top. Appl. Earth Obs. Remote Sens.* **2021**, *14*, 7869–7880. [CrossRef]
13. Song, Y.; Li, H.; Zhai, G.; He, Y.; Bian, S.; Zhou, W. Comparison of multichannel signal deconvolution algorithms in airborne LiDAR bathymetry based on wavelet transform. *Sci. Rep.* **2021**, *11*, 16988. [CrossRef]

14. Zhang, Y. A Novel Lidar Signal Denoising Method Based on Convolutional Autoencoding Deep Learning Neural Network. *Atmosphere* **2021**, *12*, 1403.
15. Gangping, L.; Ke, J. Dense and Residual Neural Networks for Full-waveform LiDAR Echo Decomposition. In Proceedings of the Imaging Systems and Applications 2021, Washington, DC, USA, 19–23 July 2021; p. IF4D.3. [CrossRef]
16. Liu, G.; Ke, J.; Lam, E.Y. CNN-based Super-resolution Full-waveform LiDAR. In Proceedings of the Imaging and Applied Optics Congress, Washington, DC, USA, 22–26 June 2020; Optica Publishing Group: Washington, DC, USA, 2020; p. JW2A.29. [CrossRef]
17. Bhadani, R. AutoEncoder for Interpolation. *arXiv* **2021**, arXiv:2101.00853
18. Chen, X.; Yang, H. Full Waveform Inversion Based on Wavefield Correlation. *IOP Conf. Ser. Mater. Sci. Eng.* **2019**, *472*, 012069. [CrossRef]
19. Hu, B.; Zhao, Y.; Chen, R.; Liu, Q.; Wang, P.; Zhang, Q. Denoising method for a lidar bathymetry system based on a low-rank recovery of non-local data structures. *Appl. Opt.* **2022**, *61*, 69–76. [CrossRef]
20. Ma, H.; Zhou, W.; Zhang, L.; Wang, S. Decomposition of small-footprint full waveform LiDAR data based on generalized Gaussian model and grouping LM optimization. *Meas. Sci. Technol.* **2017**, *28*, 045203. [CrossRef]
21. Pan, Z.; Glennie, C.; Hartzell, P.; Fernandez-Diaz, J.C.; Legleiter, C.; Overstreet, B. Performance Assessment of High Resolution Airborne Full Waveform LiDAR for Shallow River Bathymetry. *Remote Sens.* **2015**, *7*, 5133–5159. [CrossRef]
22. Ding, K.; Li, Q.; Zhu, J.; Wang, C.; Guan, M.; Chen, Z.; Yang, C.; Cui, Y.; Liao, J. An Improved Quadrilateral Fitting Algorithm for the Water Column Contribution in Airborne Bathymetric Lidar Waveforms. *Sensors* **2018**, *18*, 552. [CrossRef]
23. Abady, L.; Bailly, J.S.; Baghdadi, N.; Pastol, Y.; Abdallah, H. Assessment of Quadrilateral Fitting of the Water Column Contribution in Lidar Waveforms on Bathymetry Estimates. *IEEE Geosci. Remote Sens. Lett.* **2014**, *11*, 813–817. [CrossRef]
24. Ma, Y.; Zhang, J.; Zhang, Z.; Zhang, J.Y. Bathymetry Retrieval Method of LiDAR Waveform Based on Multi-Gaussian Functions. *J. Coast. Res.* **2019**, *90*, 324–331. [CrossRef]
25. Qi, C.; Ma, Y.; Su, D.; Yang, F.; Liu, J.; Wang, X.H. A Method to Decompose Airborne LiDAR Bathymetric Waveform in Very Shallow Waters Combining Deconvolution With Curve Fitting. *IEEE Geosci. Remote Sens. Lett.* **2022**, *19*, 7004905. [CrossRef]
26. Shen, X.; Li, Q.Q.; Wu, G.; Zhu, J. Decomposition of LiDAR waveforms by B-spline-based modeling. *ISPRS J. Photogramm. Remote Sens.* **2017**, *128*, 182–191. [CrossRef]
27. Wang, C.; Li, Q.; Liu, Y.; Wu, G.; Liu, P.; Ding, X. A comparison of waveform processing algorithms for single-wavelength LiDAR bathymetry. *ISPRS J. Photogramm. Remote Sens.* **2015**, *101*, 22–35. [CrossRef]
28. Kogut, T.; Bakuła, K. Improvement of Full Waveform Airborne Laser Bathymetry Data Processing based on Waves of Neighborhood Points. *Remote Sens.* **2019**, *11*, 1255. [CrossRef]
29. Guo, K.; Li, Q.; Wang, C.; Mao, Q.; Liu, Y.; Ouyang, Y.; Feng, Y.; Zhu, J.; Wu, A. Target Echo Detection Based on the Signal Conditional Random Field Model for Full-Waveform Airborne Laser Bathymetry. *IEEE Trans. Geosci. Remote Sens.* **2022**, *60*, 5705421. [CrossRef]
30. Xing, S.; Wang, D.; Xu, Q.; Lin, Y.; Li, P.; Jiao, L.; Zhang, X.; Liu, C. A Depth-Adaptive Waveform Decomposition Method for Airborne LiDAR Bathymetry. *Sensors* **2019**, *19*, 5065. [CrossRef] [PubMed]
31. Liu, Y.; Yue, J.; Shi, P.; Wang, Y.; Gao, H.; Feng, B.; Liu, Z.; Li, H. A deep learning method for LiDAR bathymetry waveforms processing. In Proceedings of the 2021 International Conference on Neural Networks, Information and Communication Engineering, Qingdao, China, 27–29 August 2021; Zhang, Z., Ed.; International Society for Optics and Photonics, SPIE: Bellingham, WA, USA, 2021; Volume 11933, p. 119331S. [CrossRef]
32. Asmann, A.; Stewart, B.; Wallace, A.M. Deep Learning for LiDAR Waveforms with Multiple Returns. In Proceedings of the 2020 28th European Signal Processing Conference (EUSIPCO), Amsterdam, The Netherlands, 18–21 January 2021.
33. Shanjiang, H.; Yan, H.; Bangyi, T.; Jiayong, Y.; Weibiao, C. Classification of sea and land waveforms based on deep learning for airborne laser bathymetry. *Infrared Laser Eng.* **2019**, *48*, 1113004. [CrossRef]
34. Liu, X.; Liu, X.; Wang, Z.; Huang, G.; Shu, R. Classification of Laser Footprint Based on Random Forest in Mountainous Area Using GLAS Full-Waveform Features. *IEEE J. Sel. Top. Appl. Earth Obs. Remote Sens.* **2022**, *15*, 2284–2297. [CrossRef]
35. Yang, C.L.; Chen, Z.X.; Yang, C.Y. Sensor Classification Using Convolutional Neural Network by Encoding Multivariate Time Series as Two-Dimensional Colored Images. *Sensors* **2020**, *20*, 168. [CrossRef]
36. Hu, B.; Zhao, Y.; He, J.; Liu, Q.; Chen, R. A Classification Method for Airborne Full-Waveform LiDAR Systems Based on a Gramian Angular Field and Convolution Neural Networks. *Electronics* **2022**, *11*, 4114. [CrossRef]
37. Geng, Z.; Yan, H.; Zhang, J.; Zhu, D. Deep-Learning for Radar: A Survey. *IEEE Access* **2021**, *9*, 141800–141818. [CrossRef]
38. Leng, Z.; Zhang, J.; Ma, Y.; Zhang, J. ICESat-2 Bathymetric Signal Reconstruction Method Based on a Deep Learning Model with Active dash Passive Data Fusion. *Remote Sens.* **2023**, *15*, 460. [CrossRef]
39. Wang, H.; Liu, Z.; Ai, T. Long-range Dependencies Learning Based on Non-Local 1D-Convolutional Neural Network for Rolling Bearing Fault Diagnosis. *J. Dyn. Monit. Diagn.* **2022**, *1*, 148–159. [CrossRef]
40. Magruder, L.A.; Neuenschwander, A.L.; Marmillion, S.P. Lidar waveform stacking techniques for faint ground return extraction. *J. Appl. Remote Sens.* **2010**, *4*, 043501. [CrossRef]
41. Wang, X.; Girshick, R.; Gupta, A.; He, K. Non-local Neural Networks. In Proceedings of the 2018 IEEE/CVF Conference on Computer Vision and Pattern Recognition, Salt Lake City, UT, USA, 18–23 June 2018; pp. 7794–7803. [CrossRef]

42. Chang, J.; Zhu, L.; Li, H.; Fan, X.; Yang, Z. Noise reduction in Lidar signal using correlation-based EMD combined with soft thresholding and roughness penalty. *Opt. Commun.* **2018**, *407*, 290–295. [CrossRef]
43. Han, H.; Wang, H.; Liu, Z.; Wang, J. Intelligent vibration signal denoising method based on non-local fully convolutional neural network for rolling bearings. *ISA Trans.* **2022**, *122*, 13–23. [CrossRef] [PubMed]
44. Wang, P.; Chen, P.; Yuan, Y.; Liu, D.; Huang, Z.; Hou, X.; Cottrell, G. Understanding Convolution for Semantic Segmentation. In Proceedings of the 2018 IEEE Winter Conference on Applications of Computer Vision (WACV), Lake Tahoe, NV, USA, 12–15 March 2018.

Journal of
Marine Science and Engineering

MDPI

Article

Underwater Geomagnetic Localization Based on Adaptive Fission Particle-Matching Technology

Huapeng Yu [1], Ziyuan Li [1,2,3,4,*], Wentie Yang [2,4], Tongsheng Shen [1], Dalei Liang [1] and Qinyuan He [1]

1 National Innovation Institute of Defense Technology, Beijing 100071, China
2 Hubei Key Laboratory of Marine Electromagnetic Detection and Control, Wuhan 430064, China
3 Science and Technology on Underwater Vehicles Laboratory, Harbin Engineering University, Harbin 150001, China
4 Wuhan Second Ship Design and Research Institute, Wuhan 430064, China
* Correspondence: liziyuan@hrbeu.edu.cn

Abstract: The geomagnetic field constitutes a massive fingerprint database, and its unique structure provides potential position correction information. In recent years, particle filter technology has received more attention in the context of robot navigation. However, particle degradation and impoverishment have constrained navigation systems' performance. This paper transforms particle filtering into a particle-matching positioning problem and proposes a geomagnetic localization method based on an adaptive fission particle filter. This method employs particle-filtering technology to construct a geomagnetic matching positioning model. Through adaptive particle fission and sampling, the problem of particle degradation and impoverishment in traditional particle filtering is solved, resulting in improved geomagnetic matching positioning accuracy. Finally, the proposed method was tested in a sea trial, and the results show that the proposed method has a lower positioning error than traditional particle-filtering and intelligent particle-filtering algorithms. Under geomagnetic map conditions, an average positioning accuracy of about 546.44 m is achieved.

Keywords: autonomous underwater vehicle; underwater localization; geomagnetic matching; fission particle filter

Citation: Yu, H.; Li, Z.; Yang, W.; Shen, T.; Liang, D.; He, Q. Underwater Geomagnetic Localization Based on Adaptive Fission Particle-Matching Technology. *J. Mar. Sci. Eng.* **2023**, *11*, 1739. https://doi.org/10.3390/jmse11091739

Academic Editors: Yan-Tsung Peng, Wenqi Ren, Jingchun Zhou and Qiuping Jiang

Received: 22 July 2023
Revised: 31 August 2023
Accepted: 31 August 2023
Published: 4 September 2023

1. Introduction

Navigation and positioning systems are the core technologies of autonomous underwater vehicles (AUVs) [1,2]. However, due to the rapid attenuation of Global Positioning System (GPS) signals in water, autonomous underwater robots cannot rely on GPSs for accurate navigation and positioning [3,4]. Inertial navigation systems (INSs) are currently the main forms of navigation equipment employed in underwater vehicles [5]. However, due to the continuous accumulation of measurement errors from gyroscopes and accelerometers over time, inertial navigation eventually leads to the divergence of positioning errors [6]. Effective positioning correction methods are still a popular and challenging topic in the field of underwater navigation [7].

Geomagnetic fields can provide pose correction references for underwater navigation systems. Inspired by biological geomagnetic localization, researchers have developed a series of geomagnetic positioning methods [8–11], such as geomagnetic contour matching algorithms (MAGCOMs) [12], iterative closest contours point (ICCP) [13], simultaneous localization and mapping (SLAM) of the geomagnetic field [14,15], and multi-parameter search without a magnetic map [16]. Wu proposed using interval knowledge of geomagnetic field measurements to overcome the uncertainty in measurement for practical applications of geomagnetic positioning, and underwater experiments showed that the root-mean-square error of the proposed method reached 139.3 m [17]. Li et al. proposed a dual-feature matching algorithm combining geomagnetic total intensity and its gradient to solve problems such as poor matching accuracy in areas with low geomagnetic roughness using only magnetic field total intensity as a feature. The results of a simulation experiment showed that compared with a traditional correlation matching algorithm, the positioning accuracy of the proposed algorithm could reach within 20 m [18]. A MAGCOM generally requires vehicles to accumulate a segment of trajectory and compares the correlation between the magnetic survey sequence and the magnetic map sequence in the matching area to obtain accurate position information. Compared with MAGCOMs, the ICCP algorithm enhances the ability of a rotation search based on a translational search, thereby improving the algorithm's accuracy. These methods have been effective with regard to geomagnetic positioning to some extent. However, the sparsity of geomagnetic characteristics in marine environments often leads to problems such as low effective matching rates for these algorithms within the preset matching area. Expanding the search and matching range precipitates higher computational resource consumption.

In recent years, terrain matching navigation based on particle-filtering technology has been applied [19,20]. The corresponding algorithms used in this process introduce the idea of probability estimation, which can effectively compensate for the shortcomings of geomagnetic matching algorithms based on correlation measurement. Among these algorithms, the particle-filtering method based on Bayesian estimation has shown strong performance in processing nonlinear problems [21]. Quintas et al. demonstrated that particle filtering is robust in geomagnetic navigation problems [22]. As the iteration process progresses, the impoverishment and degradation of traditional particle-filtering methods lead to particle swarm clustering and the inability to identify the best matching point. Ultimately, an unsatisfactory position correction source was obtained.

To solve the problem of particle degradation and impoverishment, this article proposes an adaptive fission particle-filtering geomagnetic matching localization algorithm. During the execution of particle matching and positioning, the current particles undergo a splitting operation and generate new particles. The newly developed particles are called "offspring" particles, while the original particles are known as "parent" particles. The degree of particle fission is judged based on the particle weight, and it is proposed that the sampling of "offspring" particles should consider both the degree of particle fission of the parent particles and the sampling variance of the "parent" particles. By redefining the sampling of the offspring particles, the distribution of the particle set becomes more reasonable, and the method can be explained in terms of generality, thus improving the probability of obtaining a correct match in geomagnetic positioning. Our contributions can be summarized as follows:

- Particle-matching technology is employed to realize underwater geomagnetic localization.
- An adaptive fission particle-filtering algorithm is proposed to solve the problem of particle degeneration and particle impoverishment. Compared with advanced intelligent particle-filtering methods, our method achieves better localization accuracy.
- The proposed method was tested in a marine environment, and the results show that our proposed geomagnetic localization method can effectively achieve underwater navigation error correction.

The remainder of this paper is organized as follows. Section 2 introduces related works. Section 3 presents the problems and methods. Section 4 describes the experiments. Section 5 draws conclusions from the study.

2. Principle of Geomagnetic Matching Localization

The principle of geomagnetic matching is to store the geomagnetic feature map of the planned trajectory area in advance on a computer. When vehicles navigate to this area, the current geomagnetic field matching feature quantity is obtained in real time through the onboard geomagnetic measuring sensor. Then, the real-time measured geomagnetic data are correlated with the stored geomagnetic map on the computer, and the matched point with a high degree of correlation is selected as the current real position of the vehicles. Afterwards, the geographic coordinates of the position are investigated using the geomagnetic map, providing reliable position information for correcting the navigation trajectory of the vehicles [23].

In this study, a geomagnetic matching localization algorithm based on particle filters was developed, the principles of which are shown in Figure 1. The vehicle employed in this study has a spherical array of magnetic sensors that can obtain real-time measurements of 16-channel, three-axis geomagnetic vector data. Firstly, each magnetometer's vector magnetic field value is preprocessed to obtain characteristic parameters that can be used for geomagnetic matching calculations. In addition, the vehicle's dead reckoning (DR) navigation system can provide rough position information. Based on the error setting of the dead reckoning navigation system, the range of particle movement is determined. Afterward, the difference between the map value of the characteristic geomagnetic parameter falling in the corresponding geomagnetic grid and the measurement value is used to update the particle weight. Then, through continuous resampling and other steps, an estimate of the vehicle's current position is obtained.

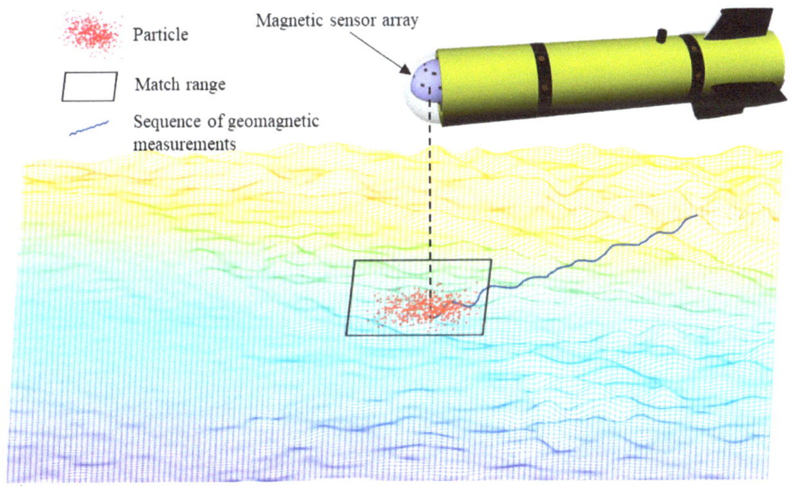

Figure 1. Schematic diagram of particle filter geomagnetic matching localization principle.

Geomagnetic positioning systems based on filtering technology can yield a continuous position output, making them superior to the above positioning methods in terms of real-time performance, and they have received attention from researchers in recent years [24]. Typical methods used in this domain include the geomagnetic/inertial positioning method with Kalman filtering, which is the core method used, and the geomagnetic positioning method with particle filtering [25]. The former draws on the Sandia inertial-geomagnetic navigation system, employs a linearized geomagnetic field model as an observation quantity, and, finally, achieves system's position or velocity error correction. However, how highly non-linear geomagnetic models are linearized constitutes a crucial factor affecting the accuracy of this method. The latter particle-filtering method based on Bayesian estimation shows strong performance in dealing with non-linear problems, requires low magnetic field measurement accuracy, allows for measurement errors, and has strong robustness. Zhang et al. used particle filtering to achieve underwater terrain matching navigation [26]. In practical applications, as long as the filter does not diverge, the geomagnetic positioning error can always be maintained within a certain range. Therefore, geomagnetic positioning methods based on filtering technology have great developmental potential in future geomagnetic navigation applications.

3. Problems and Methods

3.1. Particle Filter

In a geomagnetic matching navigation system, the state space model can be defined as follows:

$$x_k = f(x_{k-1}, u_k) \tag{1}$$

$$z_k = g(h(\theta), x_k, v_k) \tag{2}$$

In the Equation (1), x_k represents the position outputs of INS, where $x_k = \begin{bmatrix} \varphi_k & \lambda_k \end{bmatrix}^{\mathrm{T}}$. z_k represents the observation vector. $h(\theta)$ represents the magnetic field intensity at any position on the geomagnetic map. u_k and v_k represent the state noise and observation noise at time k, respectively, and the two types of noise are independent of each other and follow a Gaussian distribution.

In a particle filter algorithm, assuming that the system process follows an m-order Markov process, the state updating of the system can be achieved based on the posterior probability density recursively derived from observations. However, in reality, it is difficult to directly obtain an accurate posterior probability distribution of a target in a nonlinear system. The importance-sampling technique generates a set of particles $\hat{x}^i \sim q(x)(i = 1, 2, \ldots, N)$ via introducing a probability density function with known distribution characteristics and easy sampling characteristics. The choice of the importance probability density function has a significant impact on the accuracy of the algorithm. The detailed theoretical derivation can be found in [27]. Typically, in standard particle-filtering algorithms, the importance density function is set to the prior probability density function, namely

$$q\left(x_k^i \middle| x_{0:k-1}^i, z_{1:k}\right) = p\left(x_k \middle| x_{k-1}^i\right) \tag{3}$$

where $x_{0:k-1}^i$ represents the state variables from time 0 to $k-1$, and $z_{1:k}$ represents the observed variables from time 1 to k. The recursive update formula for particle weights is simplified as

$$w_k^i \propto w_{k-1}^i p\left(z_k \middle| x_k^i\right) \tag{4}$$

In the problem of magnetic field matching localization, the following must be defined:

$$p\left(z_k \middle| x_k^i\right) = \frac{1}{\sqrt{2\pi\tau}} \exp\left(\frac{-(\theta_k - \theta_m)^2}{2\tau}\right) \tag{5}$$

In Equation (5), τ is the variance of the magnetic field measurement error, θ_k is the total intensity value of the magnetic field measured by the magnetometer at time k, and θ_m is the magnetic map value corresponding to the grid where the particle is located.

Normalize the weights

$$\hat{w}_k^i = \frac{w_k^i}{\sum\limits_{i=1}^{N} w_k^i} \tag{6}$$

where $\sum\limits_{i=1}^{N} w^i = 1$. Thus, the particles' posterior probability density and corresponding weights are obtained. However, after several iterations, except for a few particles with large weights, the weights of the remaining particles are so small that they can be ignored. Particle degradation is a common problem faced when using sequential importance-sampling particle filters [28]. In engineering, particle-resampling techniques are commonly used to solve the problem of particle degradation. By adding a resampling calculation step after importance sampling, low-weight particles are eliminated, and high-weight particles are replicated, thereby facilitating the redistribution of particle weights. The three commonly used basic resampling schemes are multinomial resampling, stratified resampling, and systematic resampling. Resampling techniques solve the problem of particle degradation in particle filtering, but they also introduce new problems; replicating only weighted particles reduces the diversity of particles, leading to particle impoverishment [21]. To solve these problems, some adaptive particle-filtering algorithms have been proposed, such as intelligent particle filtering [29] and genetic particle filtering [30].

3.2. Geomagnetic Localization with Adaptive Particle Fission

In response to the problems of particle degradation and impoverishment with respect to traditional particle-filtering algorithms, this paper proposes an adaptive fission particle-filtering geomagnetic matching localization method to correct the dead reckoning error.

In the particle-filtering geomagnetic matching algorithm, the state variables of each particle are set as longitude, latitude, and total magnetic field strength. During initialization, particles are drawn from their prior state distribution and assigned initial weights of $w = 1/N$, where N is the total number of particles. Then, iterative calculations such as importance sampling are performed. In traditional particle filtering, high-weight particles are copied multiple times during resampling, leading to a need for more diversity among particles. Additionally, continuous iterations cause particles to gather in local areas of the geomagnetic map, resulting in only locally optimal solutions rather than global optimal solutions. As a result, significant positioning errors arise in the wrong matching area.

In the adaptive fission particle-filtering algorithm proposed in this paper, the particles before resampling are employed as "parent" particles, and all "parent" particles generate "offspring" particles after updating their weights. The "parent" particles and "offspring" particles are then mixed, ranked in descending order according to weight, and only the top N particles are retained, while the rest are discarded. This process continuously updates the particle population to enrich its diversity without increasing computational complexity and avoids local optimal solutions due to particle clustering. Assume that the number of "offspring" particles generated by each "parent" particle is m_k^i.

$$m_k^i = \text{round}\left[N \times w_k^i\right] + 2 \tag{7}$$

In the equation above, N is the total number of particles, w_k^i is the weight of the i-th particle at time k, and round$[x]$ is the rounding function. It can be seen that the number of "offspring" particles is determined by the weight of the "parent" particles. High-quality particles with high weights will generate more "offspring", while low-weight particles can produce at least two "offspring" particles. Therefore, in the iterative calculation process, the diversity of the particles can be maintained.

Next, samples are taken from a Gaussian distribution for the "offspring" particles. The primary purpose of adaptive fission particle filtering is to retain high-weight particles and perturb low-weight particles, moving them to other target areas. Therefore, the sampling of "offspring" particles should satisfy a normal distribution with a mean value of the "parent" particle state and a variance of $\boldsymbol{\mu}_k^i$, as follows:

$$\tilde{\boldsymbol{x}}_k^{ij} \sim N\left(\boldsymbol{x}_k^i, \boldsymbol{\mu}_k^i\right), j = \left[1, m_k^j\right] \tag{8}$$

Reference [31] defines the particle fission factor a_k^i as the variance of the samples taken for "offspring" particles.

$$a_k^i = \frac{1}{\left(1 + \exp\left(\frac{w_k^i - w_k^{\text{avg}}}{w_k^{\max} - w_k^{\text{avg}}}\right)\right)} \tag{9}$$

In Equation (9), w_k^{avg} and $w_k^{\max}$ represent the average and maximum weight of the particles at time k. Figure 2 shows the relationship between the weight of the "parent" particles and the fission factor [31]. From Figure 2, it can be seen that "parent" particles with smaller weights have a higher fission degree. However, it is not appropriate to directly use the fission factor as the variance for sampling "offspring" particles. As shown in Figure 2, regardless of whether the "parent" particle has a large or small weight, the sampling variance of the "offspring" particles satisfies $0 < a_k^i < 1$. For example, if the fission factor is 0.23 and the coordinate of the "parent" particle is (120° E, 30° N), then most of the generated "offspring" particles will be within the range of (120° ± 1.5° E, 30° ± 1.5° N). This distribution of "offspring" particles covers an area of nearly 300 × 300 km, which obviously does not match actual situations. The method proposed in reference [31] is only applicable to an amplitude of seismic wave signals no greater than 10 V at each time interval and has a high degree of contingency.

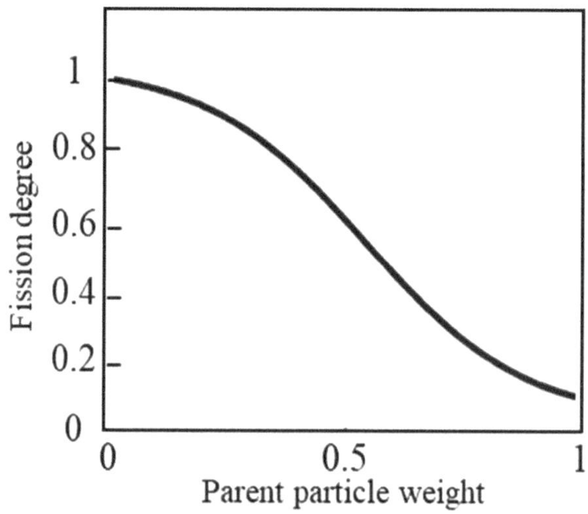

Figure 2. Relationship between parent particle weight and fission degree.

This paper indicates that the "offspring" particles generated from the fission of the "parent" particles must inherit some characteristics of the "parent" particles. Thus, the sampling of "offspring" particles should be based on the "parent" particles. Assuming that the sampling distribution variance of the "parent" particles is μ_k^i, then the variance of the sampling of the "offspring" particles should be

$$\sigma_k^i = \lambda \mu_k^i a_k^i = \frac{\lambda \mu_k^i}{\left(1 + \exp\left(\frac{w_k^i - w_k^{\mathrm{avg}}}{w_k^{\max} - w_k^{\mathrm{avg}}}\right)\right)} \tag{10}$$

In the equation, λ is the scale factor used to control the range of movement of the "offspring" particles. It is an empirical value, and researchers can set it based on the specific context of the problem being addressed. Equation (10) reflects that, under the consideration of the motion characteristics of the "parent" particles, the "offspring" particles fission adaptively based on the weights of the "parent" particles to obtain better state values. This is achieved by adapting the distribution characteristics of the "parent" particles around the distribution centered on the "parent" particles according to the fission factor size. In Figure 3, the light blue circles represent the "parent" particles, and the blue asterisks represent the "offspring" particles they generate. Each "offspring" particle is distributed around its 'parent' particle to explore new optimal solutions. Figure 4 compares the particle diversity between the proposed and traditional particle-filtering methods after 250/417 iterations. It can be seen from Figure 4 that even when the experiment is nearly 60% complete, the particles of the adaptive fission particle-filtering method remain dispersed and have good diversity. In contrast, the particles of the traditional particle-filtering method gather together. Therefore, the proposed adaptive fission particle-filtering method improves the quality of particles and aids the discovery of the best geomagnetic matching point.

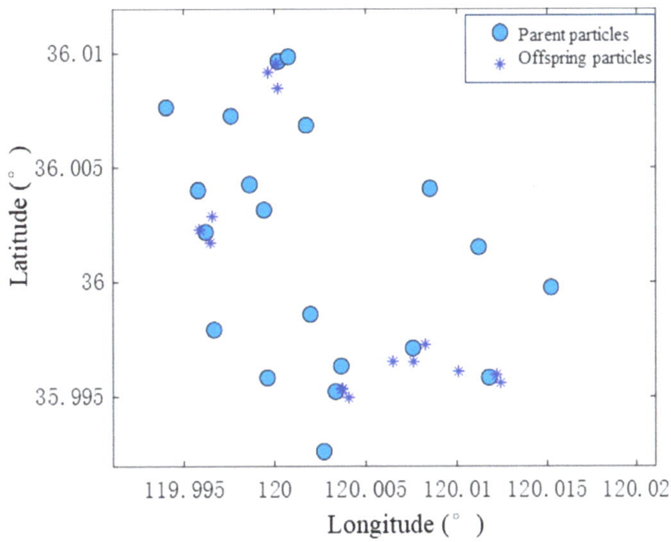

Figure 3. Schematic diagram of particle fission.

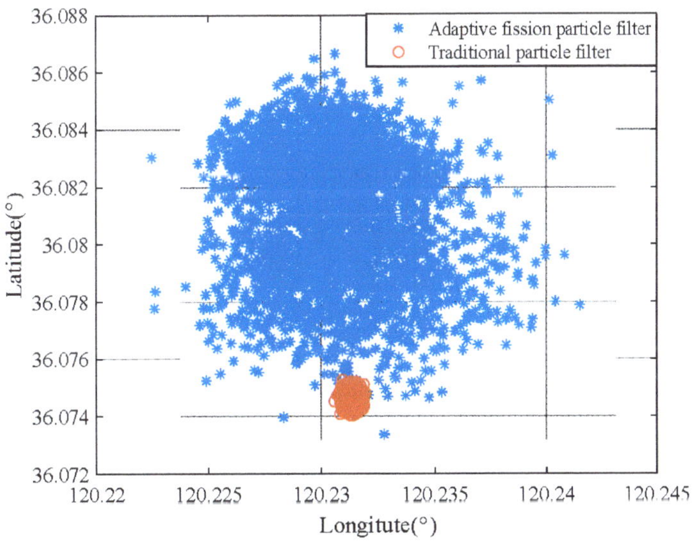

Figure 4. Comparison of particle diversity.

The newly generated "offspring" particles $\tilde{x}_k^{ij}$ update their weights according to Equation (4) based on the difference between the geomagnetic field reading values in their state space and the measurement values. Then, the "parent" particles and "offspring" particles constitute the particle set, sorted in descending order according to the weight of particles, and the top particles are selected as the new particle swarm to participate in the following iteration calculation. Finally, the particle weights are normalized, and the optimal matching position is calculated according to Equation (11) based on the states and weights of all particles.

$$x_k = \sum_{i=1}^{N} \left(x_k^i \overline{w}_k^i \right) \tag{11}$$

The workflow of the adaptive fission particle-filtering geomagnetic matching localization algorithm as Algorithm 1 shows:

Algorithm 1: The adaptive fission particle-filtering geomagnetic matching localization

1. Initialization: $k = 0$, The initialization-state particles $x_0^i \sim P(x_0), i = 1, 2, \ldots, N$ are extracted from the prior distribution $P(x_0)$. Initialize particle weights $w_0^i = 1/N$
2. Importance sampling: $x_k^i \sim q\left(x_k \middle| x_{k-1}^i, z_{1:k}\right)$
3. Calculate particle weights $w_k^i \propto w_{k-1}^i p\left(z_k \middle| x_k^i\right), p\left(z_k \middle| x_k^i\right) = \frac{1}{\sqrt{2\pi\tau}} \exp\left(\frac{-(\theta_k - \theta_m)^2}{2\tau}\right)$.
4. Normalize weights $\hat{w}_k^i = w_k^i / \sum_{i=1}^{N} w_k^i$
5. Particle fission:
   - 5.1 Calculate the number of offspring $m_k^i = \text{round}\left[N \times w_k^i\right] + 2$
   - 5.2 Calculate the state value of the "offspring" particle $\tilde{x}_k^{ij} \sim N\left(x_k^i, \mu_k^i\right), j = \left[1, m_k^j\right]$
   - 5.3 Update offspring particle weights, as in step 3.
   - 5.4 Sort all particles by weight in descending order and choose the top N particles to form a new particle swarm for the subsequent iteration calculation $\left\{x_k^i, \tilde{w}_k^i\right\}_{i=1}^{N}$.
6. Normalize weights $\overline{w}_k^i = \tilde{w}_k^i / \sum_{i=1}^{N} \tilde{w}_k^i$
7. Calculate state estimates $x_k = \sum_{i=1}^{N} \left(x_k^i \overline{w}_k^i \right)$

---

4. Experiments

4.1. Experimental Setup

This section reports the results of a sea trial performed to validate the proposed geomagnetic localization method. The vehicle used for the sea trial is shown in Figure 5 [32]. This aluminum alloy vehicle can be divided into a main cabin and a spherical bow. The components of the vehicle can be categorized into a power supply system, a perception system, and a central control system. The power supply system consists of a power supply source and a power management module, which are responsible for providing energy support to the entire system, voltage regulation, and circuit switching. The perception system consists of sensors, including a magnetometer, an inertial measurement unit (IMU), a satellite receiver, and a pressure sensor, and the performance of the corresponding sensors is shown in Table 1. The IMU is an essential sensor of the INS. Together, the INS and the GPS form an integrated navigation unit receiving data from a satellite signal, which provides reference position information for the test system. The central control system consists of an NVIDIA TX2 core board and uses a Linux operating system to read and store data uploaded by various sensors in real time. Each sensor communicates with the central control system through RS232 and USB interfaces.

In this study, two sea trials were conducted in the Jiaozhou Bay area of Qingdao on 22 June and 26 June 2022. The total distance covered in the trial 1 was 9.63 km, and the total distance covered in trial 2 was 14.37 km, for which the average speed was 5 m/s. Data on parameters such as the characteristics of the geomagnetic field, motion acceleration and angular velocity, attitude angle, GPS position, and true heading were collected during the trials. The magnetometer sampling rate was set to 10 Hz during the tests. In comparison, the acceleration and angular velocity sampling rate was set to 100 Hz, and the attitude angle, heading angle, and position data sampling rates were set to 10 Hz. The data from the IMU and magnetometer were saved separately, with a file saved every 10 min. Each data stream was timestamped based on the system read time to facilitate offline data alignment.

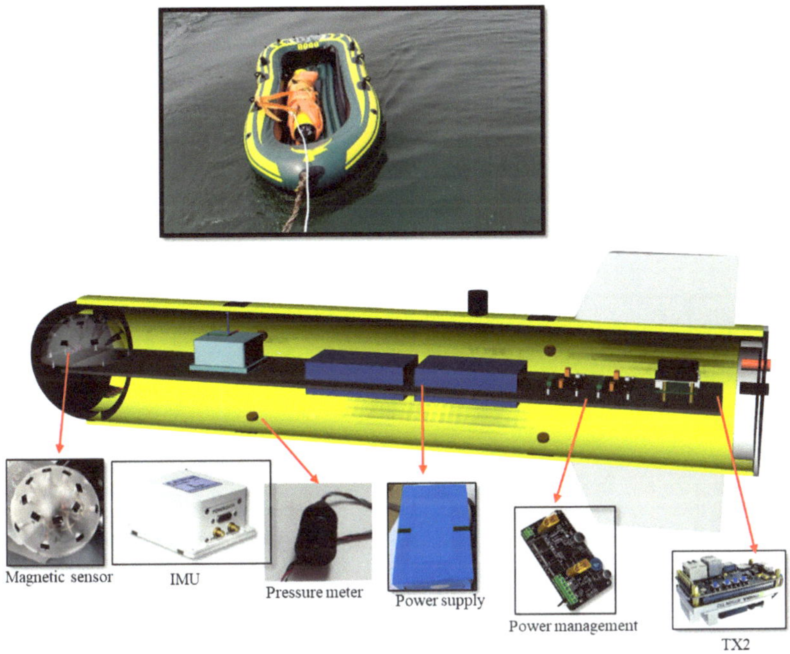

Figure 5. The test vehicle's structure.

Table 1. Parameters of main sensors.

Magnetometer		**Inertial Measurement Unit (IMU)**		**Integrated Navigation**	
Accuracy/axis	0.5% Reading ±0.1% FS	Acceleration zero-bias stability	≤0.1 mg	Heading accuracy	0.1°
Range	±100 μT	Acceleration range	±5 g	Attitude accuracy	0.1° (1σ)
Orthogonal error	<0.1°	Gyroscope zero-bias stability	10°/h	Position accuracy	≤1.2 m
Resolution	0.1 nT	Gyroscope range	±500°/s	Velocity accuracy	0.02 m/s
Rate	10 Hz	Rate	100 Hz	Rate	10 Hz

Prior to verifying the performance of the proposed method, we had the vehicle establish a sparse geomagnetic map with dimensions of 9.2 × 3.5 km along the lawn mower trajectory indicated by the black line in Figure 6. The trajectories were spaced approximately 500 m apart in the east–west direction. Then, linear interpolation was used to encrypt the measured geomagnetic data, forming a grid map with a resolution of 50 m. It is well known that the geomagnetic field undergoes long-term variations and short-term diurnal changes [33]. Long-term diurnal variations can be disregarded during geomagnetic navigation, and updating the geomagnetic map every 3–5 years is sufficient. As for short-term diurnal changes, it is advisable to conduct geomagnetic measurement experiments when the geomagnetic field is stable, i.e., around noon [18,34].

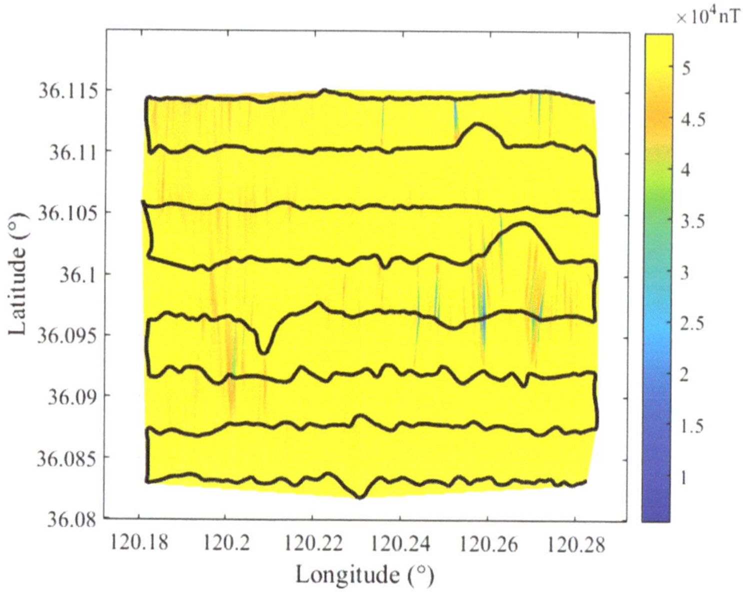

Figure 6. Total geomagnetic field intensity map.

4.2. Results and Discussions

After obtaining the geomagnetic map of the experimental area, the adaptive fission particle filter geomagnetic matching localization method proposed in this section was used to perform further position correction for the dead reckoning results of the vehicle. In the DR algorithm, the motion step and direction of the carrier are estimated based on the information provided by the accelerometer and gyroscope, and the two-dimensional position of the carrier can be calculated using known initial conditions [35].Considering that the geomagnetic field is a large-scale physical field and the magnetic field strength values change very slightly at locations that are close to each other, in cases where the measurement environment is not ideal, the interference noise amplitude may be much larger than the amplitude of geomagnetic field changes, leading to a large number of mismatches. Therefore, in this paper, position correction was performed once when the distance between the front and back exceeded 1 km. During the experiment, the particle sampling variances in the longitudinal and latitudinal directions were set to $\mathrm{diag}\left(1.6454 \times 10^{-4}, 1.6454 \times 10^{-4}\right)$, unit in degree^2, and $\tau = 100{,}000$; the scaling factor was $\lambda = 0.001$; and there were 3000 particles. At the initial time, all particles had equal weights, that is, $1/3000$. In order to highlight the performance advantages of the adaptive fission particle filter algorithm in relation to geomagnetic positioning, this paper compared it with the traditional particle filter (PF) algorithm and the intelligent particle filter (IPF) algorithm improved by Shen et al. [29]. The results are shown in Figures 7–10.

Figures 7 and 8 show that the blue, dashed line represents the dead reckoning system trajectory. In contrast, the black, dotted line is the reference trajectory provided by the GPS installed in the AUV. It can be seen from Figures 7 and 8 that after several successful particle-matching processes, the calculated trajectory is gradually corrected, approaching the true trajectory. The absolute position errors are shown in Figures 9 and 10. It can be seen that the DR algorithm disperses the position errors due to the continuous accumulation of errors. However, PF, IPF, and the proposed method show a stepwise decrease in absolute position error due to the use of the geomagnetic field to correct the DR positioning results. However, for Experiment 2, the correction of the DR navigation results via geomagnetic positioning is less effective than in Experiment 1, particularly for the PF algorithm. This is because the performance of geomagnetic matching positioning algorithms is strongly correlated with geomagnetic features. Most geomagnetic field intensity values are relatively similar in areas with sparse geomagnetic features, making it difficult for particles to match the correct geomagnetic feature points. In addition, as the program progresses, the particle set gradually degenerates into a cluster in the PF algorithm, as shown in Figure 4. At this point, particles only search for matching points in a limited local area, thereby enabling an in improvement in the geomagnetic matching positioning performance of the PF algorithm, which is also the problem this paper aims to solve. In Figure 9, for Test 1, after three consecutive, valid matches, the accumulated position error is constrained, and the corrected trajectory is almost identical to the true trajectory.

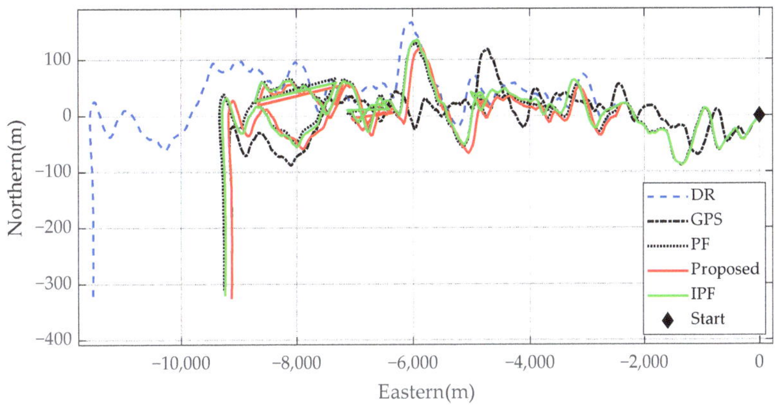

Figure 7. Comparison of geomagnetic positioning results achieved using the adaptive fission particle filter in test 1.

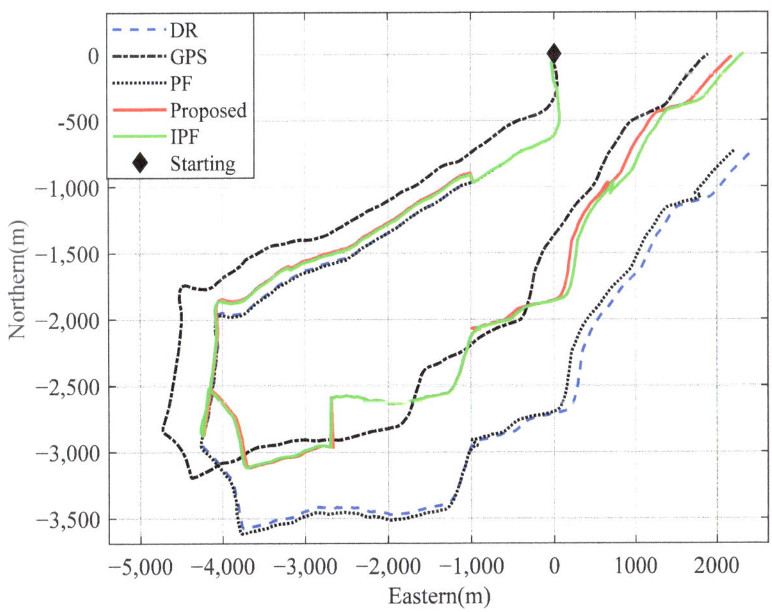

Figure 8. Comparison of geomagnetic positioning results achieved using the adaptive fission particle filter in test 2.

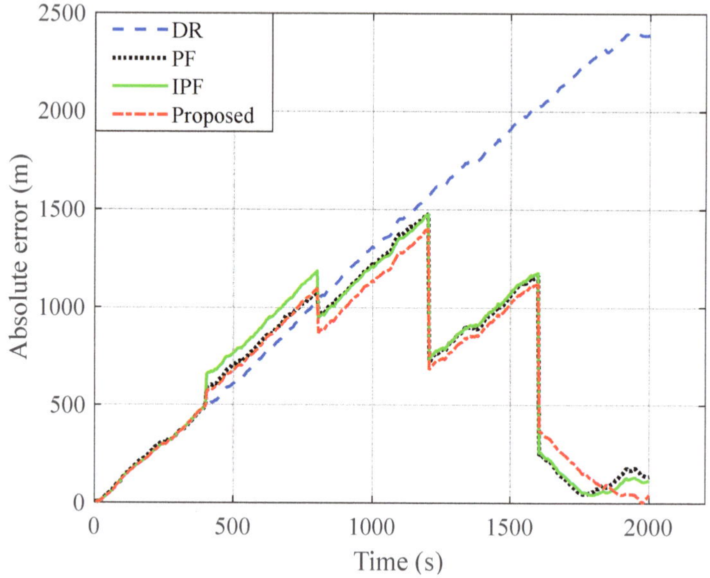

Figure 9. Geomagnetic positioning error in test 1.

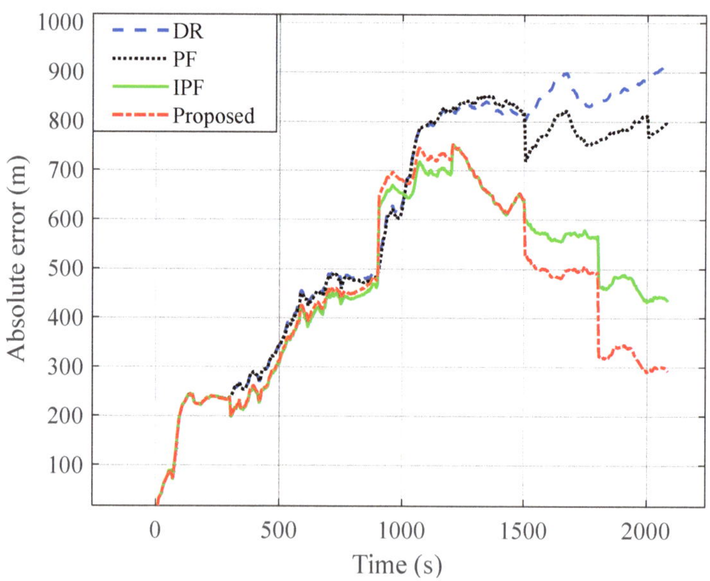

Figure 10. Geomagnetic positioning error in test 2.

In addition, after combining the results of the two tests shown in Figures 9 and 10, it was found that effective geomagnetic positioning occurred in the latter half of the voyage. The error accumulation during navigation calculation in the initial stage was small, resulting in a small distance between the dead-reckoning-indicated position and the true position, and the geomagnetic field strength values at the two positions were close. Therefore, it was difficult for the particles to distinguish the degree of geomagnetic similarity within the exploration range, and most particles eventually had similar weights. As the voyage continued, the accumulated error in the dead reckoning further increased. When there was a clear distinction between the geomagnetic fields at the predicted and true navigation positions, the particles could accurately match the correct position in the motion space through similarity calculations and then perform a correction on the DR navigation results.

Table 2 summarizes the position error results for the three particle-filtering methods in the two experiments. The table shows that the method proposed in this paper outperforms the compared methods in terms of average position error and endpoint error. In the two experiments, the dead reckoning trajectory based on heading and displacement information resulted in absolute position errors of 2391.7 m and 911.15 m, respectively. The adaptive fission particle filter method proposed in this paper can maintain particle diversity throughout the iteration process. It increases the probability of matching the best position, which leads to the geomagnetic positioning results being closer to the true position. After correction using the adaptive fission particle filter geomagnetic positioning method, the absolute position errors at the end of the task were reduced by 98.17% and 67.94%, respectively.

Table 2. Absolute position error statistics (m).

	Traditional Particle Filter		Intelligent Particle Filter		Proposed Method	
	Test 1	Test 2	Test 1	Test 2	Test 1	Test 2
RMSE	804.64	631.75	819.42	501.50	767.18	482.40
Mean positioning error	674.06	582.18	685.08	468.61	647.99	444.89
Error at the end	138.08	794.93	119.02	433.23	43.68	292.08

The first two rows of Table 2 are the root-mean-square error and average positioning error, which were obtained by comprehensively considering the positioning error of the entire trajectory. Figures 9 and 10 show that the navigation time of 1600 s in Figure 9 and the performance of the method proposed in this paper before 1500 s in Figure 10 are almost equivalent to those of IPF. Subsequently, due to the better particle diversity of the method proposed in this article, particle matching yielded better matching points than the IPF method, resulting in a significant reduction in positioning error compared to the IPF method (at 1500 s in Figure 10). At around 1800 s, the method proposed in this paper obtained even better matching points based on the original error. So, in the end, the positioning error of the method proposed in this article is smaller than that of the IPF method.

Meanwhile, the geomagnetic matching localization method based on traditional particle filtering reduced the positioning error by 94.23% and 12.76% in the two experiments. The intelligent-particle-filtering-based geomagnetic matching localization method reduced the absolute position errors by 95.02% and 52.45% in the two experiments. The average positioning errors of the proposed method in this paper were 546.44 m for the two experiments. The mean values of the traditional-particle-filtering and intelligent-particle-filtering-based geomagnetic positioning were 628.12 m and 576.85 m, respectively.

5. Conclusions

This paper studied the error accumulation problem in long-duration AUV tasks using the dead reckoning principle by combining displacement and heading. Using sparse geomagnetic maps, a method was proposed to correct the dead reckoning results using the geomagnetic field, thereby achieving the autonomous and covert navigation and positioning of the AUVs in satellite-restrictive environments. This paper proposed an adaptive fission particle-filtering-based geomagnetic positioning method that allows for the creation of "parent" particles before resampling to generate "offspring" particles. The "offspring" particles are sampled according to the fission degree and motion variance of the "parent" particles, ensuring that the particle set maintains diversity during the iteration process. This method solves the problems of particle degradation and impoverishment that occur with traditional particle filtering as the iteration progresses and improves the accuracy of geomagnetic positioning. After sea trials, the proposed adaptive fission particle-filtering-based geomagnetic positioning algorithm effectively corrected the dead reckoning error. The average positioning error after geomagnetic positioning correction was 546.44 m, which is a 41.7% improvement over that of dead reckoning.

Future work will focus on the effect of the resolution of the geomagnetic map grid on the geomagnetic positioning effect. Our team aims to conduct research on geomagnetic navigation under the condition of sparse-resolution geomagnetic maps.

Author Contributions: H.Y.: conceptualization, project administration, validation, supervision, funding acquisition. Z.L.: Conceptualization, methodology, formal analysis, data curation, writing—original draft, writing. W.Y.: review and editing, visualization. T.S.: supervision, formal analysis. D.L.: software, edition. Q.H.: data curation. All authors have read and agreed to the published version of the manuscript.

Funding: This research was funded by National Natural Science Foundation of China No. 61803381.

Institutional Review Board Statement: Not applicable.

Informed Consent Statement: Not applicable.

Data Availability Statement: This research did not report any data.

Conflicts of Interest: The authors declare no conflict of interest.

References

1. Ma, T.; Ding, S.; Li, Y.; Fan, J. A review of terrain aided navigation for underwater vehicles. *OcEng* **2023**, *281*, 114779–114795. [CrossRef]
2. Zhou, J.; Pang, L.; Zhang, D.; Zhang, W. Underwater Image Enhancement Method via Multi-Interval Subhistogram Perspective Equalization. *IJOE* **2023**, *48*, 474–488. [CrossRef]
3. Paull, L.; Saeedi, S.; Seto, M.; Li, H. AUV Navigation and Localization: A Review. *IJOE* **2014**, *39*, 131–149. [CrossRef]
4. Mu, X.; He, B.; Wu, S.; Zhang, X.; Song, Y.; Yan, T. A practical INS/GPS/DVL/PS integrated navigation algorithm and its application on Autonomous Underwater Vehicle. *Appl. Ocean Res.* **2021**, *106*, 102441. [CrossRef]
5. Zhou, J.; Sun, J.; Zhang, W.; Zifan, L. Multi-view underwater image enhancement method via embedded fusion mechanism. *Eng. Appl. Artif. Intell.* **2023**, *121*, 105946. [CrossRef]
6. Maurelli, F.; Krupiński, S.; Xiang, X.; Petillot, Y. AUV localisation: A review of passive and active techniques. *Int. J. Intell. Robot. Appl.* **2021**, *6*, 246–269. [CrossRef]
7. Minligareev, V.T.; Sazonova, T.V.; Arutyunyan, D.A.; Tregubov, V.V.; Khotenko, Y.N. Geophysical Support of Advanced Autonomous Magnetometric Navigation Systems. *Gyroscopy Navig.* **2020**, *11*, 350–356. [CrossRef]
8. Xie, W.; Li, Q.; Huang, L.; Qu, Z.; Wang, Z. A Robust Geomagnetic Matching Algorithm Based on L1 Norm. In Proceedings of the 2018 Eighth International Conference on Instrumentation & Measurement, Computer, Communication and Control (IMCCC), Harbin, China, 19–21 July 2018; pp. 1209–1214.
9. Li, H.; Liu, M.Y.; Liu, K. Bio-inspired geomagnetic navigation method for autonomous underwater vehicle. *J. Syst. Eng. Elec.* **2017**, *28*, 1203–1209. [CrossRef]
10. Bhat, P.G.; Subudhi, B.N.; Veerakumar, T.; Laxmi, V.; Gaur, M.S. Multi-Feature Fusion in Particle Filter Framework for Visual Tracking. *IEEE Sens. J.* **2020**, *20*, 2405–2415. [CrossRef]
11. Karshakov, E.V.; Pavlov, B.V.; Tkhorenko, M.Y.; Papusha, I.A. Promising Map-Aided Aircraft Navigation Systems. *Gyroscopy Navig.* **2021**, *12*, 38–49. [CrossRef]
12. Wang, A.; Ou, X. PDR/geomagnetic fingerprint indoor positioning method based on particle filter. *Bull. Surv. Mapp.* **2021**, *1*, 24–28.
13. Chen, Z.; Zhang, Q.; Pan, M.C.; Chen, D.X.; Wan, C.B.; Wu, F.H.; Liu, Y. A New Geomagnetic Matching Navigation Method Based on Multidimensional Vector Elements of Earth's Magnetic Field. *IEEE Geosci. Remote Sens. Lett.* **2018**, *15*, 1289–1293. [CrossRef]
14. Viset, F.; Helmons, R.; Kok, M. An Extended Kalman Filter for Magnetic Field SLAM Using Gaussian Process Regression. *Sensors* **2022**, *22*, 2833–2852. [CrossRef]
15. Li, Z.; Yu, H.; Shen, T.; Li, Z. Segmented Matching Method of Multi-Geophysics Field SLAM Data Based on LSTM. In Proceedings of the 2020 3rd International Conference on Unmanned Systems (ICUS), Harbin, China, 27–28 November 2020; pp. 147–151.
16. Hong, L. *Research on the Geomagnetic Bio-Inspired Navigation for AUV Based on Optimization Searching Strategy*; Northwestern Polytechnical University: Xi'an, China, 2018.
17. Wu, Z.; Hu, X.; Wu, M.; Mu, H.; Cao, J.; Zhang, K.; Tuo, Z. An experimental evaluation of autonomous underwater vehicle localization on geomagnetic map. *Appl. Phys. Lett.* **2013**, *103*, 104102. [CrossRef]
18. Li, X.; Cheng, D.; Zhou, Z. A matching Algorithm Based on the Gradient of the Total Geomagnetic. *Chin. J. Sens. Actuators* **2018**, *30*, 1869–1875.

19. Zhang, Q.; Li, Y.; Ma, T.; Cong, Z.; Zhang, W. Bathymetric Particle Filter SLAM With Graph-Based Trajectory Update Method. *IEEE Access* **2021**, *9*, 85464–85475. [CrossRef]
20. Stepanov, O.A.; Toropov, B. Nonlinear filtering for map-aided navigation. Part 1. An overview of algorithms. *Gyroscopy Navig.* **2015**, *6*, 324–337. [CrossRef]
21. Kuptametee, C.; Aunsri, N. A review of resampling techniques in particle filtering framework. *Measurement* **2022**, *193*, 110836. [CrossRef]
22. Quintas, J.a.; Cruz, J.; Pascoal, A.; Teixeira, F.C. A Comparison of Nonlinear Filters for Underwater Geomagnetic Navigation. In Proceedings of the 2020 IEEE/OES Autonomous Underwater Vehicles Symposium (AUV), St. Johns, NL, Canada, 30 September–2 October 2020.
23. Solin, A.; Särkkä, S.; Kannala, J.; Rahtu, E. Terrain navigation in the magnetic landscape: Particle filtering for indoor positioning. In Proceedings of the 2016 European Navigation Conference (ENC), Helsinki, Finland, 30 May–2 June 2016.
24. Zhou, J.; Yang, T.; Zhang, W. Underwater vision enhancement technologies: A comprehensive review, challenges, and recent trends. *Appl. Intell.* **2022**, *53*, 3594–3621. [CrossRef]
25. Lu, L.; Wei, D.; Ji, X.; Yuan, H. Review of Geomagnetic Positioning Method. *Navig. Position Timing* **2022**, *9*, 118–130.
26. Zhang, Q.; Li, Y.; Ma, T.; Cong, Z.; Zhang, W. Bathymetric Particle Filter SLAM Based on Mean Trajectory Map Representation. *IEEE Access* **2021**, *9*, 71725–71736. [CrossRef]
27. Doucet, A.; Godsill, S.; Andrieu, C. On Sequential Monte Carlo Sampling Methods for Bayesian filtering. *Stat. Comput.* **2000**, *10*, 197–208. [CrossRef]
28. Arulampalam, M.S.; Maskell, S.; Gordon, N.; Clapp, T. A Tutorial on Particle Filters for Online Nonlinear/Non-Gaussian Bayesian Tracking. *IEEE Trans. Signal Process.* **2002**, *50*, 174–188. [CrossRef]
29. Yin, S.; Zhu, X. Intelligent Particle Filter and Its Application on Fault Detection of Nonlinear System. *IEEE Trans. Ind. Electron.* **2015**, *62*, 3852–3861. [CrossRef]
30. Sun, M.; Wang, Y.; Xu, S.; Cao, H.; Si, M. Indoor Positioning Integrating PDR/Geomagnetic Positioning Based on the Genetic-Particle Filter. *Appl. Sci.* **2020**, *10*, 668. [CrossRef]
31. Xue, H.; Hongbo, L.; Yue, L.; Haitao, M.; Xian, Z. Adaptive Fission Particle Filter for Seismic Random Noise Attenuation. *IEEE Geosci. Remote Sens. Lett.* **2015**, *12*, 1918–1922. [CrossRef]
32. Li, Z.; Yu, H.; Shen, T.; Li, Y.; Zhang, W. Bionic Magnetic Compass Algorithm Based on Radical Pair Theory. *IEEE Sens. J.* **2022**, *22*, 23812–23820. [CrossRef]
33. Chulliat, A.; Brown, W.; Alken, P.; Beggan, C.; Nair, M.; Cox, G.; Woods, A.; Macmillan, S.; Meyer, B.; Paniccia, M. *The US/UK World Magnetic Model for 2020–2025: Technical Report*; NOAA: Silver Spring, MD, USA, 2020.
34. Available online: http://www.sepc.ac.cn/cosmicRays1.php (accessed on 1 January 2023).
35. Asraf, O.; Shama, F.; Klein, I. PDRNet: A Deep-Learning Pedestrian Dead Reckoning Framework. *IEEE Sens. J.* **2022**, *22*, 4932–4939. [CrossRef]

Journal of Marine Science and Engineering

Article

Underwater Image Translation via Multi-Scale Generative Adversarial Network

Dongmei Yang [1], Tianzi Zhang [1], Boquan Li [2,*], Menghao Li [1], Weijing Chen [1], Xiaoqing Li [1] and Xingmei Wang [1,3,*]

[1] College of Computer Science and Technology, Harbin Engineering University, Harbin 150001, China; yangdongmei@hrbeu.edu.cn (D.Y.); zhangtianzi@hrbeu.edu.cn (T.Z.); limenghao@hrbeu.edu.cn (M.L.); chenweijing@hrbeu.edu.cn (W.C.); lixiaoqing@hrbeu.edu.cn (X.L.)
[2] School of Computing and Information Systems, Singapore Management University, Singapore 178902, Singapore
[3] National Key Laboratory of Underwater Acoustic Technology, Harbin Engineering University, Harbin 150001, China
* Correspondence: boquanli@smu.edu.sg (B.L.); wangxingmei@hrbeu.edu.cn (X.W.)

Abstract: The role that underwater image translation plays assists in generating rare images for marine applications. However, such translation tasks are still challenging due to data lacking, insufficient feature extraction ability, and the loss of content details. To address these issues, we propose a novel multi-scale image translation model based on style-independent discriminators and attention modules (SID-AM-MSITM), which learns the mapping relationship between two unpaired images for translation. We introduce Convolution Block Attention Modules (CBAM) to the generators and discriminators of SID-AM-MSITM to improve its feature extraction ability. Moreover, we construct style-independent discriminators that enable the discriminant results of SID-AM-MSITM to be not affected by the style of images and retain content details. Through ablation experiments and comparative experiments, we demonstrate that attention modules and style-independent discriminators are introduced reasonably and SID-AM-MSITM performs better than multiple baseline methods.

Keywords: underwater image translation; generative adversarial network; convolution block attention module; style-independent discriminator

Citation: Yang, D.; Zhang, T.; Li, B.; Li, M.; Chen, W.; Li, X.; Wang, X. Underwater Image Translation via Multi-Scale Generative Adversarial Network. *J. Mar. Sci. Eng.* **2023**, *11*, 1929. https://doi.org/10.3390/jmse11101929

Academic Editors: Fausto Pedro García Márquez, Jingchun Zhou, Wenqi Ren, Qiuping Jiang and Yan-Tsung Peng

Received: 31 August 2023
Revised: 27 September 2023
Accepted: 2 October 2023
Published: 6 October 2023

1. Introduction

Underwater images play critical roles in diverse marine-related military and scientific applications, such as seabed sediment classification [1], submarine cable detection [2], and mine recognition [3]. However, the complex underwater environment limits the use of camera devices, including Kinect units [4] and binocular stereo cameras [5], which makes it difficult to obtain real underwater images. Intuitively, image translation [6] provides a viable direction to obtain such scarce data. Specifically, image translation methods translate source-domain non-underwater images into target-domain underwater ones, which reassigns particular attributes of underwater images. The translated underwater images are valuable for advanced visual tasks such as target detection, 3D reconstruction, and target segmentation [7,8].

Existing image translation methods are generally categorized into two groups, i.e., conventional and Generative Adversarial Network (GAN)-based [9] methods. First, conventional methods [10,11] extract low-level features to transfer input images' texture or devise various Convolutional Neural Network-based (CNN) [12], such as image style transfer [13], to make use of semantic content for image translation. Second, GAN-based methods, such as supervised models including Pix2Pix [14] and Pix2PixHD [15], and unsupervised models including StyleGAN [16] and StarGAN [17], use generators to translate images from one image domain to another image domain. By comparison, GAN-based methods do not require researchers to design complex loss functions, which saves manpower.

In view of the immense potential of GAN, researchers attempt to apply it to underwater image translation tasks. Li et al. [18] propose an unsupervised WaterGAN that uses in-air RGB images and depth maps to generate corresponding realistic underwater images. Wang et al. [19] use an unsupervised image translation method that also takes in-air RGB-D images to generate realistic underwater images. Li et al. [20] work to generate images with underwater style using in-air RGB images.

Although existing methods have achieved a certain success, they still face multiple challenges. (1) Data lacking. The necessary paired in-air and depth images are too scarce to train translation models. In the absence of data, using the general image translation methods, it is difficult to achieve good results. (2) Insufficient feature extraction ability. Underwater optics images and underwater sonar images present obvious colors, which reduce the visibility of objects in translated images and reduce the quality of the translated images. These translated images limit the performance of subsequent advanced computer vision tasks [21]. Therefore, the colors of the underwater images pose challenges to the feature extraction ability of image translation. (3) Loss of content details. GAN models are sensitive to the style of images (such as color and texture) [22], which makes image translation models ignore the content information of images. Similar to the lack of feature extraction ability, the loss of content details also limits the performance of subsequent advanced computer vision tasks.

With the aim of addressing the above challenges, in this paper, we propose a multi-scale underwater image translation model based on style-independent discriminators and attention modules (SID-AM-MSITM). Specifically, our contributions mainly include the following:

1. In response to the data lacking challenge, we construct the backbone model of SID-AM-MSITM based on a fundamental image translator, TuiGAN [23]. TuiGAN conducts image translation tasks based on only two unpaired images, and we thus make further improvements on its encoders and decoders.
2. In response to the challenge of insufficient feature extraction ability, we propose to apply Convolution Block Attention Modules (CBAM) [24] to the generators and discriminators of SID-AM-MSITM. CBAM assigns the weight distribution of feature maps in the two dimensions of channel and space and increases the weight of important features, so as to make SID-AM-MSITM pay attention to meaningful information.
3. In response to the loss of content details, we further improve SID-AM-MSITM by constructing style-independent discriminators. The discriminators give similar results when discriminating images with the same content and different styles, so as to make SID-AM-MSITM focus on the content information instead of the style information.
4. We conduct systematical experiments based on multiple datasets, including submarine, underwater optics, sunken ship, crashed plane, and underwater sonar images. Compared with multiple baseline models, SID-AM-MSITM improves the ability to access effective information and retain content details.

The rest of this paper is organized as follows: Section 2 details the methodology of SID-AM-MSITM. Section 3 presents our ablation and comparative experiments, and their corresponding analysis. Section 4 concludes this work.

2. Methodology

In this section, we will present our proposed SID-AM-MSITM in detail. Based on TuiGAN as a backbone architecture, SID-AM-MSITM improves its generators and discriminators by introducing CBAM and makes further improvements by devising style-independent discriminators. Figure 1 shows the architecture of SID-AM-MSITM and the process of translating a non-underwater image into an underwater image.

In the underwater image translation task, the source domain image means the non-underwater image I_X, and the target domain image means the underwater image I_Y. We use SID-AM-MSITM to translate non-underwater images into underwater images, also known as generating underwater images. Using SID-AM-MSITM, we also reconstruct translated underwater images into non-underwater images. The original image represents the initial image that has not been processed by SID-AM-MSITM.

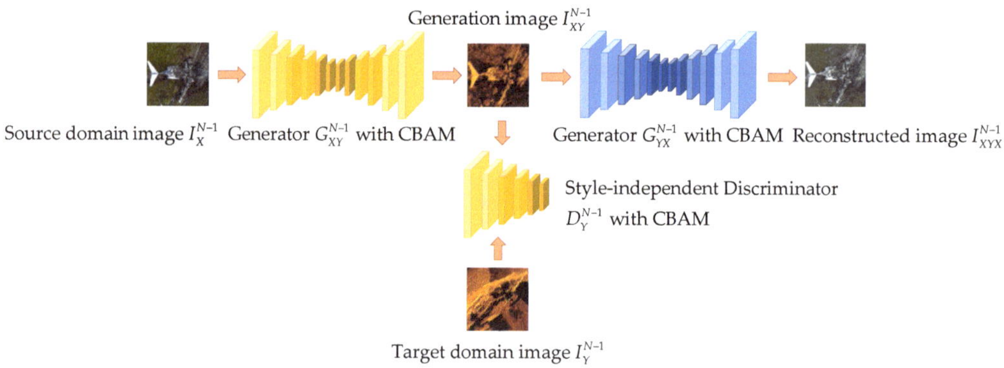

Figure 1. The architecture of SID-AM-MSITM (the process of translating a non-underwater image into an underwater image).

As in TuiGAN, generally, SID-AM-MSITM downsamples two images into different scales $\{I_X^0, I_X^1, ...I_X^N. I_Y^0, I_Y^1, ...I_Y^N\}$, and each scale corresponds to two generators $\{G_{XY}^n, G_{YX}^n\}$ and two discriminators $\{D_Y^n, D_X^n\}$. The generators $\{G_{XY}^0, G_{XY}^1, ...G_{XY}^{N-1}\}$ utilize the down-sampled source domain images $\{I_X^0, I_X^1, ...I_X^{N-1}\}$ as well as their previous-scale upsampled generated images $\{I_{XY}^{1\uparrow}, I_{XY}^{2\uparrow}, ...I_{XY}^{N\uparrow}\}$ to generate new images. At the lowest scale N, the previous-scale upsampled generated image is replaced with an image with pixel values of 0.

The discriminators $\{D_Y^0, D_Y^1, ...D_Y^N\}$ learn the distribution of the target domain using a variety of loss functions for model training, including adversarial loss WGAN-GP [25], cycle-consistency loss, identity loss, and total variation loss [26]. Among them, the cycle-consistency loss helps SID-AM-MSITM to avoid the mode collapse, the identity loss helps it to align colors and textures, and TV loss smooths the generated images. Finally, the translated underwater image I_{XY}^0 is obtained at the highest scale. In Figure 1, the discriminator processes images translated by a generator of the same color as it.

In order to obtain the generators $\{G_{YX}^0, G_{YX}^1, ...G_{YX}^N\}$, we also train the generators $\{G_{YX}^0, G_{YX}^1, ...G_{YX}^N\}$ and discriminators $\{D_X^0, D_X^1, ...D_X^N\}$ in a similar way.

2.1. Generators and Discriminators with CBAM Modules

We start with presenting generators and discriminators with CBAM modules. CBAM enables SID-AM-MSITM to focus on critical features in a given image, so as to improve the quality of generated images [27].

As illustrated in Figure 2, each CBAM contains two modules, a channel attention module [28] and a spatial attention module. Specifically, the channel attention module enables SID-AM-MSITM to focus on critical features in a given image, so as to obtain accurate weights of channel features. The spatial attention module performs Max Pooling and Average Pooling on the spatial dimension of compressed features. The yellow blocks represent the input features of the source domain, and the blue blocks represent the input features of the target domain.

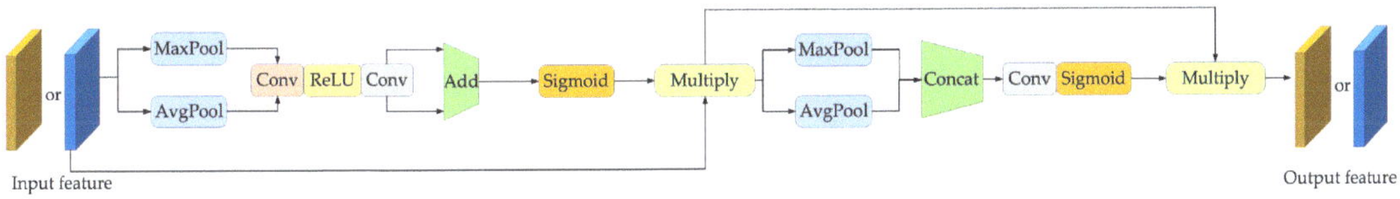

Figure 2. The structure of CBAM modules. CBAM represents the Convolution Block Attention Module. Conv represents convolution operations.

Figure 3 shows the generator and discriminator of SID-AM-MSITM, where the generator G^n_{XY} implements the translation of a source domain image I^n_X to a generated image I^n_{XY}. Firstly, SID-AM-MSITM simply processes I^n_X from source domain X to obtain an intermediate image $I^n_{XY,\phi}$ through the CBAM module and convolution operations. Then, SID-AM-MSITM utilizes $I^n_{XY,\phi}$, I^n_X, and an upsampled image after generating at the previous scale $I^{n+1\uparrow}_{XY}$ to concatenate in the direction of the channel, and obtain a mask image X^n through the CBAM module and convolution operations. Finally, a generated image I^n_{XY} is obtained using the linear combination of X^n, $I^n_{XY,\phi}$, and $I^{n+1\uparrow}_{XY}$. I^n_{XY} and the target domain image I^n_Y are input into the discriminator D^n_Y to obtain discriminant results for model training, where $0 \leq n < N$.

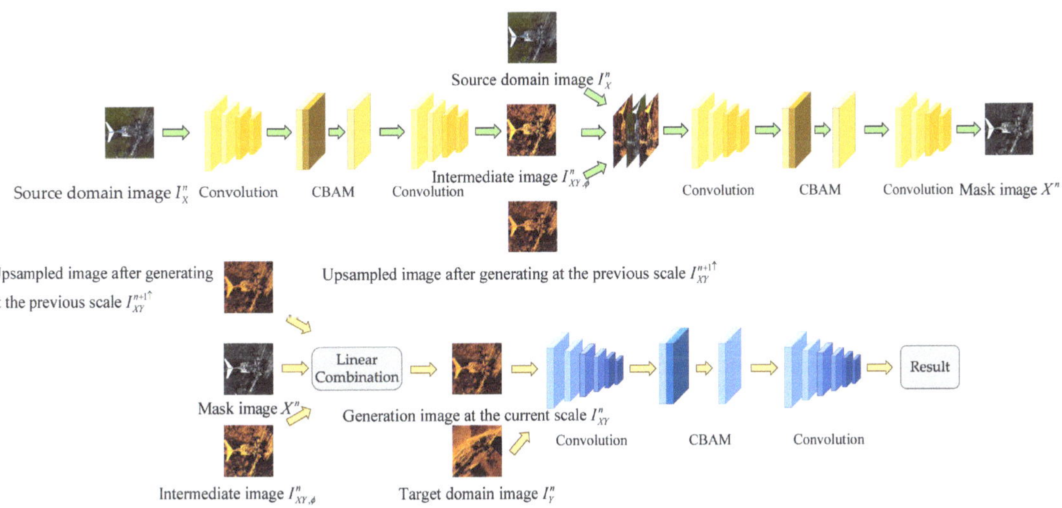

Figure 3. Generator and discriminator of SID-AM-MSITM (the process of translating a source domain image I^n_X to a generated image I^n_{XY}).

G^n_{XY} and G^n_{YX} share the same architecture but with different weights. The working principle of G^n_{XY} is as follows:

$$I^n_{XY,\phi} = \phi(I^n_X), \tag{1}$$

$$X^n = A^n\left(I^n_{XY,\phi}, I^n_X, I^{n+1\uparrow}_{XY}\right), \tag{2}$$

$$I^n_{XY} = X^n \otimes I^{n+1\uparrow}_{XY} + (1 - X^n) \otimes I^n_{XY,\phi}, \tag{3}$$

where $0 \leq n < N$, $\otimes$ represents pixel-level multiplication. At the lowest scale N, I^{n+1}_{XY} is replaced with an image with pixel values of 0. First, SID-AM-MSITM uses the encoder ϕ to preprocess I^n_X to $I^n_{XY,\phi}$. Then, SID-AM-MSITM uses the encoder A^n to generate mask X^n. Finally, SID-AM-MSITM uses the linear combination to obtain output I^n_{XY}.

Similarly, the implementation of the translation of $I_Y \rightarrow I_{YX}$ at scale n is as follows:

$$I^n_{YX,\phi} = \phi'(I^n_Y), \tag{4}$$

$$Y^n = A'^n\left(I^n_{YX,\phi}, I^n_Y, I^{n+1\uparrow}_{YX}\right), \tag{5}$$

$$I^n_{YX} = Y^n \otimes I^{n+1\uparrow}_{YX} + (1 - Y^n) \otimes I^n_{YX,\phi}, \tag{6}$$

where $0 \leq n < N$. At the lowest scale N, I^{n+1}_{YX} is also replaced with an image with pixel values of 0.

In this way, the generators focus on the regions that synthesize current scale details in the images. Meanwhile, it maintains the previously learned global structures as unaffected.

2.2. Style-Independent Discriminators

Next, we present our proposed style-independent discriminators, which focus on the images' content information rather than their style information, so as to enable SIM-AM-MSITM to avoid losing the content details in non-underwater images.

When two sets of images share the same content but different styles, it is ideal to make discriminators give similar discriminant results to the images. Thus, SID-AM-MSITM uses instance-level as well as vector-level style difference losses to train style-independent discriminators.

Figure 4 illustrates style and content differences. As illustrated in the figure, the first two generated images share the same content information, while the latter two share the same style information. s_x and s_y represent the style information of images x and y respectively. c_x and c_y represent the content information of images x and y, respectively. $G(s, c)$ indicates the image generated using style information s and content information c. $D(G(s, c))$ represents the discriminant result of $G(s, c)$ given by a discriminator.

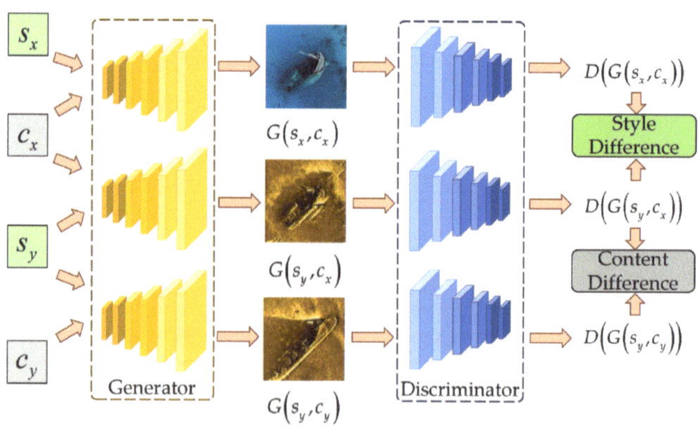

Figure 4. The illustration of style and content differences.

Figure 5 shows a style-independent discriminator D^n_Y of SIM-AM-MSITM, which requires a source domain image I^n_X, a generation image at current scale I^n_{XY}, an instance-level mixed style image $\hat{I}^n_X$, and a vector-level mixed style image $I^{n\prime}_X$ to make the discriminator D^n_Y style-independent.

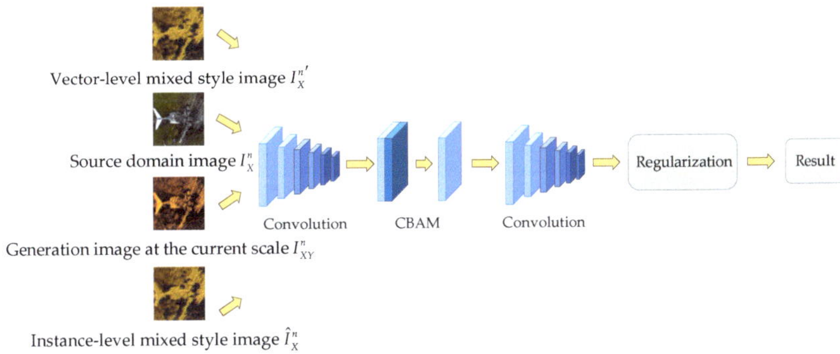

Figure 5. The training process of SID-AM-MSITM's style-independent discriminator D_Y^n.

Discriminator D_X^n has a similar structure and requires a target domain image I_Y^n, a generation image at current scale I_{YX}^n, an instance-level mixed style images $\hat{I}_Y^n$, and a vector-level mixed style image $I_Y^{n\prime}$, where $0 \leq n \leq N$.

Then, we will describe how style-independent discriminators eliminate style differences at the instance level as well as the vector level, respectively. Instance-level style difference refers to the style difference between the image obtained by stylizing its pixels and the original image. Vector-level style difference refers to the style difference between the image obtained by stylizing its encoded vectors and the original image.

2.2.1. Instance-Level Style-Independent Discriminators

Instance-level style-independent discriminators use a special regularization term, so as to reduce style differences between the images obtained by stylizing its pixels and the original images.

We first adjust weight α to gradually increase the proportion of generated images among the mixed ones at multi-scales. Then, we make discriminators to reduce the differences between the original non-underwater images or the underwater images and the final mixed images, which are constrained by a consistency loss. Such progress is formulated as follows:

$$\hat{I}_X^n = \alpha I_X^n + (1-\alpha) I_{XY}^n, 0 \leq n \leq N, \tag{7}$$

$$\mathcal{L}_{con} = \left\| D_Y^n(I_X^n) - D_Y^n(\hat{I}_X^n) \right\|_1, \tag{8}$$

$$\hat{I}_Y^n = \alpha I_Y^n + (1-\alpha) I_{YX}^n, 0 \leq n \leq N, \tag{9}$$

$$\mathcal{L}_{con} = \left\| D_X^n(I_Y^n) - D_X^n(\hat{I}_Y^n) \right\|_1, \tag{10}$$

where $0 \leq n \leq N, 0 \leq \alpha < 1$. I_X^n and I_Y^n represent the source-domain and target-domain images at the current scale, respectively. I_{XY}^n and I_{YX}^n denote the generation images at the current scale. α indicates the weight of the linear combination and gradually becomes smaller as the scale rises. $\mathcal{L}_{con}$ uses an L_1 paradigm to process the instance-level style-independent loss, and $D(\cdot)$ represents the discriminant results of discriminators.

As the scale rises, the style of instance-level mixed-style images $\hat{I}_X^n$ is closer to the target-domain ones and away from the source-domain ones. The style of instance-level mixed-style images $\hat{I}_Y^n$ is closer to the source-domain ones and away from the target-domain ones. Discriminators penalize the distances between the source-domain image outputs or the target-domain image outputs and the mixed-style image outputs.

Figure 6 shows the training process of instance-level style-independent discriminators D_Y. $\uparrow$ and $\downarrow$ indicate the value rising and descending as the scale rises, respectively.

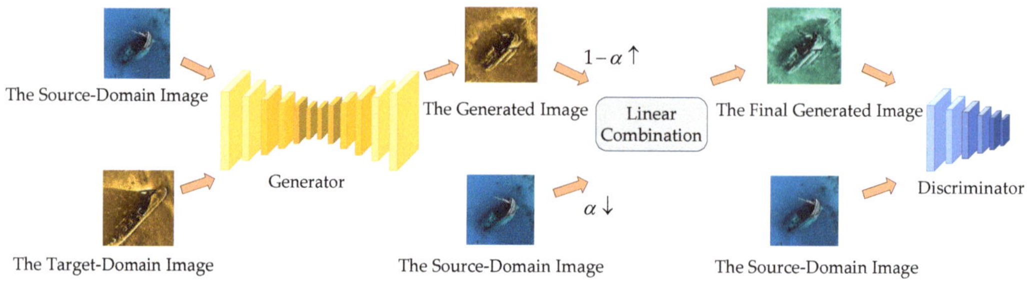

Figure 6. The training process of instance-level style-independent discriminators.

2.2.2. Vector-Level Style-Independent Discriminators

Based on the above instance-level discriminators, it is not enough to generate images since this is limited by style-independent pixels. Therefore, we devise vector-level style-independent discriminators that further mix the encoded vectors of the source-domain and target-domain images at each scale. We put the mixed encoded vectors into a decoder, and utilize its generated images as well as the source-domain ones or the target-domain ones for model training.

First, we encode the source domain-images and the target-domain images, respectively using VGG 19 [29] and then process them using AdaIN [30]. The results obtained are linearly combined with the encoded vectors of the source- or target-domain images. Then, we put the results of the linear combinations into a decoder to get the vector-level mixed-style images $I_X^{n\prime}$ and $I_Y^{n\prime}$. The decoder is a convolutional network that is symmetric to VGG 19 and upsamples the mixed encoded vectors into images. Finally, we utilize discriminators to penalize the distances between the source-domain image outputs or the target-domain image outputs and the mixed-style image outputs. Such progress is formulated as follows:

$$I_X^{n\prime} = Decoder(\alpha Encoder(I_X^n) + (1-\alpha)AdaIN(Encoder(I_X^n), Encoder(I_Y^n))), \tag{11}$$

$$\mathcal{L}_{con} = \left\| D_Y(I_X^n) - D_Y\left(I_X^{n\prime}\right) \right\|_1, \tag{12}$$

$$I_Y^{n\prime} = Decoder(\alpha Encoder(I_Y^n) + (1-\alpha)AdaIN(Encoder(I_Y^n), Encoder(I_X^n))), \tag{13}$$

$$\mathcal{L}_{con} = \left\| D_X(I_Y^n) - D_X\left(I_Y^{n\prime}\right) \right\|_1, \tag{14}$$

where $0 \le n \le N, 0 \le \alpha < 1$. I_X^n and I_Y^n represent the source-domain and target-domain images at the current scale, respectively. $Encoder(\cdot)$ is VGG 19 and $Decoder(\cdot)$ is symmetric to VGG 19. α is the weight coefficient that becomes smaller as the scale rises. $\mathcal{L}_{con}$ uses an L_1 paradigm to process the vector-level style-independent loss. $D(\cdot)$ represents the discriminant results of discriminators.

Figure 7 shows the training process of vector-level style-independent discriminators. $\uparrow$ and $\downarrow$ indicate the value rising and descending as the scale rises, respectively.

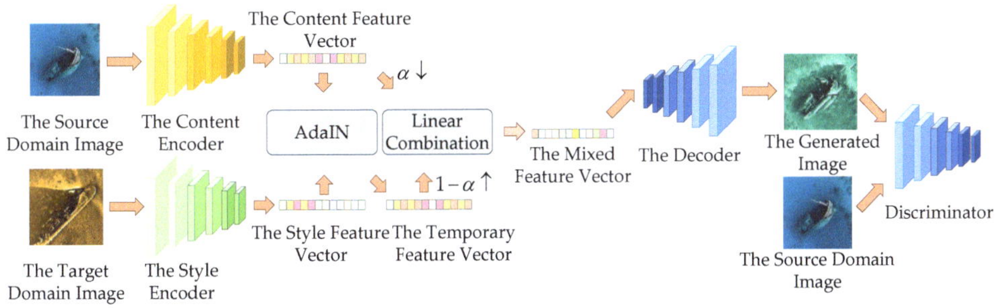

Figure 7. The training process of vector-level style-independent discriminators.

2.3. Implementation

To implement SID-AM-MSITM, we utilize Adam [31] as its optimizer and LeakyReLU [32] as its activation function. At the lowest scale, images of the model are 100 × 100-pixel ones. And at the highest scale, the size of images is 250 × 250 pixels. The model uses 6 scales.

3. Experiment and Result Analysis

In this section, we will present our experiments and the corresponding results analysis. We first introduce the evaluation metrics and then present the ablation and comparative experiments, respectively.

3.1. Evaluation Metric

We utilize four metrics for quantitative evaluation, including peak signal-to-noise ratio (PSNR) [33], structure similarity index measure (SSIM) [34], information entropy (Entropy) [35], and single image Fréchet Inception distance (SIFID) [36].

(1) PSNR: PSNR measures the distance between the distributions of two images. We use PSNR to calculate the distance between the source-domain images and reconstructed images. A larger PSNR value indicates a smaller difference between the two images.
(2) SSIM: SSIM measures the similarity of two images. The value of SSIM is between 0 and 1, and a larger SSIM indicates a better reconstruction effect, which suggests the translation effect of an image translation model.
(3) Entropy: Information entropy measures the complexity of an image. Larger information entropy indicates complex images that contain more information.
(4) SIFID: Single Image Fréchet Inception Distance (SIFID) is a special type of Fréchet Inception distance (FID) [37]. It measures the deviation between the feature distribution of two single images, and smaller SIFID indicates the better effect of generated images.

3.2. Ablation Experiment

We use five different datasets, including submarine, underwater optics, sunken ship, crashed plane, and underwater sonar datasets. The underwater optics images are from the URPC2020 dataset [38]. These images are difficult to collect and are not large in number. Specifically, the submarine, sunken ship, and crashed plane images are content categories, and the underwater sonar and underwater optics images are style ones. Meanwhile, the submarine, sunken ship, and crashed plane images are non-underwater images, and the underwater sonar and underwater optics images are underwater ones.

Figure 8 presents the utilized datasets, which are grouped into six different combinations, i.e., (1) sunken ships with underwater sonars, (2) sunken ships with underwater optics, (3) crashed planes with underwater sonars, (4) crashed planes with underwater optics, (5) submarines with underwater sonars, and (6) submarines with underwater optics.

Figure 8. Datasets.

Based on the above six combinations of images, we perform ablation experiments on four modules, including (1) TuiGAN only, (2) TuiGAN with CBAM, (3) TuiGAN with style-independent discriminators, and (4) SID-AM-MSITM, so as to comprehensively evaluate the improvements we have made.

Figures 9–14, respectively, present the generated and reconstructed images based on different combinations of datasets. In the figures, the first-column and second-column images are source-domain and target-domain ones, respectively. The third to the tenth columns, respectively, present the images generated or reconstructed using TuiGAN, TuiGAN with CBAM modules, TuiGAN with style-independent discriminators, and SID-AM-MSITM.

Figure 9. Generated and reconstructed images using the sunken ships and the underwater sonars.

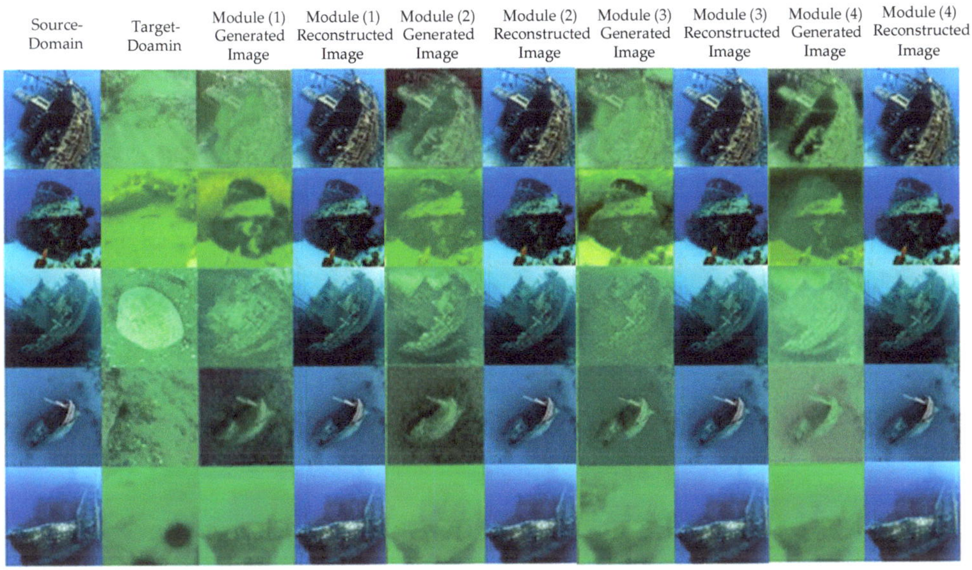

Figure 10. Generated and reconstructed images using the sunken ships and the underwater optics.

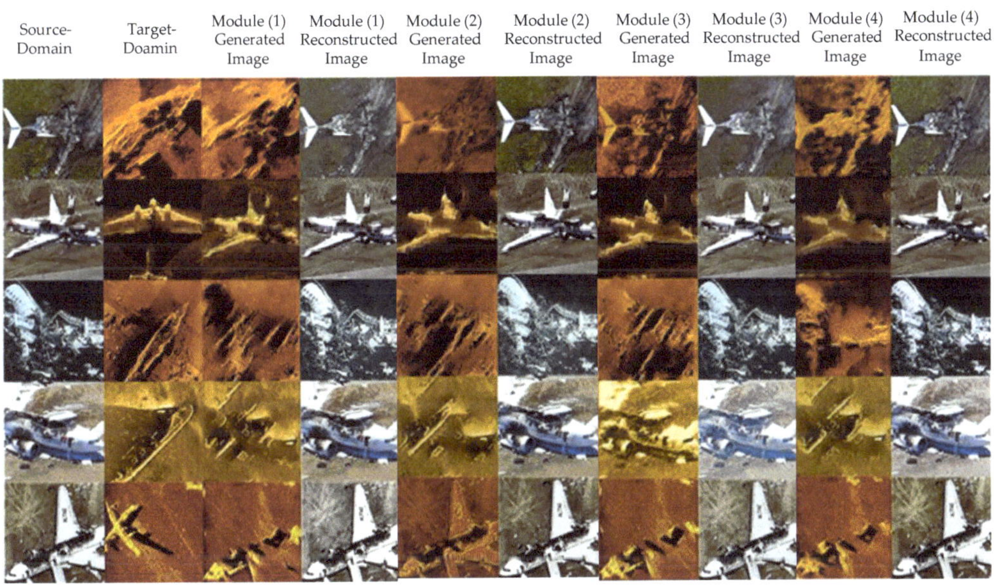

Figure 11. Generated and reconstructed images using the crashed planes and the underwater sonars.

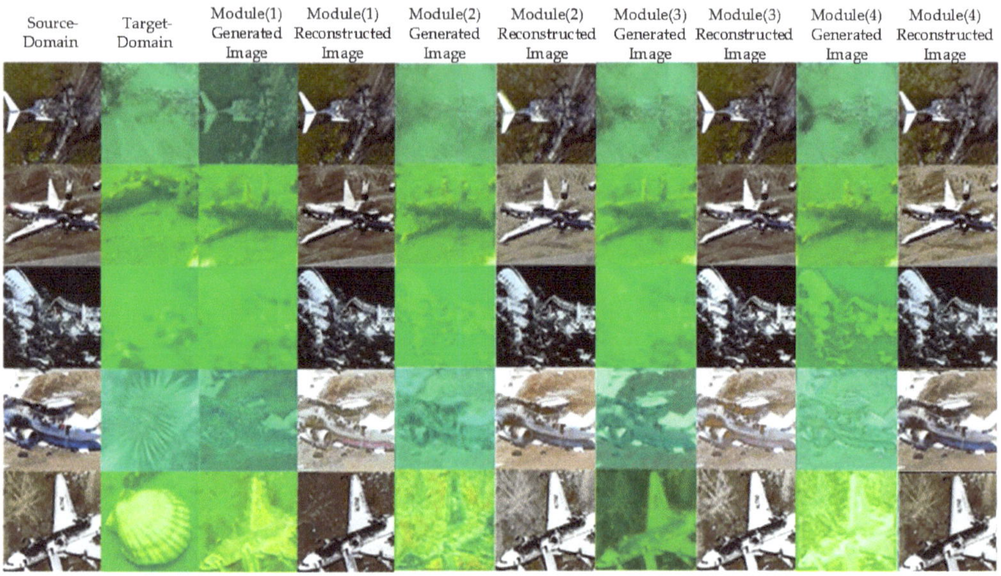

Figure 12. Generated and reconstructed images using the crashed planes and the underwater optics.

It is observed that SID-AM-MSITM has the ability to translate non-underwater images into underwater sonar images and underwater optics images, and objects such as submarines, crashed planes, and sunken ships are evident in underwater images. Meanwhile, SID-AM-MSITM is also capable of reconstructing translated underwater images into non-underwater images with little difference from the original non-underwater images.

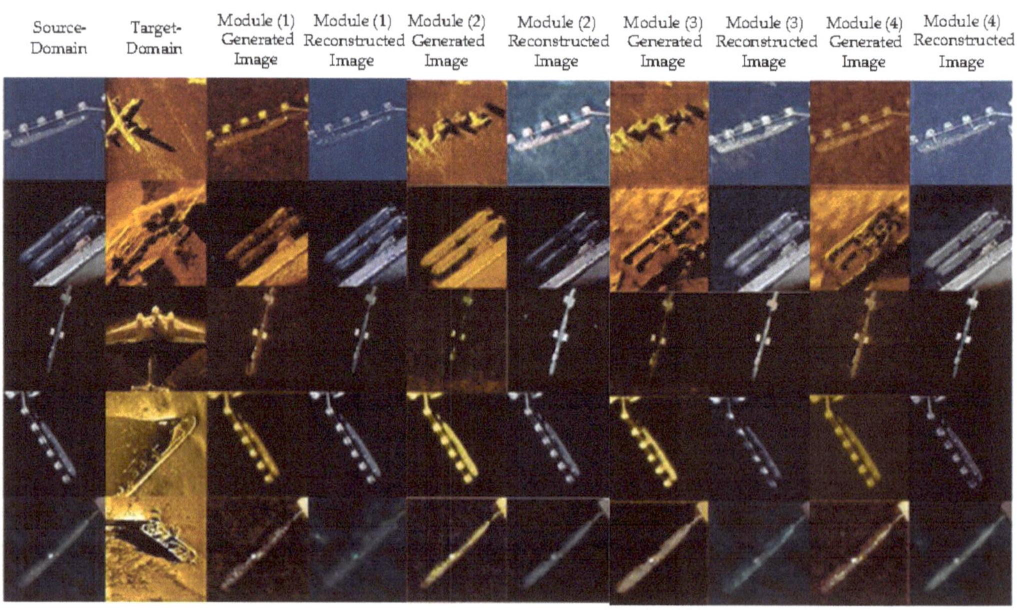

Figure 13. Generated and reconstructed images using the submarines and the underwater sonars.

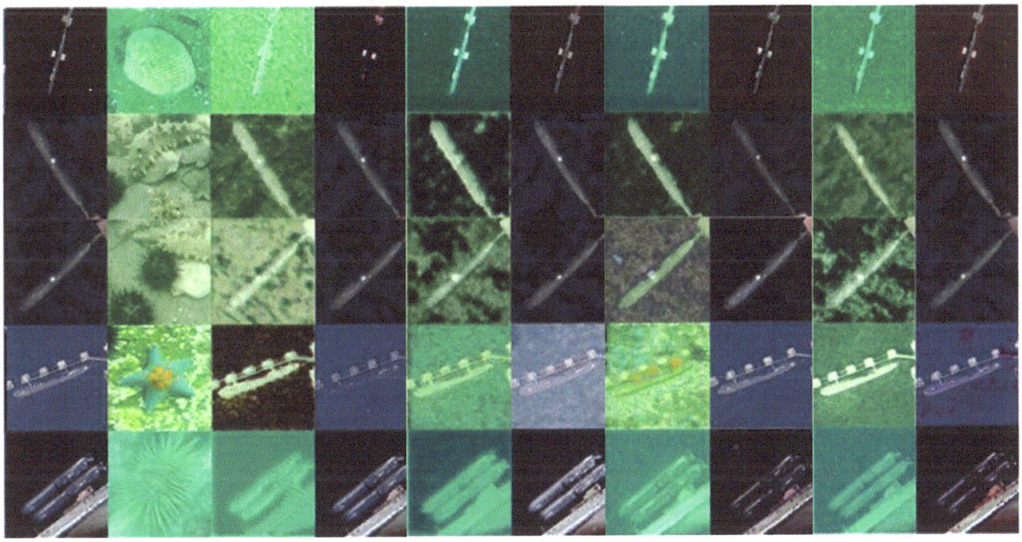

Figure 14. Generated and reconstructed images using the submarines and the underwater optics.

Table 1 presents the PSNR results of each model. It is observed that the PSNR values of the images reconstructed using the TuiGAN with CBAM modules on the three combinations of the datasets are higher than that of TuiGAN, and the maximum difference reaches 8.63. The PSNR values of the images reconstructed using TuiGAN with style-independent discriminators on the five combinations of datasets are higher than that of TuiGAN, and the maximum difference reaches 4.7. The PSNR values of the images reconstructed using SID-AM-MSITM on all combinations of the datasets are not less than that of TuiGAN, and the maximum difference reaches 4.58. The promising results indicate that the combination of CBAM modules and style-independent discriminators significantly improves the effective information acquisition ability of backbone TuiGAN and is suitable for all combinations of datasets.

Table 1. Ablation experiments on different datasets (PSNR).

Category	TuiGAN	TuiGAN with CBAM Modules	TuiGAN with Style-Independent Discriminators	SID-AM-MSITM
Sunken Ship + Sonar	17.20	20.28	19.53	22.77
Sunken Ship + Optics	21.24	18.91	19.98	22.87
Crashed plane + Sonar	20.02	23.00	20.50	24.26
Crashed plane + Optics	26.46	25.04	29.17	26.46
Submarine + Sonar	27.27	25.88	31.11	31.85
Submarine + Optics	23.20	31.83	27.90	25.96

Table 2 presents the SSIM results of each model. SSIM is also a metric to measure the effect of model reconstruction. It is observed that the SSIM results of the images reconstructed using TuiGAN with CBAM modules on four combinations of datasets are higher than that of TuiGAN, and the maximum difference reaches 0.17. The SSIM results of the images reconstructed using TuiGAN with style-independent discriminators on all combinations of datasets are not less than that of TuiGAN, and the maximum difference reaches 0.09. The SSIM values of the images reconstructed using SID-AM-MSITM on all combinations of datasets are higher than that of TuiGAN, and the maximum difference reaches 0.15. These promising results also indicate that CBAM modules and style-independent discriminators improve the ability to access effective information.

Table 2. Ablation experiments on different datasets (SSIM).

Category	TuiGAN	TuiGAN with CBAM Modules	TuiGAN with Style-Independent Discriminators	SID-AM-MSITM
Sunken Ship + Sonar	0.68	0.82	0.75	0.83
Sunken Ship + Optics	0.85	0.88	0.87	0.90
Crashed plane + Sonar	0.83	0.91	0.83	0.90
Crashed plane + Optics	0.91	0.89	0.92	0.92
Submarine + Sonar	0.85	0.84	0.88	0.89
Submarine + Optics	0.70	0.87	0.79	0.84

Table 3 presents the Entropy results of each model. It is observed that the Entropy result of the images generated using TuiGAN with CBAM modules on only one combination of datasets is higher than that of TuiGAN, and the difference reaches 0.21. The Entropy results of the images generated using TuiGAN with style-independent discriminators on four combinations of datasets are higher than that of TuiGAN, and the maximum difference reaches 0.86. The Entropy results of the images reconstructed using SID-AM-MSITM on all combinations of datasets are higher than that of TuiGAN, and the maximum difference reaches 0.78. These promising results indicate that style-independent discriminators improve the diversity of generated images. The style-independent discriminators improve TuiGAN's ability to retain content details and are suitable for the combinations of all datasets.

In summary, based on the above ablation results, our proposed SID-AM-MSITM achieves promising underwater image translation performance in terms of PSNR, SSIM, and Entropy. The ablation experiments demonstrate that CBAM modules enhance the feature extraction ability of the network, so as to enhance the ability to access effective information. Moreover, we prove that style-independent discriminators improve the diversity of the generated images without weakening the reconstruction performance, which indicates SID-AM-MSITM retains the content details of non-underwater images.

Table 3. Ablation experiments on different datasets (Entropy).

Category	TuiGAN	TuiGAN with CBAM Modules	TuiGAN with Style-Independent Discriminators	SID-AM-MSITM
Sunken Ship + Sonar	6.75	6.70	7.12	7.00
Sunken Ship + Optics	6.00	6.21	6.86	6.78
Crashed plane + Sonar	7.31	6.53	7.23	7.38
Crashed plane + Optics	5.57	5.53	5.70	5.63
Submarine + Sonar	6.47	5.54	6.96	6.59
Submarine + Optics	6.32	6.29	5.44	6.33

3.3. Comparative Experiment

The above ablation experiments demonstrate the overall effect of SID-AM-MSITM. In the following, we further compare it with multiple advanced image translation models, including CycleGAN [39], FUNIT [40], AdaIN [30], and SinDiffusion [41]. These models are selected as baselines since they present promising performance and cover general image translation models, CycleGAN, FUNIT, and AdaIN, as well as the emerging SinDiffusion.

(1) CycleGAN: CycleGAN is one of the most typical translation models using cycle consistency. The model assumes the potential correspondence between source-domain and target-domain images.

(2) FUNIT: FUNIT is an unsupervised few-shot image translation model that achieves satisfactory performance based on limited data.
(3) AdaIN: AdaIN is an image translation model that achieves real-time and arbitrary style transfer.
(4) SinDiffusion: SinDiffusion is a diffusion model that works on a single natural image.

Figure 15 presents the comparison results between the images translated using SID-AM-MS- ITM and other baseline models. Through visual effect comparison, it is observed that SID-AM-MSITM has learned the style of target-domain images and retains the content of source-domain images. Moreover, the images translated using SID-AM-MSITM show little difference between adjacent pixels as well as excellent smoothness, which is superior to CycleGAN which shows obvious adjacent pixels difference after amplification. Compared with FUNIT and AdaIN, SID-AM-MSITM retains the content of source-domain images and learns better texture and color information from the target domain.

Next, we use SIFID to quantitatively compare SID-AM-MSITM with these baselines. Table 4 shows the SIFID results. It is observed that SID-AM-MSITM achieves the best (smallest) SIFID values. For example, the SIFID values of the images translated using SID-AM-MSITM are roughly 0.02×10^{-2} to 0.058×10^{-2} smaller than that of CycleGAN, 17.408×10^{-2} to 17.55×10^{-2} smaller than that of FUNIT, 9.31×10^{-2} to 9.418×10^{-2} smaller than that of AdaIN, 0.002×10^{-2} to 0.018×10^{-2} smaller than that of TuiGAN, and 1.118×10^{-2} to 1.25×10^{-2} smaller than that of SinDiffusion. This demonstrates that the images translated using SID-AM-MSITM are closer to the source-domain images and retain more content information than other models.

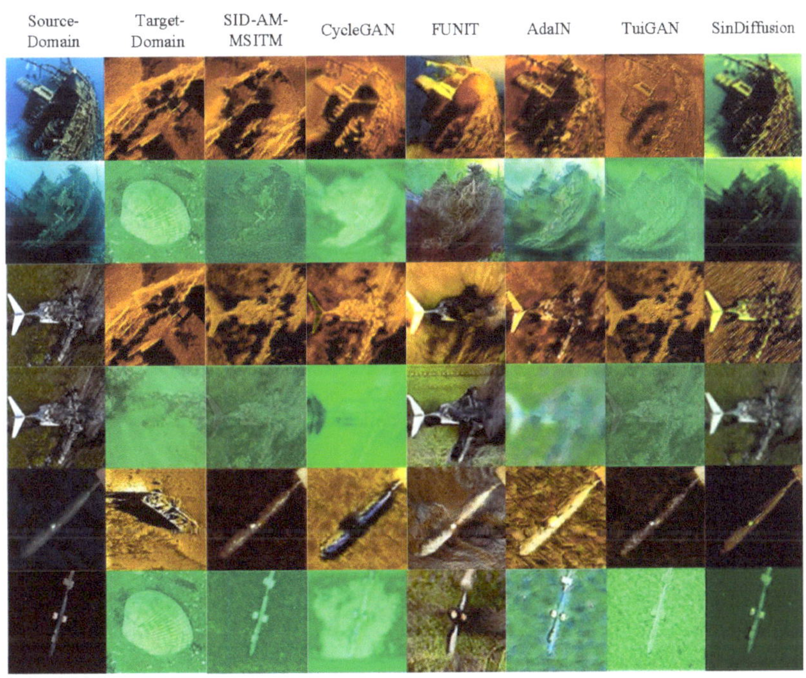

Figure 15. The comparison results of the images generated using SID-AM-MSITM and other models.

Table 4. SIFID comparison of underwater images generated using SID-AM-MSITM and other baseline models ($\times 10^{-2}$).

Our Model	CycleGAN	FUNIT	AdaIN	TuiGAN	SinDiffusion
0.092	0.130	17.5	9.51	0.101	1.21
0.054	0.080	17.6	9.41	0.072	1.23
0.050	0.108	17.6	9.36	0.052	1.30
0.015	0.035	17.5	9.35	0.017	1.20

In summary, SID-AM-MSITM is superior to multiple baseline models in improving the ability to access effective information and avoiding the loss of content details.

4. Conclusions

In this work, we propose a novel multi-scale image translation model with attention modules and style-independent discriminators (SID-AM-MSITM), to complete the underwater image translation task. We use a multi-scale generative adversarial network, TuiGAN, to construct a backbone architecture, which translates images from low scales to high scales. We introduce CBAM modules into the generators and discriminators at multi-scales and devise style-independent discriminators to improve the generative and discriminant effects. Based on systematical ablation and comparative experiments, we demonstrate that SID-AM-MSITM has the ability to acquire effective information and retain the content details of non-underwater images during the underwater image translation process, and it requires only two unpaired images to complete the image translation.

However, there are still some problems in the current research. In the use of style-independent discriminators, SID-AM-MSITM uses the number between 0 and 1 in the linear combination to achieve the translation from the source domain to the target domain. We will continue to study whether there is a more appropriate interval to train style-independent discriminators. We only select several source-domain and target-domain images as the dataset, which has certain limitations. In order to measure the performance of the model comprehensively, we will use other underwater target images to verify the versatility of SID-AM-MSITM, such as the UIEB database [42].

Author Contributions: Conceptualization, D.Y., T.Z. and M.L.; Data curation, M.L. and X.W.; Formal analysis, T.Z. and M.L.; Funding acquisition, D.Y. and X.W.; Investigation, M.L., W.C. and X.L.; Methodology, D.Y., T.Z., M.L. and X.W.; Project administration, B.L. and X.W.; Resources, M.L. and X.W.; Software, M.L. and W.C.; Supervision, B.L. and X.W.; Validation, T.Z. and M.L.; Visualization, M.L.; Writing—original draft, D.Y. and M.L.; Writing—review and editing, T.Z., B.L., W.C., X.L. and X.W. All authors have read and agreed to the published version of the manuscript.

Funding: This work is supported by a grant from the Key Laboratory of Avionics System Integrated Technology, the Fundamental Research Funds for the Central Universities in China, Grant No. 3072022JC0601, and the Ministry of Industry and Information Technology High-tech Ship Project [2019] No. 331.

Institutional Review Board Statement: Not applicable.

Informed Consent Statement: Not applicable.

Data Availability Statement: The data presented in this study are available from the corresponding author upon reasonable request.

Acknowledgments: The authors are grateful to the editors and anonymous reviewers for their constructive comments.

Conflicts of Interest: The authors declare no conflict of interest.

Abbreviations

The following abbreviations are used in this manuscript:

SID-AM-MSITM	multi-scale image translation model based on style-independent discriminators and attention modules
CBAM	convolution block attention module
GAN	generative adversarial network
CNN	convolutional neural network
LeakyReLU	leaky rectified linear unit
CycleGAN	cycle-consistent adversarial network
TV loss	total variation loss
PSNR	peak signal-to-noise ratio
SSIM	structure similarity index measure
Entropy	information entropy
AdaIN	adaptive instance normalization
CycleGAN	cycle-consistent adversarial networks
FID	the Fréchet Inception distance
SIFID	single image Fréchet Inception distance

References

1. Zhao, Y.; Zhu, K.; Zhao, T.; Zheng, L.; Deng, X. Small-Sample Seabed Sediment Classification Based on Deep Learning. *Remote. Sens.* **2023**, *15*, 2178. [CrossRef]
2. Chen, B.; Li, R.; Bai, W.; Zhang, X.; Li, J.; Guo, R. Research on recognition method of optical detection image of underwater robot for submarine cable. In Proceedings of the 2019 IEEE 3rd Advanced Information Management, Communicates, Electronic and Automation Control Conference (IMCEC), Chongqing, China, 11–13 October 2019; pp. 1973–1976.
3. Teng, B.; Zhao, H. Underwater target recognition methods based on the framework of deep learning: A survey. *Int. J. Adv. Robot. Syst.* **2020**, *17*, 1729881420976307. [CrossRef]
4. Cruz, L.; Lucio, D.; Velho, L. Kinect and rgbd images: Challenges and applications. In Proceedings of the IEEE 2012 25th SIBGRAPI Conference on Graphics, Patterns and Images Tutorials, Ouro Preto, Brazil, 22–25 August 2012; pp. 36–49.
5. Yang, L.; Wang, B.; Zhang, R.; Zhou, H.; Wang, R. Analysis on location accuracy for the binocular stereo vision system. *IEEE Photonics J.* **2017**, *10*, 1–16. [CrossRef]
6. Lin, E. Comparative Analysis of Pix2Pix and CycleGAN for Image-to-Image Translation. *Highlights Sci. Eng. Technol.* **2023**, *39*, 915–925. [CrossRef]
7. Multi-view underwater image enhancement method via embedded fusion mechanism. *Eng. Appl. Artif. Intell.* **2023**, *121*, 105946. [CrossRef]
8. Zhou, J.; Liu, Q.; Jiang, Q.; Ren, W.; Lam, K.M.; Zhang, W. Underwater camera: Improving visual perception via adaptive dark pixel prior and color correction. *Int. J. Comput. Vis.* **2023**. [CrossRef]
9. Goodfellow, I.; Pouget-Abadie, J.; Mirza, M.; Xu, B.; Warde-Farley, D.; Ozair, S.; Courville, A.; Bengio, Y. Generative adversarial nets. In Proceedings of the Advances in Neural Information Processing Systems, Montreal, QC, USA, 8–13 December 2014; Volume 27.
10. Hertzmann, A.; Jacobs, C.E.; Oliver, N.; Curless, B.; Salesin, D.H. Image analogies. In Proceedings of the 28th Annual Conference on Computer Graphics and Interactive Techniques, Los Angeles, CA, USA, 12–17 August 2001; pp. 327–340.
11. Resales; Achan; Frey. Unsupervised image translation. In Proceedings of the 9th IEEE International Conference on Computer Vision, Nice, France, 14–17 October 2003; pp. 472–478.
12. Szegedy, C.; Liu, W.; Jia, Y.; Sermanet, P.; Reed, S.; Anguelov, D.; Erhan, D.; Vanhoucke, V.; Rabinovich, A. Going deeper with convolutions. In Proceedings of the IEEE Conference on Computer Vision and Pattern Recognition, Boston, MA, USA, 7–12 June 2015; pp. 1–9.
13. Gatys, L.A.; Ecker, A.S.; Bethge, M. Image style transfer using convolutional neural networks. In Proceedings of the IEEE Conference on Computer Vision and Pattern Recognition, Las Vegas, NV, USA, 27–30 June 2016; pp. 2414–2423.
14. Isola, P.; Zhu, J.Y.; Zhou, T.; Efros, A.A. Image-to-image translation with conditional adversarial networks. In Proceedings of the IEEE Conference on Computer Vision and Pattern Recognition, Honolulu, HI, USA, 21–26 July 2017; pp. 1125–1134.
15. Wang, T.C.; Liu, M.Y.; Zhu, J.Y.; Tao, A.; Kautz, J.; Catanzaro, B. High-resolution image synthesis and semantic manipulation with conditional gans. In Proceedings of the IEEE Conference on Computer Vision and Pattern Recognition, Salt Lake City, UT, USA, 18–23 June 2018; pp. 8798–8807.
16. Karras, T.; Laine, S.; Aila, T. A style-based generator architecture for generative adversarial networks. In Proceedings of the IEEE/CVF Conference on Computer Vision and Pattern Recognition, Long Beach, CA, USA, 15–20 June 2019; pp. 4401–4410.
17. Choi, Y.; Choi, M.; Kim, M.; Ha, J.W.; Kim, S.; Choo, J. Stargan: Unified generative adversarial networks for multi-domain image-to-image translation. In Proceedings of the IEEE Conference on Computer Vision and Pattern Recognition, Salt Lake City, UT, USA, 18–23 June 2018; pp. 8789–8797.

18. Li, J.; Skinner, K.A.; Eustice, R.M.; Johnson-Roberson, M. WaterGAN: Unsupervised generative network to enable real-time color correction of monocular underwater images. *IEEE Robot. Autom. Lett.* **2017**, *3*, 387–394. [CrossRef]
19. Wang, N.; Zhou, Y.; Han, F.; Zhu, H.; Yao, J. UWGAN: Underwater GAN for real-world underwater color restoration and dehazing. *arXiv* **2019**, arXiv:1912.10269.
20. Li, N.; Zheng, Z.; Zhang, S.; Yu, Z.; Zheng, H.; Zheng, B. The synthesis of unpaired underwater images using a multistyle generative adversarial network. *IEEE Access* **2018**, *6*, 54241–54257. [CrossRef]
21. Zhou, J.; Li, B.; Zhang, D.; Yuan, J.; Zhang, W.; Cai, Z.; Shi, J. UGIF-Net: An Efficient Fully Guided Information Flow Network for Underwater Image Enhancement. *IEEE Trans. Geosci. Remote. Sens.* **2023**, *61*, 1–17. [CrossRef]
22. Geirhos, R.; Rubisch, P.; Michaelis, C.; Bethge, M.; Wichmann, F.A.; Brendel, W. ImageNet-trained CNNs are biased towards texture; increasing shape bias improves accuracy and robustness. *arXiv* **2018**, arXiv:1811.12231.
23. Lin, J.; Pang, Y.; Xia, Y.; Chen, Z.; Luo, J. Tuigan: Learning versatile image-to-image translation with two unpaired images. In Proceedings of the 16th European Conference of Computer Vision (ECCV 2020), Glasgow, UK, 23–28 August 2020; Proceedings, Part IV 16; Springer: Cham, Switzerland, 2020; pp. 18–35.
24. Woo, S.; Park, J.; Lee, J.Y.; Kweon, I.S. Cbam: Convolutional block attention module. In Proceedings of the European Conference on Computer Vision (ECCV), Munich, Germany, 8–14 September 2018; pp. 3–19.
25. Gulrajani, I.; Ahmed, F.; Arjovsky, M.; Dumoulin, V.; Courville, A.C. Improved training of wasserstein gans. In Proceedings of the Advances in Neural Information Processing Systems, Long Beach, CA, USA, 4–9 December 2017; Volume 30.
26. Mahendran, A.; Vedaldi, A. Understanding deep image representations by inverting them. In Proceedings of the IEEE Conference on Computer Vision and Pattern Recognition, Boston, MA, USA, 7–12 June 2015; pp. 5188–5196.
27. You, Q.; Wan, C.; Sun, J.; Shen, J.; Ye, H.; Yu, Q. Fundus image enhancement method based on CycleGAN. In Proceedings of the 2019 41st Annual International Conference of the IEEE Engineering in Medicine and Biology Society (EMBC), Berlin, Germany, 23–27 July 2019; pp. 4500–4503.
28. Hu, J.; Shen, L.; Sun, G. Squeeze-and-excitation networks. In Proceedings of the IEEE Conference on Computer Vision and Pattern Recognition, Salt Lake City, UT, USA, 18–23 June 2018; pp. 7132–7141.
29. Simonyan, K.; Zisserman, A. Very deep convolutional networks for large-scale image recognition. *arXiv* **2014**, arXiv:1409.1556.
30. Huang, X.; Belongie, S. Arbitrary style transfer in real-time with adaptive instance normalization. In Proceedings of the IEEE International Conference on Computer Vision, Venice, Italy, 22–29 October 2017; pp. 1501–1510.
31. Kingma, D.P.; Ba, J. Adam: A method for stochastic optimization. *arXiv* **2014**, arXiv:1412.6980.
32. Xu, J.; Li, Z.; Du, B.; Zhang, M.; Liu, J. Reluplex made more practical: Leaky ReLU. In Proceedings of the 2020 IEEE Symposium on Computers and Communications (ISCC), Rennes, France, 7–10 July 2020; pp. 1–7.
33. Najafipour, A.; Babaee, A.; Shahrtash, S.M. Comparing the trustworthiness of signal-to-noise ratio and peak signal-to-noise ratio in processing noisy partial discharge signals. *IET Sci. Meas. Technol.* **2013**, *7*, 112–118. [CrossRef]
34. Khadtare, M.S. GPU based image quality assessment using structural similarity (SSIM) index. In *Emerging Research Surrounding Power Consumption and Performance Issues in Utility Computing*; IGI Global: Hershey, PA, USA, 2016; pp. 276–282.
35. Xu, N.; Zhuang, J.; Xiao, J.; Peng, C. Regional Differential Information Entropy for Super-Resolution Image Quality Assessment. *arXiv* **2021**, arXiv:2107.03642.
36. Shaham, T.R.; Dekel, T.; Michaeli, T. Singan: Learning a generative model from a single natural image. In Proceedings of the IEEE/CVF International Conference on Computer Vision, Seoul, Republic of Korea, 27 October–2 November 2019; pp. 4570–4580.
37. Heusel, M.; Ramsauer, H.; Unterthiner, T.; Nessler, B.; Hochreiter, S. Gans trained by a two time-scale update rule converge to a local nash equilibrium. In Proceedings of the Advances in Neural Information Processing Systems, Long Beach, CA, USA, 4–9 December 2017; Volume 30.
38. Zhang, J.; Zhang, J.; Zhou, K.; Zhang, Y.; Chen, H.; Yan, X. An Improved YOLOv5-Based Underwater Object-Detection Framework. *Sensors* **2023**, *23*, 3693. [CrossRef] [PubMed]
39. Zhu, J.Y.; Park, T.; Isola, P.; Efros, A.A. Unpaired image-to-image translation using cycle-consistent adversarial networks. In Proceedings of the IEEE International Conference on Computer Vision, Venice, Italy, 22–29 October 2017; pp. 2223–2232.
40. Liu, M.Y.; Huang, X.; Mallya, A.; Karras, T.; Aila, T.; Lehtinen, J.; Kautz, J. Few-shot unsupervised image-to-image translation. In Proceedings of the IEEE/CVF International Conference on Computer Vision, Seoul, Republic of Korea, 27 October–2 November 2019; pp. 10551–10560.
41. Wang, W.; Bao, J.; Zhou, W.; Chen, D.; Chen, D.; Yuan, L.; Li, H. Sindiffusion: Learning a diffusion model from a single natural image. *arXiv* **2022**, arXiv:2211.12445.
42. Zhou, J.; Pang, L.; Zhang, D.; Zhang, W. Underwater Image Enhancement Method via Multi-Interval Subhistogram Perspective Equalization. *IEEE J. Ocean. Eng.* **2023**, *48*, 474–488. [CrossRef]

Journal of
Marine Science and Engineering

MDPI

Article

New Insights into Sea Turtle Propulsion and Their Cost of Transport Point to a Potential New Generation of High-Efficient Underwater Drones for Ocean Exploration

Nick van der Geest *, Lorenzo Garcia *, Roy Nates and Fraser Borrett

BioDesign Lab, Auckland University of Technology, Auckland 1010, New Zealand
* Correspondence: nicky.van.der.geest@aut.ac.nz (N.v.d.G.); lorenzo.garcia@aut.ac.nz (L.G.)

Abstract: Sea turtles gracefully navigate their marine environments by flapping their pectoral flippers in an elegant routine to produce the required hydrodynamic forces required for locomotion. The propulsion of sea turtles has been shown to occur for approximately 30% of the limb beat, with the remaining 70% employing a drag-reducing glide. However, it is unknown how the sea turtle manipulates the flow during the propulsive stage. Answering this research question is a complicated process, especially when conducting laboratory tests on endangered animals, and the animal may not even swim with its regular routine while in a captive state. In this work, we take advantage of our robotic sea turtle, internally known as Cornelia, to offer the first insights into the flow features during the sea turtle's propulsion cycle consisting of the downstroke and the sweep stroke. Comparing the flow features to the animal's swim speed, flipper angle of attack, power consumption, thrust and lift production, we hypothesise how each of the flow features influences the animal's propulsive efforts and cost of transport (COT). Our findings show that the sea turtle can produce extremely low COT values that point to the effectiveness of the sea turtle propulsive technique. Based on our findings, we extract valuable data that can potentially lead to turtle-inspired elements for high-efficiency underwater drones for long-term underwater missions.

Keywords: sea turtles; underwater robots; underwater flight; soft robotics; biomimicry; animal biomechanics; CFD; fluid dynamics

Citation: van der Geest, N.; Garcia, L.; Nates, R.; Borrett, F. New Insights into Sea Turtle Propulsion and Their Cost of Transport Point to a Potential New Generation of High-Efficient Underwater Drones for Ocean Exploration. *J. Mar. Sci. Eng.* **2023**, *11*, 1944. https://doi.org/10.3390/jmse11101944

Academic Editor: Diego Villa

Received: 27 August 2023
Revised: 18 September 2023
Accepted: 29 September 2023
Published: 9 October 2023

1. Introduction

Sea turtles navigate their marine environments by gracefully flapping their pectoral wings/flippers to produce a visually enchanting locomotive pattern. This flapping motion allows the sea turtle migration of thousands of kilometres to reach favourable breeding or feeding grounds [1–5]. The flapping motion has typically been described as asymmetric, with the downstroke approximately twice as fast as the upstroke [6–8]. In recent work by van der Geest et al. [6], the flapping motion was described three-dimensionally for the Green sea turtle (*Chelonia mydas*), including the soft twisting of the flipper. The authors described the flipper motion by breaking it up into five segments consisting of the Downstroke (DS), Sweep stroke (SS), Recovery stroke one (RS1), Upstroke (US) and, finally, Recovery stroke two (RS2) (Figure 1). It is understood that during the Green turtle's general flapping routine, the upstroke does not generate any thrust [6,8–10]; however, during this time, the animal's drag coefficient is lowered to help reduce swim speed losses [10]. To quantify how the drag is reduced during the upstroke, van der Geest et al. [10] conducted dedicated work to uncover the flow features generated by the flipper during this period. Through dye visualisation of a scale turtle model in a towing tank, they found the flipper enters a near-equilibrium state that produces near-constant pressure across the entire flipper surface [10] (Movie S1). The constant pressure across the surface of the flipper then cancels out any flow mixing due to pressure differences, including the wing tip vortex. However, though this work is insightful, it does not cover what flow features occur during the sea turtles

(*Chelonia mydas*) propulsive cycle consisting of the downstroke and sweep stroke. The propulsion cycle in sea turtles has been previously described as only occurring during the downstroke period, with peak thrust occurring at the end of the downstroke [8,9], with the most recent works taking very different approaches to uncover the propulsive cycle. David T. Booth [9] found the propulsive cycle by studying green turtle hatchlings in a flume, while van der Geest et al. [8] developed a full-scale robotic sea turtle based on the green turtle that could reproduce the natural animals swimming patterns. Though both these works offered comparable insights into thrust production and/or energy consumption, they did not detail the flow features and fluid mechanical mechanisms responsible for the propulsion. David T. Booth [9] hypothesised the downstroke likely produces both lift-based and drag-based propulsion depending on the flipper angle of attack; however, what does lift-based or drag-based propulsion in sea turtles look like? And is this hypothesis accurate? To the best of our knowledge, no research details the flow features and fluid mechanical interactions sea turtles utilise during their downstroke using genuine sea turtle kinematics. However, work has been produced that analysed simplified two-dimensional turtle-inspired flow features [11,12]. Though these two-dimensional examples may offer insight, they fail to reproduce three-dimensional effects such as spanwise flow and Coriolis effects that have been shown as essential factors in biological flapping wings [13].

Figure 1. The wild sea turtle (*Chelonia mydas*) flipper pattern during the animal's regular swimming routine obtained from van der Geest et al. [6].

For the last 20 years, it has been well understood that the flow feature responsible for high-performance force production in biological flapping wings is the leading-edge vortex (LEV) [14–16]. The LEV has been shown to occur across all categories of animal species [14,15,17,18], with insect flight first believed to be a paradox before its discovery [14]. However, although the LEV has been heavily studied in flapping wings, to the best of our knowledge, no research exists for LEV generation during the downstroke in sea turtles that applies genuine and accurate sea turtle kinematics.

Recent studies into the propulsion methods of sea lions demonstrated that the sea lion's flippers create additional thrust by applying a clapping motion [19,20]. The clapping motion entrains fluid momentum on the low-pressure side of the flipper (dorsal side) that later develops into complex vortex shedding to increase thrust [19]. It is now understood that sea turtles also create a clapping motion referred to as the sweep stroke (Figure 1). However, the fluid interaction during the sea turtle's sweep stroke is entirely unknown.

Obtaining the flow features of sea turtles requires solving two significant complications. First, it is necessary to obtain animal ethical approval to conduct the test on endangered species; second, the animal may not even swim with its regular swim pattern while in a captive state [6,8,10]. To overcome such hurdles, we take advantage of our robotic sea turtle (Cornelia). Cornelia is the world's first and only robotic sea turtle that accurately produces the sea turtle's natural form and function, as detailed in our previous work [8]. This makes

Cornelia an invaluable tool for studying the fluid-structure interactions of turtles without the need to trouble the actual animal.

In this work, with the help of Cornelia, we break down each of the observed flow features of the turtle's flippers during the propulsive cycle (Figure 2). To the best of our knowledge, this is the first study to show insight into the flow features of the sea turtle during the animal's propulsive cycle. We compare the observed flow features against the turtle's thrust and lift forces flipper angle of attack (AoA), flipper velocity and power consumption, to offer insight into the ways in which each feature influences the animal's propulsion effort and cost of transport (*COT*). We compare the *COT* obtained by Cornelia against the current state-of-the-art swimming robotics [21–29], and we find Cornelia to produce extremely low values for the *COT*, pointing to the effectiveness of the sea turtle propulsive strategy.

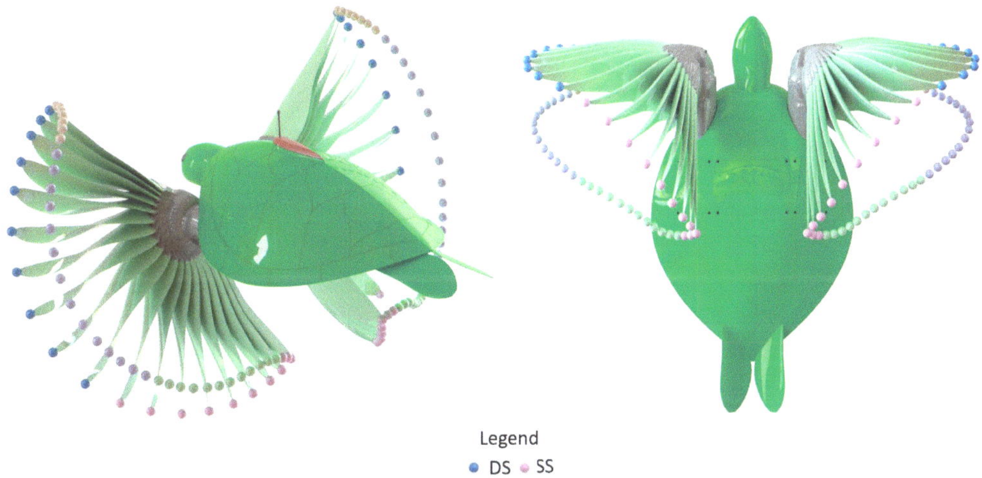

Figure 2. The robotic sea turtle (*Cornelia*) illustrating the propulsive cycle consisting of the downstroke and sweep stroke [8]. Also, see Movie S2.

Based on our findings, we hypothesise what practical aspects of the turtle's locomotion pattern could be developed and optimised to enhance the next generation of underwater drones and robotic technologies.

2. Methods

2.1. Method Overview

All tests were performed using our ad hoc testing rig, internally known as the "turtle dyno", as shown in Figure 3. Testing involved towing the robot quickly up to speed before the robot taking over to propel itself. The turtle dyno recorded lift, drag, thrust, swim velocity and power consumption simultaneously during each test. The design and specification for the turtle dyno, along with a detailed analysis of the force production during the regular swimming routine, can be found in our previous work [8], so we do not cover this in detail here.

Due to its cost effectiveness and ease of application, individual flow features were observed using dye visualisation with our in-house developed dye application tools. CFD was additionally used to help complement the field tests and provide a deeper comprehension of the flow field characteristics.

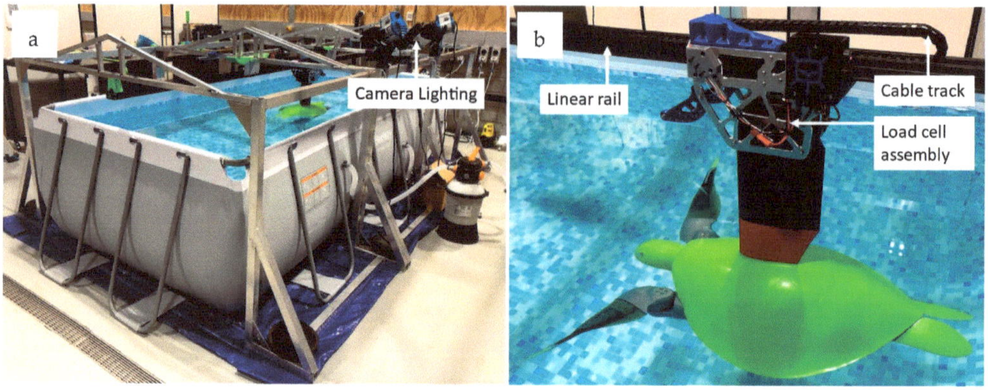

Figure 3. Turtle dyno. (**a**) Complete dyno assembly showing camera lighting arrangement. (**b**) Close-up of robot attached to load cell and linear rail assembly.

2.2. CFD Calculations

In parallel with laboratory experiments, commercial CFD tools were used to help better comprehend the flow features observed during physical testing with ANSYS Fluent (ANSYS 2021 R2, Canonsburg, PA, USA). Simulations only involved studying the flow around the rear flippers and during the sea turtle downstroke. The sweep stroke was not simulated due to its complex motion coupled with the complex wing morphing during this part of the locomotion pattern, thus creating high computational expense that was not available for this study. Additionally, it must be noted that the CFD simulations from this study were conducted not to produce highly accurate results, but to help complement the results from our laboratory experiments.

Two separate simulations were set up with the $k\omega$ SST model used to study the ways in which the flow from the turtle's carapace travels downstream to meet the rear flippers, and the realisable $k\varepsilon$ model was used for simulating the downstroke due to its lower computational expense. The $k\omega$ model had the mesh refined down to a y^+ of 0.75, with the $k\varepsilon$ model using a y^+ of 13.15 with the addition of scalable wall functions. As the turtle's downstroke applies a relatively constant wing twist [10] and a simple rotation motion, the simulation was simplified into two separate domains: a rotating domain with the flipper using a rigid body and a sliding mesh interface paired with a static domain (Figure S1a). The rotational domain angular velocity and velocity inlet values were established based on the values achieved by sea turtles during the downstroke period. The computational domain that used with the $k\omega$ model can be seen in Figure S1b, with a body of influence for mesh refinement added around the turtle body and further downstream to capture the wake produced by the turtle body. A symmetry boundary condition was used to substantially lower computational expense with a constant velocity inlet defined based on the turtle's average swimming velocity.

2.3. Dye Visualisation

To visualise the individual flow features during the regular swimming routines, we operated our in-house developed dye visualisation tools (Figure 4). The tools have been successfully used in our previous studies [10]; however, the streamline tool, as seen in Figure 4a, was further developed for this study, introducing up to 3 dye streamlines. The central pylon section of the tool used a NACA 0010 cross-section with each of the three stacked bodies using a 360° revolution of the NACA 0010 cross-section. The tool ran on a linear rail parallel to the turtle swim path and could have the dye accurately injected when required. To ensure the tool did not generate a significant disturbance in its wake, tests were performed to inject a cloud of dye into its path and record the disturbance in the wake (Figure 4c and Movie S3). Our testing suggested that the tool created insignificant disturbance compared to the disturbance an animal in the wild would likely encounter, so we deemed the tool satisfactory for use. Flow features were recorded using high-speed underwater photography (Chronos 2.1HD 32GB, Kron Technologies Inc, Burnaby, BC, Canada) at full HD 1000 FPS and an action camera (GoPro Hero 10, GoPro, San Mateo, CA, USA) at full HD 240 FPS. The Chronos cameras were installed into waterproof housings (Salty surf housings, North Wollongong, NSW, Australia) and equipped with a Sigma 18–35 mm lens (Sigma Corporation, Kawasaki, Kanagawa, Japan).

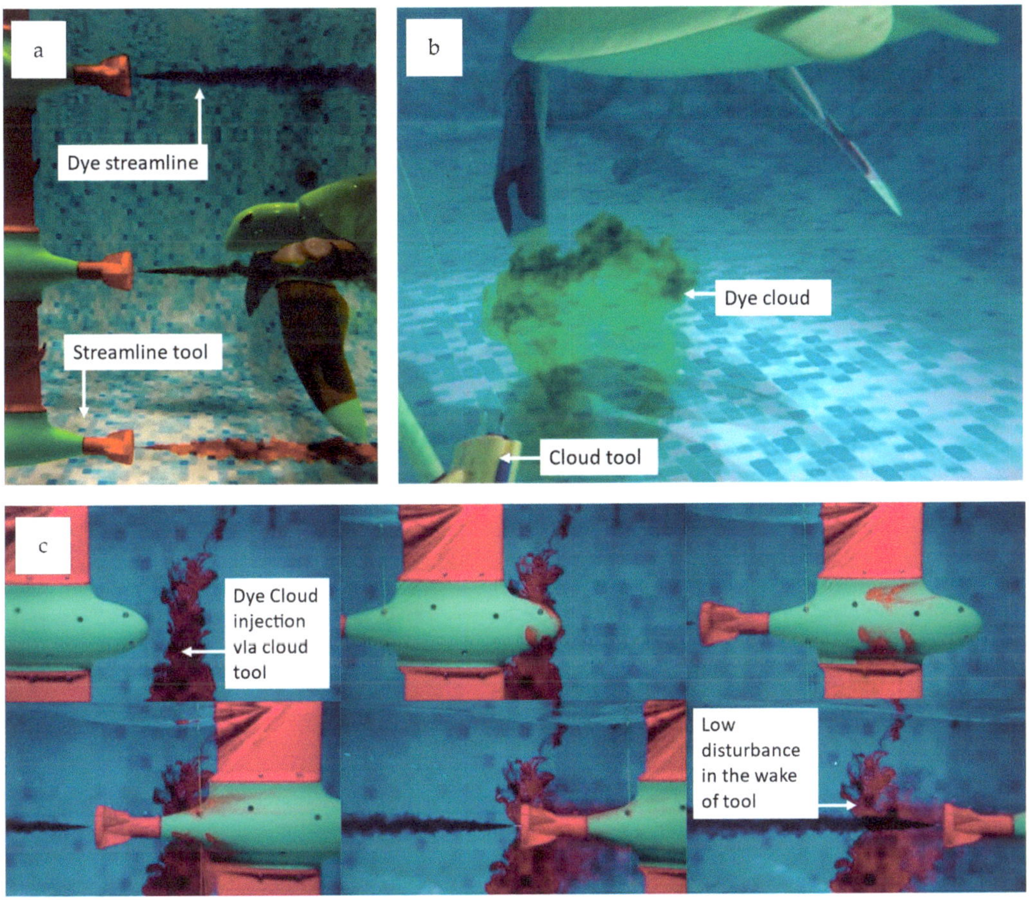

Figure 4. Dye visualisation tools. (**a**) Streamline tool in use. (**b**) Cloud tool in use. (**c**) Streamline tool wake disturbance testing. Also, see Movie S3.

3. Results and Discussion

3.1. Results Overview

As observed in Figure 5, all test results for thrust, lift, AoA, power, swim speed, and flipper tip velocity are detailed for the sea turtles DS and SS, with the corresponding flow features observed at each time interval detailed in Figure 5g. All tests were performed with the flapping frequency remaining constant at 0.23 Hz based on the average flapping observed in wild green sea turtles [6,8,30].

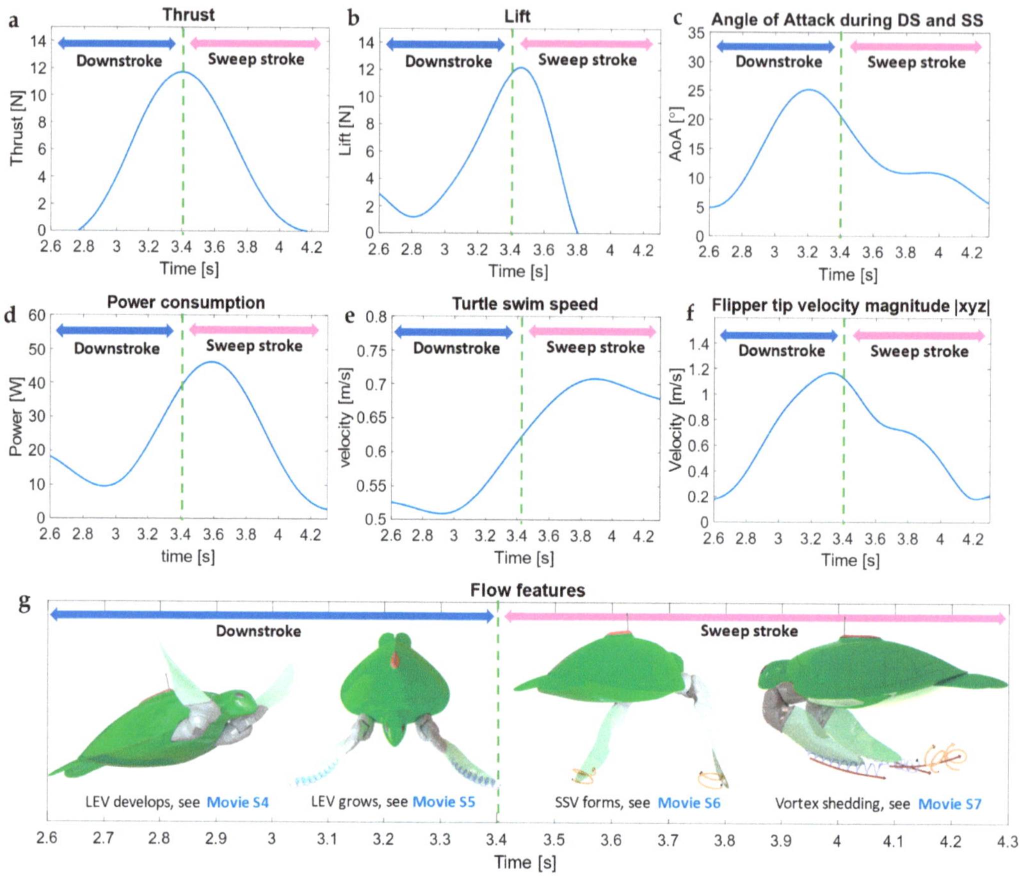

Figure 5. Plots of swimming performance of Cornelia for the Green sea turtle's regular swimming routine. (**a**) Thrust production during the downstroke and the sweep stroke obtained from van der Geest et al. [8]. (**b**) Lift production during the downstroke and the sweep stroke obtained from van der Geest et al. [8]. (**c**) The average Angle of Attack across wingspan. See Figure S3 for exact AOA values across the flipper span. (**d**) Power consumption during the downstroke and the sweep stroke obtained from van der Geest et al. [8]. (**e**) Turtle swim speed during the downstroke and the sweep stroke obtained from van der Geest et al. [8]. (**f**) The flipper tip velocity magnitude during the downstroke and the sweep stroke. (**g**) For the timing of the observed flow features, see Movies S4–S7.

Testing was conducted by applying the sea turtle's regular swimming routine at a Reynolds number of 367,000, defined as

$$Re = \frac{uD_{SCL}}{v}.$$

Re was based on the average swim velocity (u) and straight carapace length (D_{SCL}). As the Reynolds number is established simply on steady, time-independent conditions [31], the Periodic Swimming Number (P) was also considered in this study, defined as

$$P = \frac{10u}{\sqrt{4\pi f v}},$$

where f is the flapping frequency and v is the kinematics viscosity. The Periodic Swimming Number (P) was first introduced by Gurka et al. [31] as an adaptation of the Reynolds number to eliminate the need to choose a characteristic length scale and incorporate the animal's periodic motion. Applying this, we found that the sea turtle swims at a value of 3537. This puts sea turtles approximately in the same range of P as Macaroni and Adelie penguins (3729–3882), along with Harp and Ringed seals (3330–3569) [31]. Additionally, the Strouhal number (St) was calculated to be 0.24 and defined as

$$St = \frac{D_{pp}f}{u},$$

where D_{pp} is the sea turtle's flipper tip peak-to-peak distance during its regular swimming routine. This value of the Strouhal number puts sea turtles into a range of 0.2 to 0.4, as found in other swimming and flying animals tuned for high power efficiency [32–34].

3.2. Flipper Angle of Attack (AoA)

To help understand the flow feature contribution based on the relative flow around the turtle flippers during the downstroke and the sweep stroke, the AoA of the turtle's flipper was defined as

$$\theta_{AoA} = \theta_p \pm \theta_f,$$

where θ_p is the spanwise twisting of the turtle's flipper given as a linear piecewise function with respect to time as

$$\theta_p = \begin{cases} a_{p1}t, & 0 \le t < t_1 \\ a_{p2}, & t_1 \le t < t_2 \\ a_{p3}t + b_{p3}, & t_2 \le t < t_3 \\ a_{p4}t + b_{p4}, & t_3 \le t < t_4 \\ a_{p5}, & t_4 \le t < t_5 \\ a_{p6}t + b_{p6}, & t_5 \le t < t_6 \end{cases},$$

where a_{pn} and b_{pn} are the function constants. The relative flow direction θ_f on the turtle's flipper was added or subtracted depending on the stage of motion that the flipper was in (upstroke or downstroke). This was done to provide a positive AoA for the relative flow acting on the ventral side of the flipper and a negative AoA when acting at the dorsal side (Figure S2). θ_f was calculated with

$$\theta_f = arctan\left(\frac{\sqrt{\dot{y} + \dot{z}}}{V_s + \dot{x}}\right),$$

where V_s represents the swimming speed of the turtle, while $\dot{x}$, $\dot{y}$ and $\dot{z}$ signify the velocity components at any given point on the turtle's flipper. These velocity components are obtained by taking the time derivative of the flipper position function, which was formulated using a Fourier series with

$$\dot{x} = V_f\left(\sum_{i=1}^{n} -iw_x a_{ix} sin(iw_x t) + iw_x b_{ix} cos(iw_x t)\right),$$

$$\dot{y} = V_f\left(\sum_{i=1}^{n} -iw_y a_{iy} sin(iw_y t) + iw_y b_{iy} cos(iw_y t)\right),$$

$$\dot{z} = V_f\left(\sum_{i=1}^{n} -iw_z a_{iz} sin(iw_z t) + iw_z b_{iz} cos(iw_z t)\right),$$

where n is set to eight terms, a_i and b_i are the Fourier coefficients and w is the fundamental frequency. The velocity modifier (V_f) to correct the velocity for any point along the span of the turtle's flipper was represented with $V_f = \frac{x_s}{s}$, x_s representing any point along the flipper span (s). As the twisting of the flipper is a linear relationship [10], the exact amount of wing twist at any point along the flipper span (s) was caluculated with $\theta(x) = \frac{\theta_p x_s}{s}$. Shown in Figure 5c, the average AOA is plotted by calculating each value at various points along the flipper span.

3.3. Downstroke

During the initial stages of the DS, there was no reliable evidence of any substantial vortex formation on the turtle's flippers with relatively smooth flow conditions during this phase in time. This is predominately due to the low AoA during the early DS and low flipper tip velocity, resulting in low thrust, lift and power consumption. At an approximately 2.8 s mark, clear evidence of a LEV forming along the turtle's wing can be seen along with substantial spanwise flow from the wing root to the wing tip (Figure 6 and Movie S4). As the downstroke progresses, the wing tip velocity increases to reach a maximum at the end of the downstroke, where the LEV is at its most forceful stage, with thrust and lift reaching their maximum values (Movie S5). This finding differs from past research hypotheses that depict the large force production at the end of the sea turtle downstroke as being drag-based due to high AoA [9]. Additionally, in Figure 5c,f, the wing AoA begins to bleed off before the flipper reaches its maximum velocity and force production, revealing that high force production is more accurately associated with higher wing velocities and more aggressive LEV formation. Additionally, as the LEV delays wing stall [15,18,35] by forcing the flow to reattach to the low-pressure/dorsal side (Figure 6a–d and Movie S4), this suggests the entire downstroke is completely lift-based propulsion during the sea turtle's regular swimming routine.

3.4. Sweep Stroke

The sweep stroke begins at approximately 3.4 to 3.5 s into the turtle flapping routine, with the LEV remaining attached during the sweep strokes duration. During the entire sweep stroke, the AoA, flipper velocity, power consumption, thrust and lift begin to lower, with the turtle reaching a maximum swim speed approximately 50% into the sweep stroke stage. At a roughly 3.6 to 3.7 s mark, a vortex forms that is almost immediately shed into the turtle's wake (Figure 5g and Movie S6). We name this vortex the sweep stroke vortex (SSV), and in contrast to the LEV, the SSV rotates in the opposite direction and is produced by the wing's ventral side (high-pressure side).

Near the end of the sweep stroke, the flippers are brought parallel beneath the carapace to create a clapping motion similar to the sea lion [19,20]. At this point, the LEV is shed from the wing's dorsal side into the wake to follow behind the SSV (Figure 5g and Movie S7). Just before the LEV is shed into the wake, it entrains fluid momentum on the dorsal side of the flipper (Movie S7), similar to the sea lion [19]. In sea lions, this helps contribute to downstream momentum when the vortex structure is shed to add additional thrust [19]. Based on our observed flow features, this downstream momentum can also be assumed to happen with sea turtles, additionally, as the thrust curve towards the end of the stroke bleeds off rather than simply dropping off like the lift forces (Figure 5a,b). At this point, the sea turtle enters a glide that lasts for 70% of the overall limb beat cycle [8,10]. During the glide, the sea turtle shapes its flippers to generate a passive upstroke to recover its flippers into a position ready for the downstroke to help with energy expenditure [8,10].

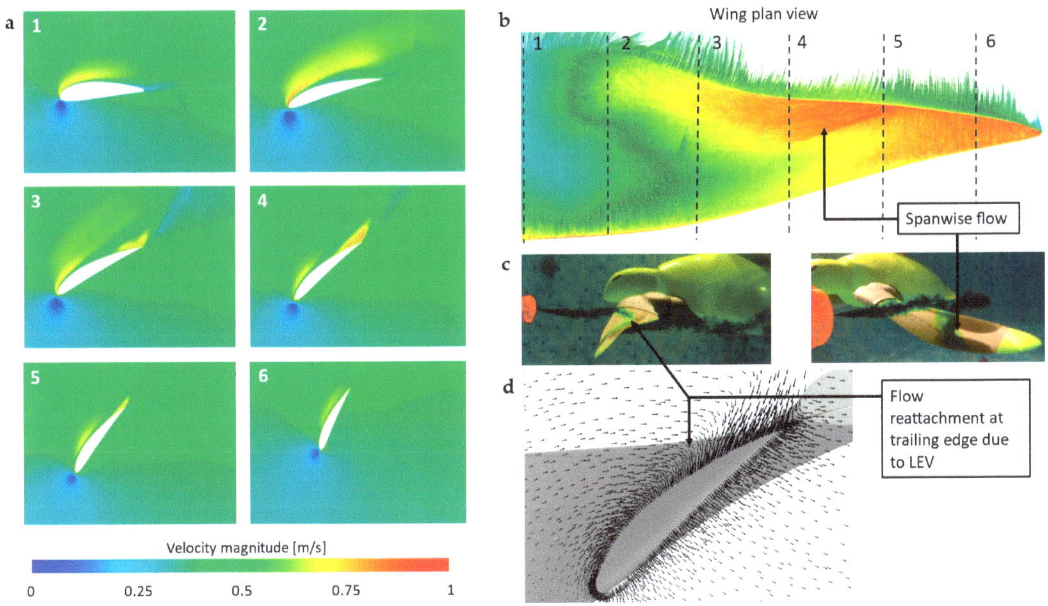

Figure 6. Downstroke flow features. (**a**) Velocity plots from various cross-sections along the turtle's wingspan from CFD. The numbers 1–6 in the top left of each cross-section correlate to the dashed lines shown in Figure 6b. (**b**) Plan view of the turtle wing showing cross-section locations and velocity streamlines obtained from CFD. (**c**) Dye visualisation testing shows flow reattachment towards the wing trailing edge and the spanwise flow demonstrated by dye being transported towards the wing tip. (**d**) Vector plot from CFD showing flow reattachment.

3.5. Rear Flippers

During the turtle's regular swimming routine, van der Geest et al. [6] documented that the rear flippers are seen to tuck in behind the carapace with the flipper tips pointing backwards and near motionless as per Figure 7. Our CFD and field test results show that towards the rear of the carapace, the flow detaches from shell to create a low energy zone directly where the rear flippers are positioned (Figure 7c,d and Movie S8). This volume of low energy flow helps lower the form and friction drag on the turtle's rear flippers, thus improving the animal's drag coefficient for the gliding stage. This also helps explain why the flippers remain almost motionless, as any changes to the flipper's position within this low energy zone may not generate any significant directional control for the turtle.

3.6. Turtle Swimming Efficiency and Cost of Transport

As observed in Figure 8, the power consumption, thrust production and swim speed data are plotted from the experimental swimming tests for the complete swimming cycle. Additionally, a curve of input power (Figure 8a) divided by output thrust (Figure 8b) is displayed for the down- and the sweep strokes in Figure 8e with the cost of transport (COT) for the complete swimming cycle detailed in Table 1 and plotted against time in Figure 8d. The cost of transport was calculated with

$$COT = \frac{P_{in}}{mgu},$$

where P_{in} is the input power (Figure 8a), m is the mass of Cornelia, g is the acceleration due to gravity and u is the swimming velocity (Figure 8c). During the regular swimming routine, Cornelia produced an average COT for the entire swimming cycle of only 0.072

to generate one of the lowest *COT* values in literature for a swimming robot (Table 1). This is largely due to the propulsion strategy, where the sea turtle produces propulsion for approximately 30% of the limb beat cycle, with the remaining 70% producing a power-saving glide that does not reduce swimming velocity substantially due to the animal's large mass and low drag coefficient [8]. This points to the effectiveness of this swimming strategy and helps explain the ability of sea turtles to swim such vast distances with minimal energy intake.

Cornelia demonstrated that the most energy-efficient point during the propulsion stage was at the 3.1 s mark, generating a power-to-thrust ratio of approximately 2 W/N or 7 N of thrust for 14 W electrical input power (Figure 8e). At this point, the AoA was almost at its maximum value, and the sea turtle had already begun accelerating its velocity from its power-saving glide. Additionally, the LEV continued to grow, with the lift forces producing approximately 5 N of upward force.

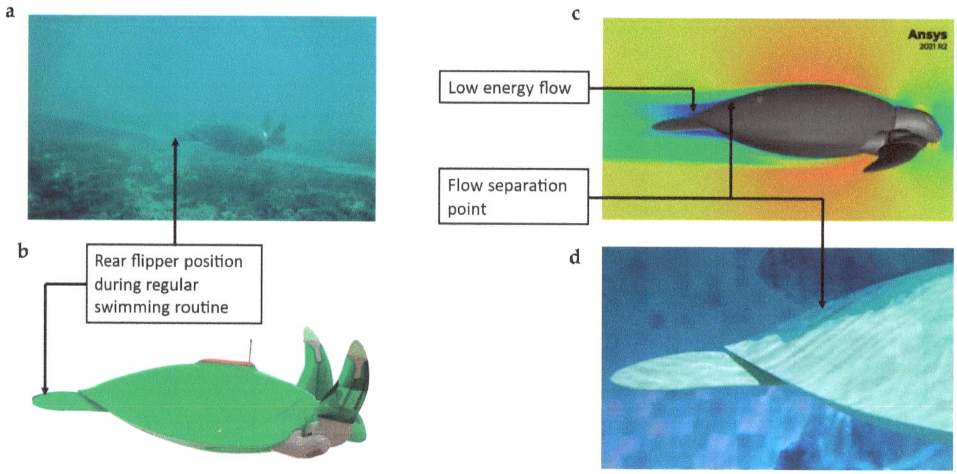

Figure 7. Flow over the sea turtle's rear flippers during its regular swimming routine. (**a**) A wild sea turtle producing the 5-stage locomotion cycle, demonstrating the rear flipper position. (**b**) Cornelia replicates the wild sea turtle in (**a**). (**c**) CFD results showing a velocity contour of the flow around the rear the flippers. (**d**) Dye visualisation tests showing flow separation point. Also see Movie S8.

Table 1. Cost of transport of recent state-of-the-art swimming robots from the literature.

COT in Recent State-of-the-Art Swimming Robot	*COT*	Data Obtained From
Cornelia	0.072	Results from this current study
ART	3	Baines et al. [24]
Eel inspired robot	10.72	Nguyen et al. [21]
Flexible swimming robot	2.5	Kwak et al. [22]
FINBOT	8.2	Berlinger et al. [23]
Squid-inspired robot	0.087	Bujard et al. [25]
Flexible robotic fish	0.293	Lu et al. [26]
Tunabot	2.83	Zhu et al. [27]
Tunabot flex	1.876	White et al. [28]
HASEL jellyfish	1.619	Wang et al. [29]

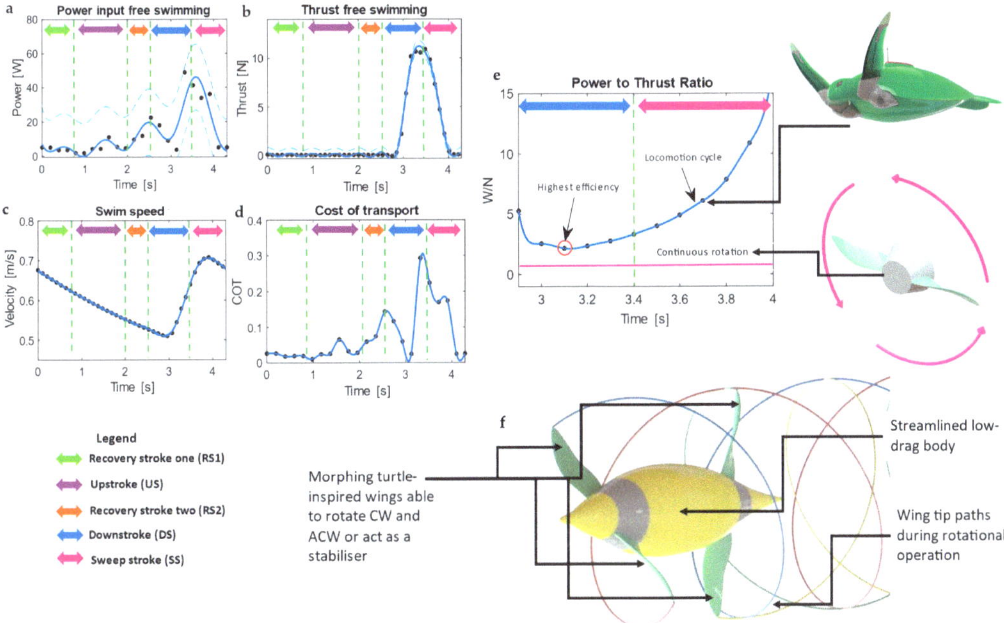

Figure 8. Turtle swimming efficiency. (**a**) Power input data for the complete swimming cycle obtained from van der Geest et al. [8]. (**b**) Thrust production for the complete swimming cycle obtained from van der Geest et al. [8]. (**c**) Turtle swim speed for complete swim cycle obtained from van der Geest et al. [8]. (**d**) Cost of transport plotted against time. (**e**) The power-to-thrust ratio plotted for the downstroke and the sweep stroke compared to the power-to-thrust ratio of a continuous rotating turtle wing. (**f**) Turtle-inspired propulsion applied to a low-drag drag streamlined body. Diagram illustrating a tandem configuration with both sets of wings/flippers generating propulsion (also see Movie S9).

Overall, we found the downstroke was more efficient than the sweep stroke; however, this could be due to the sweep stroke requiring all six servo motors to run simultaneously, contrary to the downstroke, which only required two servo motors to run heavily. Additionally, the motors used in Cornelia's robotic limbs are hobby-grade servo motors that we believe may have low mechanical efficiency.

Though the *COT* obtained is impressive, employing a flapping winged machine in a commercial drone or device for ocean exploration is far from practical, and the multi-degree of freedom wings produce complex maintenance procedures coupled with highly complex manufacturing. For the findings produced here to be valuable, practicable and obtainable for industry-level technology, we combined the essential variables consisting of wing twist, wingtip velocity and wing shape to generate a CFD simulation of a continuously rotating turtle wing to continuously harness the most efficient section of the turtle locomotive cycle, as previously mentioned at the 3.1 s mark. Our results demonstrated that it was possible to achieve a maximum sustained power-to-thrust ratio of 0.5 W/N or 8 N of thrust for 4 W mechanical input power (Figure 8e).

When comparing the thrust values of the continuously rotating turtle wing against the sea turtle locomotive cycle, it can be observed that the thrust values are comparable with the CFD results producing 8 N and Cornelia producing 7 N during the standard sea turtle locomotive cycle. However, there are variations when comparing the power values, as the CFD results do not include the overall electrical efficiency of the servo motors and electronics. Therefore, the significant difference in power consumption likely originates from two main factors: first, the efficiency of the electro-mechanical system, and second, as the turtle's flipper is accelerating at this point, it creates additional power consumption when compared to the constant velocity rotating model.

The continuously rotating turtle wing model could offer significant potential for enhancing propulsion technologies, especially in multi-functional applications. Beyond the clear energy-saving merits, incorporating a morphing rotating propulsor reveals an array of advantages for aquatic navigation and energy harvesting. Illustrated in Figure 8f and further elucidated in Movie S9, applying a set of morphing sea turtle-inspired propulsors in a tandem orientation attached to a low-drag streamlined fuselage could facilitate a multi-purpose underwater drone. While one set of wings concentrates on propulsion, the other functions as a stabiliser. This configuration promotes consistent and controlled motion, bolstering the vessel's stability—a crucial attribute for peak performance across diverse aquatic conditions.

Furthermore, as the wings morph, they can transition into a counter-rotating setup. Such an arrangement is paramount for neutralising the rotational forces exerted on the vessel's fuselage due to the torque from a singular propellor set. This ensures that the vessel's trajectory remains unaffected by undesired rotations. Additionally, the concept of torque vectoring can be explored; by dynamically adjusting the Angle Of Attack (AOA) of each wing or flipper at precise moments, the vessel may achieve unparalleled underwater agility.

Taking cues from the biomechanics of sea turtles, the device has the potential to function as a sea glider. In certain conditions, energy can be harnessed by back-spinning the propellors. This mechanism is reminiscent of how sea turtles leverage their upstroke to optimise energy use. Thus, this could evolve beyond its foundational propulsion capabilities to also serve as a renewable energy harvester, seamlessly integrating navigation proficiency with sustainable energy solutions.

4. Conclusions and Future Work

In conclusion, this study examines the sea turtle's propulsive cycle considering the downstroke and the sweep stroke during the animal's regular swimming routine. The findings reveal a critical characteristic that may account for their highly efficient swimming performance, including their capacity to generate considerable thrust and lift forces during the downstroke phase, with a continuous LEV formation during both downstroke and sweep stroke, until it is shed into the wake at the end of the sweep stroke to hypothetically contribute towards downstream momentum similarly to sea lions [19].

Additionally, the study highlights that the Green sea turtle robot, Cornelia, produces one of the lowest Cost of Transport (*COT*) values in the literature for a swimming robot, indicating the effectiveness of the sea turtle swimming strategy for long-distance swimming with minimal energy intake. This underscores the potential for the incorporation of these principles into the design and operation of marine robots and other aquatic devices. Their low *COT* values are likely due to their efficient energy usage through a combination of active propulsion and passive gliding stages. This, coupled with the rear flippers' tucking motion into a zone of low energy flow, can reduce the form and friction drag the turtle experiences, thus improving its drag coefficient for the gliding stage.

Despite the energy-efficient flapping cycle exhibited by sea turtles, applying these findings to commercial drones or ocean exploration devices remains a challenge due to the complexity of their locomotion. Yet, by capturing the most efficient section of the turtle's locomotion cycle and simulating a continuously rotating turtle wing, our study offers promising avenues for developing industry-level technology.

Though this work brings new insight into the flow features during the sea turtle's propulsive cycle, it is difficult to pinpoint the exact effect of each flow feature and how these features interact with each other to generate the animal's propulsion. A deeper understanding of this can be achieved in future work with the utilisation of a high-level PIV system. Additionally, as these findings are for regular straight-line swimming, our robot Cornelia can be programmed to study the ways in which the animal creates its manoeuvring techniques by building in the required control systems.

In summary, this research provides novel insights into the flow features and *COT* of sea turtle locomotion and offers valuable guidance for the future development of efficient aquatic propulsion systems.

Supplementary Materials: The following supporting information can be downloaded at: https://www.mdpi.com/article/10.3390/jmse11101944/s1, Supplementary Figures S1 to S3; Supplementary Movies S1 to S9.

Author Contributions: Conceptualisation: N.v.d.G., L.G., R.N. and F.B.; Methodology: N.v.d.G., L.G. and R.N.; Investigation: N.v.d.G., L.G., R.N. and F.B.; Visualisation: N.v.d.G., L.G. and R.N.; Funding acquisition: L.G.; Project administration: L.G. and R.N.; Supervision: L.G. and R.N.; Writing—original draft: N.v.d.G., L.G., R.N. and F.B.; Writing—review and editing: N.v.d.G., L.G., R.N. and F.B. All authors have read and agreed to the published version of the manuscript.

Funding: This work was partially funded by the Science for Technological Innovation project, AUTX2101 Bio-inspired Underwater Robot for Ocean Surveillance and Protection PROP-80135-NSCSEED-AUT, Ministry of Business, Innovation and Employment, New Zealand.

Institutional Review Board Statement: Not applicable.

Informed Consent Statement: Not applicable.

Data Availability Statement: All data sets for the current study are available from the authors on reasonable request via contacting the corresponding authors.

Acknowledgments: To Nick's family, friends and lab colleagues (Gary van der Geest, Bronwyn van der Geest, Lena Straub, Keegan van der Geest, Corry van der Geest, Trystan van der Geest, Anton van der Geest, Hannah Pyles, Mike Noakes, Adam Murly, Bastian Busch, Mike Norris, Harsimran Singh and Ricky Liang) for spending their weekends with the research team to conduct data collection and testing. To MAG Assembly LTD and Grant Burrell for their expert craftsmanship in painting our robotic sea turtle with a newly formulated colour named "Pearlescent Turtle Green".

Conflicts of Interest: The authors declare no conflict of interest.

References

1. Hays, G.C.; Scott, R. Global patterns for upper ceilings on migration distance in sea turtles and comparisons with fish, birds and mammals. *Funct. Ecol.* **2013**, *27*, 748–756. [CrossRef]
2. Eckert, S.A. High-use oceanic areas for Atlantic leatherback sea turtles (*Dermochelys coriacea*) as identified using satellite telemetered location and dive information. *Mar. Biol.* **2006**, *149*, 1257–1267. [CrossRef]
3. Heaslip, S.G.; Iverson, S.J.; Bowen, W.D.; James, M.C. Jellyfish Support High Energy Intake of Leatherback Sea Turtles (*Dermochelys coriacea*): Video Evidence from Animal-Borne Cameras. *PLoS ONE* **2012**, *7*, e33259. [CrossRef]
4. Alerstam, T.; Hedenström, A.; Åkesson, S. Long-distance migration: Evolution and determinants. *Oikos* **2003**, *103*, 247–260. [CrossRef]
5. Luschi, P.; Hays, G.C.; Del Seppia, C.; Marsh, R.; Papi, F. The navigational feats of green sea turtles migrating from Ascension Island investigated by satellite telemetry. *Proc. R. Soc. Lond. Ser. B Biol. Sci.* **1998**, *265*, 2279–2284. [CrossRef]
6. van der Geest, N.; Garcia, L.; Nates, R.; Godoy, D.A. New insight into the swimming kinematics of wild Green sea turtles (*Chelonia mydas*). *Sci. Rep.* **2022**, *12*, 18151. [CrossRef]
7. Davenport, J.; Munks, S.A.; Oxford, P.J. A Comparison of the swimming of Marine and Freshwater Turtles. *R. Soc. London. Ser. B Biol. Sci.* **1984**, *220*, 447–475. [CrossRef]
8. van der Geest, N.; Garcia, L.; Borret, F.; Nates, R.; Gonzalez, A. Soft-robotic green sea turtle (*Chelonia mydas*) developed to replace animal experimentation provides new insight into their propulsive strategies. *Sci. Rep.* **2023**, *13*, 11983. [CrossRef]
9. Booth, D.T. Kinematics of swimming and thrust production during powerstroking bouts of the swim frenzy in green turtle hatchlings. *Biol. Open* **2014**, *3*, 887–894. [CrossRef]
10. van der Geest, N.; Garcia, L.; Nates, R.; Gonzalez-Vazquez, A. Sea Turtles Employ Drag-Reducing Techniques to Conserve Energy. *J. Mar. Sci. Eng.* **2022**, *10*, 1770. [CrossRef]
11. Izraelevitz, J.S.; Triantafyllou, M.S. Adding in-line motion and model-based optimisation offers exceptional force control authority in flapping foils. *J. Fluid Mech.* **2014**, *742*, 5–34. [CrossRef]
12. Licht, S.C.; Wibawa, M.S.; Hover, F.S.; Triantafyllou, M.S. In-line motion causes high thrust and efficiency in flapping foils that use power downstroke. *J. Exp. Biol.* **2010**, *213*, 63–71. [CrossRef] [PubMed]
13. Jardin, T. Coriolis effect and the attachment of the leading edge vortex. *J. Fluid Mech.* **2017**, *820*, 312–340. [CrossRef]

14. Johansson, L.C.; Engel, S.; Kelber, A.; Heerenbrink, M.K.; Hedenstrom, A. Multiple leading edge vortices of unexpected strength in freely flying hawkmoth. *Sci. Rep.* **2013**, *3*, 3264. [CrossRef]
15. Nabawy, M.R.A.; Crowther, W.J. The role of the leading edge vortex in lift augmentation of steadily revolving wings: A change in perspective. *J. R. Soc. Interface* **2017**, *14*, 20170159. [CrossRef]
16. Birch, J.M.; Dickinson, M.H. Spanwise flow and the attachment of the leading-edge vortex on insect wings. *Nature* **2001**, *412*, 729–733. [CrossRef]
17. Menzer, A.; Gong, Y.; Fish, F.E.; Dong, H. Bio-Inspired Propulsion: Towards Understanding the Role of Pectoral Fin Kinematics in Manta-like Swimming. *Biomimetics* **2022**, *7*, 45. [CrossRef]
18. Videler, J.J.; Stamhuis, E.J.; Povel, G.D.E. Leading-Edge Vortex Lifts Swifts. *Science* **2004**, *306*, 1960–1962. [CrossRef]
19. Kashi, E.; Kulkarni, A.A.; Perrotta, G.; Leftwich, M.C. Flowfields produced by a robotic sea lion foreflipper starting from rest. *Bioinspir. Biomim.* **2020**, *15*, 035002. [CrossRef]
20. Liu, Y.; Li, H.; Deng, S.; Wang, S.; Liu, S.; Wang, Z. Biomimetic Robotic Sea Lion Foreflippers: Design, Modeling, and Experimentation. *IEEE ASME Trans. Mechatron.* **2022**, *27*, 5679–5689. [CrossRef]
21. Nguyen, D.Q.; Ho, V.A. Anguilliform Swimming Performance of an Eel-Inspired Soft Robot. *Soft Robot.* **2022**, *9*, 425–439. [CrossRef] [PubMed]
22. Kwak, B.; Choi, S.; Bae, J. Development of a Stiffness-Adjustable Articulated Paddle and its Application to a Swimming Robot. *Adv. Intell. Syst.* **2023**, *5*, 2200348. [CrossRef]
23. Berlinger, F.; Saadat, M.; Haj-Hariri, H.; Lauder, G.V.; Nagpal, R. Fish-like three-dimensional swimming with an autonomous, multi-fin, and biomimetic robot. *Bioinspir. Biomim.* **2021**, *16*, 026018. [CrossRef] [PubMed]
24. Baines, R.; Patiballa, S.K.; Booth, J.; Ramirez, L.; Sipple, T.; Garcia, A.; Fish, F.; Kramer-Bottiglio, R. Multi-environment robotic transitions through adaptive morphogenesis. *Nature* **2022**, *610*, 283–289. [CrossRef] [PubMed]
25. Bujard, T.; Giorgio-Serchi, F.; Weymouth, G.D. A resonant squid-inspired robot unlocks biological propulsive efficiency. *Sci. Robot.* **2021**, *6*, eabd2971. [CrossRef]
26. Lu, B.; Zhou, C.; Wang, J.; Zhang, Z.; Tan, M. Toward Swimming Speed Optimization of a Multi-Flexible Robotic Fish With Low Cost of Transport. *IEEE Trans. Autom. Sci. Eng.* **2023**, *20*, 1–12. [CrossRef]
27. Zhu, J.; White, C.; Wainwright, D.K.; Di Santo, V.; Lauder, G.V.; Bart-Smith, H. Tuna robotics: A high-frequency experimental platform exploring the performance space of swimming fishes. *Sci. Robot.* **2019**, *4*, eaax4615. [CrossRef]
28. White, C.H.; Lauder, G.V.; Bart-Smith, H. Tunabot Flex: A tuna-inspired robot with body flexibility improves high-performance swimming. *Bioinspir. Biomim.* **2021**, *16*, 026019. [CrossRef]
29. Wang, T.; Joo, H.J.; Song, S.; Hu, W.; Keplinger, C.; Sitti, M. A versatile jellyfish-like robotic platform for effective underwater propulsion and manipulation. *Sci. Adv.* **2023**, *9*, eadg0292. [CrossRef]
30. Yasuda, T.; Arai, N. Changes in flipper beat frequency, body angle and swimming speed of female green turtles *Chelonia mydas*. *Mar. Ecol. Prog. Ser.* **2009**, *386*, 275–286. [CrossRef]
31. Gurka, R.; Nafi, A.S.; Weihs, D. On an adaptation of the Reynolds number, applicable to body-caudal-fin aquatic locomotion. *Front. Mar. Sci.* **2022**, *9*, 914214. [CrossRef]
32. Taylor, G.K.; Nudds, R.L.; Thomas, A.L.R. Flying and swimming animals cruise at a Strouhal number tuned for high power efficiency. *Nature* **2003**, *425*, 707–711. [CrossRef] [PubMed]
33. Eloy, C. Optimal Strouhal number for swimming animals. *J. Fluids Struct.* **2012**, *30*, 205–218. [CrossRef]
34. Triantafyllou, G.S.; Triantafyllou, M.S.; Grosenbaugh, M.A. Optimal Thrust Development in Oscillating Foils with Application to Fish Propulsion. *J. Fluids Struct.* **1993**, *7*, 205–224. [CrossRef]
35. Carr, L.W.; Chandrasekhara, M.S. Compressibility effects on dynamic stall. *Prog. Aerosp. Sci.* **1996**, *32*, 523–573. [CrossRef]

Journal of
Marine Science and Engineering

MDPI

Article

Underwater Object Detection in Marine Ranching Based on Improved YOLOv8

Rong Jia, Bin Lv *, Jie Chen, Hailin Liu, Lin Cao and Min Liu

Institute of Oceanographic Instrumentation, Qilu University of Technology (Shandong Academy of Sciences), Qingdao 266000, China
* Correspondence: lvbin@qlu.edu.cn

Abstract: The aquaculture of marine ranching is of great significance for scientific aquaculture and the practice of statistically grasping existing information on the types of living marine resources and their density. However, underwater environments are complex, and there are many small and overlapping targets for marine organisms, which seriously affects the performance of detectors. To overcome these issues, we attempted to improve the YOLOv8 detector. The InceptionNeXt block was used in the backbone to enhance the feature extraction capabilities of the network. Subsequently, a separate and enhanced attention module (SEAM) was added to the neck to enhance the detection of overlapping targets. Moreover, the normalized Wasserstein distance (NWD) loss was proportionally added to the original CIoU loss to improve the detection of small targets. Data augmentation methods were used to improve the dataset during training to enhance the robustness of the network. The experimental results showed that the improved YOLOv8 achieved the mAP of 84.5%, which was an improvement over the original YOLOv8 of approximately 6.2%. Meanwhile, there were no significant increases in the numbers of parameters and computations. This detector can be applied on platforms for seafloor observation experiments in the field of marine ranching to complete the task of real-time detection of marine organisms.

Keywords: underwater vision; seafloor observation; object detection; deep learning; YOLO

Citation: Jia, R.; Lv, B.; Chen, J.; Liu, H.; Cao, L.; Liu, M. Underwater Object Detection in Marine Ranching Based on Improved YOLOv8. *J. Mar. Sci. Eng.* **2024**, *12*, 55. https://doi.org/10.3390/jmse12010055

Academic Editors: Yan-Tsung Peng, Wenqi Ren, Jingchun Zhou and Qiuping Jiang

Received: 27 November 2023
Revised: 20 December 2023
Accepted: 22 December 2023
Published: 25 December 2023

1. Introduction

Oceans are a "blue granary" that provide humans with access to high-end foods and high-quality proteins. Marine ranching, which is a new form of marine economy, allows for the conservation of biological resources and the repair of the ecological environment. This is an important way to realize the recovery of China's offshore fishery resources, the harmonious development of the ecosystem, and the use of the "blue carbon sink". With the increase in the world's population, food, resource, and environmental problems have become prominent. Thus, effective habitat restoration and resource conservation measures must be developed. Meanwhile, the construction of modernized marine ranching systems can effectively restore marine fishery resources and marine ecosystems [1].

The construction of a marine ranching system requires a significant investment. Can the marine ranching systems that are constructed serve as habitats for target organisms? Is the marine life in them healthy? These questions are directly related to the economic benefits of marine ranching and fisheries. Therefore, there is a strong need for monitoring biodiversity in marine ranching. It is of undoubted importance and urgency to realize the continuous online monitoring of the marine environment and biological resources through seafloor observation networks and to provide high-quality data support for the scientific management of marine pastures and the real-time monitoring of animal resources [2].

One of the major tasks in a seafloor observation network is the provision of long-term continuous real-time observation and monitoring of seafloor organisms. Traditional observations, however, rely mainly on staff to make visual observations and record them, which is inefficient and error prone. To improve the efficiency of the observation of organisms associated with marine ranching, the use of computer vision technology for target detection and assistance in the observation of marine organisms has important research value and application prospects.

Underwater images are different from normal land images. The quality of underwater images is significantly degraded due to uncertainties in the water environment, the absorption and scattering of light by water, and the various media contained in water [3]. With the rise and development of artificial intelligence technology, the introduction of deep learning-based target detection and classification techniques has enabled accurate and fast target detection in complex underwater environments.

There are two main categories of current deep learning-based target detection methods, namely, two-stage detection models and one-stage detection models. Among others, the most prominent two-stage models are R-CNN [4], Fast-RCNN [5], and Faster-RCNN [6]. The main features of two-stage models are the initial generation of a region proposal network with specialized modules, followed by movement to the foreground and adjustment of the bounding box. The model structure is more complex, large, and slow, but it has some advantages in detection accuracy. Lin et al. [7] designed the RoIMix data enhancement method based on Faster-RCNN to solve the problem of having more overlapping, occluded, and blurred targets in underwater images. Their experiments showed that this method could significantly improve the detection performance of Faster-RCNN.

The main representative of the one-stage models is YOLO [8–11]. Its main feature is the direct input of images into the detection model and the output of results. The main advantages are its simple structure, small size, and high speed. It is more suitable for underwater target detection in marine ranching. For underwater target detection in the field of one-stage modeling, Han et al. [12] first used a combination of max-RGB and shades of gray methods to enhance underwater images. Then, a deep convolutional neural network method was used for underwater target recognition, and good results were achieved. Chen et al. [13] improved YOLOv4 by replacing the upsampling module with a deconvolution module, adding depth-separable convolution, and finally, augmenting the data with an improved mosaic. Zhao et al. [14] reduced the parameters of the model by replacing the backbone network with MobileNetV3. Deformable convolution was also added to improve detection accuracy. Sun et al. [15] proposed LK-YOLO, which improved the performance of the model by introducing a large kernel convolution into the backbone network, thus improving the detection head, as well as the sample matching strategy. Currently, the application of transformers in computer vision tasks is also a popular research direction. Zhang et al. [16] proposed the YOLO-SWFormer, which introduced the Swin-Transformer into the backbone of the model. This effectively improved the detection accuracy of the model. However, at the same time, the detection speed was slow, and the model structure was relatively bloated.

In recent years, attention mechanisms have become an integral part of target detection tasks. Attention mechanisms stem from the study of human vision and its ability to sift through large amounts of information to find important data. Shen et al. [17] proposed the crisscross global interaction strategy (CGIS) for versions of YOLO detectors in order to minimize the interference of the underwater background with the detected target. Yu et al. [18] proposed YOLOv7-net, which added bi-level routing attention (BRA) and a new coordinated attention module (RFCAConv) to YOLOv7. This improved the detection of broken nets in complex marine environments. Lv et al. [19] improved YOLOv5 by adding ASPP structures and a CBAM module combined with the FOCAL loss function. A small target detection head was also added. Li et al. [20] used the RGHS algorithm to improve the image quality. The performance was then improved by adding a triplet attention mechanism and an additional small target detection header. Li et al. [21] improved YOLOv5 by using a Res2Net residual structure with a coordinate attention mechanism and applied it to fish detection. These target detection models had high recognition accuracy, fast detection speed, good robustness, and high practicality.

Based on the above analysis, to accurately and quickly recognize target marine organisms in complex underwater environments, this study proposes an improved YOLOv8 detector. Firstly, the InceptionNeXt block was used in the backbone network. This improved the feature extraction abilities of the model without increasing its number of parameters. Secondly, the SEAM attention mechanism was added to the neck. This enhanced the detection of overlapping targets by increasing the focus on the region of the detected object in the image and weakening the background region. Finally, NWD loss was added to the original CIoU loss to improve the ability to detect small targets. Data augmentation methods were used to improve the dataset during the training process, thus enhancing the robustness of the network. The main research and innovations of this study can be summarized as follows:

(1) Aiming at the characteristics of underwater image features that are not obvious, the backbone network of YOLOv8 was improved by using the InceptionNeXt block, which enhanced its ability to extract image features while maintaining its lightweight advantage.
(2) For the characteristics of underwater images with more overlapping targets, the SEAM attention mechanism was added to the neck, and experimental comparisons were made with two other classical attention mechanisms, which proved that the SEAM was the most effective.
(3) In view of the characteristics of underwater images containing more small targets, NWD loss was added on the basis of the original CIoU loss, and the most suitable ratio of the two functions was found through experiments, which improved the accuracy of small targets detections without causing a loss of detection accuracy for medium and large targets.
(4) In response to the insufficient number of underwater datasets, data from three parts were used to form the final dataset that was used. The dataset was augmented with a combination of Mosaic and MixUp to create the training set during the training process, which improved the generalization ability of the model and avoided the overfitting of the model.

The remainder of this study is organized as follows: In Section 2, we focus on the main structure of the video monitoring system in the seafloor observation network and on the analysis of the specific improvement strategies for the detection model. Section 3 focuses on a general analysis of the dataset and training strategy, as well as the design of the experiments and a discussion of the results. Section 4 provides final conclusions and directions for future work.

2. Materials and Methods

2.1. Design of the Seafloor Video System

2.1.1. General Structural Design

A seafloor video monitoring system can be regarded as an important observation subsystem of a seafloor observation network. The seafloor observation network system used here was designed with a seafloor observation platform as the core. There was two-way transmission of power and information through optoelectronic composite cables. According to functional divisions, a complete seafloor observation network is mainly composed of a seafloor observation subsystem, a power–information transmission subsystem, and a human–computer interaction and information management subsystem in the control center according [22,23]. The human–machine interaction and information management subsystem in the control center mainly consists of various servers and control hosts. They are mainly responsible for the management of observation equipment and data. The core component of the power–information transmission subsystem is the shore-based control unit. This is responsible for delivering energy and transmitting information to various subsea observation instruments. The seafloor observation subsystem is the core part of the whole seafloor observation network. All observation equipment is deployed on the seafloor observation platform. The general architecture of a typical seafloor observation network is shown in Figure 1.

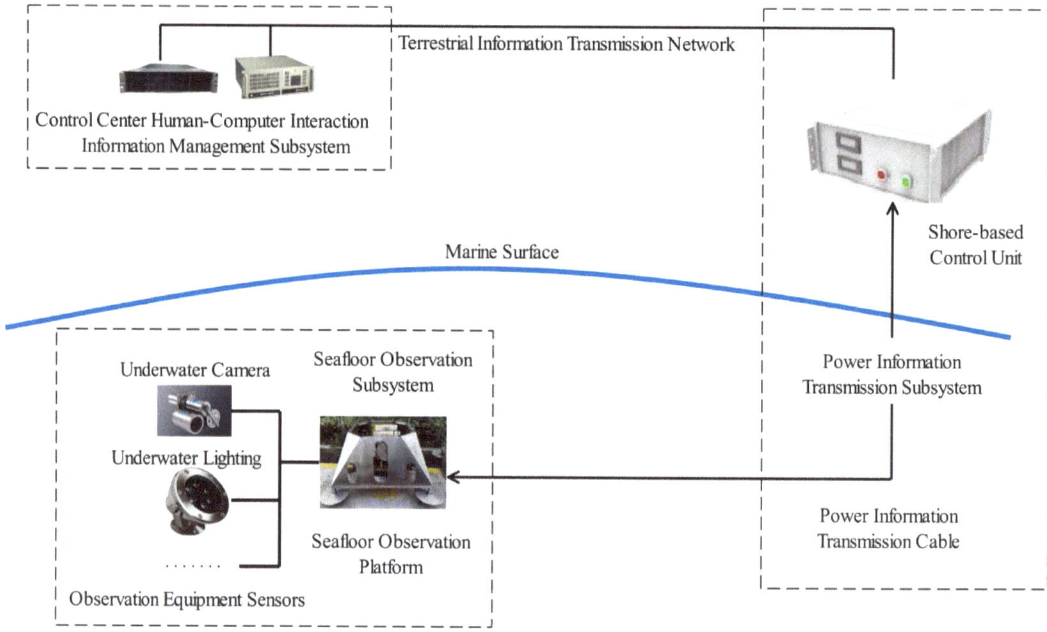

Figure 1. General architecture of a submarine observation network.

2.1.2. Design of the Video Monitoring System

Video monitoring systems for marine ranching can be divided into four main parts: the sensing layer, acquisition layer, application layer, and service layer. The sensing layer is mainly composed of various types of surveillance cameras and lighting equipment, and it is responsible for sensing dynamic information on the marine environment. The acquisition layer collects real-time ocean observation data in the field and forwards the information between the service layer and the sensing layer. The service layer manages various types of information and provides a set of operations related to remote control. The application layer is a layer for scenarios with various user requirements, and it uses different information to meet the project's requirements. The layers are relatively functionally independent from each other, and the interface among them is of a standard form. Each layer uses the services of the adjacent underlying layer and provides services to its adjacent upper layers [24]. A diagram of the video surveillance system's architecture is shown in Figure 2.

The workflow of the entire video monitoring system for marine ranching started with an underwater camera integrated with underwater lighting and a cloud terrace to obtain video and image information of the seafloor for the acquisition of original data, followed by the processing of the image data on the network video server for efficient image compression and coding of the image data. Next, the photoelectric composite cable and TCP/IP video data transmission protocol of the seafloor observation network were used in real time, and the video-image data were transmitted to the upper computer server. Finally, the received video data were decoded and stored to achieve real-time video monitoring of the deep seafloor [25].

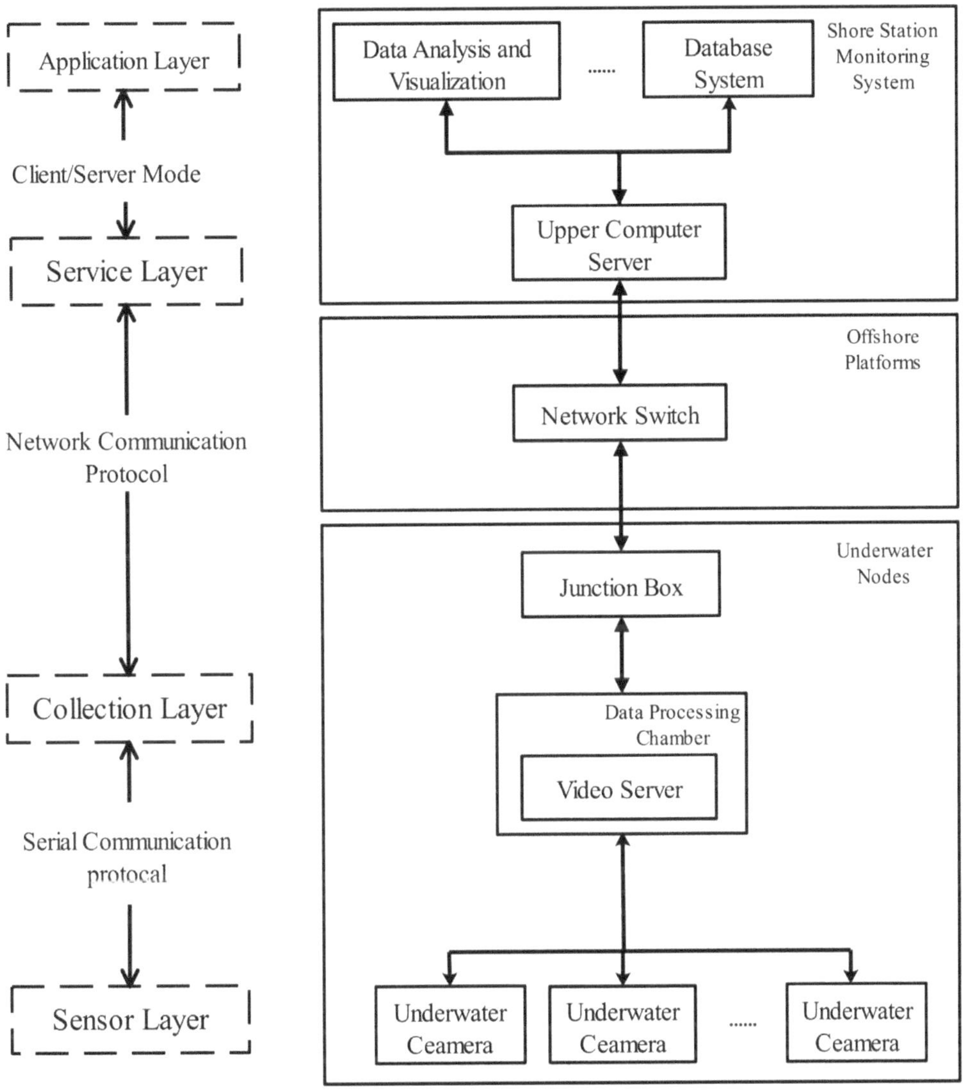

Figure 2. Video monitoring system architecture diagram.

2.2. Structure of the Detector

The target detector used in this study was mainly based on YOLOv8. YOLOv8 is the latest version of YOLO. It was refactored on the basis of YOLOv5, and many small strategies for improving the performance of the whole network were added. The authors provided a total of five detectors. In this study, we used the smallest of these: YOLOv8n. We attempted to improved it on the basis of the original detector with respect to the problem of there being more small targets and serious target obscuration when observing marine life. The whole model can be divided into the backbone, neck, and YOLO head. The structure of the whole model is shown in Figure 3.

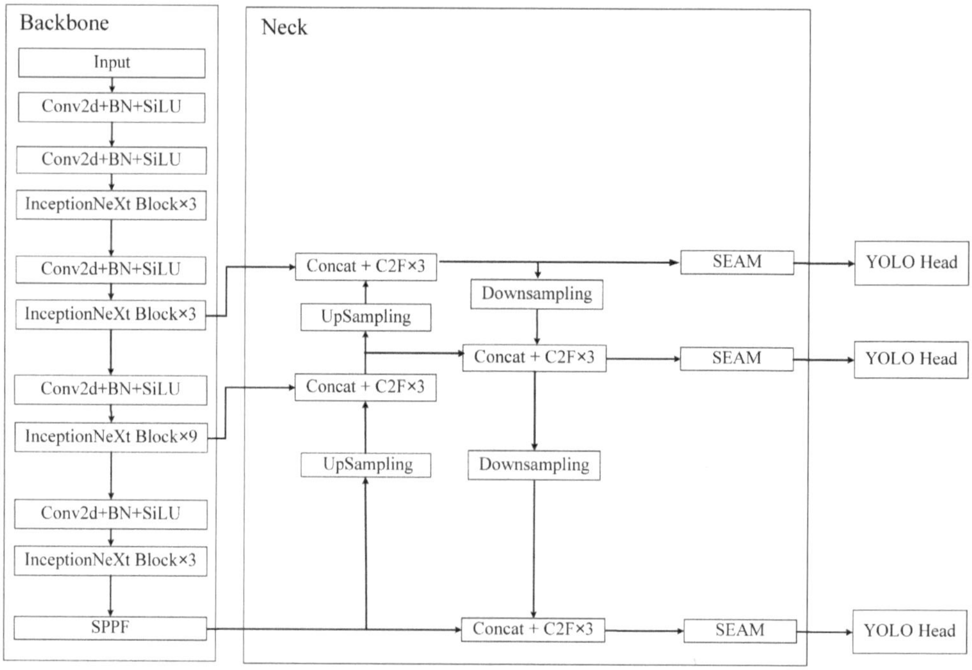

Figure 3. Improved YOLOv8 network structure diagram.

2.2.1. Backbone

The pre-processed images were fed into the backbone for feature extraction. A major improvement point in the whole feature extraction network was the introduction of the InceptionNeXt block [26] to replace the original C2F block [27], thus enhancing the extraction of the input image features. The InceptionNeXt block is mainly based on ConvNeXt [28] and the idea of Inception [29–33]. The depthwise convolution of the large kernel convolutions in ConvNeXt was decomposed into four parallel branches according to the channel dimension. One-third of the channels were kerned at 3×3, one-third of the channels were kerned at 1×11, and the remaining third of the channels were kerned at 11×1; finally, a constant mapping was added. This decomposition not only reduced the number of parameters and the computational effort, but it also retained the advantages of large kernel depthwise convolution, i.e., it expanded the field of perception and improved the model performance.

After that, the image features were extracted by the MLP block. The main difference from the previous version was the replacement of the original two layers of the fully connected network with two 1×1 convolution layers. Finally, the present structure decomposed large convolutional kernels in a simple and quick manner while maintaining comparable performance, achieving a better balance among accuracy, speed, and the number of parameters. The main structure of the InceptionNeXt block is shown in Figure 4.

2.2.2. Neck

The PANet [34] structure is most commonly used in the neck part of YOLOv8. Iterative extraction occurs, and the output contains features from three dimensions. The problem of occlusion is greater when considering marine organisms, and occlusion between different organisms can lead to misalignment, local blending, and missing features. To address these issues, the separated and enhancement attention module (SEAM) [35] was added to emphasize the object detection region in the image and weaken the background region, thus enhancing the detection of marine organisms in the presence of occlusion. The SEAM was first used for the detection of occluded faces, and a diagram of its structure is shown in Figure 5.

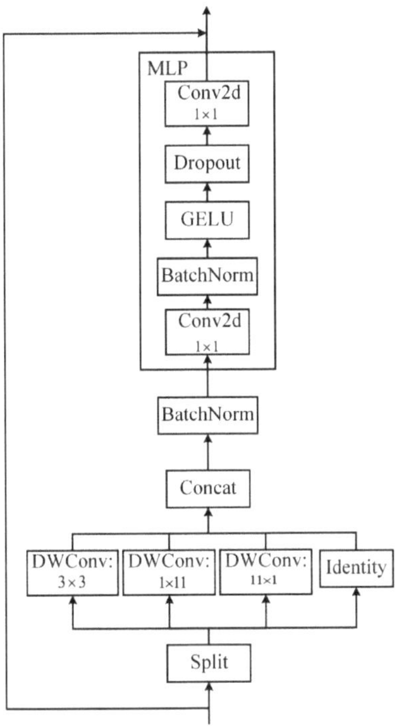

Figure 4. InceptionNeXt block structure diagram.

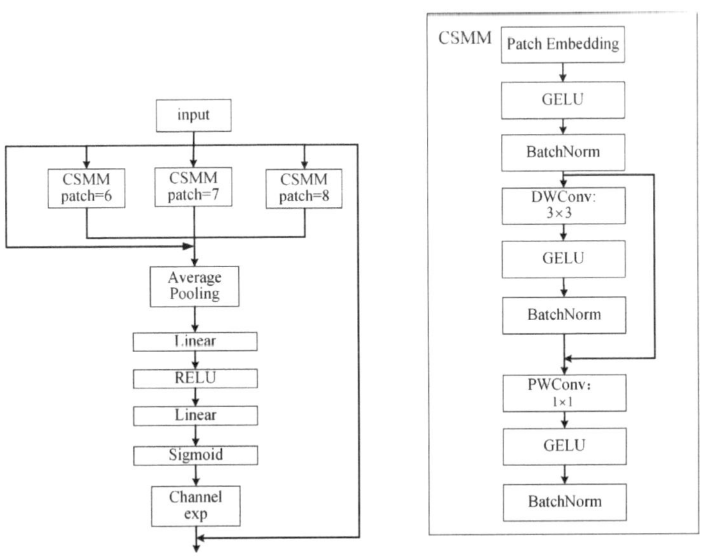

Figure 5. Illustration of SEAM.

First, the input feature maps were passed through the channel and spatial mixing module (CSSM) to learn the correlations of spatial dimensions and channels. In the CSMM, the input feature map was first sliced into a number of image sequence blocks by using the patch embedding operation, and it was linearly mapped and flattened into a one-dimensional vector. Then, there was a 3 × 3 depthwise convolution with residual connections. The depthwise convolution was operated depth-by-depth, i.e., there was a channel-by-channel separation of the convolutions. Thus, although the depthwise convolution could be used to learn the importance of different channels and reduce the number of parameters, it ignored the relationships of information between channels.

To compensate for this loss, the outputs of the different depth convolutions were subsequently combined through a 1 × 1 pointwise convolution. A two-layer fully connected network was then used to fuse the information from each channel. In this way, the network could strengthen the connections between all channels. After that, the range of values for the logits output from the fully connected layers was [0,1]. Then, the exponential function $y = e^x$ was used expand it to [1,e]. This exponential normalization provided a monotonic mapping relationship that made the results more tolerant of positional errors. Finally, the output of the SEAM was multiplied by the original features as attention so that the model could handle the occlusion of the detected targets more effectively.

2.2.3. YOLO Head

In comparison with the previous generation of YOLOv5, the biggest difference in YOLOv8 was that the head part had changed from the original coupled head based on anchors to a decoupled head without anchors; thus, the categorization task was decoupled from the regression task, and, at the same time, the objectness branch was eliminated. The structure of the YOLO head in YOLOv8 is shown in Figure 6. The loss function of YOLOv8 was mainly composed of two parts: classification loss and regression loss.

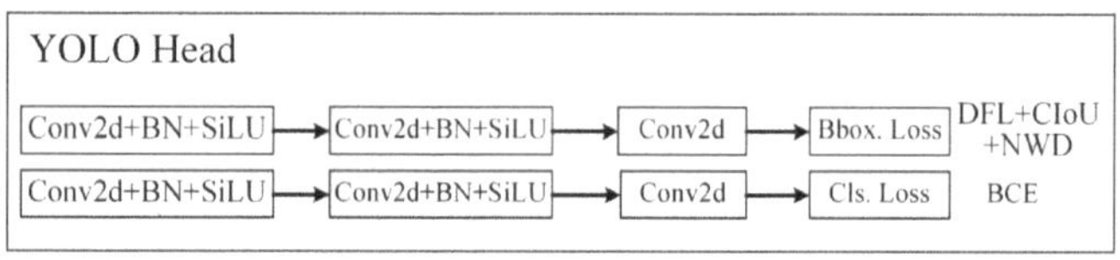

Figure 6. Illustration of YOLO head in YOLOv8.

The classification loss still used the BCE loss. The regression loss used the distribution focal loss and CIoU loss because it needed to be bound to the integral-form representation proposed in the distribution focal loss. The three loss functions were weighted with a ratio of 0.5:1.5:7.5. CIoU is an upgraded version of DIoU. Adding the aspect ratio of the prediction box to DIoU improved the regression accuracy.

The CIoU formula is expressed using Equation (1):

$$\mathrm{CIoU} = \mathrm{IoU} - \frac{\rho^2(\mathrm{b}, \mathrm{b}^{\mathrm{gt}})}{\mathrm{c}^2} - \alpha\,\mathrm{v} \quad (1)$$

The three terms in the formula correspond to the calculation of the IoU, center-point distance, and aspect ratio, respectively. $\rho^2(\mathrm{b}, \mathrm{b}^{\mathrm{gt}})$ represents the Euclidean distance between the center points of the prediction frame and the real frame, and c represents the diagonal distance of the smallest closed area that can contain both the predicted and real boxes. The equations for α and v are Equations (2) and (3):

$$\alpha = \frac{\mathrm{v}}{1 - \mathrm{IoU} + \mathrm{v}} \quad (2)$$

$$\mathrm{V} = \frac{4}{\pi^2}\left(\arctan\frac{\mathrm{w}^{\mathrm{gt}}}{\mathrm{h}^{\mathrm{gt}}} - \arctan\frac{\mathrm{w}}{\mathrm{h}}\right)^2 \quad (3)$$

Here, w, h and w^{gt},h^{gt} represent the height and width of the predicted box and the real box, respectively. The final loss is expressed using Equation (4):

$$LOSS_{CIoU} = 1 - IoU + \frac{\rho^2(b, b^{gt})}{c^2} + \alpha v \quad (4)$$

However, CIoU also has its limitations. In particular, it is very sensitive to the deviation in the positions of small targets, which seriously reduces its detection performance for such targets. To improve the detection performance for small targets while retaining the CIoU, the normalized Wasserstein distance (NWD) loss [36] was added. The main process of NWD is to first model the enclosing frame as a 2D Gaussian distribution and then use the Wasserstein distance to calculate the similarity between the corresponding Gaussian distributions. Compared with the traditional IoU, the advantages of the NWD are, firstly, that it can measure the distribution similarity regardless of the overlap between small targets and, secondly, that it is insensitive to targets of different scales and more suitable for measuring the similarities between small targets. The formula for the NWD loss is expressed using Equation (5):

$$NWD(N_a, N_b) = \exp(-\frac{\sqrt{w_2^2(N_a, N_b)}}{c}) \quad (5)$$

Here, $W_2^2(N_a, N_b)$ is the distance measure, N_a is the Gaussian distribution of the prediction frame, and N_b is the Gaussian distribution of the GT frame. C is a constant related to the dataset. In this study, we set C to the average absolute size of the targets in dataset. The NWD loss is expressed using Equation (6):

$$LOSS_{NWD} = 1 - NWD(N_a, N_b) \quad (6)$$

3. Results and Discussion

3.1. Experimental Environment and Datasets

The hardware environment for this study was the following: a laptop with 32 GB RAM, an AMD R9 5900HX CPU, and a 16 GB GeForce RTX 3080 graphics card. All tests were performed in Windows 11.

The dataset used in this study is divided into three main parts. The first was the URPC2021 dataset, which is a publicly available dataset from the 2021 Underwater Robot Picking Contest in China, and it mainly contains four kinds of creatures: echinus, holothurians, starfish, and scallops. The second part was the Wild Fish Marker dataset [37], which was sourced from the National Oceanic and Atmospheric Administration (NOAA) dataset, consisting of more than 1000 tagged fish. Finally, there were several videos and images of marine life taken from the video observations of the Luhaifeng and Laizhou Bay Marine Ranches in Shandong Province, China in 2021. Five types of marine organisms, namely, echinus, holothurians, starfish, scallops, and fish, were detected in this study. First, we needed to intercept and label the marine organisms in the observation videos and pictures. Finally, a corresponding XML configuration file was generated. Among others, this file included the image names, dimensions, information about the location of the labeled box, and the corresponding species of marine organisms. It should be noted that the software used rectangular boxes to label the detection targets, and many marine organisms are extremely irregular in shape. Their locations are dense and overlapping, and they are difficult to strictly separate. Therefore, the labeling process in this study focused on the main part of the animal and did not pay strict attention to its minutiae, such as the fins of fish, the tentacles of holothurians, and the spines of echinus.

Figure 7 shows the basic information of the training set as a part of the entire dataset. It was divided into four main sections. The upper-left panel shows the number for each detection category. The upper-right panel shows the length and width of each target box, as well as the overall number of boxes and the range of variation. The lower-left panel shows the position of the target's center point relative to the whole figure. The lower-right panel shows the height-to-width ratio of the target relative to the whole image. By synthesizing the four charts, it was found that the whole dataset was more difficult due to the uneven numbers of detection categories, which had more targets and greater variations in size, as well as more small targets.

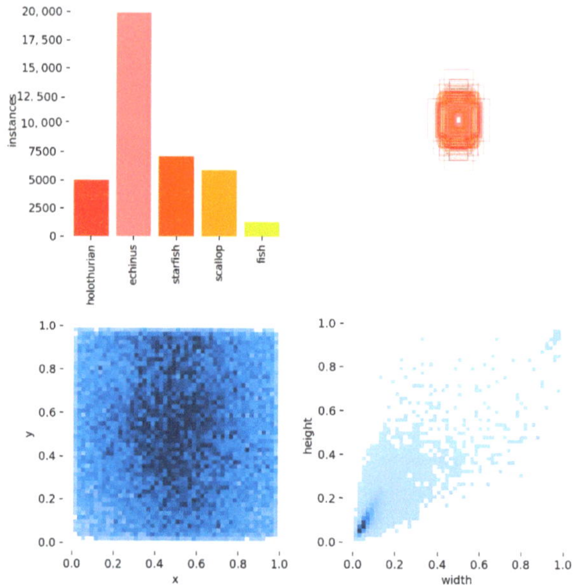

Figure 7. Basic infographic of training set.

3.2. Analysis of the Training Strategies

The dataset also needs to be pre-processed before starting the training. Firstly, all data were randomly divided at a ratio of 8:1:1 among the training set, validation set, and test set. To address the problem of the insufficient quantity and poor quality of marine organism datasets, data enhancement operations were also performed on the training set before training. The enhancement of the training data in this study consisted of three main parts: traditional data enhancement, mosaic data enhancement, and MixUp data enhancement. Traditional data enhancement mainly refers to random image flipping, scaling, and color gamut transformation operations. The steps for the mosaic data enhancement involved randomly combining four images into one. The MixUp enhancement step involved mixing two images at random. Of course, mosaic data enhancement also has its shortcomings because the distribution of the enhanced images was far from the true distribution of natural images and the large number of cutting operations affected the accuracy of the label boxes. Therefore, data augmentation was turned off in the last 30 epochs of training, which were the main reference in YOLOX [38].

The optimizer used for training was AdamW. Its main advantage is that it is very easy to use, and its gradient drop is fast. The corresponding learning rate was 0.001, and the final learning rate was 0.0001 when using the cosine learning rate adjustment strategy during training. The whole training lasted 300 epochs with a batch size of 16. If the training data did not improve within 50 epochs, the training was stopped early. A warmup training [39] strategy was used at the beginning to gradually increase the learning rate, with 10 warmup training epochs.

3.3. Comparison of the Detectors' Complexity

Currently, there are two main types of target detectors: one-stage detectors and two-stage detectors. Therefore, the models used in this study were the two-stage detectors (Faster-RCNN based on Resnet 50) and similar types of one-stage detectors (YOLOv5n, YOLOv7-tiny, and YOLOv8n). First, the complexity of each model was compared. The two main metrics for complexity analysis in deep learning are the number of computations (FLOPs) and the number of parameters (Params). FLOPs refer to the number of floating-point operations per second, which corresponds to the time complexity. Params refer to the total number of parameters to be trained in the network model, which corresponds to the spatial complexity. Then, the weights of the final trained model were obtained. The main data are shown in Table 1.

Table 1. Detector complexity comparison chart.

Detection Network	FLOPs/G	Params/M	Weights/MB
Faster-RCNN	370.2	137	105.7
YOLOv5n	4.1	1.7	3.7
YOLOv7-tiny	13.1	6.0	11.7
YOLOv8n	8.1	3.006	6.09
Improved YOLOv8	8.0	3.098	6.12

The comparison of the complexity showed that the two-stage detectors were much more complex than the one-stage detectors. Among the one-stage detectors, YOLOv5n had the lowest complexity. YOLOv8n had a significant increase in complexity over that of YOLOv5n. There was not much difference between the improved YOLOv8 and YOLOv8n. The highest complexity was that of YOLOv7-tiny. The number of parameters, the amount of computation, and the sizes of the weights were much higher than those of the other two detectors.

3.4. Performance Evaluation

The detection performance of the models was compared. The main evaluation indicators used in this study were the precision, recall, AP, and mAP. The PR curve is a curve with precision as the vertical axis and recall as the horizontal axis. In general, precision and recall are mutually constraining metrics. Therefore, plotting the PR curve can allow one to explore the comprehensive performance of a model. The observation curve can reflect the performance of a deep learning model. The PR curves of the model are shown in Figure 8. By comparing the PR curves, it can be seen that the curve of the improved YOLOv8 completely wrapped around those of the other detectors; therefore, the improved version had better performance.

AP refers to the average precision of each class to be detected, and the average of AP values for all classes is the average precision of the whole model (mAP). In the performance evaluation in this study, the mAP@0.5 was calculated. This indicates what the value of mAP is for an IoU threshold of 0.5. The predicted performance metrics for each class in the performance evaluation of these detectors are shown in Table 2.

Other performance indicators were also compared. It can be seen that the detection FPS values were similar for all one-stage detectors with a batch size of 1, with that of YOLOv5n being slightly higher. However, the two-stage detectors had lower FPS values and poorer real-time functioning. According to the mAP, the two-stage detector Faster-RCNN had a slight advantage. Among the one-stage detectors, YOLOv7-tiny had the highest complexity and the most complicated network structure, but this did not result in a performance improvement. YOLOv5n had the lowest complexity, and its mAP was also about 1.9% lower than that of YOLOv8n. The best performance on the data was that of the improved YOLOv8. Compared to those of the original YOLOv8n, the AP of each category and the total mAP were significantly improved. The most obvious boost was for holothurians, with a boost of about 9.7%. This was because holothurians presented the smallest targets and the most serious phenomenon of obscuration. The holothurians in marine ranches mostly inhabit the fine sand in the shallows. Others are in the crevices of reefs. Therefore, the improvement strategies used here were most effective for holothurians.

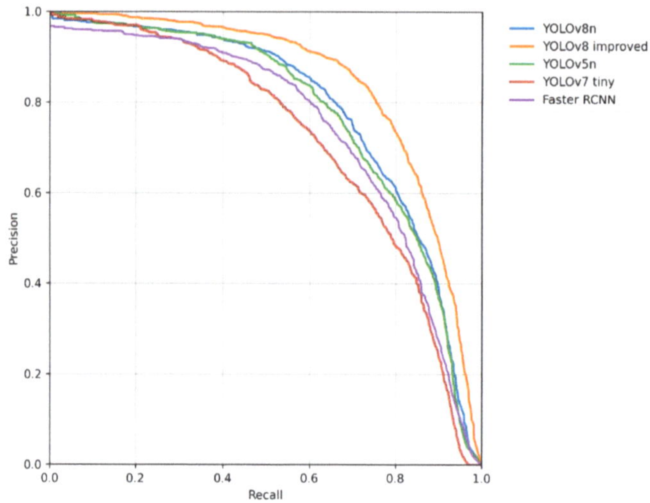

Figure 8. PR curve comparison chart.

Table 2. Predicted performance indicators of marine organism classification.

Detection Network	Echinus AP	Fish AP	Holothurian AP	Scallop AP	Starfish AP	mAP	FPS
Faster-RCNN	84.1%	76.3%	68.7%	55.6%	82.9%	73.5%	10
YOLOv5n	86%	77.8%	62%	70.7%	85.6%	76.4%	72
YOLOv7-tiny	85.8%	78.4%	49.5%	62.9%	82%	71.7%	70
YOLOv8n	87%	82%	63.7%	72.4%	86.3%	78.3%	68
Improved YOLOv8	89.9%	89.5%	73.4%	81.5%	88.4%	84.5%	65

At the end, an example of video detection was conducted while using the improved YOLOv8, and the results are shown in Figure 9. It can be seen that the whole process had excellent detection results. The FPS value was stable at around 40. This indicates that this system is competent in detecting marine organisms in seafloor videos in real time.

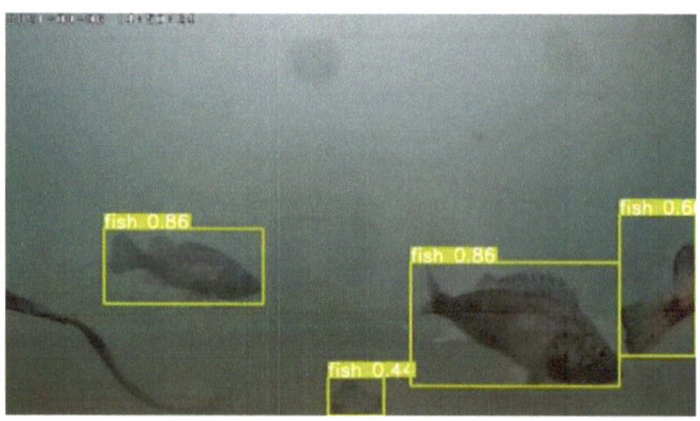

Figure 9. One example of video detection effect.

Overall, although the two-stage detector Faster-RCNN had a slight advantage in terms of the mAP, its structure was complex and functioned poorly in real time, which made it unsuitable for video monitoring systems in seafloor observation network. The one-stage model of the improved YOLOv8 had the best performance indicators. Its performance was improved without essentially changing its complexity. It is the most suitable for applications in video monitoring systems in seafloor observation networks for the detection of marine organisms.

3.5. Comparison of the Testing Results

To compare the actual results of detection, we chose four groups of more complex images with small and overlapping targets to explore the actual performance of the two detection networks.

A comparison of the first two sets of detection results is shown in Figure 10. We have used blue circles to mark the misdetections and omissions. The first set of detection images contained a large number of overlapping targets at medium to close range. By comparing the first set of test images, we found that the improved YOLOv8 detected three more holothurians but missing an echinus. The second set of detection images were dominated by a large number of small overlapping targets at a distance. By counting the detected objects in the second group of images, it was seen that the improved YOLOv8 detected a total of 49 scallops (an improvement by 10), 4 starfish (an improvement by 1), 26 echini (an improvement by 2), and 8 holothurians (an improvement by 2). At the same time, the accuracy of target detection—especially for overlapping targets—was significantly improved.

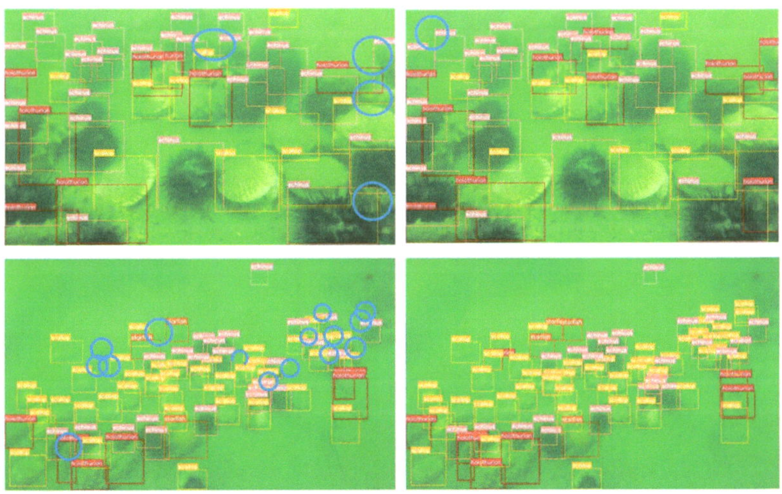

(a) (b)

Figure 10. Comparison of detections 1: (**a**) detection by YOLOv8; (**b**) detection by improved YOLOv8.

A comparison of the detection results of the latter two groups is shown in Figure 11. We have used red circles to mark the misdetections and omissions. The third and fourth groups of images mainly contained dense schools of fish. It could be seen that in the third group, the improved YOLOv8 detected sixteen fish, which was two more heavily obscured fish than the ordinary version of the detector found. In the fourth set of images, the improved YOLOv8 detected a total of 54 fish. Compared to the normal version, six more items were detected, and there was one missed item. This experiment proved that in the face of the small- and medium-sized targets and greater amount of overlap in marine ranch environment, the improved YOLOv8 performed better than the ordinary YOLOv8 and was more suitable for the detection of marine organisms under such conditions.

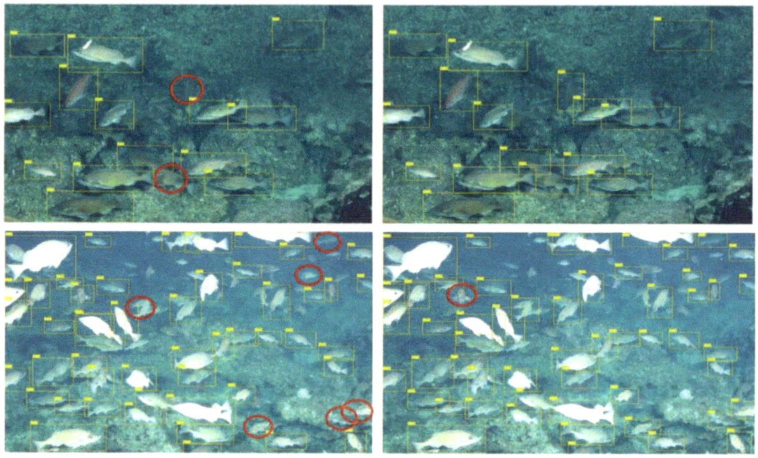

(a) (b)

Figure 11. Comparison of detections 2: (**a**) detection by YOLOv8; (**b**) detection by improved YOLOv8.

3.6. Ablation Study

In this section, we evaluate the impact of each part on the overall performance by separately conducting experiments on each improvement module. The whole process of improving the experiments is also shown.

3.6.1. InceptionNeXt Block

Here, we focused on replacing the C2F block at different positions in YOLOv8 with the InceptionNeXt block and experimentally comparing the model performance. From there, the most appropriate improvement was found. A comparison of the effects of replacing these positions is shown in Table 3. The experiment was divided into four groups: the original YOLOv8, the C2F block that replaced only the neck, the C2F block that replaced only the backbone, and all of them. The replacement positions are shown in parentheses. It is worth noting that, at first, we tried to replace all of the C2F blocks in the model with InceptionNeXt blocks, but the results were not good. This was likely because the changes were excessive and destabilized the model. So, we tried other programs separately. Ultimately, replacing only the backbone portion of the C2F block worked the best, and there was an mAP improvement of about 2.1%.

Table 3. Comparison of replacing positions.

Detection Network	Echinus AP	Fish AP	Holothurian AP	Scallop AP	Starfish AP	mAP
YOLOv8	87%	82%	63.7%	74.4%	84.3%	78.3%
YOLOv8(Neck)	87.4%	83.2%	65.3%	75.5%	84.2%	79.1%
YOLOv8(All)	86.7%	81.4%	63.2%	73.6%	83.5%	77.7%
YOLOv8(Backbone)	87.6%	84.8%	67.6%	77.5%	84.5%	80.4%

3.6.2. Attention Mechanisms

Undoubtedly, attention mechanisms have a significant impact on the performance of target detection models. They can improve a model's ability to extract effective features for learning, thus improving the performance of the whole model. Therefore, we chose the classical attention mechanisms SE [40] and CBAM [41] for a comparison. The SEAM was the most effective. The corresponding losses of occluded marine organisms could be compensated by enhancing the response of nonoccluded marine organisms. The mAP was increased by about 1.7%. A comparison of the different attention mechanisms is shown in Table 4.

Table 4. Comparison of different attention mechanisms.

Detection Network	Echinus AP	Fish AP	Holothurian AP	Scallop AP	Starfish AP	mAP
YOLOv8	87%	82%	63.7%	74.4%	84.3%	78.3%
YOLOv8+SE	87.1%	83.4%	64.5%	75.3%	84.5%	79%
YOLOv8+CBAM	87.3%	83.7%	64.8%	75.9%	84.6%	79.3%
YOLOv8+SEAM	87.4%	84.3%	66.2%	77.5%	84.6%	80%

3.6.3. Loss Function

Finally, by adding the NWD loss to the original CIoU loss to enhance the detection performance for small targets, the mAP was improved by about 2.0%. It is worth noting that, at the beginning of the experiment, we tried to use the NWD loss to completely replace the original CIoU loss. However, the effect was not ideal, and the detection performance was not increased but decreased. This was likely because the NWD loss reduced the detection performance for medium and large targets. Therefore, we chose to retain the original CIoU loss and adjust the proportions of the two loss functions to find the optimal combination. The experimental results are shown in Table 5.

Table 5. Loss function comparison.

CIoU	NWD	Echinus AP	Fish AP	Holothurian AP	Scallop AP	Starfish AP	mAP
1	0	87%	82%	63.7%	74.4%	84.3%	78.3%
0.6	0.4	86.2%	84.6%	65.5%	75%	84.4%	79.1%
0.5	0.5	86.9%	85.7%	66.3%	77.7%	84.8%	80.3%
0.4	0.6	86.5%	81.6%	62.4%	73.2%	83.5%	77.4%
0	1	86%	80.7%	61.5%	72.8%	82.4%	76.7%

4. Conclusions

This study aimed to improve the efficiency of monitoring target marine organisms in marine ranches. At the same time, the workload of staff can be reduced, and a new way of thinking for the efficient management of relevant aquatic organisms in marine ranches is provided. To achieve this goal, we attempted to improve the YOLOv8 detector as the basis of the study. Firstly, the InceptionNeXt block was used in the backbone to replace the original C2F block, which improved the feature extraction capabilities of the network while keeping the number of parameters basically unchanged. Secondly, the SEAM was incorporated into the neck to enhance the detection of overlapping targets by increasing the attention to the detected object regions in images and weakening the background regions. Finally, the NWD loss was added to the original CIoU loss, and the proportion of the two functions was adjusted through experimentation. This resulted in improved detection of small targets without compromising the detection performance for medium and large targets. The traditional enhancement method of performing several types of random transformations on images and a data enhancement method combining mosaic and MixUp were used to improve the dataset during the training process, which enhanced the robustness of the network in an attempt to obtain good results with limited resources. Overall, the improved YOLOv8 in this study achieved a mAP of 84.5%, which was an increase of 6.2%. Meanwhile, there was no significant increase in the number of parameters and computations, so a balance between detection performance and model volume was achieved. With its fair performance, it can be applied in seafloor observation platforms in marine ranches to complete the task of the real-time detection of marine organisms. However, there are still some areas that can be improved, including the following.

First, the dataset can be further improved. The dataset used here still suffered from a small and uneven sample size. In the future, we can consider acquiring more videos and images for model training and testing. There was also a serious imbalance in the number of individual detection categories in the dataset, so we can consider balancing the number of samples. Second, underwater images are different from land images because of the presence of low-contrast, non-uniform illumination, blurring, bright spots, and high noise due to a variety of complicating factors. The images in the dataset can be enhanced with image enhancement algorithms to improve their clarity and facilitate subsequent work. Finally, further improvements and test models can be considered to make this system more lightweight and faster so that it can be better adapted to embedded devices on experimental platforms, thus opening it to a wider range of applications.

Author Contributions: Conceptualization, R.J.; Methodology, R.J. and L.C.; Formal analysis and investigation, M.L. and J.C.; Writing—original draft preparation, R.J.; Writing—review and editing, B.L. and H.L. All authors have read and agreed to the published version of the manuscript.

Funding: This study is supported in part by Qilu University of Technology (Shandong Academy of Sciences) Pilot Project of Science, Education, and Industry Integration Major Innovation Special Project "Project of Unveiling System", Pivotal Technologies for Ocean Intelligent Sensing and Information Processing Based on End-to-End Cloud Architecture [No.2023JBZ02], the National Natural Science Foundation of China (42106172), Project Plan of Pilot Project of Integration of Science, Education and Industry of Qilu University of Technology (Shandong Academy of Sciences) (2022GH004, 2022PY041).

Institutional Review Board Statement: Not applicable.

Informed Consent Statement: Not applicable.

Data Availability Statement: The data presented in this study are available on request from the corresponding author.

Conflicts of Interest: The authors declare that they have no conflicts of interest or competing financial and/or nonfinancial interests in relation to this work.

References

1. Agardy, T. Effects of fisheries on marine ecosystems: A conservationist's perspective. *ICES J. Mar. Sci.* **2000**, *57*, 761–765. [CrossRef]
2. Greenville, J.; MacAulay, T. Protected areas in fisheries: A two-patch, two-species model. *Aust. J. Agric. Resour. Econ.* **2006**, *50*, 207–226. [CrossRef]
3. Hu, K.; Weng, C.; Zhang, Y.; Jin, J.; Xia, Q. An Overview of Underwater Vision Enhancement: From Traditional Methods to Recent Deep Learning. *J. Mar. Sci. Eng.* **2022**, *10*, 241. [CrossRef]
4. Girshick, R.; Donahue, J.; Darrell, T.; Malik, J. Rich feature hierarchies for accurate object detection and semantic segmentation. In Proceedings of the IEEE Conference on Computer Vision and Pattern Recognition (CVPR), Columbus, OH, USA, 23–28 June 2014; pp. 580–587. [CrossRef]
5. Girshick, R. Fast R-CNN. In Proceedings of the IEEE International Conference on Computer Vision, Santiago, Chile, 7–13 December 2015; pp. 1440–1448. [CrossRef]
6. Ren, S.; He, K.; Girshick, R.; Sun, J. Faster R-CNN: Towards Real-Time Object Detection with Region Proposal Networks. *IEEE Trans. Pattern Anal. Mach. Intell.* **2017**, *39*, 1137–1149. [CrossRef] [PubMed]
7. Lin, W.; Zhong, J.; Liu, S.; Li, T.; Li, G. ROIMIX: Proposal-Fusion Among Multiple Images for Underwater Object Detection. In Proceedings of the International Conference on Acoustics, Speech, and Signal Processing, Barcelona, Spain, 4–8 May 2020. [CrossRef]
8. Redmon, J.; Divvala, S.; Girshick, R.; Farhad, A. You Only Look Once: Unified, Real-Time Object Detection. In Proceedings of the Computer Vision & Pattern Recognition, Las Vegas, NV, USA, 26 June–1 July 2016. [CrossRef]
9. Redmon, J.; Farhadi, A. YOLOv3: An Incremental Improvement. *arXiv* **2018**, arXiv:1804.02767. [CrossRef]
10. Bochkovskiy, A.; Wang, C.; Liao, H. YOLOv4: Optimal Speed and Accuracy of Object Detection. *arXiv* **2020**, arXiv:2004.10934. [CrossRef]
11. Wang, C.; Bochkovskiy, A.; Liao, H. YOLOv7: Trainable bag-of-freebies sets new state-of-the-art for real-time object detectors. *arXiv* **2022**, arXiv:2207.02696. [CrossRef]

12. Han, F.; Yao, J.; Zhu, H.; Wang, C. Underwater Image Processing and Object Detection Based on Deep CNN Method. *J. Sens.* **2020**, *2020*, 6707328. [CrossRef]
13. Chen, L.; Zheng, M.; Duan, S.; Luo, W.; Yao, L. Underwater Target Recognition Based on Improved YOLOv4 Neural Network. *Electronics* **2021**, *10*, 1634. [CrossRef]
14. Zhao, S.; Zhang, S.; Lu, J.; Wang, H.; Feng, Y.; Shi, C.; Li, D.; Zhao, R. A lightweight dead fish detection method based on deformable convolution and YOLOV4. *Comput. Electron. Agric.* **2022**, *198*, 107098. [CrossRef]
15. Sun, S.; Xu, Z. Large kernel convolution YOLO for ship detection in surveillance video. *Math. Biosci. Eng. MBE* **2023**, *20*, 15018–15043. [CrossRef] [PubMed]
16. Zhang, Q.; Li, Y.; Zhang, Z.; Yin, S.; Ma, L. Marine target detection for PPI images based on YOLO-SWFormer. *Alex. Eng. J.* **2023**, *82*, 396–403. [CrossRef]
17. Shen, X.; Wang, H.; Li, Y.; Gao, T.; Fu, X. Criss-cross global interaction-based selective attention in YOLO for underwater object detection. *Multimed. Tools Appl.* **2023**. [CrossRef]
18. Yu, G.; Su, J.; Luo, Y.; Chen, Z.; Chen, Q.; Chen, S. Efficient detection method of deep-sea netting breakage based on attention and focusing on receptive-field spatial feature. *Signal Image Video Process.* **2023**. [CrossRef]
19. Lv, C.; Cao, S.; Zhang, Y.; Xu, G.; Zhao, B. Methods studies for attached marine organisms detecting based on convolutional neural network. *Energy Rep.* **2022**, *8*, 1192–1201. [CrossRef]
20. Li, Y.; Bai, X.; Xia, C. An Improved YOLOV5 Based on Triplet Attention and Prediction Head Optimization for Marine Organism Detection on Underwater Mobile Platforms. *J. Mar. Sci. Eng.* **2022**, *10*, 1230. [CrossRef]
21. Li, L.; Shi, G.; Jiang, T. Fish detection method based on improved YOLOv5. *Aquac. Int.* **2023**, *31*, 2513–2530. [CrossRef]
22. Favali, P.; Beranzoli, L. Seafloor observatory science: A review. *Ann. Geophys.* **2006**, *49*, 515–567. [CrossRef]
23. Matabos, M.; Best, M.; Blandin, J.; Hoeberechts, M.; Juniper, K.; Pirenne, B.; Robert, K.; Ruhl, H.; Sarrazin, J.; Vardaro, M. *Seafloor Observatories: Clark/Biological Sampling in the Deep Sea*; John Wiley & Sons, Ltd.: Hoboken, NJ, USA, 2016.
24. Chen, J.; Liu, H.; Lv, B.; Liu, C.; Zhang, X.; Li, H.; Cao, L.; Wan, J. Research on an Extensible Monitoring System of a Seafloor Observatory Network in Laizhou Bay. *J. Mar. Sci. Eng.* **2022**, *10*, 1051. [CrossRef]
25. Lv, B.; Chen, J.; Liu, H.; Chao, L.; Zhang, Z.; Zhang, X.; Gao, H.; Cai, Y. Design of deep-sea chemical data collector for the seafloor observatory network. *Mar. Georesour. Geotechnol.* **2022**, *40*, 1359–1369. [CrossRef]
26. Yu, W.; Zhou, P.; Yan, S.; Wang, X. InceptionNeXt: When Inception Meets ConvNeXt. In Proceedings of the IEEE Conference on Computer Vision and Pattern Recognition (CVPR), Vancouver, BC, Canada, 18–22 June 2023. [CrossRef]
27. Wang, C.; Liao, H.; Wu, Y.; Chen, P.; Hsieh, J.; Yeh, I. CSPNet: A new backbone that can enhance learning capability of CNN. In Proceedings of the IEEE/CVF Conference on Computer Vision and Pattern Recognition Workshops (CVPRW), Seattle, WA, USA, 14–19 June 2020. [CrossRef]
28. Liu, Z.; Mao, H.; Wu, C.; Feichtenhofer, C.; Darrell, T.; Xie, S. A ConvNet for the 2020s. In Proceedings of the IEEE Computer Vision and Pattern Recognition (CVPR), New Orleans, LA, USA, 18–24 June 2022. [CrossRef]
29. Chollet, F. Xception: Deep Learning with Depthwise Separable Convolutions. In Proceedings of the IEEE Conference on Computer Vision and Pattern Recognition (CVPR), Honolulu, HI, USA, 21–26 July 2017. [CrossRef]
30. Ioffe, S.; Szegedy, C. Batch Normalization: Accelerating Deep Network Training by Reducing Internal Covariate Shift. In Proceedings of the 32nd International Conference on Machine Learning, Lille, France, 6–11 July 2015. [CrossRef]
31. Szegedy, C.; Vanhoucke, V.; Ioffe, S.; Shlens, J.; Wojna, Z. Rethinking the inception architecture for computer vision. In Proceedings of the IEEE Conference on Computer Vision and Pattern Recognition, Las Vegas, NV, USA, 27–30 June 2016; pp. 2818–2826. [CrossRef]
32. Szegedy, C.; Ioffe, S.; Vanhoucke, V.; Alemi, A. Inception-v4, Inception-ResNet and the Impact of Residual Connections on Learning. *arXiv* **2016**, arXiv:1602.07261. [CrossRef]
33. Szegedy, C.; Liu, W.; Jia, Y.; Pierre, S.; Scott, R.; Dragomir, A.; Dumitrue, E.; Vincent, V.; Andrew, R. Going deeper with convolutions. In Proceedings of the IEEE Conference on Computer Vision and Pattern Recognition (CVPR), Boston, MA, USA, 7–12 June 2015. [CrossRef]
34. Liu, S.; Qi, L.; Qin, H.; Shi, J.; Jia, J. Path aggregation network for instance segmentation. In Proceedings of the IEEE/CVF Conference on Computer Vision and Pattern Recognition, Salt Lake City, UT, USA, 18–23 June 2018. [CrossRef]
35. Yu, Z.; Huang, H.; Chen, W.; Su, Y.; Liu, Y.; Wang, X. YOLO-FaceV2: A Scale and Occlusion Aware Face Detector. In Proceedings of the IEEE Conference on Computer Vision and Pattern Recognition (CVPR), New Orleans, LA, USA, 18–24 June 2022. [CrossRef]
36. Wang, J.; Xu, C.; Yang, W.; Lei, Y. A Normalized Gaussian Wasserstein Distance for Tiny Object Detection. In Proceedings of the IEEE Conference on Computer Vision and Pattern Recognition, Nashville, TN, USA, 20–25 June 2021. [CrossRef]
37. Cutter, G.; Stierhoff, K.; Zeng, J. Automated Detection of Rockfish in Unconstrained Underwater Videos Using Haar Cascades. In Proceedings of the Applications and Computer Vision Workshops (WACVW), Waikoloa Beach, HI, USA, 5–9 January 2015. [CrossRef]
38. Ge, Z.; Liu, S.; Wang, F.; Li, Z.; Sun, J. YOLOX: Exceeding YOLO Series in 2021. *arXiv* **2021**, arXiv:2107.08430. [CrossRef]
39. He, K.; Zhang, X.; Ren, S.; Sun, J. Deep residual learning for image recognition. In Proceedings of the IEEE Conference on Computer Vision and Pattern Recognition, Las Vegas, NV, USA, 26 June–1 July 2016; pp. 770–778. [CrossRef]

40. Hu, J.; Shen, L.; Sun, G. Squeeze-and-Excitation Networks. In Proceedings of the IEEE/CVF Conf Computer Vision Pattern Recognition, Salt Lake City, UT, USA, 18–23 June 2018; pp. 7132–7141. [CrossRef]
41. Woo, S.; Park, J.; Lee, J.-Y.; Kweon, S.I. CBAM: Convolutional block attention module. In Proceedings of the European Conference on Computer Vision (ECCV), Munich, Germany, 8–14 September 2018; pp. 3–19. [CrossRef]

Journal of
Marine Science and Engineering

MDPI

Article

G-Net: An Efficient Convolutional Network for Underwater Object Detection

Xiaoyang Zhao [1], Zhuo Wang [2], Zhongchao Deng [1,*] and Hongde Qin [2]

1 Science and Technology on Underwater Vehicle Technology Laboratory, Harbin Engineering University, Harbin 150001, China; zhaoxiaoyang@hrbeu.edu.cn
2 Qingdao Innovation and Development Center, Harbin Engineering University, Qindao 266000, China; wangzhuo@hrbeu.edu.cn (Z.W.); qinhongde@hrbeu.edu.cn (H.Q.)
* Correspondence: dengzhongchao@hrbeu.edu.cn

Abstract: Visual perception technology is of great significance for underwater robots to carry out seabed investigation and mariculture activities. Due to the complex underwater environment, it is often necessary to enhance the underwater image when detecting underwater targets by optical sensors. Most of the traditional methods involve image enhancement and then target detection. However, this method greatly increases the timeliness in practical application. To solve this problem, we propose a feature-enhanced target detection network, Global-Net (G-Net), which combines underwater image enhancement with target detection. Different from the traditional method of reconstructing enhanced images for target detection, G-Net realizes the integration of image enhancement and target detection. In addition, our feature map learning module (FML) can effectively extract defogging features. The test results in a real underwater environment show that G-Net improves the detection accuracy of underwater targets by about 5%, but also has high detection efficiency, which ensures the reliability of underwater robots in seabed investigation and aquaculture activities.

Keywords: image enhancement; image reconstruction; underwater object detection; feature enhancement

Citation: Zhao, X.; Wang, Z.; Deng, Z.; Qin, H. G-Net: An Efficient Convolutional Network for Underwater Object Detection. *J. Mar. Sci. Eng.* **2024**, *12*, 116. https://doi.org/10.3390/jmse12010116

Academic Editor: Sergei Chernyi

Received: 3 December 2023
Revised: 3 January 2024
Accepted: 5 January 2024
Published: 7 January 2024

1. Introduction

In recent years, research on underwater intelligent sensing technology has become increasingly popular due to the rapid development of modern technologies, such as the internet and artificial intelligence. Underwater unmanned vehicles perform underwater information detection, underwater aquaculture, and underwater rescue tasks with the assistance of intelligent perception technology. These tasks depend heavily on the quality of captured images [1]. However, due to the complex underwater environment, underwater images obtained from optical imaging devices cannot be directly used for target identification. These underwater images are blurred and color distorted due to scattering and absorption by water, which seriously affects the performance of underwater target detection. Some research works have been presented in the literature for underwater image enhancement [1–8]. More specifically, underwater image enhancement can be seen as an image defogging problem, and a defogging method with minimum information loss and histogram distribution prior is proposed in [2]. To better represent underwater images, an improved underwater image model was proposed in [6]. The model uses ocean monitoring data to derive the physical effective space of backscattering, which will be conducive to restoring image enhancement of complex scenes. Both [7,8] employed depth images to enhance underwater image. A lightweight adaptive feature fusion network is proposed in [5] for underwater image enhancement. The simplified U-Net was used to enhance the paired underwater images in [3]. An algorithm based on color feature fusion is proposed in [4], which adopts multi-channel feature extraction strategy to achieve underwater image enhancement.

With the widespread use of convolutional neural networks, the research on target detection techniques has been greatly improved, such as a series of faster one-stage target detection algorithms Single Shot MultiBox Detector (SSD) [9], You Only Look Once (YOLO) [10], RetinaNet [11], Fully Convolutional One-Stage Object Detector (FCOS) [12], and more accurate two-stage target detection algorithms Regions with CNN features (RCNN) [13], Fast RCNN [14], Faster RCNN [15], and Cascade RCNN [16]. These detection methods extract features through the backbone network and then classify extracted features and perform bounding box regression through the head network. However, underwater target detection remains a challenging task. These methods are only applicable to clear datasets and have difficulty detecting underwater degraded images. Moreover, underwater image enhancement methods restore degraded images to clear images and perform target detection on clear images. The traditional method firstly enhance the underwater degradation image and then detect the objects. However, the difficulty of underwater target detection is the degradation of image features extracted by backbone network, which makes it difficult for the detector to classify the target and perform boundary regression. Ref. [17] improved Fast RCNN and adversarial occlusion network for underwater target detection. Ref. [18] improved RCNN for underwater target detection. Ref. [19] improved one-stage detector yolov5 for underwater target detection. Ref. [20] improved yolox and tested it on underwater data sets. Also, image enhancement networks aim to enhance image sharpness and contrast and color correction, which may not necessarily be applicable to target detection networks. Furthermore, the efficiency of reconstructing clear images and performing target detection is inefficient, and it is difficult to reconstruct clear images and perform target detection in real time during underwater operations. To solve these two issues, the underwater target detection task is divided into two subtasks in G-Net, i.e., underwater image feature enhancement and enhanced target detection. Previous studies typically separate the two without considering the impact of enhanced images on subsequent higher-order vision tasks, but underwater enhanced image reconstruction seriously affects the operational efficiency of underwater target detection. Therefore, we construct an end-to-end underwater target detection method that does not require the reconstruction of enhanced images.

The main contributions of this work are summarized as follows:

- We propose a data-driven approach based on an end-to-end target detection model. It fuses image enhancement with target detection in the feature extraction part and enables accurate detection of target information of underwater blurred images based on enhanced features, which can be generalized to real-world underwater scenarios.
- In order to simplify the process of image enhancement, feature extraction, object classification and boundary regression in traditional methods, image enhancement and feature extraction for object detection are combined to realize the integration of image enhancement and object detection. By inputting hazy images, our G-Net network can enhance the detection features of degraded images and directly output the target detection results. The perception efficiency of the underwater unmanned boat is greatly improved.
- In order to better capture the degradation features, we propose a feature map learning (FML) module, using clear image features to guide the network to enhance the detection features of degraded images.
- Our proposed lightweight neural network not only exhibits good performance on the dataset but also performs well on real underwater environment images. It has significant performance improvement compared with other underwater object detection algorithms.

The remainder of this paper is organized as follows. Section 2 briefly describes the current research status on underwater target detection. Section 3 presents the network structure and loss function of the proposed novel lightweight neural network and the FML learning module combining feature enhancement and target detection. Section 4 compares and analyzes the experiments of G-Net and existing methods. The experimental results are summarized in Section 5.

2. Related Works

In this section, we will briefly introduce the development of deep learning-based target detection and the related content of underwater target detection.

2.1. Object Detection Based on Deep Learning

Target detection, as one of the most fundamental and important tasks in computer vision, has received widespread attention in recent years [21]. Traditional manual feature-based detection frameworks, including the Viola–Jones detector [22], histogram of gradients (HoG) [23], and deformable models [24], have been gradually replaced by neural networks.

Deep learning-based methods have achieved success in perception tasks [25–28]. With the development of deep learning, deep learning-based target detection can be divided into two categories: one-stage target detection represented by the YOLO series [29–32] and two-stage target detection represented by Faster RCNN. The two-stage detection network first forms candidate regions and then detects targets in the candidate regions. The advantage of two-stage target detection is its higher accuracy, and the advantage of one-stage target detection is its faster speed. However, the accuracy of the one-stage detector gradually becomes higher than that of the two-stage detector with development, which indicates its wider industrial application.

2.2. Underwater Object Detection Based on Deep Learning

Deep learning techniques have also developed rapidly in underwater target detection. For example, the R-CNN-based fish detection method proposed in [33], the classification of underwater plankton using deep residual networks [34], and the lightweight neural network for underwater fish detection [35]. Li et al. [36] improved the YOLOv4 target detection network by gradually using MobileNetv2 [37] and proposed a multiscale attentional feature fusion mechanism to improve the detection accuracy of underwater small targets. Yeh [38] et al. used a color conversion module and detection module jointly trained to enhance underwater target detection through the joint training of color conversion and detection modules. The underwater target single aggregation network was proposed in [39] by using multiscale features and complementary context information [40] proposed a fast underwater target detection network [41] fine-tuned YOLOv2 and tested it on the underwater dataset.

3. Proposed Methods

The traditional underwater image enhancement and target detection process is inefficient, and the detection performance is insufficient, which can not meet the needs of underwater target detection. Therefore, we propose a framework that integrates image enhancement and target detection. The enhanced network no longer needs to rebuild a clear image before detection, as shown in Figure 1. This will greatly improve the efficiency of underwater target detection. In this section, we will focus on G-Net.

3.1. Model Workflow

The flow chart of the proposed G-Net network structure is shown in Figure 1. G-Net consists of an Object Detection Feature Map Enhancement (ODFME) module for image feature enhancement and a Detect Target and Output Result (DTR) module for classification and regression, as shown in Figure 2. In the proposed FML learning module, the ODFME module learns feature maps of clear images without reconstructing the enhanced images, which enables the integration of underwater image enhancement and detection. The ODFME module outputs the enhanced detection features, and the DTR module inputs enhanced features for the regression of bounding boxes and target classifications. Compared with the traditional independent tasks of underwater image enhancement and target detection, it can be better applied to underwater target detection.

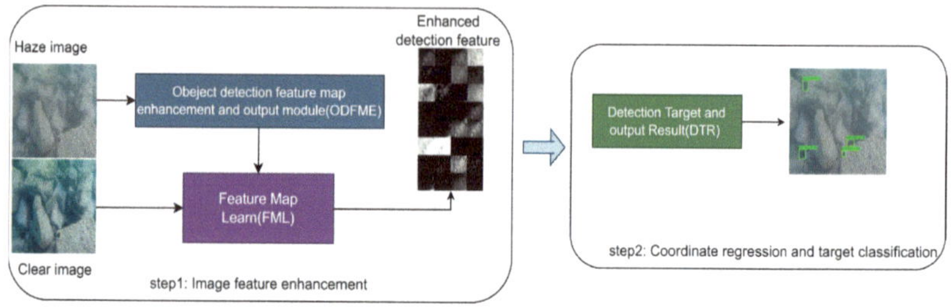

Figure 1. G-Net framework flow.

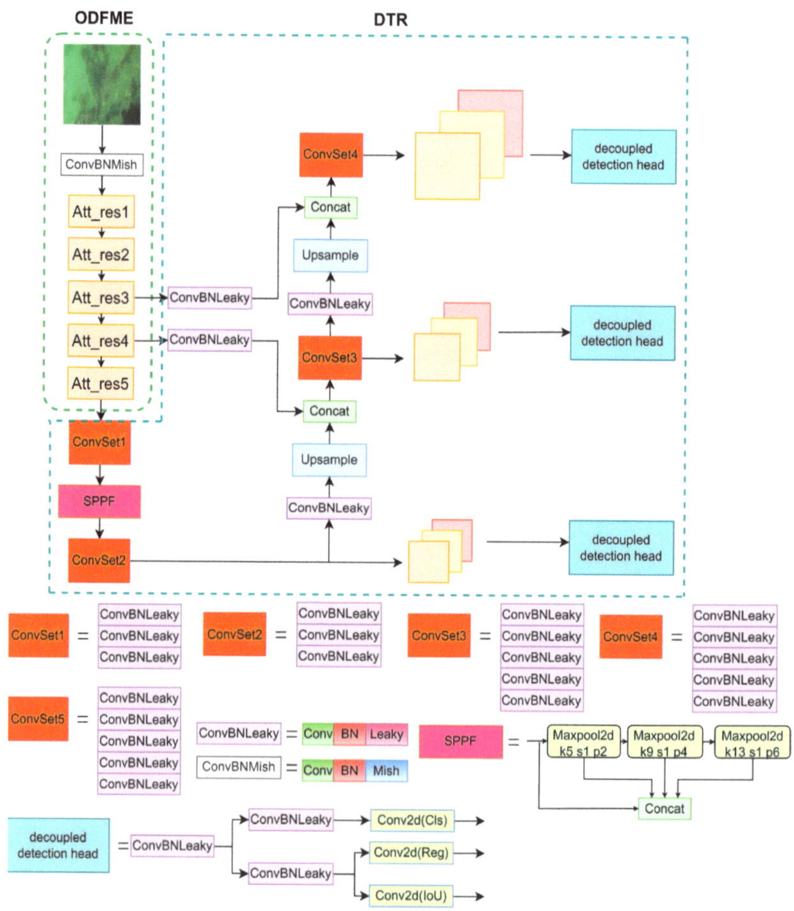

Figure 2. The image on the left shows the ODFME module and enhanced features. The ODFME module consists of five Att_res blocks. On the right is the DTR structure for coordinate regression and target classification. Att_res indicates attention residual block, Conv and Conv2d indicate convolution, BN indicates batch normalization, and Leaky and Mish indicate activation function. SPPF means spatial pyramid pooling-faster.

3.2. ODFME Module

The G-Net network structure consists of an Object detection feature map enhancement and output (ODFME) module and a detect target and output (DTR) module, as shown in Figure 2. ConBNLeaky consists of Conv2d, Batch normalization, Leaky. ConvBNMish consists of Conv2d, BN, Mish. ConvSet consists of ConvBNLeaky. SPPF consists of parallel Maxpool2d. Where Conv2d denotes the convolution, BN denotes Batch Normalization, Mish denotes Mish activation function. Leaky denotes Leaky activation function. Since our feature enhancement module does not need to reconstruct a clear underwater image but uses the enhanced feature map directly for coordinate regression and classification, our network design focuses on the ODFME part.

Our ODFME module is designed based on the CSP-DarkNet model. The main structure of the network is shown in Figure 2. Our ODFME module is mainly composed of five Attention Resual Blocks (Att_res Block). The structure of Att_res block is shown in Figure 3 (five Att_res blocks only differ in the number of attention resistance block (Aresblock), and the rest are exactly the same). Att_res module adds an attention resistance block (AresBlock) among the three ConvBNMish. It adopts serial channel attention and spatial attention, which can extract and enhance degradation features. AResBlock Concat operation can fuse shallow information with deep information. Then, parallel channel attention (CA) and spatial attention (PA) modules encode the transmission value and global atmospheric light value of the fused image, respectively. The multi-layer perceptron (MLP) module is used to re-fit the enhanced dehazing features.

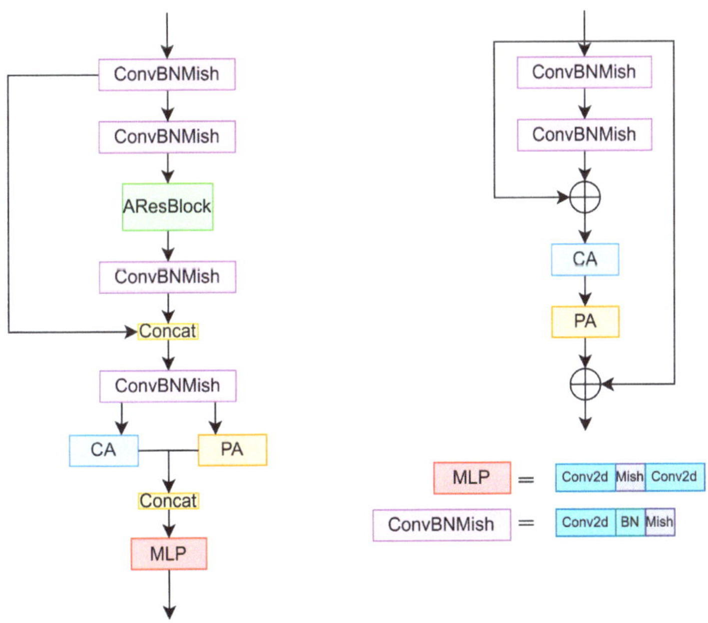

Figure 3. The network of the Att_res block and Aresblock. On the left is the Att_res block network structure. The feature map is enhanced by series-parallel channel attention and spatial attention. The image on the right shows the structure of AResBlock, which is enhanced with local residual and tandem channel attention and spatial attention. CA means channel attention, PA means spatial attention, MLP means multi-layer perceptron. AresBlock means attention resistance block. ⊕ means point-wise addition.

According to the image degradation model widely used in [42–45], the underwater image degradation formula can be expressed as

$$I(x) = J(x)t(x) + A(1 - t(x)) \tag{1}$$

where $I(x)$ represents underwater degradation image, $J(x)$ white represents clear image, $t(x)$ represents transmission value and A represents global atmospheric light value.

We believe that transmission value $t(x)$ in the underwater image degradation Formula (1) is a location-related local variable, and the global atmospheric light value A is a global shared variable. Meanwhile, most image enhancement works treat channel and pixel features equally and cannot process images with uneven distributions of underwater degradation and weighted channels. Inspired by FFA-Net, AResBlock adopts a local residual structure and a combination of a serial channel attention module and spatial attention module, which can address different features and pixel regions unequally and provide more flexibility when processing different types of information. We believe that the channel attention mechanism can better obtain the global shared variable A, and the spatial attention mechanism can better obtain the local variable t related to position. Therefore, in addition to the serial attention module used in AResBlock, we use parallel channel attention and spatial attention at the end of the Att_res structure to enhance different channel and pixel features, respectively, and the MLP module to adjust the number of channels and combine different enhancement features. We believe that the parallel use of the channel attention module and spatial attention module can prevent features from being overenhanced and can better extract the global shared variable A and the location-related local variable $t(x)$ from the original features.

The channel attention structure is shown in Figure 4. Let X be the feature map. According to the gating mechanism in [46], our channel attention can be expressed as

$$\begin{gathered} X_w = Sigmoid(Conv2d(Relu(Conv2d(GAP(X))))) \\ X_{out} = X_w \otimes X \end{gathered} \tag{2}$$

where the GAP means Global average pooling, $Relu$ means activation function, and $\otimes$ refers to the Hadamard product.

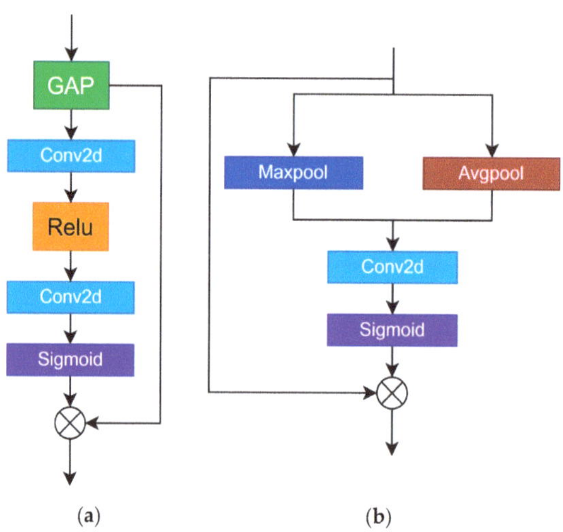

Figure 4. Channel attention and spatial attention structure. (**a**) represents the channel attention module, and (**b**) represents the spatial attention module. GAP means global average pooling. Sigmoid means activation function. $\otimes$ means Hadamard product. Maxpool means max pooling; Avgpool means average pooling.

We use global averaging pooling, Conv2d, ReLU functions, and sigmoid functions to obtain its weight on the channel and then multiply the corresponding elements with x.

The structure of spatial attention is shown in Figure 5. The gating mechanism is used as the main content of the spatial attention mechanism, the left branch is used as the feature branch, and the right branch is used as the spatial pixel selection communication number. According to [47], if the input feature graph is x, the spatial attention mechanism can be expressed as

$$\begin{gathered} W = Sigmoid(Conv2d(Avgpool(X) \oplus maxpool(X))) \\ X_{out} = X \otimes W \end{gathered} \quad (3)$$

where the $\oplus$ means point-wise addition, $Avgpool$ means average pooling, and $maxpool$ means max pooling.

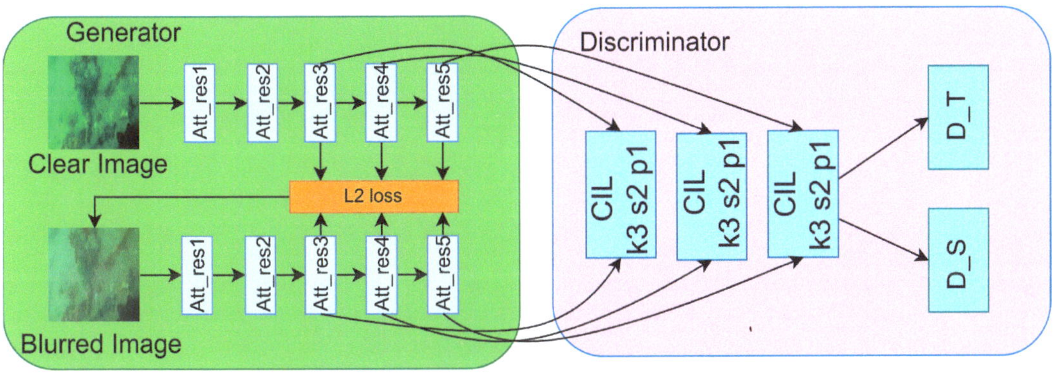

Figure 5. The FML module contains a generator and discriminator.

3.3. DTR Detection Module

The DTR structure is improved on the basis of YOLOv4. Multiple convolution blocks are used in DTR to detect feature information on features of different scales, and the up-sampled low-resolution features are combined with high-resolution features in the channel dimension to enrich the semantic and spatial information in high-resolution features. In the DTR structure, we use the SPPF module to replace the original SPP module, which can pool different feature maps without changing the size of the feature map, to capture the details of the target at different scales. It can also reduce the calculation amount of the model and improve the reasoning speed. The model structure of SPPF is shown in Figure 2. For the detection header of YOLOv4, the decoupling header can extract target location information and category information, which can effectively reduce the number of parameters and computational complexity and enhance the generalization ability and robustness of the model. The structure of the decoupling header is shown in Figure 2. In the G-Net proposed in this paper, since the ODFME module has completed the enhancement of degraded image detection features, DTR can directly perform accurate target classification and coordinate regression according to ODFME output features, which greatly improves the detection efficiency. Therefore, we did not make much improvement on the DTR part, and our improvement mainly lies in the enhanced feature extraction part of ODFME.

3.4. FML Module

The FML module proposed by us can be regarded as a new loss, and the FML learning module enables the ODFME module to better obtain the feature mapping of clear images. The concrete structure of the FML net is shown in Figure 5. As a whole, our learning module network is similar to gan. In the generator, we freeze the DTR part of G-Netnd and then let ODFME module learn the features of the corresponding clear image (the clear image is used as the input of G-Net and then trained to obtain the model and frozen). The generator outputs three kinds of characteristic maps with different scales, and the enhanced network is trained by gradient back propagation of $L2$ loss. As for the discriminator, our discriminator adopts the design of patch gan, and the input of different scales is converted into the feature map with the size of 4×4 by full convolution method, so that the discriminator can more accurately identify whether the feature map comes from a clear underwater image or a fuzzy underwater image. In the discriminator, we use the clear image output under ODFME module as the true value. Through iterative training, the feature mapping of underwater blurred image generated by ODFME enhancement network is closer to clear images. FML learning module only participates in the training phase of the model, but not in the reasoning phase of the model. Through the FML module, our ODFME module can obtain clearer detection features, which plays an important role in the following target classification and boundary regression.

3.5. Loss Function

In the training stage, we first train our G-Net network, then freeze the DTR part of the G-Net network and use the FML learning module to further train the ODFME module.

In the first phase, G-Net uses exactly the same loss functions as yolov4 (bounding box loss, confidence loss, and classification loss).

During FML module training, in the generator, we use an ODFME network with clear image as input to instruct the ODFME network with the haze image as input to learn image degradation features. According to [48], we use $L_{2\mathrm{loss}}$ as the generator's loss function. $L_{2\mathrm{loss}}$ can be formulated as:

$$L_{2loss}[X, Y] = \sum_{i=1,j=1}^{M,N} [X(i,j) - Y(i,j)]^2 \tag{4}$$

where X and Y correspond to the feature maps of paired clear and blurred underwater images, respectively; M and N correspond to the width and height of the feature maps, respectively; and i and j denote pixel points.

The loss function of the discriminator can be expressed intuitively as

$$L_{dis}[D_s, D_t] = ([D_s - 0] + [D_t - 1])/2 \tag{5}$$

where D_s and D_t indicate whether the discriminator identifies the input feature map as coming from a clear or degraded image.

4. Experiment

4.1. Datasets

It is difficult to obtain clear and degraded underwater images simultaneously. Meanwhile, to simulate the real environment as much as possible, we added haze to the underwater dataset based on the underwater imaging model based on Equation (6). To generate different concentrations of haze, the global atmospheric light value is set to (0.5, 0.95), and the transmission map is set to (0.3, 0.95). Our clear underwater dataset (UPRC) applies the data from real offshore environments and includes a total of 5542 images of four objects: holothurian, echinus, scallop, and starfish, with a total of 5542 images, as shown in Figure 6. Among them, 4987 images are used for training, and 555 images are used for testing. To reduce the memory consumption during training, our image size is set to (256, 256). Although G-Net functions include two parts, underwater image feature enhancement and object detection, underwater image enhancement (detection feature enhancement) is designed to improve the accuracy of object detection. Therefore, the experiment mainly verifies the target detection performance of G-Net.

Figure 6. Samples of underwater objects (holothurian, echinus, and scallop, and starfish) mainly considered to be detected in this article.

4.2. Evaluation Metric

To evaluate the target detection performance, the average accuracy mAP is applied to measure the detection performance of the network, and the IOU is set to 0.5. The mAP equation is expressed as

$$mAP = \frac{AP}{num\_classes} \tag{6}$$

where AP is the detection accuracy of each class of targets, and num_classes is the number of classes.

The IOU can be denoted by:

$$IOU = \frac{B_d \cap B_{gt}}{B_d \cup B_{gt}} \tag{7}$$

As shown in Figure 7, the green box indicates B_d, and the blue box indicates B_{gt}. B_d represents the detected bounding box, and B_{gt} represents the real bounding box. If the IOU of B_d and B_{gt} is greater than 0.5 and belongs to the same category, the test result is a true positive sample. Otherwise, it is a false positive sample. The intersection over union (IOU) is shown in Figure 7.

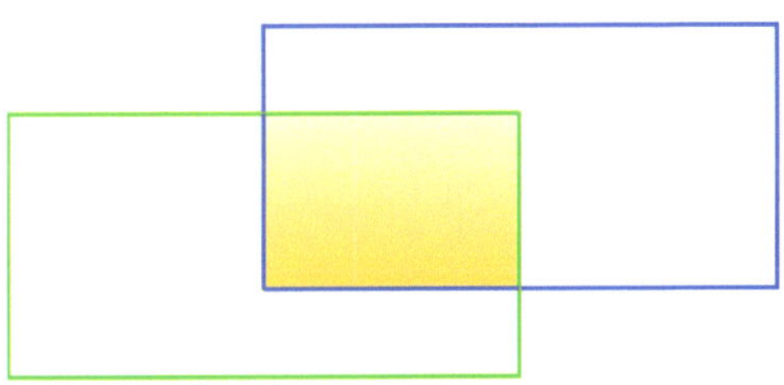

Figure 7. Intersection over union (IOU). The yellow part indicates the intersection.

The *Precision* can be expressed as

$$Precision = \frac{TP}{TP + FP} \tag{8}$$

where TP indicates a correct prediction as a true value and FP indicates an incorrect prediction as a true value. The details are shown in Table 1.

Table 1. TP denotes true positive samples, FP denotes false-positive samples, FN denotes false-negative samples, and TN denotes true negative samples.

	True Detect	False Detect
True ground	TP	FN
False ground	FP	TN

4.3. Implementation Details

All experiments are built on the PyTorch framework using a single NVIDIA GTX 4090 GPU and an Intel Core i9-13900 CPU. The resolution of the experimental image is 256 × 256. To better fit the training data and make full use of the GPU, we use a batch size of bit 32, a learning rate of 0.0001, and an Adam optimizer with a total of 300 epochs.

4.4. Contrast Experiment

The underwater degraded image feature enhancement and target detection included in G-Net are aimed at improving the accuracy of underwater target detection. Therefore, our comparison experiments mainly verify the target detection performance of G-Net. Since our G-Net was improved based on the YOLOv4 network, we adopted YOLOv4 as the target detection network for comparative testing. In this section, we first employ YOLOv4 to test different underwater enhancement methods to explore the effectiveness of our proposed method. Next, ablation experiments are conducted to investigate the effects of different components of our method using qualitative and quantitative approaches.

Underwater degraded images severely affect visibility. To verify the effectiveness of G-Net in real underwater environments, we compare the detection results of different advanced underwater degradation image enhancement methods through YOLOv4. UDCP, Ugan, CycleGan and PUIE were used as image enhancement networks, and YOLOv4 was used as a detection network to perform comparative experiments with G-Net. Table 2 demonstrates that compared to using ordinary detectors to detect underwater degraded images with the lowest detection accuracy, our G-Net has the highest detection accuracy of approximately 75.46% for the overall mAP. It can visually demonstrate the importance of G-Net in underwater degraded images without reconstructing the enhanced images and directly detecting the enhanced features. Although the parameters of G-Net are slightly higher than those of CycleGan and PUIE, but the time only needs 7.1 ms, which is lower than others, and overall, our performance is the best.

To better display the detection results of G-Net, the detection results of different enhancement algorithms are shown in Figure 8. Figure 8a is the detection result of YOLOv4 on clear images, and Figure 8b–d denote the detection results after image enhancement using the U-Gan, CycleGan, and PUIE methods, respectively. Figure 8e is the detection result of G-Net. In the second column, three different image enhancement algorithms of Figure 8b–d have missed detection behavior in holothurian detection. When detecting scallops in the third column, Figure 8b,c were misdetected; when detecting starfish in the fourth column, Figure 8b–d were also missed. Only Figure 8e can successfully detect all results.

Table 2. The detection results of traditional methods on underwater degraded images and G-Net detection results. "Params" is the total number of parameters of underwater image enhancement methods and detection methods. "FLOPs" is the number of floating-point operations of different algorithms. "Time" is the time needed for enhancement and detection by different methods. The second rows "C1" to "C4" are holothurian, echininus, scallop, and starfish.

Image Enhance Method	Detection Method	mAP(%)	AP(%)				Params (M)	FLOPs (G)	Time (ms)
			C1	C2	C3	C4			
-	YOLOv4	70.92	86.67	52.86	67.19	76.96	63.98	22.72	4.5
UDCP	YOLOv4	71.62	86.74	53.54	64.30	81.89	63.98	22.72	12.0
UGan	YOLOv4	70.64	83.86	53.96	70.48	74.27	105.81	58.85	8.2
CycleGan	YOLOv4	72.49	87.29	54.43	70.29	77.49	78.12	113.75	7.7
PUIE	YOLOv4	74.02	87.94	58.38	71.48	78.27	65.38	82.69	7.3
G-Net		75.46	87.08	59.63	74.02	81.11	78.75	33.41	7.1

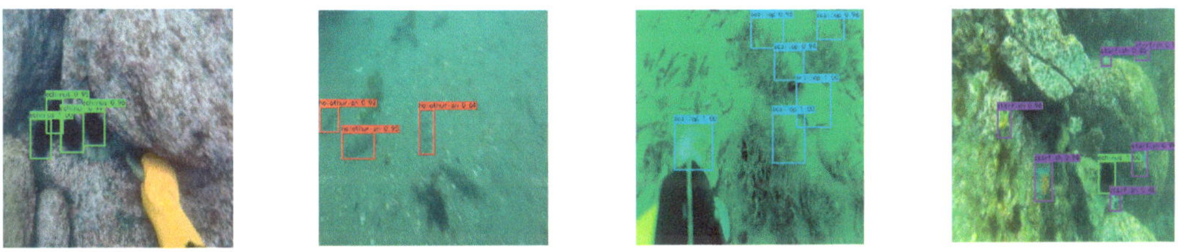

(a)

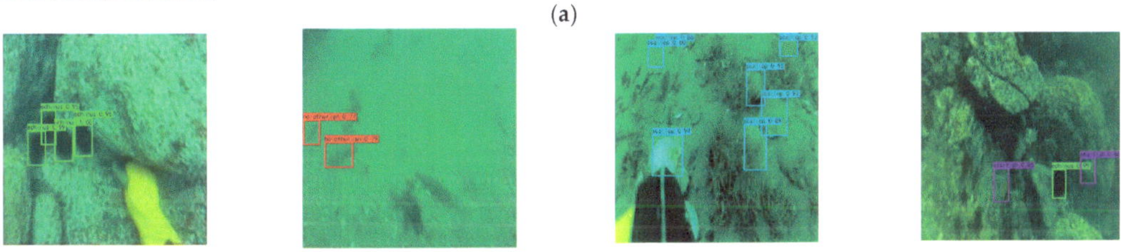

(b)

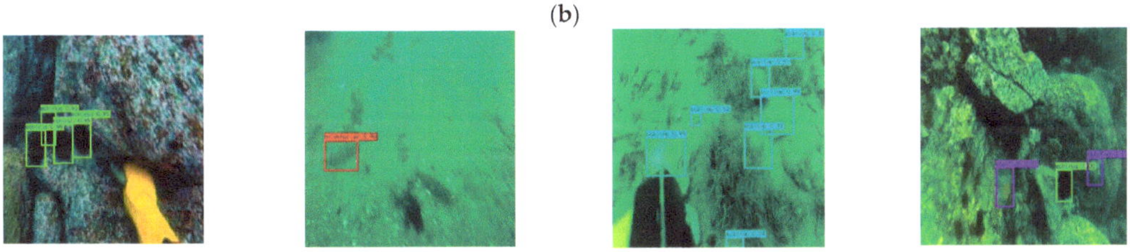

(c)

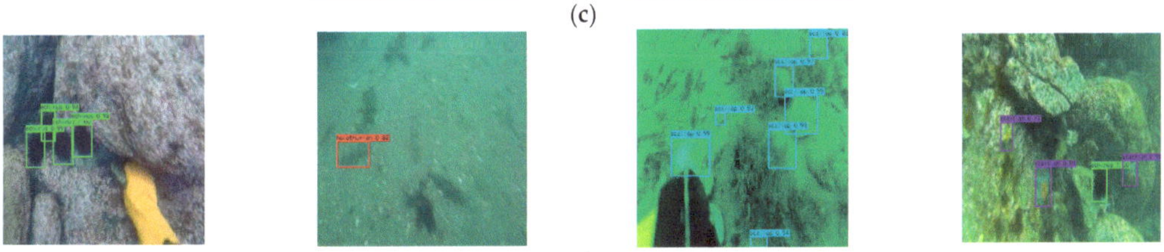

(d)

Figure 8. *Cont.*

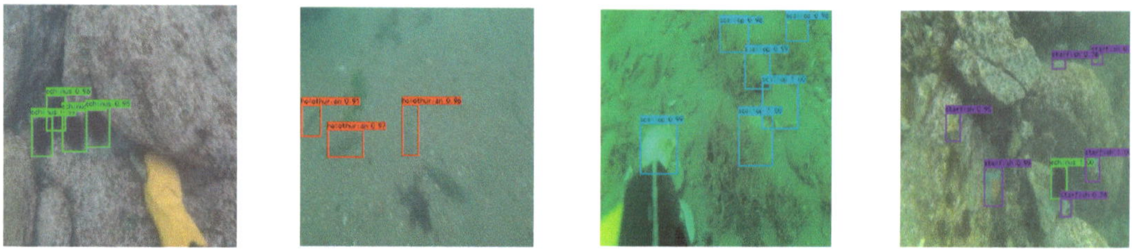

(e)

Figure 8. Detection result. (**b–d**) denote the detection results after image enhancement using the U-Gan, CycleGan, and PUIE methods, respectively. (**a**) is the detection result of YOLOv4 on clear images. (**e**) is the detection result of G-Net.

The combination of traditional image enhancement and detection has resulted in missed and false detection. The detection results of the G-Net network are very close to those of the clear image, and there is no need to rebuild clear images, which further proves the effectiveness of the proposed G-Net network.

4.5. Ablation Study

Qualitative and quantitative methods are used to validate the effectiveness of the FML learning module. We use the same dataset to compare G-Net with and without FML learning modules separately. The results in Table 3 demonstrate that G-Net with the FML learning module has the highest average detection accuracy. G-Net has a 75.46 mAP. Except for the detection accuracy of holothurian and scallop, which is slightly lower than that of G-Net without the FML module, the detection accuracy of echinus, scallop, and starfish is higher than that of G-Net without the FML module. Furthermore, the FML learning module does not participate in the forward inference of the model, so there is no increase in the number of parameters and the model time. When the backbone network does not use our attention structure, the number of parameters and the complexity of the model are reduced, the reasoning speed is relatively increased, but the detection accuracy is decreased. As shown in Table 3, the number of parameters, FLOPs, and runtime of our model are the same regardless of whether the FML module is used. The results show that the FML module can improve the detection accuracy of the G-Net network without reducing the speed. The attention structure of the backbone network also shows that we can improve our detection accuracy with a small increase in inference time.

Table 3. Experimental results of G-Net with or without the FML module. "Params" represents the number of parameters of the model. "FLOPs" indicates the complexity of the model. "C1" to "C4" and "Time" are the same as those in Table 2.

FML Module	Att_res Module	mAP(%)	AP(%)				Params (M)	FLOPs (G)	Time (ms)
			C1	C2	C3	C4			
✔		74.86	88.06	58.90	73.40	79.08	65.031	27.351	6.3
	✔	74.52	87.43	58.62	75.30	79.28	78.75	33.41	7.1
✔	✔	75.46	87.08	59.63	74.02	81.11	78.75	33.41	7.1

5. Conclusions

To reduce the interference of underwater degraded images on target detection performance and to improve the underwater detection efficiency, we propose an image feature enhancement detection network, G-Net. It simultaneously completes feature enhancement and detection tasks of underwater images in a single network, achieving the unification of underwater image enhancement and detection, and greatly improving underwater detection efficiency. Moreover, the FML unsupervised learning module uses an unsupervised approach to extract clear underwater image features, which guide the ODFME module for learning. It enables the ODFME module to learn clear underwater image features even in degraded underwater conditions. The experimental results demonstrate that our G-Net effectively reduces the interference of underwater degraded images and achieves high-accuracy target detection, which is crucial for tasks such as underwater grasping and surrounding obstacle detection.

In the follow-up study, due to the complexity and variety of underwater scenes, the visual interference caused by fog only being a part of it, as well as the effects of motion blur and light intensity, we should improve the FML module, so that it can learn different kinds of degradation features. Therefore, in the future, we will study the ODFME module and FML learning module with more general and better performance, so that they can better serve underwater target detection. At the same time, we will also try to combine some newer detectors with our G-Net to investigate more feasibility.

Author Contributions: Conceptualization, X.Z. and Z.D.; methodology, X.Z.; software, X.Z.; validation, X.Z. and Z.D.; formal analysis, X.Z.; investigation, X.Z.; resources, Z.D. and Z.W.; data curation, X.Z.; writing—original draft preparation, X.Z.; writing—review and editing, X.Z.; visualization, X.Z.; supervision, Z.D., Z.W. and H.Q.; project administration, Z.D., Z.W. and H.Q.; funding acquisition, H.Q. All authors have read and agreed to the published version of the manuscript."

Funding: This research was funded by the National Natural Science Foundation of China under Grant 52025111, China.

Institutional Review Board Statement: Not applicable.

Informed Consent Statement: Not applicable.

Data Availability Statement: All the data that support the findings in this study can be obtained by contacting the corresponding author.

Conflicts of Interest: The authors declare no conflicts of interest.

References

1. Zhang, S.; Zhao, S.; An, D.; Liu, J.; Wang, H.; Feng, Y.; Li, D.; Zhao, R. Visual SLAM for Underwater Vehicles: A Survey. *Comput. Sci. Rev.* **2022**, *46*, 100510. [CrossRef]
2. Li, C.-Y.; Guo, J.-C.; Cong, R.-M.; Pang, Y.-W.; Wang, B. Underwater Image Enhancement by Dehazing With Minimum Information Loss and Histogram Distribution Prior. *IEEE Trans. Image Process.* **2016**, *25*, 5664–5677. [CrossRef]
3. Islam, M.J.; Xia, Y.; Sattar, J. Fast Underwater Image Enhancement for Improved Visual Perception. *IEEE Robot. Autom. Lett.* **2020**, *5*, 3227–3234. [CrossRef]
4. Gong, T.; Zhang, M.; Zhou, Y.; Bai, H. Underwater Image Enhancement Based on Color Feature Fusion. *Electronics* **2023**, *12*, 4999. [CrossRef]
5. Yang, H.-H.; Huang, K.-C.; Chen, W.-T. LAFFNet: A Lightweight Adaptive Feature Fusion Network for Underwater Image Enhancement. In Proceedings of the 2021 IEEE International Conference on Robotics and Automation (ICRA), Xi'an, China, 30 May 2021; pp. 685–692.
6. Akkaynak, D.; Treibitz, T. A Revised Underwater Image Formation Model. In Proceedings of the 2018 IEEE/CVF Conference on Computer Vision and Pattern Recognition, Salt Lake City, UT, USA, 18–23 June 2018; pp. 6723–6732.
7. Akkaynak, D.; Treibitz, T. Sea-Thru: A Method for Removing Water from Underwater Images. In Proceedings of the 2019 IEEE/CVF Conference on Computer Vision and Pattern Recognition (CVPR), Long Beach, CA, USA, 15–20 June 2019; pp. 1682–1691.
8. Ueda, T.; Yamada, K.; Tanaka, Y. Underwater Image Synthesis from RGB-D Images and Its Application to Deep Underwater Image Restoration. In Proceedings of the 2019 IEEE International Conference on Image Processing (ICIP), Taipei, Taiwan, 22–25 September 2019; pp. 2115–2119.
9. Liu, W.; Anguelov, D.; Erhan, D.; Szegedy, C.; Reed, S.; Fu, C.-Y.; Berg, A.C. SSD: Single Shot MultiBox Detector. In Proceedings of the Computer Vision–ECCV 2016: 14th European Conference, Amsterdam, The Netherlands, 11–14 October 2016; Volume 9905, pp. 21–37.
10. Reis, D.; Kupec, J.; Hong, J.; Daoudi, A. Real-Time Flying Object Detection with YOLOv8 2023. *arXiv* **2023**, arXiv:2305.09972.
11. Lin, T.-Y.; Goyal, P.; Girshick, R.; He, K.; Dollar, P. Focal Loss for Dense Object Detection. In Proceedings of the 2017 IEEE International Conference on Computer Vision (ICCV), Venice, Italy, 22–29 October 2017; pp. 2999–3007.

12. Mieske, S.; Hilker, M.; Infante, L. Fornax Compact Object Survey FCOS: On the Nature of Ultra Compact Dwarf Galaxies. *Astron. Astrophys.* **2004**, *418*, 445–458. [CrossRef]
13. Girshick, R.; Donahue, J.; Darrell, T.; Malik, J. Rich Feature Hierarchies for Accurate Object Detection and Semantic Segmentation. In Proceedings of the 2014 IEEE Conference on Computer Vision and Pattern Recognition, Columbus, OH, USA, 23–28 June 2014.
14. Girshick, R. Fast R-CNN. In Proceedings of the 2015 IEEE International Conference on Computer Vision (ICCV), Santiago, Chile, 7–13 December 2015; pp. 1440–1448.
15. Ren, S.; He, K.; Girshick, R.; Sun, J. Faster R-CNN: Towards Real-Time Object Detection with Region Proposal Networks. *IEEE Trans. Pattern Anal. Mach. Intell.* **2017**, *39*, 1137–1149. [CrossRef]
16. Cai, Z.; Vasconcelos, N. Cascade R-CNN: Delving Into High Quality Object Detection. In Proceedings of the 2018 IEEE/CVF Conference on Computer Vision and Pattern Recognition, Salt Lake City, UT, USA, 18–23 June 2018; pp. 6154–6162.
17. Wang, Z.; Chen, H.; Qin, H.; Chen, Q. Self-Supervised Pre-Training Joint Framework: Assisting Lightweight Detection Network for Underwater Object Detection. *J. Mar. Sci. Eng.* **2023**, *11*, 604. [CrossRef]
18. Lei, F.; Tang, F.; Li, S. Underwater Target Detection Algorithm Based on Improved YOLOv5. *J. Mar. Sci. Eng.* **2022**, *10*, 310. [CrossRef]
19. Song, P.; Li, P.; Dai, L.; Wang, T.; Chen, Z. Boosting R-CNN: Reweighting R-CNN Samples by RPN's Error for Underwater Object Detection. *Neurocomputing* **2023**, *530*, 150–164. [CrossRef]
20. Zeng, L.; Sun, B.; Zhu, D. Underwater Target Detection Based on Faster R-CNN and Adversarial Occlusion Network. *Eng. Appl. Artif. Intell.* **2021**, *100*, 104190. [CrossRef]
21. Zou, Z.; Chen, K.; Shi, Z.; Guo, Y.; Ye, J. Object Detection in 20 Years: A Survey. *Proc. IEEE* **2023**, *111*, 257–276. [CrossRef]
22. Viola, P.; Jones, M. Robust Real-Time Face Detection. In *Proceedings Eighth IEEE International Conference on Computer Vision. ICCV 2001*; IEEE Computer Society: Vancouver, BC, Canada, 2001; Volume 2, p. 747.
23. Dalal, N.; Triggs, B. Histograms of Oriented Gradients for Human Detection. In Proceedings of the 2005 IEEE Computer Society Conference on Computer Vision and Pattern Recognition (CVPR'05), San Diego, CA, USA, 20–25 June 2005; Volume 1, pp. 886–893.
24. Felzenszwalb, P.F.; Girshick, R.B.; McAllester, D.; Ramanan, D. Object Detection with Discriminatively Trained Part-Based Models. *IEEE Trans. Pattern Anal. Mach. Intell.* **2010**, *32*, 1627–1645. [CrossRef]
25. LeCun, Y.; Bengio, Y.; Hinton, G. Deep Learning. *Nature* **2015**, *521*, 436–444. [CrossRef] [PubMed]
26. Yeh, C.-H.; Huang, C.-H.; Kang, L.-W. Multi-Scale Deep Residual Learning-Based Single Image Haze Removal via Image Decomposition. *IEEE Trans. Image Process.* **2020**, *29*, 3153–3167. [CrossRef] [PubMed]
27. Yeh, C.-H.; Lin, M.-H.; Chang, P.-C.; Kang, L.-W. Enhanced Visual Attention-Guided Deep Neural Networks for Image Classification. *IEEE Access* **2020**, *8*, 163447–163457. [CrossRef]
28. Lin, C.-Y.; Tao, Z.; Xu, A.-S.; Kang, L.-W.; Akhyar, F. Sequential Dual Attention Network for Rain Streak Removal in a Single Image. *IEEE Trans. Image Process.* **2020**, *29*, 9250–9265. [CrossRef]
29. Redmon, J.; Divvala, S.; Girshick, R.; Farhadi, A. You Only Look Once: Unified, Real-Time Object Detection. In Proceedings of the 2016 IEEE Conference on Computer Vision and Pattern Recognition (CVPR), Las Vegas, NV, USA, 27–30 June 2016; pp. 779–788.
30. Redmon, J.; Farhadi, A. YOLOv3: An Incremental Improvement. *arXiv* **2018**, arXiv:1804.02767.
31. Bochkovskiy, A.; Wang, C.-Y.; Liao, H.-Y.M. YOLOv4: Optimal Speed and Accuracy of Object Detection. *arXiv* **2020**, arXiv:2004.10934.
32. Wang, C.-Y.; Bochkovskiy, A.; Liao, H.-Y.M. YOLOv7: Trainable Bag-of-Freebies Sets New State-of-the-Art for Real-Time Object Detectors. *arXiv* **2022**, arXiv:2207.02696.
33. Li, X.; Shang, M.; Qin, H.; Chen, L. Fast Accurate Fish Detection and Recognition of Underwater Images with Fast R-CNN. In Proceedings of the OCEANS 2015—MTS/IEEE Washington, Washington, DC, USA, 19–22 October 2015; pp. 1–5.
34. Li, X.; Cui, Z. Deep Residual Networks for Plankton Classification. In Proceedings of the OCEANS 2016 MTS/IEEE Monterey, Monterey, CA, USA, 19–23 September 2016; pp. 1–4.
35. Li, X.; Tang, Y.; Gao, T. Deep But Lightweight Neural Networks for Fish Detection. In Proceedings of the OCEANS 2017—Aberdeen, Aberdeen, UK, 19–22 June 2017; pp. 1–5.
36. Jiang, Y.; Li, W.; Zhang, J.; Li, F.; Wu, Z. YOLOv4-dense: A Smaller and Faster YOLOv4 for Real-time Edge-device Based Object Detection in Traffic Scene. *IET Image Process.* **2023**, *17*, 570–580. [CrossRef]
37. He, K.; Zhang, X.; Ren, S.; Sun, J. Spatial Pyramid Pooling in Deep Convolutional Networks for Visual Recognition. In Proceedings of the Computer Vision—ECCV 2014, Zurich, Switzerland, 6–12 September 2014; pp. 346–361. Available online: https://link.springer.com/chapter/10.1007/978-3-319-10578-9_23 (accessed on 2 December 2023).
38. Yeh, C.-H.; Lin, C.-H.; Kang, L.-W.; Huang, C.-H.; Lin, M.-H.; Chang, C.-Y.; Wang, C.-C. Lightweight Deep Neural Network for Joint Learning of Underwater Object Detection and Color Conversion. *IEEE Trans. Neural Netw. Learn. Syst.* **2022**, *33*, 6129–6143. [CrossRef]
39. Deng, J.; Pan, Y.; Yao, T.; Zhou, W.; Li, H.; Mei, T. Single Shot Video Object Detector. *IEEE Trans. Multimed.* **2021**, *23*, 846–858. [CrossRef]
40. Yu, K.; Cheng, Y.; Tian, Z.; Zhang, K. High Speed and Precision Underwater Biological Detection Based on the Improved YOLOV4-Tiny Algorithm. *J. Mar. Sci. Eng.* **2022**, *10*, 1821. [CrossRef]
41. Redmon, J.; Farhadi, A. YOLO9000: Better, Faster, Stronger. In Proceedings of the 2017 IEEE Conference on Computer Vision and Pattern Recognition (CVPR), Honolulu, HI, USA, 21–26 July 2017; pp. 6517–6525.

42. Zhang, Y.; Tian, Y.; Kong, Y.; Zhong, B.; Fu, Y. Residual Dense Network for Image Super-Resolution. In Proceedings of the 2018 IEEE/CVF Conference on Computer Vision and Pattern Recognition, Salt Lake City, UT, USA, 18–23 June 2018; pp. 2472–2481.
43. Peng, Y.-T.; Cosman, P.C. Underwater Image Restoration Based on Image Blurriness and Light Absorption. *IEEE Trans. Image Process.* **2017**, *26*, 1579–1594. [CrossRef]
44. Peng, Y.-T.; Cao, K.; Cosman, P.C. Generalization of the Dark Channel Prior for Single Image Restoration. *IEEE Trans. Image Process.* **2018**, *27*, 2856–2868. [CrossRef]
45. Chiang, J.Y.; Chen, Y.C. Underwater Image Enhancement by Wavelength Compensation and Dehazing. *IEEE Trans. Image Process.* **2012**, *21*, 1756–1769. [CrossRef]
46. Hu, J.; Shen, L.; Sun, G. Squeeze-and-Excitation Networks. In Proceedings of the 2018 IEEE/CVF Conference on Computer Vision and Pattern Recognition, Salt Lake City, UT, USA, 18–23 June 2018; pp. 7132–7141.
47. Woo, S.; Park, J.; Lee, J.-Y.; Kweon, I.S. CBAM: Convolutional Block Attention Module. In *Computer Vision—ECCV 2018*; Ferrari, V., Hebert, M., Sminchisescu, C., Weiss, Y., Eds.; Lecture Notes in Computer Science; Springer International Publishing: Cham, Switzerland, 2018; Volume 11211, pp. 3–19. ISBN 978-3-030-01233-5.
48. Zhao, H.; Gallo, O.; Frosio, I.; Kautz, J. Loss Functions for Image Restoration With Neural Networks. *IEEE Trans. Comput. Imaging* **2017**, *3*, 47–57. [CrossRef]

remote sensing

MDPI

Article

A Statistical Evaluation of the Connection between Underwater Optical and Acoustic Images

Rebeca Chinicz [1] Roee Diamant [1,2,*]

[1] Hatter Department of Marine Technologies, University of Haifa, Haifa 3103301, Israel; rchinicz@campus.haifa.ac.il

[2] Faculty of Electrical Engineering and Computing, University of Zagreb, 10000 Zagreb, Croatia

* Correspondence: roee.d@univ.haifa.ac.il

Abstract: The use of Synthetic Aperture Sonar (SAS) in autonomous underwater vehicle (AUV) surveys has found applications in archaeological searches, underwater mine detection and wildlife monitoring. However, the easy confusability of natural objects with the target object leads to high false positive rates. To improve detection, the combination of SAS and optical images has recently attracted attention. While SAS data provides a large-scale survey, optical information can help contextualize it. This combination creates the need to match multimodal, optical–acoustic image pairs. The two images are not aligned, and are taken from different angles of view and at different times. As a result, challenges such as the different resolution, scaling and posture of the two sensors need to be overcome. In this research, motivated by the information gain when using both modalities, we turn to statistical exploration for feature analysis to investigate the relationship between the two modalities. In particular, we propose an entropic method for recognizing matching multimodal images of the same object and investigate the probabilistic dependency between the images of the two modalities based on their conditional probabilities. The results on a real dataset of SAS and optical images of the same and different objects on the seafloor confirm our assumption that the conditional probability of SAS images is different from the marginal probability given an optical image, and show a favorable trade-off between detection and false alarm rate that is higher than current benchmarks. For reproducibility, we share our database.

Keywords: SAS object detection; SAS–optical multimodal; feature descriptors; entropy metrics; image matching

Citation: Chinicz, R.; Diamant, R. A Statistical Evaluation of the Connection between Underwater Optical and Acoustic Images. *Remote Sens.* **2024**, *16*, 689. https://doi.org/10.3390/rs16040689

Academic Editors: Jingchun Zhou, Wenqi Ren, Qiuping Jiang and Yan-Tsung Peng

Received: 7 January 2024
Revised: 8 February 2024
Accepted: 13 February 2024
Published: 15 February 2024

1. Introduction

1.1. Overview

Autonomous underwater vehicles (AUVs) are efficient tools for surveying the seabed for target detection, e.g., for identifying mines, exploring shipwrecks and monitoring marine fauna. In the past, sonar was the preferred sensor for these investigations. However, due to their higher resolution, optical cameras provide better information for target classification. The combination of the two modalities can therefore offer an advantage. For example, multimodal sonar and optical sensors have proven effective in underwater navigation [1], object classification [2] and coastal characterization [3]. However, this combination poses a challenge for the comparison of sonar and optical images.

The matching of objects between sonar and optical data can be seen as a kind of multimodal sensing, where the main challenge is to overcome the different physical properties of the two modalities when viewing the same object. Sonar images are generated by the reflection of acoustic signals from the object and its surroundings and contain highlights and shadow regions [4] for the direct reflections from the object and the area blocked by the object, respectively. The sonar image also contains reflections from the area around the object (the background) and has a relatively low pixel resolution. The sonar image provides details about the height of the object (by shadow measurement), its material composition (by spectral analysis) and the general shape and size of the object. However, due to the low resolution (around 2 cm per pixel for high-precision Synthetic Aperture Sonar (SAS) systems [2]), no fine details of the object are captured. The optical image, on the other hand, provides millimeter resolution at short distances of a few meters, as well as texture and color data, but requires the observer to be close to the object and its quality is affected by the turbidity of the water. Differences between SAS and optical information can also be observed in the distribution of pixel intensity. For example, sonar reflections can be modeled as Beta- or K-distribution [5], while the pixels in optical images are considered as a Gaussian or Rayleigh distribution [6,7]. This is because the SAS image is created by beamforming and matched filtering of the received reflections, while optical images convert the light reflections into RGB values. Given this challenge, the combination of optical and SAS images is associated with object matching.

Object matching refers to the characterization of a complete mapping process between images acquired by different sensors or at different times. The available methods can be divided into two main approaches: area-based or feature-based. In the area-based approach, a template is matched to the different images using a similarity metric, such as cumulative cross entropy or residual entropy [8]. In feature-based approaches, relevant features are extracted from both images and matched, such as the Scale-Invariant Feature Transform (SIFT) algorithm [9] and its inheritors. In this method, the image is transformed into a collection of features that are fully scale-invariant, as well as translationally and rotationally invariant. In this transformation, a scale space is constructed and Gaussian differences are computed to form common feature descriptors for both images. Both the area-based and feature-based methods have found applications in areas such as optical and Synthetic Aperture Radar (SAR) registration [10] and matching between different optical, SAR and Light Detection and Ranging (LiDAR) images [11], with the primary goal of object detection and classification. However, recent works [2] showed that the above approaches fail when matching optical and sonar images due to the different pixel distribution and structure. Therefore, feature extraction is still an essential part of most object matching methods.

1.2. State of the Art

In the case considered in this paper, full registration is not required to align SAS and optical images. Instead, we focus on image matching: the aim is to check whether the same object is represented in both the SAS and the optical modality. In image matching, the features extracted from the object help to recognize the object, since it is assumed that the basic shape of the object is preserved in both modalities. One of the most influential feature descriptors for optical images is the Scale Invariant Feature Transform (SIFT) [9]. However, matching optical and SAS images using SIFT is more challenging than matching images of the same modality or even specifically the multimodal case of matching optical and SAR images, since the appearance of the objects is different in the two modalities. An example of this can be found in Figure 1, where the structural similarities between optical and SAR images are more apparent than in a pair of optical and SAS images of an object on the seafloor.

To overcome the challenges of matching between optical and SAS images, ref. [12] proposes the use of Convolutional Neural Networks (CNNs) to extract content and style features from sonar and optical images, respectively, and attempts to build a conversion scheme from sonar and optical images of a submerged panel of numbers and letters in an experimental pool. However, this approach is limited to a specific use case of character conversion between the two modalities, and requires a large amount of data. In an oceanic environment, it is more difficult to obtain optical and especially SAS images of different objects, especially image pairs, so training CNNs to match such images is more challenging. Recently, geometric features have been proven to be efficient to describe both SAS and optical images [2]. Notable geometric features for both optical and SAS modalities include contour-based features, such as the solidity of an object, eccentricity and normalized central moments, and region-based features, such as roughness and compactness [13]. With the absence of a large database, feature-based matching is a common approach for multimodal combination.

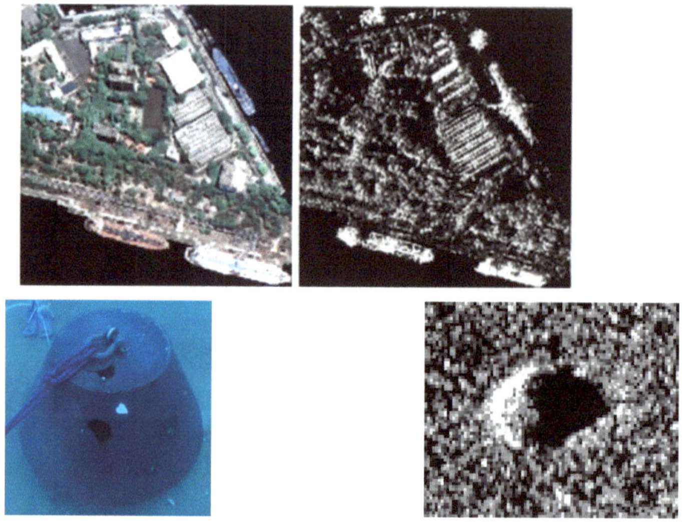

Figure 1. Optical and SAR images of the same structure, from [11] (**top panels**), and, for comparison, optical and SAS images of an underwater object (**bottom panels**). Similarities can be observed between the land images, whereas the marine-based images appear very different.

Recent work has focused on improving navigation methods by fusing visual and acoustic information. A fusion of acoustic DVL measurements and stereo imaging is offered in [14] for Simultaneous Localization And Mapping (SLAM) by formulating a joint utility function that also incorporates observations from a gyroscope and a depth sensor. In [15], a visual odometry system is proposes for underwater unmanned vehicles. The method filters out unreliable points from the 3D reconstruction of a scene provided by stereo cameras augmented by depth information from a single-beam sonar. Another multimodal SLAM is considered in [16], where monocular images are merged with images from a forward-looking sonar. The features from both modalities are extracted separately and matched in a maximum likelihood estimation model. However, this requires that the images from both sensors are acquired simultaneously and from the same vehicle, otherwise the matching will fail.

The aim of this work is to quantify the likelihood that an object identified in an SAS image is the same object identified in an optical image. We investigate the use of state-of-the-art feature descriptors, compute their distribution, and evaluate the statistical relationship between the descriptors of the two modalities in terms of a concept we call *mutual entropy*, which provides insights into the potential benefits of combining SAS and optical images. In other words, mutual entropy quantifies whether the information embedded in the optical image can be used to characterize the object in the SAS image and vice versa. This study provides metrics for the comparison of optical and SAS images, as well as statistical evidence that the multimodal combination of SAS and optical images is beneficial.

In the following, we refer to matched SAS–optical image pairs, i.e., pairs of images of the same object, as *positive* samples, and unmatched image pairs as *negative* samples. To test the performance of our entropy-based combination metric, we use a dataset of 1217 pairs of SAS and optical images we have collected in several sea experiments with our A18 ECA-robotics AUV, which contains a two-sided Kraken-based SAS and high-resolution optical cameras. To create a dataset of SAS–optical pairs, we compared the objects recognized in SAS images and optical images. The SAS images and the optical images were not acquired at the same time, position and orientation. The reason for this is the different observation range of SAS and optical: SAS requires a distance of tens of meters above the seafloor, while optical images require a small distance of the camera to the object (about 5 m). Therefore, we matched our SAS and optical observations by: (1) location of the object and (2) manual recognition of the object. The dataset contains 185 positive samples and 1032 negative samples. Our results show that entropy metrics, which quantify the information embedded in SAS and optical images by some feature descriptors, are effective in detecting SAS–optical similarities and that there is indeed a statistical relationship between the two modalities. In particular, the results show a favorable trade-off between the detection and false alarm rates, which is much better than the chance level and represents an improvement compared to benchmark methods. To ensure reproducibility, we present our database of matched and unmatched SAS and optical files in: https://drive.google.com/file/d/1ggz8BA0W6CtRXH-48XTfy9eO23-Ag1Qt/view?usp=sharing, accessed on 14 February 2024.

Although we have made considerable efforts to collect the above database with several sea experiments involving AUV and scuba divers, its size is still small. For this reason, we refrain from offering a deep learning approach and focus on statistical analysis instead. Statistics-based approaches also benefit from more data, but are more intuitively understandable despite the size of the dataset and therefore help in this initial exploration of the relationship between optical and acoustic images. The main contributions of this work are:

1. A first demonstration of the statistical relationship between underwater optical and acoustic images.
2. A statistics-based method for validating optical and SAS image pairs as matching or not.
3. A shared database of manually reviewed and labeled underwater optical and SAS images in which objects have already been recognized and segmented.

The rest of the paper is structured as follows: In Section 2, we provide our system model with our main assumptions and preliminaries for feature descriptors and entropy measures. Section 3 presents the methodologies of our solution to quantify the similarities between SAS–optical pairs, and Section 4 describes the exploration of the statistical relations between SAS and optical images. Results are discussed in Section 5, and conclusions are drawn in Section 6.

2. System Model

Referring to the illustration in Figure 2, the scenario under consideration is an AUV searching an area for a target object with its SAS. As soon as a target of interest is detected, e.g., a wreck, gas sip or a submerged mine, the AUV approaches the detected target to obtain optical images for target verification. This process can involve (1) matching an object found in the optical image with the object in the SAS image for target verification, or (2) matching an object found in the optical image with an object found in the SAS image as a navigation aid. The two scenarios considered are illustrated in Figure 2, and the latter scenario is also explained in detail in [17]. As a central tool for both objectives, we focus in this paper on the comparison of an object from an optical image with an object from an SAS image. We clarify that our solution is not specifically tailored for, e.g., navigation or target tracking, but rather focus on the backbone of the task of determining if an object found in an SAS image and an object found in an optical image are the same.

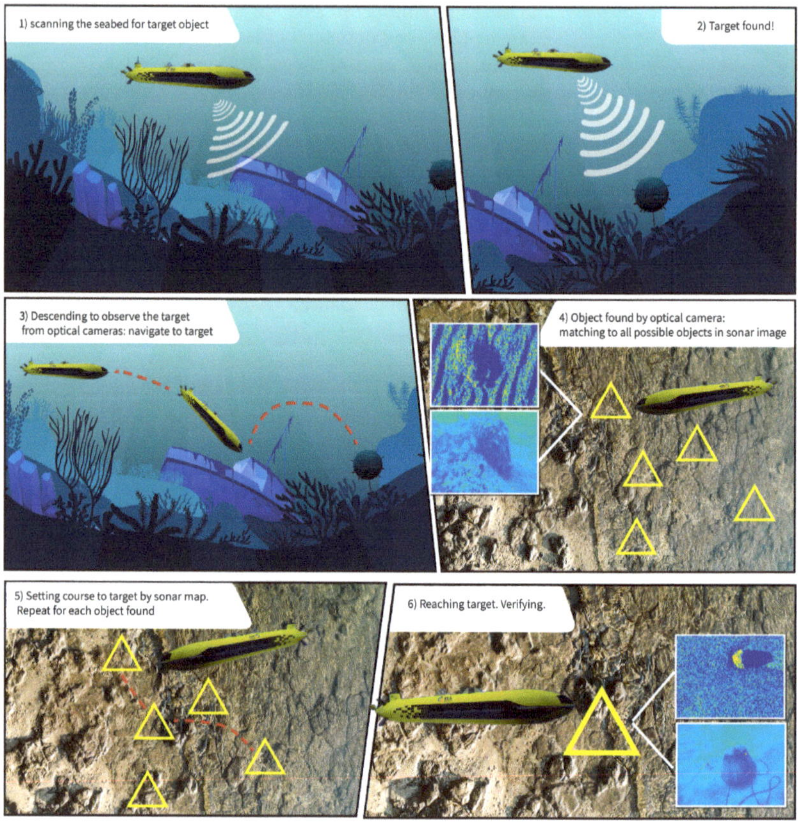

Figure 2. Demonstration of the considered scenario. Triangles represent location of targets.

2.1. Main Assumptions

We assume that several objects are found in the SAS image and that the SAS image acquisition takes place at a different time and at a different distance than the optical image acquisition. This means that the process of matching between the objects in the SAS image and an object found in an optical image should be insensitive to the viewing angle, size and shape of the object. Examples for the contour of such rotated images are given in Figure 3. Instead, such a matching procedure requires a statistical relationship between the objects in the images generated by the two modalities. Here, we assume that the relationship between SAS and optical images can be explored through the statistical distribution of the features of the objects. The preprocessing steps required for our solution are listed below.

We assume an underlying process that identifies a single object in both the SAS and optical images. This detection leads to regions of interest (ROIs), which are assumed to contain a signal object. These can be obtained by segmentation, which separates potential targets from their surrounding background. While several detectors are offered for SAS and for optical images, we choose the segmentation scheme presented in [4] for SAS and the algorithms in [18] for optical images. The former performs fuzzy clustering, the latter involves the use of Markov Random Fields (MRFs). We believe that these methods are well suited for our multimodal matching problem, as they provide robust results at a relatively low computational cost. See Section 3 below for more details. Another set of tools we use are feature descriptors and entropy matrices. Some preliminary remarks on these tools follow.

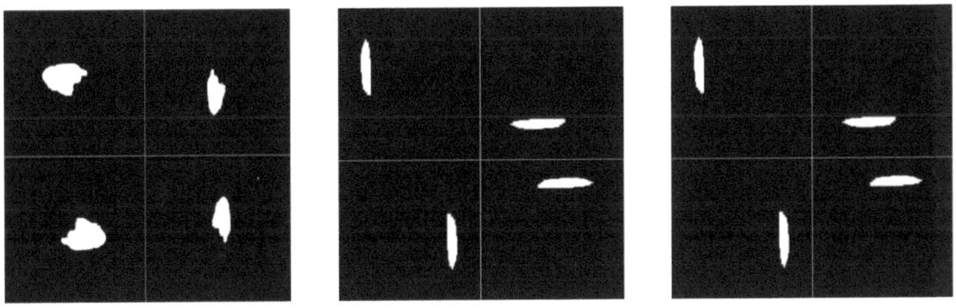

(a) (b) (c)

Figure 3. Augmentations performed in optical, SAS highlight and SAS shadow contour, in order to obtain the feature distributions. The contour in each figure belongs to the same object, a cylinder. Each figure above is a square grid with the original contour, and three rotations: 90, 180 and 270 degrees. (**a**) Contour of rotated optical images. (**b**) Contour of SAS-highlight images. (**c**) Contour of SAS-shadow images.

2.2. Preliminaries

2.2.1. Feature Descriptors

Our SAS–optical matching scheme relies on comparing features of the two objects. Given the two very different modalities physics, we avoid shape-based feature descriptors such as SIFT. Instead, we rely on geometry-based features of local curves to describe the objects within the images from the two modalities. A local curve refers to adjacent points on the contour, and is represented by a polynomial function of the range and angle of the curve, relative to the centroid of the contour. However, considering that the SAS- and optical-based objects are acquired at different times, distances and orientations, we use only angle-independent features; ones that avoid matching the two objects by the angle-of-view. In addition, region- and contour-based features are extracted, including the perimeter of the contour (P_c), its solidity, eccentricity, compactness and circularity, the FFT-based low-frequency density and the skewness of the discrete Fourier transform (DFT), as well as the central moments and the newly proposed entropy-angle feature [2]. Table 1 summarizes the definitions of the individual extracted features. The relationship between the features can be quantified using entropy metrics.

Table 1. Summary of features extracted.

Name	Definition	Observations
Ecc	Eccentricity $= \frac{l_{\text{major}}}{l_{\text{minor}}}$	l_{major} and l_{minor} are equal to the two eigenvalues of the co-variance matrix [13]
Perimeter	Perimeter of the object's contour	
Comp	Compactness $= \frac{P_c}{A}$	A is the area of the contour and P_c is the perimeter
cir	Circularity $= \frac{A}{A_c}$	A_c is the area of the circle having the same length as the object's perimeter
Solidity	Solidity $= \frac{A}{A_{\text{convex hull}}}$	$A_{\text{convex hull}}$ is the area of the convex hull [13]

Table 1. *Cont.*

Name	Definition	Observations
roughness	$\text{Roughness} = \frac{P_c}{P_{\text{convex hull}}}$	$P_{\text{convex hull}}$ is the perimeter of the convex hull [13]
sigma$_{ij}$ and l_k	$\bar{\zeta}_{ij} = \frac{\zeta_{ij}}{\zeta_{00}^l}, \quad l = 1 + \frac{i+j}{2}, \quad \zeta_{ij} = \sum_u \sum_v (u-\bar{u})^i (v-\bar{v})^j I(u,v)$	Normalized central moment is $\bar{\zeta}_{ij}$, for every pixel (u,v), center mass $(\bar{u},\bar{v})$, $I(u,v) \in [0,1]$ is 1 if (u,v) is within the object's region, and each $sigma_{ij}$ refers to a central moment ζ_{ij} and l to the normalized version of lth calculated central moment [2]
Low Freq Den	$LowFrequencyDensity = \frac{1}{N_{\text{LF}}} \sum_{n_{\text{DFT}}=1}^{N_{\text{LF}}} D_{\text{cen}}(n_{\text{DFT}})$	D_{cen} is the magnitude of the Fourier coefficients of the centroid distance function and the DFT is implemented with N_{DFT} points
DFT-skewness	$\frac{\frac{1}{N_{\text{DFT}}} \sum_{n_{\text{DFT}}=1}^{N_{\text{DFT}}} (D_{\text{cen}}(n_{\text{DFT}}) - \mu_{\text{cen}})^3}{(\frac{1}{N_{\text{DFT}}} \sum_{n_{\text{DFT}}=1}^{N_{\text{DFT}}} (D_{\text{cen}}(n_{\text{DFT}}) - \mu_{\text{cen}})^2)^{1.5}}$	$\mu_{\text{cen}} = \frac{1}{N_{\text{DFT}}} \cdot \sum_{n_{\text{DFT}}=1}^{N_{\text{DFT}}} D_{\text{cen}}(n_{\text{DFT}})$
localCur$_i$	Local curve, polynomial coefficient i [2]	
Hist-BAS	Entropy-Angle Feature (EAF) [2]	

2.2.2. Entropy Measures

The Shannon entropy (H) for a dataset X is defined as:

$$H(X) = -\sum_{x \in X} p(x) \log p(x) \quad (1)$$

A direct calculation of this metric may be too computationally expensive and difficult to derive in its exact form. Instead, several alternatives are explored.

The Mutual Information provides knowledge about the reduction of uncertainty in one variable, given observations from another. For two datasets x, y, it is computed by:

$$I(X;Y) = -\sum_{x \in X, y \in Y} \log(\frac{p(x,y)}{p(y)\,p(x)})\, p(x,y)\,. \quad (2)$$

The Differential Entropy provides insight on the expected uncertainty in one variable, given the values of another. It is calculated by:

$$h(X;Y) = -\sum_{x \in X, y \in Y} \log(\frac{p(x,y)}{p(y)})\, p(x,y)\,. \quad (3)$$

The Transfer Entropy and the Normalized Transfer Entropy are, respectively, defined by:

$$T_{X \to Y} = H(Y_t \mid Y_{t-1:t-L}) - H(Y_t \mid Y_{t-1:t-L}, X_{t-1:t-L}) \quad (4)$$

$$\frac{T_{X \to Y}}{H(Y_t \mid Y_{t-1:t-L})}\,. \quad (5)$$

and are calculated by the compressed transfer entropy (cTE) [19]. The two measures are useful to determine dependencies between time series, as a form of mutual information that also takes into account the transition probabilities between the ordered elements of the data sets. Vector entropy is used to describe the complexity of a signal and takes into account non-linear behavior. Formally define a constant γ and denote Γ as the Gamma function. The method for calculating the vector entropy is presented in Algorithm 1.

Algorithm 1 Vector Entropy KL

Input: feature vectors from the SAS and optical images, X **and** Y

$z \leftarrow X$ concatenated with Y
$n \leftarrow$number of rows in z ▷ the size of both X and Y
$p \leftarrow$number of columns in z
$D \leftarrow$distances between the $K = 4$ nearest neighbors between X and Y based on a KNN search
$n \leftarrow$ size of D

$$\text{Output} \leftarrow \frac{p*\text{mean}(\log D)+\log(\frac{\pi^{\frac{p}{2}}}{\Gamma(\frac{p}{2}+1)})+\gamma+\log(n-1)}{\log 2}$$

3. Methodology

3.1. Key Idea

The input to our scheme are two regions of interest (ROIs) containing possibly the same object; one acquired by SAS and the other by an optical camera. The scheme augment the two ROIs by rotation and scaling to calculate the statistics of extracted features of the two ROIs. Comparison of this statistics via entropy measures then determines if the two objects are indeed the same. A block diagram illustrating our process is shown in Figure 4. We distinguish between the path of detection (red) and the path of information exploration (blue). In the first step, we perform ROI detection and ROI segmentation. Next, in the detection route, each segmented image is expanded to l ROIs by rotating and rescaling the image. We then extract key features for each of the augmented ROIs to form a dataset with M descriptors for each extracted feature. This dataset is used to evaluate the distribution of the feature for each ROI. This step eliminates the need to learn the general statistics of each feature and contributes to the robustness of the method. The feature distributions of the SAS and optical ROIs are then compared using an entropy metric. The result is then thresholded to obtain a binary detection decision for a *positive* match for ROIs containing the same object and vice versa for *negative*. To determine which feature entropy metric is most effective for our similarity comparison, we quantify the overlap between the distributions of positive and negative matches using K-Means Clustering [20] accuracy.

Our goal is to divide the original ROIs from SAS and optical images into positive (matched) and negative (mismatched). Formally, given an ROI from an SAS image S, and an ROI from an optical image O, we determine whether $P(S|O) = P(S,O)/P(O) \neq P(S)$, or whether $P(O|S) = P(S,O)/P(S) \neq P(O)$. The former states that O provides valuable information about S, while the latter states that S is related to O. In both cases, the conclusion is that S and O contain the same object. This is explored via the information exploration route (blue lines), where we define feature vectors in terms of matching and non-matching optical and SAS data points, which we directly compare via an entropy measure and their conditional and marginal probabilities.

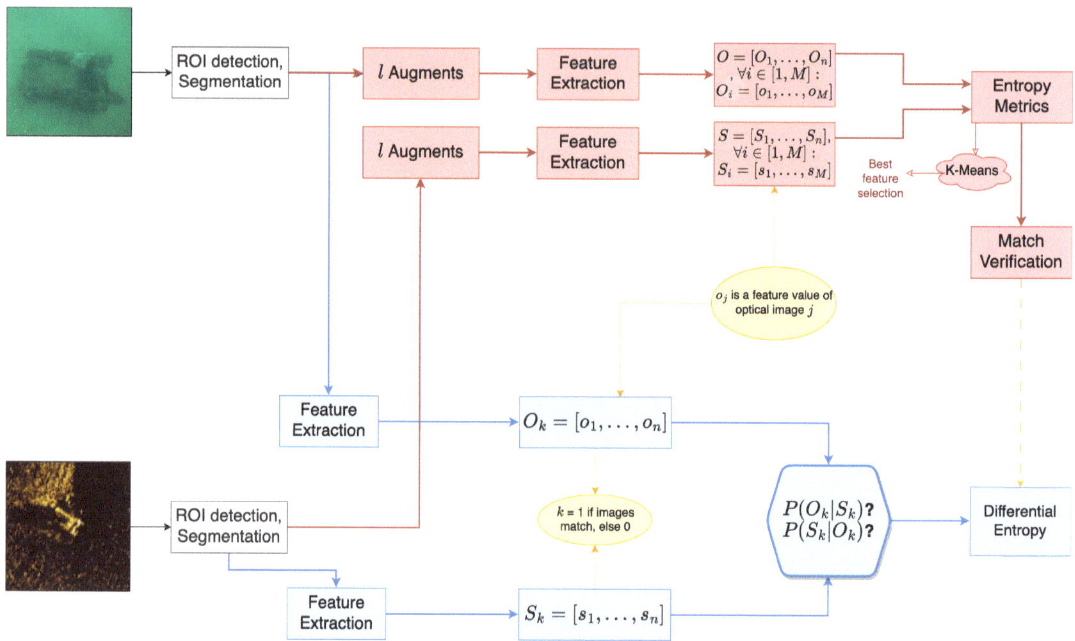

Figure 4. Diagram summarizing the steps of our proposed SAS–optical comparison approach. The detection process involves the steps on the top side of the diagram (red lines), logic steps (yellow lines) and the bottom side gives an overview of the steps taken to explore the statistical connection between the images (blue lines).

3.2. Entropy Matching Decision

Joint entropy measures can express the information exchange between two feature vectors. In this paper, we investigate the use of differential entropy, mutual information, transfer entropy and normalized transfer entropy, and vector entropy over the concatenation of two feature vectors. We chose these metrics because of their efficiency in identifying the exchange of information between statistical populations. The above entropy measures take as input pairs of features derived from the ROIs of the SAS and the optical images. The entropy is then calculated after the distribution of each feature set is computed. Note that since the entropy measures are not symmetric, we perform the analysis both from the SAS to the optical side and from the optical to the SAS direction. In addition, the analysis is performed separately for the shadow and highlight regions in the SAS ROI. We leave the investigation of a possible merging of the two regions to future work.

The entropy-based matching method is based on the distribution function of the features extracted from the SAS ROI and the optical ROI. Depending on the direction of exploration, from SAS to optical or vice versa, the two distributions are computed and labeled as $p(x)$ and $p(y)$. These are then fed into one of the entropy measures listed in Section 2.2.2, the result of which is called a soft decision. Crossing a threshold for this value would result in a positive or negative decision for each pair of SAS and optical ROIs. This process is applied separately for the shadow and highlights segments of the SAS ROIs and separately for the SAS to optical and optical to SAS directions. A positive match is determined if one of these tests leads to a positive decision. In the following sections, we provide details on how to obtain the distribution of the individual features.

3.3. Feature Extraction

The feature extraction process begins with a segmentation of the ROI to determine the position of the object's pixels within the ROI. For SAS segmentation, we choose the method in [4], which relies on kernel-based fuzzy clustering for segmentation. The process includes a denoising step that contributes to the segmentation process. The result is a three-grade segmentation, where the pixels of the ROI are divided into contiguous regions of background, highlights and shadows. For optical segmentation, we chose the method in [18], as it is a low complexity approach that incorporates spatial information to segment images via a Markov Random Fields (MRF)-based mixture model. From each segmented image, we extract a set of feature descriptors from the list described in Section 2.2 to express geometric information from both optical and SAS images.

The entropy detection process described above requires the calculation of the distribution of the feature. Since there is no probabilistic model for the feature descriptors, we turn to a numerical evaluation of the distribution. This is obtained by augmenting each ROI by rotation and scaling operations. Formally, for images defined as a two-dimensional matrix, these two operations are obtained by multiplying the image by an affine transformation matrix. For each pixel (x, y), we perform Rotation and Scaling.

3.3.1. Rotation

Considering that the SAS- and optical-based matched objects are most probably obtained at different (any) orientations, the angle-of-view does not contain valuable information that may affect performance. We thus use rotation to augment our dataset. This is performed by

$$\begin{bmatrix} x' \\ y' \\ 1 \end{bmatrix} = \begin{bmatrix} \cos\alpha & \sin\alpha & 0 \\ -\sin\alpha & \cos\alpha & 0 \\ 0 & 0 & 1 \end{bmatrix} \begin{bmatrix} x \\ y \\ 1 \end{bmatrix}, \tag{6}$$

where α as the specific angle of rotation.

3.3.2. Scaling

$$\begin{bmatrix} x' \\ y' \\ 1 \end{bmatrix} = \begin{bmatrix} s_x & 0 & 0 \\ 0 & s_y & 0 \\ 0 & 0 & 1 \end{bmatrix} \begin{bmatrix} x \\ y \\ 1 \end{bmatrix}, \tag{7}$$

where s_x, s_y are the scaling factors in the x, y dimensions, respectively. Note that in this case, we use the same scale factor in both dimensions, that is $s_x = s_y$.

The augmentation process leads to a series of 89 augmentations per ROI. A single descriptor is drawn from each augmented ROI to obtain a set of 89 features for each ROI. This process is performed separately for both the SAS and optical ROIs. To demonstrate the effectiveness of this augmentation step, we show in Figure 5 an example feature set drawn from the ROI of an SAS and an optical image of a cylinder, as shown in Figures 6 and 7. We observe a variability in the feature values that reflects a change in the ROI due to the augmentation procedure. However, as the differences between the values show, a direct comparison between the feature distribution of the SAS and the optical ROIs is not possible for the task of matching the two, and a deeper statistical investigation through the concept of information exchange using joint entropy is required.

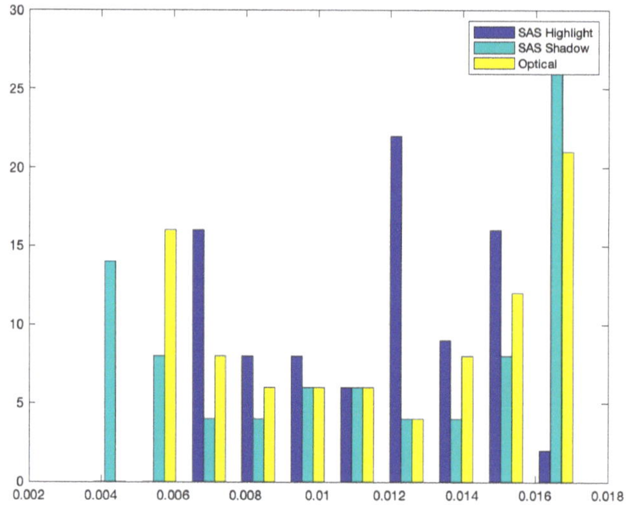

Figure 5. Distribution (histogram) of central moment with $i = 0$, $j = 2$ of SAS image of cylinder vs. optical image of cylinder.

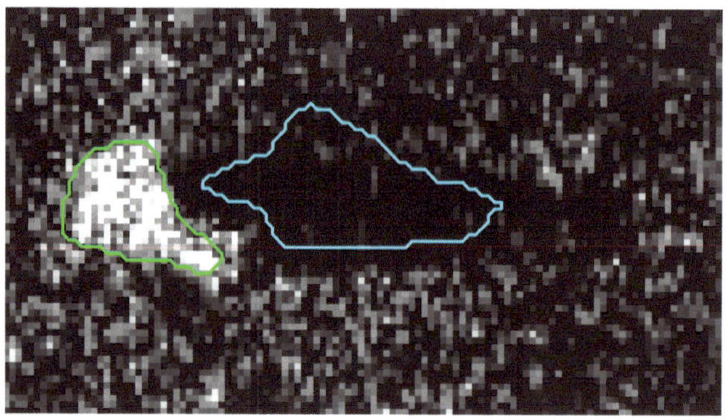

Figure 6. Original ROI of the SAS image of the cylinder segmented into highlight in green and shadow in blue.

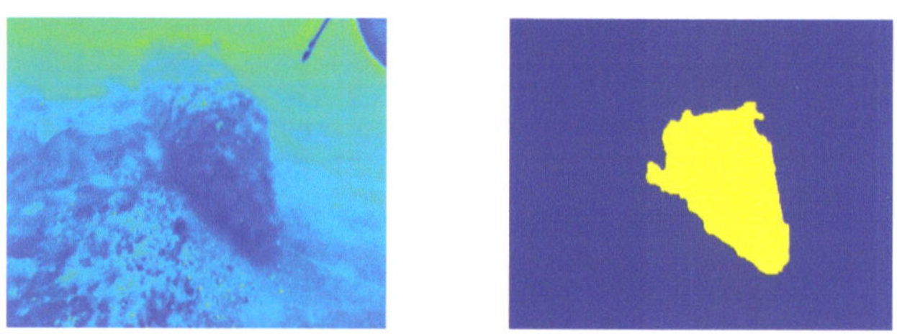

Figure 7. Original ROI of the optical image of the cylinder and its segmentation.

4. Exploration of Statistical Relations between SAS and Optical Images

We now turn to investigate whether there is indeed a relationship between optical and SAS images that can be used for matching, comparing or, even better, classifying a detected object. To this end, we are looking for a statistical relationship in the sense of an exchange of information between the optical and sonar images. The exploration of statistical relationships between data sets can be performed by calculating correlation and covariance measures, such as the Pearson correlation coefficient, under certain conditions, such as linearity [21]. In this paper, we turn again to testing the relationship between SAS and optical images by using joint entropy measures to infer the statistical relationship between a set of features from an SAS ROI and a set of features from an optical ROI. To complete this analysis, we explore the direct calculation of the conditional probabilities $P(S|O)$ and $P(O|S)$.

Exploring the statistical relationships involves extracting the same feature from a set of ROIs derived from SAS and optical images. Some of these image pairs contain the same object and some different objects. We denote the positive (i.e., matched objects) dataset for each feature as $S_1 = [s_1, ..., s_m]$, $H_1 = [h_1, ..., h_m]$ and $O_1 = [o_1, ..., o_m]$, and the negative dataset as $S_0 = [s_1, ..., s_n]$, $H_0 = [h_1, ..., h_n]$ and $O_0 = [o_1, ..., o_n]$, where S, H and O represent the SAS-based ROI with the segmented shadow, the SAS-based ROI with the segmented highlight and the segmented ROI of the optical images, respectively. Each member in the S, H and O groups reflects the result of the selected feature over a particular ROI.

5. Results

Our goal is to compare a pair of optical and SAS images to determine whether they depict the same object. For this reason, we compare the performance of our approach with that of recent work [17], we refer to as *Abu-2023*. This benchmark scheme quantifies the likelihood that an SAS and an optical image contain the same object using a generic Gaussian radial basis function, which is known to improve robustness to image noise [22].

5.1. Dataset

Our dataset contains sonar images collected with our ECA robotics A18D AUV. The AUV is equipped with a Kraken-manufactured SAS sensor and a pair of optical cameras. The data were collected during four sea trials off the coasts of Caesarea and Haifa, Israel. The optical images of the objects found were obtained either from the AUV's cameras or from handheld optical cameras operated by divers. The ROIs were determined according to the scheme in [2] and checked manually.

The dataset contains images of a cylinder, a manta mine, a box and a variety of unclassified natural objects (rocks, corals, etc.). The natural objects are not labeled in either the SAS images or the optical images, and are therefore not matched. In addition, there were only optical images of the box. Therefore, the positive (matched) sonar-optical pairs were only formed with combinations of images of the cylinder and the manta objects, and the rest were only used to generate more negative (unmatched) samples. Figure 8 shows examples of optical and SAS images of the objects. With a total of 1217 samples—185 positive samples formed by pairing multiple images of the same objects (cylinder and manta mine) and 1032 negative samples—Table 2 quantifies the set of images in each modality per object type.

Table 2. Overview of images in the dataset.

Object Type	SAS	Optical
Cylinder	9	9
Manta Mine	8	13
Box	0	6
Natural	25	14

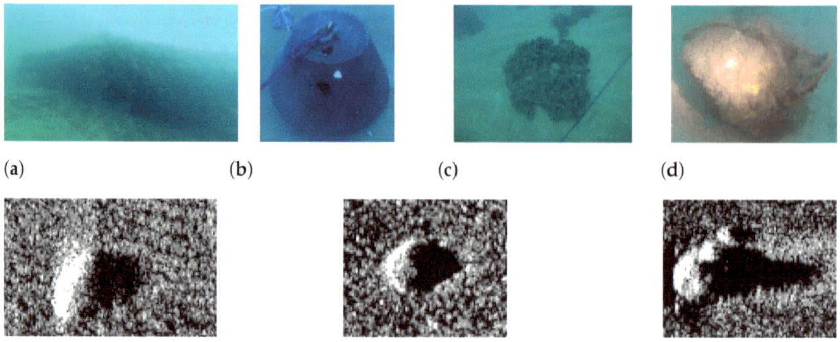

(a) (b) (c) (d) (e) (f) (g)

Figure 8. Examples of images from each type of object in the dataset. (**a**) Optical image of cylinder. (**b**) Optical image of manta mine. (**c**) Optical image of natural object. (**d**) Optical image of box. (**e**) SAS image of cylinder. (**f**) SAS image of manta mine. (**g**) SAS image of natural object.

5.2. Feature Analysis

To quantify how well each feature's entropy measure separates between a positive and a negative match, we use the K-Means Clustering algorithm. It aims to divide a number of observations into K clusters. In our case, $K = 2$, and we assume that the feature whose entropy measures are most correctly clustered should be used for identifying matches. This choice of $K = 2$ is due to the fact that here we cluster the entropy values comparing optical–SAS image pairs into either "matching" or "non-matching", which is a binary task. For the SAS optical matching case, the accuracy of the K-Means clustering is used to indicate for each direction (from SAS to optical and from optical to SAS), for each entropy measure, and for each selected feature descriptor whether the positive and negative cases are well observed and distinguished from each other.

To determine the best feature for the similarity test, we show the accuracies of the K-Means clusterings over all tested features and entropy measures for both positive and negative matches in Figure 9. To account for the known distribution of positive and negative samples in the dataset, we set a threshold, λ, on the ratio between the sizes of the two clusters. The threshold takes into account the extreme case where, for example, all observations would be clustered in the negative cluster and we would obtain a high clustering accuracy. Nevertheless, the detection rate of matches would be low due to the imbalance between the number of positive and negative samples. This threshold was empirically set to 0.2, and if the criterion was not met, an accuracy of 0 was assigned for better visual discrimination. Table 3 summarizes which feature had the best accuracy, and was therefore selected for the matching procedure, for each entropy measure and direction, i.e., optical to SAS and SAS to optical, for SAS highlights (HL) and shadows (SH).

Table 3. Highest K-Means accuracy feature per entropy and direction of comparison. See the feature preliminaries in Section 2.2 for each feature's definition.

Direction / Entropy	**Optical to SAS HL**	**SAS HL to Optical**	**Optical to SAS SH**	**SAS SH to Optical**
Differential Entropy	sigma20	localCur6	l2	l4
Mutual Information	l4	l4	sigma20	sigma11
Transfer Entropy	localCur1	localCur4	l2	localCur4
Normalized Transfer Entropy	sigma02	Solidity	l2	Solidity
Vector Entropy	DFT skewness	DFT skewness	roughness	roughness

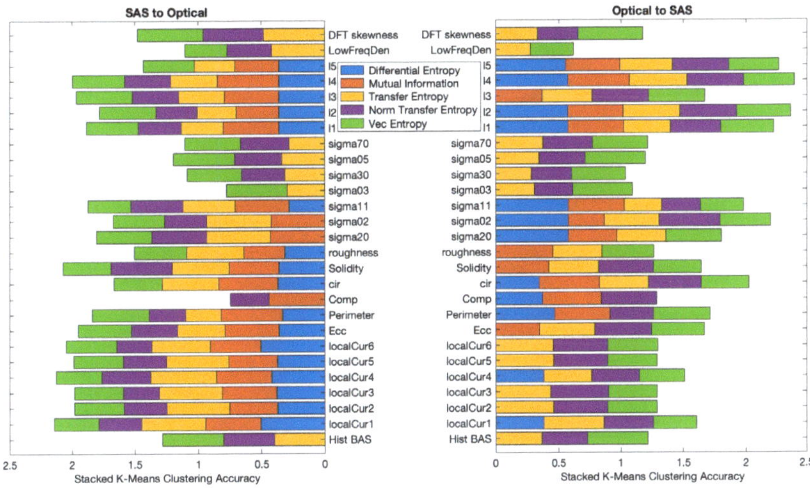

(**a**)

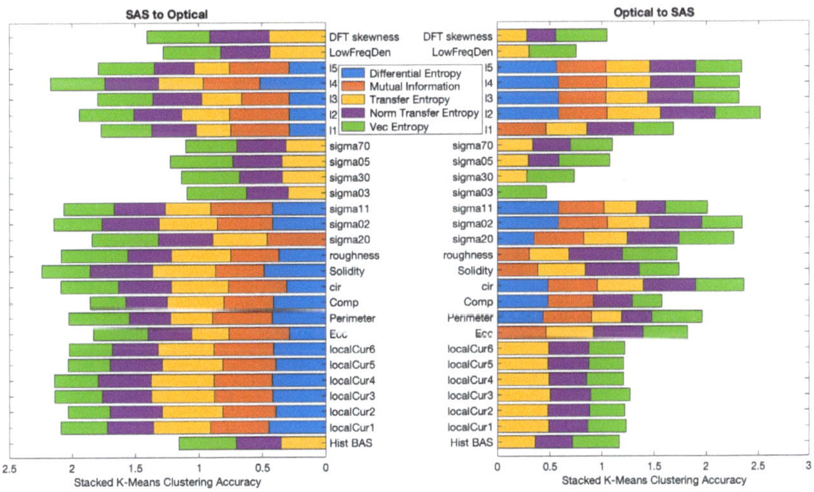

(**b**)

Figure 9. Stacked K-Means clustering accuracies of each entropy type, in different colors (X-axis), as tested with each each of the 27 features (Y-axis). The accuracy here refers to the accuracy of the resulting clusters at splitting the positive and negative image pairs (their entropy comparison values) (**a**) K-Means accuracies for entropy measures by feature with SAS highlight only. (**b**) K-Means accuracies for entropy measures by feature with SAS shadow only.

5.3. Entropy Matching

For each selected feature, we now examine the results of the entropy matching procedure. The results are measured using the receiver operating characteristics (ROC) curve to observe the trade-off between the detection rate and the false alarm rate. Detection is defined here as the correct assignment of a positive match, while a false alarm refers to the case of a positive decision on a non-similar object pair. The results are shown in Figure 10, and are compared to the work of [17] as a benchmark. We report that the highest clustering accuracy was achieved with differential entropy. We compute the ROC for this entropy measure in all possible directions, i.e., from optical to SAS HL and to SAS SH and from SAS HL and SAS SH to optical.

As can be seen from Figure 10, the detection was not successful when the entropy measures were examined from SAS to optical, while in the other direction, the differential entropy provided a match far above the chance level. This was the case for both the highlights and the shadow regions, indicating that both the highlights and the shadows in SAS may provide relevant shape information that is statistically related to the shape information extracted from the optical images.

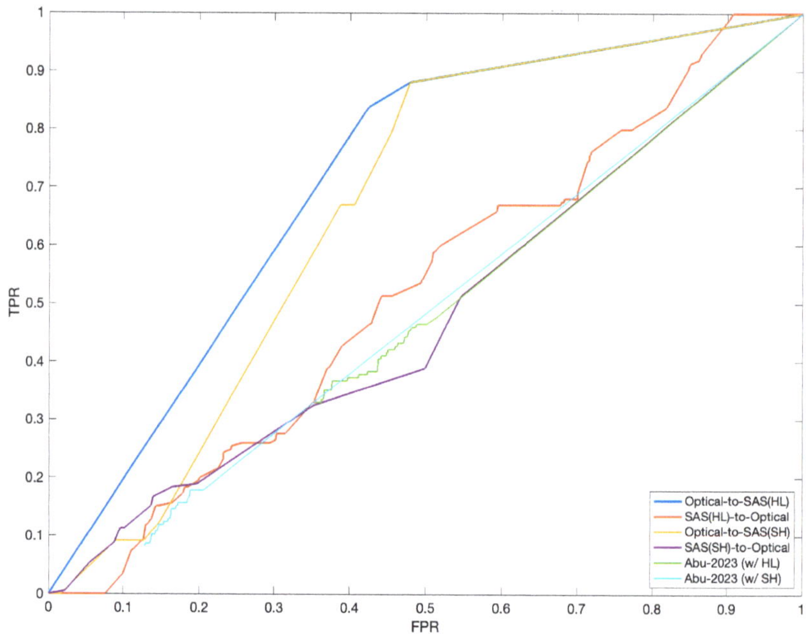

Figure 10. ROC for match detection between all directions with Differential Entropy, as well as benchmark, with SAS highlight (HL) and with SAS shadow (SH) segmentation. We note that there was little variation across over 10,000 threshold values tested, which may lead the resulting curves to contain points concentrated in specific parts of the curve only.

5.4. Information Exchange

Our final analysis examines the statistical relationship between the SAS and the optical images. In Table 4, we report the differential entropy values for the set of positive and negative matches. We conclude that the information from optical and SAS images is indeed statistically related, with values of approximately 3 and 5 for positive and negative series, respectively, compared to roughly 3 and 4 from the SAS to optical direction. As for the highlight and shadow effects, respectively, we find that there is little difference when comparing the two with the optical features.

Table 4. Values of differential entropy between optical–SAS (HL: highlight only, SH: shadow only) pairs, for the most appropriate features (see Table 3).

Optical to SAS			
Positive (HL)	**Negative (HL)**	**Positive (SH)**	**Negative (SH)**
3.0744	5.1850	3.3481	5.2553
SAS to Optical			
Positive (HL)	**Negative (HL)**	**Positive (SH)**	**Negative (SH)**
3.4682	4.4457	3.4682	4.4457

To calculate the joint entropy and conditional probabilities, we estimate the probability density function of each data set using a numerical histogram. We find that the entropy between matched optical and SAS datasets is consistently lower than the entropy between unmatched optical and SAS datasets, for all features. This means that there is indeed more information flowing between optical and SAS images of the same object than in images of different objects.

Finally, we examine the conditional probability of the feature vectors to determine whether $P(O|S) = P(S,O)/P(S) \neq P(O)$. To do this, we calculate the conditional probabilities $P(O_1|S_1), P(O_0|S_0)$ and the marginal probabilities $P(O_1), P(O_0)$, and determine their distance using the Kullback–Leibler divergence (KLD) [23]. Formally, the KLD for two distributions P and Q over one variable X, the KLD is derived as follows:

$$D_{\mathrm{KL}}(P \parallel Q) = \sum_{x \in X} P(x) \log\left(\frac{P(x)}{Q(x)}\right). \tag{8}$$

In Figure 11, we show the resulting KLDs, both when the SAS feature vector comes from the highlight and when it comes from the shadow segmentation. We find that, for all features, the divergence between the conditional and marginal probabilities of the matched sonar-optical feature vectors in the optical-to-SAS direction is significantly higher than for unmatched feature vectors. While only small differences can be seen between SAS highlight and shadow, the differences between the later features, including those selected for the similarity test, sigma20 and l2, are larger. Regarding the SAS to the optical direction, smaller deviations and a smaller difference between matched and mismatched deviations are observed. This is to be expected, as was also seen in the matching test, where this direction did not provide much relevant information flow. An exception is the localCur features from the SAS shadow, which showed a much higher divergence than all other features in the SAS-to-optical direction. This seems consistent with the fact that these features also had the highest K-Means accuracy for some entropy measures in this direction, such as differential entropy and transfer entropy, although no entropy measure was successful in detecting positives above chance level, likely due to the lack of information that can flow from SAS to optical compared to the reverse direction.

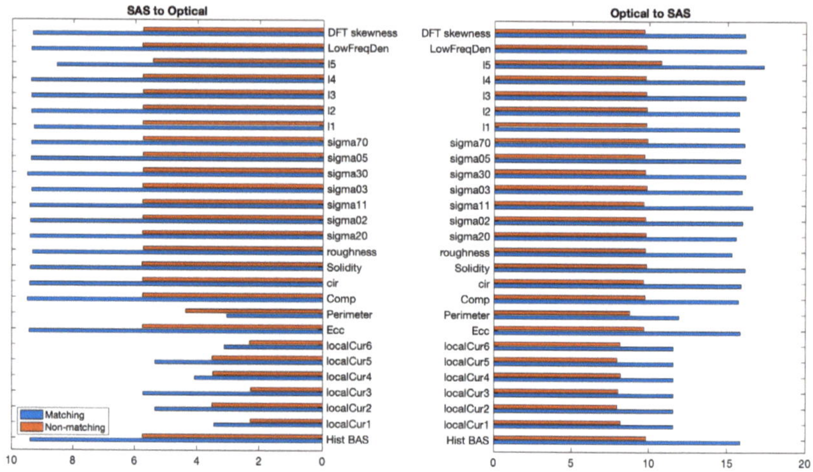

(**a**)

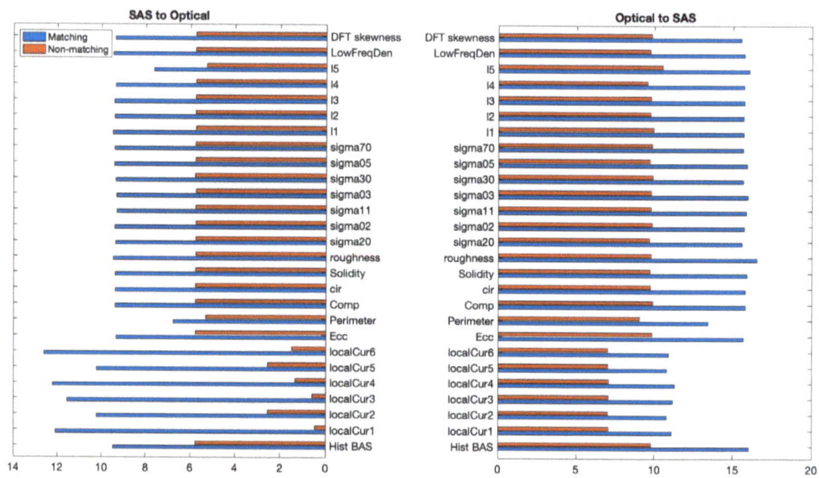

(**b**)

Figure 11. KLD for each feature, between optical and SAS feature vectors, matching (blue) and non-matching (red). (**a**) KLD between conditional and marginal with SAS highlight only. (**b**) KLD between conditional and marginal with SAS shadow only.

5.5. Discussion

An interesting result is that the detection performance depends on the direction of the comparison, i.e., from optical to SAS or from SAS to optical. In particular, better performance is obtained in the optical to SAS direction. This is to be expected since the optical images contain more information due to their much higher resolution and color coding. The results of the statistical relation exploration support this observation by showing a higher differential entropy for the optical to SAS direction than vice versa. Another observation in this context concerns the performance when considering the highlight vs. the shadow ROI. The results suggest that, at least for our dataset, there is generally little difference when only one or the other is considered. This means that both can correctly express the geometric information from the SAS image relative to the geometric information from the optical image, at least when considered separately. Further work can be derived from our results to explore the significance of this information gain. In other words: which areas of the object contribute most to the similarities between optical and SAS images?

Another consideration for our system is the resolution of the SAS image. The higher the resolution of the SAS image, the better the object matching performance is likely to be. This is because a higher resolution is directly reflected in a better representation of the object features. Possible methods for high-resolution SAS can be found in [24,25]. In our system, we used a two-sided SAS system manufactured by Kraken on an AUV with a resolution of 2 cm per pixel and a one-sided aperture of 100 m.

We recognize that the statistical nature of our approach is compromised by the few pairs of optical and SAS images. However, since, to our knowledge, there is no analytical model for directly converting or comparing these two modalities, this statistical approach provides a simple and intuitive way to detect matched multimodal optical and SAS data. Furthermore, this method does not require the images of both modalities to be transformed or filtered, which could lead to a loss of relevant information, but instead examines the information from the image of each modality as it is. It should also be noted that the acoustic and optical images in our database were recorded from different angles. This might affect the results when comparing them directly, but to obtain a robust method, we indeed wish to have different representations of the same object. We apply a number of enhancements (rotations and scaling) to the images to obtain different representations and assume that these cover as many different angles as possible in order to be able to compare the images as statistical distributions.

6. Conclusions

In this work, we have used statistical measures and tests to evaluate and identify the relationship between optical and SAS images of different objects. In particular, we examined the performance of an entropy-based matching test and investigated the differential entropy and the divergence between the conditional and marginal probabilities of optical and SAS feature vectors. Despite the limited data available for this study, the results suggest a statistical relationship between matching optical and SAS image pairs. These results could serve as a basis and stimulus for further research on combining these two modalities.

Author Contributions: Conceptualization, R.D.; methodology, R.C. and R.D.; software, R.C.; validation, R.C.; formal analysis, R.C. and R.D.; investigation, R.C.; resources, R.D.; data curation, R.C. and R.D.; writing—review and editing, R.C. and R.D.; visualization, R.C. and R.D.; supervision, R.D.; project administration, R.D.; funding acquisition, R.D. All authors have read and agreed to the published version of the manuscript.

Funding: This research was supported by the Horizon Europe programme of the European Union under the UWIN-LABUST project (project #101086340).

Data Availability Statement: Dataset is available on https://drive.google.com/file/d/1ggz8BA0W6CtRXH-48XTfy9eO23-Ag1Qt/view?usp=sharing, accessed on 14 February 2024.

Conflicts of Interest: The authors declare no conflicts of interest. The funders had no role in the design of the study; in the collection, analyses, or interpretation of data; in the writing of the manuscript, or in the decision to publish the results.

References

1. Chantler, M.; Lindsay, D.; Reid, C.; Wright, V. Optical and acoustic range sensing for underwater robotics. In Proceedings of the OCEANS'94, Brest, France, 13–16 September 1994; Volume 1, pp. 205–2010.
2. Abu, A.; Diamant, R. Feature set for classification of man-made underwater objects in optical and SAS data. *IEEE Sensors J.* **2022**, *22*, 6027–6041. [CrossRef]
3. Fumagalli, E.; Bibuli, M.; Caccia, M.; Zereik, E.; Del Bianco, F.; Gasperini, L.; Stanghellini, G.; Bruzzone, G. Combined acoustic and video characterization of coastal environment by means of unmanned surface vehicles. *IFAC Proc. Vol.* **2014**, *47*, 4240–4245. [CrossRef]
4. Abu, A.; Diamant, R. Enhanced fuzzy-based local information algorithm for sonar image segmentation. *IEEE Trans. Image Process.* **2019**, *29*, 445–460. [CrossRef] [PubMed]

5. Gubnitsky, G.; Diamant, R. A multispectral target detection in sonar imagery. In Proceedings of the OCEANS 2021: San Diego–Porto, San Diego, CA, USA, 20–23 September 2021; pp. 1–5.
6. Schettini, R.; Corchs, S. Underwater image processing: State of the art of restoration and image enhancement methods. *EURASIP J. Adv. Signal Process.* **2010**, *2010*, 1–14. [CrossRef]
7. Ghani, A.S.A.; Isa, N.A.M. Underwater image quality enhancement through integrated color model with Rayleigh distribution. *Appl. Soft Comput.* **2015**, *27*, 219–230. [CrossRef]
8. Wang, F.; Vemuri, B.C. Non-rigid multi-modal image registration using cross-cumulative residual entropy. *Int. J. Comput. Vis.* **2007**, *74*, 201–215. [CrossRef] [PubMed]
9. Lowe, G. Sift-the scale invariant feature transform. *Int. J.* **2004**, *2*, 2.
10. Ye, Y.; Shen, L.; Hao, M.; Wang, J.; Xu, Z. Robust optical-to-SAR image matching based on shape properties. *IEEE Geosci. Remote Sens. Lett.* **2017**, *14*, 564–568. [CrossRef]
11. Ye, Y.; Bruzzone, L.; Shan, J.; Bovolo, F.; Zhu, Q. Fast and robust matching for multimodal remote sensing image registration. *IEEE Trans. Geosci. Remote Sens.* **2019**, *57*, 9059–9070. [CrossRef]
12. Jang, H.; Kim, G.; Lee, Y.; Kim, A. CNN-based approach for opti-acoustic reciprocal feature matching. In Proceedings of the ICRA Workshop on Underwater Robotics Perception, Montreal, QC, Canada, 24 May 2019; Volume 1.
13. Fei, T. Advances in Detection and Classification of Underwater Targets Using Synthetic Aperture Sonar Imagery. Ph.D. Thesis, Technische Universität, Berlin, Germany, 2015.
14. Xu, S.; Luczynski, T.; Willners, J.S.; Hong, Z.; Zhang, K.; Petillot, Y.R.; Wang, S. Underwater visual acoustic SLAM with extrinsic calibration. In Proceedings of the 2021 IEEE/RSJ International Conference on Intelligent Robots and Systems (IROS), Prague, Czech Republic, 27 September–1 October 2021; pp. 7647–7652.
15. Xu, Z.; Haroutunian, M.; Murphy, A.J.; Neasham, J.; Norman, R. An Integrated Visual Odometry System With Stereo Camera for Unmanned Underwater Vehicles. *IEEE Access* **2022**, *10*, 71329–71343. [CrossRef]
16. Cardaillac, A.; Ludvigsen, M. Camera-Sonar Combination for Improved Underwater Localization and Mapping. *IEEE Access* **2023**, *11*, 123070–123079. [CrossRef]
17. Abu, A.; Diamant, R. A SLAM Approach to Combine Optical and Sonar Information from an AUV. *IEEE Trans. Mob. Comput.* **2023**. https://doi.org.10.1109/TMC.2023.3336697. [CrossRef]
18. Nguyen, T.M.; Wu, Q.J. Fast and robust spatially constrained Gaussian mixture model for image segmentation. *IEEE Trans. Circuits Syst. Video Technol.* **2012**, *23*, 621–635. [CrossRef]
19. Faes, L. cTE—Matlab Tool for Computing the Corrected Transfer Entropy. Available online: http://www.lucafaes.net/cTE.html (accessed on 28 July 2023).
20. MacQueen, J. Some methods for classification and analysis of multivariate observations. In *Proceedings of the Fifth Berkeley Symposium on Mathematical Statistics and Probability*; University of California Press: Oakland, CA, USA, 1967; Number 14, pp. 281–297.
21. Wackerly, D.; Mendenhall, W.; Scheaffer, R.L. *Mathematical Statistics with Applications*; Cengage Learning: Singapore, 2014.
22. Shang, R.; Tian, P.; Jiao, L.; Stolkin, R.; Feng, J.; Hou, B.; Zhang, X. A spatial fuzzy clustering algorithm with kernel metric based on immune clone for SAR image segmentation. *IEEE J. Sel. Top. Appl. Earth Obs. Remote Sens.* **2016**, *9*, 1640–1652. [CrossRef]
23. Kullback, S.; Leibler, R.A. On information and sufficiency. *Ann. Math. Stat.* **1951**, *22*, 79–86. [CrossRef]
24. Zhang, X.; Wu, H.; Sun, H.; Ying, W. Multireceiver SAS imagery based on monostatic conversion. *IEEE J. Sel. Top. Appl. Earth Obs. Remote Sens.* **2021**, *14*, 10835–10853. [CrossRef]
25. Yang, P. An imaging algorithm for high-resolution imaging sonar system. *Multimed. Tools Appl.* **2023**, 1–17. [CrossRef]

Journal of
Marine Science and Engineering

Article

An Underwater Localization Method Based on Visual SLAM for the Near-Bottom Environment

Zonglin Liu [1], Meng Wang [1,*], Hanwen Hu [1], Tong Ge [1] and Rui Miao [1,2]

[1] School of Naval Architecture, Ocean and Civil Engineering, Shanghai Jiao Tong University, Shanghai 200240, China; liuzonglin@sjtu.edu.cn (Z.L.); tongge@sjtu.edu.cn (T.G.); miaorui@sjtu.edu.cn (R.M.)
[2] State Key Laboratory of Ocean Engineering, Shanghai Jiao Tong University, Shanghai 200240, China
* Correspondence: bob00@sjtu.edu.cn

Abstract: The feature matching of the near-bottom visual SLAM is influenced by underwater raised sediments, resulting in tracking loss. In this paper, the novel visual SLAM system is proposed in the underwater raised sediments environment. The underwater images are firstly classified based on the color recognition method by adding the weights of pixel location to reduce the interference of similar colors on the seabed. The improved adaptive median filter method is proposed to filter the classified images by using the mean value of the filter window border as the discriminant condition to retain the original features of the image. The filtered images are finally processed by the tracking module to obtain the trajectory of underwater vehicles and the seafloor maps. The datasets of seamount areas captured in the western Pacific Ocean are processed by the improved visual SLAM system. The keyframes, mapping points, and feature point matching pairs extracted from the improved visual SLAM system are improved by 5.2%, 11.2%, and 4.5% compared with that of the ORB-SLAM3 system, respectively. The improved visual SLAM system has the advantage of robustness to dynamic disturbances, which is of practical application in underwater vehicles operated in near-bottom areas such as seamounts and nodules.

Keywords: underwater visual SLAM; underwater raised sediments environment; image pre-processing; color recognition; adaptive median filter

Citation: Liu, Z.; Wang, M.; Hu, H.; Ge, T.; Miao, R. An Underwater Localization Method Based on Visual SLAM for the Near-Bottom Environment. *J. Mar. Sci. Eng.* **2024**, *12*, 716. https://doi.org/10.3390/jmse12050716

Academic Editor: Christos Tsabaris

Received: 20 March 2024
Revised: 23 April 2024
Accepted: 25 April 2024
Published: 26 April 2024

1. Introduction

Underwater inspection and surveys are important underwater applications such as seafloor resource exploration. Visual technology is widely used for Underwater inspection and surveys. Deep-sea mining and seafloor oil and gas exploration utilized by AUVs are popular topics to research [1–3]. Wang uses a robust Real-Time AUV Self-Localization method for deep-sea exploration [4]. Hong presents a portable autonomous underwater vehicle (AUV) named Shark for vision-based underwater inspection [5]. Chemisky conducts a review of the close-range optical methods for the underwater oil and gas industry [6]. Stenius presents the application of AUVs for seaweed farm inspection [7]. Underwater visual localization technology such as underwater visual SLAM is one of the key technologies for underwater inspection tasks. Underwater visual SLAM is utilized for the trajectory localization of underwater vehicles and the construction of the surrounding environment by feature matching and tracking the captured video images in the underwater scene [8,9]. Underwater navigation is necessary for the operation of autonomous underwater vehicles [10]. The position of the underwater vehicle is a prerequisite for underwater navigation [11]. Due to the absence of GPS information in the underwater environment, underwater localization is difficult and has been extensively investigated. Multi-sensor information fusion is commonly applied to obtain the position information of autonomous underwater vehicles. A passive inverted Ultra-Short Baseline (piUSBL) positioning system is proposed by Wang [12], which provides accurate and instantaneous positioning for small Autonomous Underwater Vehicles (AUVs) by single-beacon tracking at low cost and power consumption. The acoustic image processing based on multi-beam bathymetric sonar data is utilized in underwater terrain-aided navigation, which is more stable when direction error is more significant than 10°, and the accuracy is approximately 50% better. At the same time, noise and scale vary in the real-time images compared with the terrain contour matching algorithm [13]. In addition to using additional sensor information to aid navigation, improved underwater navigation algorithms are also proposed for underwater localization [14–16]. However, accumulated errors are unavoidable in traditional integrated navigation methods, and devices such as DVL and USBL fail in near-bottom environments. Machine vision can work steadily for long periods with tiny cumulative time errors [17,18]. Thus, underwater visual SLAM has been developed and applied for location awareness of the underwater environment and assisted navigation in recent years, which has excellent potential for unmanned surveys and free cruising applications [19–23]. The application of underwater SLAM is widely studied. Issartel uses SLAM technology for the underwater military to achieve underwater hiding for tasks [24]. Zhang utilizes BSLAM (Bathymetric Particle Filter SLAM) which is accurate and fast for oceanographic surveys, demining, and seabed mappings [25]. Yang proposes a SLAM localization algorithm using forward-looking sonar for deep-sea mining [26]. Mahajan proposed a pilot aid using visual SLAM for seabed surveying applications [27].

Joshi verifies and analyzes multiple visual algorithms in the underwater environment, such as OKVIS, SVO, ROVIO, VINS-Mono, and ORB-SLAM3, based on the datasets tested [28]. The Fugu-f (Fugu flexible) system is presented to provide visual localization in submarine tasks such as navigation, surveying, and mapping under good visibility with the main advantages of robustness and flexibility [29]. An omnidirectional and positioning-tolerant miniaturized prototype AUV docking system based on the integrated visual navigation and docking algorithm is proposed to solve the planar-type docking issues in a transparent water environment [30]. Although underwater visual SLAM has been used for AUV navigation tasks, it is not always feasible for all cases due to limitations in underwater image quality. A keyframe-based monocular visual odometry method is proposed by adding a re-tracking mechanism to enhance optical flow tracking, realizing a robust vision-based underwater localization in the turbid underwater environment [31]. However, underwater raised sediments sometimes occur in near-bottom environments. The feature matching of visual SLAM is affected by the randomness of motion direction of the underwater raised sediments. There are few studies on this influence.

When visual SLAM is affected by the external environment, there are two main solutions: adding sensors or image pre-processing [32]. Since the role of visual SLAM is auxiliary rather than central in underwater navigation, the solution of adding sensors for visual SLAM is not adopted in underwater navigation. Image pre-processing for visual SLAM includes two parts: image classification and image denoising.

Because the raised sediment phenomenon is occasional and does not always exist, image classification can reduce the computational effort to increase real-time performance, which is essential for visual SLAM. Image classification methods use underwater image features such as color, texture, shape, and spatial distribution to classify images. Mittal uses deep learning and image color analysis to classify underwater photographs and recognize numerous things, such as fish, plankton, coral reefs, submarines, and the gestures of sea divers [33]. Mahmood proposes a new image feature (called ResFeats) extracted from images' textures and shapes. ResFeats has state-of-the-art classification accuracies on MLC, Benthoz15, EILAT, and RSMAS datasets compared with the traditional CNN method [34]. Lopez-Vazquez designs a pipeline using integrated spatial distribution and temporal dynamics information to perform well in mobile and sessile megafauna recognition and classification tasks [35]. The accuracy value of the classification method reaches 76.18% in deep-sea videos taken at 260 m depth in the Barents Sea. As the underwater raised sediments have the characteristics of noticeable color difference with seawater and strong randomness of shape and spatial distribution, the color features of the underwater image are utilized for image classification. However, the color of the underwater raised sediments is similar to that of the sea floor in the near-bottom environment, affecting image classification. There are few studies for image classification based on image color features in near-bottom environments.

The images that need to be denoised are obtained through image classification. The image-denoising methods include learning-based and filtering-based [36]. Deep learning techniques such as convolutional neural networks (CNN) are widely utilized for the image-denoising method of learning [37]. Pang proposed a data augmentation technique called corrupted-to-corrupted (R2R) to achieve unsupervised image denoising. The method is competitive to representative supervised image denoising [38]. Li proposes a self-supervised image denoising (SSID) method for real-world sRGB images to seek spatially adaptive supervision on real-world sRGB photographs [39]. Dasari uses GAN architecture and histogram equalization to enhance the underwater images. The 2186 real-world underwater images are used for verification [40]. Raj uses SURF (Speeded-Up Robust Features) and SVM (Support Vector Machines) algorithms to attain maximum accuracy in underwater image classification [41]. Moghimi uses a two-step image enhancement method which includes color correction and a convolutional neural network (CNN) with deep learning capability to realize the underwater image quality enhancement [42].

However, underwater raised sediments are often random and unknown during underwater operations. The background has also changed due to the movement of underwater vehicles. There are not enough sample sets to train and learn underwater image classification and denoising in an underwater survey task when the operating area is unknown. Terrestrial training models are directly used whose results are not good. Therefore, filtering-based methods are utilized for image denoising. There are extensive studies on filtering-based image-denoising methods [43]. Kumar proposes different median filter methods to eliminate salt-and-pepper noise [44]. Sagar presents a circular adaptive median filter (CAMF) to denoise salt-and-pepper noise of varying noise densities for magnetic resonance imaging (MRI) images [45]. It can be seen that the primary filter-based methods are effective for salt-and-pepper noise. The underwater raised sediments are similar to salt-and-pepper noise in terms of significant color differences. However, there is a big difference in size and shape. There is little research on underwater raised sediments denoised through filter-based methods.

In this paper, an improved visual SLAM system is proposed to reduce the impact of the underwater raised sediments to the feature matching of the visual SLAM to improve the robustness of the visual SLAM. The weights of pixel position are added to improve the color recognition method in HSV color space for image classification to reduce the interference of similar colors on the seabed to improve the real-time of the visual SLAM. An improved adaptive median filtering method is proposed by utilizing the mean value of the window border pixels as a filtering criterion, which enhances the retained feature information of the classified images to retain more original features of the images to improve the success rate of feature matching. The filtered images are finally processed by the tracking module to obtain the trajectory of underwater vehicles and the seafloor maps. The video datasets captured in the western Pacific Ocean at 3000 m depth are processed by the improved visual SLAM system. Keyframes, mapping points, and feature point matching pairs are extracted from the improved visual SLAM system, which improved by 5.2%, 11.2%, and 4.5%, respectively. The improved visual SLAM system has the advantage of robustness to dynamic disturbances such as underwater raised sediments, water bubbles, etc., which is of practical application in underwater vehicles operated in near-bottom areas such as seamounts, rockfall, and nodules.

This paper is organized as follows. Section 2 describes the underwater raised sediments phenomenon and proposes a novel visual SLAM system in the underwater raised sediments environment. Section 3 presents the image classification and denoising methods to achieve image pre-processing. Then, image classification and quality evaluation results are obtained to verify the effectiveness of the methods. Section 4 shows the experimental tests and results. Section 5 presents the conclusions of the paper.

2. The Visual SLAM System for Underwater Raised Sediments Environment Establishment

Underwater images taken by the autonomous underwater vehicles while working at a depth of 3000 m in the western Pacific seamount area are shown in Figure 1. Underwater no-raised sediment images that expressed different areas during the movement and operation of autonomous underwater vehicles are shown in Figure 1, respectively. The seamount area is shown in Figure 1a, the rockfall area is shown in Figure 1b, and the nodules area is shown in Figure 1c. The images of the underwater different areas are clear and rich in texture detail. When the autonomous underwater vehicles operate in the seamount area near the bottom, the localization of the low-cost autonomous underwater vehicles is realized generally by an inertial navigation system (INS) with IMU as the core sensor and integrated navigation assisted by underwater acoustic equipment such as Doppler velocity log(DVL) and ultra-short baseline (USBL). However, there is a dead band due to the installation position of the Doppler velocity log(DVL) on the low-cost autonomous underwater vehicles that are too close to the seabed. The ultra-short baseline (USBL) is disturbed by bubbles generated by propeller disturbance. Underwater acoustic equipment fails when it moves and inspects underwater near-bottom seamount areas. Because the images taken in the underwater seamount area are clear and texture features are sufficient, the visual localization method is utilized instead of underwater acoustic equipment to assist integrated navigation.

(a) (b) (c)

Figure 1. No raised sediment environment in the underwater area. (**a**) The seamount area; (**b**) the rockfall area; and (**c**) the nodules area.

Due to the movement of the underwater vehicle and the disturbance of the propeller near the bottom, the underwater raised sediments will sometimes be generated in near-bottom areas in Figure 2. The degrees of the underwater raised sediments are different in different areas. The underwater raised sediment in the seamount area is light degree shown in Figure 2a, the underwater raised sediment occupies a small part of the images, and most of the feature information of the underwater images is retained compared with the origin images; the underwater raised sediment in the rockfall area is medium degree shown in Figure 2b, the underwater raised sediment takes up most of the images, and most of the feature information of the underwater images are influenced by the underwater raised sediments; and the underwater raised sediment in the area of the nodule is heavy degree shown in Figure 2c, and there is fog dust apart from line dust. Few of the feature information is retained in underwater images. The impact of underwater raised sediments on visual localization techniques such as ORB-SLAM3 is mainly divided into two parts: the original images are obscured by the underwater raised sediments, reducing the feature information. Image recovery techniques are generally used to recover characteristics, but image recovery techniques require accurate image information, which is often unknown in the underwater near-bottom environment; the direction of motion of underwater raised sediments is random and different from the motion direction of underwater vehicles. When the degree of underwater dust increases, it will cause a reduction in the number of feature point-matching pairs due to the directional consistency detection of the tracking module. Therefore, image pre-processing is necessary to remove raised sediments which can increase feature point matching pairs and increase the robustness of visual SLAM.

Figure 2. Different degrees of the raised sediments in different areas. (**a**) Light degree in the seamount area; (**b**) medium degree in the rockfall area; and (**c**) heavy degree in the nodules area.

An improved visual SLAM system is proposed for visual localization in the underwater raised sediments environment. The block diagram of the improved underwater visual SLAM system is shown in Figure 3. The monocular video is extracted frame by frame into an image stream, and each image is classified as to whether or not it has to be pre-processed. The improved adaptive median filtering algorithm is then utilized to perform image denoising on the raised sediment images. The ORB feature points are retrieved from pre-processed images, and the matching between the initial frame and the current frame is achieved by performing monocular initialization using the Homography matrix or the Fundamental matrix. The pose of the initialization is obtained by Epipolar Geometry. The matching feature point pairs are then projected into 3D map points using triangulate. Via tracking the motion model or key frame, feature matching is conducted. Then, the pose of the current frame is estimated by PnP (Perspective-n-Point) such as DLT (Direct Linear Transform), and optimized by the Back-end Optimization such as BA (Bundle Adjustment). The Loop Closure Detection is not necessary, as the underwater vehicle does not return to its starting point in the underwater exploration task.

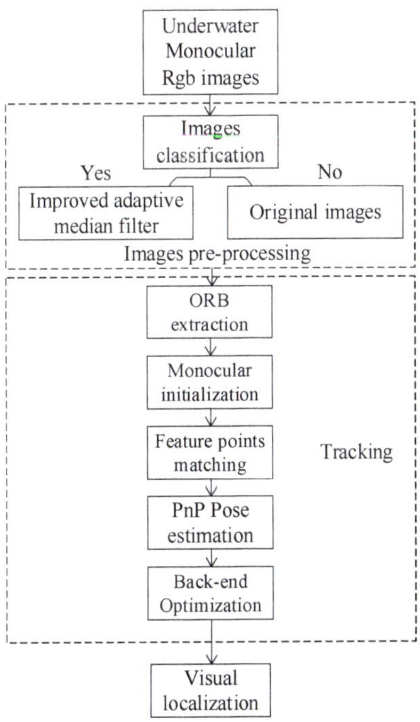

Figure 3. The block diagram of the improved underwater visual SLAM system.

3. Underwater Raised Sediments Image Pre-Processing Method

The underwater raised sediments image pre-processing method consists of image classification and image denoising, which removes dynamic interference in underwater images. The proposed image classification method is presented in Section 3.1. The underwater images are classified based on the color recognition method in HSV color space to obtain the images that need to be denoised by adding the weights of pixel location to reduce the interference of similar colors on the seabed. The improved adaptive median filtering method is proposed in Section 3.2. The improved adaptive median filter method is proposed to denoise the classified images by using the mean value of the filter window border as the discriminant condition to reduce the disturbance of underwater raised sediments and to retain the original features of the image. The filtered image quality assessment is shown in Section 3.3 through Mean Gradient (MG), Structural Similarity (SSIM), and Peak Signal-to-Noise Ratio (PSNR) methods.

3.1. The Proposed Image Classification Method

The flowchart of the proposed image classification method is shown in Figure 4, where the dotted box indicates the proposed image classification method. The original underwater images are first converted to HSV color space. The location weight values are set by the application scenes added in color recognition to reduce the interference of similar colors on the seabed. When the color recognition value of the image exceeds the discriminant threshold, the image needs to be filtered; otherwise, the original image is retained. The classified images are entered into the filter module, and the remaining images are entered directly into the tracking module.

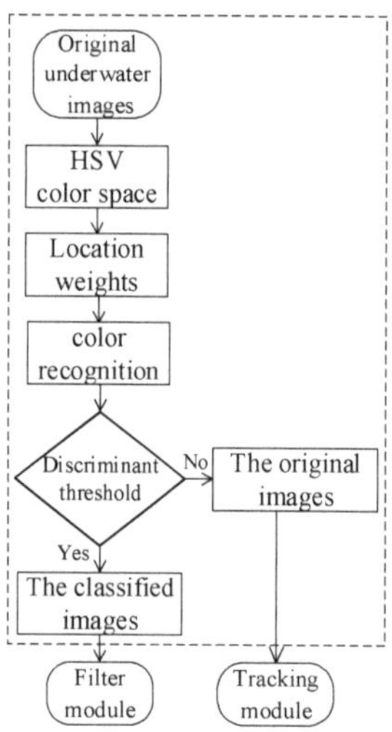

Figure 4. The flowchart of the proposed image classification method.

The color space of an image includes RGB (Red, Green, and Blue) color space, CMY (Cyan, Magenta, and Yellow) color space, and HSV (Hue, Saturation, and Value) color space, etc. The CMY color space is used to represent a printed image and the digital images commonly use RGB color space and HSV color space. The RGB color space is the most used way to describe electronic images, but parameter changes in RGB can cause significant color changes. Therefore, it is not suitable for classifying images by color. Conversely, the HSV color space can be used to classify underwater images by setting a parameter range for the color.

Images are classified based on the color and location of the underwater raised sediments to determine if the images need to be denoised. The color of the underwater raised sediments is different from the water, so the image classification can be realized through color recognition. However, since the seabed's color is similar to that of the underwater raised sediments, location is also necessary to determine the color weights. Depending on the camera mounting angle and distance from the bottom, underwater-raised sediments in near-bottom images suspended in seawater are present in the image's upper half, not the seafloor's lower half. Therefore, the yellow pixel weight for the seawater is ω_a, and the yellow pixel weight for the seabed is ω_b, $\omega_a \gg \omega_b$, The size of the photo is $m * n$, and the pixel point location is expressed by (i, j), and the location weight ω is expressed in Equation (1):

$$\omega = \begin{cases} \omega_a & 0.4m < i < m \\ \\ \omega_b & 0 < i < 0.4m \end{cases} \tag{1}$$

The images captured by the underwater camera are stored in RGB color space. RGB color space uses a linear combination of three-color components to represent color. But in color recognition, any color is highly correlated with these three components, so it is not intuitive to continuously change colors, and these three components need to change to adjust the color of the image. Therefore, we need to convert the RGB into HSV color space expressed in Equation (2). The color component value of a pixel point is R, G, B, respectively; max is the maximum of the three color components, min is the minimum of the three color components, V is the luminance Value, S is the Saturation, and H is the hue. Color is only highly correlated with Hue. Adjusting Saturation and Value will result in similar colors.

$$\begin{cases} max = max(R, G, B) \\ min = min(R, G, B) \\ V = max(R, G, B) \\ S = (max - min)/max \\ if(R = max)H = (G - B)/(max - min) * 60 \\ if(G = max)H = 120 + (B - R)/(max - min) * 60 \\ if(B = max)H = 240 + (R - G)/(max - min) * 60 \\ if(H < 0)H = H + 360 \end{cases} \tag{2}$$

The original purpose of image classification was to reduce the amount of computation. The purpose of the increase in position weights is to increase the accuracy of image classification based on color. The limitations of the positional weights are such that it is not able to correctly classify all images, but the ORB-SLAM3 system itself is robust to images that are not correctly classified. The range of values for the color of underwater raised sediments is set in Equation (3):

$$\begin{cases} 0.12 < H < 0.15 \\ S < 0.3 \\ 0.5 < V < 0.81 \end{cases} \tag{3}$$

where H is expressed using radians.

k is a Boolean value, if the HSV value of the pixel satisfies Equation (3), the value k_{ij} is 1; otherwise, it is 0. ω is the position weight, K is the number of pixels identified by adding the position weight, and ρ is the discriminant threshold.

$$K = \sum \omega k_{ij} \tag{4}$$

When $K > \rho$, the image is considered to need image noise denoising, otherwise the original image is kept.

For the underwater videos of the different areas, 2000 underwater images were extracted at 15 fps, respectively. Let discriminant threshold $\rho = 10, 15, 20, 25, 30$, there are classification results shown in Tables 1–3. The 'real' respects the true results which are used to compare. The title of Need-Denoising shows the number of classified images. The title of

Original shows the number of the remaining images. Accuracy is obtained by the number of correctly detected images divided by the total number of images.

Table 1. Classification results of the 2000 underwater images in the seamounts area.

Discriminant Threshold	Need-Denoising	Original	Accuracy
10	868	1132	75.4%
15	454	1546	96.1%
20	296	1704	95.9%
25	112	1888	86.7%
30	23	1977	82.3%
Real	377	1623	-

Table 2. Classification results of the 2000 underwater images in the rockfall area.

Discriminant Threshold	Need-Denoising	Original	Accuracy
10	1267	733	64.8%
15	942	1158	81.1%
20	603	1704	98.0%
25	430	1570	93.4%
30	224	1776	83.1%
Real	563	1437	-

Table 3. Classification results of the 2000 underwater images in the nodules area.

Discriminant Threshold	Need-Denoising	Original	Accuracy
10	184	1816	84.8%
15	112	1888	81.2%
20	47	1953	78.0%
25	32	1968	77.2%
30	2	1998	75.7%
Real	488	1437	-

The image classification in the seamount area has high accuracy, when $\rho = 15 or 20$. The real number of Need-Denoising images in the rockfall area is more than that in the seamount area. The number of Need-Denoising images in the rockfall area is more than the real number because the underwater raised sediment takes up most of the images. During the underwater operation of an underwater vehicle, underwater raised sediments are not present at every moment, so not all the images need to be denoised. The image classification method proposed in this paper can significantly reduce the computational effort and retain original image features.

3.2. *The Improved Adaptive Median Filtering Method*

The flowchart of the improved adaptive median filtering method is shown in Figure 5, where the dotted box indicates the improved adaptive median filtering method. One pixel in the classified image is chosen, and the filter window length is initialized (set in 3). The mean value of the window border is compared with the mean value of the background, which is the mean value of the image. The window length is determined through the compared result based on the Pauta criterion. The mean value of the window border is utilized for the filter discriminant condition, which is compared with the value of the chosen pixel to decide whether to filter or not. The median value of the filter window is used to replace the filtered pixel. Otherwise, the original value is retained. Then, the next pixel repeats the same steps until the end of the loop. The filtered image is entered in the tracking module at last.

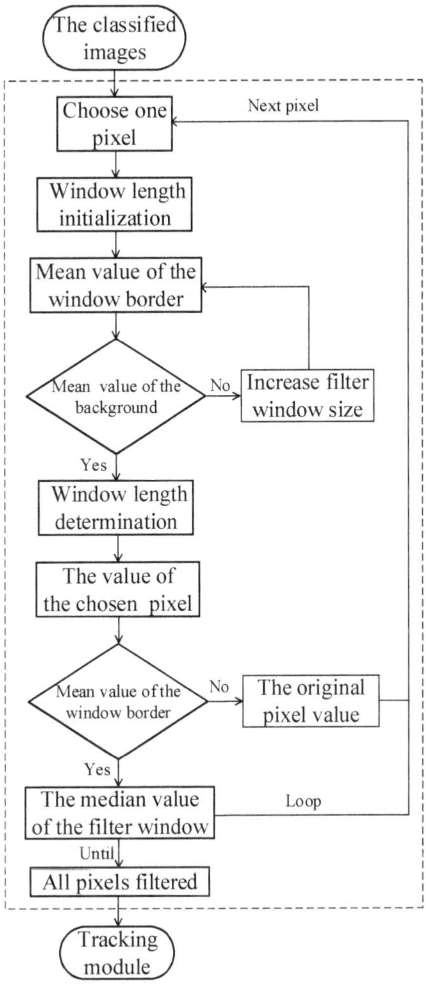

Figure 5. The flowchart of the improved adaptive median filtering method.

Underwater-raised sediments are small in the image, and the color is significantly different from seawater. Due to the relative motion of underwater raised sediments and underwater vehicles, there is a smear in the underwater image, as shown in Figure 2. The smear can be seen as a kind of line salt-and-pepper noise. Adaptive median filtering can effectively filter out salt-and-pepper noise of different sizes through adaptive window size. The original adaptive median filter is more suitable for granular noise. This paper proposes an improved adaptive median filter for line noise. The window size is determined according to the mean pixel value of the window border compared with the mean pixel value of the background. Then, the center point is compared with the mean pixel value of the window border to decide whether to filter or retain. If the filter is decided, the filtered pixel points are replaced by the median value within the window. The improved adaptive filtering has a better effect of denoising the line noise.

The underwater raised sediments are small in the image, and the color is significantly different from seawater. Due to the relative motion of underwater raised sediments and underwater vehicles, there is a smear in the underwater image, as shown in Figure 2. The smear can be seen as a kind of line salt-and-pepper noise. Adaptive median filtering can effectively filter out salt-and-pepper noise of different sizes through adaptive window size. The original adaptive median filter is more suitable for granular noise. This paper proposes an improved adaptive median filter for line noise. The window size is determined according to the mean pixel value of the window border compared with the mean pixel value of the background. Then, the center point is compared with the mean pixel value of the window border to decide whether to filter or retain. If the filter is decided, the filtered pixel points are replaced by the median value within the window. The improved adaptive filtering has a better effect of denoising the line noise.

1. Filter window size determination

The size of the filter window should be chosen to be as small as possible to retain more feature information about the underwater images. Thus, an adaptive filter method for the selection of filter window size is applied. The window is a square, and the initial value of the window length n_w is 3. The gray value of the center point p_{ij} is shown in the cell of the window, as shown in Figure 6. The gray value of the center point p_{ij} is 171, and the pixels are sorted from most minor to most significant, as shown in Figure 7. The maximum gray value $Z_{\max}$ of the window is 171, the maximum gray value $Z_{\min}$ of the window is 113, and the median gray value Z_{med} of the window is 118. The mean gray value of the window border $\overline{w}_{ij}$ is 139.5. The mean of the background grayscale value is u_b, and the standard deviation of the background grayscale value is σ_b. According to the Pauta criterion, if $\overline{w}_{ij} - u_b < 3\sigma_b$, determine the window length n_w and enter the filtering session. Otherwise, add 2 to the window length n_w and perform a new cycle until the window length n_w is determined. The maximum value of the window length is $n_{\max}$. When $n_w = n_{\max}$, the filtering session is entered directly.

113	114	113
121	171	129
117	118	120

Figure 6. The pixel value of window length $n_w = 3$.

113	113	114	117	118	120	121	129	171

Figure 7. The sequence of window length $n_w = 3$.

2. Filtering session

The method of mean value filtering is a common method for image denoising. However, the method of median filtering has less computational effort which increases the real-time performance of ORB-SLAM3, and the image processed by median filtering retains more feature information compared to mean filtering to improve the stability of the ORB-SLAM3. Therefore, the method of median filtering is applied for the underwater image denoising. The gray value of the center point p_{ij} is g_{ij}, the mean gray value of the window border is u_w in Figure 8, and the standard deviation of the background grayscale value is σ_w. According to the Pauta criterion, if $g_{ij} - u_w < 3\sigma_w$, the gray value of the center point g_{ij} is replaced by the median gray value of the window Z_{med}, otherwise the original value g_{ij} is retained.

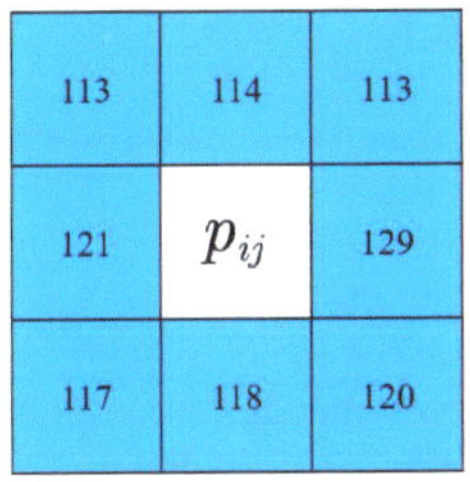

The window border pixels is shown in blue background. u_w is the mean value of the window border pixels.

Figure 8. The mean gray value u_w of the window border.

3.3. The Filtered Image Quality Assessment

The assessment of image quality focuses on three aspects. Firstly, measuring whether the sharpness and contrast of the images are effectively improved, is generally evaluated by the Mean Gradient (MG). Secondly, detecting whether the enhanced images retain the information of the original image as much as possible, which generally uses Structural Similarity (SSIM) and Peak Signal-to-Noise Ratio (PSNR) to calculate the structural similarity of the images. Finally, visually analyze the denoising effect by observing the images before and after processing.

(1) Mean Gradient (*MG*) is used to measure the contrast of images, and the larger the mean gradient, the greater the contrast.

$$MG = \frac{\sum_{i=1}^{H-1}\sum_{j=1}^{W-1}\sqrt{\left(p_{i,j}-p_{i+1,j}\right)^2+\left(p_{i,j}-p_{i,j-1}\right)^2}}{\sqrt{2}(H-1)(W-1)} \tag{5}$$

where $p_{i,j}$ denotes the pixel value at position (i,j) and the image size is $H * W$.

(2) Structural Similarity (SSIM) is applied to evaluate the pixel correlation between the processed and original images.

$$\text{SSIM} = \frac{(2\mu_x\mu_y + C_1)(2\sigma_{xy} + C_2)}{\left(\mu_x^2 + \mu_y^2 + C_1\right)\left(\sigma_x^2 + \sigma_y^2 + C_2\right)} \tag{6}$$

where μ_x and μ_y are the mean of the two images, σ_x and σ_y are the standard deviations, while σ_{xy} is the covariance of the two images, and C_1 C_2 are constants.

(3) Peak Signal-to-Noise Ratio (*PSNR*) reflects the degree of similarity between the processed and original images and is similar to the SSIM function.

$$PSNR = 10\lg\frac{(2^{\varepsilon}-1)^2}{MSE} \tag{7}$$

MSE is the Mean Square Error (MSE) of the two images before and after processing and ϵ is the number of pixel bits in binary, which is taken as 8.

The assessment of image quality focuses on three aspects. Firstly, measuring whether the sharpness and contrast of the images are effectively improved, is generally evaluated by the Mean Gradient (MG). Secondly, detect whether the enhanced images retain the information of the original image as much as possible, which generally uses Structural Similarity (SSIM) and Peak Signal-to-Noise Ratio (PSNR) to calculate the structural similarity of the images. Finally, visually analyze the denoising effect by observing the images before and after processing.

Because the degree of underwater raised sediments is severe in the rockfall and nodules areas, the feature matching of ORB-SLAM3 is affected leading to initialization failure. The effectiveness of image pre-processing and the enhancement of ORB-SLAM3 is validated in the seamount area.

An original color image of underwater raised sediments is shown in Figure 9a, and its grayscale image is shown in Figure 9b. The results of the traditional adaptive median filter (TAMF) and improved adaptive median filter (IAMF) on the original grayscale image are shown in Figures 9c and 9d, respectively. The image quality assessment results are shown in Table 4. The metrics are the three assessment methods. The TAMF and IAMF are the abbreviations of the two filter methods. The improvement is calculated by the difference value of the two filter methods divided by the value of the traditional adaptive median filter. The image contrast is significantly improved by 106.7%. Image similarity is improved by 4.6%, and image quality by 1.1%. More image similarity means more original information preserved, which can be seen by observing the images directly. The improved adaptive median filter has a better denoising effect on the line noise than the traditional adaptive median filter.

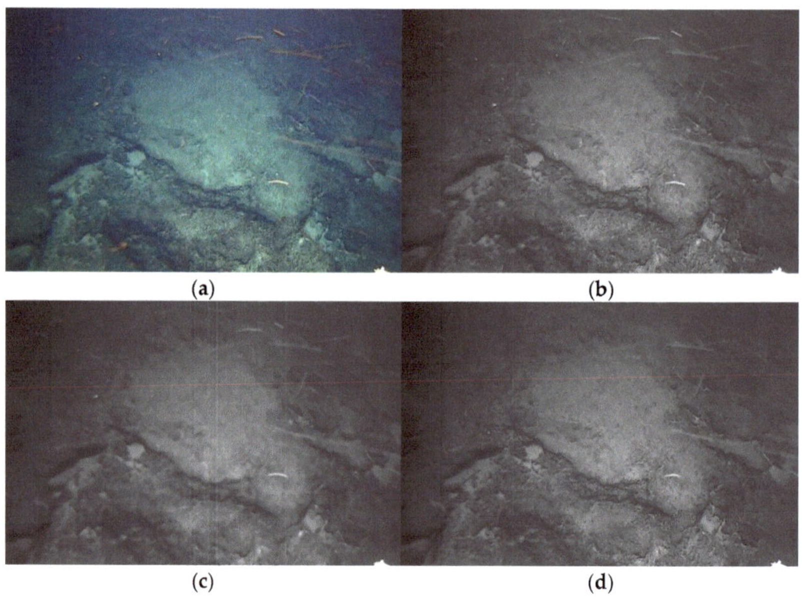

Figure 9. Improved adaptive median filtering results in the seamount area. (**a**) Original color image; (**b**) original grayscale image; (**c**) traditional adaptive median filtering; and (**d**) improved adaptive median filtering.

Table 4. Image quality assessment results in the seamount area.

Metrics	TAMF	IAMF	Improvement
MG	1.3761	2.8451	106.7%
SSIM	0.9164	0.9591	4.6%
PSNR	81.60	85.10	1.1%

4. Experimental Verification and Analysis

The experimental environment is shown in Section 4.1. The experimental procedures and results are shown in Section 4.2. The datasets of seamount areas captured in the western Pacific Ocean are processed by the improved visual SLAM system. The initialization is recorded, which proves that the improved system is easy to succeed. The keyframes, mapping points, and feature point matching pairs extracted from the improved visual

SLAM system are improved by 5.2%, 11.2%, and 4.5% compared with that of the ORB-SLAM3 system, respectively. The improved visual SLAM system has the advantage of robustness to dynamic disturbances such as underwater raised sediments, water bubbles, etc., which is of practical application in underwater vehicles operated in near-bottom areas such as seamounts, rockfall, and nodules.

4.1. The Experimental Environment for the Seamount Images

The experimental environment is shown in Table 5. ORB-SLAM3 is the popular visual SLAM method, which is selected for the comparison system. The SLAM operating system is Ubuntu 20.04, and the image-processing operating system is Windows 10. The image processing program software is MatLab R2022a, and the computer CPU is Ryzen7.

Table 5. Experimental test environment for the seamount images.

Related Devices	Model
Visual SLAM	ORB-SLAM3
SLAM operating system	Ubuntu 20.04
Image processing operating system	Windows 10
Image processing program software	MatLab R2022a
CPU	Ryzen7

4.2. Experimental Procedures and Results for the Seamount Images

The experimental tests were conducted using the videos captured by ROV in the seamount area at a frame rate of 15 fps, with 2000 consecutive frames each to form image datasets. ORB-SLAM3 is the famous monocular vision SLAM system being used for comparison. The datasets are processed under proposed visual SLAM systems. The initialization phase, mapping, and trajectory are recorded. The number of keyframes, matched point pairs, and map points are extracted. The analysis was performed according to the experimental results.

The initialization phase is recorded in Figures 10 and 11. The tests are carried out several times, where Test 1 and Test 2 are the two representative tests. Initialization failure occurred in the initialization phase due to the influence of underwater raised sediments under the ORB-SLAM3 system in Figure 10. There are not enough feature points matched to finish the initialization in Figure 10. The feature of the seamount image is not richer than the terrestrial environment. Initialization failure occurs when other dynamic disturbances exist, such as water bubbles and underwater raised sediments. Initialization was rapidly successful due to image pre-processing for the underwater raised sediments under the proposed system in Figure 11. Initialization under the proposed system is easy to succeed in the underwater raised sediments environment.

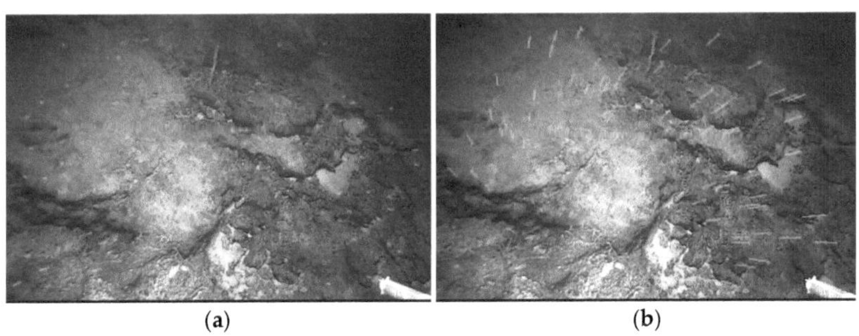

Figure 10. Initialization failure under ORB-SLAM3 system. (**a**) Initialization failure in Test 1. (**b**) Initialization failure in Test 2.

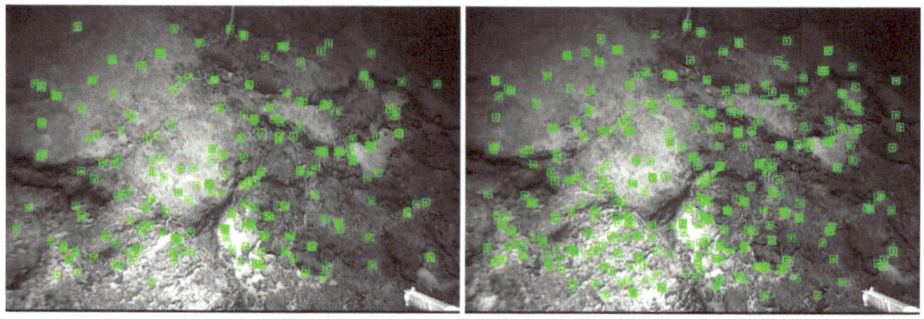

(**a**) (**b**)

Figure 11. Initialization success under the proposed system. (**a**) Initialization success in Test 1. (**b**) Initialization success in Test 2.

Mapping and trajectory in the initialization phase under the proposed system were recorded in Figure 12. Mapping and trajectory in the end phase under the ORB-SLAM3 system were recorded in Figure 13. Mapping and trajectory in the end phase under the proposed system were recorded in Figure 14. Different representative moments were recorded continuously such as moment 1 and moment 2 in Figures 12–14. Mapping and trajectory under the proposed system are more obtained than the ORB-SLAM3 system, which can be seen from the number of keyframes and map points. The underwater raised sediment images in the datasets processed by the proposed system caused matching point pairs to increase. Increasing matched point pairs provides more accurate tracking, which is proved by more keyframes and mapping points obtained.

(**a**) (**b**)

Figure 12. Mapping and trajectory in the initialization phase under the proposed system. (**a**) Moment 1. (**b**) Moment 2.

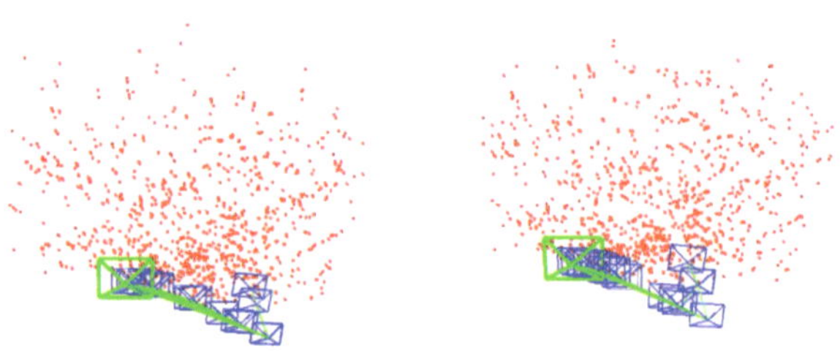

(**a**) (**b**)

Figure 13. Mapping and trajectory in the end phase under the ORB-SLAM3 system. (**a**) Moment 1. (**b**) Moment 2.

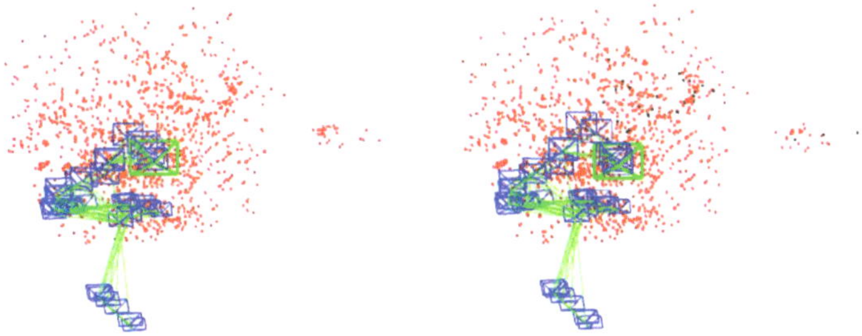

(a) (b)

Figure 14. Mapping and trajectory in the end phase under the proposed system. (**a**) Moment 1. (**b**) Moment 2.

The number of match point pairs (Matches) under both systems is shown in Figure 15. The number of match point pairs of the proposed system is shown in Figure 15a; the number of match point pairs of the ORB-SLAM3 system is shown in Figure 15b. The statistical results of match point pairs are shown in Table 6. The title of Max is the maximum value of the match point pairs; the title of Min is the minimum value of the match point pairs; the title of Average is the average value of the match point pairs; and the improvement is calculated by the difference value of the two systems divided by the corresponding value of the ORB-SLAM3. The proposed system decreased the impact of the underwater raised sediments on the matching phase. The average of the match point pairs under the proposed system improved by 4.5% compared with ORB-SLAM3. Due to the rapid initialization speed, the running time is long under the same datasets. The improvement of the match point pairs proves the effectiveness of the improved system in reducing the impact of the underwater raised sediments environment.

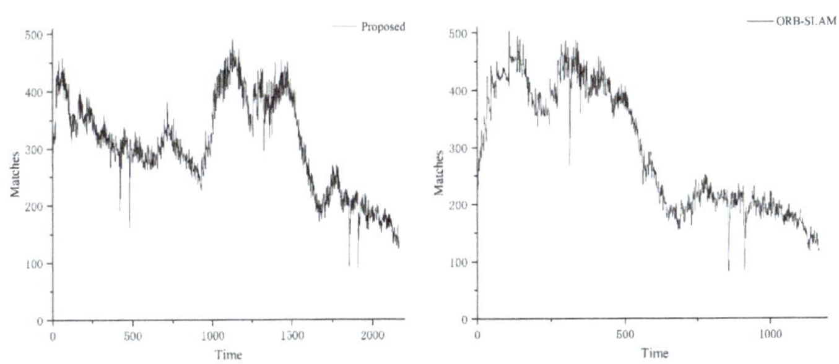

(a) (b)

Figure 15. The number of match point pairs under both systems. (**a**) The proposed system. (**b**) ORB-SLAM3 system.

Table 6. Statistical results of match point pairs.

Number	ORB-SLAM3	Proposed
Max	503	490
Min	82	90
Average	292.05	305.14
Improvement	-	4.5%

The number of mapping points (MPs) and keyframes (KFs) under both systems is shown in Figures 16 and 17, respectively. The statistical results of mapping points and keyframes are shown in Tables 7 and 8, respectively. The length of available data under the proposed system is 2167, and the length of available data under ORB-SLAM3 is 1171. It means the proposed system has a faster initialization than ORB-SLAM3 with the same datasets captured in the underwater raised sediments environment. The number of mapping points improved by 11.5%, and the number of mapping points improved by 5.2%. More matching point pairs provide more rich information for the mapping phase resulting in more mapping points obtained. The number of keyframes has increased less because the selection of keyframes is rigorous. More mapping points and keyframes mean the proposed system has robustness in the underwater raised sediments environment.

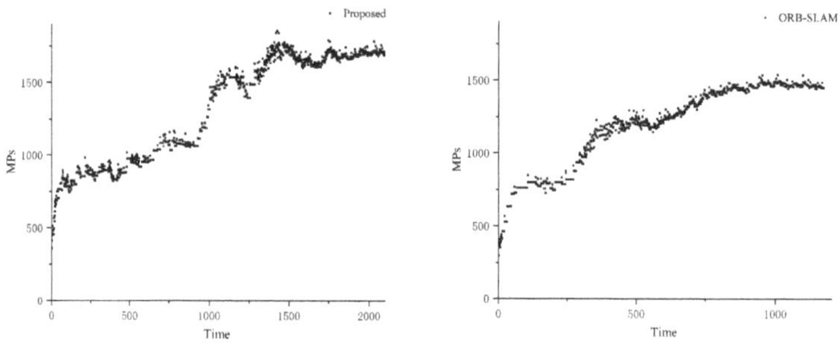

(a) (b)

Figure 16. The number of mapping points under both systems. (**a**) The proposed system. (**b**) ORB-SLAM3 system.

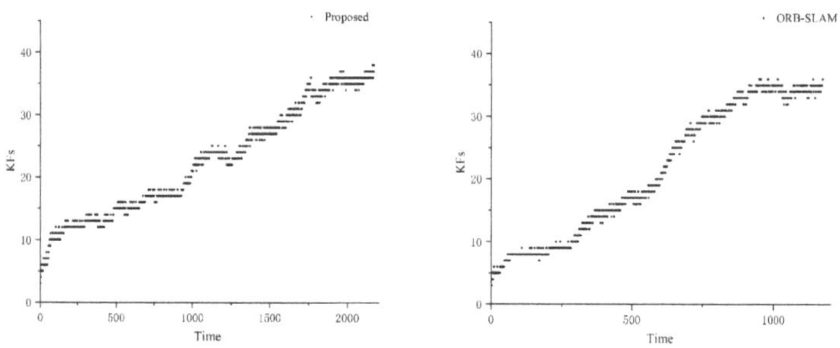

(a) (b)

Figure 17. The number of keyframes under both systems. (**a**) The proposed system. (**b**) ORB-SLAM3 system.

Table 7. Statistical results of mapping points.

Number	ORB-SLAM3	Proposed
Max	1538	1855
Min	296	358
Average	1181.06	1316.59
Improvement	-	11.5%

Table 8. Statistical results of keyframes.

Number	ORB-SLAM3	Proposed
Max	36	38
Min	3	3
Average	21.30	22.42
Improvement	-	5.2%

5. Conclusions

The underwater images are classified by the improved color recognition method to reduce the computation of image pre-processing to improve the real-time of the proposed SLAM system. The improved adaptive median filtering is proposed to denoise the classified images to reduce the effect of underwater raised sediments on feature matching of the SLAM system to improve the robustness of the proposed SLAM system. The MG of the filtered images is improved by 106.7% compared with those filtered by the traditional adaptive median filtering, SSIM by 4.6%, and PSNR by 1.1%, resulting in more information on the original features being retained compared with the traditional adaptive median filter. The filtered images are finally processed by the tracking module to obtain the trajectory of underwater vehicles and the seafloor maps. The datasets of the video captured from the seamount of the western Pacific Ocean at 3000 m depth are processed in the improved visual SLAM system. Keyframes, mapping points, and feature point matching pairs are extracted from the improved visual SLAM system by 5.2%, 11.2%, and 4.5% compared with ORB-SLAM3, respectively. The improved visual SLAM system has robustness in near-bottom environments such as seamounts, rockfall, and nodules, which is less impacted by dynamic disturbances such as water bubbles and underwater raised sediments.

In future work, the parameters of image classification and image denoising are adaptive for different underwater investigation tasks. The parameters of the proposed method are prior and set by the known underwater operating environments and the mounting locations of cameras. However, it is difficult to cope with an unknown environment underwater. The proposed SLAM is a loose-coupling system, in which the visual localization is realized by the pre-processed images imported into the tracking methods. The tight-coupling system will be studied in future work, in which the impact of underwater raised sediments is reduced by optimizing the feature matching phase within SLAM.

Author Contributions: This study is the result of collaborative teamwork. Conceptualization, Z.L. and M.W.; validation, Z.L.; writing—original draft preparation, Z.L.; writing—review and editing, M.W. and R.M.; supervision, H.H. and T.G. All authors have read and agreed to the published version of the manuscript.

Funding: The research carried out in this paper was partly supported by the National Natural Science Foundation of China with grant No. 52231011, 71971139.

Institutional Review Board Statement: Not applicable.

Informed Consent Statement: Not applicable.

Data Availability Statement: Data are contained within the article.

Conflicts of Interest: The authors declare no conflicts of interest.

References

1. Mattioli, M.; Bernini, T.; Massari, G.; Lardeux, M.; Gower, A.; De Baermaker, S. Unlocking Resident Underwater Inspection Drones or AUV for subsea autonomous inspection: Value creation between technical requirements and technological development. In Proceedings of the Offshore Technology Conference, Houston, TX, USA, 2–5 May 2022; p. D021S024R004.
2. Marini, S.; Gjeci, N.; Govindaraj, S.; But, A.; Sportich, B.; Ottaviani, E.; Márquez, F.P.G.; Bernalte Sanchez, P.J.; Pedersen, J.; Clausen, C.V. ENDURUNS: An integrated and flexible approach for seabed survey through autonomous mobile vehicles. *J. Mar. Sci. Eng.* **2020**, *8*, 633. [CrossRef]
3. Vamråk Solheim, A.; Lesage, M.; Asbjørnslett, B.E.; Erikstad, S.O. Deep sea mining: Towards conceptual design for underwater transportation. In Proceedings of the International Conference on Offshore Mechanics and Arctic Engineering, Fort Lauderdale, FL, USA, 28 June–3 July 2020; p. V06BT06A050.
4. Wang, Y.; Gu, D.; Ma, X.; Wang, J.; Wang, H. Robust real-time AUV self-localization based on stereo vision-inertia. *IEEE Trans. Veh. Technol.* **2023**, *72*, 7160–7170. [CrossRef]
5. Hong, L.; Wang, X.; Zhang, D.-S.; Zhao, M.; Xu, H. Vision-Based Underwater Inspection with Portable Autonomous Underwater Vehicle: Development, Control, and Evaluation. *IEEE Trans. Intell. Veh.* **2023**, *9*, 2197–2209. [CrossRef]
6. Chemisky, B.; Menna, F.; Nocerino, E.; Drap, P. Underwater survey for oil and gas industry: A review of close range optical methods. *Remote Sens.* **2021**, *13*, 2789. [CrossRef]

7. Stenius, I.; Folkesson, J.; Bhat, S.; Sprague, C.I.; Ling, L.; Özkahraman, Ö.; Bore, N.; Cong, Z.; Severholt, J.; Ljung, C. A system for autonomous seaweed farm inspection with an underwater robot. *Sensors* **2022**, *22*, 5064. [CrossRef] [PubMed]
8. Chen, W.; Shang, G.; Ji, A.; Zhou, C.; Wang, X.; Xu, C.; Li, Z.; Hu, K. An overview on visual slam: From tradition to semantic. *Remote Sens.* **2022**, *14*, 3010. [CrossRef]
9. Sun, C.-Z.; Zhang, B.; Wang, J.-K.; Zhang, C.-S. A review of visual SLAM based on unmanned systems. In Proceedings of the 2021 2nd International Conference on Artificial Intelligence and Education (ICAIE), Dali, China, 18–20 June 2021; pp. 226–234.
10. Wu, Y.; Ta, X.; Xiao, R.; Wei, Y.; An, D.; Li, D. Survey of underwater robot positioning navigation. *Appl. Ocean Res.* **2019**, *90*, 101845. [CrossRef]
11. Zhang, X.; He, B.; Gao, S.; Mu, P.; Xu, J.; Zhai, N. Multiple model AUV navigation methodology with adaptivity and robustness. *Ocean Eng.* **2022**, *254*, 111258. [CrossRef]
12. Wang, Y.; Huang, S.; Wang, Z.; Hu, R.; Feng, M.; Du, P.; Yang, W.; Chen, Y. Design and experimental results of passive iUSBL for small AUV navigation. *Ocean Eng.* **2022**, *248*, 110812. [CrossRef]
13. Song, Z.; Bian, H.; Zielinski, A. Application of acoustic image processing in underwater terrain aided navigation. *Ocean Eng.* **2016**, *121*, 279–290. [CrossRef]
14. Xu, C.; Xu, C.; Wu, C.; Qu, D.; Liu, J.; Wang, Y.; Shao, G. A novel self-adapting filter based navigation algorithm for autonomous underwater vehicles. *Ocean Eng.* **2019**, *187*, 106146. [CrossRef]
15. Zhang, X.; He, B.; Mu, P.; Zhang, D. Hybrid model navigation method for autonomous underwater vehicle. *Ocean Eng.* **2022**, *261*, 112027. [CrossRef]
16. Lv, P.-F.; He, B.; Guo, J.; Shen, Y.; Yan, T.-H.; Sha, Q.-X. Underwater navigation methodology based on intelligent velocity model for standard AUV. *Ocean Eng.* **2020**, *202*, 107073. [CrossRef]
17. Xu, Z.; Haroutunian, M.; Murphy, A.J.; Neasham, J.; Norman, R. A Low-Cost Visual Inertial Odometry System for Underwater Vehicles. In Proceedings of the 2021 4th International Conference on Mechatronics, Robotics and Automation (ICMRA), Zhanjiang, China, 22–24 October 2021; pp. 139–143.
18. Qin, J.; Li, M.; Li, D.; Zhong, J.; Yang, K. A survey on visual navigation and positioning for autonomous UUVs. *Remote Sens.* **2022**, *14*, 3794. [CrossRef]
19. Köser, K.; Frese, U. Challenges in underwater visual navigation and SLAM. In *AI Technology for Underwater Robots*; Springer: Cham, Switzerland, 2020; pp. 125–135.
20. Carreras, M.; Hernández, J.D.; Vidal, E.; Palomeras, N.; Ribas, D.; Ridao, P. Sparus II AUV—A hovering vehicle for seabed inspection. *IEEE J. Ocean Eng.* **2018**, *43*, 344–355. [CrossRef]
21. Abu, A.; Diamant, R. A SLAM Approach to Combine Optical and Sonar Information from an AUV. *IEEE Trans. Mob. Comput.* **2023**, 1–11. [CrossRef]
22. Özkahraman, Ö.; Ögren, P. Efficient navigation aware seabed coverage using auvs. In Proceedings of the 2021 IEEE International Symposium on Safety, Security, and Rescue Robotics (SSRR), New York, NY, USA, 25–27 October 2021; pp. 63–70.
23. Sabra, A. Cooperative Localisation in Underwater Robotic Swarms for Ocean Bottom Seismic Imaging. Ph.D. Thesis, Robert Gordon University, Aberdeen, UK, 2021.
24. Issartel, M. Towards a Robust Slam Framework for Resilient AUV Navigation. Ph.D. Thesis, Cranfield University, Bedford, UK, 2021.
25. Zhang, Q.; Li, Y.; Ma, T.; Cong, Z.; Zhang, W. Bathymetric particle filter SLAM based on mean trajectory map representation. *IEEE Access* **2021**, *9*, 71725–71736. [CrossRef]
26. Xu, W.; Yang, J.; Wei, H.; Lu, H.; Tian, X.; Li, X. A localization algorithm based on pose graph using Forward-looking sonar for deep-sea mining vehicle. *Ocean Eng.* **2023**, *284*, 114968. [CrossRef]
27. Mahajan, A.; Rock, S. A Pilot Aid for Real-Time Vision-Based Coverage Estimation for Seabed Surveying Applications. In Proceedings of the Global Oceans 2020: Singapore–US Gulf Coast, Biloxi, MS, USA, 5–30 October 2020; pp. 1–6.
28. Joshi, B.; Rahman, S.; Kalaitzakis, M.; Cain, B.; Johnson, J.; Xanthidis, M.; Karapetyan, N.; Hernandez, A.; Li, A.Q.; Vitzilaios, N. Experimental comparison of open source visual-inertial-based state estimation algorithms in the underwater domain. In Proceedings of the 2019 IEEE/RSJ International Conference on Intelligent Robots and Systems (IROS), Macau, China, 3–8 November 2019; pp. 7227–7233.
29. Bonin-Font, F.; Oliver, G.; Wirth, S.; Massot, M.; Negre, P.L.; Beltran, J.-P. Visual sensing for autonomous underwater exploration and intervention tasks. *Ocean Eng.* **2015**, *93*, 25–44. [CrossRef]
30. Wang, T.; Zhao, Q.; Yang, C. Visual navigation and docking for a planar type AUV docking and charging system. *Ocean Eng.* **2021**, *224*, 108744. [CrossRef]
31. Ferrera, M.; Moras, J.; Trouvé-Peloux, P.; Creuze, V. Real-time monocular visual odometry for turbid and dynamic underwater environments. *Sensors* **2019**, *19*, 687. [CrossRef]
32. Cheng, J.; Zhang, L.; Chen, Q.; Hu, X.; Cai, J. A review of visual SLAM methods for autonomous driving vehicles. *Eng. Appl. Artif. Intell.* **2022**, *114*, 104992. [CrossRef]
33. Mittal, S.; Srivastava, S.; Jayanth, J.P. A survey of deep learning techniques for underwater image classification. *IEEE Trans. Neural Netw. Learn. Syst.* **2022**, *34*, 6968–6982. [CrossRef]
34. Mahmood, A.; Bennamoun, M.; An, S.; Sohel, F.; Boussaid, F. ResFeats: Residual network based features for underwater image classification. *Image Vis. Comput.* **2020**, *93*, 103811. [CrossRef]

35. Lopez-Vazquez, V.; Lopez-Guede, J.M.; Marini, S.; Fanelli, E.; Johnsen, E.; Aguzzi, J. Video image enhancement and machine learning pipeline for underwater animal detection and classification at cabled observatories. *Sensors* **2020**, *20*, 726. [CrossRef]
36. Goyal, B.; Dogra, A.; Agrawal, S.; Sohi, B.S.; Sharma, A. Image denoising review: From classical to state-of-the-art approaches. *Inf. Fusion* **2020**, *55*, 220–244. [CrossRef]
37. Tian, C.; Fei, L.; Zheng, W.; Xu, Y.; Zuo, W.; Lin, C.-W. Deep learning on image denoising: An overview. *Neural Netw.* **2020**, *131*, 251–275. [CrossRef]
38. Pang, T.; Zheng, H.; Quan, Y.; Ji, H. Recorrupted-to-recorrupted: Unsupervised deep learning for image denoising. In Proceedings of the IEEE/CVF Conference on Computer Vision and Pattern Recognition, Nashville, TN, USA, 20–25 June 2021; pp. 2043–2052.
39. Li, J.; Zhang, Z.; Liu, X.; Feng, C.; Wang, X.; Lei, L.; Zuo, W. Spatially Adaptive Self-Supervised Learning for Real-World Image Denoising. In Proceedings of the IEEE/CVF Conference on Computer Vision and Pattern Recognition, Vancouver, BC, Canada, 17–24 June 2023; pp. 9914–9924.
40. Dasari, S.K.; Sravani, L.; Kumar, M.U.; Rama Venkata Sai, N. Image Enhancement of Underwater Images Using Deep Learning Techniques. In Proceedings of the International Conference on Data Analytics and Insights, Kolkata, India, 11–13 May 2023; pp. 715–730.
41. Raj, M.V.; Murugan, S.S. Underwater image classification using machine learning technique. In Proceedings of the 2019 International Symposium on Ocean Technology (SYMPOL), Ernakulam, India, 11–13 December 2019; pp. 166–173.
42. Moghimi, M.K.; Mohanna, F. Real-time underwater image resolution enhancement using super-resolution with deep convolutional neural networks. *J. Real-Time Image Process.* **2021**, *18*, 1653–1667. [CrossRef]
43. Fan, L.; Zhang, F.; Fan, H.; Zhang, C. Brief review of image denoising techniques. *Vis. Comput. Ind. Biomed. Art* **2019**, *2*, 1–12. [CrossRef]
44. Kumar, N.; Dahiya, A.K.; Kumar, K. Modified median filter for image denoising. *Int. J. Adv. Sci. Technol.* **2020**, *29*, 1495–1502.
45. Sagar, P.; Upadhyaya, A.; Mishra, S.K.; Pandey, R.N.; Sahu, S.S.; Panda, G. A circular adaptive median filter for salt and pepper noise suppression from MRI images. *J. Sci. Ind. Res.* **2020**, *79*, 941–944.

Journal of
Marine Science and Engineering

MDPI

Article

Sensing Pre- and Post-Ecdysis of Tropical Rock Lobsters, *Panulirus ornatus*, Using a Low-Cost Novel Spectral Camera

Charles Sutherland [1,*], Alan D. Henderson [1], Dean R. Giosio [1], Andrew J. Trotter [2] and Greg G. Smith [2]

1 School of Engineering, University of Tasmania, Sandy Bay, TAS 7005, Australia; alan.henderson@utas.edu.au (A.D.H.); dean.giosio@utas.edu.au (D.R.G.)
2 Institute for Marine & Antarctic Studies (IMAS), University of Tasmania, Taroona, TAS 7053, Australia; andrew.trotter@utas.edu.au (A.J.T.); gregory.smith@utas.edu.au (G.G.S.)
* Correspondence: charles.sutherland@utas.edu.au

Abstract: Tropical rock lobsters (*Panulirus ornatus*) are a highly cannibalistic species with intermoult animals predominantly attacking animals during ecdysis (moulting). Rapid, positive characterisation of pre-ecdysis lobsters may open a pathway to disrupt cannibalism. Ecdysial suture line development is considered for pre-ecdysis recognition with suture line definition compared for intermoult and pre-ecdysis lobsters emerged and immerged, using white, near ultraviolet (365 nm), near infrared (850 nm), and specialty SFH 4737 broadband IR LEDs against a reference of intermoult lobsters with no suture line development. Difficulties in acquiring suture line images prompted research into pre-ecdysis characterisation from the lobster's dorsal carapace, due to its accessibility through a culture vessel's surface. In this study, a novel low-cost spectral camera was developed by coordinating an IMX219 image sensor, an AS7265x spectral sensor, and four SFH 4737 broadband infrared LEDs through a single-board computer. Images and spectral data from the lobster's dorsal carapace were acquired from intermoult, pre-ecdysis, and post-ecdysis lobsters. For the first time, suture line definition was found to be enhanced under 850 nm, 365 nm, and SFH 4737 LEDs for immerged lobsters, while the 850 nm LED achieved the best suture line definition of emerged lobsters. Although the spectral camera was unable to characterise pre-ecdysis, its development was validated when a least squares regression for binary classification decision boundary successfully separated 86.7% of post-ecdysis lobsters. Achieving post-ecdysis characterisation is the first time the dorsal carapace surface has been used to characterise a moult stage for palinurid lobsters.

Keywords: lobster; crustacean; moulting; low-cost spectroscopy

Citation: Sutherland, C.; Henderson, A.D.; Giosio, D.R.; Trotter, A.J.; Smith, G.G. Sensing Pre- and Post-Ecdysis of Tropical Rock Lobsters, *Panulirus ornatus*, Using a Low-Cost Novel Spectral Camera. *J. Mar. Sci. Eng.* **2024**, *12*, 987. https://doi.org/10.3390/jmse12060987

Academic Editor: Sergei Chernyi

Received: 13 April 2024
Revised: 25 May 2024
Accepted: 10 June 2024
Published: 12 June 2024

1. Introduction

Tropical rock lobsters (*Panulirus ornatus*) have significant aquaculture potential; however, as a juvenile animal, they are highly cannibalistic, which provides a challenge for the large-scale propagation of this species. Cannibalism events predominantly occur for *P. ornatus* during the process of ecdysis (moulting), where the moulting animals are cannibalised by intermoult animals [1]. An element missing from current strategies is the ability to automatically identify pre-ecdysis juvenile lobsters, which is currently limited to manual inspection. Technology designed to sense pre-ecdysis may provide an opportunity to disrupt cannibalism and is thus the primary focus of this study. Achieving rapid sorting, or possibly an automated solution capable of in situ sensing of pre-ecdysis lobsters, is a desirable long-term outcome because excessive manual handling stresses lobsters, interferes with feed intake, and increases the risk of limb autotomy, which can retard the growth rate of the lobsters [2,3].

A comprehensive review of the literature found few precedent works on the subject of pre-ecdysis sensing of lobsters. Garland and Sekretta [4] found that the join between the head and thorax of a nephropid lobster, *Homarus americanus*, would darken under infrared light with increasing levels of blood protein, but no such marker has been reported for palinurid (spiny) lobsters. Sutherland et al. [5] use photographic methods to appraise markers of pre-ecdysis by comparing intermoult and pre-ecdysis lobsters using visual appraisal and digital image analysis in the HSV color space. Sutherland et al. [5] found that suture line development was a pre-ecdysis marker, but its formation was disguised by surrounding pigment when captured in images using only visible light. Sutherland et al. [6] used an exploratory approach testing five non-destructive ultrasound transducers and found a signal segment strongly associated with intermoult lobsters formed a basis to distinguish intermoult and pre-ecdysis lobsters. This study intends to expand on the foundation of pre-ecdysis sensing possibilities and inform and guide further research into pre-ecdysis sensing, rather than a thorough investigation of a single sensing opportunity.

Moult stage classifications as defined by Sutherland et al. [6] are used for this study. Pre-ecdysis juvenile lobsters are defined as those on the day of ecdysis, with fully developed suture lines, while the intermoult stage is defined as one-week post-ecdysis extending to the earliest external signs of approaching ecdysis. Sutherland et al. [5] report that early signs of approaching ecdysis are noted by ventral surface pigment absorption and darkening of the region between the thorax and abdomen, and the darkening of the pleopods and uropods. Comparative analysis is used to find distinct differences between data collected from the intermoult and pre-ecdysis groups that could form the basis of a pre-ecdysis sensor [6].

Affordability is a key requirement for industry due to foreseen replicated installation throughout a culture facility [6]. Illuminating the lobster's surface with narrowband light sources is a simple, low-cost way to explore the interaction of varying light conditions and the low-cost IMX219 NOIR (Sony Semiconductor Manufacturing Corporation, Kumamoto, Japan) image sensor chosen for use in this study [7,8].

Suture lines must develop for each moult as they are key to survival by enabling escape from the old exoskeleton [9,10]. Suture lines on small lobsters are difficult to discern visually, making pre-ecdysis identification imprecise and onerous, and requiring experience for manual identification. An image of a clear, conspicuous suture line could improve both speed and accuracy of manual identification to facilitate the separation of animals, thus reducing the load on production staff and increasing productivity [11]. Improving suture definition would also increase the likelihood of success of an in situ computer vision pre-ecdysis detector by making a clear distinction between intermoult and pre-ecdysis lobsters. Lowe [12] explains that feature extraction is simplified for images with less clutter, which highlights the advantages of processing images of well-defined features on predominantly smooth backgrounds.

Comparing the definition of the suture line against its visible light appearance will establish if any advantage of distinction is gained by using light outside the visible light spectrum. Further comparisons with lobsters prior to suture line development can enrich the understanding of how varying the light conditions affect the definition with which suture lines appear on images of juvenile lobsters. Complications for suture line detection in situ are gaining a side-perspective view of lobsters from cameras on the bottom or sides of culture vessels, and the positioning of the legs which obscures the region of suture line formation.

The noted complications associated with suture detection prompted consideration of other methods for pre-ecdysis sensing. Disconnecting the exoskeleton in preparation for moulting is a known marker of pre-ecdysis which may result in a biochemical change on the dorsal carapace surface, and near-infrared spectroscopy is a tool able to detect such changes [13]. Changes observed on the cephalothorax of *H. americanus* under infrared light support an exploratory investigation of the dorsal carapace using infrared techniques for *P. ornatus* [4]. Pre-ecdysis detection from the dorsal carapace surface of palinurid lobsters is desirable as it is accessible via entry through the culture vessel's surface [6].

A hyperspectral snapshot camera in combination with an infrared light source may be suited for infrared spectrographic sensing of the dorsal carapace surface. Infrared light above 1400 nm penetrates only millimetres through water, meaning that much of the capability of such a camera is wasted. A further key consideration is its cost of around USD 15,000. An exploratory low-cost novel spectral camera was built at a cost of USD 610 [14]. Simultaneous data collection from an IMX219 NOIR image sensor and an AS7265x spectral sensor (ams OSRAM AG, Premstätten, Austria) was coordinated with a single board computer (SBC). Using broadband infrared illumination from SFH 4737 LEDs (ams OSRAM AG, Regensburg, Germany) and placing the camera lens in the centre of the AS7265x sensors creates an exploratory, novel low-cost spectroscopy sensor to attempt pre-ecdysis detection from the dorsal carapace [14]. Aquino et al. [15] demonstrated that the combination of SFH 4737 LEDs with an AS7265x spectral sensor was able to create a low-cost tool to evaluate the fat content of olives, while Noguera et al. [16] assessed the ripeness of grapes and achieved promising results.

Post-ecdysis lobsters, defined in this study as being lobsters on the day after ecdysis, are an extra group included for comparison in testing the novel spectral camera. The post-ecdysis dorsal carapace surface is distinguished from intermoult and pre-ecdysis by being unmineralized [17,18]. Successful recognition of the post-ecdysis dorsal carapace would provide encouragement that the novel spectral camera may have broader applications in other research endeavours, and opportunistically provide a documented post-ecdysis detector.

This study aims to appraise the comparative definition of suture lines in images against baseline images of intermoult lobsters under varying lighting conditions using a IMX219 NOIR image sensor. This study then aims to investigate and report on the performance and characteristics of SFH 4737 LEDs and the AS7265x spectral sensor when operated as components in a novel spectral camera based around the IMX219 NOIR image sensor. We also aim to assess the reliability of operation, and data consistency of the novel spectral camera while being tested as a sensor of pre-ecdysis, and/or post-ecdysis from the dorsal carapace surface of *P. ornatus*.

2. Materials and Methods

2.1. Test Animals

2.1.1. Animal Husbandry

The study was undertaken at the Institute for Marine and Antarctic Studies (IMAS), University of Tasmania, Taroona, over a duration of four months. Twelve hatchery-bred and -reared juvenile *P. ornatus* were utilised in this study. Lobsters had a carapace length and weight range of 35.9–50.4 mm and 46.9–123.1 g, respectively. The lobsters were of mixed sex, with 5 females and 7 males in the population. The lobsters were maintained in a communal culture vessel (2.52 m × 0.96 m × 0.38 m—length × width × height; volume 920 L), on recirculating seawater, temperature 26 ± 0.5 °C, salinity 34.0 ± 0.8, pH 8.2 ± 0.1, and with culture vessels receiving 3 water exchanges h^{-1}. Lobsters were fed twice daily with proprietary formulated pellet at a rate of 3.5% dry weight of animal body weight, adjusted to satiation. Cleaning of the tanks and removal of uneaten feed was performed via siphon prior to each feeding event.

2.1.2. Moult Stages for Comparison

The moult stage groups for comparison are as follows: (1) Intermoult lobsters, in this instance defined as one-week post-ecdysis extending to the earliest external signs of pre-ecdysis; (2) Pre-ecdysis, lobsters on the day of ecdysis with fully developed suture lines; (3) Post-ecdysis, lobsters on the day after ecdysis. Sutherland et al. [5] provides further details on the timing of externally visible indications of approaching ecdysis and moult stage classification.

2.2. System Components and Construction

2.2.1. Host Single-Board Computer

The host SBC was a Jetson Nano development kit (Rev 2B) (NVIDIA Corporation, Santa Clara, CA, USA) running Jetpack 5.6. Nvgstcapture-1.0 (NVIDIA Corporation,

Santa Clara, CA, USA) is a Jetson image capture and camera control application supplied with the Jetpack SDK. Nvgstcapture-1.0 natively produces a live preview stream to a display and can simultaneously capture images. The system was built on to Nvgstcapture-1.0 to include control of the light sources via the system's GPIO. UART communication with the AS7265x spectral sensor (ams OSRAM AG, Premstätten, Austria) was added using the Termios libraries using programmed AT commands through a USB UART interface. Imaging via a CSI/MIPI interface and spectral data collection via USB allowed near-simultaneous (<100 ms) operation.

2.2.2. Camera

The IMX219 NOIR (Sony Semiconductor Manufacturing Corporation, Kumamoto, Japan) image sensor was used for all image collection. The sensor was mounted on an Arducam carrier board and connected to the host system via a CSI/MIPI interface. Arducam (Arducam Technology Co., Ltd., Suzhou, China) supply the IMX219 NOIR sensor with a motorised focus lens that is adjustable from the host system via the I^2C connection included in the CSI/MIPI interface specification [19]. The camera was left in its default configuration with automatic exposure mode, permitting time to adjust to test light conditions before image acquisition. Although available with a NOIR designation from Arducam and Raspberry Pi (Raspberry Pi Foundation, Cambridge, UK), the sensitivity information of this camera is incomplete. Sony's datasheet does not specify the full NOIR sensitivity of the sensor's RGB channels beyond 700 nm, with Sony indicating that this sensor is not a designated IR sensor ([20], Internal comms). Pagnutti et al. [7] independently reviewed the specifications of this sensor on a Raspberry Pi V2 fixed-focus module, but also did not report the sensitivity beyond 700 nm. A wider channel sensitivity bandwidth is reported for other Sony sensors. The IMX335 (Sony Semiconductor Manufacturing Corporation, Kumamoto, Japan) image sensor has a similar sensitivity pattern to the IMX219 NOIR, between 400 and 700 nm, with the expanded sensitivity plot showing how the three channels have overlapping sensitivity in the near infrared, just beyond 800 nm [21]. It was expected that the channel sensitivity of the IMX219 NOIR would behave similarly, albeit with reduced sensitivity levels, due to the similarity of the underlying semiconductor and RGB filter properties.

2.2.3. Light Sources for Suture Line Imaging

Four illuminating light sources for suture line imaging were LED SJ-3W-CW cool white LEDs (visible light) (Shenzhen Ipixel LED Light Co., Ltd., Shenzhen, China), LZ4-00R408 850 nm LEDs (NIR) (LED Engin, Inc., San Jose, CA, USA), LZ1-00UV0R 365 nm LEDs (NUV) (LED Engin, Inc., San Jose, CA, USA), and SFH 4737 LEDs (IR broadband) (ams OSRAM AG, Regensburg, Germany).

2.2.4. Near-Infrared Spectroscopy Light Source

SFH 4737 LEDs were used as the spectroscopy light source. The SFH 4737 LEDs operated for 3 s bursts to meet the requirements for integration of the AS7265x sensors. LED 2000 driver demonstration boards (Model STEVAL-ILL051V1, STMicroelectronics N.V., Geneva, Switzerland) were left in their default configuration for driving the SFH 4737 LEDs at 700 mA to generate a high intensity light. The operational parameters of the LEDs varied from those given in the datasheet (350 mA, 10 mS pulse) [22]. The relative emission spectrum of the LEDs under operational conditions was recorded with a SpectralEvolution RS-8800 spectrometer (Spectral Evolution Inc., Haverhill, MA, USA) off a 127 × 127 mm (5 × 5 inch) white 99% Spectralon reflectance panel (Labsphere Inc., North Sutton, NH, USA). The measured curve of the LED relative radiant intensity emission spectrum was overlaid on the characteristic relative emission spectrum from the datasheet for comparison. The SFH 4737 LEDs were mounted on purpose built aluminium PCBs for heat control.

2.2.5. Spectral Sensor

An AS7265x 18-channel spectral array was used to capture spectral data. The AS7265x sensors were set to their maximum integration time of 708.9 ms. The AS7265x gain control is a linear multiplier and was set to its maximum value of 64. Test samples were taken to ensure the 16-bit channel data registers did not saturate and cause data loss. Each aperture of the three AS7265x sensors was covered with Tsujiden D121UP diffraction film (Tsujiden Co., Ltd., Tokyo, Japan) to ensure adequate light diffusion from the target at close range.

The AS7265x datasheet shows that each channel has an associated integration function that covers a bandwidth of light wavelengths [23]. Each of the 18 integration functions is presented relative to its own peak value, resulting in a common scale between 0 and 1. This presentation overlooks the effects of relative channel sensitivity. A full calibration to a known light source is impractical with integration functions that are neither defined nor scaled to relative sensitivity. However, relative channel sensitivity can be investigated by testing with a calibrated light source.

Channel sensitivity was assessed with the low-cost spectral camera fitted in its housing. A Labsphere Helios (Model USLR-D12L-NANS, Labsphere Inc., North Sutton, NH, USA) integration sphere with a 150 W lamp at 50% power was used as the test source. Raw data from test shots taken by the AS7265x were corrected using the formula:

$$g(\lambda) = \frac{L(\lambda)}{\frac{R_{DN}^{(\lambda)total} - R_{DN}^{(\lambda)dark}}{IT}} \quad (1)$$

where $g(\lambda)$ is calibration gain, L is calibrated source radiance, R_{DN} is measured total signal or dark current of the test sensor, and IT is the integration time of the test sensor. All test data were analysed as relative values because the continuous wavelength readout from the Helios integration sphere could not be mapped to the channel outputs of the AS7265x due to the undefined channel integration functions.

Four reference values were required to relatively adjust, align, and compare the known curve of the test light source, the readings of the test light source from the AS7265x, the gain correction curve, and the gain-corrected readings of the test light source from the AS7265x. The four reference points were as follows: (1) The test light source data were made relative to the value at 940 nm as this was the highest value in the relevant wavelength domain. (2) Readings of the test light source from the AS7265x were made relative to the 810 nm channel value as this was the highest recorded value. (3) Gain correction curve values were made relative to the 810 nm value as this value was close to the median value of the gain correction curve and it also aligned with the AS7265x data reference in point 2. (4) The gain-corrected AS7265x readings of the test light source was made relative to the 940 nm channel value as this was the highest value and aligned the AS7265x corrected readings to the known test light source curve. The derived gain correction curve can be used to assess the extent to which channel sensitivity contributes to the acquired data.

2.2.6. Low-Cost Spectral Camera

The low-cost spectral camera was constructed by mounting the camera lens through a hole central to the placement of the three AS7265x sensors on the AMS AS7265x demonstration board. Four SFH 4737 LEDs surrounded the low-cost spectral camera in a purpose-built black HDPE housing with acrylic windows. Each LED was surrounded by a parabolic reflector and fitted into a separate tube. The four tubes were mounted in the housing to focus the individual light beams to a point 75 mm directly in front of the camera lens and AS7265x spectral sensors (Figure 1). A manual action button was used to trigger the following capture sequence: (1) ambient LEDs off; (2) SFH 4737 LEDs on; (3) integration delay/camera exposure adjustment; (4) near-simultaneous image and spectral capture; (5) SFH 4737 LEDs off; (6) ambient LEDs on.

Figure 1. The HDPE waterproof housing (95 × 142 mm) with glued in clear acrylic windows. The four light tubes are arranged to focus the four light sources 75 mm beneath the sensors. (**A**) A SFH 4737 LED surrounded by a parabolic reflector; (**B**) the three AS7265x chips covered with Tsujiden D121UP diffraction film with the camera lens visible through the centre hole.

2.3. Suture Line Imaging

Imaging the suture lines facilitated image comparisons under the four light sources outlined in Section 2.2.3. Suture line images from pre-ecdysis lobsters and baseline images from intermoult lobsters were collected for comparison. Each light source was assessed for definition of the suture line when compared with the baseline image. Comparative image sets were acquired from emerged and immerged lobsters.

2.3.1. Emerged Suture Line Imaging

Emerged suture line images were taken to assess suture line appearance in the circumstance of camera-assisted manual sorting. In this circumstance, only the assessment of RGB images was deemed suitable, given the simplicity of using a direct camera feed. To obtain clear images of emerged lobsters, the lobsters were secured to an elevated platform, and images were acquired from the side. The elevated platform allowed the legs to fall away from the region of suture development so its full extent could be captured in images.

2.3.2. Immerged Suture Line Imaging

Immerged suture line imaging was considered as a circumstance aligned with in situ automated detection of the suture line. Lobsters were placed in water filled 3 mm clear acrylic tubes, so the sides of the lobsters were accessible for imaging. The suture line's appearance was compared on the complete RGB image, and on each color channel presented in greyscale.

2.4. Low-Cost Spectroscopy Camera

Intermoult, pre-ecdysis, and post-ecdysis lobsters were sampled for comparative spectral and image data. The use of GPIO controlled ambient (white) lighting allowed the camera's on-screen preview to be used to align the low-cost spectral camera with distinct spines and edges on the dorsal surface of the lobster. Image and spectral data were captured from the dorsal surface of lobsters held on a platform and submerged in a blackened tank of seawater after switching to illumination from SFH 4737 LEDs. Multiple readings were taken to ensure suitably comparable readings and images were acquired from each lobster.

2.4.1. Spectral Sampling NIR Reflectance Analysis

Only the seven longest wavelength channels, which include all the NIR channels, of the AS7265x were used for analysis. The visible light channels, particularly in blue, are affected by the colored pigments of the lobster's surface, which varies naturally in a population and are not considered for analysis. The AS7265x NIR channel raw data were plotted by lobster for each of the three sample groups to assess the variability of the data between lobsters and groups. The spectral distribution from the dorsal carapace was assessed for apparent changes that occurred within the distributions of the three sample groups, while the seven long wavelength channel values were summed to assess the relative reflectance of all NIR light. Means for each group and the gain-corrected means for each group were all plotted on the same axis to assess the effect of channel sensitivity on the mean distribution shape.

2.4.2. Spectral Sampling Image Analysis

All images were compared as the complete color image and split into grayscale representations of each RGB channel to better understand the effect of the SFH 4737 emission spectrum has on image presentation at the IMX219 sensor.

Green channel image analysis of the dorsal carapace proceeded by creating a dorsal carapace ROI through setting all pixels outside the dorsal carapace boundary to black. A threshold value of 35 (out of 255) was chosen as the threshold to distinguish dark and illuminated pixels in the ROI. The green channel images were normalised to percentage of illuminated pixels using the count of illuminated pixels and the total count of ROI pixels.

2.4.3. Spectral Sampling Statistical Analysis

Achieving either pre-ecdysis or post-ecdysis characterisation using the spectral camera requires establishing that either the pre-ecdysis or post-ecdysis groupings can be statistically separable from the other groups. Statistical methods have been applied to check the separation of the three lobster groups using the NIR reflectance data, the green channel pixel percentage data, and using both data streams in combination. The statistical analysis was performed using the R programming language. One-way ANOVAs were performed for the reflectance of the summed AS7265x NIR raw channel data (Section 2.4.1), and green channel pixel percentage illumination (Section 2.4.2) across the three sample groups. All data were checked for conformance to the normal distribution with a Shapiro–Wilk test, and for homogeneity with Bartlett's test. The ANOVAs were grouped by stage, and significant results were assessed with a Tukey HSD post hoc comparison. Significance was accepted at level $p < 0.05$.

To check for correlation between the NIR reflectance data and the green channel illuminated pixel percentage data, a Pearson's correlation coefficient was performed. A correlation analysis of the combined intermoult and pre-ecdysis data was performed, with the post-ecdysis data correlated separately.

The green channel percentage of pixel illumination data was plotted against the NIR reflectance data with the stage groups as individual series. Least squares regression for binary classification was used to establish a decision boundary to separate post-ecdysis and the combined intermoult and pre-ecdysis stage groups on the plot. The model used was:

$$\delta(X) = \begin{cases} 1 & X^T\beta + \beta_0 \geq 0 \\ -1 & X^T\beta + \beta_0 < 0 \end{cases} \quad (2)$$

where X is a vector of the two independent variables of green channel pixel percentage illumination and infrared reflectance, β is a vector of slope coefficients from the least squares regression, and β_0 is the intercept coefficient.

3. Results

3.1. Emerged Suture Line Imaging

With the lobster emerged, the suture line is detectable on pre-ecdysis images under all four lighting conditions. Under the NIR and the SFH 4737 LEDs, the suture line is well defined along its entire length as the detail and contrast of other surface structures of the lobster are supressed. Visible and NUV lighting maintains the definition of non-suture line textures and contrast on the surface of the lobster (representative images are shown in Figure 2). The suture remains distinct from baseline intermoult images because the suture path between the carapace and the branchiostegite is white during intermoult and becomes dark when the suture lines form. However, the posterior section of suture development on the carapace has a similar appearance to intermoult due to similarity with a band of brown pigment normally present on the intermoult branchiostegite.

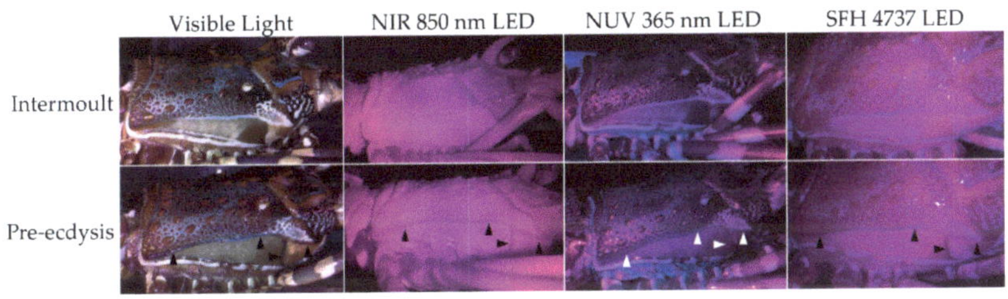

Figure 2. The appearance of suture lines of staged *Panulirus ornatus* under four light sources with image capture on a Sony IMX219 NOIR image sensor. Arrows on the pre-ecdysis images indicate the suture line.

3.2. Immerged Suture Line Imaging

With the lobster immerged and imaged using visible light, the presence of brown pigmentation on the posterior branchiostegite increases the uncertainty of suture line identification because the formed suture line is only defined by having a darker appearance when compared to the pigmentation in intermoult images. NIR, NUV, and SFH 4737 LEDs show the suture line is clear and distinct from the intermoult images, with obvious darkening occurring in the suture line's posterior section. These light sources do not reflect the brown pigmentation of the posterior branchiostegite, which improves the definition of the suture line when it is present in this region. Suture line obstruction by the legs is evident in all images, with the anterior section of the suture being most affected, supporting the preferred focus on the posterior carapace (Figure 3).

The RGB channel breakdown from the IMX219 NOIR image sensor shows little difference between the images of the three channels for visible light images. Under visible light, the posterior suture line appears slightly darker than the equivalent appearance of pigmentation present in the baseline images. Under NIR light, the suppression of surface contrast and features enhances the definition and contrast of the suture line on all color channels compared to baseline images. The green channel image is noticeably grainier than the red and blue channel images when viewed at high resolution but appears unchanged at the resolution of Figure 3. The NUV light source creates a dark suture line which contrasts with a clear white line of intact integument of the intermoult images. The blue channel is marginally brightest overall, but both the red and blue channels capture contrast and detail of the lobster's surface features, albeit with reduced definition in the red channel image. NUV lighting does not convey information in the green channel with the images being too dark for any definition in the image.

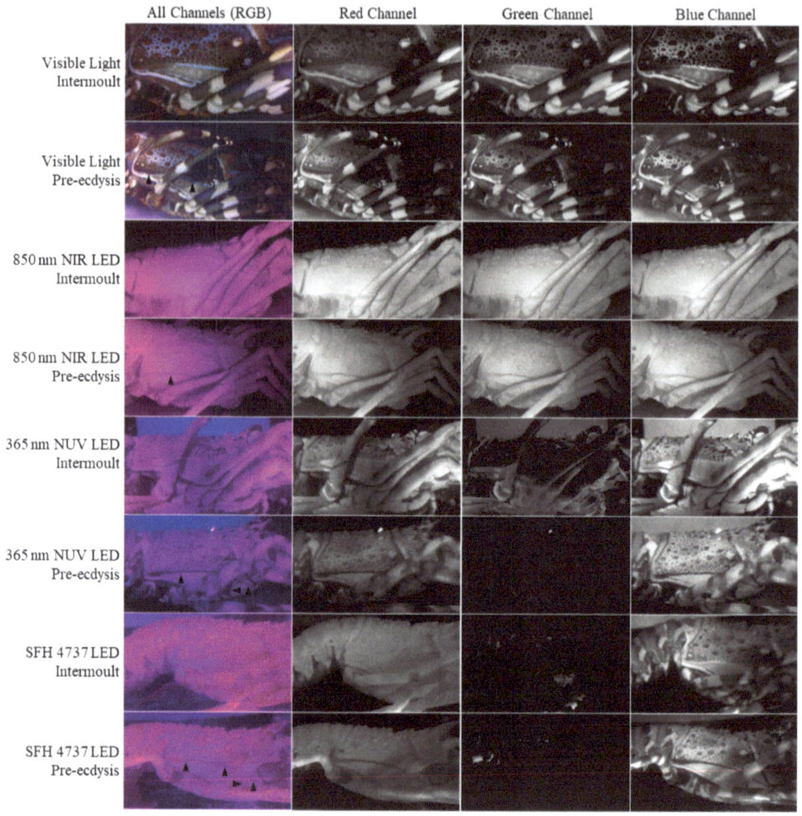

Figure 3. The appearance of the posterior suture line region of submerged *Panulirus ornatus* illuminated by four different light sources with image capture on a Sony IMX219 NOIR image sensor. Representative RGB images are broken into greyscale representations of the red, green, and blue color channels. Arrows on the pre-ecdysis RGB images indicate the suture line.

The SFH 4737 LEDs produce images on the IMX219 NOIR image sensor with a red channel that closely resembles the NIR image, and a blue channel that closely resembles the NUV image blue channel. The red channel strongly suppresses contrast and detail leaving a mostly smooth image, while the blue channel captures the full contrast and detail of the carapace surface. The green channel conveys no information about the suture line as it is too dark, although regions of pixels corresponding with spines and pigmentation bands on the legs are activated and appear "grainy".

3.3. Spectral Analysis

3.3.1. SFH 4737 Relative Emission Spectrum

The system relative emission spectrum is a close match to the emission published in the SFH 4737 product datasheet (Figure 4). The infrared performance beyond 850 nm appears slightly degraded in the configuration used for sampling. A maximum deviation of approximately 3% occurs at 950 nm. The maximum deviation between 500 and 700 nm is approximately 0.035%.

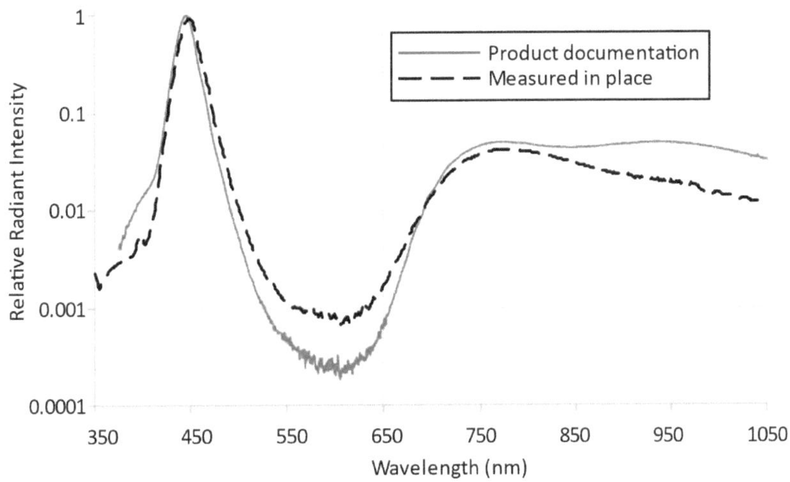

Figure 4. The relative emission spectrum of the system SFH-4737 LEDs vs. the product's stated relative emission spectrum [22]. Logarithmic Y-axis, with a maximum variation of 3% at 950 nm.

3.3.2. AS7265x Calibration

A gain correction curve to map the AS7265x channel output to a calibration light source was generated. The deviation of the gain correction curve from its reference of 1 is indicative of the relative spectral sensitivities of the channels on the AS7265x. Values greater than 1 indicate reduced relative channel sensitivity, while values less than 1 indicate heightened relative channel sensitivity. The calibration curve has increased channel sensitivity in the 410, 435, and 460 nm blue light channels. Channel sensitivity to infrared at the 900 and 940 nm channels is reduced, with the 940 nm channel being less than half as sensitive as the median level (Figure 5).

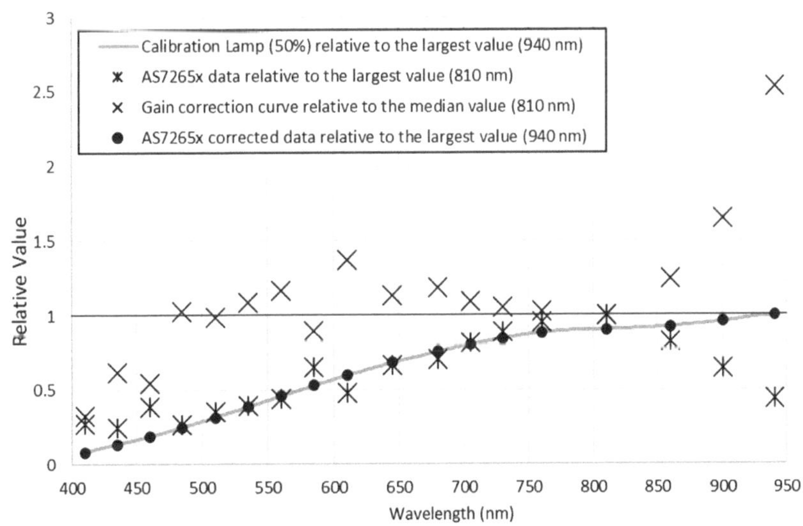

Figure 5. Fitting the AS7265x channel sensitivities to a known calibrated light source (Helios integration sphere) using relative values.

3.3.3. Dorsal Surface Imaging Using the Low-Cost Camera

The appearance of the dorsal carapace in red and blue channel images shows no obvious differences between the intermoult, pre-ecdysis, and post-ecdysis groups. Reiterating the results from suture line imaging using the SFH 4737 lights, the red channel images have strongly suppressed contrast and appear as a NIR image, while the blue channel images have high contrast and feature definition and appear as a NUV blue channel image. The green channel on images of the dorsal carapace produces a third view, where the green channel from suture line images was mostly dark (Figure 6). The intermoult and pre-ecdysis green channel images have similar pixel illumination for each lobster, but the post-ecdysis green channel image of each lobster has reduced pixel illumination levels (Figure 7).

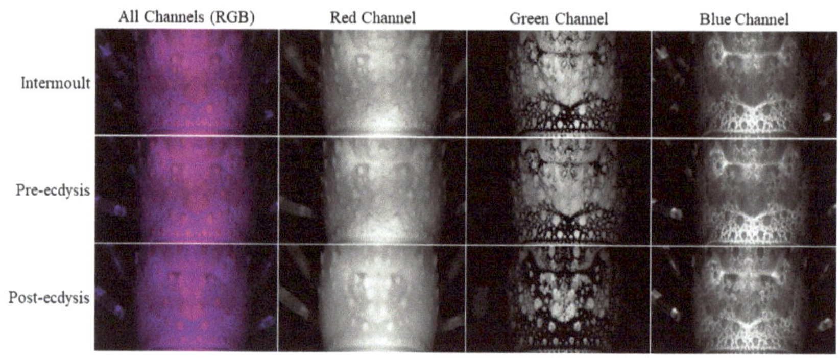

Figure 6. Close-up view of the posterior dorsal surface of a *Panulirus ornatus* lobster using four SFH 4737 LEDs for illumination with image capture on a Sony IMX219 NOIR image sensor. The RGB images are broken into greyscale representations of its red, green, and blue color channels. Each row is a separate moult cycle stage.

Overall, the one-way ANOVA result of a green channel illuminated pixel percentage value analysis was significant. The group results were as follows: intermoult 56.3% ± 17.7%; pre-ecdysis 53.9% ± 16.3%; post-ecdysis 27.3% ± 13.1%. (F = 12.47; d.f. = 2.33; and $p < 0.0001$). The Tukey HSD post hoc comparison showed significance between the post-ecdysis values and both the intermoult and pre-ecdysis values ($p = 0.0002$ and $p = 0.0006$ respectively). However, the intermoult and pre-ecdysis values were not significantly different ($p = 0.9254$). The intermoult and pre-ecdysis pixel illumination values were combined for further comparisons with the post-ecdysis values.

3.3.4. Dorsal Surface Spectral Analysis Using the Low-Cost Camera

The spectral distribution around the NIR channels of the AS7265x formed a characteristic peak at the 810 nm channel when illuminated by SFH 4737 LEDs. The level of reflectivity increases steadily from the 705 nm channel with an increasing wavelength to the 810 nm channel and then declines to the 940 nm channel. No change in the absorption characteristic of the dorsal carapace is evident because all channel values remained in a proportionally similar position to each other. The highest variation in reflectivity occurs at the central 810 nm channel, with both margins (705 and 940 channels) showing only small variability. The variability of the channels in the midpoints between the centre and each edge was proportional to their distance from the centre (Figure 8).

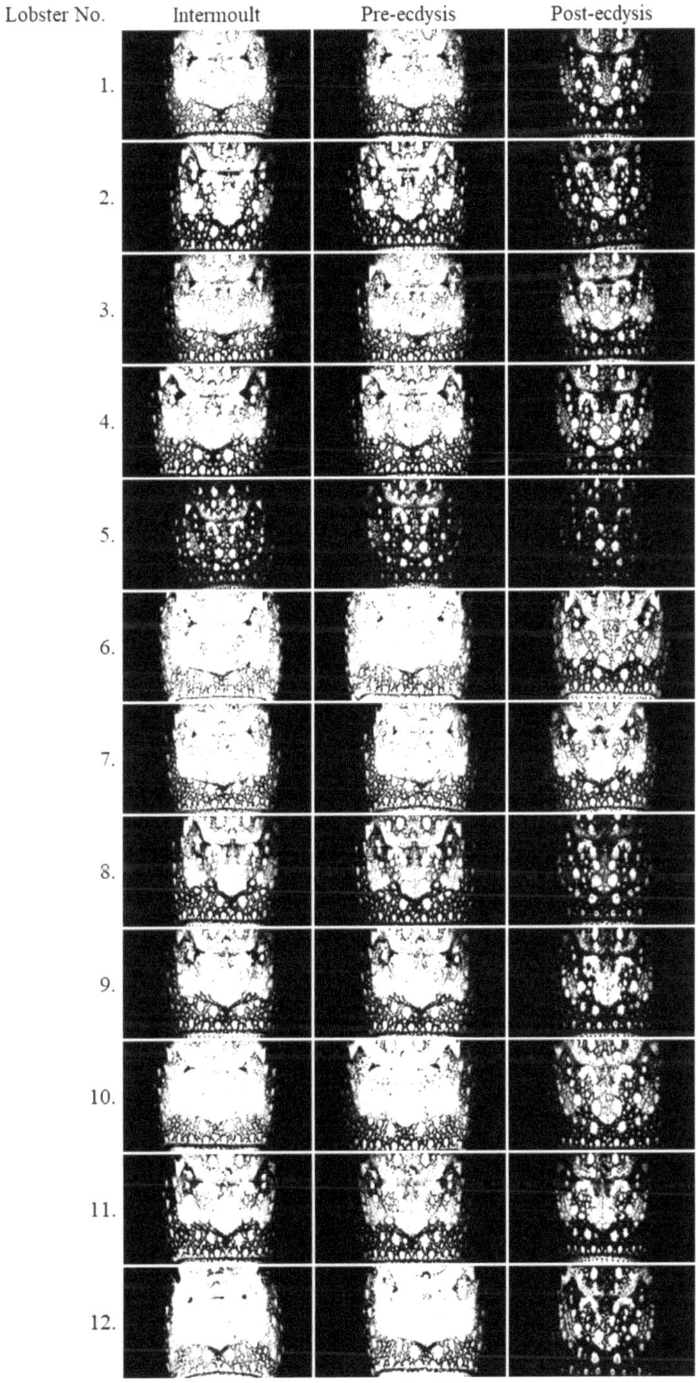

Figure 7. Representative green channel images of the dorsal carapace of the twelve sample *Panulirus ornatus* lobsters using SFH 4737 LEDs. The images have been masked outside the dorsal carapace, and a threshold of 35 (out of 255) has been applied.

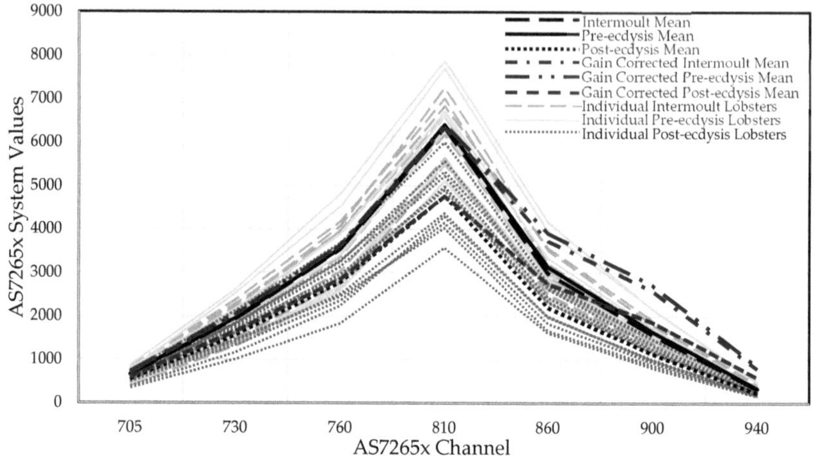

Figure 8. AS7265x NIR channel raw system value spectral distribution plots from the dorsal carapace surface of *Panulirus ornatus* lobsters during growth, pre-ecdysis, and post-ecdysis stages. High variability is evident from the individual spectral distributions.

The individual lobster traces show consistency of proportional placement of each spectral channel on the AS7265x (Figure 8). An overall change in NIR reflectivity is apparent due to the proportional scaling of all points. On average, lobsters are less reflective to NIR light at post-ecdysis. The one-way ANOVA of infrared light reflectance from the surface of lobsters showed a significant result (F = 9.35; d.f. = 2.27; and $p = 0.0008$). Group results were as follows (summed AS7265x NIR channel raw data): intermoult 17,287 $\pm$ 2184; pre-ecdysis 17,659 $\pm$ 3270; post-ecdysis 13,185 $\pm$ 2379. The Tukey HSD post hoc comparison showed significance between the post-ecdysis values and both the intermoult and pre-ecdysis values ($p = 0.0036$ and $p = 0.0021$ respectively). However, the NIR reflectance of intermoult and pre-ecdysis lobsters was not significantly different ($p = 0.9487$). The intermoult and pre-ecdysis NIR reflectivity values were combined for further comparisons with the post-ecdysis group.

Applying the gain correction leaves the distinct peak reflection at 810 nm intact and has little effect on the overall shape of the spectral curve, particularly on the lower peak sensitivity channels. Channel sensitivity has its largest influence on the 860 nm and 900 nm peak channel. The effect of gain calibration appears reduced at the 940 nm peak channel due to the relatively low values recorded. Channel sensitivity itself does not create the reflectivity peak at the 810 nm peak channel.

3.3.5. Correlation of Illuminated Pixel Percentage and NIR Abundance

Correlation between illuminated pixel percentage and NIR abundance was not seen for the combined intermoult and pre-ecdysis values ($r = -0.0034$ and $p = 0.9890$), nor the post-ecdysis values ($r = 0.0782$ and $p = 0.8191$).

3.3.6. Scatterplot of Illuminated Pixel Percentage and NIR Abundance

The scatterplot of illuminated pixel percentage values against NIR abundance values shows intermingling of the intermoult and pre-ecdysis values. The post-ecdysis values generally gather away from the intermoult and pre-ecdysis values. The least squares regression model ($R^2 = 0.5804$; RSE = 0.6581 with d.f. 27) produced a binary classification decision boundary line with formula:

$$y = -0.0059x + 126.25 \tag{3}$$

This boundary correctly classifies 26 of 30 (86.7%) of the sample lobsters (Figure 9).

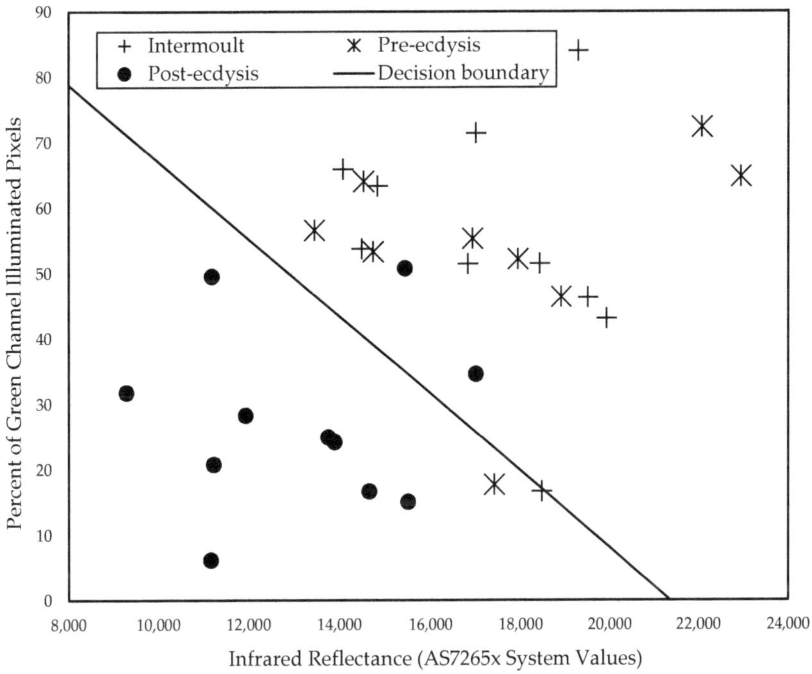

Figure 9. Scatterplot of percentage of green channel illuminated pixels and infrared reflectance by stage from the dorsal carapace of *Panulirus ornatus*. A linear regression for binary classification decision boundary was determined to separate the post-ecdysis values from the combined growth and pre-ecdysis values.

4. Discussion

Extensive stock losses due to conspecific cannibalistic interactions in culture vessels is driving a need to detect the signs of pre-ecdysis quickly and accurately, whether the lobster is in, or out, of the culture vessel. Suture line development and nutrient and mineral reabsorption are key pre-ecdysis events that may enable pre-ecdysis characterisation with a sensor. Suture line development occurs visibly, allowing assessment via manual inspection, or via a computer vision algorithm. While nutrient and mineral re-absorption does not alter the visual appearance of the dorsal carapace, it may alter the surface chemical composition and thus light absorption properties on the lobster's surface. Altered light absorption properties would create an opportunity to use spectroscopy to characterise pre-ecdysis. A low-cost spectral sensing solution is required for practical reasons. The availability of low-cost components, SBCs, and rapid development coupled with comparative analysis enable the creation and assessment of novel solutions.

Real advantages in suture line imaging were gained by testing a variety of light sources with the Sony IMX219 NOIR camera. Clarifying the presence of the suture simplifies detecting approaching ecdysis and is a step towards the ultimate goal of identifying pre-ecdysis in situ. Overall, the use of visible light is the least preferred method to create a well-defined image of the suture line. NIR light's ability to flatten contrast and detail creates a smooth background against which the suture line becomes well defined. NUV light produces a well-defined suture line for immerged lobsters while maintaining the details of the lobster's surface.

The ability of the SFH 4737 LEDs to produce three different views simultaneously on the three camera channels creates benefits for the use of this light source, particularly in conjunction with computer vision. Using the red and blue channel images could allow parallel inference from two models for improved detection accuracy. Parallel inference with re-combination is used for combining RGB image data with depth information for improved inference accuracy [24].

The low-cost camera was effective at aligning the target via the on-screen preview allowing comparable datasets to be acquired. The data generated by the low-cost camera also had high repeatability and consistency, which is supported by Ducanchez et al. [25], who report good repeatability when using the AS7265x sensors, and Pagnutti et al. [7] report that the Raspberry Pi camera module V2 has stable operational characteristics. The spectral readings consistently created a proportionally scaled output which has low variability in the proportional placement of the datapoints. The spectral distribution shape, particularly the reflectivity peak on the 810 nm channel, was unexplained either by variations in the emission spectrum from the SFH 4737 LEDs under our operational conditions, or by the channel sensitivity biases introduced by the AS7265x spectral sensor. In the absence of an alternative explanation, it appears that *P. ornatus* strongly reflects NIR light around 810 nm.

Using an SBC was beneficial in this study as it allowed the green channel of the camera and the NIR channels of the AS7265x to be captured simultaneously and combined to a single two-dimensional dataset. Dorsal surface characterisation of post-ecdysis lobsters was demonstrated using the two-dimensional dataset with the creation of a least squares regression decision boundary to correctly classify 86.7% of lobsters on the two-dimensional plane created by the AS7265x NIR reflectivity data and the camera's green channel pixel illumination percentage data. Higher classification rates are unlikely due to high variability amongst the sample lobster population, particularly of the dorsal surface excretion responsible for green channel pixel illumination. Sutherland et al. [5] noted a high variability of ventral surface color due to phenotypic and exogenic effects, which is likely applicable here.

A second benefit from the use of an SBC is control of invisible light sources. Cummins et al. [26] show that *Panulirus argus* have light sensitivity from 360 nm to approximately 600 nm, which may trigger photo avoidance behaviours. This observation coupled with the spectral reflectivity observation that NIR reaches a reflectivity peak near 810 nm from the surface of lobsters indicate that an invisible NIR light source may be most suitable for monitoring lobsters in culture vessels with a camera. We demonstrated effective on/off light control from the same Jetson Nano used for data collection using only simple additional circuits and readily available components.

The third benefit of SBCs is flexible configuration. The Jetson Nano development kit carrier board is equipped with a GPIO that has 2 PWM GPIO pins, UART (serial), I^2C, and SPI communications, and dual CSI/MIPI camera connectors. Dimming control of the lights was unused in this study, but easily implemented by swapping the GPIO output to PWM and using the dimming control input of the STEVAL-ILL051V1 LED driver boards (STMicroelectronics N.V., Geneva, Switzerland). This allows for full automation of light control with the development of object detection models. The manual action button could be substituted by an inference trigger to momentarily change the Jetson Nano's light and camera configuration to capture the best possible images for pre-ecdysis characterisation and reduce high intensity infrared light exposure while monitoring.

Upgrading both the spectral and image sensors are options to increase spectral resolution, addressing the observation that pre-ecdysis changes on the surface of the dorsal carapace were insufficient to detect using the low-cost spectral sensing system as developed. The AS7421 (ams OSRAM AG, Premstätten, Austria) has 64 NIR channels between 700 and 1000 nm [27], while image sensor technology is advancing steadily from the different vendors, including a wider variety of specialty sensors.

The Jetson Nano has dual display outputs on the development kit carrier board allowing this system to form the basis of a manual identification workstation based on suture line detection. Clarification of the suture can be used for manual sorting by production workers in the interim as development continues towards in situ detection. Clear vision of the suture lines facilitates fast and accurate sorting and reduces handling and time spent out of water which are important factors in manual sorting. Using a live stream to a computer monitor and replacing the shutter release button with a foot pedal, an operator would have two hands free to gently hold and position the lobster in front of a camera and light source, placed behind a protective screen. A system that makes manual sorting viable in a production setting could have an immediate impact in reducing losses to conspecific cannibalism.

5. Conclusions

In this study of 12 juvenile *P. ornatus*, images were taken and grouped into three moult stages measured relative to the observed day of ecdysis: intermoult, pre-ecdysis, and post-ecdysis lobsters. For the first time, it was shown that formed suture lines can be captured in images with greater definition by using light sources outside visible light with lobsters emerged and immerged.

The IMX219 NOIR image sensor and narrowband 850 nm LED combined to flatten contrast and reduce detail, as well as supress surface pigmentation in images. The suture line was made conspicuous by appearing against a mostly featureless background. The clarified suture line may simplify manual sorting and is also a step towards in situ automated pre-ecdysis characterisation.

The novel low-cost spectral camera developed specifically in this study showed promising operational characteristics collecting many comparable images and spectral samples with a high level of consistent, reproduced data. Separate interactions of reduced green channel pixel percentage illumination and reduced NIR reflectance from the dorsal surface combined to enable the characterisation of post-ecdysis from the dorsal surface of *P. ornatus* for the first time. This finding providing encouragement that the exploratory creation and testing of this novel spectral camera may have application in other research endeavours.

This study has shown that combining image, spectral data, and specialty light sources into a single two-dimension data stream, it is easily possible to re-configure and tune the system from the variety of available components. Combining different low-cost sensors on the same base platform provided a low-cost analogue of typically expensive equipment.

This innovative design of a low-cost spectral camera showed that the dorsal surface of *P. ornatus* remains stable between intermoult and pre-ecdysis despite nutrient and mineral absorption occurring within the integument. In the absence of a contradictory finding, the dorsal surface stability of twelve *P. ornatus* juveniles into pre-ecdysis excludes the spectrographic determination of pre-ecdysis, regardless of the equipment used.

Author Contributions: Conceptualization, C.S.; methodology, C.S.; software, C.S.; formal analysis, C.S.; investigation, C.S.; resources, C.S., A.D.H. and G.G.S.; data curation, C.S.; writing—original draft preparation, C.S.; writing—review and editing, C.S., A.D.H., D.R.G., A.J.T. and G.G.S.; supervision, A.D.H., D.R.G., A.J.T. and G.G.S.; project administration, C.S., A.D.H. and G.G.S.; funding acquisition, G.G.S. All authors have read and agreed to the published version of the manuscript.

Funding: This research was conducted by the Australian Research Council Industrial Transformation Hub for Sustainable Onshore Lobster Aquaculture (project number IH190100014). The views expressed herein are those of the authors and are not necessarily those of the Australian Government or the Australian Research Council.

Institutional Review Board Statement: Ethical review and approval were waived for this study due to research on invertebrates is currently exempt from ethics approval as per the current Australian code for the care and use of animals for scientific purposes. "The Code applies to the care and use of all live non-human vertebrates and cephalopods". Decapod crustaceans do not fall within these categories.

Informed Consent Statement: Not applicable.

Data Availability Statement: Data are available on request.

Acknowledgments: We would like to express appreciation for the technical assistance at IMAS, including Mathew Allan, Charlotte Levi, Jose Garcia Lafuente, Nigel Coombes, and Ross Goldsmid, and technical assistance at the School of Engineering from Andrew Bylett, Rodrigo Ximeno, Ellie Jane, Simon Hogwood, Jon Rodden, and Rick Barrett. We are grateful to Yukiko Burns from the Australia Japan Society, and Hachimure from TSUJIDEN Co., Ltd. for organising and supplying the D121UP diffusion film used in this study.

Conflicts of Interest: The authors declare no conflicts of interest. The funders had no role in the design of the study; in the collection, analyses, or interpretation of data; in the writing of the manuscript; or in the decision to publish the results.

References

1. Kelly, T.R.; Giosio, D.R.; Trotter, A.J.; Smith, G.G.; Fitzgibbon, Q.P. Cannibalism in Cultured Juvenile Lobster *Panulirus Ornatus* and Contributing Biological Factors. *Aquaculture* **2023**, *576*, 739883. [CrossRef]
2. Emery, T.J.; Hartmann, K.; Green, B.S.; Gardner, C. Handled with Care: Minimal Impacts of Appendage Damage on the Growth and Productivity of the Southern Rock Lobster (*Jasus Edwardsii*). *Fish. Res.* **2016**, *175*, 75–86. [CrossRef]
3. Frisch, A.J.; Hobbs, J.-P.A. Effects of Autotomy on Long-Term Survival and Growth of Painted Spiny Lobster (*Panulirus Versicolor*) on the Great Barrier Reef, Australia. *Mar. Biol.* **2011**, *158*, 1645–1652. [CrossRef]
4. Garland, J.J.; Sekretta, G. Imaging for Determination of Crustacean Physical Attributes. U.S. Patent US20150359205A1, 17 December 2015.
5. Sutherland, C.; Henderson, A.; Trotter, A.J.; Giosio, D.; Smith, G. Assessing Sensing Techniques for Detecting Markers of Approaching Ecdysis in Juvenile Tropical Rock Lobsters, *Panulirus ornatus*. *Aquac. Eng.* **2023**, *102*, 102342. [CrossRef]
6. Sutherland, C.; Henderson, A.; Holloway, D.; Trotter, A.J.; Giosio, D.; Smith, G. A Survey of NDT Ultrasound Transducers for Sensing Pre-Moult Tropical Rock Lobsters, *Panulirus ornatus*. *Appl. Acoust.* **2024**, *223*, 110073. [CrossRef]
7. Pagnutti, M.; Ryan, R.E.; Cazenavette, G.; Gold, M.; Harlan, R.; Leggett, E.; Pagnutti, J. Laying the Foundation to Use Raspberry Pi 3 V2 Camera Module Imagery for Scientific and Engineering Purposes. *J. Electron. Imaging* **2017**, *26*, 013014. [CrossRef]
8. Malchow, D. Imaging in the Shortwave Infrared (SWIR) for Industrial Applications: When Visible Imaging Comes up Short, SWIR Can Be the Answer. *Adv. Imaging* **2007**, *22*, 30–36.
9. Aiken, D.E. Molting and Growth. In *The Biology and Management of Lobsters*; Academic Press: New York, NY, USA, 1980; Volume 1, pp. 91–163, ISBN 0-12-177401-5.
10. Passano, L.M. Molting and Its Control. In *The Physiology of Crustacea*; Waterman, T.H., Ed.; Academic Press: New York, NY, USA, 1960; Volume 1, pp. 473–536, ISBN 978-0-12-395628-6.
11. Jones, C.M. Tropical Spiny Lobster Aquaculture Development in Vietnam, Indonesia and Australia. *J. Mar. Biol. Assoc. India* **2010**, *52*, 304–315.
12. Lowe, D.G. Distinctive Image Features from Scale-Invariant Keypoints. *Int. J. Comput. Vis.* **2004**, *60*, 91–110. [CrossRef]
13. Beć, K.B.; Grabska, J.; Huck, C.W. Near-Infrared Spectroscopy in Bio-Applications. *Molecules* **2020**, *25*, 2948. [CrossRef] [PubMed]
14. Sutherland, C.R.; Henderson, A.; Giosio, D.; Trotter, A.; Smith, G. Synchronising an Imx219 Image Sensor and As7265x Spectral Sensor to Make a Novel Low-Cost Spectral Camera. *Preprints* **2024**, 2024040897. [CrossRef]
15. Aquino, A.; Noguera, M.; Millan, B.; Mejías, A.; Ponce, J.M.; Andújar, J.M. A Preliminary Evaluation of a Low-Cost Multispectral Sensor for Non-Destructive Evaluation of Olive Fruits' Fat Content. In *XLIII Jornadas de Automática: Libro de Actas: 7, 8 y 9 de Septiembre de 2022, Logroño (La Rioja)*; Servizo de Publicacións da UDC: A Coruña, Spain, 2022; pp. 475–478, ISBN 978-84-9749-841-8.
16. Noguera, M.; Millan, B.; Andújar, J.M. New, Low-Cost, Hand-Held Multispectral Device for In-Field Fruit-Ripening Assessment. *Agriculture* **2022**, *13*, 4. [CrossRef]
17. Roer, R.; Dillaman, R. The Structure and Calcification of the Crustacean Cuticle. *Am. Zool.* **1984**, *24*, 893–909. [CrossRef]
18. Travis, D.F.; Friberg, U. The Deposition of Skeletal Structures in the Crustacea: VI. Microradiographic Studies of the Exoskeleton of the Crayfish *Orconectes virilis* Hagen. *J. Ultrastruct. Res.* **1963**, *9*, 285–301. [CrossRef] [PubMed]
19. Arducam NoIR IMX219-AF Programmable/Auto Focus IR Sensitive Camera Module for Nvidia Jetson Nano. Arducam. 2023. Available online: https://www.arducam.com/product/b0189-arducam-noir-imx219-af-programmable-auto-focus-ir-sensitive-camera-module-nvidia-jetson-nano/ (accessed on 9 June 2024).
20. Arducam IMX219 Datasheet. 2016. Available online: https://docs.arducam.com/Raspberry-Pi-Camera/Native-camera/source/IMX219DS.PDF (accessed on 20 May 2024).
21. FRAMOS FSM-IMX335 Datasheet. Available online: https://www.framos.com/wp-content/uploads/FSM-IMX335-Datasheet.pdf (accessed on 10 August 2023).
22. ams-OSRAM AG SFH 4737 Datasheet. Available online: https://look.ams-osram.com/m/576f284cd3c20cb4/original/SFH-4737.pdf (accessed on 9 June 2023).
23. ams-OSRAM AG AS7265x Smart 18-Channel VIS to NIR Spectral_ID 3-Sensor Chipset with Electronic Shutter. Available online: https://look.ams-osram.com/m/76ce4c0d80cd1565/original/AS7265x-DS000612.pdf (accessed on 9 June 2023).
24. He, L.; Wang, G.; Hu, Z. Learning Depth from Single Images with Deep Neural Network Embedding Focal Length. *IEEE Trans. Image Process.* **2018**, *27*, 4676–4689. [CrossRef] [PubMed]

25. Ducanchez, A.; Moinard, S.; Brunel, G.; Bendoula, R.; Héran, D.; Tisseyre, B. The AS7265x Chipset as an Alternative Low-Cost Multispectral Sensor for Agriculture Applications Based on NDVI. In *Proceedings of the Sense the Real Change: Proceedings of the 20th International Conference on Near Infrared Spectroscopy*; Chu, X., Guo, L., Huang, Y., Yuan, H., Eds.; Springer Nature: Singapore, 2022; pp. 201–206.
26. Cummins, D.R.; Chen, D.-M.; Goldsmith, T.H. Spectral Sensitivity of the Spiny Lobster, *Panulirus argus*. *Biol. Bull.* **1984**, *166*, 269–276. [CrossRef]
27. ams-OSRAM AG AS7421 64-Channel Hyperspectral NIR Sensor. Available online: https://look.ams-osram.com/m/1164a4e1da5c19a9/original/AS7421-DS000667.pdf (accessed on 9 June 2023).

Journal of
Marine Science and Engineering

MDPI

Article

Artificial Neural Network for Glider Detection in a Marine Environment by Improving a CNN Vision Encoder

Jungwoo Lee [1], Ji-Hyun Park [1], Jeong-Hwan Hwang [1], Kyoungseok Noh [1], Youngho Choi [1] and Jinho Suh [2,*]

[1] Smart Mobility Research Center, Korea Institute of Robotics and Technology Convergence (KIRO), Pohang 37666, Republic of Korea; ricow@kiro.re.kr (J.L.); jhpark87@kiro.re.kr (J.-H.P.); hwangjh@kiro.re.kr (J.-H.H.); ksno@kiro.re.kr (K.N.); rockboy@kiro.re.kr (Y.C.)
[2] Major of Mechanical System Engineering, Pukyong National University, Busan 48513, Republic of Korea
* Correspondence: suhgang@pknu.ac.kr

Abstract: Despite major economic and technological advances, much of the ocean remains unexplored, which has led to the use of remotely operated vehicles (ROVs) and gliders for surveying. ROVs and underwater gliders are essential for ocean data collection. Gliders, which control their own buoyancy, are particularly effective unmanned platforms for long-term observations. The traditional method of recovering the glider on a small boat is a risky operation and depends on the skill of the workers. Therefore, a safer, more efficient, and automated system is needed to recover them. In this study, we propose a lightweight artificial neural network for underwater glider detection that is efficient for learning and inference. In order to have a smaller parameter size and faster inference, a convolutional neural network (CNN) vision encoder in an artificial neural network splits an image of a glider into a number of elongated patches that overlap to better preserve the spatial information of the pixels in the horizontal and vertical directions. Global max-pooling, which computes the maximum over all the spatial locations of an input feature, was used to activate the most salient feature vectors at the end of the encoder. As a result of the inference of the glider detection models on the test dataset, the average precision (AP), which indicates the probability that an object is located within the predicted bounding box, shows that the proposed model achieves AP = 99.7%, while the EfficientDet-D2 model for comparison of detection performance achieves AP = 69.2% at an intersection over union (IOU) threshold of 0.5. Similarly, the proposed model achieves an AP of 78.9% and the EfficientDet-D2 model achieves an AP of 50.5% for an IOU threshold of 0.75. These results show that accurate prediction is possible within a wide range of recall for glider position inference in a real ocean environment.

Keywords: artificial neural network; CNN vision encoder; underwater glider; low-rank adaptation

Citation: Lee, J.; Park, J.-H.; Hwang, J.-H.; Noh, K.; Choi, Y.; Suh, J. Artificial Neural Network for Glider Detection in a Marine Environment by Improving a CNN Vision Encoder. *J. Mar. Sci. Eng.* **2024**, *12*, 1106. https://doi.org/10.3390/jmse12071106

Academic Editors: Jingchun Zhou, Wenqi Ren, Qiuping Jiang and Yan-Tsung Peng

Received: 11 June 2024
Revised: 27 June 2024
Accepted: 28 June 2024
Published: 29 June 2024

1. Introduction

A rich source of natural resources, the oceans cover a significant portion of the Earth's surface. With advances in economics and technology, ocean exploration has gained widespread attention. Remotely operated vehicles (ROVs) and underwater gliders play a critical role in ocean data collection. ROVs can operate in deep-sea environments that are difficult for humans to access and use a variety of sensors and tools to collect data. Underwater gliders are among the most effective unmanned underwater platforms for ocean observation. These gliders are designed to operate by changing the buoyancy of the surrounding water. They have advantages such as low energy consumption, long navigation range, and extended endurance. Meanwhile, gliders will explore the oceans autonomously and transmit data continuously for long periods of time.

By switching between a negative and positive lift, the gliders follow a slow sawtooth up-and-down trajectory using very little energy. This allows them to travel farther and stay open longer. As a result, they can conduct ocean sampling missions lasting hours to weeks or months, over thousands of kilometers. At the end of long missions, the glider must be recovered because it is drifting at sea and has no surface propulsion for its own return to the mothership.

The conventional method of lifting the glider onto a small boat relies on human skill and basic tools such as nets, cranes, belts, and hooks. First, the mother ship navigates close to the floating position of the glider. Workers then approach the glider in a small boat. They drop a net or hook to secure the glider and then pull it on board. The boat with the workers and the glider on board is then hoisted back to the mother ship by a crane. The experience and skill of the workers are critical to the success of this recovery operation. Adverse weather conditions can frequently complicate the operation, slowing it down and increasing the risk of injury to the workers. These traditional methods remain largely manual, despite their risks and limitations. There is a need for a safer, more efficient, and automated system of recovery.

In this work, we propose an artificial neural network to detect gliders in a maritime environment and recover them using an ROV platform, which can operate in rough seas and is capable of both human-operated and semi-autonomous control. The ROV platform uses GPS tracking to navigate from a distance to the visible location of the glider, guided by the camera sensors. To navigate long distances, the ROV relies on GPS to get within a few meters of the glider. For short-range navigation, the ROV uses a camera sensor to detect the glider within its visible range and then moves to within a meter of the glider. To facilitate this process, an artificial neural network detects the glider in the camera images, provides position coordinates, and helps control the ROV's movements based on this information.

The main contributions of this work are summarized as follows:

- We propose a lightweight, end-to-end artificial neural network model for detecting gliders with fast inference speed. To compress the weight of the model, a low-rank approximation is applied to the CNN vision encoder.
- A CNN vision encoder that divides an image of a glider at sea into several elongated variable-width patches and extracts feature vectors for each direction. These patches are overlapped to better preserve the spatial information of the pixels in the horizontal and vertical directions.

2. Related Works

Deep learning models use various image segmentation methods to perform image processing tasks. The feature pyramid network (FPN) [1] is a method that effectively uses the features extracted from different resolutions of an image to perform image segmentation tasks. To achieve accurate image segmentation results, the FPN effectively utilizes important information from multiple resolutions of the image. The FPN extracts feature maps from the input image at different resolutions, and the high-resolution feature map information is fed into low-resolution feature maps to generate feature maps with rich information. The vision transformer (ViT) [2] is a method that uses a transformer-based neural network architecture to segment images. It consists of patching, which divides the input image into smaller patches; position encoding, which adds position information to each patch; a transformer encoder, which processes the sequence of patches to learn the image context; and a segmentation head, which uses the learned features to predict the category of each pixel. The ViT can better understand the complex structure of images by learning longer-term dependencies than CNN-based models.

Methods for detecting and tracking objects like gliders in images include traditional image processing techniques and deep learning models. Conventional image processing involves object patch matching, which involves extracting a patch containing the slider from an image and then matching it to similar areas in another image to locate it. These algorithms include Tracking, Learning and Detection (TLD) [3], Kernel Correlation Filters (KCFs) [4], and Channel and Spatial Reliability (CSRT) [5]. However, this method has the drawback that it often fails to match due to variations in brightness and color in different marine environments and changes in the glider's pose. Also, as the image size increases, the complexity of the matching operation increases.

In order to identify and track the glider more efficiently, deep learning-based object detection uses advanced models. These models are typically implemented as convolutional neural networks (CNNs) and detect objects using images. One of the early successful models is the region-based convolutional neural network (R-CNN) [6], which uses a selective search to generate regions of interest (ROIs) and performs classification and location within those ROIs. An improvement on R-CNN, Fast R-CNN [7] shares the feature extraction stage and uses RPNs to efficiently generate ROIs. As a further refinement, Faster R-CNN integrates RPNs into the network, enabling end-to-end training and faster performance. The single shot multibox detector (SSD) [8] uses a single convolutional network to predict bounding boxes and class labels for each object in an image. RetinaNet [9] is a one-stage dense object detector that uses focal loss, a feature pyramid network, and dense anchor boxes to achieve high accuracy and efficiency. CenterNet [10] is also a one-stage object detector that predicts the key points of objects and regresses their sizes and offsets, which allows for fast and accurate object detection without the need to generate bounding boxes. EfficientDet [11] is a family of neural network architectures that combine depth, width, and resolution scaling to outperform other CNN models. You Only Look Once (YOLO) [12] takes a different approach by simultaneously detecting and classifying objects using a single neural network.

3. Methods

3.1. CNN Vision Encoder

The CNN vision encoder proposed in this work N-splits the input image into horizontal and vertical patches of different widths and generates a feature vector by convolving each image block. The convolution layer applies a depth-separable convolution, passes through a multi-layer perception (MLP) that non-linearizes the output of the convolution, and performs global max pooling to compress the weights of the vision encoder model.

A splitting overlapping image patches in deep learning models, such as CNNs and vision transformers, reduces information loss at the patch boundaries, maintains image continuity, and enables richer and more robust feature learning. Overlapping patches help prevent the loss of important information at the patch boundaries and better detect continuous edges and textures that span across patch boundaries more effectively. This approach mitigates the boundary effects and improves the model's spatial awareness, leading to smoother predictions and better generalization, despite the increased computational cost.

In this work, as shown in Figure 1 below, by dividing the image horizontally and vertically so that some of the patches overlap, the spatial characteristics of the pixels are preserved, and the structural information of the image is transferred to the convolutional layer. The nested CNN vision encoder processes each patch of the image and generates feature vectors.

Depthwise separable convolution is an efficient technique that can significantly reduce the size of the model and the computational cost when compared to the standard convolution operations. It applies a 1×1 filter to each input channel independently and extracts the spatial information across the channels, and then combines all the channels using a 1×1 filter. In a normal convolution operation, each input channel is convolved with a 1×1 filter, which results in the application of the same filter to all the channels. In contrast, depthwise separable convolution applies independent filters to each channel and extracts only spatial information across channels. This results in a significant reduction in the number of parameters in the model.

Low-rank approximation (LRA) [13] has emerged as a valuable technique for compressing a MLP with dense layers in neural networks. LRA can dramatically reduce the number of parameters in dense layers, leading to a substantial decrease in the model size. This translates to reduced storage requirements, faster model training, and more efficient model deployment, particularly for resource-constrained environments such as mobile devices or embedded systems. By reducing the number of parameters, LRA also leads to a significant reduction in computational complexity. This translates to faster model inference speeds, enabling real-time applications and reducing the overall computational burden. Despite parameter reduction, LRA can often maintain or even slightly improve model accuracy. This is attributed to the ability of LRA to identify and retain the most important features in the data while discarding redundant or less significant information.

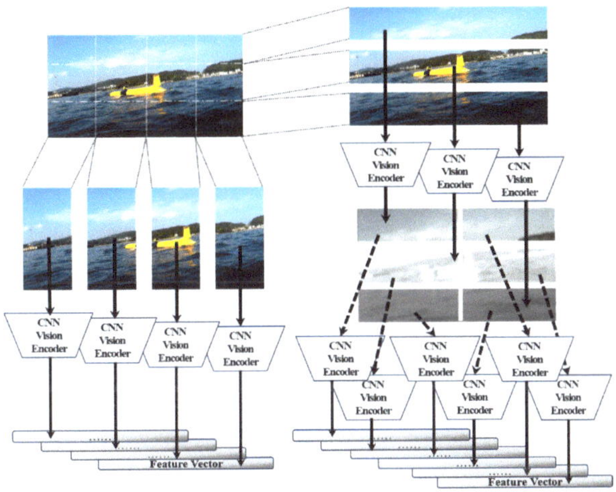

Figure 1. The process of dividing an image into horizontal and vertical directions in a CNN vision encoder.

LRA can be applied to a wide range of dense layer architectures, including fully connected layers in feedforward neural networks, recurrent layers in long short-term memory (LSTM) networks, and fully connected layers in convolutional neural networks (CNNs). Xception [14] is a deep CNN architecture that proposes efficient low-rank approximation techniques for deep CNNs. It introduces depth-wise separable convolutions and a novel depth multiplier mechanism to control the depth and width of the network. Xception also employs low-rank approximation to compress the weight matrices, enabling efficient training and inference of deep CNNs. MobileNet [15] is a lightweight CNN architecture designed for efficient operation on mobile and embedded devices. It utilizes depth-wise separable convolutions and low-rank approximation to significantly reduce the number of parameters and computational cost without sacrificing accuracy.

Global max-pooling, a technique commonly applied in convolutional neural networks (CNNs), offers several advantages that enhance the model performance. Global max-pooling selects the most prominent activations from the input feature map to generate its output. This enables the model to better capture and learn the dominant features within an image. Particularly in object recognition tasks, global max-pooling can improve the model accuracy. Unlike max-pooling, global max-pooling retains spatial information by considering all pixels within the feature map. This helps preserve the structural information of the image, making it valuable for tasks like object detection. In a previous study, Network in Network (NIN) [16] employed global max-pooling for image classification. SqueezeNet [17] is an ultra-lightweight CNN architecture that achieves the accuracy of AlexNet [18] on ImageNet with fewer parameters, making efficient use of convolutional layers and global max-pooling layers.

The diagram of the proposed CNN vision encoder is shown in Figure 2. An image patch of variable width, divided horizontally and vertically, is generated as a feature vector in latent space by depthwise separable convolution, which significantly reduces computational parameters with a separate filter for each channel and a 1×1 convolution kernel for all channels. The global max-pooling layer compresses the vision encoder output after passing through the dense layer block by low-rank adaptation.

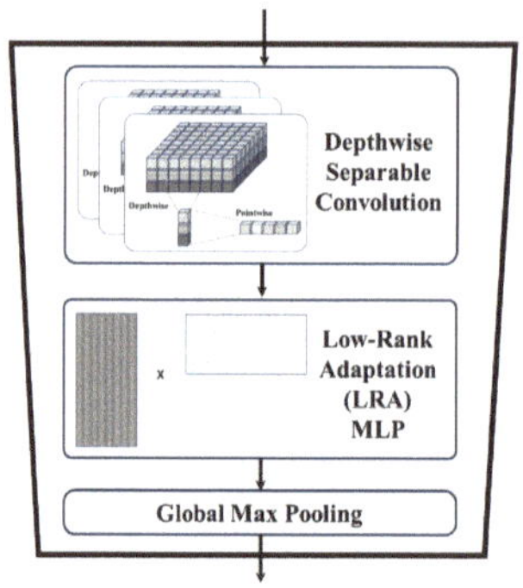

Figure 2. A diagram of the proposed CNN vision encoder.

3.2. Artificial Neural Network Model for Glider Detection

In the proposed artificial neural network model for glider detection, as shown in Figure 3, the image is divided into 2 × 2, 4 × 3, and 9 × 5 with horizontal and vertical, respectively, considering the resolution of the camera mounted on the ROV, and each image patch is converted into a feature vector by a CNN vision encoder.

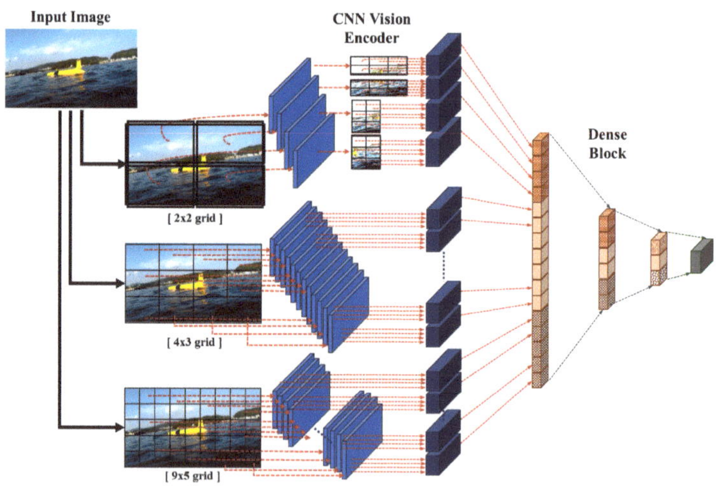

Figure 3. The proposed artificial neural network for glider detection.

Feature vectors in latent space, which are the output of nested CNN vision encoders, are concatenated according to the order of segmented positions, and the output dense layers are mapped to the bounding box and center position to estimate the glider position.

4. Experiments and Results

4.1. Collecting Data in the Marine Environment

For data collection in the marine environment [19], a mothership control system is set up in a dock at Yongho Pier in Busan, South Korea, as shown in Figure 4. The ROV is steered towards the glider to acquire video data from the camera. The sensor information and images are collected by moving the ROV platform closer to the glider as it floats on the sea surface [20]. Floating gliders have different postures, such as rolling or submerged, which are affected by waves. Using the ROV-mounted PoE camera, the internal camera, and the additional GoPro camera mounted on top of the ROV, the ROV captured video from different approaches. The tracking API of OpenCV is used to mark the position of the float in the recorded image with a bounding box and then automatically track it. The bounding box of the glider object is set wide enough to include the center of the glider for tracking purposes.

Figure 4. Experiment for the collection of image data of gliders at sea.

Automated object bounding box detection methods quickly generate tagging information for large amounts of image data. However, compared to manually setting bounding boxes by humans, the accuracy of the location information is lower, and incorrect detection information is sometimes mixed, which reduces the quality of the dataset. Datasets with an imprecise ground truth are a factor that hinders the improvement of the model's object detection performance, but we used them appropriately to balance cost and resources. The training dataset for the detection of gliders floating on the water surface has generated approximately 2,250,000 samples in a variety of environments.

4.2. Evaluation of the Inference Performance of Artificial Neural Network for Glider Detection

The intersection over union (IOU), a common metric for evaluating detection models, is used to evaluate the inference performance of the deep learning-based glider detection model. The IOU used to evaluate the inference performance of the glider detection model is the ratio of the overlap between two ground truth and predicted bounding boxes. If the value is greater than or equal to the threshold of a given value, it is considered true positive (TP), and if it is less than the threshold, it is considered false positive (FP). TP means that the prediction is actually correct and FP means that the prediction is actually wrong. If it is not possible to detect the ground truth, it is false negative (FN). For general classification problems, the thresholds of IOU are 50%, 75%, and 95%.

However, in the case of glider position tracking detection, glider detection and center position detection are more important than the need to accurately match the shape of the glider object, so the IOU threshold does not need to be high.

Furthermore, since the ground truth bounding box is imprecise when the training dataset is generated, and often only a specific part of the object is tagged instead of the whole object, the IOU threshold to measure the inference performance of the glider detection model is set to 50% and 75% for evaluation.

Precision, also known as positive predictive value (PPV), measures the proportion of true positives, or correctly predicted positive cases, among all positive predictions. It reflects the accuracy of the model's predictions and is an answer to the question of how many of the cases the model predicted would be positive were actually positive. A high PPV is an indication that the model is good at identifying true positives and does not over-predict false positives.

Recall is also known as sensitivity or a hit rate and is a measure of the proportion of true positives among all true positives. It reflects the model's ability to identify positive cases and answers the question of how many true positives the model has correctly identified. A high recall rate is an indication that the model is good at identifying the majority of true positives and that there are no misses.

$$Precision = \frac{TP}{TP+FP} = \frac{TP}{all\ detections} \tag{1}$$

$$Recall = \frac{TP}{TP+FN} = \frac{TP}{all\ ground\ truths} \tag{2}$$

The calculation formulas for precision and recall are described in Equations (1) and (2), and the confusion matrix that explains the relationship between them is shown in Figure 5.

		Predicted Value		
		Positive	**Negative**	
Actual Value	**Positive**	**TP** (True Positive)	**FN** (False Negative)	**Recall** $\frac{TP}{TP+FN}$
	Negative	**FP** (False Positive)	**TN** (True Negative)	**Specificity** $\frac{TN}{TN+FP}$
		Precision $\frac{TP}{TP+FP}$	**Negative Predictive Value** $\frac{TN}{TN+FN}$	**Accuracy** $\frac{TP+TN}{TP+TN+FP+FN}$

Figure 5. Confusion matrix.

There is a trade-off between precision and recall. That is, an improvement in one metric often comes at the expense of the other. For example, a model that is very strict in what it predicts will have high precision but low recall. This is because the model will correctly identify most positive cases but miss some. Conversely, a model that is more lenient in its predictions will have high recall but low precision because it will correctly identify most positive cases, but it will also predict many false positives.

The average precision (AP) calculates the prediction results, sorts them in descending order by the confidence score, which indicates the probability that an object is within the prediction bounding box, and creates a precision–recall (P–R) curve, which is the average of the area under the curve. In the COCO metric, the AP is obtained by 101-point interpolation, adding the precision for each 0.01-unit section of the recall and averaging. For this metric, the IOU ranges from 0.5 to 0.95 and is incremented by 0.05. In particular, an AP with an IOU of 0.50 is referred to as the PASCAL VOC metric, and an AP with an IOU of 0.75 is referred to as the strict metric. Equation (3) is the definition of the AP calculation of the COCO metric.

$$AP = \frac{1}{101} \sum_{r \in (0.0,0.01,\ldots 1)} \max_{r:r \geq r} \rho(r) \tag{3}$$

To evaluate the precision and recall of the glider detection, it is necessary to set an IOU threshold t that classifies each detection as a TP or FP. The AP is a metric for the evaluation of precision and recall at different confidence levels. Thus, it is necessary to count the number of classifications of a TP and FP at different confidence levels. Different precision and recall values can be obtained by choosing a more restrictive threshold value for the AP. When the precision and recall values are calculated using a more restrictive AP threshold, the number of FP detections significantly reduces the recall values.

We compare it with the inference results obtained by EfficientDet. For this comparison, the EfficientDet model was transfer trained using the glider detection dataset. The proposed deep learning glider detection model, SingleDet, uses two modes with a different number of internal layers and weight values, while EfficientDet uses three modes, D0, D1, and D2, depending on the size of the input image and the backbone network. EfficientDet-D0 reportedly achieved 34.3 AP and EfficientDet-D2 achieved 43.5 AP on the COCO dataset.

To verify the inference performance of the model, the test dataset collected from the ocean environment is kept separate from the training dataset. It is not used to train the model, but only to measure the inference performance of the model.

The AP values for the IOU range of the EfficientDet models and the proposed SingleDet models are compared in Table 1 below. In the result, EfficientDet models record an average AP of about 0.67 for an IOU of 0.5 for a test dataset consisting of images collected directly from the ocean environment for glider detection, which decreases exponentially as the IOU increases. In contrast, the SingleDet model records an AP of about 0.78 or higher up to the strict metric with an IOU of 0.75. On average, the SingleDet model performs 50% better than the AP of the EfficientDet model. A graph comparing the AP of different models used in the evaluation by IOU value is shown in Figure 6.

Table 1. Comparison of AP between EfficientDet and SingleDet models in the IOU range.

Model	IOU										mAP
	0.50	0.55	0.60	0.65	0.70	0.75	0.80	0.85	0.90	0.95	
EfficientDet-D0	0.670	0.635	0.593	0.550	0.515	0.454	0.371	0.266	0.112	0.083	0.425
EfficientDet-D1	0.656	0.629	0.594	0.555	0.507	0.437	0.351	0.240	0.094	0.053	0.412
EfficientDet-D2	0.692	0.659	0.628	0.601	0.556	0.505	0.426	0.318	0.134	0.029	0.455
SingleDet-01	0.997	0.993	0.976	0.938	0.879	0.789	0.663	0.517	0.288	0.217	0.726
SingleDet-02	0.989	0.978	0.955	0.916	0.865	0.786	0.655	0.459	0.258	0.092	0.695

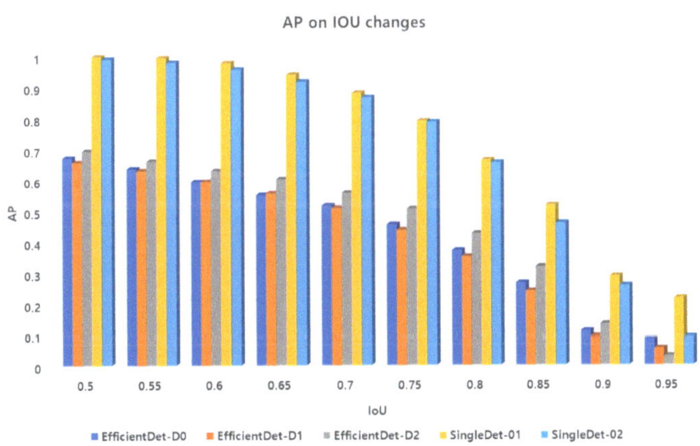

Figure 6. A graphical representation comparing the AP of models by IOU.

The graphical representation of the P–R curve for the inference of the SingleDet glider detection models evaluated for the PASCAL VOC metric at IOU of 0.50 and the strict metric at IOU of 0.75 are as Figure 7. In the P–R curve, the precision of the SingleDet model group tends to be maintained constant even when the recall is increased, which means that the model increases the detection rate while retaining the precision.

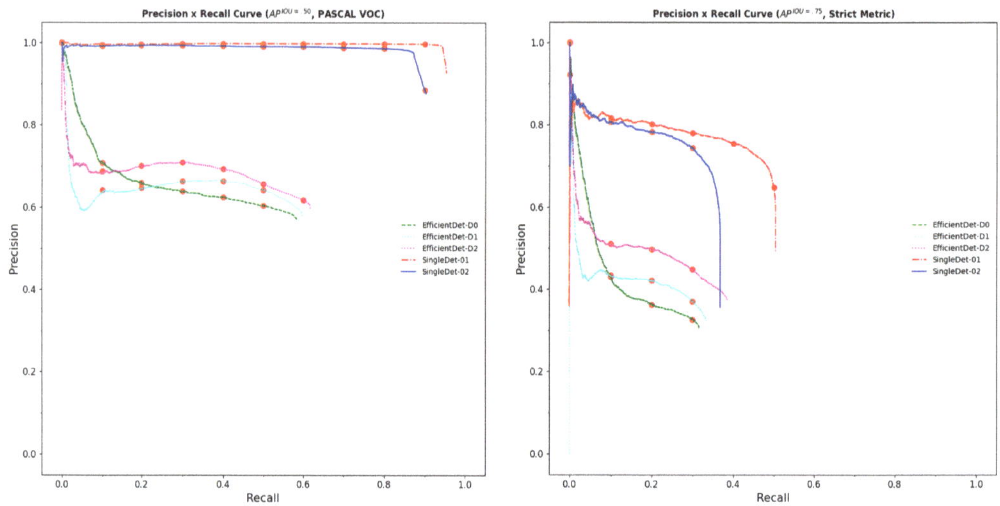

(a) (b)

Figure 7. Graph of the precision–recall curve ((**a**) $IOU_{threshold} = 0.50$, (**b**) $IOU_{threshold} = 0.75$).

For the SingleDet model group, using a less restrictive IOU threshold (t = 0.5) leads to higher recalls with the highest precision. That is, the inference of the Singledet-01 model can predict approximately 99.7% of the total ground truth without missing any detections.

The SingleDet-01 model achieves AP = 99.7% while the EfficientDet-D2 model achieves AP = 69.2% at an IOU threshold of t = 0.5. Similarly, for an IOU threshold of t = 0.75, the SingleDet-01 model achieves an AP of 78.9% and the EfficientDet-D2 model achieves an AP of 50.5%. When we use the IOU threshold of t = 0.75, the inference of the glider detection model becomes more sensitive to different confidence levels. This can be explained by the degree to which the curve goes up and down.

A comparison of the inference performance of the SingleDet and EfficientDet glider detection models is shown in Table 2. The computer specifications consist of an Intel i9-9980 CPU and an Nvidia RTX A3000 GPU used to perform the model inference. The results of the comparison show that the SingleDet set of models has more than 1.5 times the average precision of the EfficientDet set and uses about half the number of weight parameters, resulting in a faster inference speed.

Table 2. Comparison of SingleDet and EfficientDet models' AP, parameter size, and prediction time.

Model	Average Prediction (%)			#Parameters		Predict Time
	AP_{50}	AP_{75}	AP_{90}	Params	Ratio	
SingleDet-01	99.7	78.9	28.8	2.5 M	1.0×	177 ms
SingleDet-02	98.9	78.6	25.8	2.9 M	1.2×	314 ms
EfficientDet-D0	67.0	45.4	11.2	3.9 M	1.6×	183 ms
EfficientDet-D1	65.6	43.7	9.4	6.6 M	2.6×	534 ms
EfficientDet-D2	69.2	50.5	13.4	8.1 M	3.3×	732 ms

The results of glider detection using different artificial neural network detection models by operating the ROV platform in the marine environment are shown in Figure 8 below.

(a) (b) (c) (d) (e)

Figure 8. Results of the inference of artificial neural network models for the detection of gliders in the marine environment ((**a**) EfficientDet-D0, (**b**) EfficientDet-D1, (**c**) EfficientDet-D2, (**d**) SingleDet-01, (**e**) SingleDet-02).

5. Conclusions

Underwater gliders use long missions to explore the oceans. Unlike other underwater vehicles, they do not have a propulsion system. As a result, recovery of these gliders at the end of their missions is currently a manual process that can be dangerous depending on weather conditions.

In this study, we improve the CNN vision encoder of an artificial neural network model for detecting a glider floating on the water from camera images during the stage of performing glider recovery operations using the ROV platform, when the ROV and the glider are in close proximity.

The proposed artificial neural network glider detection model divides the input image horizontally and vertically into a number of variable-width patches and extracts feature maps of different latent space scales by depthwise separable convolution. The output of the glider detection model is information about the center position and bounding box of the detected object. The proposed SingleDet-01 model showed an average precision of 99.7% when comparing the inference performance of the other detection models on the IOU thresholds set to 0.5. It also had a tendency to maintain precision as recall increased, so the actual detection rate is judged to be high over a wide range.

For future works, this artificial neural network model will be used to assist the ROV platform in glider recovery. The time required for each unit task and the success rate of the operation will be evaluated compared to when a human operator performs the recovery operation with manual control alone. Our goal is to provide feedback on the performance of the work support in the real marine environment and to advance an artificial neural network model to a level where it can be used in practice.

Author Contributions: Conceptualization, J.L. and Y.C.; methodology, J.L. and J.-H.H.; software, J.L., J.-H.H. and K.N.; validation, J.L., Y.C. and J.S.; formal analysis, J.L. and K.N.; investigation, J.L. and J.-H.P.; resources, J.L.; data curation, J.L.; writing—original draft preparation, J.L. and J.-H.H.; writing—review and editing, J.L., Y.C. and J.S.; visualization, J.L., J.-H.H. and K.N.; supervision, J.S.; project administration, J.S.; funding acquisition, J.S. All authors have read and agreed to the published version of the manuscript.

Funding: This research was supported by the Korea Institute of Marine Science & Technology Promotion (KIMST), funded by the Ministry of Ocean and Fisheries (2020048213, Development of the core technology and establishment of the operation center for underwater gliders).

Institutional Review Board Statement: Not applicable.

Informed Consent Statement: Not applicable.

Data Availability Statement: The original contributions presented in the study are included in the article, further inquiries can be directed to the corresponding author.

Acknowledgments: All authors have read and agreed to the published version of the manuscript. The authors would like to thank all researchers of the smart mobility research center in the Korea Institute of Robotics and Technology Convergence, and all reviewers for very helpful comments and suggestions.

Conflicts of Interest: The authors declare no conflicts of interest.

References

1. Lin, T.-Y.; Belongie, S. Feature Pyramid Networks for Object Detection. In Proceedings of the IEEE Conference on Computer Vision and Pattern Recognition (CVPR), Honolulu, HI, USA, 21–26 July 2017; pp. 936–944. [CrossRef]
2. Dosovitskiy, A. An Image is Worth 16 × 16 Words: Transformers for Image Recognition at Scale. *arXiv* **2020**, arXiv:2010.11929.
3. Kalal, Z.; Mikolajczyk, K.; Matas, J. Tracking-Learning-Detection. *IEEE Trans. Pattern Anal. Mach. Intell.* **2012**, *34*, 1409–1422. [CrossRef] [PubMed]
4. Henriques, J.F.; Caseiro, R.; Martins, P.; Batista, J. High-Speed Tracking with Kernelized Correlation Filters. *arXiv* **2014**, arXiv:1404.7584. [CrossRef] [PubMed]
5. Lukežič, A.; Vojíř, T.; Čehovin, L.; Matas, J.; Kristan, M. Discriminative Correlation Filter with Channel and Spatial Reliability. *arXiv* **2016**, arXiv:1611.08461. [CrossRef]
6. Girshick, R.; Donahue, J.; Darrell, T.; Malik, J. Region-Based Convolutional Networks for Accurate Object Detection and Segmentation. *IEEE Trans. Pattern Anal. Mach. Intell.* **2016**, *38*, 142–158. [CrossRef] [PubMed]
7. Ren, S.; He, K.; Girshick, R.; Sun, J. Faster R-CNN: Towards Real-Time Object Detection with Region Proposal Networks. *IEEE Trans. Pattern Anal. Mach. Intell.* **2017**, *39*, 1137–1149. [CrossRef] [PubMed]
8. Liu, W.; Anguelov, D.; Erhan, D.; Szegedy, C.; Reed, S.; Fu, C.-Y.; Berg, A.C. SSD: Single Shot MultiBox Detector. In *Lecture Notes in Computer Science*; Springer: Berlin/Heidelberg, Germany, 2016; Volume 9905, pp. 21–37. [CrossRef]
9. Lin, T.-Y.; Goyal, P.; Girshick, R.; He, K.; Dollar, P. Focal loss for dense object detection. In Proceedings of the 2017 IEEE International Conference on Computer Vision (ICCV), Venice, Italy, 22–29 October 2017. [CrossRef]
10. Zhao, Z.-Q.; Zheng, P.; Xu, S.-T.; Wu, X. Object detection with deep learning: A review. *IEEE Trans. Neural Netw. Learn. Syst.* **2019**, *30*, 3212–3232. [CrossRef] [PubMed]
11. Tan, M.; Pang, R.; Le, Q.V. EfficientDet: Scalable and Efficient Object Detection. *arXiv* **2019**, arXiv:1911.09070.
12. Redmon, J.; Divvala, S.; Girshick, R.; Farhadi, A. You only look once: Unified, real-time object detection. In Proceedings of the IEEE Conference on Computer Vision and Pattern Recognition (CVPR), Las Vegas, NV, USA, 27–30 June 2016; pp. 779–788. [CrossRef]
13. Iyer, C.; Gittens, A.; Carothers, C.; Drineas, P. Iterative Randomized Algorithms for Low Rank Approximation of Tera-scale Matrices with Small Spectral Gaps. In Proceedings of the IEEE/ACM 9th Workshop on Latest Advances in Scalable Algorithms for Large-Scale Systems (scalA), Dallas, TX, USA, 12 November 2018; pp. 33–40. [CrossRef]
14. Chollet, F. Xception: Deep Learning with Depthwise Separable Convolutions. In Proceedings of the IEEE Conference on Computer Vision and Pattern Recognition (CVPR), Honolulu, HI, USA, 21–26 July 2017; pp. 1800–1807. [CrossRef]
15. Howard, A.G.; Zhu, M.; Chen, B.; Kalenichenko, D.; Wang, W.; Weyand, T.; Andreetto, M.; Adam, H. MobileNet: Efficient Convolutional Neural Networks for Mobile Vision Applications. *arXiv* **2017**, arXiv:1704.04861.
16. Lin, M.; Chen, Q.; Yan, S. Network in network. *arXiv* **2013**, arXiv:1312.4400.
17. Iandola, F.N.; Han, S.; Dally, M.W.; Keutzer, K. SqueezeNet: AlexNet-level accuracy with 50x fewer parameters and <0.5 MB model size. *arXiv* **2016**, arXiv:1602.07360.
18. Hinton, G.E.; Srivastava, N.; Krizhevsky, A.; Sutskever, I.; Salakhutdinov, R.R. Improving neural networks by preventing co-adaptation of feature detectors. *arXiv* **2012**, arXiv:1207.0580.
19. Huynh, T.; Tran, M.-T.; Lee, M.; Kim, Y.-B.; Lee, J.; Suh, J.-H. Development of Recovery System for Underwater Glider. *J. Mar. Sci. Eng.* **2022**, *10*, 1448. [CrossRef]
20. Kumar, R.P.; Dasgupta, A.; Kumar, C.S. Robust Tracking Control of Underwater Vehicles using Time-Delay Control in Discrete-Time Domain. In Proceedings of the OCEANS 2006—Asia Pacific, Singapore, 16–19 May 2006; pp. 1–5. [CrossRef]

Journal of Marine Science and Engineering

Article

Enhanced YOLOv7 for Improved Underwater Target Detection

Daohua Lu [1,2,*], Junxin Yi [1] and Jia Wang [1]

1 School of Mechanical Engineering, Jiangsu University of Science and Technology, Zhenjiang 212003, China; 15161085985@163.com (J.Y.); wjjzhb@just.edu.cn (J.W.)
2 Marine Equipment and Technology Institute, Jiangsu University of Science and Technology, Zhenjiang 212003, China
* Correspondence: ludaohua_just@126.com

Abstract: Aiming at the problems of the underwater existence of some targets with relatively small size, low contrast, and a lot of surrounding interference information, which lead to a high leakage rate and low recognition accuracy, a new improved YOLOv7 underwater target detection algorithm is proposed. First, the original YOLOv7 anchor frame information is updated by the K-Means algorithm to generate anchor frame sizes and ratios suitable for the underwater target dataset; second, we use the PConv (Partial Convolution) module instead of part of the standard convolution in the multi-scale feature fusion module to reduce the amount of computation and number of parameters, thus improving the detection speed; then, the existing CIou loss function is improved with the ShapeIou_NWD loss function, and the new loss function allows the model to learn more feature information during the training process; finally, we introduce the SimAM attention mechanism after the multi-scale feature fusion module to increase attention to the small feature information, which improves the detection accuracy. This method achieves an average accuracy of 85.7% on the marine organisms dataset, and the detection speed reaches 122.9 frames/s, which reduces the number of parameters by 21% and the amount of computation by 26% compared with the original YOLOv7 algorithm. The experimental results show that the improved algorithm has a great improvement in detection speed and accuracy.

Keywords: underwater target detection; YOLO7; loss function; attention mechanism

Citation: Lu, D.; Yi, J.; Wang, J. Enhanced YOLOv7 for Improved Underwater Target Detection. *J. Mar. Sci. Eng.* **2024**, *12*, 1127. https://doi.org/10.3390/jmse12071127

Academic Editors: Yan-Tsung Peng, Wenqi Ren, Jingchun Zhou and Qiuping Jiang

Received: 6 June 2024
Revised: 28 June 2024
Accepted: 3 July 2024
Published: 4 July 2024

1. Introduction

Occupying a large part of the earth's area, the ocean is an important source of oil, natural gas, and mineral resources, attracting extensive attention from some adventurers and researchers, which inevitably leads to an increasing number of ocean exploration activities [1]. As an important technology for marine exploration activities, underwater target detection is widely used in archaeology, marine environment monitoring, underwater navigation, fish farming, and other fields, and has received continuous attention [2–7]. However, the harsh marine environment makes underwater target detection still face various challenges.

The main challenges we are currently facing in underwater target detection are as follows: first, we have found from existing underwater datasets and images from real applications for which wavelength-dependent absorption and scattering [8] degrade the quality of underwater images, causing visibility, weak contrast, and color variations, which make the underwater targets blurry. Then, because some underwater organisms have swarming habits and prefer to attach to objects such as mud, sand, and coral reefs, this causes the underwater target and the background area to obscure each other, making the detection accuracy suffer. Finally, because some embedded devices have limited computational power, which leads to the fact that some network models with large parameter counts cannot be applied to underwater embedded devices, so people are also actively pursuing underwater detection devices that can be applied to large parameters [9].

In recent years, underwater target detection methods based on deep learning have been widely studied and gradually applied in the field of underwater biological detection. Deep learning-based underwater target detection is based on learning features iteratively, taking the output of each layer as the input of the next layer, and transforming the detailed features of the lower layer into the detailed features of the higher layer through nonlinear mapping between the lower layer and the higher layer. However, due to the relatively small dataset for underwater object detection, the available learning features are limited, and most underwater organisms occur in groups and are relatively small and fuzzy. Current deep learning-based detection algorithms are unable to effectively detect small objects, which poses a great challenge to the target detection task. To cope with this challenge, the YOLO series of algorithms now exist, including YOLOv1 [10], YOLO9000 [11], YOLOv3 [12], YOLOv4 [13], YOLOv5 [14], YOLOv6 [15], YOLOv7 [16], YOLOv8 [17], etc. The YOLO (You Only Look Once) series comprises typical single-stage target detection algorithms, which have faster detection speed and wider application scope than two-stage target detection algorithms such as RCNN [18], Fast-RCNN [19], Faster RCNN [20], Mask-RCNN [21], Cascade-RCNN [22], and SSD [23]. In order to adapt to different application scenarios and improve the detection accuracy for different detection objects, many researchers have successively proposed a variety of improved detection methods based on the YOLO series of algorithms. The literature [24] has proposed an underwater target detection algorithm, YOLOv5s-CA, based on an improved YOLOv5, to improve the detection accuracy by embedding a Coordinate Attention (CA) module and a Squeeze-and-Excitation (SE) module. The literature [25] also proposes a lightweight algorithm based on an improved YOLOv4, aiming to make the model have a smaller number of parameters and smaller size by combining MobileNetv2 and depth-separable convolution.

However, the target size of the underwater target detection studied in this paper is relatively small, and the previous YOLOv3, YOLOv4, and YOLOv5 algorithms are less effective at detecting small targets, and only the YOLOv7 algorithm has a better detection performance in small target detection at present. Therefore, for the different characteristics of underwater organisms, an underwater target detection algorithm based on the improved YOLOv7 is proposed, with the following four main improvements:

(1) The K-Means algorithm is used to re-cluster the underwater target dataset, and the anchor frames produced by the clustering are more in line with the smaller size of the underwater targets studied in this paper, which accelerates the convergence speed of the model and improves the detection accuracy of small-sized targets.
(2) Pconv (Partial Convolution) is introduced to optimize the multi-scale feature fusion module, which reduces the parameter count and computational workload while improving the detection speed.
(3) The ShapeIou_NWD loss function is used instead of the CIou loss function, which effectively solves the problem of slow convergence and reduced prediction accuracy during the training process by ignoring the shape and scale of the bounding box itself, as well as the possibility of detecting targets that are too small.
(4) Introducing the SimAM attention mechanism after the multi-scale feature fusion module enhances the detection accuracy of the network model without parameter increase.

Finally, several comparative experiments and ablation experiments are conducted to prove the effectiveness of the improved algorithm in this paper.

2. Materials and Methods

2.1. YOLOv7 Model

Compared with its variants YOLOv7-D6, YOLOv7-E6, YOLOv7-E6E, YOLOv7-W6, and YOLOv7-X, YOLOv7 has the smallest number of parameters, the fastest detection speed, and is most suitable to be applied to underwater target detection. Therefore, YOLOv7 is selected as the base algorithm to be improved in this paper. The network structure of YOLOv7 is shown in Figure 1.

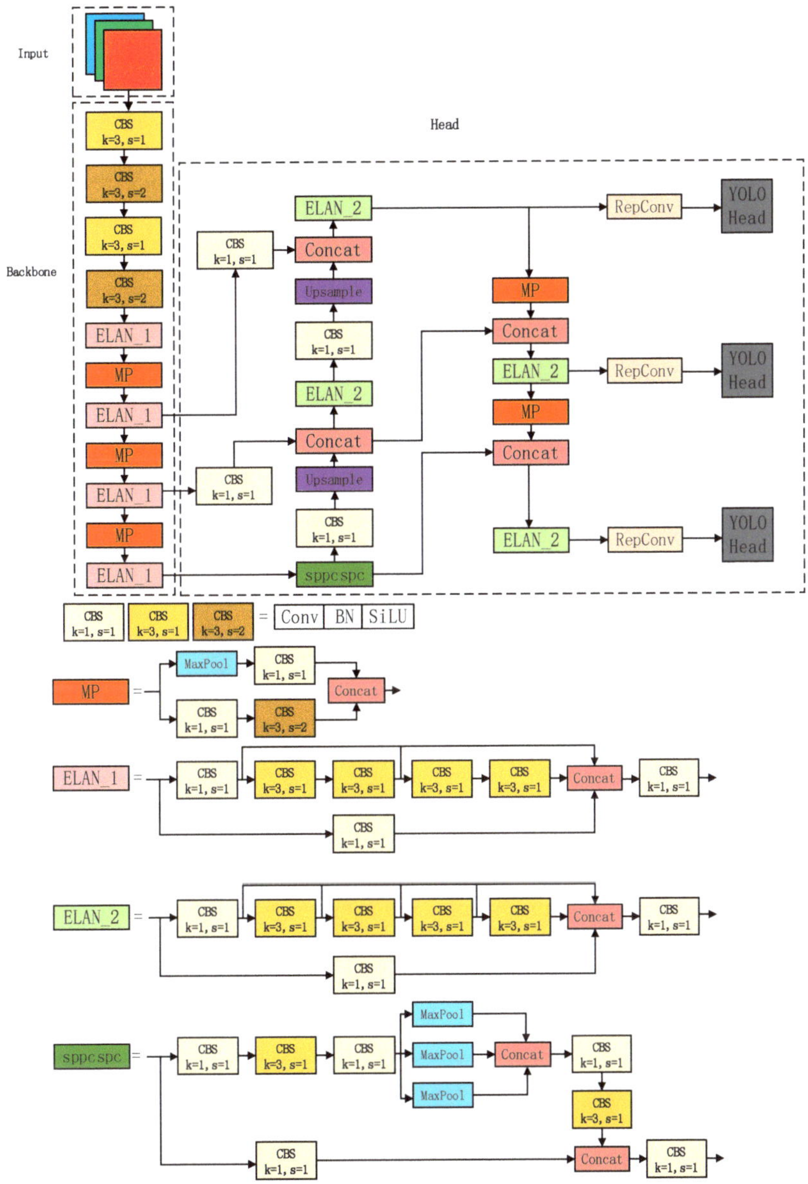

Figure 1. Illustration of the YOLOv7 network structure.

As can be seen from Figure 1, the network structure of YOLOv7 consists of three parts: Input, Backbone, and Head. Input scales the image to be detected to a fixed size after inputting the image to fulfill the input demands of the Backbone, and then carries out the feature extraction through the Backbone, which contains three structures: CBS (Conv + BN + SiLU), ELAN_1, and MP. The CBS mainly uses convolutional layers for feature extraction, and ELAN_1, as a kind of efficient layer aggregation network, greatly improves the learning ability of the detected objects and enriches the diverse feature learning. The MP structure adds a MaxPool layer on top of the CBS, and the upper and lower layers are contacted. The MP structure adds the MaxPool layer on top of the CBS, which greatly improves the feature extraction ability by contacting the upper and lower layers for feature fusion of the features extracted from the branches. In the Head part, the SPPCSPC pyramid structure is employed to broaden the receptive field and make the Head network suitable for multi-size inputs, and then the bottom information is passed upwards from the bottom to the top through the pyramid network structure, so as to realize the fusion of feature information of different scales, and after fusing semantic information and spatial information at multiple scales, three target feature layers of different scales are outputted, which are respectively reused through the RepConv structure. The three obtained feature layers are reparametrized by the RepConv structure to adjust the number of channels, then the preliminary prediction results are obtained by the YOLO Head, and finally the preliminary prediction results are subjected to some post-processing operations, such as confidence filtering, NMS (Non-Maximum Suppression), and so on, in order to obtain the final results.

2.2. Kmeans

The a priori frame sizes used in YOLOv7 were obtained by clustering on the MS COCO dataset using the K-Means [26] algorithm. The MS COCO dataset contains about 41% small targets (area < 32 × 32), and the rest are medium vs. large targets. However, in the marine life dataset, marine organisms are predominantly small- to medium-sized targets, which is significantly different from the size of the objects in the COCO dataset. Therefore, the original anchor frame data size is not suitable for the dataset in this paper. In order to improve the matching probability between the underwater targets and anchor frames, the anchor frame size was redesigned using the K-means clustering algorithm. The basic process is described as follows:

- Randomly select k samples from the dataset as initial clustering centers $c = \{c_1, c_2, \ldots, c_k\}$.
- For each sample in the dataset, calculate its distance from the K cluster centers and assign it to the class corresponding to the cluster center with the smallest distance.
- For each category c_i, recalculate its clustering center $c_i = \frac{1}{|c_i|}\sum_{x \in c_i} x$ (i.e., the center of mass of all samples belonging to the class).
- Repeat steps 2 and 3 until the position of the clustering center no longer changes.

Compared with the K-Means++ [27] algorithm, the K-Means algorithm is simple in principle and easy to implement, only one hyperparameter k needs to be adjusted, and the K-Means++ algorithm relies on the already selected centroids each time the next centroids are selected.

Therefore, in this paper, the K-Means algorithm is selected to recluster the anchor frames. The anchor frames after reclustering using K-Means are presented in Table 1 below:

Table 1. Optimized K-Means algorithm for clustering anchor frame parameters.

Feature Map Size	80 × 80	40 × 40	20 × 20
YOLOv7	(21, 17) (28, 24) (35, 32)	(52, 35) (44, 46) (57, 56)	(80, 51) (82, 79) (140, 117)

2.3. ELAN_PC

ELAN [28], mainly composed of VoVNet [29] and CSPNet [30], is an efficient layer aggregation network. It facilitates the network to acquire more features by regulating the shortest and longest gradient pathways. ELAN is mainly composed of two branches, the first branch mainly doing the change of channel number through the convolution of 1 × 1, and the second branch firstly doing the change of channel number through the convolution of 1 × 1, then doing the feature extraction through the four convolutional modules of 3 × 3, and finally superimposing the results of the two branches together. The ELAN can then effectively alleviate the problem of gradient disappearance when the model reaches a certain depth. However, the optimization of the ELAN network in terms of the number of parameters and the amount of computation is not ideal, so in this paper, while ensuring the structural integrity of the ELAN network, PConv is introduced to construct the ELAN_PC_1 and ELAN_PC_2 network modules, which use PConv to replace the convolution kernel of 3 × 3 convolutional layers in the ELAN network. The ELAN_PC_1 and ELAN_PC_2 network structures are shown in Figure 2.

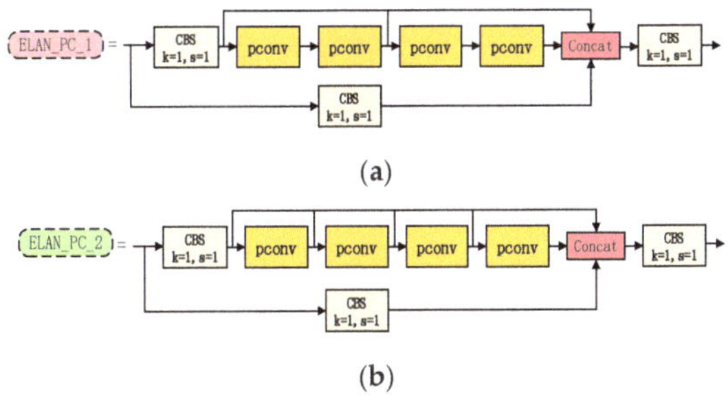

Figure 2. Improved ELAN structure; (**a**) ELAN_PC_1; (**b**) ELAN_PC_2.

PConv [31] is a new lightweight convolution module that reduces computational redundancy while reducing memory accesses. In this module, we employ a convolutional operation on a subset of the input channels to avoid excessive redundancy in the feature map. This approach, illustrated in Figure 3, ensures that the convolutional operation is applied to a select set of channels while the remaining channels remain unchanged.

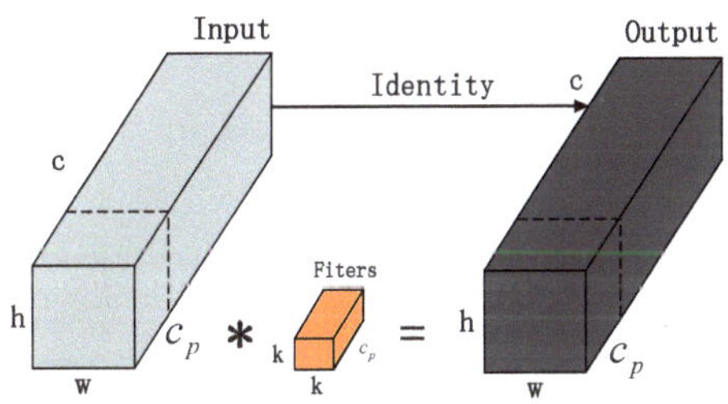

Figure 3. The structure diagram of PConv module.

For continuous or regular memory accesses, the input or output c_p channels are computed as representative of the entire feature map. The PConv is computed as $h \times w \times k^2 \times c_p^2$, while the regular convolution is computed as $h \times w \times k^2 \times c^2$, the memory accesses for the PConv are $h \times w \times 2c_p$, and the memory accesses for the regular convolution are $h \times w \times 2c$. If $c_p = c/4$, then the PConv is computed as $1/16$ of the regular convolution, and the memory accesses are $1/4$.

It can be seen that the introduction of the PConv convolution module into the ELAN module can significantly reduce the amount of computation and memory access, thus making the model lightweight and speeding up the inference.

2.4. ShapeIoU_NWD

The YOLOv7 model employs the CIOU [32] loss function, which is designed to account for the overlap area, centroid distance, and aspect ratio of the bounding box regression. However, this loss function does not consider the influence of the inherent properties of the bounding box itself, such as shape and scale. Consequently, the CIOU loss function may prevent the model from optimizing the similarity when the aspect ratio is the same [33]. To solve this problem, this paper adopts ShapeIoU [34], a bounding box regression method that focuses on the shape and scale of the bounding box itself. This method can calculate the loss by focusing on the shape and scale of the bounding box itself, which makes the bounding box regression more accurate. The parameter schematic of ShapeIoU is presented in Figure 4.

$$\mathrm{IoU} = \frac{|B \cap B^{gt}|}{|B \cup B^{gt}|} \tag{1}$$

$$ww = \frac{2 \times (w^{gt})^{scale}}{(w^{gt})^{scale} + (h^{gt})^{scale}} \tag{2}$$

$$hh = \frac{2 \times (h^{gt})^{scale}}{(w^{gt})^{scale} + (h^{gt})^{scale}} \tag{3}$$

$$\mathrm{distance}^{shape} = hh \times (x_c - x_c^{gt})^2 / c^2 + ww \times (y_c - y_c^{gt}) / c^2 \tag{4}$$

$$\Omega^{shape} = \sum_{t=w,h} (1 - e^{-\omega_t})^{\theta}, \theta = 4 \tag{5}$$

$$\begin{cases} \omega_w = hh \times \frac{|w - w^{gt}|}{\max(w, w^{gt})} \\ \omega_h = ww \times \frac{|h - h^{gt}|}{\max(h, h^{gt})} \end{cases} \tag{6}$$

where B represents the prediction frame, B^{gt} represents the real frame, w^{gt} and h^{gt} represent the width and height of the real frame respectively, scale is the scale factor, which is related to the scale of the target in the dataset, ww and hh are the weight coefficients in the horizontal and vertical directions, respectively, and their values are related to the shape of the real frame. Its corresponding bounding box regression loss is as follows:

$$L_{ShapeIoU} = 1 - IoU + \mathrm{distance}^{shape} + 0.5 \times \Omega^{shape} \tag{7}$$

In order to further improve the accuracy of underwater small target detection, we have introduced the Normalized Wasserstein Distance [35]. In this approach, the Gaussian distributions N_a and N_b, modeled for the two bounding boxes $A = (c_{xa}, c_{ya}, w_a, h_a)$ and $B = (c_{xb}, c_{yb}, w_b, h_b)$, can be expressed as follows:

$$W_2^2(N_a, N_b) = \left\| \left(\left[cx_a, cy_a, \frac{w_a}{2}, \frac{h_a}{2} \right]^T, \left[cx_b, cy_b, \frac{w_b}{2}, \frac{h_b}{2} \right]^T \right) \right\|_2^2 \tag{8}$$

However, since $W_2^2(N_a, N_b)$ is a distance measure and not a similarity measure, it cannot be directly used as such. Therefore, in order to address this limitation, it is necessary to normalize the distance by transforming $W_2^2(N_a, N_b)$ into a value between 0 and 1. This process results in the normalized Gaussian Wasserstein distance (NWD), which enables more effective and meaningful comparisons and evaluations in the context of detecting small underwater objects. The formula is as follows:

$$NWD(N_a, N_b) = \exp\left(-\frac{\sqrt{W_2^2(N_a, N_b)}}{C} \right) \tag{9}$$

Here, C is a constant related to the dataset.

Therefore, the loss of our *ShapeIoU_NWD* can be obtained by taking the form of a weighted summation based on the introduced $_{ShapeIoU}$ loss function and *NWD* metric with the following formula:

$$L_{ShapeIoU\_NWD} = (1-r) \times (1 - NWD(N_a, N_b)) + r \times L_{ShapeIoU} \tag{10}$$

where r is a scaling factor.

In this paper, we use the ShapeIoU_NWD loss function instead of the CIOU loss function, which takes into account both the effects of changes in the shape and scale of the bounding box itself, as well as the sensitivity of small target displacements, and provides a significant improvement in the detection accuracy of small- and medium-sized targets.

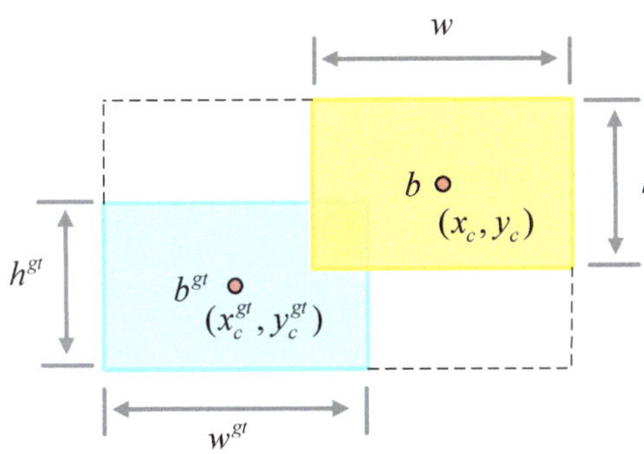

Figure 4. ShapeIou parameter diagram.

2.5. SimAM

The size of underwater targets is relatively small, and because of the presence of some mud, sand, and some other interfering background information, it occupies less information in the whole image. In order to improve the accuracy of small target detection and reduce the interference of background information, this paper adopts the attention mechanism to adaptively focus on the detail information related to the small target, and reduces the attention to other interference information. In contrast to the SE [36] (Squeeze-and-Excitation) channel attention mechanism, which solely considers the internal channel information, and the CBAM [37] (Convolutional Block Attention Module), which focuses on the local spatial location range, the SimAM [38] attention mechanism does not introduce additional network parameters for feature maps, thereby deriving 3D attention weights. Furthermore, it is a plug-and-play feature that can be integrated into any position within the model. Consequently, in this paper, three SimAM attention mechanisms are incorporated after the multi-scale feature fusion module with the objective of enhancing the detection accuracy of the model. The structure of the SimAM attention mechanisms is depicted in Figure 5.

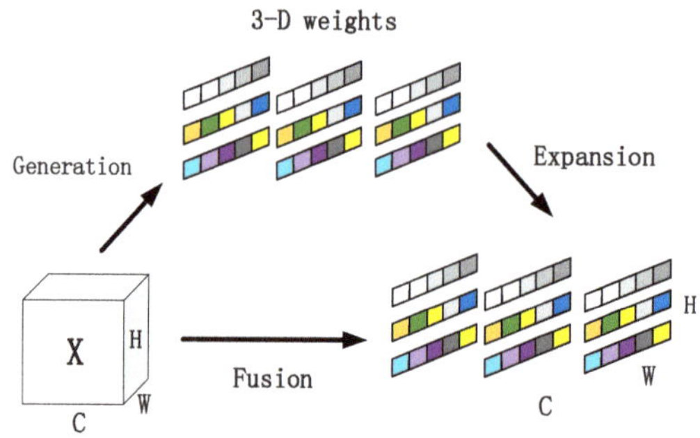

Figure 5. SimAM attention mechanism structure.

The core idea of SimAM is based on the local self-similarity of images. In an image, neighboring pixels usually have strong similarity to each other, while the similarity between distant pixels is weak. SimAM takes advantage of this property to generate attention weights by calculating the similarity between each pixel in the feature map and its neighboring pixels. The formula is shown below:

$$\dot{X} = \text{sigmoid}\left(\frac{1}{E}\right) \odot X \tag{11}$$

$$E = \frac{4(\sigma^2 + \lambda)}{(t-\mu)^2 + 2\sigma^2 + 2\lambda} \tag{12}$$

$$\mu = \frac{1}{M}\sum_{i=1}^{M} x_i \tag{13}$$

$$\sigma^2 = \frac{1}{M}\sum_{i=1}^{M} (x_i - \mu)^2 \tag{14}$$

where X is the input feature, E is the energy function on each channel. In order to prevent the possibility of too large a value for E, a sigmoid function is used to limit it; t is the value of the input feature, λ is a constant value, which is 1×10^{-4}, μ and σ^2 denote the mean and variance on each channel in X, respectively, and M = H $\times$ W denotes the number of values on each channel.

2.6. Proposed Improved Algorithm

In comparison to other one-stage target detection algorithms, such as YOLOv3 and YOLOv4, YOLOv7 exhibits superior performance in detecting small targets. However, the detection effect is less satisfactory when there are problems such as occlusion and low contrast of the target. Therefore, the following improvements are made to YOLOv7 to address these problems. Figure 6 illustrates the network structure of the improved YOLOv7 algorithm.

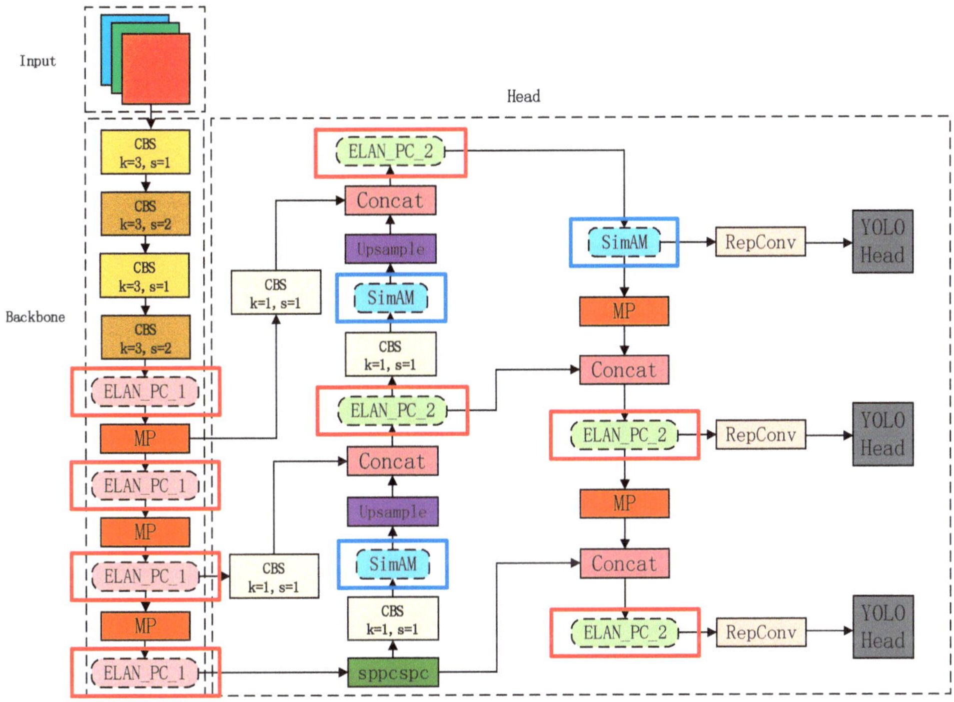

Figure 6. Improved YOLOv7 network structure diagram.

3. Experiments

3.1. Experimental Dataset

The images for underwater target detection studied in this paper are from the 2020 National Underwater Robotics Professional Competition (URPC) dataset, which consists of 5543 images, with an image size of 640 × 640. Based on the definition of small, medium, and large targets in the COCO dataset, each type of target was divided into small, medium, and large targets, where the number of holothurian tags was 5537, in which the number of small targets was 61, the number of medium targets was 3487, and the number of large targets was 1989; the number of echinus tags was 22,343, in which the number of small targets was 2788, the number of medium targets was 13,696, and the number of large targets was 5859; the number of scallop tags was 6720, with the number of small targets 603, the number of medium targets was 1359, and the number of large targets 4758; and the number of starfish tags 6841, with the number of small targets 588, the number of medium targets 4059, and the number of large targets 2194. The results are shown in Figure 7.

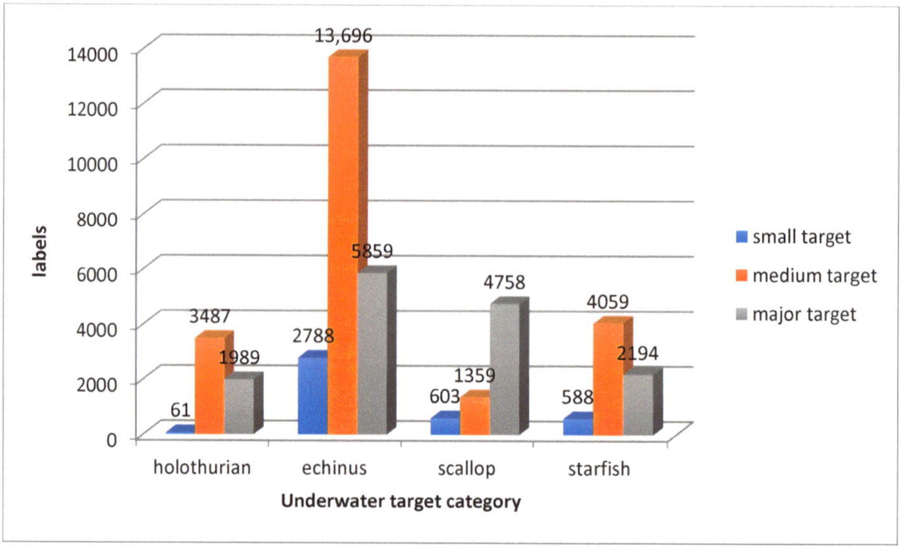

Figure 7. Number of tags for each type of target in the underwater target data set.

The sample images, labeled with location and category information, were subsequently stored in PASCAL VOC format. The dataset was randomly divided into a training set of 4434 images and a validation set of 1109 images according to the corresponding marine organism category in a ratio of 8:2.

3.2. Experimental Environment and Parameterization

This experiment is implemented in the ubuntu20.04 operating system based on the PyTorch deep learning framework, the GPU selection for the size of the memory 12 G NVIDIA GeForce RTX 3080Ti, the CPU configuration is a 12-core AMD Ryzen 9 5900X, PyTorch version 2.0.1, CUDA version 11.7, and the python language environment is 3.8.17.

The hyperparameters for this experiment are configured as follows: in the model training phase, the parameters are tuned using the SGD optimizer, with the initial learning rate set to 0.01 and momentum to 0.937, and the learning rate decayed using warm up, with the weight decay coefficient set to 0.0005. In addition, the batch size is set to 8, and a total of 150 rounds are trained.

3.3. Experimental Design

3.3.1. Evaluation Metrics

This experiment focuses on underwater target detection algorithms, which should satisfy both real-time and good detection performance, so the values of FPS, FLOPS, Params, mAP, precision and recall are used as evaluation indexes to compare the algorithms. FPS represents the frame rate, indicating the number of images processed per second. FLOPS represents the number of floating-point operations executed, serving as a measure of the model's computational complexity, Params is the sum of the model parameters, which are used to evaluate the size of the model, and mAP is the average value of the precision of each type of underwater target detection. The formula for mAP is as follows:

$$mAP = \frac{\sum_{i=0}^{n} AP(i)}{n} \tag{15}$$

where n is the number of underwater target classes and AP (Average Precision) is the precision value of each class.

Additionally, the precision and recall values are derived through the following calculations:

$$Precision = \frac{TP}{TP + FP} \tag{16}$$

$$Recall = \frac{TP}{TP + FN} \tag{17}$$

where TP is the number of positive samples predicted to be positive (true positive); FP is the number of negative samples predicted to be positive (false positive); FN is the number of positive samples predicted to be negative (false negative).

3.3.2. Experimental Results

Three images are extracted from the dataset for comparison. The three original images extracted are shown in Figure 8a. Using YOLOv7 and this paper's algorithm to detect these three pictures, the results will be detected for comparison, and the comparison results are presented in Figure 8b,c.

As illustrated in Figure 8, the YOLOv7 algorithm is more prone to miss detection and partially occluded cases are not recognized or recognized with lower confidence values compared to this paper's algorithm, whereas this paper's algorithm is able to detect as accurately as possible all types of underwater targets on the map.

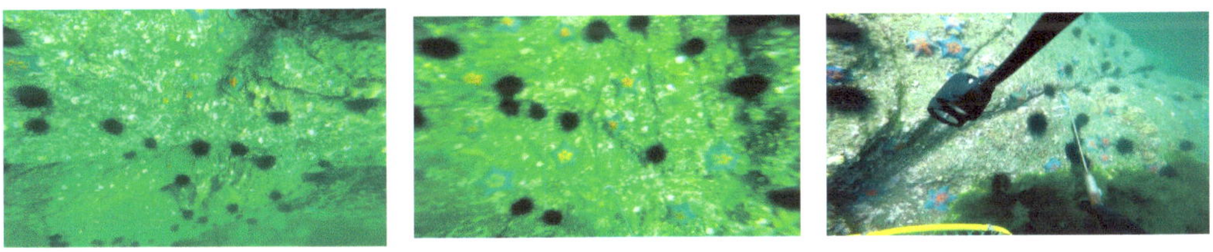

(**a**)

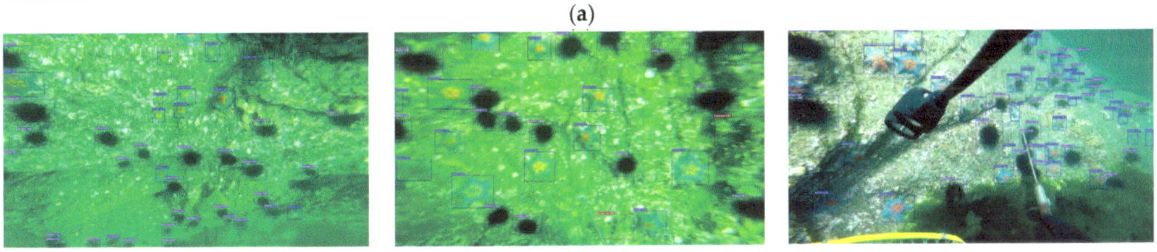

(**b**)

Figure 8. *Cont.*

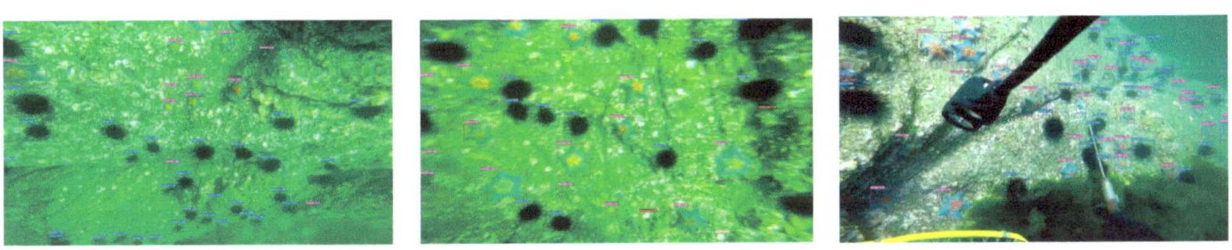

(**c**)

Figure 8. Comparison chart of detection results of two algorithms; (**a**) The raw image; (**b**) YOLOv7 algorithm detection results; (**c**) Improved YOLOv7 algorithm detection results.

Figure 9 illustrates the precision-recall (P-R) curves of the original YOLOv7 algorithm and the modified YOLOv7 algorithm after improving each module, which were trained on the identical underwater target dataset. Specifically, Figure 9a illustrates the P-R curves of the YOLOv7 algorithm, Figure 9b represents the P-R curves of the YOLOv7_kmeans, Figure 9c represents the P-R curves of the YOLOv7_kmeans with the addition of the ELAN_PC module, and Figure 9d represents the P-R curves of the YOLOv7_kmeans with the addition of the ELAN_PC module and the P-R curve of the ShapeIou NWD loss function. Figure 9e represents the P-R curve for the final addition of the SimAM attention mechanism. As can be seen from Figure 9a,e, the AP of holothurian increased by 1.1%, the AP of echinus increased by 0.8%, the AP of scallop increased by 0.4%, and the AP of starfish increased by 1.6%.

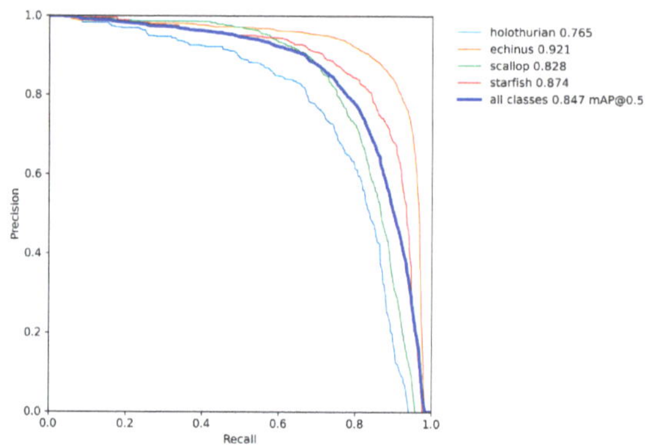

(a)

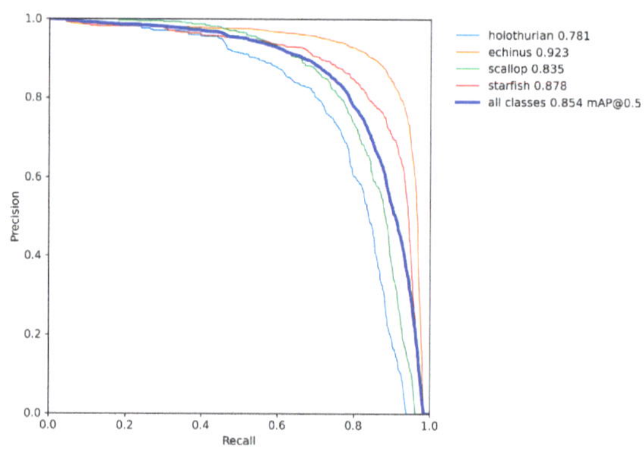

(b)

Figure 9. *Cont.*

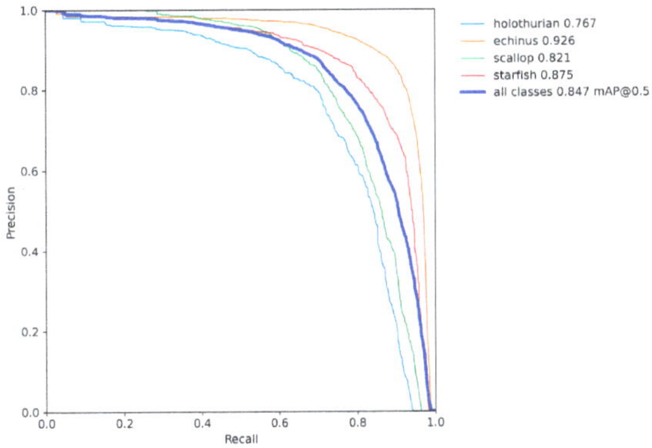

(**c**)

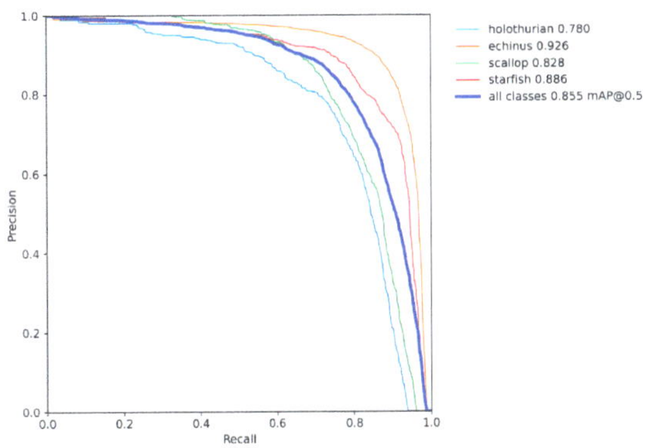

(**d**)

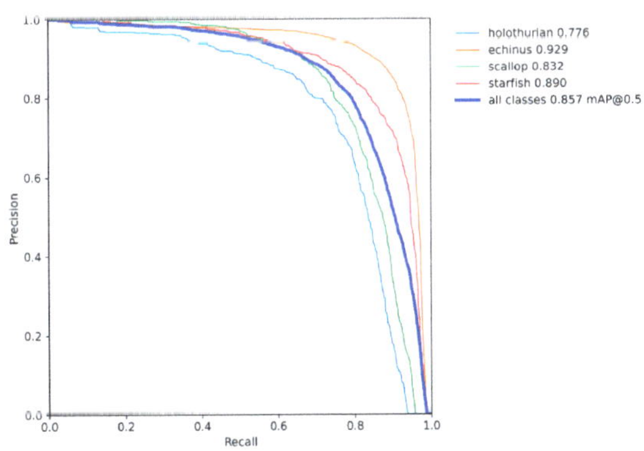

(**e**)

Figure 9. (**a**) The P-R curves of the original YOLOv7 algorithm; (**b**) P-R curve for the YOLOv7_kmeans; (**c**) P-R curve of the ELAN_PC module added to YOLOv7_kmeans; (**d**) P-R curves with the ELAN_PC module and the ShapeIoU_NWD loss function added to the YOLOv7_kmeans; (**e**) Final improved YOLOv7 algorithm.

4. Discussion

4.1. Ablation Experiments

CBAM, CPCA, CA, GAM, and SimAM are introduced after the multi-scale feature fusion module, and the network is trained on the basis of the K-Means algorithm, the ELAN_PC structure, and the ShapeIou_NWD, the obtained detection results are compared according to the average accuracy value, and the comparison results are presented in Table 2.

As illustrated in Table 2, it is evident that the introduction of attention mechanisms such as CBAM, CPCA, CA, and GAM reduced the average accuracy value compared to the original algorithms that did not incorporate an attention mechanism, and the 85.5% accuracy value of the algorithms that did not incorporate an attention mechanism was reduced by 0.2%, 1.1%, 0.2%, and 2.7%, respectively. By integrating the SimAM attention mechanism, the average accuracy value witnessed a 0.2% increase. In summary, the utilization of the SimAM attention mechanism demonstrates a more pronounced impact on enhancing the detection accuracy of small targets.

Table 2. The results of the attention mechanism ablation experiments.

Attention Mechanism	Holothurian (%)	Echinus (%)	Scallop (%)	Starfish (%)	mAP (%)
CBAM	77.3	92.7	83.1	88.3	85.3
CPCA	77.8	92.1	80.1	87.8	84.4
CA	77.5	92.3	83.1	88.5	85.3
GAM	77.3	85.6	79.8	88.6	82.8
SimAM	77.6	92.9	83.2	89.0	85.7

Through the ablation experiments, the impact of the different modules in the improved algorithm was examined, and the results are summarized in Table 3.

Table 3. The results of the ablation experiments.

Algorithm	Params (M)	FLOPs (G)	mAP (%)	FPS (frame/s)
YOLOv7	36.5	103.2	84.7	112.5
YOLOv7 + Kmeans	36.5	103.2	85.4	113.2
YOLOv7 + Kmeans + ELAN_PC	28.3	75.4	84.7	126.3
YOLOv7 + Kmeans + ELAN_PC + ShapeIoU_NWD	28.3	75.4	85.5	125.3
YOLOv7 + Kmeans + ELAN_PC + ShapeIoU_NWD + SimAM	28.7	76.6	85.7	122.9

As can be seen from Table 3, by adding the K-means clustering algorithm, the average accuracy is improved by 0.7%; by adding the ELAN_PC structure, although the accuracy value decreases by 0.7%, the number of parameters decreases by 22%, the amount of computation decreases by 27%, and the speed of detection is improved by 12%; and later on the ShapeIou_NWD loss function is utilized to increase the accuracy of detection to 85.5% by keeping the number of parameters and the amount of computation constant. Finally, the detection accuracy is improved to 85.7% using the SimAM attention mechanism. Therefore, compared with the original YOLOv7 algorithm, the whole improved algorithm increases the average accuracy value of underwater target detection by 1% and the detection speed by 9.2%.

4.2. Comparative Experiments

The improved YOLOv7 model was compared to these algorithms including Faster RCNN, SSD, YOLOv5, YOLOv7, YOLOv7-W6, YOLOv7-E6E and YOLOv8 algorithms on an underwater target dataset using the aforementioned evaluation metrics. The comparison results are presented in Table 4.

Table 4. Comparison of the improved algorithm with several mainstream algorithms.

Algorithm	Holothurian (%)	Echinus (%)	Scallop (%)	Starfish (%)	mAP (%)	FPS (frame/s)
Faster RCNN	56.0	82.0	52.0	79.0	67.5	40.7
SSD	63.0	77.0	46.0	74.0	65.0	167.9
YOLOv5	73.7	91.4	80.6	85.1	82.7	270.0
YOLOv7	76.5	92.1	82.8	87.4	84.7	112.5
YOLOv7-W6	74.2	90.8	75.2	87.1	81.8	114.2
YOLOv7-E6E	74.6	89.7	49.2	87.6	75.3	51.9
YOLOv8	74.9	91.4	80.3	88.3	83.7	131.9
Ours	77.6	92.9	83.2	89.0	85.7	122.9

From Table 4, we can see that our improved YOLOv7 algorithm has the highest detection accuracy in each class of underwater targets and the highest mAP value in all classes, which is 18.2% higher than the two-stage Faster RCNN algorithm, compared with the single-stage algorithms SSD, YOLOv5, YOLOv7, YOLOv7-W6, YOLOv7- E6E, and YOLOv8, and the mAP of the improved algorithm is improved by 20.7%, 3%, 1%, 3.9%,10.4%, and 2%, respectively. In addition, although the detection speed of the SSD algorithm, the YOLOv5 algorithm and the YOLOv8 algorithm is slightly higher than that of the improved YOLOv7 algorithm, the detection accuracy is much different from the improved algorithm in this paper, so the comprehensive comparison of this paper's algorithm has a great advantage over other algorithms.

From Table 5, we can see that the total accuracy of our improved algorithm is 38.8% higher compared to the two-stage Faster RCNN algorithm, and for each class of underwater targets, the accuracy value of our improved algorithm is higher. In addition, compared to other one-stage algorithms, other algorithms, such as YOLOv5, YOLOv7, YOLOv7-W6, and YOLOv7-E6E, are 1.1%, 1%, 3%, and 11.2% less accurate than ours, respectively, except for the SSD algorithm and the YOLOv8 algorithm, which are 1% and 0.6%, respectively, more accurate than our algorithm.

Table 5. Precision comparison results for different algorithms.

Algorithm	Holothurian (%)	Echinus (%)	Scallop (%)	Starfish (%)	All (%)
Faster RCNN	35.4	53.2	37.8	51.5	44.5
SSD	80.6	89.0	83.1	84.4	84.3
YOLOv5	76.5	88.3	83.4	80.5	82.2
YOLOv7	75.1	88.0	84.6	81.5	82.3
YOLOv7-W6	75.5	86.3	79.7	79.6	80.3
YOLOv7-E6E	79.9	88.6	34.8	85.2	72.1
YOLOv8	77.8	89.0	85.6	83.4	83.9
Ours	78.0	88.7	85.1	81.6	83.3

As can be seen from Table 6, the improved YOLOv7 algorithm has the largest value of Total Recall, improving 4% over the two-stage Faster RCNN algorithm and 32.9%, 1.9%, 0.6%, 3.2%, 6%, and 3.6% over the one-stage SSD, YOLOv5, YOLOv7, YOLOv7-W6, YOLOv7-E6E, and YOLOv8, respectively.

Table 6. Recall comparison results for different algorithms.

Algorithm	Holothurian (%)	Echinus (%)	Scallop (%)	Starfish (%)	All (%)
Faster RCNN	65.6	88.2	61.5	85.1	75.1
SSD	50.5	51.4	27.7	55.1	46.2
YOLOv5	70.1	86.0	73.3	79.5	77.2
YOLOv7	71.8	86.4	72.9	82.8	78.5

Table 6. *Cont.*

Algorithm	Holothurian (%)	Echinus (%)	Scallop (%)	Starfish (%)	All (%)
YOLOv7-W6	68.5	85.9	66.5	82.7	75.9
YOLOv7-E6E	66.3	82.4	64.1	79.6	73.1
YOLOv8	68.4	83.1	68.4	82.0	75.5
Ours	73.3	87.4	72.5	83.3	79.1

5. Conclusions

In this paper, an underwater target detection algorithm based on an improved YOLOv7 is proposed for underwater targets with some smaller sizes, complex backgrounds, and low contrast. By introducing the SimAM attention mechanism, the improved ELAN_PC structure and the ShapeIou_NWD loss function are used to improve the ability to extract features for smaller underwater targets and to reduce the loss of feature information. Meanwhile, in order to enhance the robustness of the algorithm in this paper, the K-Means anchor frame clustering algorithm is used to enhance the performance of the algorithm. Several comparison experiments and ablation experiments show that the improved YOLOv7 target detection algorithm achieves an average accuracy value of 85.7%, which is 1% higher than the original YOLOv7, and the speed reaches 122.9 frames/s, which is a good balance between detection speed and accuracy. Afterwards, the main feature extraction part of the model will be improved by using a lighter weight module to allow the algorithm to increase the inspection accuracy of underwater targets while being lighter weight.

Author Contributions: Conceptualization, J.W. and J.Y.; methodology, J.W. and J.Y.; software, J.Y.; validation, J.Y.; formal analysis, J.W. and D.L.; investigation, J.Y.; data curation, J.Y.; writing—original draft preparation, J.Y.; writing—review and editing, J.W. and D.L.; visualization, J.Y.; supervision, J.W. and D.L.; project administration, J.W. and D.L.; funding acquisition, J.W. and D.L. All authors have read and agreed to the published version of the manuscript.

Funding: This research was made possible by the Key Research and Development Program of Jiangsu Province (SBE2022010137).

Institutional Review Board Statement: Not applicable.

Informed Consent Statement: Not applicable.

Data Availability Statement: Related improvements have been posted at https://github.com/hero259/yolov7-main-underwater (accessed on 1 June 2024).

Acknowledgments: Thanks to each of the authors for their dedication to the experiment and technical support.

Conflicts of Interest: The authors confirm that they have no conflicts of interest to report in relation to the present study.

References

1. Zhou, X.; Ding, W.; Jin, W. Microwave-assisted extraction of lipids, carotenoids, and other compounds from marine resources. In *Innovative and Emerging Technologies in the Bio-Marine Food Sector*; Academic Press: Cambridge, MA, USA, 2022; pp. 375–394.
2. Wang, S.; Liu, X.; Yu, S.; Zhu, X.; Chen, B.; Sun, X. Design and Implementation of SSS-Based AUV Autonomous Online Object Detection System. *Electronics* **2024**, *13*, 1064. [CrossRef]
3. Yu, G.; Cai, R.; Su, J.; Hou, M.; Deng, R. U-YOLOv7: A network for underwater organism detection. *Ecol. Inform.* **2023**, *75*, 102108. [CrossRef]
4. Jia, R.; Lv, B.; Chen, J.; Liu, H.; Cao, L.; Liu, M. Underwater Object Detection in Marine Ranching Based on Improved YOLOv8. *J. Mar. Sci. Eng.* **2023**, *12*, 55. [CrossRef]
5. Wu, B.; Liu, C.; Jiang, F.; Li, J.; Yang, Z. Dynamic identification and automatic counting of the number of passing fish species based on the improved DeepSORT algorithm. *Front. Environ. Sci.* **2023**, *11*, 1059217. [CrossRef]
6. Zhao, H.; Cui, H.; Qu, K.; Zhu, J.; Li, H.; Cui, Z.; Wu, Y. A fish appetite assessment method based on improved ByteTrack and spatiotemporal graph convolutional network. *Biosyst. Eng.* **2024**, *240*, 46–55. [CrossRef]
7. Liu, Y.; An, D.; Ren, Y.; Zhao, J.; Zhang, C.; Cheng, J.; Liu, J.; Wei, Y. DP-FishNet: Dual-path Pyramid Vision Transformer-based underwater fish detection network. *Expert Syst. Appl.* **2024**, *238*, 122018. [CrossRef]

8. Sahu, P.; Gupta, N.; Sharma, N. A survey on underwater image enhancement techniques. *Int. J. Comput. Appl.* **2014**, *87*, 333–338. [CrossRef]
9. Christensen, L.; de Gea Fernández, J.; Hildebrandt, M.; Koch, C.E.S.; Wehbe, B. Recent advances in ai for navigation and control of underwater robots. *Curr. Robot. Rep.* **2022**, *3*, 165–175. [CrossRef]
10. Redmon, J.; Divvala, S.; Girshick, R.; Farhadi, A. You only look once: Unified, real-time object detection. In Proceedings of the IEEE Conference on Computer Vision and Pattern Recognition, Las Vegas, NV, USA, 27–30 June 2016; pp. 779–788.
11. Redmon, J.; Farhadi, A. YOLO9000: Better, faster, stronger. In Proceedings of the IEEE Conference on Computer Vision and Pattern Recognition, Honolulu, HI, USA, 21–26 July 2017; pp. 7263–7271.
12. Redmon, J.; Farhadi, A. Yolov3: An incremental improvement. *arXiv* **2018**, arXiv:1804.02767.
13. Bochkovskiy, A.; Wang, C.Y.; Liao, H.Y.M. Yolov4: Optimal speed and accuracy of object detection. *arXiv* **2020**, arXiv:2004.10934.
14. Zhu, X.; Lyu, S.; Wang, X.; Zhao, Q. TPH-YOLOv5: Improved YOLOv5 based on transformer prediction head for object detection on drone-captured scenarios. In Proceedings of the IEEE/CVF International Conference on Computer Vision, Montreal, BC, Canada, 11–17 October 2021; pp. 2778–2788.
15. Li, C.; Li, L.; Jiang, H.; Weng, K.; Geng, Y.; Li, L.; Wei, X. YOLOv6: A single-stage object detection framework for industrial applications. *arXiv* **2022**, arXiv:2209.02976.
16. Wang, C.Y.; Bochkovskiy, A.; Liao, H.Y.M. YOLOv7: Trainable bag-of-freebies sets new state-of-the-art for real-time object detectors. *arXiv* **2022**, arXiv:2207.02696.
17. Jocher, G. YOLOv8 by Ultralytics. 2023. Available online: https://github.com/ultralytics/ultralytics (accessed on 15 February 2023).
18. Girshick, R.; Donahue, J.; Darrell, T.; Malik, J.; Berkeley, U.C.; Malik, J. Rich feature hierarchies for accurate object detection and semantic segmentation. In Proceedings of the IEEE Conference on Computer Vision and Pattern Recognition, Columbus, OH, USA, 23–28 June 2014; pp. 580–587.
19. Girshick, R. Fast r-cnn. In Proceedings of the IEEE International Conference on Computer Vision, Santiago, Chile, 7–13 December 2015; pp. 1440–1448.
20. Ren, S.; He, K.; Girshick, R.; Sun, J. Faster r-cnn: Towards real-time object detection with region proposal networks. In Proceedings of the International Conference on Neural Information Processing Systems (NIPS), Montreal, QC, Canada, 7–12 December 2015; pp. 91–99.
21. He, K.; Gkioxari, G.; Dollár, P.; Girshick, R. Mask r-cnn. In Proceedings of the IEEE International Conference on Computer Vision, Venice, Italy, 22–29 October 2017; pp. 2961–2969.
22. Cai, Z.; Vasconcelos, N. Cascade r-cnn: Delving into high quality object detection. In Proceedings of the IEEE Conference on Computer Vision and Pattern Recognition, Salt Lake City, UT, USA, 18–22 June 2018; pp. 6154–6162.
23. Liu, W.; Anguelov, D.; Erhan, D.; Szegedy, C.; Reed, S.; Fu, C.Y.; Berg, A.C. SSD: Single shot multibox detector. In Proceedings of the Computer Vision–ECCV 2016: 14th European Conference, Proceedings Part I 14, Amsterdam, The Netherlands, 11–14 October 2016; Springer International Publishing: Cham, Switzerland, 2016; pp. 21–37.
24. Wen, G.; Li, S.; Liu, F.; Luo, X.; Er, M.-J.; Mahmud, M.; Wu, T. Yolov5s-ca: A modified yolov5s network with coordinate attention for underwater target detection. *Sensors* **2023**, *23*, 3367. [CrossRef] [PubMed]
25. Zhang, M.; Xu, S.; Song, W.; He, Q.; Wei, Q. Lightweight Underwater Object Detection Based on YOLO v4 and Multi-Scale Attentional Feature Fusion. *Remote Sens.* **2021**, *13*, 4706. [CrossRef]
26. Sinaga, K.P.; Yang, M. Unsupervised K-Means Clustering Algorithm. *IEEE Access* **2020**, *8*, 80716–80727. [CrossRef]
27. Arthur, D.; Vassilvitskii, S. K-means++: The advantages of careful seeding. In Proceedings of the Eighteenth Annual ACM-SIAM Symposium on Discrete Algorithms, SODA 2007, New Orleans, LA, USA, 7–9 January 2007; pp. 1027–1035.
28. Zhang, X.; Zeng, H.; Guo, S.; Zhang, L. Efficient long-range attention network for image super-resolution. In Proceedings of the Computer Vision–ECCV 2022: 17th European Conference, Tel Aviv, Israel, 23–27 October 2022; Part XVII. Springer: Cham, Switzerland, 2022; pp. 649–667.
29. Lee, Y.; Hwang, J.W.; Lee, S.; Bae, Y.; Park, J. An Energy and GPU-Computation Efficient Backbone Network for Real-Time Object Detection. In Proceedings of the IEEE/CVF Conference on Computer Vision and Pattern Recognition (CVPR) Workshops, Long Beach, CA, USA, 16–17 June 2019.
30. Wang, C.Y.; Mark Liao, H.Y.; Wu, Y.H.; Chen, P.Y.; Hsieh, J.W.; Yeh, I.H. CSPNet: A new backbone that can enhance learning capability of cnn. In Proceedings of the IEEE Conference on Computer Vision and Pattern Recognition (CVPR 2020), Washington, DC, USA, 14–19 June 2020; pp. 390–391.
31. Chen, J.; Kao, S.-H.; He, H.; Zhuo, W.; Wen, S.; Lee, C.-H.; Chan, S.-H.G. Run, Don't walk: Chasing higher FLOPS for faster neural networks. In Proceedings of the IEEE/CVF Conference on Computer Vision and Pattern Recognition, Vancouver, BC, Canada, 18–22 June 2023.
32. Zheng, Z.; Wang, P.; Ren, D.; Liu, W.; Ye, R.; Hu, Q.; Zuo, W. Enhancing Geometric Factors in Model Learning and Inference for Object Detection and Instance Segmentation. *arXiv* **2020**, arXiv:2005.03572. [CrossRef] [PubMed]
33. Zhang, Y.-F.; Ren, W.; Zhang, Z.; Jia, Z.; Wang, L.; Tan, T. Focal and Efficient IOU Loss for Accurate Bounding Box Regression. *arXiv* **2021**, arXiv:2101.08158. [CrossRef]
34. Zhang, H.; Zhang, S. Shape-IoU: More Accurate Metric considering Bounding Box Shape and Scale. *arXiv* **2023**, arXiv:2312.17663.

35. Wang, J.; Xu, C.; Yang, W.; Yu, L. A normalized Gaussian Wasserstein distance for tiny object detection. *arXiv* **2021**, arXiv:2110.13389.
36. Hu, J.; Shen, L.; Sun, G. Squeeze-and-excitation networks. In Proceedings of the IEEE Conference on Computer Vision and Pattern Recognition, Salt Lake City, UT, USA, 18–23 June 2018; pp. 7132–7141.
37. Woo, S.; Park, J.; Lee, J.Y.; Kweon, I.S. CBAM: Convolutional Block Attention Module. *arXiv* **2018**, arXiv:1807.06521.
38. Yang, L.; Zhang, R.Y.; Li, L.; Xie, X. SimAM: A Simple, Parameter-Free Attention Module for Convolutional Neural Networks. In Proceedings of the International Conference On Machine Learning (ICML), Virtual Event, 18–24 July 2021; pp. 11863–11974.

Journal of
Marine Science and Engineering

MDPI

Article

Grabbing Path Extraction of Deep-Sea Manganese Nodules Based on Improved YOLOv5

Chunlu Cui , Penglei Ma *, Qianli Zhang, Guijie Liu * and Yingchun Xie

Department of Mechanical and Electrical Engineering, Ocean University of China, Qingdao 266100, China; cuichunlu@stu.ouc.edu.cn (C.C.); zhangqianli@ouc.edu.cn (Q.Z.); xieyc@ouc.edu.cn (Y.X.)
* Correspondence: mapenglei@ouc.edu.cn (P.M.); liuguijie@ouc.edu.cn (G.L.)

Abstract: In an effort to enhance the efficiency and accuracy of deep-sea manganese nodule grasping behavior by a manipulator, a novel approach employing an improved YOLOv5 algorithm is proposed for the extraction of the shortest paths to manganese nodules targeted by the manipulator. The loss function of YOLOv5s has been improved by integrating a dual loss function that combines IoU and NWD, resulting in better accuracy for loss calculations across different target sizes. Additionally, substituting the initial C3 module in the network backbone with a C2f module is intended to improve the flow of gradient information while reducing computational demands. Once the geometric center of the manganese nodules is identified with the improved YOLOv5 algorithm, the next step involves planning the most efficient route for the manipulator to pick up the nodules using an upgraded elite strategy ant colony algorithm. Enhancements to the ACO algorithm consist of implementing an elite strategy and progressively decreasing the number of ants in each round. This method reduces both the number of iterations and the time required for each iteration, while also preventing the occurrence of local optimal solutions. The experimental findings indicate that the improved YOLOv5s detection algorithm boosts detection accuracy by 2.3%. Furthermore, when there are fewer than 30 target planning points, the improved algorithm requires, on average, 24% fewer iterations than the ACO algorithm to determine the shortest path. Additionally, the speed of calculation for each iteration is quicker while still providing the optimal solution.

Keywords: manganese nodule; YOLOv5; path extraction; ant colony optimization

Citation: Cui, C.; Ma, P.; Zhang, Q.; Liu, G.; Xie, Y. Grabbing Path Extraction of Deep-Sea Manganese Nodules Based on Improved YOLOv5. *J. Mar. Sci. Eng.* **2024**, *12*, 1433. https://doi.org/10.3390/jmse12081433

Academic Editor: Marco Cococcioni

Received: 14 June 2024
Revised: 13 August 2024
Accepted: 17 August 2024
Published: 19 August 2024

1. Introduction

The ocean is rich in mineral resources, one of which is manganese nodules. These nodules are a form of ore that forms on the seabed, characterized by a black or brown surface and a spherical or bulky shape. They contain over 30 different metal elements, with manganese, copper, cobalt, and nickel being the most commercially valuable for extraction [1]. The extraction of deep-sea manganese nodules is primarily reliant on the utilization of deep-sea manipulators. Currently, the autonomous operation systems of vision-based manipulators exhibit challenges related to accuracy and efficiency. A significant focus in addressing these challenges is the improvement in both the detection success rate and the efficiency of grasping manganese nodules. Notably, advancements have been made by researchers in this domain. For instance, Bazeille et al. employed color features for the detection of underwater targets, with experimental findings suggesting that suboptimal lighting conditions—whether insufficient or excessive—negatively impact detection efficacy [2]. Christian et al. implemented an underwater target detection technique utilizing active contour methods, which delineates the target region by leveraging three distinct features: color, direction, and brightness. The integration of statistical approaches alongside active contour methodologies significantly mitigates the dependence on initial parameters for target detection. Nonetheless, it is important to note that the efficacy of detection may be compromised when the background color closely resembles that of the target [3].

Given the intricate and variable lighting conditions and scenes present on the seafloor, deep learning-based recognition methods demonstrate significant advantages. Currently, deep learning detection algorithms are categorized into two types: one-stage target detection algorithms and two-stage target detection algorithms. The two-stage target detection algorithms, in contrast to their one-stage counterparts, provide benefits such as enhanced classification accuracy and improved precision in detection box localization. A seminal contribution to the field was made by Girshick et al. with the introduction of the R-CNN algorithm, which marked the first application of convolutional neural networks for target detection [4]. Building upon this, Girshick et al. and Ren et al. introduced Fast R-CNN and Faster R-CNN algorithms, establishing a series of R-CNN algorithms [5,6]. The two-stage target detection algorithm is currently in the nascent phase of development within the field of underwater target detection, with numerous researchers actively working to refine the R-CNN series of algorithms. Yuan et al. introduced a secondary transfer learning approach that builds upon the Faster R-CNN framework, incorporating enhancements through the multi-scale retinex with color restoration (MSRCR) technique. Initially, the Open Images fish dataset was processed utilizing the ImageNet model to establish a preliminary network. Subsequently, an underwater fish dataset was collected, followed by a second transfer learning phase to produce the final network. Ultimately, the MSRCR algorithm was employed to improve the congruence between the underwater dataset and the Open Images fish dataset, effectively mitigating the challenges associated with the degradation of image quality in underwater environments [7]. Yang et al. proposed the QueryDet target detection algorithm, which enhances both the inference speed and the accuracy of the model by introducing the CSQ mechanism. This offers a new direction for future research [8].

The one-stage target detection algorithm does not generate candidate regions to directly predict regions during the detection process. Compared to the two-stage target detection method, the detection speed is faster. The one-stage target detection algorithm has better detection speed and accuracy. Therefore, it has more engineering application value. The main representative of the one-stage target detection algorithm is the YOLO series algorithm. Wang et al. proposed an improved YOLOv2 algorithm and applied it to detect fish images. It changed the last convolutional layer of the network model from 7×7 to 9×9. Furthermore, in accordance with the specific requirements, the quantity of filters in the final convolutional layer was decreased. This modification markedly improved the detection accuracy of YOLOv2 for small fish [9]. Muksit et al. introduced an advanced version of the YOLOv3 model, designated as YOLO-Fish-1, which significantly enhanced the recognition accuracy of small target fish by optimizing the detection step size. Following this, they developed YOLO-Fish-2, which incorporated an increase in the spatial pyramid pooling of YOLO-Fish-1. This modification not only bolstered the robustness of the network model but also augmented its recognition accuracy in dynamic environments [10]. Chen et al. introduced an enhanced version of the YOLOv4 algorithm, which optimizes the feature extraction capabilities of CSPDarknet53 (cross-stage partial network Darknet53), the foundational architecture of the YOLOv4 network. This enhancement enables the algorithm to acquire weighted multi-scale features, subsequently utilizing the most pertinent features for the detection of underwater targets. Verification using the Brackish dataset demonstrated an improvement in average accuracy by 5.03% while achieving a detection speed of 15 frames per second [11]. Xu et al. introduced the PP-YOLOE target detection algorithm, which incorporates several enhancements to both the training strategy and inference speed. These modifications result in a significant increase in inference speed and training efficiency while preserving high accuracy. Consequently, the model demonstrates enhanced competitiveness in practical applications [12]. Wang et al. introduced the YOLOv7 algorithm, which integrates an ELAN module within its network architecture. This integration significantly enhances the model's ability to capture long-range dependencies within images. Additionally, the convolutional approach employed, known as RepConvN, serves to decrease both the complexity of the model and its computational demands, all while maintaining a high level of accuracy [13]. Cai et al. introduced the

Gold-YOLO algorithm, which incorporates a gather-and-distribute mechanism alongside a pre-training approach inspired by the masked autoencoder (MAE) framework. This innovative methodology significantly enhances the model's ability to fuse multi-scale information, resulting in state-of-the-art (SOTA) performance across various datasets [14]. Wang et al. introduced the YOLOv9 algorithm, which has been optimized comprehensively in terms of network architecture and loss function. This optimization markedly enhances the model's detection performance in complex environments, positioning it among the most advanced target detection algorithms currently available [15].

Concurrently, advancements in research utilizing the Transformer model have been notable. Huang et al. introduced a two-stage target detection algorithm for AD-DETR, which markedly enhances the accuracy of target detection while simultaneously decreasing the model's inference speed. This improvement is achieved through the incorporation of multi-scale feature integration, alongside enhancements to the training objectives and matching strategies [16]. Liu et al. introduced an enhanced version of the DAB-DETR algorithm through the development of a DETR algorithm. This new approach integrates self-attention and cross-attention mechanisms within a two-layer framework, thereby significantly enhancing the precision of target feature extraction in intricate environments [17].

In comparison to one-stage algorithms, two-stage target detection algorithms exhibit superior performance in terms of accuracy and localization. However, the computational speed and cost constraints associated with two-stage algorithms render them unsuitable for scenarios that require real-time processing. The evolution of target detection algorithms has resulted in incremental enhancements in the detection accuracy of one-stage algorithms; however, this progress has concurrently led to a substantial increase in the number of parameters and computational complexity, thereby diminishing their applicability for real-time detection and processing tasks. The challenge that arises is how to optimize the model for real-time detection scenarios by minimizing its weight without sacrificing accuracy. The YOLOv5 algorithm represents a lightweight model that maintains high accuracy while providing rapid inference speeds, making it particularly well-suited for real-time scene processing. In the context of current underwater operations, the identification and manipulation tasks performed by manipulators predominantly rely on manual identification and positioning, which lack autonomy and are characterized by inefficiency and time consumption. To mitigate these challenges, this study proposes a method for the autonomous recognition and grasping of manganese nodules. This method incorporates a lightweight algorithm with high inference speed and enhances it to further boost accuracy and grasping efficiency. Furthermore, the elite strategy ant colony algorithm is employed to determine the shortest grasping path from a single-frame image, thereby reducing the time required for grasping. This approach offers a conceptual framework for the autonomous operation of underwater manipulators.

2. Materials and Methods

Stereolabs ZED

The apparatus employed in this study is the ZED 2 binocular stereo camera manufactured by Stereolabs. This camera features a resolution of 3840 × 1080 pixels (1080P) and operates at a refresh rate of 30 Hz. The sealing treatment applied to the exterior of the camera is illustrated in Figure 1, where (1) denotes the Stereolabs ZED camera and (2) indicates the sealing structure.

In the course of the experiment, the ZED binocular camera and the manipulator are configured in an eye-to-hand placement mode, as illustrated in Figure 1. This configuration entails that both the camera and the manipulator are stationary, thereby maintaining a consistent coordinate transformation relationship between the camera and the base of the manipulator. Communication between the ZED binocular camera and the manipulator is facilitated via a handheld controller. The comprehensive communication process of the entire system is depicted in Figure 2.

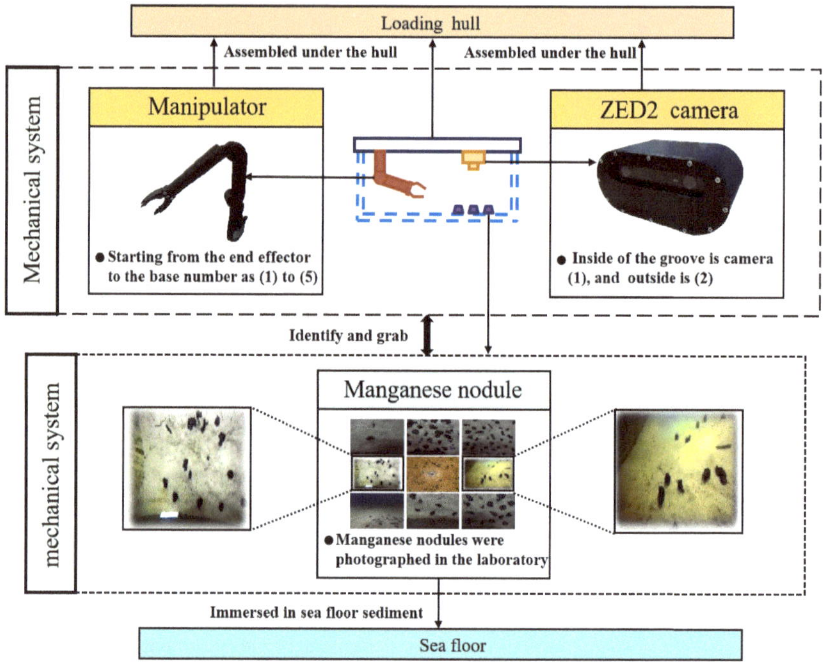

Figure 1. Grab system position diagram.

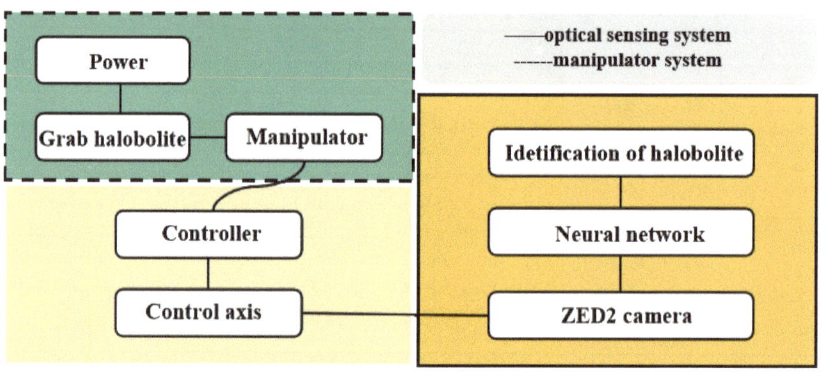

Figure 2. Grab system connection diagram.

3. Manipulator Grasping Method Based on Binocular Vision

Feature extraction for underwater targets typically involves the utilization of color, texture, and shape features derived from enhanced underwater imagery. These extracted features are subsequently classified using a designated classifier. The practical application outcomes of these methodologies are illustrated in Figure 3. However, the aforementioned methods encounter several challenges in the feature extraction process. Notably, the histogram of the extracted color features fails to adequately represent the spatial distribution information of the image. In instances of color similarity, the degree of waveform coincidence is elevated, leading to comparable two-dimensional color histograms, which complicates classifier recognition. Furthermore, relying solely on shape features does not effectively capture the spatial information of the image, and variations such as target rotation and occlusion can adversely affect the recognition rate. While texture feature extraction demonstrates greater robustness, the irregularities in underwater illumination may produce misleading textures of the target. Additionally, the target may exhibit diverse texture features at varying resolutions, which can further influence the recognition rate. Traditional methods also face significant difficulties in the identification of manganese nodules.

Traditional methods have proven inadequate for the effective identification of manganese nodules. This study introduces a novel approach utilizing deep learning techniques for the recognition of manganese nodules. Specifically, the YOLOv5 model has been optimized to enhance the detection rate of manganese nodules, thereby facilitating the identification of a greater number of geometric centers associated with these nodules. Furthermore, to improve the efficiency of the manipulator and minimize energy consumption, an enhanced elite strategy ant colony algorithm is employed subsequent to the recognition of geometric centers. This algorithm is utilized to determine the path characterized by the highest pheromone concentrations, thereby facilitating the extraction of the shortest route for the manipulator to grasp the manganese nodules.

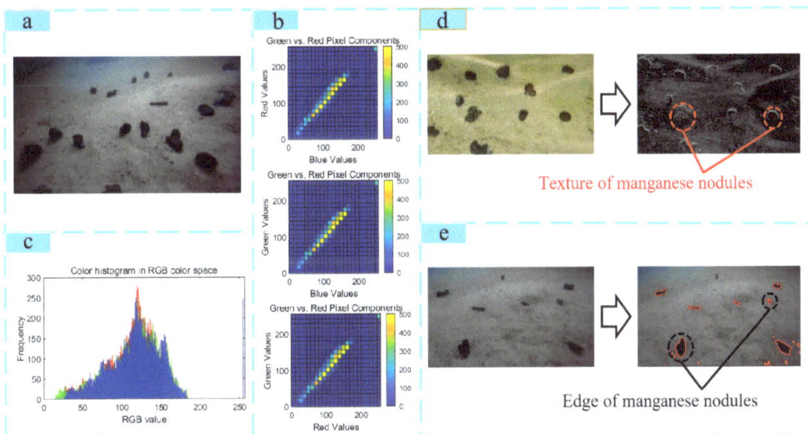

Figure 3. (**a**) Initial picture, (**b**) two-dimensional color histogram, (**c**) RGB color histogram, (**d**) texture of manganese nodules, and (**e**) edge of manganese nodules.

4. Improved YOLOv5 for Manganese Nodule Detection

4.1. Data Acquisition and Selection

4.1.1. Data Acquisition

The dataset was compiled in the underwater robotics laboratory at the Ocean University of China on 18 October 2023. The images were captured using a ZED2 binocular stereo camera, San Francisco, USA with a resolution of 672 × 376 pixels. To ensure a diverse range of samples, between 5 and 60 nodules were randomly positioned in the pool, with portions of them submerged in sediment. Various levels of brightness and angles of illumination were employed during the sampling process to further enhance sample diversity. Following a selection process, 1200 images were retained, and the dataset was subsequently augmented to include a total of 2500 images through techniques such as mosaic creation, rotation, and the introduction of noise. The dataset was partitioned into a training set and a validation set in a 7:3 ratio. Image labeling was conducted using Labelimg, with the type and coordinate information of the labeled results stored in *.txt format.

4.1.2. Data Selection

Currently, the availability of open-source images depicting manganese nodules from actual seabed environments is quite limited. Consequently, this study utilizes datasets derived from simulated laboratory environments. To effectively replicate the recognition context of the marine environment, this research integrates various datasets and identifies the most appropriate combinations through a series of comparative experiments. The experimental groups are defined as follows:

(1) Group A consists of both the training set and the validation set sourced from laboratory images;

(2) Group B comprises a training set derived from laboratory images, while the validation set is obtained from publicly accessible images;

(3) Group C involves a combination of laboratory images and open-source images at a 1:1 ratio, with both the training and validation sets being formed from this integrated dataset.

In this paper, the three datasets were trained using the same YOLOv5 framework, and the experimental data are presented in Table 1.

Table 1. Dataset comparison experimental result.

Comparison Groups	Average Precision/%
A	94.1
B	36.4
C	72.2

It can be seen from the data that the AP value of comparison group B is relatively low. This indicates that the images taken by the laboratory make it difficult to identify the real seabed images from the open-source network. In order to further verify the above conclusions, this paper compares the training weights of group A to identify real seabed images and finds that the training weights of group A are not effective in identifying real seabed images. It can be observed that the seabed environment is complex, with changing light and scenery. Therefore, we set the dataset as the comparison group C, added some real seabed images into the training process, and supplemented the image features that some laboratory images do not have so as to better identify the manganese nodules in real-world environments.

4.2. Training Environment

The system for training runs on Windows 11 and is equipped with a 12th Gen Intel®Core™ i5-12400 2.50 GHz CPU, 32 GB of memory, and two NVIDIA GeForce RTX 3060 graphics cards. The training framework is PyTorch, and Anaconda is used to establish the environment configuration for related software.

The proposed algorithm is implemented using Python 3.9, and the code is compiled with PyTorch 2.0.

5. Improved YOLOv5

5.1. YOLOv5 Model's Specific Modifications and Performance Testing

The YOLO series [18–22] is a one-stage object detection algorithm characterized by a framework comprising four key components: the input section, the trunk section, the neck section, and the prediction section. Notably, YOLOv5 distinguishes itself from other models within the YOLO series by its streamlined architecture, which facilitates enhanced detection speed and greater flexibility in deployment. A significant feature of YOLOv5 is its implementation of mosaic data augmentation, which enhances the dataset's diversity by combining four randomly selected images. The model employs a feature extraction structure that includes CSPDarknet53 and an SPP layer, with the extracted features subsequently integrated using PANet [23]. YOLOv5 is available in five distinct variants: YOLOv5n, YOLOv5s, YOLOv5m, YOLOv5l, and YOLOv5x. The variant examined in this study is an improved version of YOLOv5s, primarily tailored for object detection in intricate deep-sea environments. Figure 4 illustrates the structural design of the improved YOLOv5 model.

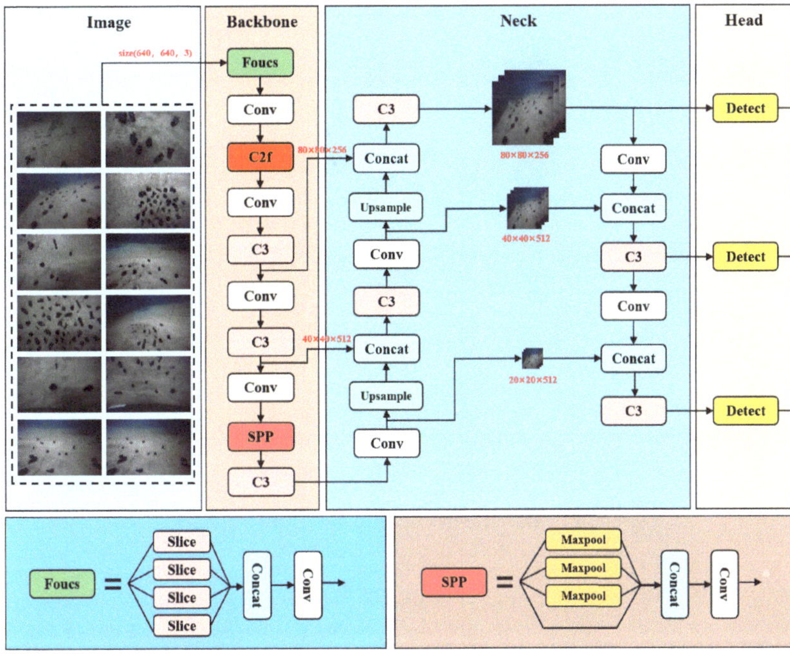

Figure 4. Enhanced network structure.

Through experiments, it has been found that the YOLOv5s model still exhibits low accuracy when applied to the identification of manganese nodule datasets. Therefore, the model has been modified in the following two aspects:

(1) The C3 module is improved to the C2f module.

The architecture of the C2f (cross-stage partial network) module [24] has been enhanced based on the C3 module. Certain aspects of its design bear a resemblance to the ELAN architecture, which facilitates the parallelization of multiple gradient flow branches, thereby enabling the acquisition of more comprehensive gradient flow information while maintaining a lightweight model. This approach aims to enhance both the training efficacy and convergence speed of the model. To further minimize computational demands and improve efficiency, the number of Bottleneck input channels in the C2f module has been reduced to 50% of that in the preceding level, and the kernel size of the initial convolutional layer has been modified from 6 × 6 to 3 × 3. Additionally, a segmentation has been introduced between the CBS and Bottleneck components to partition the feature map.

The structure of the C2f module is illustrated in Figure 5. Within this module, the Bottleneck component consists of two 1 × 1 convolutional layers and one 3 × 3 convolutional layer. The primary function of the two 1 × 1 convolutional layers is to modify the dimensions of the input and output layers, thereby establishing the 3 × 3 convolutional layer as the bottleneck in terms of input/output dimensions. This Bottleneck architecture effectively decreases the number of parameters and enhances computational efficiency while maintaining the original level of accuracy. Through a series of experiments involving various placements of the C2f module and differing quantities of replacements, it was determined that the optimal AP value was attained by substituting the initial C3 module of the Darknet53 network backbone with a C2f module.

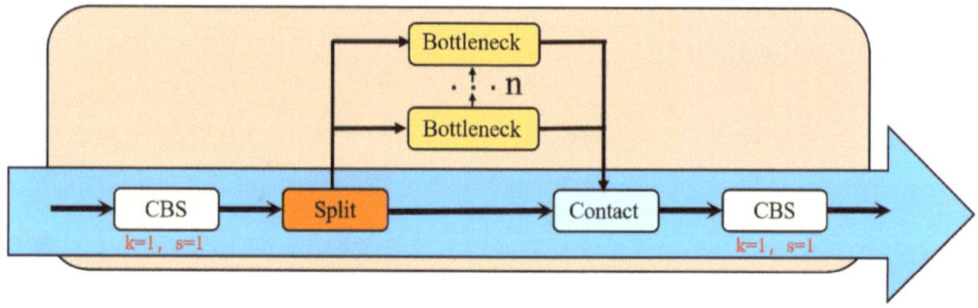

Figure 5. C2f module structure diagram.

(2) NWD + IoU double loss function

To address the challenge of balancing the computation of the loss function for targets of varying scales, we propose the NWD+IoU double loss function. The IoU (intersection over union) loss function is widely recognized as the predominant loss function utilized within the YOLO series of algorithms. Nevertheless, it exhibits significant limitations in the detection of small targets and in the context of multi-scale fusion detection. Conversely, the NWD (noise-contrastive estimation with discretized representations) is less sensitive to variations in object scale, rendering it more effective for assessing the similarity of small objects. To improve the recognition accuracy of the manganese nodule dataset, we have augmented the loss function to incorporate the NWD + IoU double loss function, thereby facilitating a more comprehensive calculation of the total loss associated with the target.

In contrast to the IoU loss function, the NWD loss function [25] is more adept at assessing the similarity of small objects characterized by a Gaussian distribution. The fundamental principle underlying this approach is to enhance the similarity between positive and negative samples by minimizing the KL (Kullback–Leible) divergence. This is achieved by optimizing the model through a comparative analysis of the similarities between the positive and negative samples. In this context, the positive sample represents the original input data, while the negative sample is generated by introducing noise to the original representation.

Given that the majority of objects do not conform to standard rectangular shapes, the process of delineating the small target boundary from the background frequently results in ambiguity. To enhance the precision of the loss function, the NWD loss function incorporates a two-dimensional Gaussian distribution, which allocates the maximum weight to the central point of the small target, with the weight progressively diminishing towards the periphery. For the purpose of this discussion, let us consider a bounding box with a size of $S = (ax, ay, w, h)$, where x and y represent the coordinates of the center point, and w and h denote the width and height of the bounding box. The interior elliptic equation can be expressed as follows (1):

$$\frac{(x-\mu_x)^2}{\sigma_x^2} + \frac{\left(y-\mu_y\right)^2}{\sigma_y^2} = 1 \tag{1}$$

where $(\mu x, \mu y)$ is the center coordinate of the ellipse. $\sigma x, \sigma y$ is the half-axis length along the x, y axis. Where, $\mu x = ax, \mu y = ay, \mu x = w^2, \mu y = h^2$

When $(x-\mu)^{\top}\Sigma^{-1}(x-\mu) = 1$ is satisfied, the probability density function of the two-dimensional Gaussian distribution can be expressed as Equation (2), and its probability is the degree function:

$$f(x \mid \mu, \Sigma) = \frac{\exp\left(-\frac{1}{2}(x-\mu)^T\Sigma^{-1}(x-\mu)\right)}{2\pi|\Sigma|^{\frac{1}{2}}} \tag{2}$$

where μ and Σ are, respectively, the following (3) and (4):

$$\mu = \begin{bmatrix} c_x \\ c_y \end{bmatrix} \quad (3)$$

$$\Sigma = \begin{bmatrix} \frac{w^2}{4} & 0 \\ 0 & \frac{h^2}{4} \end{bmatrix} \quad (4)$$

NWD calculates the distribution distance using the Wasserstein distance. For two two-dimensional Gaussian distributions $\mu 1 = N(m1, \Sigma 1)$ and $\mu 2 = N(m2, \Sigma 2)$, the second-order Wasserstein distance between $\mu 1$ and $\mu 2$ can be simplified as follows:

$$NWD(N_a, N_b) = \exp\left(-\frac{\sqrt{W_2^2(N_a, N_b)}}{G_J \text{ Zivang}} \right) \quad (5)$$

The detailed procedure for the fusion of NWD and IOU is outlined as follows: first, the Wasserstein distance is computed between the predicted bounding box and the actual bounding box, which is then condensed into a one-dimensional tensor. Next, a scaling factor is established to equilibrate the Wasserstein loss with the IOU loss, with empirical evidence indicating that the AP achieves its maximum value when the scaling factor is set to 0.5. Following this, the overall loss value is determined. Upon the integration of the NWD loss function into the framework, the overall loss function can be represented as follows (6):

$$L_{\text{total}} = \left(1 - NWD_{(N_a N_b)}\right) * NWD_{\text{ratio}} + (1 - NWD_{\text{ratio}}) * (1 - IoU) \quad (6)$$

Among them, L_{total} is the total loss, NWD_{ratio} is the ratio of the NWD loss function, and IoU is the ratio of the intersection and union of the real box and the prediction box.

The recognition rate of the enhanced YOLOv5 network model has shown improvement. Figure 6 presents eight recognition cases that encompass a diverse range of object categories, sizes, and scene complexities, thereby providing a comprehensive assessment of the model's generalization capabilities and robustness. The cases illustrate that the enhanced model demonstrates accuracy and effective localization performance in detecting various targets. Notably, in complex environments characterized by variations in illumination, occlusions, targets of differing scales, or background interference, the improved YOLOv5 is capable of accurately identifying the primary targets within the image and delivering precise bounding boxes. In this context, yellow labels represent actual seabed data, while purple labels denote a self-constructed dataset.

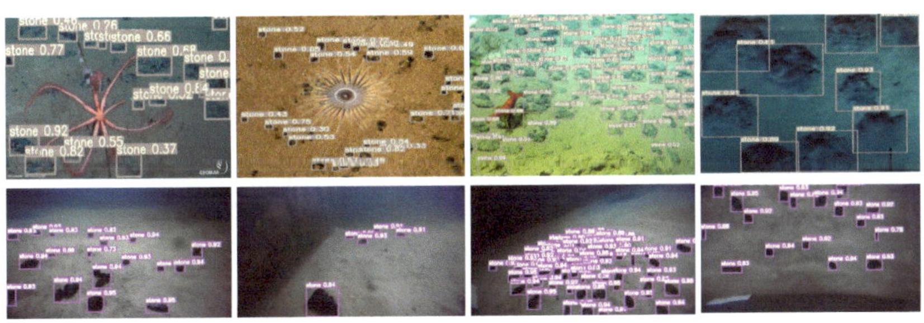

Figure 6. Detection diagram of manganese nodules.

To enhance the assessment of the model's performance, images of manganese nodules exhibiting overlapping regions and masking were identified. The following Figure 7 displays the results predicted by the enhanced algorithm. The figure illustrates that the target can be accurately recognized when the overlapping part is small. However, accurate recognition becomes challenging when the overlapping part is large and the boundary is more blurred. The masked target can still be recognized, but the position of the prediction box may deviate to some extent when the mask is too large.

Figure 7. Detection diagram of overlap and masking.

5.2. Analysis of the Computational Complexity and Resource Requirements of the Improved Model

YOLOv5's initial model has a floating-point operation count of 21 GFLOPS and 9 million parameters on the dataset used in this study. In comparison, the improved model has increased the floating-point operation count by 7 GFLOPS and the parameter count by 4.6 million. Additionally, in the feature layer where C2f is located, the parameter count has increased from 18,000 to 38,000. This indicates that the improved model has increased computational complexity, but still maintains a significant lightweight advantage compared to models like YOLO8. While the YOLOv5 model is relatively lightweight in terms of computational resources, deep learning-based object detection algorithms still require GPU support, leading to the need for high hardware specifications for real-time detection of the YOLOv5 model. Moreover, differences in lighting conditions and the presence of more complex background interference in the actual scenarios may pose limitations during deployment.

6. The Shortest Grasping Path Extraction of the Manipulator

In the context of real-time video transmission, the camera captures multiple objects within each frame. Strategic planning of the sequence in which these targets are grasped can significantly reduce the time required for grasping and enhance the overall efficiency of the operation. The procedure for frame-by-frame grasping path planning is delineated as follows:

Step 1: Identify the center point of the target object within each frame and record the corresponding coordinates.

Step 2: Employ an improved elite strategy ant colony algorithm to devise a path based on the identified center point coordinates.

Step 3: Integrate the planned path with the actual image to facilitate the manipulation of the manipulator's rotation.

The specific implementation steps of the visual part are illustrated in Figure 8.

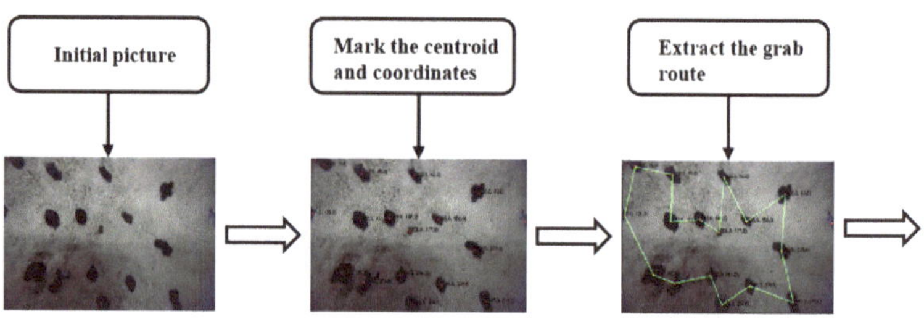

Figure 8. From left to right, is the initial picture, coordinate labeling picture, and shortest path planning pictures.

6.1. Basic Ant Colony Optimization Algorithm

To address the challenge of path extraction among various targets within a single image frame, we propose the implementation of the ACO algorithm [26–28]. ACO is a heuristic optimization technique designed to tackle pathfinding issues. In their natural foraging behavior, ants typically select paths at random. Upon traversing a particular route, ants deposit a chemical substance known as pheromones, which facilitates communication among the ant population. Other ants, upon encountering these pheromones, can detect their concentration through their antennae and are inclined to favor paths with higher pheromone levels. Given that shorter paths require less time for traversal, the frequency of ant passage along these routes increases, resulting in a greater accumulation of pheromones. This positive feedback loop encourages an increasing number of ants to follow the paths with elevated pheromone concentrations, ultimately leading to the identification of the optimal route. The probability of an ant moving from point a to point b at time t is as follows:

$$P_{ab}^{k}(t) = \begin{cases} \frac{[\tau_{ab}(t)]^{\alpha}\cdot[\eta_{ab}(t)]^{\beta}}{\sum_{c\in S(k)}[\tau_{ac}(t)]^{\alpha}\cdot[\eta_{ac}(t)]^{\beta}}, b \in S(k) \\ 0, \quad otherwise \end{cases} \tag{7}$$

where $S(k)(k = 1, 2, \cdots, m)$ is the set of the next locations that the ant needs to traverse, m is the number of ants, and k is the number of locations that the ant has traversed, η_{ab} is heuristic information, with the specific value being the reciprocal of the distance between point a and point b, α, β is the influence degree of pheromone and heuristic pheromone on ant path selection, and n is the total number of points. $\tau_{ab}(t)$ is the number of pheromones between corresponding points a and b at time t. When the ant traverses all the points, the pheromone corresponding to each path is updated as follows (8):

$$\tau_{ab}(t+1) = (1-\delta)\tau_{ab}(t) + \Delta_{ab} \tag{8}$$

where Δ_{ab} is the pheromone left between a and b after k cycles, and $\delta \in (0,1)$ is the degree of attenuation of the pheromone.

6.2. Enhanced Elite Strategy Ant Colony Algorithm

The ant colony optimization algorithm continues to encounter challenges related to its relatively slow speed in identifying the shortest path. To address this issue and to improve the efficiency of manipulator grasping, we propose an enhanced elite strategy ant colony algorithm [29,30]. This elite strategy augments the pheromone levels within the framework of the ant colony optimization algorithm. The fundamental principle underlying this approach is that when an ant identifies the optimal path, the pheromone concentration along that path is increased, thereby promoting a higher pheromone density on the most favorable route and facilitating quicker convergence. The elite strategy ant colony algorithm incorporates an additional positive feedback component into Equation (10), which is derived from the original remaining pheromone represented in Equation (9).

$$\Delta\tau_{ab} = \sum_{k=1}^{m} \Delta\tau_{ab}^{k} \tag{9}$$

$$\Delta\tau_{ab} = \sum_{k=1}^{m} \Delta\tau_{ab} + EPFV \tag{10}$$

where $\Delta\tau_{ab}$ is the total residual pheromone, $\Delta\tau_{ab}^{k}$ is the residual pheromone of ant k between a and b, and EPFV (extra positive feedback value) is the additional positive feedback value, which can be expressed as Equation (11):

$$EPFV = \begin{cases} \frac{c}{L_{bp}}, (a,b) \in BP \\ 0, \ otherwise \end{cases} \tag{11}$$

where c is the parameter to adjust the additional feedback value, L_{bp} is the length of the best path, and BP (the best path) is the current best path.

In addition to the introduction of the elite strategy, we also made a decreasing improvement in the number of ant colonies and proposed an improved elite strategy ant colony algorithm. On the premise of avoiding the local optimal solution, the number of ant colonies decreases in the round-by-round traversal, which can be expressed as follows (12):

$$m_n = m_{n-1} - \alpha(n-1) \quad (12)$$

where n $(n = 1, 2, 3 \cdots)$ is the number of rounds traversed by ants, m_n is the number of ants in the round n, and α is the attenuation coefficient of the number of ants. The decreasing number of ants helps to further reduce the extraction time of the optimal path and improve the grasping efficiency of the manipulator.

The initial number of ants should not be set too large or too small. An excessively large value will result in slow convergence of the algorithm, directly impacting the response speed of the manipulator. Conversely, a value that is too small will increase the likelihood of obtaining a local optimal solution. By testing the initial number of ants from small to large, we found that when the initial number of ants is 1.3 times the number of manganese nodules, there will be no local optimal solution (50 tests). At the same time, to ensure clarity and recognition accuracy, the number of manganese nodules in a single frame of a manganese nodule image should not exceed 30. When the quantity of manganese nodules surpasses 30, the quality of the shortest path extraction diminishes, leading to an increased likelihood of encountering local optimal solutions during experimentation. In certain instances, even after more than 1000 iterations, the global optimal solution remains elusive. Concurrently, the blurring of image boundaries intensifies, resulting in inaccuracies in the delineation of the target's prediction box, which adversely impacts the localization of the central point. This suggests that the optimal number of points for traversal by the ants should be limited to fewer than 30.

6.3. Algorithm Flow and Performance Test

The ant colony optimization algorithm plays a pivotal role in establishing the initial quantity of ants and the pheromone evaporation coefficient. Generally, the initial number of ants is set between 10 and 50, while the pheromone evaporation coefficient typically ranges from 0.1 to 0.9. To optimize traversal time and improve computational efficiency, it is recommended to reduce both the initial number of ants and the pheromone evaporation coefficient. However, excessively low values for the initial number of ants may result in prolonged traversal times for the shortest path and yield unstable results. Likewise, a very low pheromone evaporation coefficient can lead to the algorithm's tendency to repeatedly traverse previously established paths, thereby increasing the risk of converging on a local optimum. Due to its pronounced sensitivity, extensive experimentation has indicated that configuring the initial number of ants to 1.3 times the target value and setting the pheromone evaporation coefficient to 0.2 can substantially decrease computation time while preserving the quality of the solutions obtained.

The initialization parameters encompass the following elements: the initial quantity of ant colonies is established at 1.3 times the desired number of manganese nodules. The termination criterion is defined as the situation in which only one ant remains. The information evaporation coefficient is assigned a value of 0.1, while the supplementary feedback value for the residual pheromone is determined to be 0.2, in accordance with the target quantity. Furthermore, the selection of the attenuation coefficient for the number of ant colonies must satisfy the termination condition when the number of iterations exceeds 30. The flowchart illustrating the enhanced elite ant colony algorithm is presented in Figure 9.

Figure 10 shows the effect diagram of the enhanced elite ant colony algorithm. It can be seen that by reducing the number of ant colonies and increasing the information residue, it is still possible to extract the shortest path for obtaining manganese nodules.

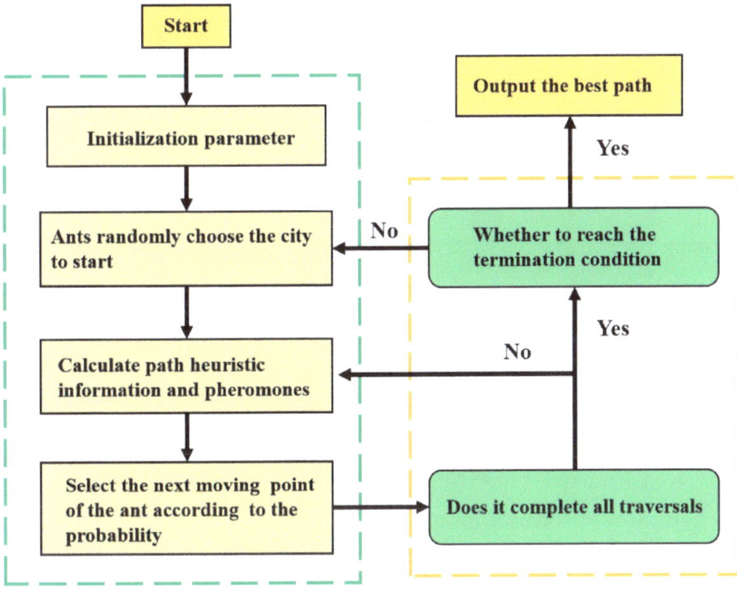

Figure 9. Enhanced elite ant colony algorithm flow chart.

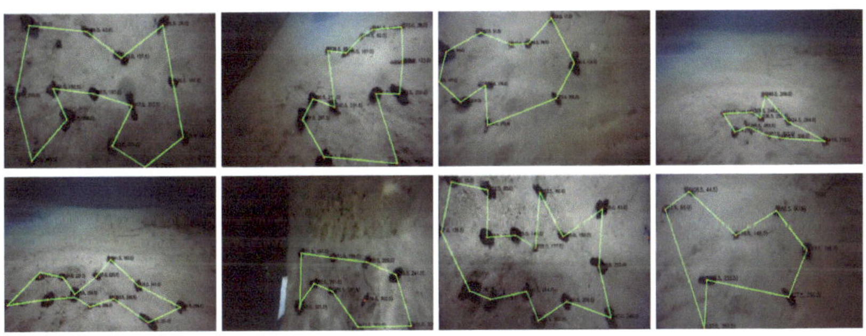

Figure 10. Path extraction effect diagram.

7. Experimental Evaluation Methods and Conclusions

7.1. Detection of Manganese Nodules Based on Enhanced YOLOv5

In this study, the detection of manganese nodules is evaluated based on precision (P), recall (R), mean average precision (mAP), and average precision (AP). The calculation method is as follows (13):

$$\begin{aligned} P &= \frac{1P}{TP+FP} \times 100\% \\ P &= \frac{TP}{TP+FP} \times 100\% \\ AP &= \int_0^1 p(r)dr \\ mAP &= \frac{1}{m}AP_i \end{aligned} \tag{13}$$

where TP is the number of prediction boxes with correct position recognition, FP is the number of prediction boxes with wrong position recognition, and FN is the number of prediction boxes with wrong position recognition. Table 2 shows the important hyperparameter settings for training the improved YOLOv5 model.

Table 2. Setting of hyperparameters.

Parameter Name	Parameter Values
Depth multiple	0.5
Width multiple	0.65
Lr0	0.01
Lrf	0.2
Batch-size	20

To assess the efficacy of the validation enhancement strategy, the influence of each improvement approach on the model was evaluated through ablation experiments. The outcomes of these enhancements were measured using the AP value as a benchmark. The findings are detailed in Table 3. The data presented in the table indicate that the improvement strategy employed in this study yields the highest AP value and demonstrates the most substantial effect.

Table 3. Results of ablation experiment.

C2f	NWD	AP%
×	×	72.2
×	✓	73.7
✓	×	72.9
✓	✓	74.5

"✓" indicates that the current module was used, and "×" indicates that it was not used.

In the present dataset, there exists a singular object category designated for detection, resulting in mAP being equivalent to AP value. The mAP for the enhanced YOLOv5 model is recorded at 74.5%, with a recall rate of 83% and a precision rate of 67.2%, indicating a notable enhancement relative to the pre-enhanced model. To assess the efficacy of the improved YOLOv5 model, a comparative analysis is conducted against the original model's performance. As illustrated in Figure 11, the validation outcomes for the enhanced YOLOv5 model demonstrate reduced box regression loss and confidence loss in comparison to the original model.

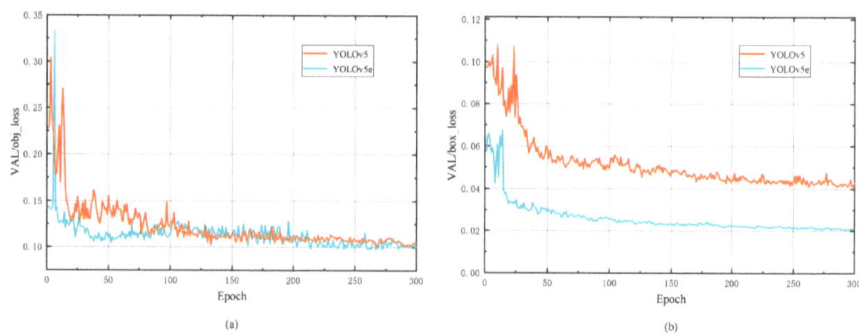

Figure 11. The loss comparison between the improved model and the original model. (**a**) The box regression loss represents the validation results, and (**b**) the confidence loss represents the validation results.

Figure 12 shows the comparison between the accuracy of the improved model and that of the original model. It can be seen from the figure that the AP of the improved model is higher than that of the original model.

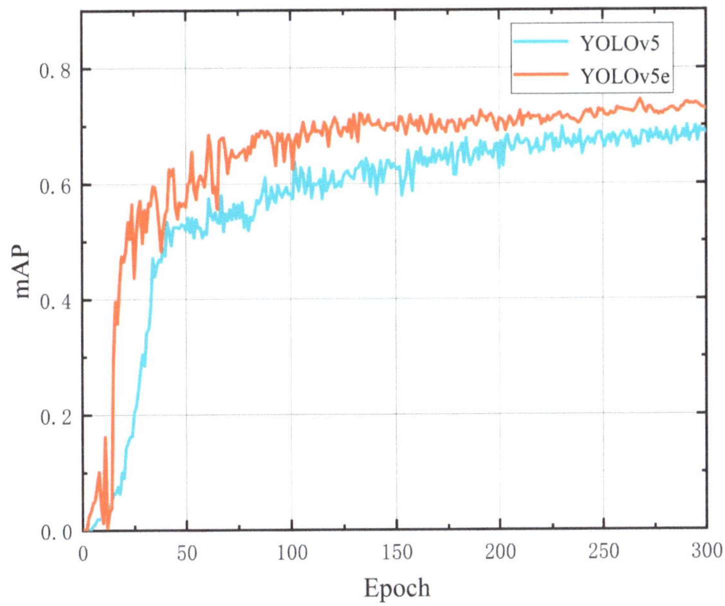

Figure 12. The AP comparison between the improved model and the original model.

To further examine the influence of illumination on the detection of manganese nodules, we performed a series of comparative experiments by modifying the brightness levels of all images within the dataset to 0.2 times, 0.5 times, and 1.5 times their original values. The experimental data presented in Table 4 below were obtained through training the same model.

Table 4. Different brightness training results.

Brightness Ratio	AP/%
0.2	72.5
0.5	74.3
1.0	74.5
1.5	73.7

The experimental data indicate that the model's detection accuracy is somewhat influenced by variations in brightness; however, the reduction in AP value is minimal. The subsequent four images, as illustrated in Figure 13, present the prediction outcomes across different brightness levels. The results clearly demonstrate that manganese nodules remain identifiable even under conditions of substantially reduced brightness. This observation implies that the model exhibits a degree of robustness to fluctuations in brightness.

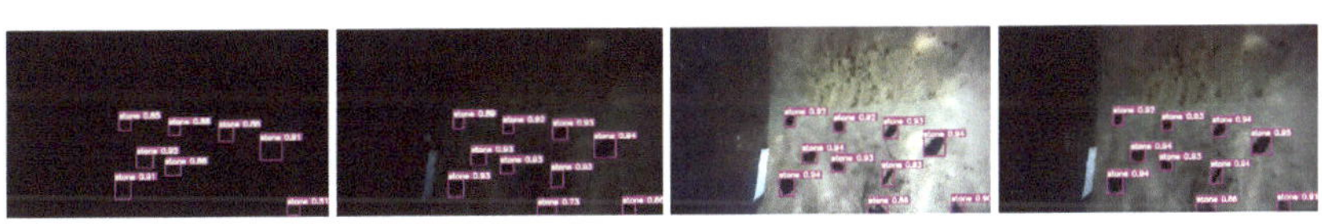

Figure 13. Brightness detection result comparison for 0.2, 0.5, 1.0, 1.5.

Table 5 summarizes the accuracy, recall, and precision of MobileNetV3, TOOD, YOLOv4, Faster RCNN, YOLOv7-tiny, YOLOv8, YOLOv5s, and YOLOv5enhanced at a confidence threshold of 0.5. Among these models, only YOLOv8 has a higher AP value than YOLOv5enhanced. However, the YOLOv8 model has a significantly larger number of parameters and high computational complexity, making it unsuitable for real-time processing applications.

Table 5. Different model training results.

Algorithm	AP/%	P/%	R/%
MobileNetV3	67.2	78.7	61.7
TOOD	73.4	83.7	67.9
YOLOv4	68.4	80.7	61.3
Faster R-CNN	73.7	86.0	68.5
YOLOv7-tiny	73.8	83.3	67.4
YOLOv8	78.1	85.7	72.3
YOLOv5s	72.2	83.5	66.1
YOLOv5enhanced	74.5	85.2	67.1

7.2. Path Extraction Based on Improved Elite Ant Colony Algorithm

A total of 15 images, each with designated coordinates, were randomly selected to assess the efficacy of the enhanced algorithm. The concentration of manganese nodule targets within these images ranged from 15 to 25. The results of the experiments are presented in Table 6. A series of ten path extraction experiments were performed on images depicting various manganese nodules, with the highest and lowest values being excluded from the analysis. The average value represents the number of iterations required for optimal path extraction. The first column of the table indicates the number of manganese nodules present in each individual image. The data reveal that, on average, the number of iteration rounds required by the improved algorithm has been reduced by 24%.

Table 6. Path extraction results.

Number of Manganese Nodules	Optimal Path Length	Basic Rounds	Improve Rounds	Relative Error
7	1211	1	1	0
8	1531	2.3	1.5	0
9	1471	3	2	0
10	752	32	17.4	0
11	1547	3.5	3	0
12	9883	9.6	8.8	0
13	1293	4.3	3.3	0
14	1772	9.3	7.8	0
16	1891	7.5	7.2	0
17	10,468	23.4	20	0
18	9219	17.8	14	0
20	14,512	35.3	29.9	1.4%
22	6251	25.3	21.5	0
24	12,130	22.5	20.5	2.1%
26	12,093	27.6	19.3	2.6%

8. Conclusions

This study presents a vision-based methodology for the extraction of grasping paths for deep-sea manganese nodules, offering a viable solution for manipulators tasked with this objective. The approach incorporates four enhancements to the YOLOv5 model and the ant colony optimization algorithm. Firstly, the implementation of a dual loss function effectively balances the loss calculations across targets of varying scales. Secondly, the C2f module enhances the flow of gradient information. Additionally, the number of ants is reduced round by round and the elite strategy is introduced to speed up the pheromone accumulation of the best path. Validation through a custom dataset and real seabed photographic experiments indicate a 2.3% improvement in detection accuracy compared to the pre-enhancement model. Furthermore, the average number of iterations required for path extraction is reduced by 24%, alongside a decrease in the duration of individual iterations, thereby demonstrating that the proposed method achieves superior efficiency and accuracy.

Currently, there are fewer cases of underwater manipulator operations, and there are still many uncertainties. The objective of this study is to decrease computational time while maintaining recognition accuracy to facilitate improved applications in underwater operations. However, challenges arise when the quantity of manganese nodules within a single frame is excessively high, leading to potential issues such as target omission during detection. Furthermore, the extraction of the shortest path may result in a local optimal solution, thereby prolonging computation time. Consequently, future research should explore the integration of path planning methodologies, such as reinforcement learning, with YOLO series algorithms to optimize planning for individual targets. Additionally, the implementation of multimodal fusion and the incorporation of sensors to support localization and recognition may significantly enhance the success rate of grasping operations. The deployment of the model is a critical factor that warrants careful consideration. Discrepancies between the experimental environment and the actual deployment context can be mitigated through the application of domain adaptation techniques, which adjust the source domain model to better correspond with the data distribution in the target domain. This approach aims to minimize the differences between the two environments and improve the overall performance of the model.

Author Contributions: C.C.: conceptualization, methodology, experimental demonstration, data processing, writing—original draft. P.M.: project management, writing—review and editing, funding acquisition. Q.Z.: methodology, writing—review and edition. G.L.: project management, funding acquisition. Y.X.: project management, funding acquisition. All authors have read and agreed to the published version of the manuscript.

Funding: The authors gratefully acknowledge the support of the Laoshan Laboratory (LSKJ202203500), the Taishan Scholars Program of Shandong Province (No. tstp20231215), and China Postdoctoral Science Foundation (No. 2021M693020).

Institutional Review Board Statement: Not applicable

Informed Consent Statement: Not applicable

Data Availability Statement: The data presented in this study are available on request from the first author. These data are not publicly available due to the need for future work.

Conflicts of Interest: The authors declare that they have no known competing financial interests or personal relationships that could have appeared to influence the work reported in this paper.

Abbreviations

The following abbreviations are used in this manuscript:

ACO ant colony optimization

References

1. Yu, L.; Zhang, P.; Xiao, G.; Zhang, L. Experimental Research on Cobaltic Existence State and Distill of Ocean Manganese Nodule. *J. Jilin Univ. (Earth Sci. Ed.)* **2012**, *39*, 1475–1481.
2. Bazeille, S.; Quidu, I.; Jaulin, L. Identification of underwater man-made object using a colour criterion. In Proceedings of the Conference on Detection and Classification of Underwater Targets, Edinburgh, UK, 18–19 September 2007; Volume 29.
3. Chienyao, W.; Phlypo, R.T. A Fully Automated Method to Detect and Segment a Manufactured Object in an Underwater Color Image. *EURASIP J. Adv. Signal Process.* **2010**, *2010*, 568092.
4. Girshick, R.; Donahue, J.; Darrell, T. Rich feature hierarchies for accurate object detection and semantic segmentation. In Proceedings of the 27th IEEE Conference on Computer Vision and Pattern Recognition (CVPR), Columbus, OH, USA, 23–28 June 2014; pp. 580–587.
5. Girshick, R. Fast R-CNN. *arXiv* **2015**, arXiv:1504.08083.

6. Ren, S.; He, K.; Girshick, R.; Sun, J. Faster R-CNN: Towards Real-Time Object Detection with Region Proposal Networks. *IEEE Trans. Pattern Anal. Mach. Intell.* **2017**, *39*, 1137–1149. [CrossRef] [PubMed]
7. Zeng, L.; Sun, B.; Zhu, D. Underwater target detection based on Faster R-CNN and adversarial occlusion network. *Eng. Appl. Artif. Intell.* **2021**, *100*, 104190. [CrossRef]
8. Yang, C.; Huang, Z.; Wang, N. QueryDet: Cascaded Sparse Query for Accelerating High-Resolution Small Object Detection. *arXiv* **2022**, arXiv:2013.09136.
9. Wang, M.; Liu, M.; Zhang, F.; Lei, G.; Guo, J.; Wang, L. Fast Classification and Detection of Fish Images with YOLOv2. In Proceedings of the 2018 OCEANS-MTS/IEEE Kobe Techno-Oceans (OTO), Kobe, Japan, 28–31 May 2018; pp. 1–4.
10. Redmon, J.; Farhadi, A. YOLOv3: An Incremental Improvement. *arXiv* **2018**, arXiv:1804.02767.
11. Chen, L.; Liu, Z.; Tong, L.; Jiang, Z.; Wang, S.; Dong, J.; Zhou, H. Underwater object detection using Invert Multi-Class Adaboost with deep learning. In Proceedings of the J2020 International Joint Conference on Neural Networks (IJCNN), Glasgow, UK, 19–24 July 2020; pp. 1–8.
12. Xu, S.; Wang, X.; Lv, W.; Chang, Q.; Cui, C.; Deng, K.; Wang, G.; Dang, Q.; Wei, S.; Du, Y.; et al. PP-YOLOE: An evolved version of YOLO. *arXiv* **2022**, arXiv:2203.16250.
13. Wang, C.-Y.; Bochkovskiy, A.; Liao, H.-Y. YOLOv7: Trainable Bag-of-Freebies Sets New State-of-the-Art for Real-Time Object Detectors. In Proceedings of the 2023 IEEE/CVF Conference on Computer Vision and Pattern Recognition (CVPR), Vancouver, BC, Canada, 17–24 June 2023; pp. 7464–7475.
14. Wang, C.; He, W.; Nie, Y.; Guo, J.; Liu, C.; Wang, Y.; Han, K. Gold-YOLO: Efficient Object Detector via Gather-and-Distribute Mechanism. *arXiv* **2023**, arXiv:2309.11331.
15. Wang, C.-Y.; Yeh, I.-H.; Liao, H.-Y. YOLOv9: Learning What You Want to Learn Using Programmable Gradient Information. *arXiv* **2024**, arXiv:2402.13613.
16. Huang, Y.; Yuan, G. AD-DETR: DETR with asymmetrical relation and decoupled attention in crowded scenes. *Math. Biosci. Eng. MBE* **2023**, *20*, 14158–14179. [CrossRef] [PubMed]
17. Liu, S.; Li, F.; Zhang, H.; Yang, X.; Qi, X.; Su, H.; Zhu, J.; Zhang, L. DAB-DETR: Dynamic Anchor Boxes are Better Queries for DETR. *arXiv* **2022**, arXiv:2201.12329.
18. Redmon, J.; Divvala, S.; Girshick, R.; Farhadi, A. You Only Look Once: Unified, Real-Time Object Detection. *arXiv* **2016**, arXiv:1506.02640.
19. Redmon, J.; Farhadi, A. YOLO9000: Better, Faster, Stronger. In Proceedings of the 2017 IEEE Conference on Computer Vision and Pattern Recognition (CVPR), Honolulu, HI, USA, 21–26 July 2017; pp. 6517–6525.
20. Dang, T.L.; Nguyen, G.T.; Cao, T. Object Tracking Using Improved Deep_Sort_YOLOv3 Architecture. In Proceedings of the 2017 IEEE Conference on Computer Vision and Pattern Recognition (CVPR), Honolulu, HI, USA, 21–26 July 2020; pp. 961–969.
21. Chen, W.; Lu, S.; Liu, B.; Li, G.; Qian, T. Detecting Citrus in Orchard Environment by Using Improved YOLOv4. *Sci. Program.* **2020**, *2020*, 8859237. [CrossRef]
22. Dong, X.; Yan, S.; Duan, C. A lightweight vehicles detection network model based on YOLOv5. *Eng. Appl. Artif. Intell.* **2022**, *113*, 104914. [CrossRef]
23. Mei, Y.; Fan, Y.; Zhang, Y.; Yu, J.; Zhou, Y.; Liu, D.; Fu, Y.; Huang, T.S.; Shi, H. Pyramid Attention Network for Image Restoration. *Int. J. Comput. Vis.* **2023**, *131*, 3207–3225. [CrossRef]
24. Reis, D.; Kupec, J.; Hong, J.; Ahmad, D. Real-Time Flying Object Detection with YOLOv8. *arXiv* **2024**, arXiv:2305.09972.
25. Wang, J.; Chang, X.; Yang, W. A Normalized Gaussian Wasserstein Distance for Tiny Object Detection. *arXiv* **2022**, arXiv:2110.13389.
26. Konatowski, S.; Pawłowski, P. Application of the ACO algorithm for UAV path planning. *Prz. Elektrotech.* **2019**, *95*, 117–121. [CrossRef]
27. Jie, Z.; Xiuqim, P. *Path Planning for Mobile Robots in Complex Environments Based on Improved ant Colony Algorithm*; Springer Nature: Cham, Switzerland, 2022; pp. 3–13.
28. Liu, Z.; Liu, J. Improved ant colony algorithm for path planning of mobile robots based on compound prediction mechanism. *J. Intell. Fuzzy Syst.* **2022**, *44*, 1–16. [CrossRef]
29. Meng, X.; Zhu, X.; Zhao, J. Obstacle Avoidance Path Planning Using the Elite Ant Colony Algorithm for Parameter Optimization of Unmanned Aerial Vehicles. *Arab. J. Sci. Eng.* **2023**, *48*, 2261–2275. [CrossRef]
30. Zhang, J.; Yang, J.G.; Qin, W.; Li, H.; Xu, Z.G.. An Improved Ant Colony Algorithm Based Dynamic Scheduling Method in Job Shop with Parallel Machines. *Adv. Mater. Res.* **2012**, *628*, 304–309. [CrossRef]

Journal of
Marine Science
and Engineering

MDPI

Article

DA-YOLOv7: A Deep Learning-Driven High-Performance Underwater Sonar Image Target Recognition Model

Zhe Chen [1,2], Guohao Xie [1,2,3], Xiaofang Deng [1,2,*], Jie Peng [1,2] and Hongbing Qiu [1,2,*]

1 School of Information and Communication, Guilin University of Electronic Technology, Guilin 541004, China; chenzhe@mail.nwpu.edu.cn (Z.C.); 22172301007@mails.guet.edu.cn (G.X.); pengjie@guet.edu.cn (J.P.)
2 Cognitive Radio and Information Processing Key Laboratory Authorized by China's Ministry of Education Foundation, Guilin University of Electronic Technology, Guilin 541004, China
3 School of Ocean Engineering, Guilin University of Electronic Technology, Beihai 536000, China
* Correspondence: xfdeng@guet.edu.cn (X.D.); qiuhb@guet.edu.cn (H.Q.)

Abstract: Affected by the complex underwater environment and the limitations of low-resolution sonar image data and small sample sizes, traditional image recognition algorithms have difficulties achieving accurate sonar image recognition. The research builds on YOLOv7 and devises an innovative fast recognition model designed explicitly for sonar images, namely the Dual Attention Mechanism YOLOv7 model (DA-YOLOv7), to tackle such challenges. New modules such as the Omni-Directional Convolution Channel Prior Convolutional Attention Efficient Layer Aggregation Network (OA-ELAN), Spatial Pyramid Pooling Channel Shuffling and Pixel-level Convolution Bilat-eral-branch Transformer (SPPCSPCBiFormer), and Ghost-Shuffle Convolution Enhanced Layer Aggregation Network-High performance (G-ELAN-H) are central to its design, which reduce the computational burden and enhance the accuracy in detecting small targets and capturing local features and crucial information. The study adopts transfer learning to deal with the lack of sonar image samples. By pre-training the large-scale Underwater Acoustic Target Detection Dataset (UATD dataset), DA-YOLOV7 obtains initial weights, fine-tuned on the smaller Smaller Common Sonar Target Detection Dataset (SCTD dataset), thereby reducing the risk of overfitting which is commonly encountered in small datasets. The experimental results on the UATD, the Underwater Optical Target Detection Intelligent Algorithm Competition 2021 Dataset (URPC), and SCTD datasets show that DA-YOLOV7 exhibits outstanding performance, with mAP@0.5 scores reaching 89.4%, 89.9%, and 99.15%, respectively. In addition, the model maintains real-time speed while having superior accuracy and recall rates compared to existing mainstream target recognition models. These findings establish the superiority of DA-YOLOV7 in sonar image analysis tasks.

Keywords: deep learning; underwater images; underwater target recognition; sonar images; improved YOLO

Citation: Chen, Z.; Xie, G.; Deng, X.; Peng, J.; Qiu, H. DA-YOLOv7: A Deep Learning-Driven High-Performance Underwater Sonar Image Target Recognition Model. *J. Mar. Sci. Eng.* **2024**, *12*, 1606. https://doi.org/10.3390/jmse12091606

Academic Editors: Yan-Tsung Peng, Wenqi Ren, Jingchun Zhou and Qiuping Jiang

Received: 6 August 2024
Revised: 7 September 2024
Accepted: 7 September 2024
Published: 10 September 2024

1. Introduction

In underwater target detection, there is an increasing demand for high-precision recognition in marine resource development, underwater construction, and marine ecological monitoring. Sonar image target identification plays a crucial role [1–4]. However, traditional image recognition algorithms face challenges due to the complex underwater environment, low-resolution sonar image data, and small sample sizes, which result in difficulties in achieving accurate recognition. Therefore, there is a need to develop more effective methods to improve the performance of sonar image target recognition.

This research aims to tackle these challenges by leveraging deep learning techniques. Specifically, we strive to build a high-performance underwater sonar image target recognition model. This model should be able to handle the complexities of the underwater environment, enhance the accuracy of target recognition, and solve the problem of limited sample sizes. The novelty of this research lies in leveraging deep learning techniques to build a high-performance underwater sonar image target recognition model, namely the Dual Attention Mechanism YOLOv7 model (DA-YOLOv7). This model incorporates new modules such as the Omni-Directional Convolution Channel Prior Convolutional Attention Efficient Layer Aggregation Network (OA-ELAN), Spatial Pyramid Pooling Channel Shuffling and Pixel-level Convolution Bilateral-branch Transformer (SPPCSPCBiFormer), and Ghost-Shuffle Convolution Enhanced Layer Aggregation Network-High performance (G-ELAN-H) to enhance the model's ability to handle the complexities of the underwater environment, improve the accuracy of target recognition, and address the issue of limited sample sizes. By doing so, we hope to significantly contribute to underwater target detection and provide more reliable and efficient solutions for various applications.

Inherent in sonar imagery lies its origin in imaging sonars. When operating as an active sonar system, the process unfolds through the following steps: (I) The sonar system initiates the emission of sound waves; (II) these waves traverse through water, bouncing off underwater targets and returning; (III) the reflected echoes retrace their path back to the sonar system; and (IV) image formation ensues from the sophisticated processing of these echoes. The imaging procedure is susceptible to medium effects. Due to the complexity and inherent uncertainty of the underwater environment, echo signals often encounter challenges such as attenuation and distortion, resulting in lower contrast, reduced resolution, blurred target boundaries, and scarcity of discernible features in the generated sonar images [5–7].

Traditional sonar image target identification methodologies predominantly employ pixel-based features, grayscale values, or prior assumptions about the targets [8–12], often resulting in limited accuracy. Recently, inspired by the exceptional performance of deep convolutional neural networks (DCNNs) in optical image object detection [13–16], researchers have extensively investigated the application of deep learning in enhancing sonar image recognition. For instance, Fan and colleagues [17] designed a 32-layer deep residual network, substituting the Residual Network (Resnet50/101) in the Mask Regions with Convolutional Neural Network features (R-CNN) to enhance detection efficiency while minimizing trainable parameters, with implications for real-time operations and embedded systems. Zhu and co-authors [18] advanced this by integrating the Swin Transformer and Deformable Convolutional Networks (DCN) to create a Swin Transformer Based Anchor-Free Network (STAFNet). This no-anchor detection model surpasses conventional CNN-based solutions like Faster R-CNN and Fully Convolutional One-Stage Object Detection (FCOS) in detecting victims, vessels, and aircraft within their forward-facing sonar dataset. Zhou et al. [19] enhanced the detection and recognition of underwater biological targets in the Underwater Optical Target Detection Intelligent Algorithm Competition 2021 Dataset (URPC) through the fusion of image enhancement techniques, expanded Visual Geometry Group 16-layer network (VGG16) feature extraction, and a Faster R-CNN incorporating feature maps. Chen and collaborators [20] introduced IMA (Invert Multi-Class AdaBoost), a weighting scheme based on sample distribution, to mitigate noise-induced degradation in detection accuracy. Qiao and his team [21] developed a real-time and precise classifier for underwater targets, utilizing a combination of Local Wavelet Acoustic Pattern (LWAP) and Multilayer Perceptron (MLP) networks to tackle the complexities of underwater target classification. While these methods leverage CNNs to extract features, cascade convolutional layers, pool dimensions, and classify them through fully connected layers, they still exhibit room for improvement in accuracy when confronted with intricate sonar imagery.

Additionally, some scholars have adopted the YOLO (You Only Look Once) framework, reframing the sonar image target recognition problem as a regression task that directly predicts target locations and categories, optimizing recognition speed and precision. Notable examples include the work of [22,23], which integrated YOLOv3's principles by incorporating feature pyramids for multi-scale feature aggregation. Fan and his team [24] built upon the Adaptive Spatial Feature Fusion (ASFF) concept [25] to refine the YOLOv4 backbone, enhancing the feature fusion capabilities. Zhang et al. [26] further enhanced the YOLOv5 backbone, enhancing detection speed. Cheng et al. [27] studied underwater target recognition in the context of small datasets, proposing a new approach that combines diffusion models with YOLOv7. Zheng [28] improved YOLOv8 by introducing the Scale and Channel Efficient Module Attention (ScEMA) module, enhancing the model's sensitivity to small targets and objects across various scales. Despite the algorithm's advantages in speed, YOLO has been found to occasionally miss detections or produce false positives, particularly in complex environments and with limited datasets, raising concerns about its stability.

Traditional image recognition algorithms have a relatively complex process to achieve accurate recognition when dealing with low-resolution sonar image data and small samples. In addition, the existing deep learning-based models still have room for improvement in accuracy when handling complex sonar images. For example, the YOLO framework has problems with omissions and false detections in complex environments and limited datasets and lacks stability. Meanwhile, with the continuous advancement in technology, although YOLOv10 shows an excellent performance in the field of optical images, in the field of sonar images, because underwater sonar targets are usually small in scale, YOLOv7 has more advantages due to its excellent recognition ability for small targets. However, the insufficiency of available public sonar image datasets severely limits the application of deep learning models in this field. To address these challenges, the researchers of this study have decided to make improvements based on YOLOv7 and propose to use DA-YOLOv7 to solve these problems.

Our approach addresses the drawbacks of low-resolution sonar imagery, unclear target features, and limited sample availability by introducing the Dual Attention Mechanism YOLOv7 model, abbreviated as DA-YOLOv7. To address the drop in accuracy in complex environments, we develop the OA-ELAN module, integrating Omni-Directional Convolution (ODConv) and Channel Prior Convolutional Attention (CPCA) attention mechanisms, thereby enhancing the model's capacity for capturing crucial local features and improving the recognition of object shapes and edges. Focusing on the intricacy of sonar image targets, we devise the SPPCSPCBiFormer and G-ELAN-H modules, leveraging the ability of the Transformer to handle long-range dependencies. These innovations enhance the model's adaptability to multi-scale targets and reduce computational demands while improving the detection accuracy for small and dense targets. Transfer learning is employed to counteract the scarcity of sonar image samples. We put the data from the diverse Underwater Acoustic Target Detection Dataset (UATD) [29] into the DA-YOLOv7 model for pre-training. During this process, the model learns to extract features and make predictions based on these data. After the training, the pre-trained weights optimized for the UATD dataset are obtained. The pre-trained model can be used for transfer learning. In this case, fine-tuning the pre-trained weights on the smaller Common Sonar Target Detection Dataset (SCTD) [30] can alleviate the overfitting issues typically associated with small datasets. To verify the effectiveness of our proposed method, we conducted rigorous comparative evaluations on various real-world sonar image datasets, including UATD, SCTD, and URPC [31].

To conclude, the core innovations of this paper are embodied in the following key contributions:

- The development of the DA-YOLOv7 model represents a significant advancement, striking a balance between computational efficiency and enhanced feature extraction capabilities. By systematically refining YOLOv7's modules and incorporating innovative elements such as the OA-ELAN, SPPCSPCBIFormer, and G-ELAN-H units, the model not only fortifies its ability to discern crucial information but also streamlines multi-scale target processing and integrates long-range dependencies seamlessly. These enhancements collectively foster enhanced generalization, diversification, and robustness within the overall architecture of the model.
- In response to the lack of datasets encountered in sonar image target recognition tasks, this investigation employs a transfer learning training approach. DA-YOLOv7

initiates by acquiring pre-trained weights through an extensive pretraining phase on the UATD dataset. These pre-trained weights are then strategically employed to refine the model's training on the smaller SCTD dataset, thereby effectively addressing the common issue of diminished recognition accuracy due to the scarcity of data in the small datasets.

- Our analysis meticulously investigates its performance across various scenarios to strengthen the credibility of YOLOv7's enhanced capabilities for underwater sonar image target recognition. Our proposed method includes rigorous testing on low-resolution images sourced from the UATD dataset and color images from the URPC dataset, showcasing its dependable and versatile nature in different imaging circumstances.

The structure of the remainder of this paper is as follows: Section 2 mainly introduces YOLOv7 and the various modules for its improvement, including OA-ELAN, SPPCSPCBiFormer, G-ELAN-H, etc. The improvements in these modules aim to enhance the model's performance when handling the underwater sonar image target recognition task. Section 3 elaborates on the structure and improvements in the DA-YOLOv7 network. Through the upgrades of multiple modules, DA-YOLOv7 is committed to addressing the existing problems in YOLOv7 in underwater sonar image target recognition and enhancing the performance and adaptability of the model. Section 4 is dedicated to the comparative analysis of DA-YOLOv7 with leading sonar image recognition technologies, presenting the results on multiple real datasets. The summary and conclusion of our investigation results are presented in Section 5.

2. Related Works

We selected YOLOv7 for our research because it has shown promising performances in various object detection tasks. However, we modified this model to better suit the underwater sonar image target recognition requirements. The newer versions of YOLO may have their advantages, but YOLOv7 provides a solid foundation that allows us to make targeted improvements to address the unique challenges in this domain. Our modifications include adding the OA-ELAN, SPPCSPCBiFormer, and G-ELAN-H modules to enhance the model's feature extraction, target recognition, and generalization capabilities in the underwater context.

2.1. YOLOv7

Figure 1 depicts the network structure diagram of YOLOv7, encompassing the input layer, backbone, head, and prediction layer. The adaptive bounding box calculation approach is employed in the input layer to ensure that the input color image is uniformly scaled to the 640 $\times$ 640 size specification. The backbone comprises the Convolutional Block with Convolution-Batch Normalization-SiLU activation function module (CBS), the Efficient Layer Aggregation Network module (ELAN), and the Multi-scale Layer (MP). The input image undergoes 3 $\times$ 3 convolutions with strides of 1 and then with strides of 2 successively to compress the spatial dimension and increase the number of channels. The ELAN module consists of multiple CBSs, which enhances feature extraction by enlarging the receptive field. The MP layer is accountable for adjusting the channel ratio, among which MP1 utilizes max pooling to reduce the number of channels, and MP2 compresses the space and increases the number of channels via convolution and downsampling. This design enables the ELAN and MP layers to be alternately reused multiple times, progressively expanding the receptive field and enriching the feature expression. Eventually, the backbone constructs a multi-scale feature pyramid, and these feature maps are passed to different prediction heads, each focusing on detecting a specific target size and generating the corresponding bounding box, category probability, and confidence through the convolutional layer.

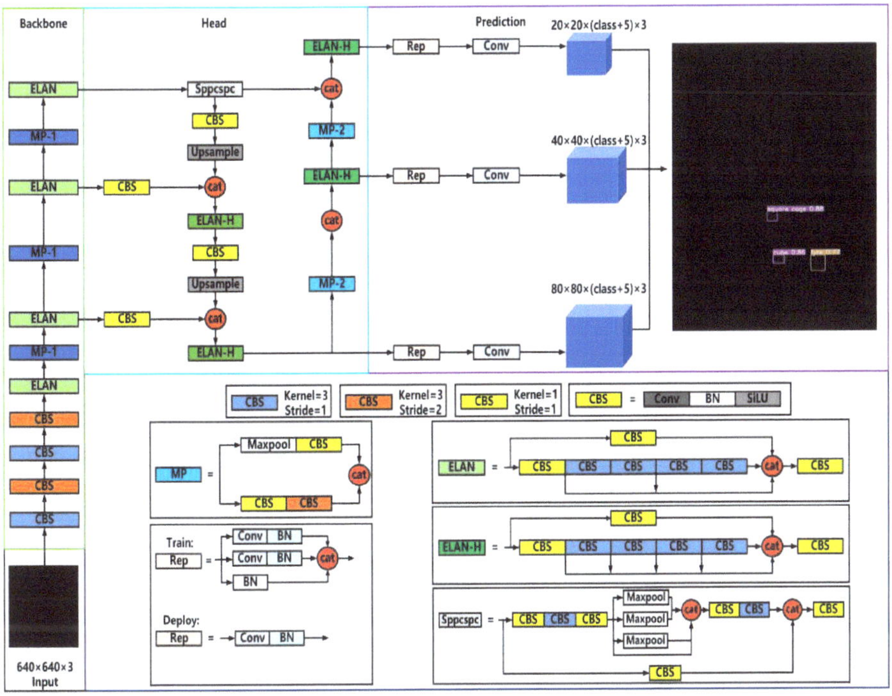

Figure 1. Structure of the YOLOv7.

2.2. OA-ELAN

The effect of YOLOv7 in processing optical images with high contrast and apparent target features is exceptionally excellent. However, problems of false recognition and missed recognition are prone to occur when processing sonar images with low contrast and blurred target features. For this reason, we designed a new OA-ELAN module. Specifically, we replaced the ordinary convolution in the CBS module after the cat operation in the original ELAN module with the ODConv module and incorporated the innovative CPCA attention mechanism.

This change is mainly reflected in the following two aspects: First, in the CBS module after the cat operation in the ELAN module, we utilized the advanced ODConv module to replace the traditional convolution operation. The ODConv module, through its parallel strategy and the combination of a multi-attention mechanism, can learn a more abundant and flexible four-dimensional convolution kernel space, significantly enhancing the model's feature extraction ability, especially in dealing with small targets. Secondly, we introduced a brand-new CPCA attention mechanism. Through its unique design, the CPCA mechanism can flexibly project attention among different channels and regions, enabling the model to precisely focus on crucial single-channel information and deeply understand and ingeniously utilize the inherent interaction relationships between the different channels, further optimizing the feature representation. Our approach has greatly enhanced the accuracy of target recognition and the stability of the model. Especially when facing the complex and changeable background of sonar images, it plays a significant role in effectively reducing false recognitions and missed recognitions.

2.2.1. ODConv

To solve the problems of false recognition, missed recognition, and low recognition accuracy, the limitations of dealing with multi-scale targets, being interfered with by background noise, inaccurate target positioning, and poor performance in the complex and changeable underwater environment existing in the object recognition of underwater sonar images by YOLOv7, we newly added the convolutional operation method of ODConv (Figure 2). ODConv can divide the input signal into high-frequency and low-frequency parts and, through processing with different convolutional kernels, it can better capture the local details and global information of the image, enhance the model's understanding and processing ability for complex images, and improve the recognition accuracy of the targets; it can enable the model to learn different features, especially for small target recognition, and the accurate detection of underwater sonar targets of different scales; its anti-noise ability can filter out background noise by separating high- and low-frequency information, allowing the model to focus on the target itself and reducing the occurrence of false recognition and missed recognition; the depth understanding ability of ODConv helps the model understand the depth differences of the objects and improves the accuracy of target positioning, further improving the recognition performance; in addition, ODConv has solid environmental adaptability and flexibility, can maintain a good performance in different underwater environments, enhance the robustness of object recognition, and ensure the stable operation of the model.

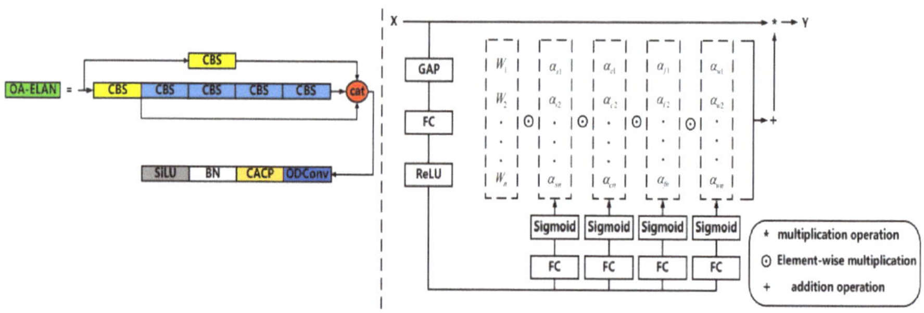

Figure 2. (**left**): OA-ELAN structure diagram, (**right**): ODConv Structure diagram.

2.2.2. CPCA Attention Mechanism

The Channel Prior Convolutional Attention Module is depicted in Figure 3, which sequentially undertakes channel and spatial attention. With an intermediate feature map, $F \in R^{C \times H \times W}$, provided as the input, the channel attention module (CA) initially infers a 1D channel attention map, $M_c \in R^{C \times 1 \times 1}$. Following the procedure, the operation of element-wise multiplication between M_c and input feature, F yields channel attention values broadcast along the spatial dimensions to generate a refined feature, $F_c \in R^{C \times H \times W}$, enriched with channel-specific focus. Subsequently, the spatial attention module (SA) applies its processing on F_c to yield a three-dimensional spatial attention map, $M_s \in R^{C \times H \times W}$. The final output feature, $\hat{F} \in R^{C \times H \times W}$, is computed by the element-wise multiplication of M_s with F_c, where C signifies the number of channels, H represents the height, and W denotes the width. In summary, the entire attention mechanism is encapsulated within the following formulaic description:

$$F_c = CA(F) \otimes F \tag{1}$$

$$\hat{F} = SA(F_c) \otimes F_c \tag{2}$$

where $\otimes$ means the element-by-element multiplication.

The channel attention module is central in generating a channel-wise attention map to decipher the complex interdependencies within feature channels. Employing average and max pooling operations effectively consolidates the feature maps' spatial context, thereby generating two unique spatial context descriptors. These descriptors are then processed through a shared MLP, characterized by a single hidden layer of fixed dimension, $R^{c/r\times 1\times 1}$, with r denoting the reduction ratio to ensure efficient parameter utilization. The computation of the channel attention map is completed through the integration of MLP outputs using element-wise summation, its systematic process being mathematically formalized as follows:

$$CA(F) = \sigma(MLP(AvgPool(F)) + MLP(MaxPool(F))) \tag{3}$$

where σ represents the sigmoid function.

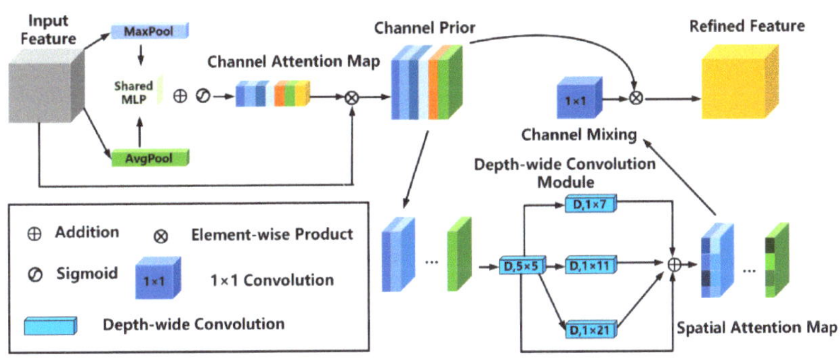

Figure 3. The CPCA attention mechanism.

Spatial attention maps are generated by a process that involves extracting the spatial relationships facilitated by the deep convolution layers that simultaneously preserve inter-channel correlations and capture intricate spatial dependencies. A multi-scale architecture is adopted to optimize this, allowing for convolution operations to effectively discern spatial relationships without compromising computational efficiency. The spatial attention module concludes with a 1×1 convolutional layer, which mixes channels and produces a more refined attention map. The mathematical description of the spatial attention calculation proceeds as follows:

$$SA(F) = Conv_{1\times 1}(\sum_{i=0}^{3} Branch_i(DwConv(F))) \tag{4}$$

The model architecture incorporates Depthwise Convolution ($DwConv$), a deep convolutional component, alongside branches designated as $Branch_i$ and $i \in \{0,1,2,3\}$, collectively forming branch *i-th*. Notably, $Branch_0$ constitutes a direct connection path, functioning as a shortcut that omits any intermediate transformations or processing, allowing the input to flow uninterrupted to the output. $Conv_{1\times 1}$ is a 1×1 convolution. This design choice contributes to the overall architectural integrity while maintaining computational efficiency.

In response to the challenges faced by YOLOv7 during underwater sonar image object recognition, such as limited feature extraction, vulnerability to noise and interference, and inadequate adaptation to diverse target dimensions, we employed a series of strategic improvements. Primarily, we replaced the ELAN module in the backbone with the advanced OA-ELAN, enhancing its structural robustness. The introduction of the ODConv module within the Contextual CBS bolstered the model's capacity to detect objects across multiple scales and locations, reducing false positives and missing recognitions in complex scenarios with multi-scale objects. It facilitated the dynamic capture of spatial and channel-specific details thus optimizing feature representation, particularly for precise small target identification.

The OA-ELAN module is a novel design that replaces the ordinary convolution in the original ELAN module with the ODConv module and incorporates the CPCA attention mechanism. This innovation enhances the model's feature extraction ability, especially for small targets. It reduces false and missed recognitions, a significant improvement over the traditional methods that struggle with the low contrast and blurred target features of sonar images.

The CPCA attention mechanism further improves the feature expression ability of the model, facilitating the extraction of critical features, emphasizing target significance, and enhancing the model's understanding of underwater sonar imagery. Our method improved recognition and recognition accuracy, reduced noise and interference resilience, and enhanced robustness in complex underwater environments. Additionally, the mechanism adaptively adjusted attention weights based on target size and shape, enabling more effective recognition across a spectrum of target dimensions. The model's transfer learning and generalization capabilities were significantly enhanced by fostering general feature representations.

Notably, these enhancements were achieved without compromising computational efficiency, as both the ODConv and CPCA mechanisms maintained high computational effectiveness, ensuring the model's runtime speed. Consequently, these modifications substantially improved YOLOv7's underwater sonar image object recognition performance, particularly in tackling complex backgrounds, noise, and small target recognition tasks.

2.3. SPPCSPCBiFormer Module

To better recognize and understand the target in complex scenes, we have incorporated the SPPCSPCBiFormer module (Figure 4). This module is integrated with the Spatial Pyramid Pooling Channel Shuffling and Pixel-level Convolution (SPPCSPC) module and the Bilateral-branch Transformer (BiFormer) module.

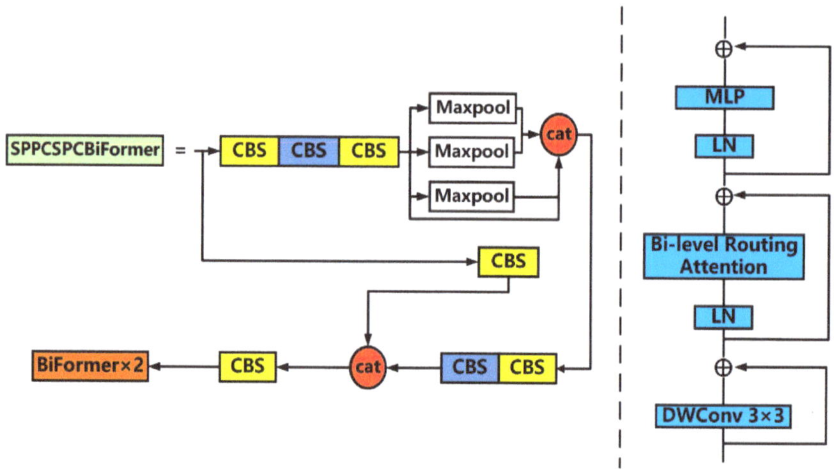

Figure 4. Left: SPPCSPC structure, **Right**: BiFormer structure.

Among them, the Spatial Pyramid Pooling (SPP) in the SPPCSPC module generates multi-scale feature maps by conducting pooling operations of different scales on the input image, thereby effectively handling the variations in the input size and enhancing the invariance in the model to image scaling, rotation, and other transformations; Channel Shuffling and Pixel-level Convolution (CSPC) incorporates channel shuffling to promote the interaction between channels and pixel-level convolution to extract local features, which contributes to improving the model's ability to represent features of high-dimensional data.

SPPCSPCBiFormer not only inherits the advantage of the SPPCSPC module in its ability to better understand the diversity and complexity of the target in complex scenes but also integrates the strength of the self-attention mechanism of the BiFormer module in understanding the complex relationships between targets, further enriching the feature representation and enabling the model to understand the input data from multiple perspectives and levels.

This combination of multiple modules boosts the model's generalization ability, enabling it to adapt to targets of various scales and handle complex dependency relationships. It integrates multi-scale feature extraction, long-distance dependency capture, and efficient feature fusion, significantly enhancing the model's ability to recognize and understand the target.

As illustrated in Figure 4, the BiFormer architecture commences with a Depthwise Convolution, which inherently encodes spatial relationships. Following this, the model employs the Bi-directional Relationship Aggregation (BRA) module, followed by a two-layer MLP with an expansion rate of e, the latter of which is dedicated to modeling cross-position relationships and generating per-position embeddings, thereby enriching the feature representation.

A feedforward neural network layer is deployed after the multi-head attention layer to enhance the expressive power of the extracted features. Residual connections are strategically employed to mitigate the issue of vanishing gradients and optimize the model's training efficiency.

The BRA module is the core part of the BiFormer module. It processes the input features through multiple parallel attention heads and each attention head can learn different feature representations, thereby improving the flexibility and expression ability of the model. The steps are as follows:

Region partitioning and input projection: Given an input feature map $X \in R^{H\times W\times C}$, we first partition it into $S \times S$ non-overlapping regions, such that each region contains $\frac{HW}{S^2}$ feature vectors. This step is accomplished by reshaping X into $X^R \in R^{S^2\times \frac{HW}{S^2}\times C}$. Then, we use a linear projection to derive the query, key, and value tensors Q, K, $V \in R^{S^2\times \frac{HW}{S^2}\times C}$:

$$Q = W^r W^q, K = X^r W^k, V = X^r W^v \quad (5)$$

where W^q, W^q, $W^v \in R^{C\times C}$ are the projection weights of query, keys, and values.

- First, the regional-level queries and keys Q^r, $K^r \in R^{S^2\times C}$ are derived by applying the average value of each region to Q and K, respectively. Then, we derived the adjacency matrix $A^r \in R^{S^2\times S^2}$ of the region-to-region affinity graph through the matrix multiplication between Q^r and the transpose of K^r as follows:

$$A^r = Q^r (k^r)^T \quad (6)$$

Among them, the semantic relevance of two regions is measured in the adjacency matrix A^r.

The core step that we undertake next is to prune the affinity graph by merely retaining the top-k connections of each region. Specifically, we employ the row-wise *topk* operator to obtain the routing index matrix $I_r \in N^{S^2\times K}$ as follows:

$$I^r = topkIndex(A^r) \quad (7)$$

- Token-level Attention: Our approach harnesses the region-to-region routing index matrix I^r to implement a meticulous token-to-token attention mechanism. Each query token within region i extends its attention to all the key–value pairs that are found within the aggregated routing regions indexed by $I^r_{(i,1)}, I^r_{(i,2)}, \ldots, I^r_{(i,k)}$, representing the union of k regions. The process of attention computation begins with the collection of the key and value tensors, which are fundamental components in this procedure, as follows:

$$K^g = gather(K, I^r), V^g = gather(V, I^r) \quad (8)$$

where $K^g, V^g \in R^{S^2 \times \frac{kHW}{S^2} \times C}$ is the clustered key–value tensor.

We can then focus our attention on the collected key–value pairs:

$$O = Attention(Q, K^g, V^g) + LCE(V) \quad (9)$$

Here, we introduce the local context enhancement terms $LCE(V)$, as shown in [32]. The function $LCE(\cdot)$ is parameterized using a deep convolution, and we set the kernel size to 5.

The SPPCSPCBIFormer module enhances the ability to handle targets of different scales, enabling a more comprehensive understanding of the features of targets in complex scenes, thereby improving recognition accuracy. Regarding long-range dependency capture, the Transformer structure helps handle dense or overlapping targets. In terms of enhancement of the generalization ability, introducing multiple attention mechanisms and Transformer structures enables the model to adapt to the variability of the underwater environment and consistently maintain good performance.

2.4. G-ELAN-H

To overcome the issues of inadequate target recognition accuracy, weak generalization ability, and high computational cost existing in the YOLOv7 model, we substituted some of the Convs in all the ELAN-H modules of YOLOv7 with Ghost-Shuffle Convolution (GSConv), thereby constituting the G-ELAN-H module. As shown in Figure 5, the structure of the G-ELAN-H module reveals its design. In this manner, GSConv can assist the model in learning features more effectively, significantly enhancing the target recognition accuracy, and the recognition effect is particularly notable for small targets or densely arranged targets; it can strengthen the model's processing capability for targets of diverse shapes and sizes and enhance its generalization ability; and it can decrease the computational cost, accelerate the running speed of the model, and achieve faster image processing.

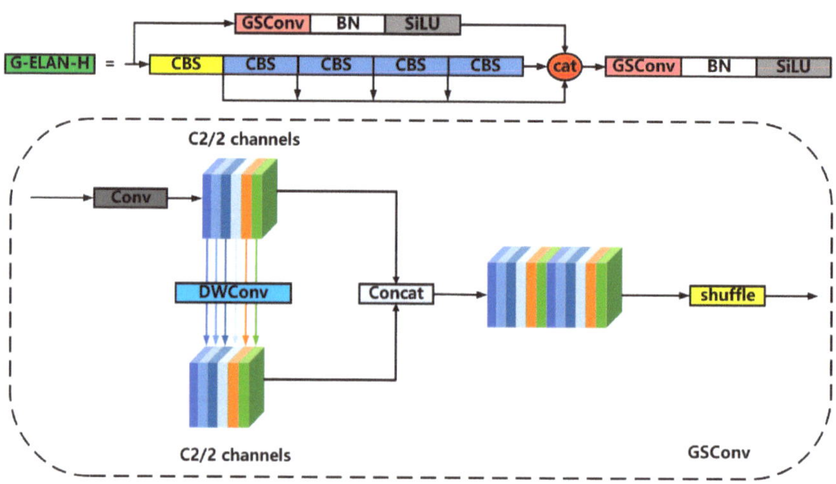

Figure 5. Structure diagram of G-ELAN-H.

3. Proposed Method

3.1. DA-YOLOv7 Network

The DA-YOLOv7 model, as shown in Figure 6, aims to address the problems in underwater sonar image target recognition of YOLOv7 and enhance the performance and adaptability of the model. Through improvements in the multiple modules, it strives to overcome the limitations of YOLOv7 in handling sonar images with low contrast and blurred target features, as well as the issues of insufficient target recognition accuracy, poor generalization ability, and high computational cost.

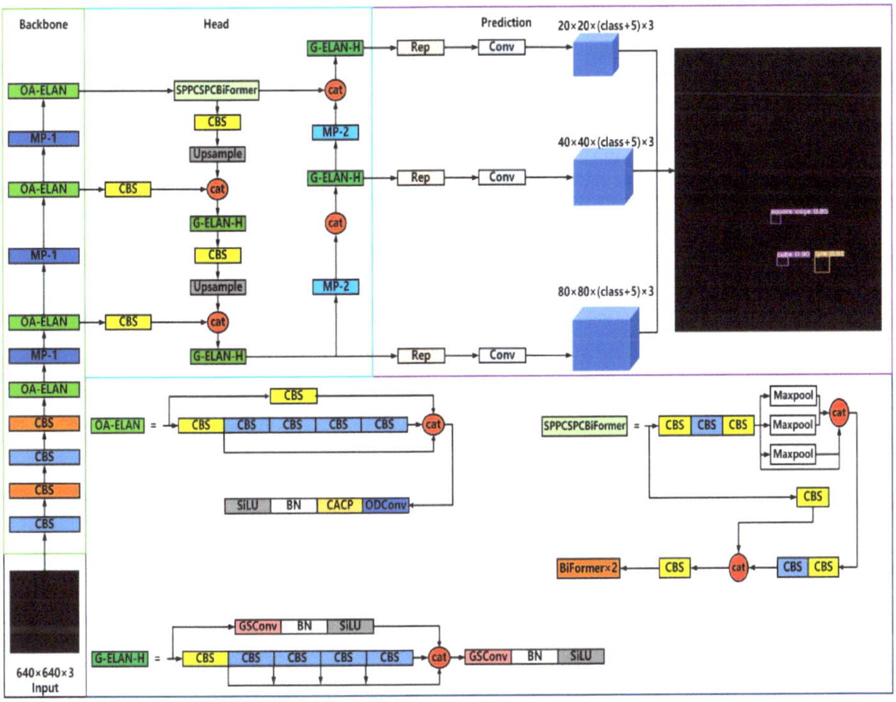

Figure 6. The DA-YOLOv7 network.

In the OA-ELAN module, we made significant modifications. We replaced the ordinary convolution in the CBS module after the cat operation in the original ELAN module with the ODConv module and incorporated the CPCA attention mechanism. This change aims to enhance the model's feature extraction ability, especially for small targets. The ODConv module can better capture the image's local details and global information, reducing the problems of false recognition and missed recognition in sonar images with low contrast and blurred target features. The CPCA attention mechanism helps the model to precisely focus on crucial information, improving the accuracy of target recognition and the stability of the model.

The SPPCSPCBiFormer module integrates the SPPCSPC and the BiFormer modules to improve the model's ability to identify and understand targets in complex scenes. The SPPCSPC module generates multi-scale feature maps and enhances the model's invariance to image transformations. In contrast, the BiFormer module leverages the self-attention mechanism to handle the complex relationships between targets. This integration enables the model to understand the input data from multiple perspectives and levels, enhancing its processing and generalization ability for targets of different scales.

In the G-ELAN-H module, we substituted some of the Convs in all the ELAN-H modules of YOLOv7 with Ghost-Shuffle Convolution (GSConv). This modification helps the model learn features more effectively, significantly enhancing the target recognition accuracy, especially for small or densely arranged targets. It also strengthens the model's processing capability for targets of diverse shapes and sizes, enhances its generalization ability, reduces the computational cost, and speeds up the running speed of the model.

These comprehensive improvements enable DA-YOLOv7 to exhibit extremely high accuracy, robustness, and computing speed when detecting small targets, analyzing dense scenes, and coping with changeable environments, significantly enhancing the performance of underwater sonar image target recognition.

3.2. Comparison of Related Work

To present the characteristics and differences of the related works more clearly, Table 1 summarizes and compares the associated works of YOLOv7 and its improved models.

Table 1. Comparison Table of YOLOv7 and its Improved Models.

Related Work	Description
YOLOv7	The network features an input layer for uniform image scaling to 640 × 640, a backbone with CBS, ELAN, and an MP, constructing a multi-scale feature pyramid. The output from the previous stage feeds into various prediction heads for precise object detection.
OA-ELAN	YOLOv7's modifications target low-contrast and blurred sonar images to reduce false and missed detections. The CBS module integrates ODConv, enhancing local and global feature capture, while the CPCA attention mechanism refines feature representation, boosts recognition accuracy, and stabilizes the model.
SPPCSPCBiFormer Module	The system integrates the SPPCSPC and BiFormer modules for enhanced target recognition in complex scenes. The SPPCSPC module boosts feature representation and model invariance to image transformations through multi-scale pooling and channel shuffling. The BiFormer module leverages bidirectional feature aggregation and multi-layer perceptrons to improve multi-scale target handling and scene nderstanding.
G-ELAN-H	To address YOLOv7's accuracy, generalization, and computational efficiency issues, GSConv replaces some convolutions in ELAN-H modules. Our approach enhances feature learning, particularly for small or clustered targets, and improves the model's handling of diverse target shapes and sizes. It also reduces computational demands and accelerates processing speed.
DA-YOLOv7 Network	Enhancements across several modules aim to tackle YOLOv7's underwater sonar image recognition challenges, enhancing model performance and adaptability. The OA-ELAN module strengthens feature extraction for small targets, minimizing false and missed detections. The SPPCSPCBiFormer module boosts multi-scale target recognition in complex scenes. The G-ELAN-H module refines accuracy, improves generalization, reduces computational costs, and speeds up image processing.

It can be seen from the table that YOLOv7 is the basic model, and the subsequent improvement works mainly focus on improving the performance of the model when processing sonar images. The OA-ELAN module enhances the model's ability to capture local features and critical information by introducing the ODConv and CPCA attention mechanisms, reducing misidentification and missed identification. The SPPCSPCBiFormer module integrates the advantages of the SPPCSPC module and the BiFormer module, improving the model's ability to handle multi-scale targets and understand complex scenes. The G-ELAN-H module improves the target recognition accuracy and generalization ability and reduces the computational cost by replacing the convolution operation. The DA-YOLOv7 network integrates these improvements, enhancing the underwater sonar image target recognition task.

4. Results and Discussion

To evaluate the effectiveness of DA-YOLOv7 in natural underwater environments, we used multiple underwater sonar image datasets, such as the lake bottom and shallow water areas of UATD, the diverse biomes of URPC, and the marine test scenarios of SCTD, to achieve comprehensive qualitative and quantitative analysis. We compared DA-YOLOv7 with the current underwater sonar image recognition models through these datasets.

4.1. Experimental Environment

We conducted rigorous experimental evaluations on the UATD, URPC, and SCTD datasets to substantiate the model's effectiveness to verify its recognition capabilities. The experimental setup included a Windows 11 operating environment, with the deep learning computations handled by PyTorch version 1.4.0. The hardware specifications comprised an Intel Core i7 12,700 H processor, 32 gigabytes of Random Access Memory (RAM), and a powerful NVIDIA GeForce GTX 3070Ti graphics processing unit (GPU).

4.2. Experimental Indicators

The assessment criteria were $Precision$, $Recall$, mAP, and FPS using the following formulas:

$$Precision = \frac{TP}{TP + FP} \quad (10)$$

$$Recall = \frac{TP}{TP + FN} \quad (11)$$

Here, TP represents predicting the correct answer, FP stands for mistakenly predicting from other classes to this class, and FN indicates that this category of labels is predicted to be of the other category of labels.

mAP is an abbreviation of average accuracy and an indicator of recognition accuracy in target recognition as follows:

$$AP = \int_0^1 P(r)dr \quad (12)$$

$$mAP = \frac{\sum_{n=1}^{N} AP_n}{N} \quad (13)$$

The following metrics are employed for evaluating the neural network's performance: precision (p), recall rate (r), a function characterized by parameter r (p), and the total number of object categories (n). The average accuracy in target identification, denoted as AP_n, is another critical aspect. The Mean Average Precision (MAP) is assessed using the following two distinct measures: $mAP@0.5$, which imposes a moderate recognition requirement, and $mAP@0.5:0.95$, which imposes a more stringent standard. These four evaluative parameters collectively determine the network's efficacy, and recognition speed is quantified through the measurement of frames per second (FPS).

4.3. UATD Dataset

The study employs the Open-Source Underwater Acoustic Target Recognition (UATD) dataset, featuring over nine thousand images captured utilizing a Tritech Gemini 1200 ik sonar, a recognized standard for MFLS data acquisition. The dataset is characterized by its extensive nature, encompassing raw sonar imagery sourced from various lake and shallow water settings. It serves as a valuable resource, featuring a diverse range of ten target objects, including cubes, spheres, cylinders, mannequins, tires, circular and square cages, metal buckets, aircraft models, and remotely operated vehicles (ROVs), thereby providing a robust empirical basis for research purposes.

4.3.1. Ablation Experiments on the UATD Dataset

We carried out comprehensive tests and ablation studies on each component of DA-YOLOv7 using the UATD dataset to delve into the impact of the modules detailed in Section 2 on the model's performance. As shown in Table 2, the notation "√" indicates the experimental outcomes when the respective module is engaged.

Table 2. Ablation comparison of model performance improvements in the UAATD dataset.

Model	OA-ELAN	SPPCSPCBiFormer	G-ELAN-H	Precision (%)	Recall(%)	mAP@0.5 (%)	mAP@0.5:0.95(%)
YOLOv7				85.7	83.0	81.2	34.4
	√			87.1	84.6	83.6	35.5
	√	√		91.2	88.9	87.2	37.2
	√	√	√	92.8	89.7	89.4	37.8

The original YOLOv7 model was taken as the baseline, with a precision of 85.7%, a recall rate of 83.0%, a mAP@0.5 of 81.2%, and a mAP@0.5:0.95 of 34.4%. When the OA-ELAN module was introduced alone, the precision increased to 87.1%, the recall rate increased to 84.6%, the mAP@0.5 increased to 83.6%, and the mAP@0.5:0.95 increased to 35.5%. This finding indicates that the OA-ELAN module is highly effective in optimizing feature extraction and classification capabilities and improving target detection accuracy under different confidence thresholds.

When both the OA-ELAN and SPPCSPCBiFormer modules were introduced simultaneously, the precision significantly increased to 91.2%, the recall rate increased to 88.9%, the mAP@0.5 increased dramatically to 87.2%, and the mAP@0.5:0.95 increased to 37.2%. This result shows the synergy of the two modules, enhancing the processing of complex features, reducing missed and false detections, and improving the detection performance in a broader range of confidence levels.

When integrating the three modules of OA-ELAN, SPPCSPCBiFormer, and G-ELAN-H, the precision reached as high as 92.8%, the recall rate reached 89.7%, the accuracy of mAP@0.5 significantly increased to 89.4%, and the mAP@0.5:0.95 increased to 37.8%. This finding proves that adding the G-ELAN-H module further improves the model architecture, enabling the model to achieve comprehensive and significant performance improvements across the entire confidence range, with more vital generalization ability and robustness. In conclusion, each module's individual and combined effects significantly improve the model performance.

To comprehensively compare YOLOv7 and our approach, we inspected the confusion matrices and precision-recall (PR) curves of the four models in question. As depicted in Figures 7 and 8, our methodology exhibits superior performance, demonstrating enhanced accuracy and a more balanced recognition capability for target and background classes.

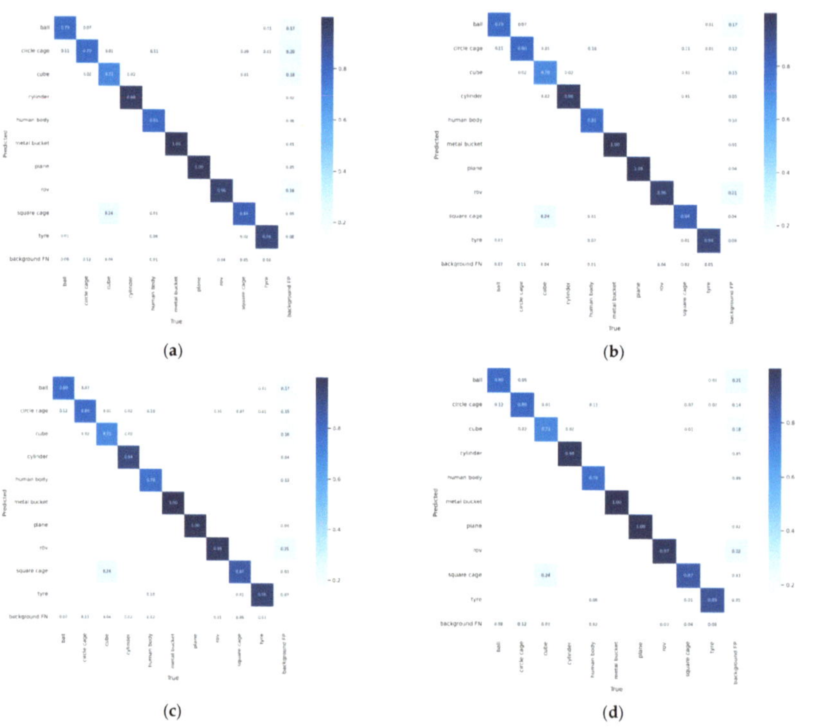

Figure 7. Confusion matrix of the ablation model: (**a**) YOLOv7; (**b**) YOLOv7 + OA-ELAN; (**c**) YOLOv7 + OA-ELAN + SPPCSPCBiFormer; (**d**) DA-YOLOv7.

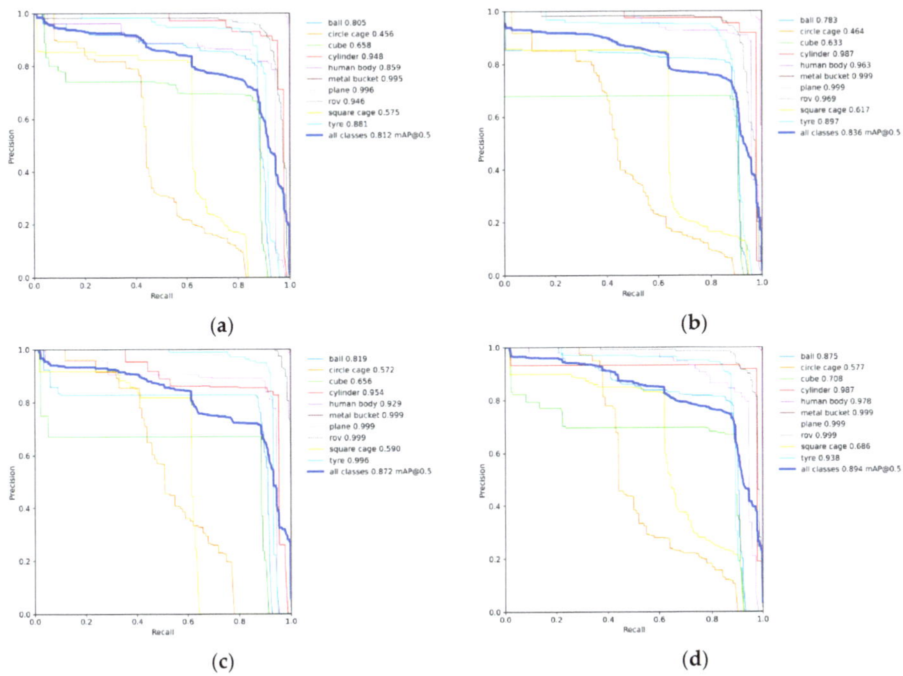

Figure 8. The PR curve: (**a**) YOLOv7; (**b**) YOLOv7 + OA-ELAN; (**c**) YOLOv7 + OA-ELAN + SPPC-SPCBiFormer; (**d**) DA-YOLOv7.

It can be observed from Figure 8 that in Figure 8a, namely YOLOv7, the precision and recall rates of various targets are at the baseline level, indicating that the original YOLOv7 model has a specific performance in handling these targets, but there is still room for improvement. In Figure 8b, namely YOLOv7 + OA-ELAN, there are some significant improvements compared to Figure 8a. For example, the precision of the circle cage has increased from 0.456 to 0.464, and the precision of the cylinder has significantly increased from 0.948 to 0.987, which shows that the OA-ELAN module plays a vital role in enhancing the recognition accuracy of specific targets.

The improvements are more prominent in Figure 8c, namely YOLOv7 + OA-ELAN + SPPCSPCBiFormer. For example, the cube has increased from 0.633 to 0.656, and the precision for the human body has also increased from 0.963 to 0.978. These results indicate that the combined effect of the SPPCSPCBiFormer and OA-ELAN modules has brought significant performance improvements and effectively optimized the recognition ability of complex targets.

Figure 8d, DA-YOLOv7, integrates all the improvement modules and performs excellently in almost all target categories. For instance, the precision of a square cage has increased from 0.617 to 0.686, and the precision of the tire has increased from 0.897 to 0.938. This finding fully demonstrates the synergy of the three modules, OA-ELAN, SPPCSPCBi-Former, and G-ELAN-H, enabling the model to recognize various targets more accurately and comprehensively.

4.3.2. Analysis of UATD Dataset Results

This experiment evaluates the DA-YOLOv7 model's accuracy and recall performance for detecting ten distinct target categories. Figure 8d illustrates the trend of changes in these metrics when employing a forward-looking sonar for recognition, with a mean average precision (mAP) at 0.5, reaching 89.4% for all categories. Moreover, Figure 7d presents a confusion matrix showcasing the DA-YOLOv7's recognition outcomes for various target classes, reinforcing the model's recognition capabilities.

While the model demonstrates strong performance in detecting various targets, it occasionally encounters background noise in forward-looking sonar images, causing the misidentification of certain background regions as targets. Therefore, further investigations into sonar image denoising is deemed essential.

Finally, we trained and tested multiple popular target recognition models along with the original YOLOv7, and the comparative performance of these models is presented in Table 3.

Table 3. Target recognition results of each model in the previsual sonar images.

Model	Backbone	mAP@0.5 (%)	FPS
FasterR-CNN	Resnet	83.9	44.1
FasterR-CNN	Resnet-50	82.9	32.9
FasterR-CNN	Resnet-101	81.8	26.6
YOLOv3	Darknnet-53	80.1	49.8
YOLOv3	MobilenetV2	78.7	93.4
YOLOv5	CSPDarknet-53	81.5	83
YOLOv7	ELAN-Net	85.3	62.11
YOLOv8	CSPDarknet-c2f	85.6	49
CCW-YOLOv5	CSPDarknet-53	85.3	54
DA-YOLOv7	OA-ELAN-Net	89.4	97.09

It can be learned from Table 3 that, in the target recognition results of forward-looking sonar images, different models have their characteristics. In the FasterR-CNN series, the mAP@0.5 value gradually decreases as the backbone network changes, and the frame rate also gradually drops. In YOLOv3, the model with the Darknet-53 backbone network has a higher accuracy than the MobilenetV2 backbone network, but the latter has a better frame rate. For YOLOv5, YOLOv7, and YOLOv8, which adopt different backbone networks, respectively, the mAP@0.5 values vary.

However, our DA-YOLOv7 model has significant advantages. When using OA-ELAN-Net as the backbone network, the model achieves a mAP@0.5 as high as 89.4%, and its accuracy rate is significantly ahead of the other models. At the same time, the frame rate reaches 97.09, and the processing speed is breakneck. Combining the roles of different modules as described before, the OA-ELAN module can capture the critical features of the target more accurately by optimizing feature extraction and classification to improve the accuracy rate. The SPPCSPCBiFormer module enhances the processing of complex features and the utilization of global information, helping the model better understand the target context and overall features and improving accuracy. The G-ELAN-H module improves the model architecture, optimizes the depth and width of the network, and promotes feature fusion. While improving the accuracy rate, it ensures the efficient operation of the model and significantly improves the processing speed. These modules work together to make DA-YOLOv7 have both high accuracy and processing speed, showing excellent comprehensive performance.

As depicted in Figure 9, the value steadily decreases as the number of iterations rises, ultimately attaining convergence after 200 iterations. This stability reflects the optimization process of the model.

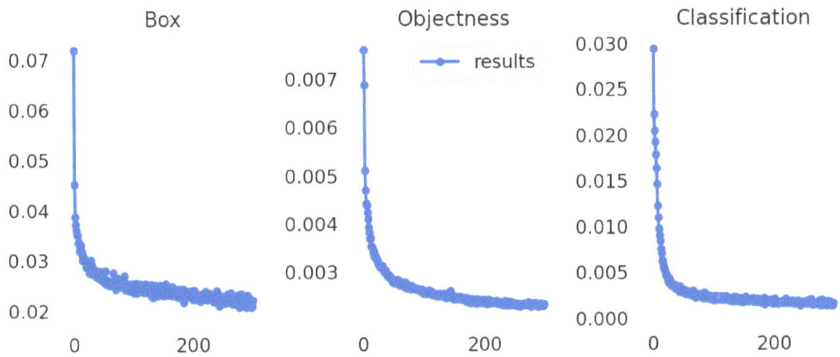

Figure 9. Curve of the change in loss value on the UATD dataset.

To visually illustrate the target recognition performance of the DA-YOLOv7 model developed in this chapter under real-world circumstances, Figure 10 presents the prediction results of various targets in multi-beam forward-looking sonar images extracted from the UATD validation set.

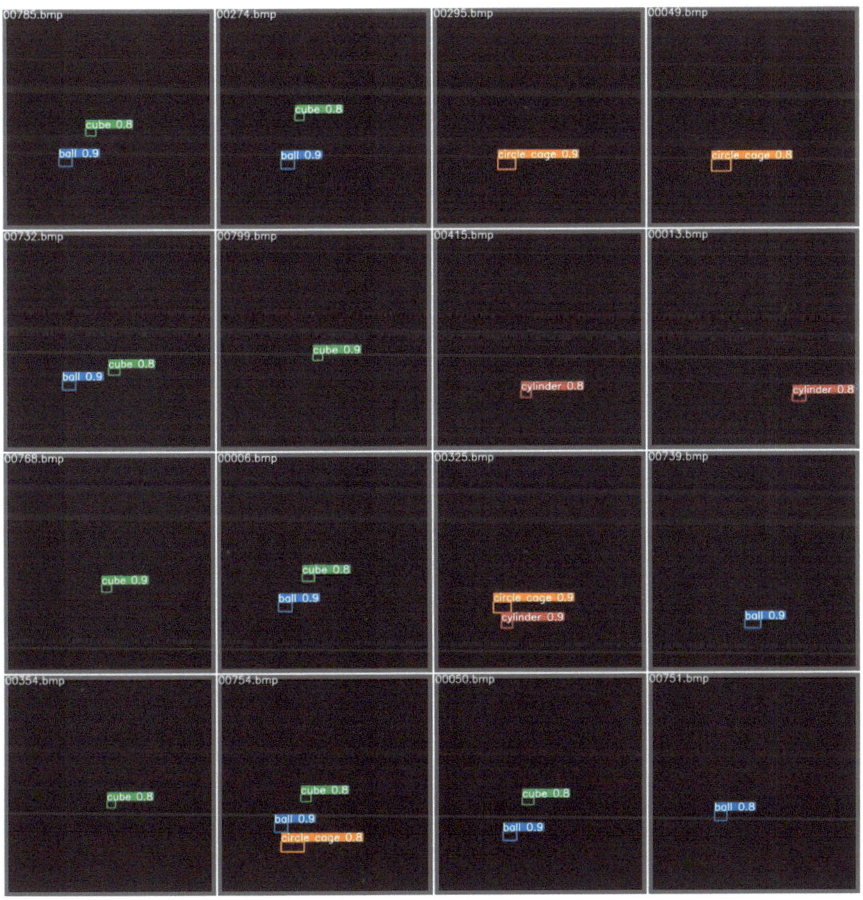

Figure 10. Prediction results of various targets in UATD multi-beam forward-looking sonar images.

Figure 10 shows many multi-beam forward-looking sonar images and their corresponding target annotations. From the figure, the advantages of our model can be observed. The model can not only accurately identify various targets, such as "ball", "cube", "cylinder", etc., but also performs well in complex target combination situations and can still make accurate judgments when multiple targets of the same or different types exist simultaneously. Moreover, it performs stably and consistently in various images. Whether a single target or a complex multi-target scene, it can maintain a high accuracy rate and effectively distinguish easily confused targets. Its strong generalization ability enables it to complete the target recognition task excellently in different multi-beam forward-looking sonar image scenarios.

4.4. SCTD Dataset

We collected an SCTD dataset showing the sonar imaging results of different targets in different underwater maritime trials to conduct image processing and recognition research. These sonar images were filtered and classified, resulting in sonar images of the following three fundamental target categories: human, ship, and airplane. We selected three images of each type for display, as shown in Figure 11.

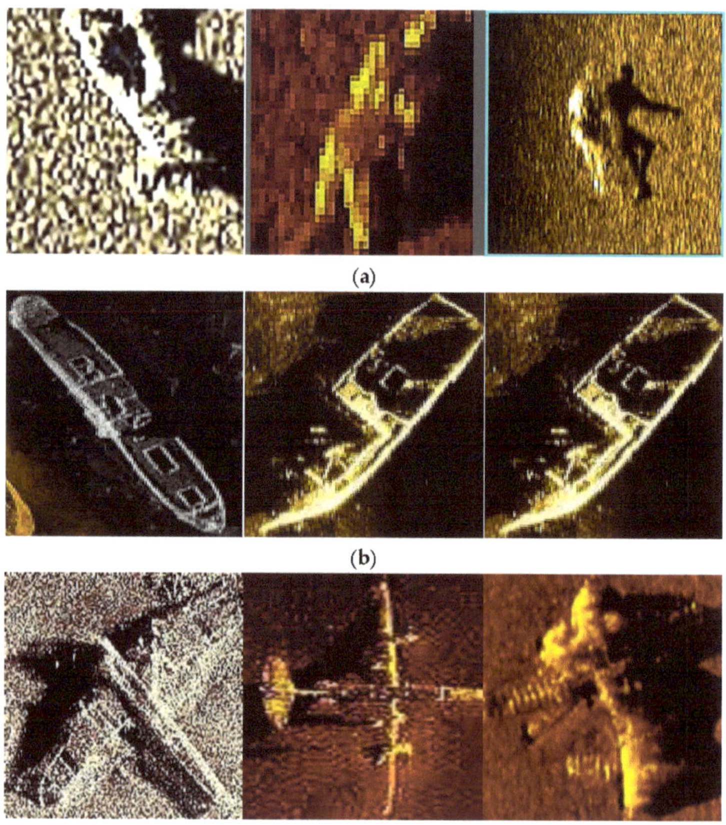

(a)

(b)

(c)

Figure 11. SCTD sonar image dataset: (**a**) human; (**b**) ship; (**c**) aircraft.

The SCTD dataset is categorized into three classes—ships, airplanes, and humans. Numerous uncertainties, such as complex backgrounds, object fragmentation, breakage, and deformation, augment the difficulty of recognition. Each represents one of the three underwater targets. These images shall be utilized as the input of the deep learning model. Through manual annotation, the target images are classified into three categories, respectively. The training set and the validation set are partitioned in a 9:1 ratio.

4.4.1. Training Strategy for the SCTD Dataset

The SCTD dataset presently encompasses a total of 357 images. Owing to the limited number of samples, we adopted a pre-trained model to tackle the problem of small sample datasets, and the flowchart is presented in Figure 12. This experiment aims to demonstrate that, by utilizing a pre-trained model, we can effectively tackle the issue of the limited number of samples in the SCTD dataset and enhance the performance and generalization capability of the model on small sample datasets.

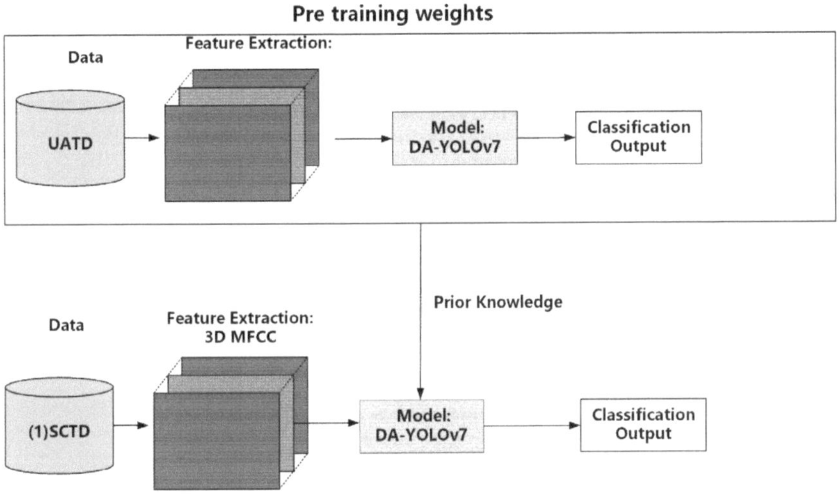

Figure 12. Flowchart of the training strategy for the SCTD dataset.

When dealing with a small sample dataset like SCTD, we adopted an innovative approach of pre-training the DA-YOLOv7 model on the UATD large dataset to obtain pre-trained weights. This approach has many advantages. Firstly, the UATD large dataset is rich and diverse, enabling DA-YOLOv7 to learn extensive and general features and patterns. When these pre-trained weights are used for training on the SCTD small dataset, the model can quickly adapt to the new data, significantly reducing the training time and computational cost. Secondly, the knowledge acquired by DA-YOLOv7 from the UATD dataset can provide valuable prior information for its learning on the SCTD small dataset, helping the model to extract more representative features from the limited data, enhancing its understanding and learning ability of the small dataset, and thereby improving the generalization performance.

Regarding the issue of low accuracy on small datasets, the pre-trained weights play a crucial role. By relying on the general feature representation learned on the UATD dataset, DA-YOLOv7 can more accurately capture the critical information when confronted with the SCTD small dataset, effectively reducing the possibility of overfitting and thereby significantly improving the accuracy. In conclusion, by leveraging the UATD large dataset to pre-train DA-YOLOv7 and then applying it to the training of the SCTD small dataset, an efficient and feasible approach is provided to address the challenges of small sample datasets.

4.4.2. Model Performance Comparison

Table 4 presents the performance comparison results between the proposed model and other outstanding recognition models on the dataset SCTD. The evaluation metrics of this model encompass AP for each category, mAP@0.5, and FPS.

Table 4. Model performance comparison on SCTD.

Model	Aircraft-AP (%)	Human-AP (%)	Ship-AP (%)	mAP@0.5 (%)	FPS
YOLOv4-tiny	88.16	79.35	59.44	75.65	199
YOLOv5I	88.37	85.95	70.64	81.66	51
EfficientDetD0	93.83	84.37	89.62	89.27	28
YOLOX-s	98.86	92.96	86.41	92.72	90
YOLOX-m	99.89	93.53	91.50	94.98	63
SDNET	99.39	93.53	90.74	95.20	138
DA-YOLOv7 (pre training)	100	100	97.00	99.15	125

As indicated in Table 4, compared to other recognition models, this model exhibits higher performance on the sonar dataset SCTD.

The DA-YOLOv7 model has significant advantages when transferred to the SCTD small dataset after pre-training with the UATD large dataset. In terms of performance improvements, after pre-training with the UATD large-scale dataset, the average precision (AP) of the DA-YOLOv7 model for the three categories of aircraft, human, and ship dramatically improves. For example, compared to the model trained only on the SCTD small dataset, aircraft-AP increased from 88.16% to 100%, human-AP increased from 79.35% to 100%, and ship-AP increased from 59.44% to 97.00%, indicating a significant enhancement in the model's ability to recognize various types of targets. At the same time, using a large-capacity UATD dataset for pretraining helps the model learn more extensive visual patterns and features, improving its generalization ability, maintaining extremely high accuracy on the SCTD small dataset, and demonstrating good adaptability to new scenes and targets.

In addition, pretraining also brings a faster convergence speed. Because the model has already learned the basic features of a large amount of data, it can achieve the desired performance faster on the SCTD small dataset, saving training time and computing resources. Moreover, due to the rich diversity of the UATD dataset, the model undergoes a large amount of noise and complex situations in the pretraining stage, making it more resistant to overfitting and able to maintain stable performance on the small-scale SCTD dataset. Although the running speed (FPS) of DA-YOLOv7 is not the fastest (125 FPS), its significant advantage in accuracy achieves a good balance between accuracy and speed. The experimental results demonstrate the novelty and superiority of DA-YOLOv7. Compared to other models, DA-YOLOv7 achieves higher accuracy and faster speed, especially on the SCTD dataset with small sample sizes. The pretraining strategy on the UATD dataset and the transfer learning to the SCTD dataset effectively address the challenge of limited samples, a novel approach in this field. Additionally, the model's performance improvements in mAP@0.5 and recall rate on the SCTD dataset showcase its excellent ability to recognize targets in complex underwater environments.

For applications with extremely high accuracy requirements, the high AP value of DA-YOLOv7 far outweighs its minor disadvantage in speed. In conclusion, through pre-training with the UATD large dataset, DA-YOLOv7 performs exceptionally well on the SCTD small dataset and is an excellent choice for object recognition tasks. Figure 13 shows the improved model's enhanced recognition effect on the SCTD dataset.

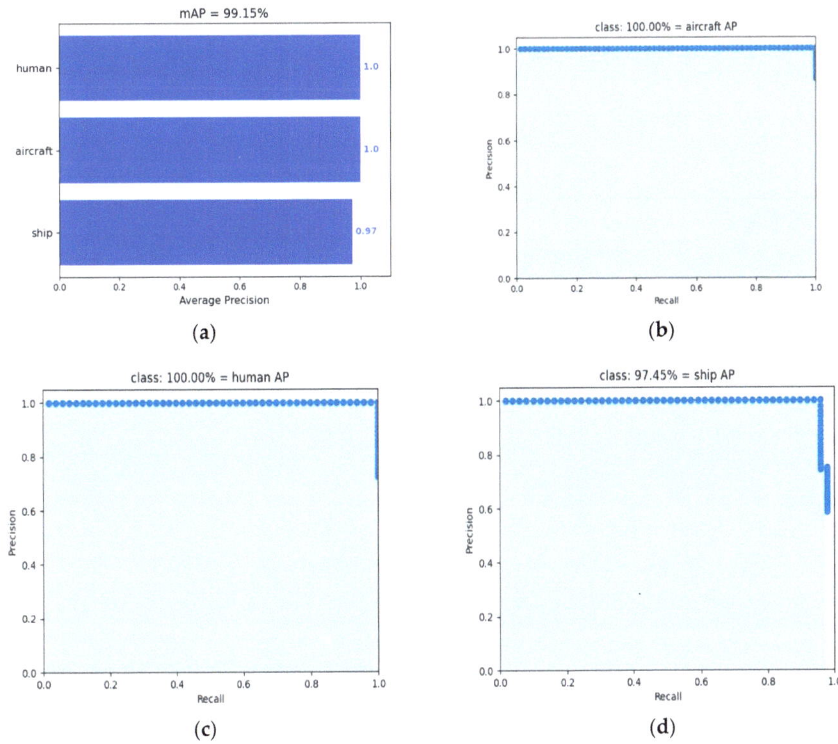

Figure 13. The effect of recognition on the SCTD dataset: (**a**) SCTD mAP Results; (**b**) SCTD aircraft-AP results; (**c**) SCTD human-AP results; (**d**) SCTD ship-AP results.

4.5. Experimental Results and Analysis of the Underwater Optical Target Detection Intelligent Algorithm Competition 2021 Dataset (URPC)

To reinforce the model's superiority and generalizability across diverse scenarios, we utilize the URPC dataset for training and evaluation. The dataset, comprising 5543 images distributed across four classes, urchins, sea cucumbers, scallops, and starfish, providing a comprehensive benchmark. The dataset is divided into a training set (80%) and a testing set (20%), totaling 4434 images for training and 1109 for testing. It captures intricate challenges, including visual occlusions due to underwater organism aggregations, variations in lighting, and motion-induced blurring, accurately reflecting the underwater environment and enhancing the model's adaptability. However, the dataset presents imbalanced category distributions and variable resolutions, posing considerable challenges during training. Figure 14a, a category statistics chart, reveals that sea urchins predominate, followed by scallops and starfish, with sea cucumbers being the least represented. The box plot indicates that the target sizes are relatively consistent, and the regularized target position map highlights the horizontal densification, contrasted with vertical dispersion. The normalized target size map further illustrates a concentration of the target sizes, mainly consisting of smaller objects. A selection of sample images from the URPC dataset is showcased in Figure 14b.

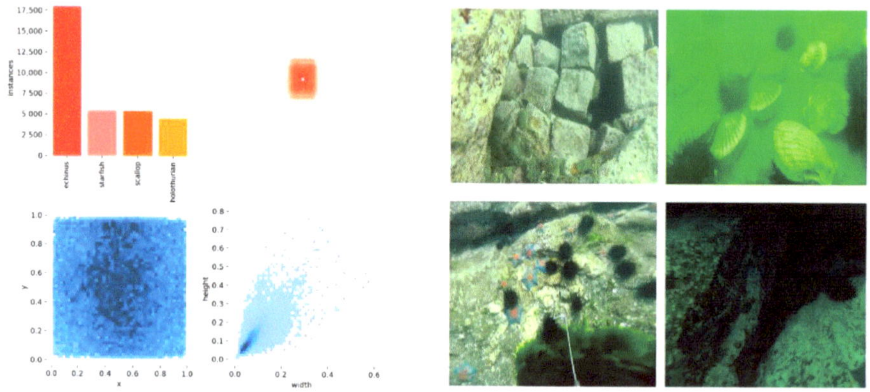

(**a**) (**b**)

Figure 14. The sample information of URPC is as follows: (**a**) Labels: The upper left corner shows the distribution of categories; the upper right corner presents the visualization of all box sizes; the lower left corner indicates the distribution of the box centroid position; the lower right corner depicts the distribution of the box aspect ratio. (**b**) Example images.

Comparative Experiments on the URPC Dataset

To further substantiate the superiority of our proposed DA-YOLOv7 model, we conducted comparative analyses with renowned object recognition models, including SSD, RetinaNet, Faster-RCNN, YOLOX, YOLOv5s, YOLOv6, YOLOv7, YOLOv8n, and YOLOv8s. Both training and testing were conducted using the URPC dataset, with performance metrics such as accuracy, recall rate, and mAP@0.5 being evaluated. The comparison outcomes are presented in the table below.

It can be seen from Table 5 that on the URPC dataset, the performance of each target recognition model varies. The indicators of traditional models such as SSD, RetinaNet, and Faster-RCNN are relatively low. Among the YOLO series, YOLOX performs poorly and, although YOLOv5s, YOLOv6, YOLOv7, YOLOv8n, and YOLOv8s gradually improve in performance, there is still a significant gap compared to our DA-YOLOv7 model.

Table 5. Performance comparison of object recognition models on the URPC dataset.

Model	Precision (%)	Recall (%)	mAp@0.5 (%)
SSD	74.2	68.7	75.4
RetinaNet	75.2	66.8	73.4
Faster-RCNN	78.8	73.1	76.1
YOLOX	73.3	64.1	69.5
YOLOv5s	78.9	75.3	80.8
YOLOv6	81.7	79.1	80.4
YOLOv7	82.9	78.3	83.2
YOLOv8n	83.8	79.2	85.7
YOLOv8s	86.4	82.1	87.1
DA-YOLOv7	90.0	84.4	89.9

Our DA-YOLOv7 model has extremely remarkable advantages. Its precision is as high as 90.0%, far exceeding other models, so it can identify targets more accurately and reduce misjudgments. The recall rate is 84.4%, indicating that it can effectively capture more real targets and reduce the situation of missed detections. The mAp@0.5 reaches 89.9%, demonstrating its stable and excellent detection performance under different thresholds. The DA-YOLOv7 model can perform outstandingly because of its unique architectural design and elaborate optimization strategy. It adopts advanced feature extraction and fusion techniques, extracting key and discriminative features from complex data, thereby achieving precise positioning and recognition of targets. At the same time, its efficient training algorithm and parameter adjustment enable the model to maintain excellent performance and generalization ability when facing various complex scenes and target changes. Overall, the DA-YOLOv7 model has shown a decisive advantage and excellent comprehensive performance, far exceeding other models on the URPC dataset.

Figure 15 vividly showcases the recognition performance of the updated model in four distinct scenarios. It demonstrates the model's remarkable capacity for precise recognition even under arduous underwater conditions. Whether dealing with sparse or dense targets, the model exhibits its superiority. In sparse target situations, it accurately identifies and locates individual targets. In dense target scenarios, it can distinguish multiple targets despite the complexity.

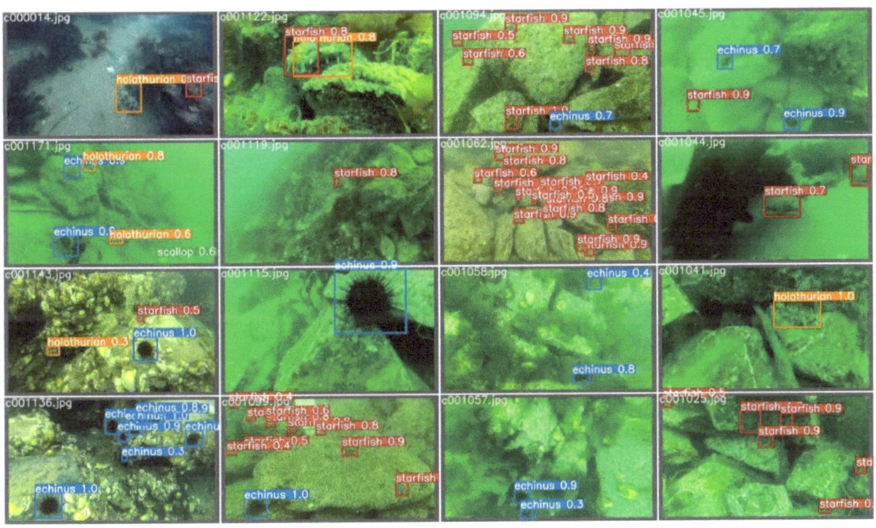

Figure 15. Recognition results in multiple underwater scenes.

The performance of the updated model in these four scenarios highlights its advanced design and training. This advanced design and training hold great promise for various applications in underwater exploration, marine biology research, and underwater robotics. The model's ability to handle different underwater conditions with precision and reliability makes it a valuable tool for these fields, enabling more accurate exploration, better understanding of marine life, and improved performance of underwater robots.

The DA-YOLOv7 model successfully identified the targets in diverse underwater scenes, manifesting its robust recognition performance. As depicted in Figure 16, with the augmentation in the number of iterations, the values exhibit a stable descending trend and eventual stabilization, attaining convergence after 200 iterations.

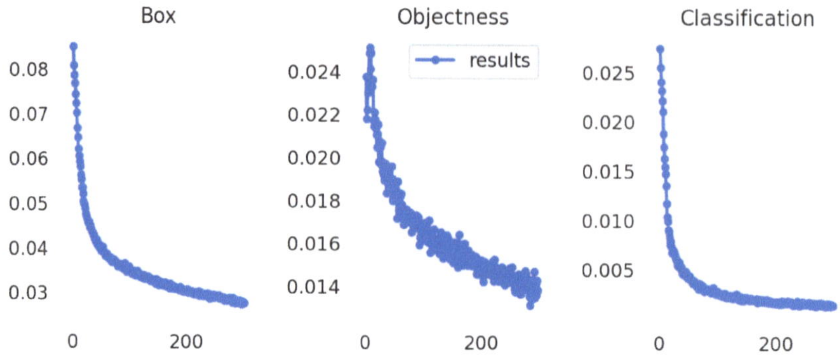

Figure 16. RCurve of loss value changes on the UPRC dataset.

5. Conclusions

This study proposed an improved DA-YOLOv7 model based on YOLOv7 to tackle the challenges in target recognition within complex underwater environments and the issue of low recognition accuracy resulting from small samples of underwater sonar images. The following significant results were obtained:

1. With innovative improvements in YOLOv7, the OA-ELAN module, the SPPCSPCBiFormer module, and the G-ELAN-H module were introduced, significantly enhancing the model's performance. The OA-ELAN module augments the ability to extract local features and capture critical information, thereby improving the recognition accuracy of features such as object shapes and edges; the SPPCSPCBiFormer module enhances the ability to capture long-range correlations and contextual information in the input feature map, enhancing the processing and generalization ability of multi-scale targets; the G-ELAN-H module boosts the model's adaptability to various target sizes and shapes, further enhancing the generalization performance.
2. For the problem of small samples of underwater sonar images, pre-training and transfer learning methods were adopted. The large-scale UATD dataset was used to pre-train DA-YOLOv7 to obtain pre-trained weights, which were then applied to the training of the small sample SCTD dataset, effectively avoiding overfitting and improving the generalization ability of small sample data.
3. Experiments on the UATD, URPC, and SCTD datasets showed that DA-YOLOv7 performed excellently in accuracy, recall rate, and running speed. Especially in the mAP@0.5 metric, it improved by 8.2% compared to YOLOv7, reaching 89.4%, and the running speed was 97.09 FPS, achieving a balance between accuracy and real-time performance, establishing a new benchmark for underwater sonar image target recognition.
4. DA-YOLOv7 demonstrated excellent robustness and accuracy in different underwater environments, such as the lake bottom and shallow water areas of UATD, the diverse biological communities of URPC, and the ocean test scenarios of SCTD, showing broad application potential.

Future work on DA-YOLOv7 includes reducing the dependence on training data, enhancing the model's adaptability to new environments and targets, improving the model's anti-noise ability and computational efficiency to adapt to resource-constrained environments, simplifying the model structure to increase maintainability, exploring more effective data augmentation and balancing strategies to enhance generalization ability, testing the model's generalization performance on a more diverse underwater sonar image dataset, and developing more effective noise suppression techniques, optimizing the model structure to reduce computational costs, and exploring data augmentation strategies to improve generalization ability and model interpretability. These efforts aim to optimize the network structure further, enhance the anti-noise ability, adapt to more diverse underwater environments, and support the ability of automated monitoring and resource management in underwater environments.

Author Contributions: Conceptualization, Z.C. and H.Q.; methodology, X.D. and G.X.; software, J.P.; validation, X.D., J.P. and H.Q.; investigation, Z.C. and G.X.; writing—original draft preparation, Z.C.; writing—review and editing, H.Q. and X.D.; funding acquisition, X.D. and H.Q. All authors have read and agreed to the published version of the manuscript.

Funding: This work is supported by Guangxi Science and Technology Base and Talent Project (No. GuikeAD21220098) and the 2021 Open Fund project of the Key Laboratory of Cognitive Radio and Information Processing of the Ministry of Education (No. CRKL210102). We also thank to the support of Guangxi Key Laboratory of Wireless Broadband Communication and Signal Processing Project (No. GXKL06240114), Beihai City Science and Technology Bureau Project (No. Bei ke He 2023158004) and the Innovation Project of Guangxi Graduate Education (No. YCSW2024344).

Institutional Review Board Statement: Not applicable.

Informed Consent Statement: Not applicable.

Data Availability Statement: The data used to support the findings of this study are available from the corresponding author upon request.

Conflicts of Interest: The authors declare no conflicts of interest.

Abbreviations

The following abbreviations are used in this manuscript:

DA-YOLOv7	The Dual Attention Mechanism YOLOv7 model
OA-ELAN	Omni-Directional Convolution Channel Prior Convolutional Attention Efficient Layer Aggregation Network
SPPCSPCBiFormer	Spatial Pyramid Pooling Channel Shuffling and Pixel-level Convolution Bilateral-branch Transformer
G-ELAN-H	Ghost-Shuffle Convolution Enhanced Layer Aggregation Network-High performance
DCNNs	Deep convolutional neural networks
R-CNN	Regions with Convolutional Neural Network features
DCN	Deformable Convolutional Networks
STAFNet	Swin Transformer Based Anchor-Free Network
URPC	The Underwater Optical Target Detection Intelligent Algorithm Competition 2021 Dataset
FCOS	Fully Convolutional One-Stage Object Detection
VGG16	Visual Geometry Group 16-layer network
IMA	Invert Multi-Class AdaBoost
LWAP	Local Wavelet Acoustic Pattern
MLP	Multilayer Perceptron
YOLO	You Only Look Once
ASFF	Adaptive Spatial Feature Fusion
ScEMA	Scale and Channel Efficient Module Attention
ODConv	Omni-Directional Convolution
CPCA	Channel Prior Convolutional Attention
UATD	Underwater Acoustic Target Detection Dataset
SCTD	Smaller Common Sonar Target Detection Dataset
CBS	Convolution-Batch Normalization-SiLU activation function
ELAN	Efficient Layer Aggregation Network
MP	The Multi-scale Layer
SPPCSPC	Spatial Pyramid Pooling Channel Shuffling and Pixel-level Convolution
BiFormer	The Bilateral-branch Transformer
SPP	Spatial Pyramid Pooling
CSPC	Channel Shuffling and Pixel-level Convolution

References

1. Yin, Z.; Zhang, S.; Sun, R.; Ding, Y.; Guo, Y. Sonar image target detection based on deep learning. In Proceedings of the 2023 International Conference on Distributed Computing and Electrical Circuits and Electronics (ICDCECE), Ballar, India, 29–30 April 2023; pp. 1–8.
2. Huang, C.; Zhao, J.; Zhang, H.; Yu, Y. Seg2Sonar: A Full-Class Sample Synthesis Method Applied to Underwater Sonar Image Target Detection, Recognition, and Segmentation Tasks. *IEEE Trans. Geosci. Remote Sens.* **2024**, *62*, 1–19. [CrossRef]
3. Steiniger, Y.; Groen, J.; Stoppe, J.; Kraus, D.; Meisen, T. A study on modern deep learning detection algorithms for automatic target recognition in sidescan sonar images. In Proceedings of the 6th Underwater Acoustics Conference and Exhibition, Virtual, 21–24 June 2021; pp. 1–6.
4. Li, J.; Chen, L.; Shen, J.; Xiao, X.; Liu, X.; Sun, X.; Wang, X.; Li, D. Improved neural network with spatial pyramid pooling and online datasets preprocessing for underwater target detection based on side scan sonar imagery. *Remote Sens.* **2023**, *15*, 440. [CrossRef]
5. Vijaya Kumar, D.T.T.; Mahammad Shafi, R. A fast feature selection technique for real-time face detection using hybrid optimized region based convolutional neural network. *Multimed. Tools Appl.* **2022**, *82*, 13719–13732. [CrossRef]
6. Girshick, R.; Donahue, J.; Darrell, T.; Malik, J. Rich feature hierarchies for accurate object detection and semantic segmentation. In Proceedings of the 2014 IEEE Conference on Computer Vision and Pattern Recognition, Columbus, OH, USA, 23–28 June 2014; pp. 580–587.
7. Girshick, R. Fast R-CNN. In Proceedings of the 2015 IEEE International Conference on Computer Vision, Santiago, Chile, 7–13 December 2015; pp. 1440–1448.
8. Chen, Z.; Wang, H.; Shen, J.; Dong, X. Underwater Object Detection by Combining the Spectral Residual and Three-Frame Algorithm. In *Advances in Computer Science and Its Applications*; Springer: Berlin/Heidelberg, Germany, 2014; pp. 1109–1114.
9. Villar, S.A.; Acosta, G.G.; Solari, F.J. OS-CFAR Process in 2-D for Object Segmentation from Side-scan Sonar Data. In Proceedings of the 2015 XVI Workshop on Information Processing and Control (RPIC), Cordoba, Argentina, 6–9 October 2015; pp. 1–6.
10. Mukherjee, K.; Gupta, S.; Ray, A.; Phoha, S. Symbolic Analysis of Sonar Data for Underwater Target Detection. *IEEE J. Ocean. Eng.* **2011**, *36*, 219–230. [CrossRef]
11. Midtgaard, O.; Hansen, R.E.; Sæbø, T.O.; Myers, V.; Dubberley, J.R.; Quidu, I. Change Detection Using Synthetic Aperture Sonar: Preliminary Results from the Larvik Trial. In Proceedings of the OCEANS'11 MTS/IEEE KONA, Waikoloa, HI, USA, 19–22 September 2011; pp. 1–6.
12. Raghuvanshi, D.S.; Dutt, I.; Vaidya, R.J. Design and analysis of a novel sonar-based obstacle-avoidance system for the visually impaired and unmanned systems. In Proceedings of the 2014 International Conference on Embedded Systems (ICES), Coimbatore, India, 3–5 July 2014; pp. 238–243.
13. Bochkovskiy, A.; Wang, C.Y.; Liao, H.Y.M. YOLOv4: Optimal speed and accuracy of object detection. *arXiv* **2020**, arXiv:2004.10934.
14. Zhu, X.; Lyu, S.; Wang, X.; Zhao, Q. TPH-YOLOv5: Improved YOLOv5 based on transformer prediction head for object detection on drone-captured scenarios. In Proceedings of the IEEE/CVF International Conference on Computer Vision, Montreal, BC, Canada, 11–17 October 2021; pp. 2778–2788.
15. Li, C.; Li, L.; Jiang, H.; Weng, K.; Geng, Y.; Li, L.; Wei, X. YOLOv6: A single-stage object detection framework for industrial applications. *J. Mar. Sci. Eng.* **2022**, *11*, 67721.
16. Wang, C.Y.; Bochkovskiy, A.; Liao, H.Y.M. YOLOv7: Trainable bag-of-freebies sets new state-of-the-art for real-time object detectors. *arXiv* **2022**, arXiv:2207.02696.
17. Fan, Z.; Xia, W.; Liu, X.; Li, H. Detection and segmentation of underwater objects from forward-looking sonar based on a modified Mask R-CNN. *Signal Image Video Process.* **2021**, *15*, 1135–1143. [CrossRef]
18. Zhu, X.; Liang, Y.; Zhang, J.; Chen, Z. STAFNet: Swin Transformer Based Anchor-Free Network for Detection of Forward-looking Sonar Imagery. In Proceedings of the 2022 International Conference on Multimedia Retrieval, Newark, NJ, USA, 27–30 June 2022. [CrossRef]
19. Zhou, H.; Huang, H.; Yang, X.; Zhang, L.; Qi, L. Faster R-CNN for marine organism detection and recognition using data augmentation. In Proceedings of the International Conference on Video and Image Processing, Singapore, 27–29 December 2017; pp. 56–62.
20. Chen, L.; Liu, Z.; Tong, L.; Jiang, Z.; Wang, S.; Dong, J.; Zhou, H. Underwater object detection using Invert Multi-Class Adaboost with deep learning. In Proceedings of the 2020 International Joint Conference on Neural Networks (IJCNN), Glasgow, UK, 19–24 July 2020; pp. 1–8.
21. Qiao, W.; Khishe, M.; Ravakhah, S. Underwater targets classification using local wavelet acoustic pattern and Multi-Layer Perceptron neural network optimized by modified Whale Optimization Algorithm. *Ocean. Eng.* **2021**, *219*, 108415. [CrossRef]
22. Yan, W. Sonar Image Target Detection and Recognition Based on Convolution Neural Network. *Mob. Inf. Syst.* **2021**, *2021*, 5589154. [CrossRef]
23. Lin, T.Y.; Dollár, P.; Girshick, R.; He, K.; Hariharan, B.; Belongie, S. Feature Pyramid Networks for Object Detection. In Proceedings of the 2017 IEEE Conference on Computer Vision and Pattern Recognition (CVPR), Honolulu, HI, USA, 21–26 July 2017; pp. 936–944.
24. Fan, X.; Lu, L.; Shi, P.; Zhang, X. A novel sonar target detection and classification algorithm. *Multimed. Tools Appl.* **2022**, *81*, 10091–10106. [CrossRef]

25. Liu, S.; Huang, D.; Wang, Y. Learning Spatial Fusion for Single-Shot Object Detection. *arXiv* **2019**, arXiv:1911.09516.
26. Zhang, H.; Tian, M.; Shao, G.; Cheng, J.; Liu, J. Target Detection of Forward-Looking Sonar Image Based on Improved YOLOv5. *IEEE Access* **2022**, *10*, 18023–18034. [CrossRef]
27. Cheng, C.; Hou, X.; Wen, X.; Liu, W.; Zhang, F. Small-Sample Underwater Target Detection: A Joint Approach Utilizing Diffusion and YOLOv7 Model. *Remote Sens.* **2023**, *15*, 4772. [CrossRef]
28. Zheng, L.; Hu, T.; Zhu, J. Underwater Sonar Target Detection Based on Improved ScEMA-YOLOv8. *IEEE Geosci. Remote Sens. Lett.* **2024**, *21*, 1–4. [CrossRef]
29. Xie, K.; Yang, J.; Qiu, K. A Dataset with Multibeam Forward-Looking Sonar for Underwater Object Detection. *Sci. Data* **2022**, *9*, 739. [CrossRef] [PubMed]
30. Zhou, Y.; Chen, S.; Wu, K.; Ning, M.; Chen, H.; Zhang, P. SCTD1.0: Common Sonar Target Detection Dataset. *Ship Sci. Technol.* **2021**, *48*, 334–339.
31. Dong, J.; Yang, M.; Xie, Z.; Cai, L. Overview of Underwater Image Object Detection Dataset and Detection Algorithms. *J. Ocean. Technol.* **2022**, *41*, 60–72.
32. Ren, S.; Zhou, D.; He, S.; Feng, J.; Wang, X. Shunted self-attention via multi-scale token aggregation. In Proceedings of the IEEE/CVF Conference on Computer Vision and Pattern Recognition, New Orleans, LA, USA, 7–8 May 2022; pp. 10853–10862.

Journal of
Marine Science and Engineering

MDPI

Article

Autonomous Underwater Vehicle Navigation Enhancement by Optimized Side-Scan Sonar Registration and Improved Post-Processing Model Based on Factor Graph Optimization

Lin Zhang, Lianwu Guan *, Jianhui Zeng * and Yanbin Gao

College of Intelligent Systems Science and Engineering, Harbin Engineering University, Harbin 150001, China; yigona@hrbeu.edu.cn (L.Z.); gaoyanbin@hrbeu.edu.cn (Y.G.)
* Correspondence: guanlianwu@hrbeu.edu.cn (L.G.); zengjianhui@hrbeu.edu.cn (J.Z.)

Abstract: Autonomous Underwater Vehicles (AUVs) equipped with Side-Scan Sonar (SSS) play a critical role in seabed mapping, where precise navigation data are essential for mosaicking sonar images to delineate the seafloor's topography and feature locations. However, the accuracy of AUV navigation, based on Strapdown Inertial Navigation System (SINS)/Doppler Velocity Log (DVL) systems, tends to degrade over long-term mapping, which compromises the quality of sonar image mosaics. This study addresses the challenge by introducing a post-processing navigation method for AUV SSS surveys, utilizing Factor Graph Optimization (FGO). Specifically, the method utilizes an improved Fourier-based image registration algorithm to generate more robust relative position measurements. Then, through the integration of these measurements with data from SINS, DVL, and surface Global Navigation Satellite System (GNSS) within the FGO framework, the approach notably enhances the accuracy of the complete trajectory for AUV missions. Finally, the proposed method has been validated through both the simulation and AUV marine experiments.

Keywords: AUVs; SSS; seabed mapping; sonar image registration; FGO; post navigation

Citation: Zhang, L.; Guan, L.; Zeng, J.; Gao, Y. Autonomous Underwater Vehicle Navigation Enhancement by Optimized Side-Scan Sonar Registration and Improved Post-Processing Model Based on Factor Graph Optimization. *J. Mar. Sci. Eng.* **2024**, *12*, 1769. https://doi.org/10.3390/jmse12101769

Academic Editor: Fabio Bruno

Received: 21 August 2024
Revised: 14 September 2024
Accepted: 17 September 2024
Published: 5 October 2024

1. Introduction

The utilization of Autonomous Underwater Vehicles (AUVs) equipped with Side-Scan Sonar (SSS) stands as a pivotal technique for seabed scanning [1]. AUVs typically utilize a navigation system that integrates data from the Strapdown Inertial Navigation System (SINS) and the Doppler Velocity Log (DVL) [2]. By amalgamating the measurements from the Side-Scan Sonar (SSS) with the navigation data, seabed acoustic mosaics are generated, which contain navigation information and the positions of significant seabed features [3]. The precision of the AUV's navigation data holds substantial sway over the accuracy of seabed mapping and the localization of seabed features. Nevertheless, conventional SINS/DVL-integrated navigation methods are susceptible to errors stemming from imprecise DVL measurements, scale factors, and mounting error angles, thereby culminating in positioning discrepancies over time. While post-processing with satellite data before and after diving might yield enhancement, this approach is constrained by the absence of positional data during the underwater phase and limitations in modeling accuracy. Based on our experimental findings, although post-processing with satellite data before and after diving could offer some enhancements, this approach is hindered by the lack of positional data during the underwater phase and limitations in modeling accuracy.

AUV utilizes the SINS/DVL-integrated navigation method to obtain navigation information underwater [4,5]. This is a dead-reckoning method that achieves positioning by fusing and integrating the measurements of DVL and SINS. However, not only the heading errors of SINS would cause overall trajectory deviations, but also there are error sources such as the change in DVL calibration due to sound speed and installation errors between

DVL and SINS in the system, leading to accumulated positioning errors of underwater AUVs [6,7].

Performing simple post-processing with GNSS measurements taken before the submerging and after the surfacing of AUV could optimize the trajectory to some extent [8,9], but there are still some issues remaining.

The first limitation is the difficulty in obtaining stable and reliable relative position measurements from Side-Scan Sonar (SSS) images: Relative position measurements from sonar image registration can complement the measurements; conventional feature-based image registration methods are limited in dull environments [10], making them prone to failure in seabed sonar images. Image registration methods based on the Fast Fourier Transform (FFT) show improved performance by leveraging overall image information [11,12], and it is already utilized in image sonar. However, the registration of SSS images presents a greater challenge. Unlike images from conventional image sonar, which typically exhibit similar perspectives, the perspectives of SSS images are usually entirely distinct. This leads to significant discrepancies between images, resulting in inaccuracies in the determination of relative positions in the output and the potential outliers.

The second limitation is that existing methods often lack the estimation of the AUV's heading and the DVL installation errors. These omissions significantly affect the quality of SSS imaging, for it is the AUV's heading, rather than its navigational course, which governs the angle of this frame in the stitched map. The conventional map stitching methods do not correct for heading, treating the heading values obtained from the SINS/DVL-integrated navigation as true values [10,13], which limits the maximum achievable accuracy. However, existing methods typically overlook the installation errors between DVL and the SINS [14]. This omission results in errors in the transmission of position correction within the method, casting suboptimal accuracy in heading estimation [15]. Although traditional filtering methods could estimate errors in time series by extending the system model, they often encounter difficulties when the intervals between positional measurements are excessively long [16]. This challenge arises from the nonlinear system, where certain states, despite being unobservable at a given moment, may still be inaccurately estimated by the filter, potentially resulting in system instability. Consequently, this might be a reason why existing methods generally do not incorporate the estimation of these errors.

This study aims to address the two previously mentioned issues in the AUV navigation information for seafloor mapping. On one hand, an improved SSS image registration method based on the FFT is designed and implemented, which enables a more stable and accurate acquisition of relative positions from the SSS. On the other hand, to concurrently estimate the state sequence of the AUV and the constant system error parameters, we propose a method based on FGO. Compared to filter-based methods, which necessitate the sequential estimation of constant states, the FGO-based method allows for the flexible modeling of states as either sequences or constants [17,18], making it particularly suitable for scenarios like this study, where large time intervals between measurements are utilized to estimate constant states such as installation errors.

Ultimately, by using FGO to fuse relative position from SSS images and position from GNSS before submersion and after surfacing, it becomes possible to simultaneously estimate navigation information such as attitude, velocity, and position as time series, along with constant error parameters like DVL scale factors and installation errors. This method offers two significant advantages: first, it allows for the estimation of more accurate AUV attitude and position, thereby enhancing the quality of seafloor images through improved attitudes and positions of the SSS. Second, the derived parameters, such as installation errors, can serve as valuable references for the AUV's subsequent missions.

The contribution of this study Can be summarized as

1. To acquire reliable relative position measurement, an improved Fourier-based image registration technique has been proposed to address the lack of features in SSS seafloor images. This method builds upon traditional registration by incorporating a Gaussian prior to eliminating outliers, and employs bandpass filtering to enhance the accuracy

after outlier removal. This approach not only significantly improves the stability of the registration process, but also requires minimal computational resources since both enhancements are applied to the normalized cross-correlation function.

2. A post-processing method based on Factor Graph Optimization (FGO) is proposed that facilitates the simultaneous estimation of the varying AUV's navigation information and constant error parameters, such as DVL scale factors and installation errors. With position measurements, this method not only allows for the optimization of trajectory information in the same manner as traditional post-processing methods, but also enables an effective optimization of heading information.

This paper includes an improved SSS registration method, an enhanced post-processing model, and an optimization implementation based on FGO. The sonar registration algorithm was validated through SSS seabed images, while the optimization method was validated through two sets of experiments using both simulated data and ocean trial data. Section 2 presents the overview, Section 3 presents the improved sonar image registration method and its validation, Section 4 proposes the integrated navigation with measurement from SSS image registration based on FGO, and Sections 5 and 6 provide comparative simulations and experiments of the existing methods and the improved methods, respectively.

2. Overview

The proposed approach is outlined in Figure 1, which comprises three primary components.

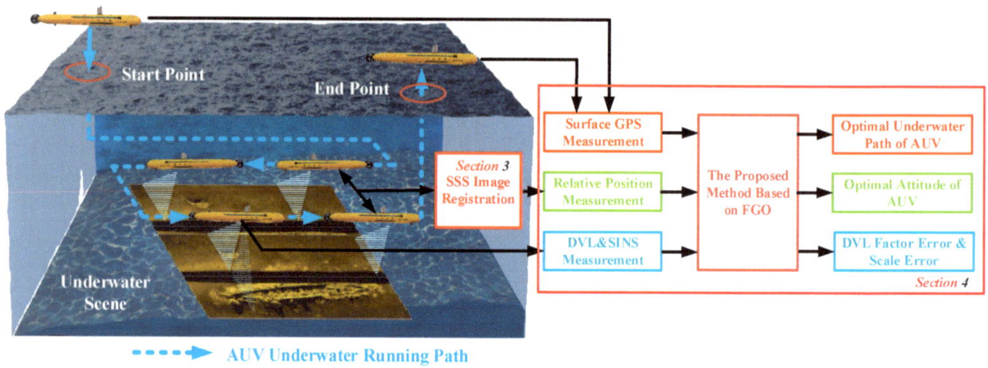

Figure 1. The framework of the proposed method.

(1) Registration of SSS images

SSS image pair selection, image pair pre-processing, and Fourier-based registration are included, aiming to establish the spatial relationship between the SSS images. This will be demonstrated with details in Section 3.

(2) Factor graph optimization

Based on the improved high-accuracy pre-integration model and DVL/SSS measurement residuals, as shown in Section 4, the state of the entire trajectory will be batch-optimized through FGO. The specifics of the FGO formulation are provided in Section 4.1. The DVL measurement model will be presented in Section 4.2. The residuals and Jacobian matrix will be demonstrated in Sections 4.3 and 4.4.

(3) Information output

After the states are estimated using FGO, the navigational information for the trajectory can be generated.

3. Fourier-Based SSS Image Registration

When the AUV navigates to a location near its previous path, the survey areas of the SSS will overlap. Pre-processing and registration can be applied to the partially overlapping sonar images to obtain relative position measurements.

This section presents an improved Fourier-based image registration technique. It builds on the standard Fourier-based SSS Image Registration method by adding two key improvements. The two improvements involve the addition of a Gaussian prior and the use of a window function on the normalized cross-correlation function, which, respectively, address significant errors and minor errors in SSS image registration. These methods will be validated using examples of SSS images.

3.1. Standard Fourier-Based SSS Registration

3.1.1. Pre-Process of SSS Images

Prior to registration, it is necessary to perform slant-range correction, essential image enhancement, and longitudinal intensity normalization for SSS images. Assuming a level seabed, the formula for slant-range correction is as follows:

$$L_{feature} = \sqrt{\left(L_{slope}\right)^2 - (H)^2} \tag{1}$$

where $L_{feature}$ and L_{slope} represent the distance from a point on the seabed to the midline of the acoustic survey path, and the diagonal distance from that point to the SSS transducer, respectively. H represents the height of the transducer relative to the seabed.

After slant-range correction and necessary image enhancement, a vertical intensity normalization is required due to the inherent vertical intensity unevenness in the images. It can be shown as

$$\begin{aligned} I'(i,j) &= I(i,j) + c_j \\ c_j &= \mu_{global} - \mu_{col}(j) \end{aligned} \tag{2}$$

where $I'(i,j)$ and $I(i,j)$, respectively, represent the pixel intensity values at the row i and column j of the intensity-balanced image and the original image; c_j represents the intensity adjustment value for column j; μ_{global} is the global mean intensity of the original image I; and $\mu_{col}(j)$ is the mean intensity of column j in the original image.

3.1.2. Fourier-Based SSS Registration

As the scanning routes are nearly parallel, it can be assumed that the two images g and f to be registered only have a translational relationship, as shown in Equation (3).

$$f(x,y) = g(x - t_x, y - t_y) \tag{3}$$

The normalized cross-power spectrum is illustrated in Equation (4). The robustness of Fourier-based registration to noise is attributed to the process-normalized process in Equation (4), which can be viewed as a pre-whitening step.

$$C(u,v) = \frac{F(u,v)G^*(u,v)}{|F(u,v)G^*(u,v)|} = e^{-i(ut_x+vt_y)} \tag{4}$$

Subsequently, through the inverse Fourier transform, the Phase Correlation Matrix (PCM) can be obtained as shown in (5):

$$P(u,v) = \mathcal{F}^{-1}C(u,v) \tag{5}$$

Finally, the position relationship is determined in Equation (6), which is the relative position measurement corrected by sonar image pairs.

$$\left(t_x, t_y\right) = \underset{(u,v)}{\operatorname{argmax}}\{P(u,v)\} \tag{6}$$

3.2. The Optimization of SSS Registration

3.2.1. Gaussian Prior-Enhanced SSS Registration

The common features present in SSS images often introduce errors in image registration. Along an AUV track, the intensity of SSS images exhibits a gradient, increasing from the port side to a peak at the centerline, followed by a decrease towards the starboard side. Additionally, the contrast fluctuates between weak and strong, reaching its peak at a moderate distance from the midline of the acoustic survey path. When seabed features are not clearly defined, these fixed characteristics of intensity and contrast can dominate the registration results, causing errors in relative position measurements.

However, it has been observed that even when the underwater features in the images are not clearly defined, the PCM frequently yields local maxima in proximity to the correct registration outcomes, albeit not globally optimal. Consequently, this study suggests leveraging the coarse relative positional data supplied by the AUV navigation system as a Gaussian prior, and integrating this Gaussian prior into the registration process to effectively derive meaningful registration results from the PCM.

When the prior image displacement is $\left(t_x^*, t_y^*\right)$, the two-dimensional normal distribution $f(u,v)$ is defined as

$$f(u,v) = \frac{1}{2\pi\sigma_u\sigma_v}\exp\left(-\frac{1}{2}\left[\frac{(u-t_x^*)^2}{\sigma_u^2} - \frac{2\rho(u-t_x^*)(v-t_y^*)}{\sigma_u\sigma_v} + \frac{(v-t_y^*)^2}{\sigma_v^2}\right]\right) \quad (7)$$

where σ_u and σ_v represent the standard deviations of $f(u,v)$ in the u and v directions, determined by the attitude holding capability of the SINS; t_x^* and t_y^* denote the prior image displacements in the horizontal and vertical directions, respectively.

The PCM with added Gaussian prior is denoted as $P^{Gaussian}(u,v)$.

$$P^{Gaussian}(u,v) = P(u,v) + f(u,v)\cdot(P_{\max} - P_{\min})\cdot k \quad (8)$$

where $P_{\max}$ and $P_{\min}$ represent the maximum and minimum values of $P(u,v)$, respectively. The parameter k represents the confidence coefficient of the prior information, with values ranging from 0 to 1, typically determined empirically.

By using $P^{Gaussian}$ instead of the original PCM, the registration results with the added Gaussian prior can be obtained.

$$(t_x, t_y) = \underset{(u,v)}{\operatorname{argmax}}\left\{P^{Gaussian}(u,v)\right\} \quad (9)$$

3.2.2. Bandpass Filter-Aided SSS Registration

Although the inclusion of prior information can reduce errors introduced by the inherent characteristics in SSS images, the presence of noise and perspective effects still compromise the precision of registration.

Bandpass filters serve to highlight the seabed features of interest, thereby improving the quality of registration. Moreover, since Fourier-based image registration operates in the frequency domain, the enhanced registration results achieved through bandpass filtering can be obtained with minimal computational effort. This is achieved by simply computing the Hadamard product of the normalized cross-power spectrum with a designed window function.

The frequency limits for FIR bandpass filters can be set independently along the horizontal and vertical axes.

The frequency limits for FIR bandpass filters can be individually set for both the horizontal and vertical dimensions. This entails defining the upper frequency limit $f_{high,row}$

and the lower frequency limit $f_{low,row}$ for the horizontal direction, as well as the upper frequency limit $f_{high,col}$ and the lower frequency limit $f_{low,col}$ for the vertical direction.

$$\begin{aligned} 0 \leq f_{low,row} < f_{high,row} \leq 1 \\ 0 \leq f_{low,col} < f_{high,col} \leq 1 \end{aligned} \tag{10}$$

Then, these parameters are used to define the row and column dimensions of the bandpass filter.

$$\begin{aligned} H_{\text{row}} &= \lfloor f_{\text{high,row}} \times m \rfloor \\ L_{\text{row}} &= \lfloor f_{\text{low,row}} \times m \rfloor \\ H_{\text{col}} &= \lfloor f_{\text{high,col}} \times n \rfloor \\ L_{\text{col}} &= \lfloor f_{\text{low,col}} \times n \rfloor \end{aligned} \tag{11}$$

where m represents the number of rows in the image, n is the number of columns in the image, and $\lfloor \cdot \rfloor$ denotes the floor function, which rounds down to the nearest integer.

Then, the window function W can be determined.

$$\begin{aligned} RowPass(u, L_{\text{row}}, H_{\text{row}}, m) &= \begin{cases} 1 & \text{if } u \in (L_{\text{row}}, H_{\text{row}}) \cup (m - H_{\text{row}} + 1, m - L_{\text{row}} + 1) \\ 0 & \text{otherwise} \end{cases} \\ ColPass(v, L_{col}, H_{col}, n) &= \begin{cases} 1 & \text{if } v \in (L_{col}, H_{\text{col}}) \cup (n - H_{\text{col}} + 1, m - L_{\text{col}} + 1) \\ 0 & \text{otherwise} \end{cases} \\ W(u,v) &= RowPass(u, L_{\text{row}}, H_{\text{row}}, m) \times ColPass(v, L_{col}, H_{col}, n) \end{aligned} \tag{12}$$

where u and v represent the indices for the rows and columns, respectively.

Subsequently, the enhanced frequency domain results can be achieved by using the Hadamard product between the window function and the normalized cross-power spectrum.

$$C^{FIR}(u,v) = C(u,v) \odot W(u,v) \tag{13}$$

where $\odot$ denotes the operation of taking the Hadamard product of two matrices.

After this step, the time-domain results, which are also the optimized PCM, can be derived through an inverse Fourier transform, following the same procedure as standard Fourier-based image registration.

$$\begin{aligned} P^{\text{FIR}}(u,v) &= \mathcal{F}^{-1} C^{FIR}(u,v) \\ (t_x, t_y) &= \underset{(u,v)}{\operatorname{argmax}} \{ P^{\text{FIR}}(u,v) \} \end{aligned} \tag{14}$$

3.3. Evaluation of Optimized Fourier-Based SSS Registration

To validate and verify the performance of the improved registration method, the following four registration approaches will be applied to the same pairs of sonar images:

1. Classic Fourier-based image registration method;
2. Fourier-based registration method optimized with Gaussian prior;
3. Fourier-based registration method optimized with bandpass filter;
4. Fourier-based registration method optimized with both Gaussian prior and band pass filter.

The SSS image pairs employed in the experimental study were meticulously chosen to comprise seabed visuals with ambiguous characteristics, acquired by an unmanned semi-submersible along contiguous survey transects. The two images only have a translational relationship between them. The pre-registered SSS image pairs, which have undergone image enhancement and intensity balancing, are shown in Figure 2. Each pixel in the image represents 0.1 m. According to GNSS measurements, in correct registration, the left half of Figure 2b should overlap with the right half of Figure 2a, indicating a minimal vertical displacement and a lateral displacement approximately equal to half the width of the image.

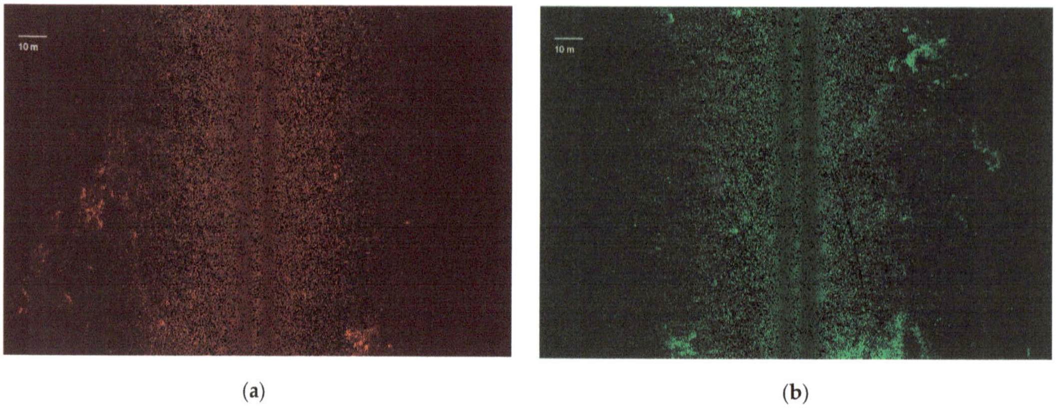

Figure 2. The original SSS image pairs: (a) The original SSS image 1; (b) The original SSS image 2.

3.3.1. Fourier-Based Image Registration

Under the classic Fourier-based image registration, the PCM and the overlapping result of the two images are shown as Figure 3.

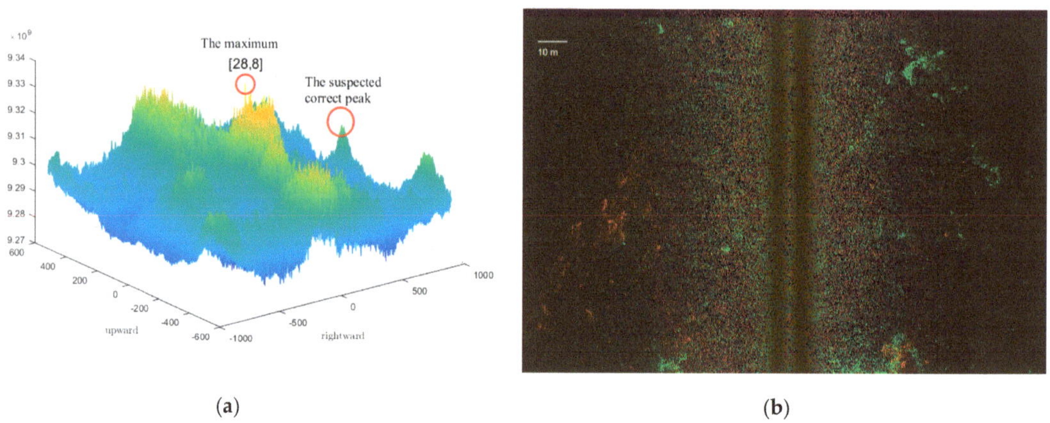

Figure 3. The result of classic Fourier-based image registration: (**a**) the PCM; (**b**) the overlapping.

This registration attempt was unsuccessful, with an error of 76.2 m, rendering it unsuitable for positional measurements.

In the classic Fourier-based registration algorithm, the coordinates of the maximum value of the normalized cross-correlation function on the upward and rightward axes represent the relative pixel displacement of the two images in the upward and rightward directions, respectively. However, as shown in Figure 3a, the maximum of the PCM is located on the ridge with a rightward displacement close to zero, rather than at the correct registration position. The overlap image of the registration result is shown in Figure 3b, where it can be observed that due to the influence of the longitudinal features, the registration algorithm considers the two images to be almost completely overlapping. This is far from the reference position provided by GNSS. This is a failed registration with an error of 76.16 m, which is unacceptable.

The two unfavorable conditions for this registration can be observed in the PCM. Firstly, there is a ridge at a rightward displacement close to zero, which is generated by the influence of residual longitudinal features in the image. Secondly, the PCM contains numerous small spikes, which are caused by high-frequency noise in the image and lead to local registration errors. The PCM's maximum value, on which this failed registration is based, corresponds to a small spike on the ridge caused by high-frequency noise due to the longitudinal features. However, at the end of the rightward axis of Figure 3a, there is a noticeable but less prominent peak, the position of which aligns with the reference provided by GNSS. This indicates that a frequency domain analysis is capable of extracting the correct displacement information, but it is overwhelmed by misleading information. This demonstrates the feasibility of optimizing the registration process.

3.3.2. Gaussian Prior-Optimized Registration

Under the registration method optimized with Gaussian prior, the PCM and the overlapping result of the two images are shown as follows.

This is a successful but less precise registration, with an error of 0.9 m as referenced by GNSS measurements.

Figure 4a shows that, compared to the PCM in the classic registration method, the PCM with Gaussian prior optimization has added convexities due to the prior, which weights the maxima near the prior. This highlighting makes the peaks, which were overwhelmed by misleading information in the classic method, stand out and become more likely to be the global maximum. Therefore, Gaussian prior optimization in registration can largely avoid gross errors caused by the subtlety of seabed features, making the output registration results more reliable. Figure 4b also illustrates this point; the overlap shown in the registration result is more similar to the reference value provided by GNSS.

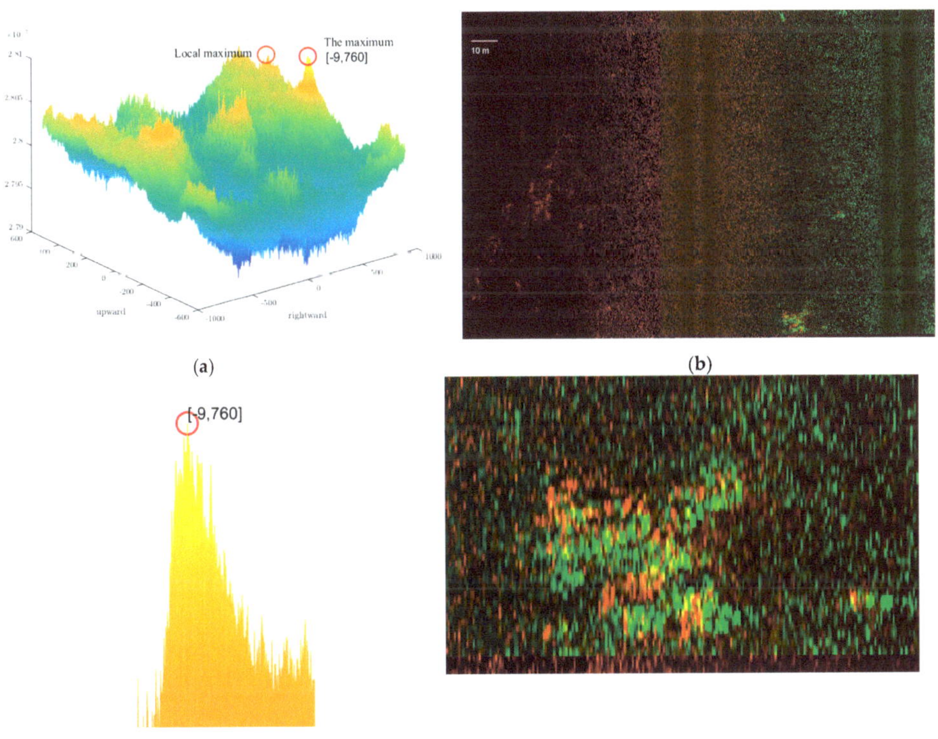

Figure 4. The result of registration optimized with Gaussian prior: (**a**) the PCM; (**b**) the overlapping; (**c**) the local area of the PCM; (**d**) the local area of the overlapping.

However, there are two shortcomings to the registration method that uses only Gaussian prior optimization. On one hand, the effectiveness of this method is inherently influenced by the accuracy of the prior information. When the confidence in the prior information is not high, the two-dimensional Gaussian distribution will strengthen the maxima of the cross-correlation function over a broader range. Since the original PCM contains multiple maxima, if the prior is close to a wrong maximum, it could also lead to an incorrect registration result. For example, there are local maxima caused by low-frequency features in Figure 4a, which might compete with the correct registration maximum when the prior information is not highly confident or is biased. On the other hand, when we focus on the local area of the PCM as shown in Figure 4c, it can be observed that due to the high-frequency noise in the acoustic imagery, there are numerous noise spikes around the maximum value, which can interfere with the accuracy of local registration. Figure 4d displays the enlarged details of the overlap, where it can be seen that, compared to the overall features, it is the small bright spots that align more precisely.

3.3.3. Bandpass Filter-Optimized Registration

Under the registration method optimized with a bandpass filter, the PCM and the overlapping result of the two images are shown as follows.

This represents a failed registration with an error of 60.07 m.

From Figure 5a, it is evident that the PCM optimized with bandpass filtering retains only two groups of peak values. These include a local maximum with a larger rightward value, which corresponds to the correct registration we expect, and another peak at a rightward displacement close to zero, which is due to the incorrect registration caused by longitudinal features. In contrast to the traditional method and the Gaussian prior optimization method, the cross-correlation function near the correct registration position in the PCM with bandpass filtering optimization is clearer. This showcases the noise suppression and peak optimization performance of the bandpass filtering.

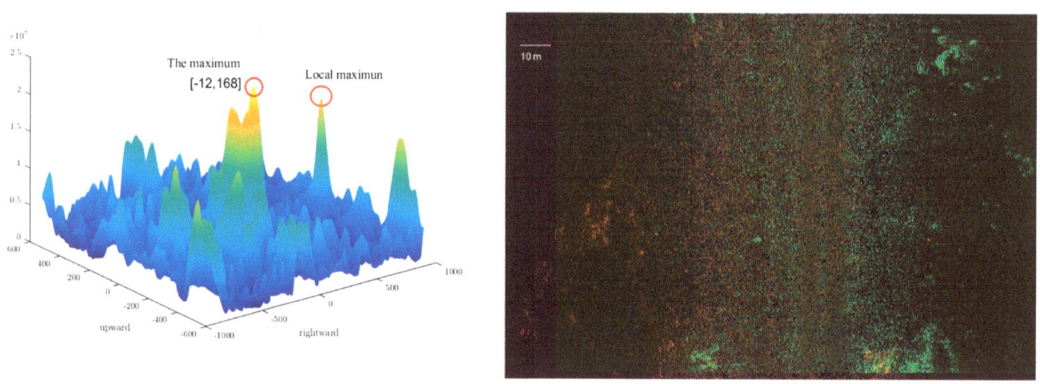

(a) (b)

Figure 5. The result of registration optimized with a bandpass filter: (**a**) the PCM; (**b**) the overlapping.

However, due to the subtle features of this image pair, the maximum value of the cross-correlation function still lies at the incorrect peak. Although bandpass optimization can filter out most of the competing erroneous registration results, it cannot guarantee that the registration of interest becomes the global maximum without individually tuning parameters for each image pair. Considering that the image pairs to be registered may not always have visually identifiable features, the effectiveness of using bandpass filtering optimization alone for registration is limited.

3.3.4. Gaussian Prior- and Bandpass Filter-Integrated Registration

Under the registration method optimized with both a Gaussian prior and bandpass filter, the PCM and the overlapping result of the two images are shown as follows.

This is a successful registration, with a reference GNSS measurement error of 0.2 m. Given that each pixel in the image represents 0.1 m, the precision of this registration is satisfactory.

In Figure 6, it can be observed that with the complementarity of the two optimization methods, the cross-correlation function value at the correct registration position successfully becomes the global maximum and is no longer affected by noise spikes and potential competing local maxima. The Gaussian prior optimization can exclude erroneous registrations with gross errors, while the bandpass optimization can refine the registration near the prior position. This results in the most accurate registration outcome.

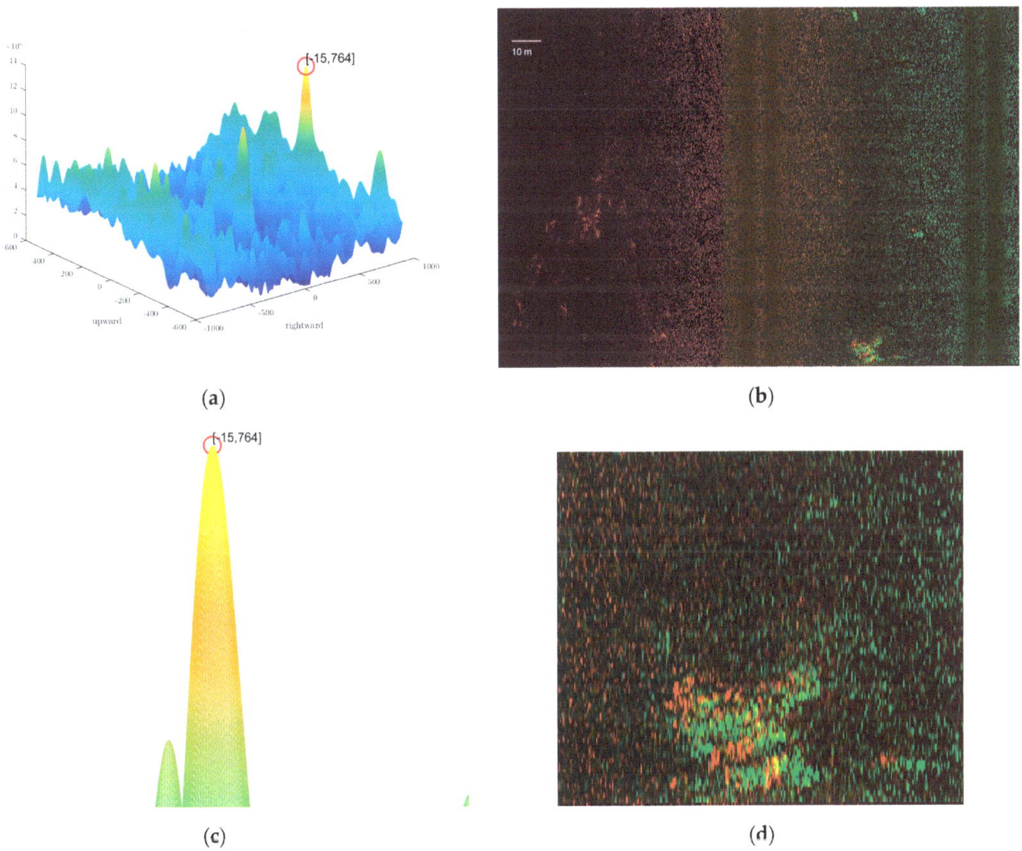

Figure 6. The result of registration optimized with both a Gaussian prior and bandpass filter: (**a**) the PCM; (**b**) the overlapping; (**c**) the local area of the PCM; (**d**) the local area of the overlapping.

The registration results for the four methods are shown in Table 1 below.

In conclusion, in the experiments with the four methods, it can be observed that the classic Fourier-based image registration is susceptible to the influence of high-frequency noise and residual longitudinal features in the SSS images, making it prone to failure when dealing with images lacking distinct features.

Table 1. The registration results for the four methods.

Registration Method	Precision
Classic Fourier-based image registration	16.2 m
Registration optimized with Gaussian prior	0.9 m
Registration optimized with bandpass filter	60.7 m
Registration optimized with both Gaussian prior and bandpass filter	0.2 m

Optimization with Gaussian prior can eliminate large errors during registration, but still can be misled by local maxima, resulting in registration errors.

Optimization with bandpass filtering can focus on the features at the desired scale in the image, reducing noise spikes and some misleading local maxima. However, it cannot guarantee that the peak value of interest in the registration result is the global maximum. Hence, it may still be influenced by the shared features in the SSS images.

By combining the optimization based on Gaussian prior and the optimization based on bandpass filtering in a single registration, the strengths of both methods can be leveraged. This approach not only eliminates gross errors to improve the likelihood of correct registration but also reduces the risk of being misled by local maxima near the prior registration position. The integrated optimization method of Gaussian prior and bandpass filtering requires minimal computational resources while greatly improving the stability of the registration process.

4. SSS-Integrated Navigation Method Based on FGO

A navigation data processing method based on FGO is introduced, which integrates SSS position measurements and incorporates estimates of DVL scale factors and installation errors. This section includes updated factor graph structures, definitions of residuals, and calculations of the Jacobian matrix. In addition, the IMU pre-integration method used in the approach is an improved method that takes into account the Earth's rotation [19]. The frame nomenclature is provided in Table 2.

Table 2. Nomenclature.

Symbol	Description
n	Ideal local-level navigation frame
b	Body frame
e	Earth frame
i	Nonrotating inertial frame

4.1. Formulation of FGO

In Figure 7, the structure of the proposed factor graph is depicted, using circles to represent the states x_k, and squares to represent the factors or the residuals. The corresponding factor is explicitly defined in the subsequent sections.

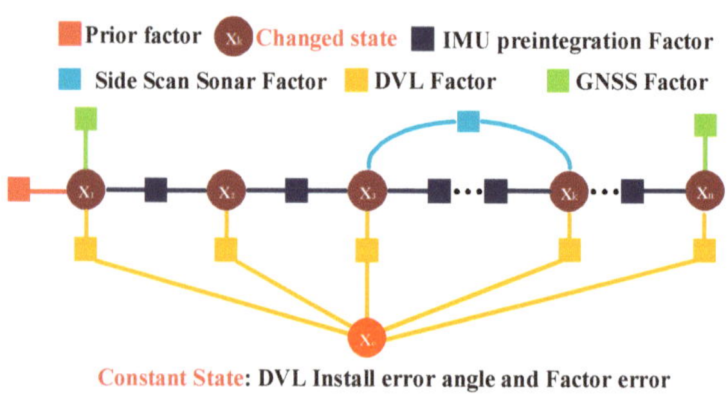

Figure 7. Factor graph structure of proposed method.

At time step k, the state x_k is defined as Equation (15),

$$x_k = \begin{bmatrix} C_{b\,k}^{n} & v_k & p_k & \varepsilon_k & \nabla_k \end{bmatrix} \tag{15}$$

where $C_{b\,k}^{n}$ represents the attitude Direction Cosine Matrix (DCM), δv_k is velocity error, δp_k is the position error, and ε_k and ∇_k are the bias of gyros and accelerators, respectively.

Then, the state encompassing each time step in the factor graph can be expressed as (16).

$$X = \begin{pmatrix} x_2 & x_2 & x_3 & \cdots & x_{n-1} & x_n & \phi_{DVL} & \delta k \end{pmatrix} \tag{16}$$

In this context, $\phi_{DVL} = \begin{bmatrix} \alpha & \beta & \gamma \end{bmatrix}^T$ denotes the DVL installation error angles consisting of the roll, heading, and pitch. δk denotes the scale factor error of the DVL. Both ϕ_{DVL} and δk are defined as time-invariant constants.

4.2. DVL Measurement Model

Errors in DVL velocity measurements can be classified into systematic errors and non-systematic errors. Systematic errors include scale factor errors and installation errors, which can be calibrated out. See Figure 8.

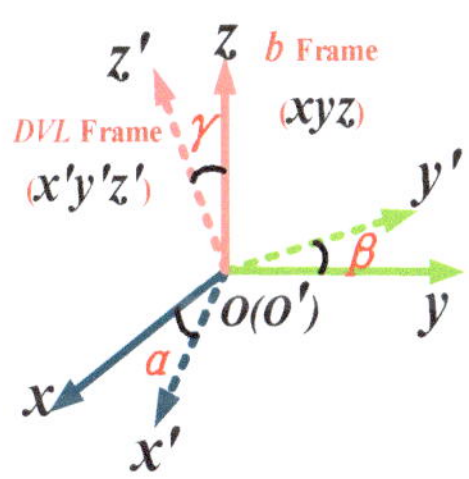

Figure 8. DVL installation angle.

Define the DVL velocity measurement as $v_{DVL} = \begin{bmatrix} v_x^d & v_y^d & v_z^d \end{bmatrix}^T$; the measurement model of the DVL can be expressed as

$$\tilde{v}_{DVL} = C_d^b(1+k)v_{DVL} = (I_{3\times3} - \phi_{DVL}\hat{})(1+\delta k)v_{DVL} + \delta v_{DVL} \tag{17}$$

The DCM for transforming from the DVL-fixed coordinate to the vehicle coordinate is denoted by C_d^b. $\tilde{v}_{DVL}$ represents the measurement obtained from the DVL, whereas δv_{DVL} is the measurement noise of DVL, typically considered as white noise. δk denotes the DVL scaling factor error; $\phi_{DVL}\hat{}$ is the skew-symmetric matrix generated from $\phi_{DVL} = \begin{bmatrix} \alpha & \beta & \gamma \end{bmatrix}^T$.

$$\phi_{DVL}\hat{} = \begin{bmatrix} 0 & -\gamma & \beta \\ \gamma & 0 & -\alpha \\ -\beta & \alpha & 0 \end{bmatrix} \tag{18}$$

4.3. Definition of Residuals

(1). Residuals of pre-integration factors

The INS residuals $r_{\Delta INS} = \begin{bmatrix} r_{\Delta R_{ij}} & r_{\Delta v_{ij}} & r_{\Delta p_{ij}} & r_{b_g} & r_{b_a} \end{bmatrix}^T$ can be expressed as (19); the $r_{\Delta R_{ij}}$, $r_{\Delta v_{ij}}$, $r_{\Delta p_{ij}}$, r_{b_g}, and r_{b_a} represent the attitude, velocity, position, accelerometers, and gyroscope residuals, respectively.

$$
\begin{aligned}
r_{\Delta R_{ij}} &= Log\left(\Delta\widetilde{R}_{ij}^{T}\left(C_{n(i)}^{n(j)}C_{b(i)}^{n(i)}\right)^{-1}C_{b(j)}^{n(j)}\right) \\
r_{\Delta v_{ij}} &= v_{en(j)}^{n(j)} - v_{en(i)}^{n(i)} - g^{n}\Delta T - \Delta\widetilde{v}_{ij} \\
r_{\Delta p_{ij}} &= \frac{1}{M_{pv}}(p_j - p_i) - v_{en(i)}^{n(i)}\Delta T - \frac{1}{2}g^{n}\Delta T^2 - \Delta\widetilde{p}_{ij} \\
r_{b_g} &= b_{g,j} - b_{g,i} \\
r_{b_a} &= b_{a,j} - b_{a,i}
\end{aligned}
\tag{19}
$$

(2). Residual of the DVL measurement factor

The DVL measurement residuals $r_{v_{DVL}}$ and the SSS measurement residuals can be expressed as (22); the $\Delta\widetilde{p}_{SSSab}$ indicates the relative position error calculated by (20).

$$
r_{v_{DVL}} = \left(v_i - C_{b(i)}^{n(i)}v_{\mathrm{DVL}}\right) \tag{20}
$$

(3). Residual of SSS measurement factor

The residuals related to the relative position measurements from the SSS are expressed as follows,

$$
r_{\Delta p_{SSSij}} = \left(\frac{1}{M_{pv}}(p_j - p_i) - \Delta\widetilde{p}_{SSSij}\right) \tag{21}
$$

where $\Delta\widetilde{p}_{SSSij} = \overline{C}_{b(i)}^{n(i)}\Delta\widetilde{p}_{SSSij}^{b(i)}$. $\overline{C}_{b(i)}^{n(i)}$ represents the rotation matrix derived from the average heading over a period of time centered at time i. The duration of this time period is determined by the length of the corresponding SSS image during image matching, which is fixed at 50 s in this paper.

(4). Surface GNSS measurement factor

$$
r_{\Delta p_{GPS}} = \frac{1}{M_{pv}}(p_i - p_{GPS}) \tag{22}
$$

Finally, the whole state can be optimally estimated by the following expression,

$$
X^* = \mathrm{argmin}_X \sum_k \|r_{\Delta INS}\|^2_{\Sigma_k^{INS}} + \|r_{v_{DVL}}\|^2_{\Sigma_k^{DVL}} + \left\|r_{\Delta p_{SSSij}}\right\|^2_{\Sigma_k^{SSS}} + \|r_{\Delta p_{GPS}}\|^2_{\Sigma_k^{GPS}} + \|r_{PRIOR}\|^2_{\Sigma_k^{PRIOR}} \tag{23}
$$

where Σ_k^{INS}, Σ_k^{DVL}, Σ_k^{SSS}, Σ_k^{GPS}, and Σ_k^{PRIOR} are all convex matrices. Σ_k^{INS} is the weight of the INS residuals, determined by the accuracy of the IMU; Σ_k^{DVL} is the weight of the DVL measurement residuals, determined by the measurement noise of the DVL; Σ_k^{SSS} is the weight of SSS measurement residuals, which is determined by the matching noise of the SSS; Σ_k^{GPS} is the weight of GPS measurement residuals and determined by the measurement noise of GPS; and Σ_k^{PRIOR} can be obtained through the marginalization or set directly.

4.4. Jacobian Matrix

To solve the nonlinear least squares problem presented in Equation (23), it is necessary to compute the detailed Jacobian matrix. The corresponding derivation of the Jacobian matrix is presented as follows.

(1). Jacobian matrix of IMU pre-integration

The Jacobian matrix of the pre-integration factor for each state is as follows:

$$
J_{IMU\_PRE} = \begin{bmatrix}
-J_r^{-1}\left(r_{\Delta\widetilde{R}_{ij}}\right)\left(C_{b(j)}^{n(j)}\right)^{-1}\left[I - T(\omega_{in}^{n})\right]C_{b(i)}^{n(i)} & 0_{3\times3} & 0_{3\times3} & -J_r^{-1}\left(r_{\Delta\widetilde{R}_{ij}}\right)\Delta\widetilde{R}_{ij}^{T}\left(\left[I - T(\omega_{in}^{n})\right]C_{b(i)}^{n(i)}\right)^{-1}J_r\left(\frac{\partial\Delta\widetilde{R}_{ij}}{\partial b_{g,i}}\right) & 0_{3\times3} & J_r^{-1}\left(r_{\Delta\widetilde{R}_{ij}}\right) & 0_{3\times3} & 0_{3\times3} & 0_{3\times3} & 0_{3\times3} \\
-\frac{\partial\Delta\widetilde{v}_{ij}}{\partial C_{b(i)}^{n(i)}} & -I_{3\times3} & 0_{3\times3} & -\frac{\partial\Delta\widetilde{v}_{ij}}{\partial b_{g,i}} & -\frac{\partial\Delta\widetilde{v}_{ij}}{\partial b_{a,i}} & 0_{3\times3} & I_{3\times3} & 0_{3\times3} & 0_{3\times3} & 0_{3\times3} \\
-\frac{\partial\Delta\widetilde{p}_{ij}}{\partial C_{b(i)}^{n(i)}} & -\Delta T & -I_{3\times3} & -\frac{\partial\Delta\widetilde{p}_{ij}}{\partial b_{g,i}} & -\frac{\partial\Delta\widetilde{p}_{ij}}{\partial b_{a,i}} & 0_{3\times3} & 0_{3\times3} & I_{3\times3} & 0_{3\times3} & 0_{3\times3} \\
0_{3\times3} & 0_{3\times3} & 0_{3\times3} & -I_{3\times3} & 0_{3\times3} & 0_{3\times3} & 0_{3\times3} & 0_{3\times3} & I_{3\times3} & 0_{3\times3} \\
0_{3\times3} & 0_{3\times3} & 0_{3\times3} & 0_{3\times3} & -I_{3\times3} & 0_{3\times3} & 0_{3\times3} & 0_{3\times3} & 0_{3\times3} & I_{3\times3}
\end{bmatrix} \tag{24}
$$

where the $\frac{\partial \Delta \tilde{v}_{ij}}{\partial C_{b(i)}^{n(i)}}$, $\frac{\partial \Delta \tilde{p}_{ij}}{\partial C_{b(i)}^{n(i)}}$, $\frac{\partial \Delta \tilde{R}_{ij}}{\partial b_{g,i}}$, $\frac{\partial \Delta \tilde{v}_{ij}}{\partial b_{g,i}}$, $\frac{\partial \Delta \tilde{p}_{ij}}{\partial b_{g,i}}$, $\frac{\partial \Delta \tilde{v}_{ij}}{\partial b_{a,i}}$, and $\frac{\partial \Delta \tilde{p}_{ij}}{\partial b_{a,i}}$ need to be obtained from recursion, as follows:

$$
\begin{aligned}
\frac{\partial \Delta \tilde{v}_{ij}}{\partial C_{b(i)}^{n(i)}} &= -\sum_{k=i}^{j-1} \left(C_{n(i)}^{n(k)} C_{b(i)}^{n(i)} \left(C_{b(k)}^{b(i)} \left(\Delta v_k + \Delta v_{\text{rot}(k)}^{b(k-1)} + \Delta v_{\text{scul}(k)}^{b(k-1)} \right) \right)^{\wedge} \right) \\
\frac{\partial \Delta \tilde{p}_{ij}}{\partial C_{b(i)}^{n(i)}} &= \sum_{k=i}^{j-1} \frac{\partial \Delta \tilde{v}_{ik}}{\partial C_{b(i)}^{n(i)}} \Delta t \\
\frac{\partial \Delta \tilde{R}_{ij}}{\partial b_{g,i}} &= -\sum_{k=i}^{j-1} \left[\Delta \tilde{R}_{k+1,j} J_{r,k} \Delta t \right] \\
\frac{\partial \Delta \tilde{v}_{ij}}{\partial b_{g,i}} &= -\sum_{k=i}^{j-1} \left[C_{n(i)}^{n(k)} C_{b(i)}^{n(i)} \Delta \tilde{R}_{ik} \Delta v_k^{\wedge} \frac{\partial \Delta \tilde{R}_{ik}}{\partial b_{g,i}} \Delta t \right] \\
\frac{\partial \Delta \tilde{p}_{ij}}{\partial b_{g,i}} &= -\sum_{k=i}^{j-1} \left[\frac{\partial \Delta \tilde{v}_{ik}}{\partial b_{g,i}} \Delta t \right] \\
\frac{\partial \Delta \tilde{v}_{ij}}{\partial b_{a,i}} &= -\sum_{k=i}^{j-1} \left[C_{n(i)}^{n(k)} C_{b(i)}^{n(i)} \Delta \tilde{R}_{ik} \Delta t \right] \\
\frac{\partial \Delta \tilde{p}_{ij}}{\partial b_{a,i}} &= -\sum_{k=i}^{j-1} \left[\frac{\partial \Delta \tilde{v}_{ik}}{\partial b_{a,i}} \Delta t \right]
\end{aligned}
\tag{25}
$$

(2). Jacobian matrix of DVL measurement

$$\frac{\partial r_{v_{DVL}}}{\partial x_k} = \left[C_{b(i)}^{n(i)} \tilde{v}_{DVL}^{\wedge} \quad I_{3\times3} \quad 0_{3\times3} \quad 0_{3\times3} \quad 0_{3\times3} \right] \tag{26}$$

$$\frac{\partial r_{v_{DVL}}}{\partial \phi_{DVL}} = -C_{b(i)}^{n(i)} ((1+\delta k) v_{DVL}) \tag{27}$$

$$\frac{\partial r_{v_{DVL}}}{\partial (\delta k)} = -C_{b(i)}^{n(i)} v_{DVL} + C_{b(i)}^{n(i)} \phi_{DVL} \hat{v}_{DVL} \tag{28}$$

(3). Jacobian matrix of SSS measurement

$$
\begin{aligned}
\frac{r_{\Delta p_{SSSij}}}{\partial x_i} &= \left[0_{3\times3} \quad 0_{3\times3} \quad -I_{3\times3} \quad 0_{3\times3} \quad 0_{3\times3} \right] \\
\frac{r_{\Delta p_{SSSij}}}{\partial x_j} &= \left[0_{3\times3} \quad 0_{3\times3} \quad I_{3\times3} \quad 0_{3\times3} \quad 0_{3\times3} \right]
\end{aligned}
\tag{29}
$$

(4). Jacobian matrix related to the surface GNSS measurements

$$\frac{\partial r_{pGPS}}{\partial x_k} = \left[0_{3\times3} \quad 0_{3\times3} \quad \frac{1}{M_{pv}} \quad 0_{3\times3} \quad 0_{3\times3} \right] \tag{30}$$

5. Simulation and Result Analysis

5.1. Setup of Simulation

The simulation models 3000 s of maneuvers, which corresponds to a typical underwater "Z" route for AUVs, with each side of the route, called a survey line, measuring 500 m. All methods incorporate an initial heading error of 2.5°.

The measurements in the simulation include IMU measurements, DVL measurements, relative position measurements from the SSS, and surface GNSS measurements. The IMU's data frequency is set to 100 Hz, with the zero biases for the three-axis gyroscopes set at 1.0°/h, 0.9°/h, and −1.1°/h, respectively. Gaussian noise with a standard deviation of 0.05°/s and 0.3 mg is introduced. The zero biases for the three-axis accelerometers are set at 0.2 mg, −0.25 mg, and 0.18 mg. Additionally, angular jitter and linear motion are incorporated across all three axes. The DVL data frequency is 1 Hz. The scale factor is configured to 0.98, and the installation errors for the DVL are set to 0.2°, −0.5°, and −0.5°, respectively. The SSS images are registered every 50 m along the survey line, with the registration results subjected to Gaussian noise with a standard deviation of 5m. The GNSS measurement frequency is 1 Hz and is only valid at the beginning and end of the simulation, with Gaussian noise having a standard deviation of 0.5 m.

A total of six methods are verified as follows:

1. EKF: SINS+DVL. This method represents the traditional EKF-based SINS/DVL-integrated navigation approach. It is used to illustrate the effectiveness of the most widely applied filtering methods for AUV navigation.
2. FGO: SINS+DVL. This method is based on FGO for SINS/DVL-integrated navigation, allowing for the batch optimization of the entire trajectory using all available SINS and DVL measurement data. It is used to demonstrate the effectiveness of batch processing methods in AUV navigation.
3. FGO: SINS+DVL+SSS. This method incorporates relative position measurements from the SSS into method 2. It serves to assess the auxiliary role of the proposed SSS relative position measurements in AUV navigation.
4. FGO: SINS+DVL+Position Constraint. This method integrates GNSS position constraints, obtained before descent and after surfacing, into the FGO-based SINS/DVL-integrated navigation model. It is used to demonstrate the effectiveness of post-processing navigation data using a traditional measurement source.
5. FGO: SINS+DVL+Position Constraint+SSS. This method incorporates relative position measurements from the SSS into method 4. It serves as a comparison to method 4, assessing the auxiliary role of the proposed SSS relative position measurements in post-processing navigation data.
6. FGO: The Proposed Method, or FGO: SINS+DVL+Position Constraint+SSS+ Improved Model. This method builds upon method 5 by incorporating the model with DVL installation errors proposed in this paper. It is used to compare with method 5, assessing the improvements in DVL installation error calibration and heading estimation brought about by the proposed model.

The EKF method is employed because traditional SINS/DVL-integrated navigation systems predominantly utilize Bayesian filtering techniques, with EKF being one of the most widely applied. The primary focus remains on the comparison between different FGO methods.

5.2. Results of Simulation

Figure 9 shows the comparison of the integrated navigation results of several methods, including trajectory comparison, position error comparison, heading angle error comparison, and gyro zero bias and accelerometer zero bias estimation effect comparison. Table 3 shows the comparison of the average position and heading errors of different methods.

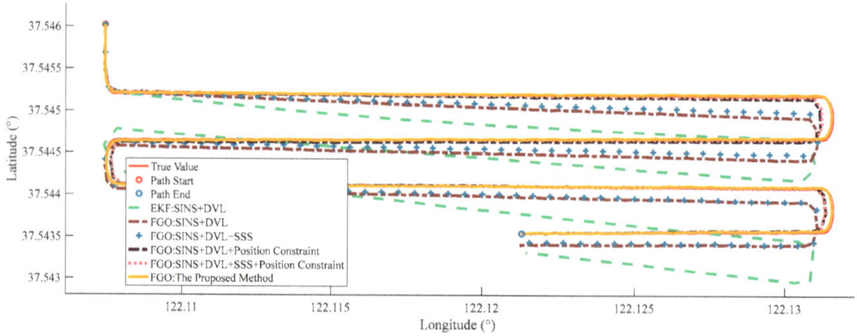

Figure 9. The trajectory comparison of different methods of the simulation.

Table 3. The comparison of average positioning and heading errors.

Method	Positioning Error (m)	Heading Error (deg)
KF: SINS+DVL	47.638	1.601
FGO: SINS+DVL	35.777	0.227
FGO: SINS+DVL+SSS	31.637	0.090
FGO: SINS+DVL+Position constraint	17.256	0.486
FGO: SINS+DVL+Position constraint+SSS	15.853	0.471
FGO: SINS+DVL+Position constraint+SSS +Improved model **(The proposed method)**	**2.234**	**0.039**

Figure 9 illustrates the trajectory comparisons of different methods. It is evident that among the real-time navigation group that does not utilize GNSS position constraints, the EKF: SINS+DVL method performs the worst, as it struggles to correct the initial heading error due to its reliance on a dead-reckoning algorithm. In contrast, the other two batch processing methods for real-time navigation, namely FGO: SINS+DVL and FGO: SINS+DVL+SSS, show slightly better performance, as they optimize information over the entire trajectory. The FGO: SINS+DVL+SSS method benefits from incorporating relative position measurements from SSS. In the post-processing methods that utilize GNSS position constraints, all methods maintain good trajectory accuracy; however, the proposed method using the enhanced model demonstrates superior performance at the end of the "Z" route.

Figure 10 and Table 3 present the details of the positioning and heading errors for each method. Figure 10a provides a clearer depiction of trajectory accuracy. For the comparative methods, while incorporating SSS position measurements and GNSS position constraints reduces position errors, these errors still display a linear trend as the AUV traverses the "Z" route. This linear variation is primarily attributed to errors in the DVL scale factor. The proposed method significantly mitigates this variation, which is further evidenced by the average position errors presented in Table 3. Figure 10b compares the heading errors of different methods, while Table 3 provides the specific values of the average heading errors. Firstly, the FGO methods, which can optimize historical navigation information, show smaller heading angle errors compared to the EKF method, which does not adjust for previous heading values. Secondly, the inclusion of SSS relative position information is found to enhance the accuracy of heading estimation. More importantly, while adding position constraints without utilizing the improved model decreases the average positioning errors from over 30 m to below 20 m, it results in an increase in the average heading error from below 0.25° to above 0.45°. This occurs due to the existing model not being adequate, leading to incorrect feedback into the heading estimates. In contrast, the proposed method addresses this issue, resulting in reductions in both positioning and heading errors.

Figure 11 and Table 4 illustrate the estimates of inertial sensor biases for the different methods. It can be seen that the inclusion of SSS measurements enhances the estimation accuracy of the Z axis gyroscope bias.

The summary of this simulation result is as follows:

1. Compared to filtering methods, batch processing methods can optimize past navigation data, significantly improving the positioning accuracy of the AUV during surveying tasks.
2. The relative position measurements provided by SSS can enhance the positioning and heading accuracy of the AUV, with a more pronounced effect when position measurements are otherwise lacking.
3. Methods that do not incorporate DVL error modeling result in GNSS position measurements improving the system's positioning accuracy at the expense of its heading accuracy. However, this issue does not occur with the model proposed in this paper, as both positioning and heading exhibit higher accuracy.

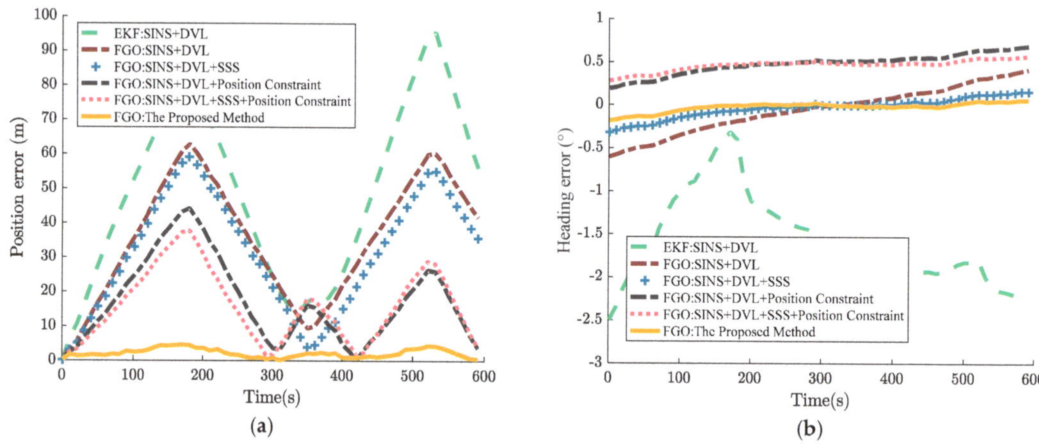

Figure 10. (**a**) Position error comparison of the simulation; (**b**) heading error comparison of the simulation.

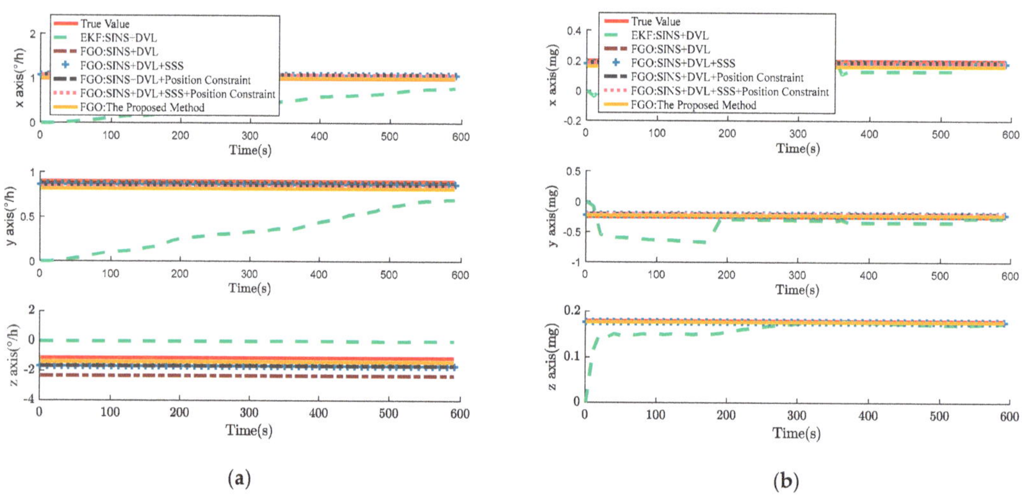

Figure 11. (**a**) Gyro bias estimation comparison; (**b**) Acc bias estimation comparison.

Table 4. Comparison of average gyroscope and accelerometer bias errors.

Methods	Gyro X Axis Bias (deg/h)	Gyro Y Axis Bias (deg/h)	Gyro Z Axis Bias (deg/h)	Acc X Axis Bias Error (mg)	Acc Y Axis Bias Error (mg)	Acc Z Axis Bias Error (mg)
KF: SINS+DVL	0.598	0.553	1.100	0.088	0.152	0.017
FGO: SINS+DVL	0.081	0.026	1.215	0.017	0.032	0.002
FGO: SINS+DVL+SSS	0.081	0.035	0.555	0.018	0.0337	0.023
FGO: SINS+DVL+Position constraint	0.083	0.055	0.572	0.023	0.403	0.003
FGO: SINS+DVL+SSS+Position constraint	0.083	0.058	0.323	0.013	0.047	0.003
FGO: SINS+DVL+SSS+Position constraint +Improved model **(The proposed method)**	**0.008**	**0.083**	**0.272**	**0.037**	**0.021**	0.003

6. AUV Marine Experiments and Result Analysis

6.1. Setup for AUV's Marine Experiments

The physical experiment took place in Sanya, Hainan, and was conducted using a semi-submersible vehicle. During operation, the main body of the robot remains underwater, unaffected by surface waves, while an antenna, approximately the same length as the AUV, is kept above the water surface. This setup allows for the real-time transmission of large volumes of data. Additionally, the antenna is equipped with a GPS module that integrates RTK technology, enabling high-precision positioning results.

The semi-submersible vehicle operates at a speed of approximately 3 knots. An initial heading error of 4° is set for the experiment. Figure 12 illustrates the AUV setup and its trajectory during the experiment. Tables 5–8 display the parameters of the sensors.

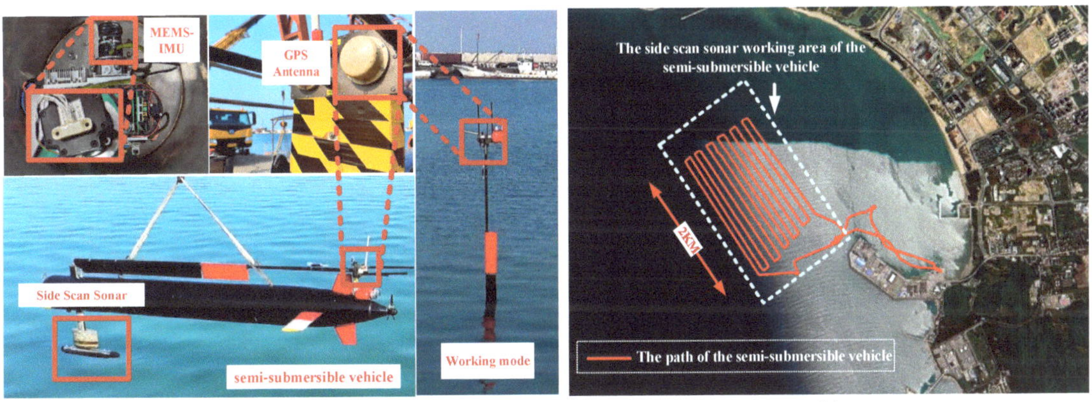

(a) (b)

Figure 12. Physical experiment setup. (**a**) The sensors equipped on the semi-submersible vehicle; (**b**) the semi-submarine vehicle's trajectory (the red lines) and the SSS recording area.

Table 5. Parameters of the MG-300B MEMS-IMU.

Parameters	Value
Gyro bias stability	0.02°/h
Angle random walk	≤0.015°/$\sqrt{h}$
Rate bias over temperature	≤1°/h (over life)
Gyro factor error	<100 ppm
Acc bias stability	<0.1 mg
Velocity random walk	<30 μg$\sqrt{Hz}$
Acc bias over Temp	<2 mg (over life)

Table 6. Parameters of the SSS ES4590.

Parameters	Value
Range	75 m (900 kHz)
Resolution	0.17 m

Table 7. Parameters of the Waterlinked a125 DVL.

Parameters	Value
Ping rate	2–15 Hz
Velocity resolution	0.1 mm/s
Long-term accuracy	±1.01%

Table 8. Parameters of the RTK GPS module K823.

Parameters	Value
Position accuracy	15 mm+ (baseline length (KM)/1,000,000) mm
Update rate	20Hz

The referenced true values for the experiment are sourced as follows

1. Position trajectory comparison and position error comparison

The GPS antenna of the semi-submersible vessel remains at the water surface at all times, and the positioning results obtained using RTK technology will be directly utilized as the true position values. The absolute position errors of the results from different methods are compared, along with their average absolute position errors.

2. Heading error comparison

For semi-submersible unmanned vessels, there is no higher-precision attitude reference installed. Therefore, the output of the smoothed result from the integrated navigation of SINS/GNSS is used as the true heading value. Since the heading angle accuracy of the SINS/GNSS integration is significantly higher than that of the SINS/DVL integration, it is reasonable to consider its results as the true values.

Similar to the simulation, an initial heading error of 4° is also introduced for all methods in the experiment. A total of six methods are verified:

1. EKF: SINS+DVL.
2. FGO: SINS+DVL.
3. FGO: SINS+DVL+SSS.
4. FGO: SINS+DVL+Position Constraint.
5. FGO: SINS+DVL+Position Constraint+SSS.
6. FGO: The Proposed Method, or FGO: SINS+DVL+Position Constraint+SSS+ Improved Model.

6.2. Results of Marine Experiments

Figure 13 displays the trajectory results for all methods.

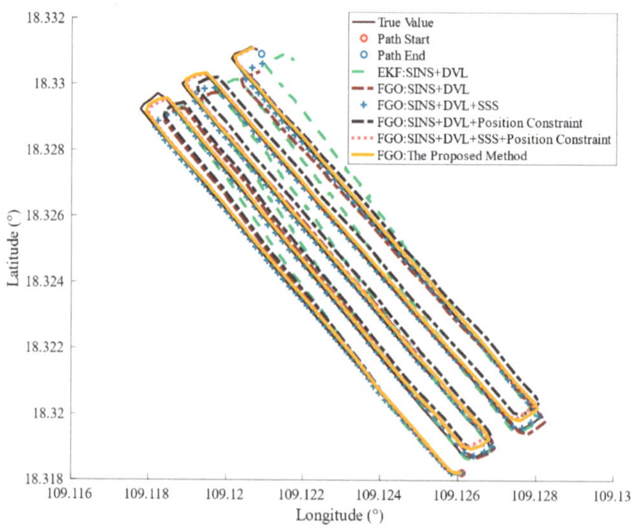

Figure 13. The trajectory comparison of different methods of marine experiments.

From Figure 13, it is evident that the EKF: SINS+DVL method exhibits significant errors, as the initial attitude error leads to uncorrected positioning errors. Among the FGO methods, FGO: SINS+DVL+SSS demonstrates superior trajectory tracking compared to FGO: SINS+DVL. The inclusion of GNSS position constraints before diving and after surfacing in FGO: SINS+DVL+Position Constraint further enhances positioning accuracy. Additionally, FGO: SINS+DVL+Position Constraint+SSS achieves even better performance. The trajectory tracking of the proposed method is comparable to that of FGO: SINS+DVL+SSS+Position Constraint.

Figure 14 presents a comparison of position and heading errors, while Table 9 displays the average values of these errors for each method. As shown in Figure 14a, the inclusion of SSS reduces position errors. However, in the absence of GNSS position constraints at the beginning and end, the vehicle's position errors fluctuate over time due to DVL scale factor errors. When GNSS position constraints are added, the overall position errors decrease. On the other hand, Figure 14b indicates that without using the improved model, the addition of GNSS position constraints does not significantly enhance heading accuracy.

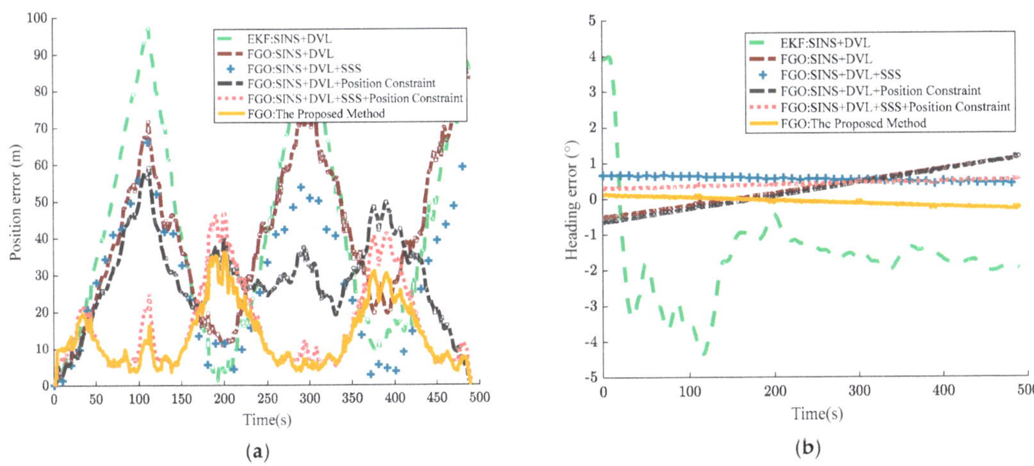

Figure 14. (**a**) Position error comparison of marine experiments; (**b**) heading error comparison of marine experiments.

Table 9. The comparison of average positioning error and heading error.

Method	Average Positioning Error (m)	Average Heading Error (deg)
KF: SINS+DVL	42.333	1.946
FGO: SINS+DVL	40.509	0.477
FGO: SINS+DVL+SSS	29.267	0.554
FGO: SINS+DVL+Position constraint	28.656	0.488
FGO: SINS+DVL+Position constraint+SSS	16.120	0.421
FGO: SINS+DVL+Position Constraint+SSS+Improved Model (The proposed method)	**11.548**	**0.133**

Table 9 provides average values that further illustrate this point. When SSS relative position measurements are added to the system, the average positioning error decreases from 40.509 m to 29.267 m. Even with GNSS position constraints at the beginning and end of the trajectory, incorporating SSS relative position measurements further reduces the average positioning error from 28.656 m to 16.120 m.

Regarding heading errors, the EKF method cannot correct past heading deviations, resulting in the largest heading error of 1.946°. After applying the FGO method to process the SINS/DVL-integrated navigation data, the heading angle error is reduced to 0.477° due to the optimization of the previous trajectory. However, adding more measurements does not lead to a further reduction in heading errors. In fact, when comparing the FGO: SINS+DVL method with the FGO: SINS+DVL+Position Constraint method, the latter exhibits a higher average heading error of 0.488°, compared to 0.477° for the former. Upon the analysis, it is concluded that the traditional modeling is not sufficiently accurate, as unaccounted factors such as scale factor errors and DVL installation angle errors contribute to position errors. This results in position residuals being incorrectly fed back into the attitude angle, ultimately leading to erroneous estimates.

In contrast, the proposed method, which employs the improved model, effectively reduces both positioning and heading errors by enhancing the overall modeling accuracy.

The summary of the experimental results is as follows:

1. The proposed method of incorporating SSS relative position measurements as a position reference into the SINS/DVL navigation system significantly improves the positioning accuracy of the integrated navigation system, particularly in the absence of position measurements.
2. The introduction of GNSS measurements before diving and after surfacing to optimize the underwater trajectory of the AUV greatly enhances positioning accuracy, especially when the accuracy of the inertial devices is slightly lower.
3. In methods utilizing the traditional model, although the addition of GNSS position constraints improves positioning accuracy, it does not enhance heading accuracy. However, the proposed method with the improved model raises both positioning and heading accuracy. Under the traditional model, residuals are incorrectly fed back into the heading; with a more robust model, these residuals are instead directed towards the DVL calibration angle and scale factor, resulting in improved heading accuracy.

7. Conclusions

This paper proposes a post-processing navigation method for underwater robots based on FGO that incorporates SSS relative position references. The method employs an improved SSS image registration method to obtain relative positions, and integrates these with other measurements from the AUV using an enhanced model within the FGO framework. This approach simultaneously optimizes the navigation information and DVL error parameters within the trajectory, providing a more accurate attitude reference for the SSS map.

The research first introduces an improved Fourier-based image registration technique that enhances measurement stability and accuracy using Gaussian priors and band-pass filtering, with only low computational resource consumption. Subsequently, an SSS-integrated navigation method based on the improved model FGO is proposed, capable of simultaneously estimating the AUV's navigation information and system error parameters, such as DVL scale factor errors, thereby optimizing position and heading information. Finally, the effectiveness of this method is validated through simulations and field experiments.

There are three principal conclusions:

1. The introduction of relative position measurements from SSS and GNSS measurements significantly enhances the position and heading accuracy of the AUV navigation system, particularly in scenarios lacking position measurements.
2. While the traditional model improves positioning accuracy with the inclusion of GNSS position constraints, it does not enhance heading accuracy. In contrast, the proposed improved model effectively mitigates the negative impact of residual errors on heading, resulting in improved accuracy for both position and heading.

3. Compared to the Kalman filter method, the batch processing approach optimizes past navigation data, leading to significant improvements in the position accuracy of AUV during survey tasks, especially under the traditional model.

Author Contributions: Conceptualization, L.Z. and L.G.; Data curation, L.Z. and J.Z.; Formal analysis, L.Z.; Funding acquisition, Y.G.; Investigation, L.Z. and J.Z.; Methodology, L.Z.; Project administration, L.G.; Resources, L.Z.; Supervision, J.Z. and Y.G.; Visualization, L.G.; Writing—original draft, L.Z.; Writing—review and editing, L.G. All authors have read and agreed to the published version of the manuscript.

Funding: This work was funded in part by the Fundamental Research Funds for the Central Universities (No. 3072024XX0406), in part by the Department of Science and Technology of Heilongjiang Province (2023ZX01A21), and in part by the National Natural Science Foundation of China (NSFC. 61803118).

Institutional Review Board Statement: Not applicable.

Informed Consent Statement: Not applicable.

Data Availability Statement: The data that support the findings of this study are available from the corresponding author upon reasonable request.

Conflicts of Interest: The funders had no role in the design of the study; in the collection, analyses, or interpretation of data; in the writing of the manuscript; or in the decision to publish the results.

References

1. Hansen, R.E.; Saebo, T.O.; Callow, H.J.; Hagen, P.E.; Hammerstad, E. Synthetic Aperture Sonar Processing for the HUGIN AUV. In Proceedings of the Europe Oceans 2005, Brest, France, 20–23 June 2005; Volume 2, pp. 1090–1094.
2. Naus, K.; Piskur, P. Applying the Geodetic Adjustment Method for Positioning in Relation to the Swarm Leader of Underwater Vehicles Based on Course, Speed, and Distance Measurements. *Energies* **2022**, *15*, 8472. [CrossRef]
3. Jaffre, F.; Littlefield, R.; Grund, M.; Purcell, M. Development of a New Version of the REMUS 6000 Autonomous Underwater Vehicle. In Proceedings of the OCEANS 2019—Marseille, Marseille, France, 17–20 June 2019; pp. 1–7.
4. Wang, J.; Tang, Y.; Li, S.; Lu, Y.; Li, J.; Liu, T.; Jiang, Z.; Chen, C.; Cheng, Y.; Yu, D.; et al. The Haidou-1 Hybrid Underwater Vehicle for the Mariana Trench Science Exploration to 10,908 m Depth. *J. Field Robot.* **2024**, *41*, 1054–1079. [CrossRef]
5. Wåhlin, A.; Alley, K.E.; Begeman, C.; Hegrenæs, Ø.; Yuan, X.; Graham, A.G.C.; Hogan, K.; Davis, P.E.D.; Dotto, T.S.; Eayrs, C.; et al. Swirls and Scoops: Ice Base Melt Revealed by Multibeam Imagery of an Antarctic Ice Shelf. *Sci. Adv.* **2024**, *10*, eadn9188. [CrossRef] [PubMed]
6. Xu, B.; Wang, L.; Li, S.; Zhang, J. A Novel Calibration Method of SINS/DVL Integration Navigation System Based on Quaternion. *IEEE Sens. J.* **2020**, *20*, 9567–9580. [CrossRef]
7. Yan, M.; Wang, Z.; Zhang, J. Online Calibration of Installation Errors of SINS/OD Integrated Navigation System Based on Improved NHC. *IEEE Sens. J.* **2022**, *22*, 12602–12612. [CrossRef]
8. Gade, K. NavLab, a Generic Simulation and Post-Processing Tool for Navigation. *MIC* **2005**, *26*, 135–150. [CrossRef]
9. Yao, Y.; Shen, Y.; Xu, X.; Deng, K.; Xu, X. A Modified Smoothing Scheme for Water Current-Aided SINS/DVL Integration System. *IEEE Sens. J.* **2023**, *23*, 26366–26374. [CrossRef]
10. Franchi, M.; Ridolfi, A.; Pagliai, M. A Forward-Looking SONAR and Dynamic Model-Based AUV Navigation Strategy: Preliminary Validation with FeelHippo AUV. *Ocean Eng.* **2020**, *196*, 106770. [CrossRef]
11. Hurtós, N.; Ribas, D.; Cufí, X.; Petillot, Y.; Salvi, J. Fourier-based Registration for Robust Forward-looking Sonar Mosaicing in Low-visibility Underwater Environments. *J. Field Robot.* **2015**, *32*, 123–151. [CrossRef]
12. Song, Y.; He, B.; Zhang, L.; Yan, T. Side-Scan Sonar Image Registration Based on Modified Phase Correlation for AUV Navigation. In Proceedings of the OCEANS 2016—Shanghai, Shanghai, China, 10–13 April 2016; pp. 1–4.
13. Hover, F.S.; Eustice, R.M.; Kim, A.; Englot, B.; Johannsson, H.; Kaess, M.; Leonard, J.J. Advanced Perception, Navigation and Planning for Autonomous in-Water Ship Hull Inspection. *Int. J. Robot. Res.* **2012**, *31*, 1445–1464. [CrossRef]
14. Zhang, L.; Zhou, H.; Gao, Y. An In-Motion Alignment Method of AUV SINS/DVL Navigation System Based on FGO. *Measurement* **2023**, *222*, 113578. [CrossRef]
15. Xu, B.; Guo, Y. A Novel DVL Calibration Method Based on Robust Invariant Extended Kalman Filter. *IEEE Trans. Veh. Technol.* **2022**, *71*, 9422–9434. [CrossRef]
16. Barfoot, T.D. *State Estimation for Robotics*, 1st ed.; Cambridge University Press: Cambridge, UK, 2017; ISBN 978-1-107-15939-6.
17. Cao, S.; Lu, X.; Shen, S. GVINS: Tightly Coupled GNSS–Visual–Inertial Fusion for Smooth and Consistent State Estimation. *IEEE Trans. Robot.* **2022**, *38*, 2004–2021. [CrossRef]

18. Qin, T.; Li, P.; Shen, S. VINS-Mono: A Robust and Versatile Monocular Visual-Inertial State Estimator. *IEEE Trans. Robot.* **2018**, *34*, 1004–1020. [CrossRef]
19. Zhang, L.; Wen, W.; Hsu, L.-T.; Zhang, T. An Improved Inertial Preintegration Model in Factor Graph Optimization for High Accuracy Positioning of Intelligent Vehicles. *IEEE Trans. Intell. Veh.* **2023**, *9*, 1641–1653. [CrossRef]

sensors

MDPI

Article

Wake Detection and Positioning for Autonomous Underwater Vehicles Based on Cilium-Inspired Wake Sensor

Xuanye Hu [1,2], Yi Yang [1,*], Zhiyu Liao [1], Xinghua Zhu [1], Renxin Wang [3], Peng Zhang [3] and Zhiqiang Hu [1]

1 State Key Laboratory of Robotics, Shenyang Institute of Automation, Chinese Academy of Sciences, Shenyang 110016, China; huxuanye@sia.cn (X.H.); liaozhiyu@sia.cn (Z.L.); zhuxinghua@sia.cn (X.Z.); hzq@sia.cn (Z.H.)
2 University of Chinese Academy of Sciences, Beijing 100049, China
3 State Key Laboratory of Dynamic Measurement Technology, North University of China, Taiyuan 030051, China; wangrenxin@nuc.edu.cn (R.W.); s202206014@st.nuc.edu.cn (P.Z.)
* Correspondence: yangyi@sia.cn

Abstract: This paper proposes a method for passive detection of autonomous underwater vehicle (AUV) wakes using a cilium-inspired wake sensor (CIWS), which can be used for the detection and tracking of AUVs. First, the characteristics of the CIWS and its working principle for detecting underwater flow fields are introduced. Then, a flow velocity sensor is used to measure the flow velocities of the "TS MINI" AUV's wake at different positions, and a velocity field model of the "TS MINI" AUV's wake is established. Finally, the wake field of the "TS MINI" AUV was measured at various positions using the CIWS. By analyzing the data, the characteristic frequency of the AUV's propeller is identified, which is correlated with the AUV's rotation speed and the number of blades. Through further analysis, a mapping model is established between the spectral amplitude of the characteristic frequency at different positions and the corresponding wake velocity. By substituting this mapping model into the AUV's wake velocity field model, the possible position range of the sensor relative to the AUV propeller can be estimated. The research provides a technical foundation for underwater detection and tracking missions based on wake detection.

Keywords: cilium-inspired wake sensor; wake detection; wake tracking; target positioning; autonomous underwater vehicles

Academic Editor: Fabio Leccese

Received: 26 November 2024
Revised: 21 December 2024
Accepted: 23 December 2024
Published: 25 December 2024

Citation: Hu, X.; Yang, Y.; Liao, Z.; Zhu, X.; Wang, R.; Zhang, P.; Hu, Z. Wake Detection and Positioning for Autonomous Underwater Vehicles Based on Cilium-Inspired Wake Sensor. *Sensors* **2025**, *25*, 41. https://doi.org/10.3390/s25010041

1. Introduction

Autonomous underwater vehicles (AUVs) offer several advantages, including operational flexibility, strong stealth capability, adaptability to complex ocean conditions, and cost-effectiveness. With the continuous development of AUV technology, the complexity and difficulty of their missions have also increased significantly, making a single AUV insufficient for meeting increasingly complex demands [1]. This has led to the inevitable trend of multiple AUVs collaborating in swarms to carry out new missions [2–4]. AUV swarms are similar to the fish swarms. Traditionally, AUV swarms use acoustic or visual communication or position methods [5–8]. However, fish rely primarily on their highly sensitive lateral line organs to sense the surrounding fluid environment, allowing them to perform essential tasks like foraging and obstacle avoidance. Inspired by biomimetics, sensors with functions similar to lateral lines can be used to detect the wakes produced by other AUVs during navigation, providing AUVs with sensory capabilities comparable to those of fish. This allows AUVs to discern other weak moving targets underwater and enables the AUV swarm formation similar to fish schooling. Lateral line sensing, compared to traditional sonar and visual detection methods, features a simpler device structure. As a passive detection technology, it offers the advantage of lower energy consumption compared to active sonar and underwater cameras. In complex underwater environments, sonar is prone to interference from surrounding objects, while visual detection relies on adequate lighting and high water clarity. In such harsh hydrological conditions, lateral line sensing technology remains effective and reliable.

Bio-inspired sensor technology has become a significant research area in recent years [9,10]. Astreinidi's [11] research explored how biological organisms use mechanical interactions to acquire information and assessed the feasibility of applying these principles to mechanical design. Sietse M. van Netten [12,13] validated the fish lateral line dynamics model through calculations and experiments and elucidated the signal-processing capabilities of the lateral line canal organ by studying its frequency response, which had proven its capability to maintain constant sensitivity to fluid acceleration at low frequencies. Debarun Sengupta [14] proposed a novel fabrication process for fabricating inexpensive yet sensitive bio-inspired cilium sensors and demonstrated their potential applications in flow velocity detection. Qiao [15] encapsulated and adapted the cilium-inspired wake sensors, making them feasible for AUV wake detection.

However, currently, no researchers have practically applied CIWSs for AUV wake detection or further AUV swarm perceptions. One of the application scenarios for the existing wake detection technology in underwater vehicles is torpedo wake guidance [16]. Using CIWSs can determine the relationship between wake velocity and sensor signal amplitude, offering higher measurement accuracy than traditional wake guidance and enabling effective underwater target detection and tracking. Unlike conventional torpedo wake guidance, which requires frequent traversals across the wake boundary to sense the wake [17–19], CIWSs can perceive the wake continuously within its range, thereby effectively reducing energy consumption during the tracking process.

In this paper, the working principle of the CIWS is analyzed and the relationship between the wake velocity and the sensor signal amplitude is established. Subsequently, the spectral data of the sensor at different positions in the wake are analyzed, and the correlation between the sensor data and the relative position in the wake is established through a wake decay model, all of which provides a theoretical foundation for subsequent wake perception and target tracking based on CIWSs.

2. CIWS Model

2.1. Flow Field Sensing Principle Based on Bio-Inspired Cilium

The lateral line system is a specialized mechanosensory system found in fish and certain amphibians. The lateral line sensory system in fish consists of superficial neuromasts and canal neuromasts(CN), both of which rely on cilium-based receptors to perform their primary functions [20]. The superficial neuromasts are positioned on the surface of the fish, directly exposed to the external flow, and contribute to flow sensing. The CNs are embedded beneath the epidermis within the lateral line canal and connect to the external water flow through small pores on the fish's skin, thereby enabling the detection of pressure fields in the water. The lateral line canal effectively filters out low-frequency noise generated by the fish's own movement, as well as other environmental noise, thereby enhancing the fish's ability to detect targets. The biomechanical model of the CN can be represented as a rigid hemisphere sliding without friction on a plane. This rigid hemisphere is coupled to a linear spring, with its stiffness provided by the cilium, as shown in Figure 1.

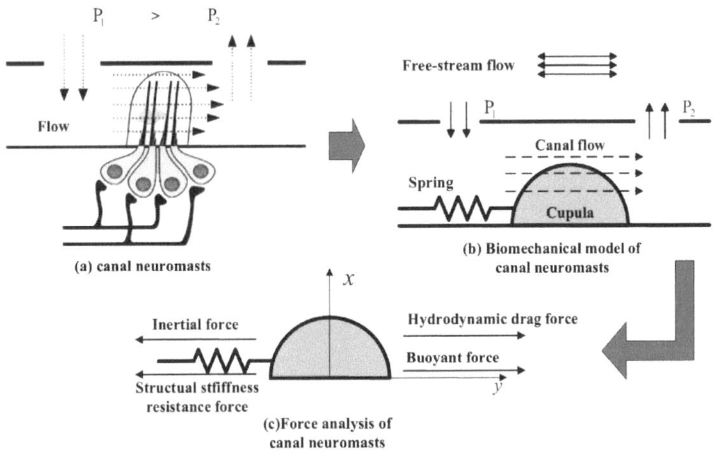

Figure 1. Schematic diagram of the biomechanics of the CN [20]. (**a**) Structural components of the CN. (**b**) Biomechanical model of the CN. (**c**) Force analysis of the CN.

Figure 1c shows the forces on the cupula of CN.Taking the hemisphere as the main body, the mechanical control equation of the CN in the lateral line system is defined as

$$F_i + F_s = F_h + F_b \tag{1}$$

where F_i represents the inertial force of the hemisphere, which can be expressed as

$$F_i = M\frac{d^2Y(t)}{dt^2} \tag{2}$$

Here, M is the mass of the hemisphere and $M = 4\pi a^3\rho/3$, a is the radius of the hemisphere, ρ is the density of the hemisphere. $Y(t)$ is the displacement of the hemisphere induced by the fluid flow, where $Y(t) = Y_0(f)\exp(i2\pi ft)$ is the steady-state oscillatory displacement. $Y_0(f)$ represents the displacement amplitude of the hemisphere, which is a function of the stimulus frequency f.

In Equation (1), F_s represents the structural stiffness force due to the elastic coupling between the hemisphere and the epithelial cells, which can be defined as

$$F_s = KY(t) \tag{3}$$

where K is the sliding coefficient, which is proportional to the number of epithelial cells.

In Equation (1), the first term on the right-hand side, F_h, represents the hydrodynamic drag force acting on the hemisphere, which can be defined as

$$F_h = D\left(\frac{dY(t)}{dt} - \frac{dW(t)}{dt}\right) \tag{4}$$

where D is the drag coefficient, and $dY(t)/dt - dW(t)/dt$ represents the relative displacement between the hemisphere and the external flow velocity. $W(t) = W_0(f)\exp(i2\pi ft)$ represents the oscillatory displacement of the external flow. $W_0(f)$ is the amplitude of the external fluid displacement, and f is the excitation frequency.

In Equation (1), F_b represents the buoyancy force acting on the hemisphere due to the pressure difference around the structure, which can be defined as

$$F_b = M\frac{d^2W(t)}{dt^2} \tag{5}$$

Thus, the mechanical control equation can also be expressed as

$$M\frac{d^2Y(t)}{dt^2} + KY(t) = D\left(\frac{dY(t)}{dt} - \frac{dW(t)}{dt}\right) + M\frac{d^2W(t)}{dt^2} \tag{6}$$

The control equation is linear and can be solved in the frequency domain. Therefore, by solving this control equation, the frequency-dependent sensitivity of the hemisphere can be obtained. Sensitivity is defined as the ratio of the displacement amplitude $Y_0(f)$ to the external fluid velocity amplitude $V_0(f)$. The external fluid velocity term can be obtained from Equation (6):

$$V(t) = \frac{dW(t)}{dt} = i2\pi f W_0(f)\exp(i2\pi ft) = V_0(f)\exp(i2\pi ft) \tag{7}$$

Thus, the frequency-dependent sensitivity of the hemisphere can be expressed as

$$S_{cn}(f) = \frac{Y_0(f)}{V_0(f)} = \frac{1}{2\pi f_t}\frac{1 + \frac{\sqrt{2}}{2}(1+i)\left(\frac{f}{f_t}\right)^{1/2} + \frac{1}{3}i\frac{f}{f_t}}{N_r + i\frac{f}{f_t} - \frac{\sqrt{2}}{2}(1+i)\left(\frac{f}{f_t}\right)^{3/2} - \frac{1}{3}i\left(\frac{f}{f_t}\right)^2} \tag{8}$$

where $f_t = \mu/2\pi\rho_w a^2$ is the transition frequency at which either viscous force ($f < f_t$) or inertial force ($f > f_t$) acts on the hemisphere. μ is the dynamic viscosity of the fluid. $N_r = Ka\rho_w/6\pi\mu^2$ is the resonance factor affecting the resonance of the hemisphere, and ρ_w is the density of water. The frequency response model can be represented by a transfer function. The transfer function is defined as the ratio of the stimulus variable to the response variable and can therefore be used as a mathematical expression for sensitivity. The frequency response of the hemisphere varies with the frequency of the external flow stimulation.

The entire process of external flow excitation acting on the hemisphere can be divided into two steps. In the first step, the velocity or acceleration of the external free flow is transformed by the canal into a local flow velocity. The external flow generates a pressure difference between the lumen, which, in turn, creates a local flow velocity in the canal. In this step, sensitivity or the transfer function is defined as the ratio of the local flow velocity to the free flow velocity, denoted as $S_{cn_0}(f)$. $S_{cn_0}(f)$ can be analytically solved using basic hydrodynamics theory and cylindrical flow theory. In the second step, the flow inside the canal generates fluid forces acting on the hemisphere, causing it to slide. The sensitivity $S_{cn}(f)$ is defined as the ratio of the displacement amplitude of the hemisphere to the flow velocity inside the canal, as shown in Equation (8). By calculating the product of the above two transfer functions, the composite frequency response of the hemisphere can be obtained, which provides the relationship between the hemisphere displacement and the external canal flow velocity.

The excitation of the hemisphere by the external water flow can be divided into the following two steps. In the first step, the speed or acceleration of the free external flow is transformed by the canal into the local flow speed. The external flow creates a pressure difference across the canal, which, in turn, generates a local flow velocity within the canal. In this step, the sensitivity or transfer function is defined as the ratio of the local flow speed to the free flow speed, which can be analytically solved using basic hydrodynamic theory and cylindrical flow theory. In the second step, the fluid flow within the canal generates a fluid force acting on the hemisphere, causing the hemisphere to slide. The sensitivity is defined as the ratio of the displacement amplitude of the hemisphere to the velocity of the flow within the canal, as shown in Equation (8). By calculating the product of these two transfer functions, the composite frequency response of the hemisphere can be obtained. Using this composite frequency response, the relationship between the displacement of the hemisphere and the external flow velocity can be determined.

2.2. CIWS

In this study, the CIWS independently developed by North University of China was selected [21]. The sensor utilizes a cilium-crossbeam stress and voltage output model, as shown in Figure 2. The model employs cylindrical cilium, with piezoresistive elements distributed at the points of maximum stress on the intersecting cantilever beams, thereby maximizing the sensitivity of the sensing units. When different flow velocities act on the cilium, the cantilever beam deforms in response to the direction of the flow velocity. This deformation changes the resistance of the piezoresistors, which can be measured by monitoring the voltage across different piezoresistors.

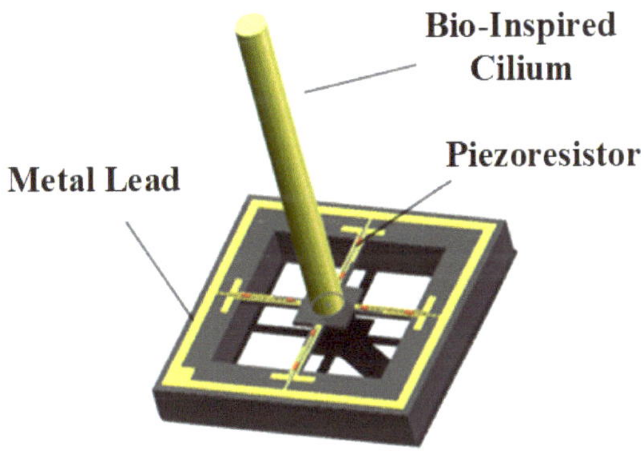

Figure 2. Cilium-Crossbeam Stress and Voltage Output Model for CIWS.

The packaging of the CIWS is shown in Figure 3. An underwater fairing featuring four evenly distributed holes around its structure is installed at the head of the sensor, directing water flow onto the cilium-crossbeam structure. The underwater fairing is mounted at the sensor head, and the deformation of the cilium generates a potential difference, which is transmitted to a conditioning circuit board to amplify the voltage in each signal channel. The amplified signals are transmitted to the signal acquisition circuit through waterproof cables. The specific parameters of the CIWS are listed in Table 1.

Table 1. The specific parameters of the CIWS.

Cilium Structure	Diameter	Length	Operating Voltage
Crossbeam	24 mm	160 mm	±5 V

From Equation (7), it can be derived that the sensitivity of the CIWS is defined as the ratio of the hemispherical displacement amplitude $Y_0(f)$ to the external flow velocity amplitude $V_0(f)$. The frequency response curve as a function of the excitation frequency is shown in Figure 4. From the figure, it can be observed that the ratio of the hemispherical displacement to the external flow velocity amplitude fluctuates around 10^0 in the low-frequency range, indicating that the hemispherical displacement is approximately proportional to the external flow velocity. Furthermore, based on the elastic mechanics formula: $F = kx$, it follows that the hemispherical displacement is directly proportional to the force acting on the hemisphere. Therefore, it can be concluded that the force acting on the hemisphere is linearly related to the external flow velocity.

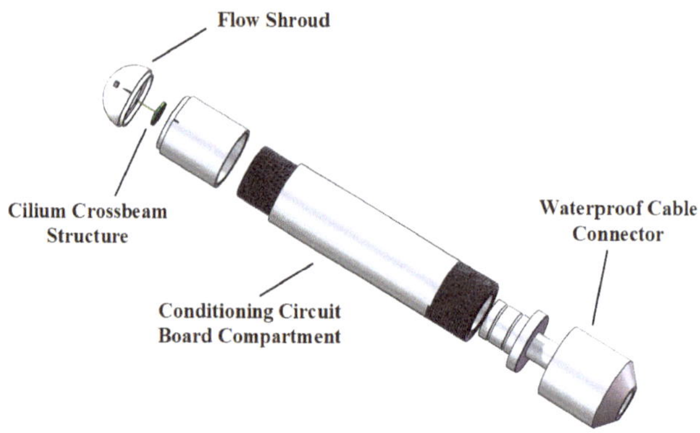

Figure 3. Structure of the CIWS.

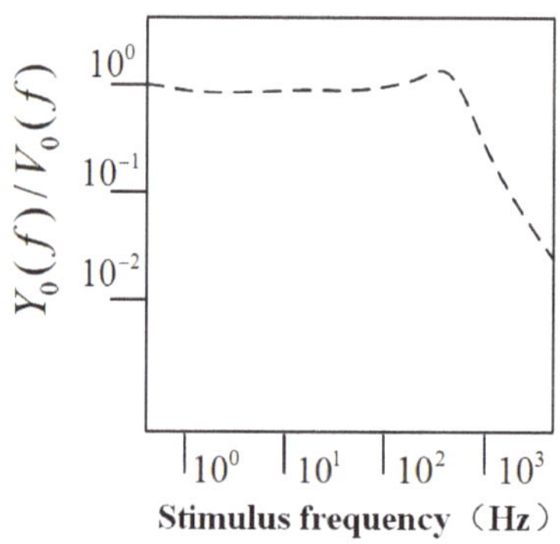

Figure 4. The frequency response curve as a function of the excitation frequency [21].

The displacement of the hemisphere is approximately proportional to the external flow velocity in the low-frequency range, meaning that the CIWS data can intuitively reflect the flow velocity at the current position. However, in addition to the vortices, the wake also contains turbulent flows, resulting in unstable local flow velocities. This leads to large fluctuations in the corresponding time-domain signal, without any distinct signal features, making typical feature matching algorithms unsuitable for time-domain analysis. Calculating the average wake velocity over a certain period can represent the average velocity at the current position. However, during AUV navigation, it is not possible for the AUV to remain at the same position for an extended period, necessitating real-time acquisition of wake velocity information. Therefore, using spectral analysis to obtain wake velocity is a feasible approach. As previously analyzed, in the low-frequency domain, the displacement of the hemisphere is linearly related to the external flow velocity. Thus, in the low-frequency part of the spectrum shown in Figure 4, it is possible to identify frequency points where the displacement of the hemisphere is linearly related to the external flow velocity. The spectral amplitude at these frequency points can then be used to reflect the flow velocity at the current position.

3. Experimental Testing and Modeling of the Flow Field of Pump-Jet Propellers

The sensitivity of the CIWS tends to stabilize at a constant value in the low-frequency range. The voltage of the sensor corresponds to the displacement of the cilium, and the displacement of the cilium is linearly related to the external flow velocity. To quantitatively analyze the relationship between the CIWS signal and the wake velocity at the current position, it is necessary to acquire the CIWS data at different positions in the wake velocity field, along with the corresponding flow velocity values.

3.1. Wake Field Generation Using Pump-Jet Propellers

In this study, the "TS MINI" AUV [22], developed by the Shenyang Institute of Automation, Chinese Academy of Sciences, was selected to generate the AUV wake, as shown in Figure 5. The propulsion system is a pump-jet propeller (PJP) with an aft stator. The specific parameters of the PJP are listed in Table 2.

Table 2. The specific parameters of the PJP.

Stator Position	Number of Rotor Blades	Number of Stator Blades	Shroud Inner Diameter	Central Shaft Diameter	Supply Voltage	Set Rotational Speed	Actual Rotational Speed
Aft Stator	Seven Blades	Nine Blades	80 mm	30 mm	24 V	1000 rpm	960 rpm

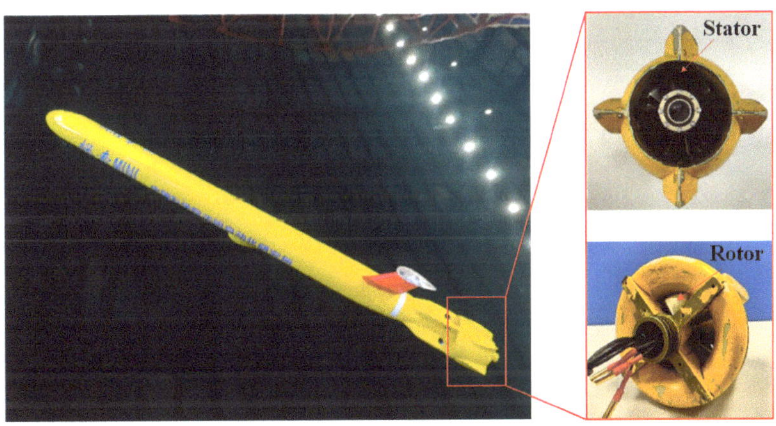

Figure 5. Photograph of the Aft Stator Pump-Jet Propeller.

To standardize the orientation of the coordinate axes and the position of the origin for subsequent analysis, an inertial reference coordinate system O-xyz is established based on the PJP model, as shown in Figure 6. The origin O is located at the center point of the plane at the downstream end of the PJP rotational axis. The y-axis points vertically upward, the z-axis is aligned with the central axis and points towards the outlet, and the x-axis follows the right-hand rule. Here, n represents the rotation speed of the rotor (with the direction of rotation defined by the right-hand rule).

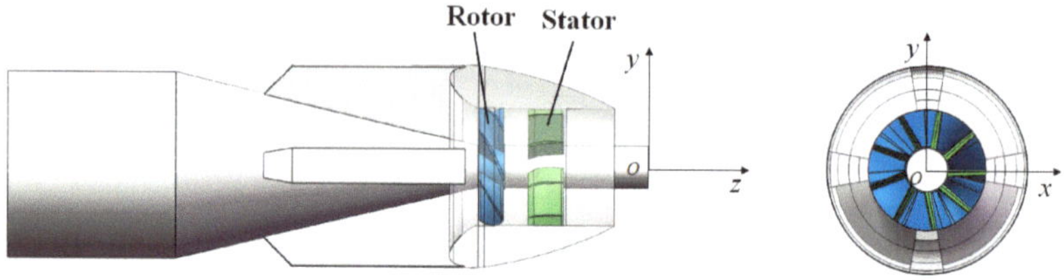

Figure 6. The PJP Model and Reference Coordinate System.

3.2. Wake Flow Field Measurement

The PJP wake comprises both turbulence and vortices, leading to fluctuations in the velocity of the wake field. To determine the average velocity at a given position, the flow velocity at a fixed position was measured over a specific period of time, and the mean value was calculated. In this experiment, the wake was generated using the "TS MINI" AUV PJP. The experimental setup consisted of a tank with dimensions of 4 m in length, 2 m in width, and 1 m in height with a water depth of 68 cm. The PJP was mounted on a frame positioned 20 cm above the bottom of the tank. A $1\,\text{m} \times 2\,\text{m}$ frame was placed behind the PJP to hold the sensors, and a ruler was attached to the frame to measure the exact coordinates of the sensor.During the experiment, the PJP operated in a moored state, and the selected AUV had a relatively low cruising speed, ensuring that the propeller wake dominated the flow field. The wake flow field under moored conditions can effectively reflect the wake characteristics during navigation. Additionally, the PJP exhibits strong jet-focused characteristics, resulting in slower lateral wake diffusion. The impact of echo effects from the wake reaching the tank walls can be considered negligible. Moreover, the length of the tank is significantly greater than the extent of the wake, rendering the axial echo effects negligible as well.

The LS300A flow meter, manufactured by Nanjing Ouka Instrument and Meter Co., Ltd. (Nanjing, China), was utilized for velocity measurements, maintaining the flow meter at the same height as the propeller. Measurements were conducted along the Oz axis, with the x-axis ranging from $-10\,\text{cm}$ to $10\,\text{cm}$ and the z-axis ranging from $10\,\text{cm}$ to $110\,\text{cm}$, resulting in 11×56 velocity measurement points. The PJP rotational speed was set to 1000 rpm (actual speed of 960 rpm), which corresponds to one of the operating speeds of the "TS MINI" AUV, with a cruising speed of 3 knots. At this speed, the wake field intensity is suitable for measurement and provides a rapid response for AUV navigation control. The flow meter measured the flow velocity at each position for one minute, and the average value was calculated to represent the mean velocity at each position. Measurements were repeated three times for each position. The experimental setup is shown in Figure 7.

The experimental measurement data are presented in Figure 8. It can be observed that due to the obstruction caused by the central shaft of the PJP, the velocity curve at a lateral offset of 0 cm is not the maximum, and the axial velocity at this point initially increases and then decreases. The data for other lateral offsets generally follow a decaying trend. The average velocity demonstrates an approximately symmetrical relationship across the lateral distances. The velocity field of the PJP is shown in Figure 9. From the figure, it can be observed that the maximum flow velocity is approximately $1.1\,\text{m/s}$. When the axial distance exceeds 100 cm, the wake velocity tends to stabilize. Additionally, beyond a lateral distance of 10 cm, the wake flow is essentially negligible.

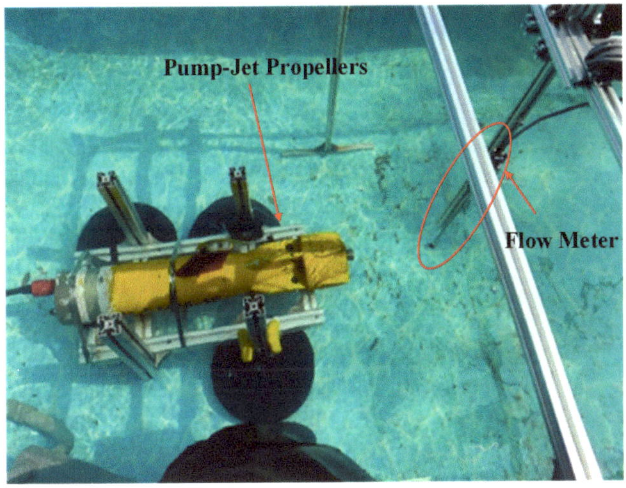

Figure 7. Measurement Site for the Average Velocity of PJP Wake.

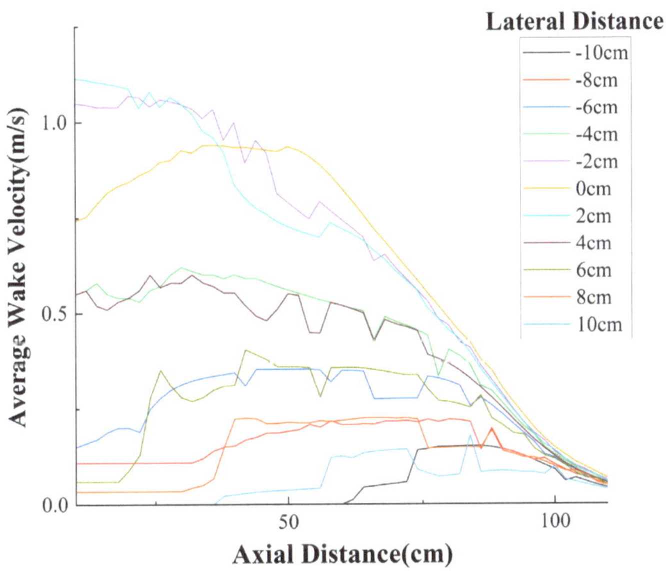

Figure 8. Relationship Between Measured Wake Velocity and Position.

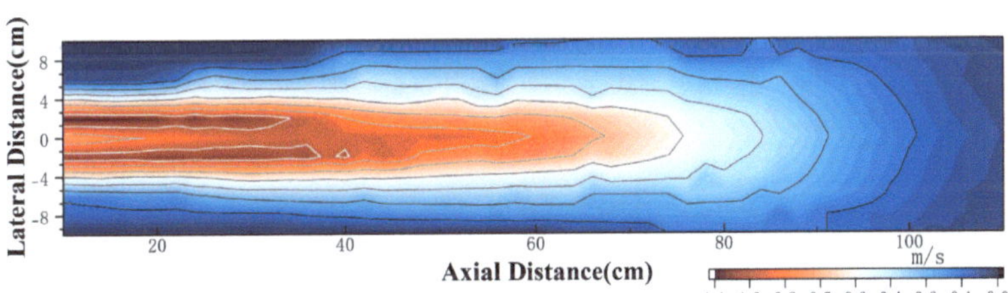

Figure 9. Iso−Velocity Contour Map of the Wake Flow Field.

4. Wake Detection Experiment Based on CIWS

In the previous section, an average velocity decay model of the wake was established based on the measurement of average velocity within the wake region of the propeller. To further investigate the relationship between the wake sensor signals and the average wake velocity, it is necessary to measure the wake sensor data under the same operating conditions within the PJP's wake region. The wake sensor utilized is a cilium-based MEMS wake sensor developed by North University of China, with the wake still generated by the "TS MINI" AUV PJP.

The PJP and sensor were placed in a tank with dimensions of 4 m in length, 2 m in width, and 1 m in height, with a water depth of 68 cm. The wake data from the "TS MINI" AUV were collected using the wake sensor. The PJP was fixed onto a frame positioned 20 cm above the bottom of the tank, while a 1 m × 2 m frame was placed behind it to fix the sensor. The frame was equipped with rulers along the z-axis and y-axis to mark the sensor's specific coordinates. The z-axis measurement range started at 10 cm and extended to 100 cm, while the effective measurement range along the y-axis spanned from −10 cm to 10 cm. This experiment was conducted under static conditions, with both the PJP and the sensor held in fixed positions. The PJP was positioned at the center of the tank, equidistant from both sides, and the sensor was used to collect data at predefined distances. The experimental setup is illustrated in Figure 10.

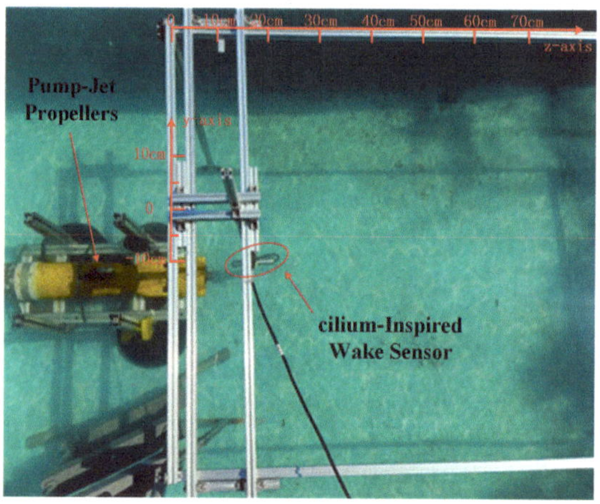

Figure 10. Data Collection Site of the CIWS.

The PJP rotation speed was set to 1000 rpm (actual speed of 960 rpm). Under these conditions, measurements were conducted for axial data along the positive z-axis at an x-axis offset of 0, and for lateral data along the x-axis at a z-axis offset of 30 cm. Specifically, for the axial data, measurements were taken from 10 cm to 100 cm at 10 cm intervals, resulting in 10 data points. For the lateral data, measurements were taken from −10 cm to 10 cm at 2 cm intervals, resulting in 11 data points. Throughout the entire measurement process, the sensor was aligned parallel to the longitudinal axis.The block diagram of the wake data acquisition experimental setup is shown in Figure 11.

The CIWS used was a cilium-crossbeam structure, which has two-dimensional sensing capability. To simplify the experiment, the y-axis offset was kept at 0 throughout the measurements, thereby enabling the assessment of the sensor's sensitivity in a single dimension. This experimental setup is consistent with the fixed-depth navigation mode of an AUV during underwater operations.

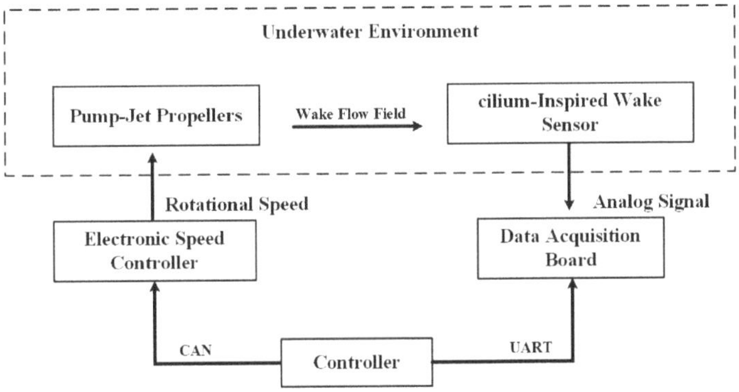

Figure 11. Block Diagram of the Wake Data Acquisition Experimental Setup.

Data collection was conducted using a signal acquisition circuit based on the WM8978 chip from Wolfson Microelectronics. The deformation of the cilium caused a change in the resistance of the piezoresistor, generating a potential difference. The signal acquisition circuit converted this voltage into digital signals through analog-to-digital conversion (ADC) and recorded the data, with a sampling frequency of 96 kHz. Given that the sensitivity of the CIWS remains stable for low-frequency components, this study focused on the low-frequency portion of the signal spectrum, for which the chosen sampling frequency was sufficient. The duration of each sampling session was 10 s, and each measurement point was sampled six times to minimize random error. During the entire measurement process, the PJP remained continuously operational. After relocating the sensor to the next measurement point, data collection commenced following a waiting period of 1 minute to reduce errors associated with movement.

The final experiment produced time-domain data for the wake across a 90 cm × 20 cm area, including one set of axial distance data and one set of lateral distance data. Each sampling point was measured six times, resulting in a total of 21 sets of 126 time-domain data samples. Figure 12 presents ten sets of time domain signals collected by the wake sensor at an x-axis offset of 0, with the z-axis offset ranging from 10 cm to 100 cm, under the PJP operating condition of 960 rpm, as well as one set of background noise signals with the PJP not working. It can be observed from the figure that the signal intensity at 10 cm is not the highest due to the obstruction of the PJP central shaft. As the z-axis offset increases, the signal intensity initially increases and then decreases. Specifically, at distances of 90 cm and 100 cm from the propeller, the signals detected by the sensor are weak and difficult to distinguish. However, the signals at both locations are still significantly higher than the background noise while the propeller is not in operation. This indicates that the cilium-based sensor has greater sensitivity to the propeller's noise compared to flow velocity. The root mean square (RMS) values of the time-domain signal amplitude shown in Figure 13 corroborate the aforementioned trend, where the signal strength initially increases and subsequently decreases with increasing axial distance.

The time-domain data from the CIWS can intuitively reflect the flow velocity at the current position. However, due to the turbulent nature of the wake, the flow is complex and difficult to predict, and as shown in Figure 12, there are no distinctive features in the time-domain signal. Therefore, subsequent analysis can be conducted through spectral analysis to determine the relationship between the spectral amplitude and the average wake velocity. Since spectral data can be obtained in real-time, the results of the spectral analysis can effectively guide the wake detection process of the AUV.

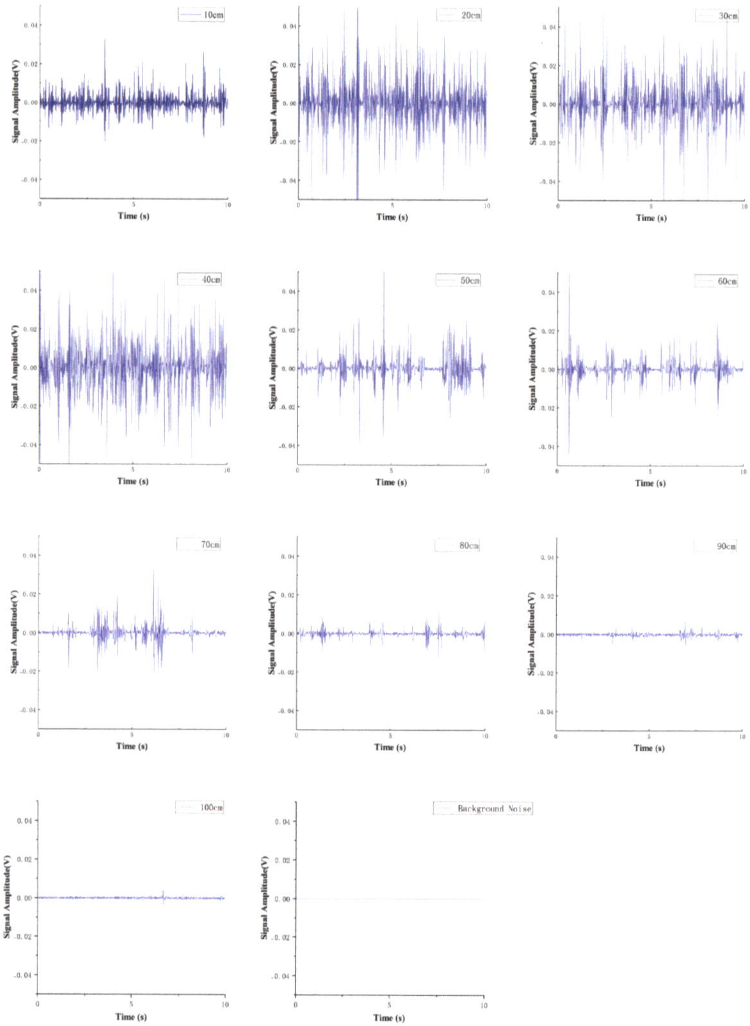

Figure 12. Time −Domain Signals Measured by the CIWS at Different Axial Distances.

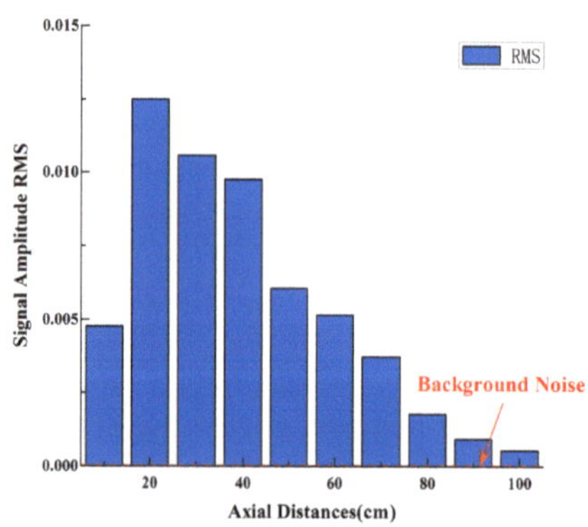

Figure 13. Time−Domain Signal Amplitude RMS at Different Axial Distances.

5. Wake Data Analysis and Positioning

5.1. Frequency Domain Analysis

In the previous section, we conducted experiments to measure the time-domain data of the CIWS at different positions. Through Fourier transform (FT), the corresponding spectral data were obtained. By performing FT on each set of time-domain data, the spectral data for all positions were derived. For the set of axial CIWS spectral data at an x-axis offset of 0 under an operating condition of 960 rpm, as shown in Figure 14a, it can be observed that the overall spectral amplitude initially increases with distance and subsequently decreases as the distance continues to increase. This trend is consistent with the attenuation pattern of the average wake velocity. The effective spectral information is mainly concentrated in the low-frequency range, while the spectral amplitudes at frequencies above 2 kHz are nearly identical for different distances, indicating limited research significance in this region.

The background noise remains stable and low in amplitude due to the absence of significant signal content. Notably, the spectrum features two characteristic frequency points at 485 Hz and 1455 Hz. Observing the spectral data beyond an axial distance of 80 cm, as shown in Figure 14a, reveals that the spectral curves tend to converge, suggesting that the sensor's ability to detect wake information is significantly diminished at axial distances greater than 80 cm.

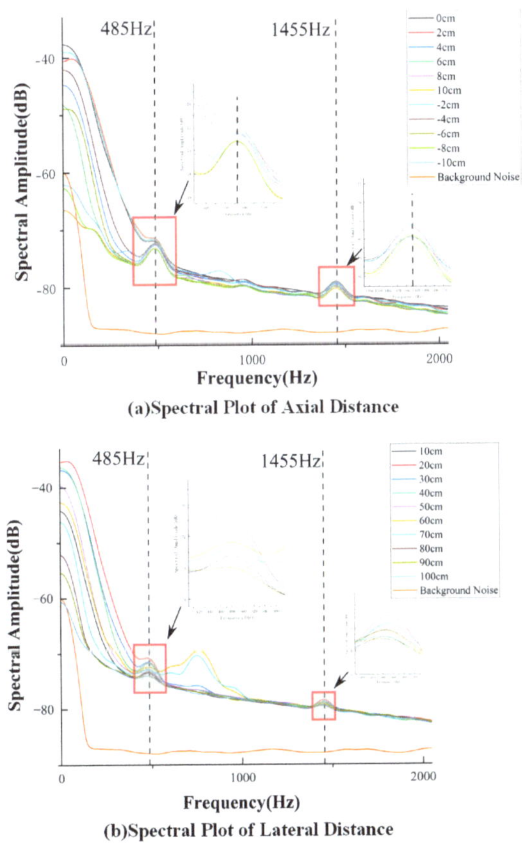

Figure 14. (**a**) Spectral Plot of Different Axial Distances at 960 rpm Operating Condition, (**b**) Spectral Plot of Different Lateral Distances at 960 rpm Operating Condition.

For the set of lateral CIWS spectral data at a z-axis offset of 30 cm under an PJP operating condition of 960 rpm, as shown in Figure 14b, it can be observed that the overall spectral amplitude is highest at a lateral offset of 0 cm. As the lateral distance increases, the spectral amplitude decreases. Beyond a lateral offset of 5 cm, the spectral curves tend to converge, indicating that the sensor's ability to detect wake information is significantly weakened for lateral offsets greater than 5 cm. Furthermore, the high-frequency portion of the spectrum is found to have limited research significance. Notably, the spectrum also shows two characteristic frequency points at 485 Hz and 1455 Hz.

5.2. Characteristic Frequency Analysis

The characteristic values present in the spectral signal of the CIWS have practical physical significance; these characteristic values correspond to the vertical pulsation frequency of the PJP and its subharmonic frequency. Furthermore, the wake detection range of the CIWS can also be derived from the spectral signal, and the rotational speed of the PJP can be inferred from the spectral data.

The two characteristic frequencies of 485 Hz and 1455 Hz, observed in Figure 14, are related to the rotation speed of the PJP. According to the previously established inertial reference coordinate system O-xyz at the rear of the PJP. The number of rotor blades is denoted by Z_R, and the number of stator blades is denoted by Z_S. In subsequent texts, the rotor and stator are also represented by R and S, respectively, with the rotor speed denoted by N.The lateral force along the x-axis is defined as F_x, the vertical force along the y-axis is defined as F_y, and the axial force along the z-axis is defined as F_z. F_t and F_r represent the tangential force and radial force of the blade, respectively. A rotating coordinate system $O - x_1y_1z_1$ is also established, aligned in the same direction as the inertial reference frame $O - xyz$. The rotational frame of reference has the same angular direction and speed as the rotor This definition is used to analyze the vibration frequency of the lateral force F_x of the PJP.

According to Rao [23], the lateral force of the rotor is given by

$$F_{x,R} = -\frac{Z_R}{2}\sum_{k=1}^{\infty} B_{r,t,k} \cdot \sin(nZ_R\theta - \beta_{rk} - \phi_{-}^{+}) \tag{9}$$

where

$$\phi_{-}^{+} = \arctan\left(\frac{\mp B_{rk} - B_{tk}\cos(\beta_{rk} - \beta_{tk})}{B_{tk}\sin(\beta_{rk} - \beta_{tk})}\right),$$

$$B_{r,t,k} = \sqrt{[\mp B_{rk} - B_{tk}\cos(\beta_{rk} - \beta_{tk})]^2 + [B_{tk}\sin(\beta_{rk} - \beta_{tk})]^2} \tag{10}$$

In the equation, B_{tk} and B_{rk} represent the amplitude of the tangential force and radial force at step k, respectively. β_{tk} and β_{rk} represent the phase angles of the tangential and radial forces, respectively, at step k. θ represents the angular position of the reference line of the 0-th rotor.The sign $\mp B_{rk}$ takes the negative sign when $kZ_S + 1 = nZ_R$ and the positive sign when $kZ_S - 1 = nZ_R$.

The lateral force of the stator and duct is given by

$$F_{x,S} = -\sum_{k=1}^{\infty}\frac{Z_S}{2}\{B_{r_1,t_1,k} \cdot \sin(kZ_R\theta - \beta_{t_1,k} - \psi_{-}^{+})\} \tag{11}$$

where

$$\psi_{-}^{+} = \arctan\left(\frac{B_{t_1,k} \pm B_{r_1,k}\cos(\beta_{r_1,k} - \beta_{t_1,k})}{\pm B_{r_1,k}\sin(\beta_{r_1,k} - \beta_{t_1,k})}\right),$$

$$B_{r_1,t_1,k} = \sqrt{[B_{t_1,k} \pm B_{r_1,k}\cos(\beta_{r_1,k} - \beta_{t_1,k})]^2 + [\pm B_{r_1,k}\sin(\beta_{r_1,k} - \beta_{t_1,k})]^2} \tag{12}$$

B_{t_1k} and B_{r_1k} represent the amplitude of the k-th order tangential force and radial force, respectively, in the rotating coordinate system O-$x_1y_1z_1$. β_{t_1k} and β_{r_1k} denote the coordinated phase angles of the tangential and radial forces, respectively, for the k-th order.The term $\pm B_{r_1,k}$ takes a positive sign when $kZ_S + 1 = nZ_R$ is satisfied and a negative sign when $kZ_S - 1 = nZ_R$ is satisfied.

It is evident that the conditions for the lateral force of both the stator and rotor are the same, i.e., $kZ_S \pm 1 = nZ_R$, and they share the same form of expression. Therefore, by adding the lateral forces of the stator and rotor, the total lateral force of the propeller can be written as

$$F_x = \sum_{k=1}^{\infty} B_k \cdot \sin(nZ_R\theta + \xi) \tag{13}$$

The duct can be considered part of the stator; thus, the derivation of the pulsation frequency of the stator's unsteady force also includes the lateral force component of the duct.

Let $t = 0$ denote the initial angular position of the 0th rotor as zero, then we have $\theta = 2\pi Nt$. Substituting into Equation (11) yields the vibration frequency of the total lateral force of the propeller:

$$f_{x,kn} = \frac{2nZ_RN\pi}{2\pi} = nZ_RN \tag{14}$$

The conditions $kZ_S + 1 = nZ_R$ or $kZ_S - 1 = nZ_R$ must be strictly satisfied, where k, n, Z_S, and Z_R are all positive integers.

For the PJP selected in this study, the number of rotor blades is $Z_R = 9$, and the number of stator blades is $Z_S = 7$. The actual rotation speed of 960 rpm corresponds to a rotor speed of $N = 16$ rps. When $k = 10$ and $n = 13$, the condition $kZ_S + 1 = nZ_R$ is satisfied, resulting in $f_{x,kn} = 1455$ Hz.

It can be observed in Figure 14 that a characteristic value exists at 1455 Hz, as well as a subharmonic frequency of $f_{x,kn}$ at 485 Hz (which is 1/3 of $f_{x,kn}$). However, the spectral amplitude at $f_{x,kn}$ is relatively low, and the degree of concentration is not as distinct as at 485 Hz. Therefore, 485 Hz is selected as the characteristic frequency for further analysis.

5.3. Detection Data and Flow Field Fitting

By substituting the positional information of the CIWS data into the wake velocity decay model in Section 2, the average velocity value corresponding to that position can be calculated. The spectral amplitude data of the sensor at different offset distances along the z-axis (axial) under the 960 rpm condition were preprocessed and fitted to the corresponding average velocity. From Figure 14, it can be observed that the data at 485 Hz exhibit greater dispersion compared to those at 1455 Hz, and there is an approximately linear relationship between the spectral amplitude and the average velocity. Therefore, the spectral amplitude at the characteristic frequency of 485 Hz was chosen for linear fitting with the corresponding average velocity using the following equation:

$$A = kv + b \tag{15}$$

where A is the spectral amplitude, and v is the average velocity.

Since the spectral data beyond an axial distance of 80 cm tend to be similar, this portion of the data negatively impacts the fitting process and was therefore excluded. The remaining valid data were fitted based on Equation (15), yielding $k = 3.85$ and $b = -75.43$, as shown in Figure 15. By intersecting the fitted line of the valid data with that of the excluded data, the intersection point $(0.39, -73.92987)$ can be obtained. This indicates that when the average velocity is less than 0.39 m/s, the spectral amplitude of the sensor no longer changes with the velocity.

The same method was used to investigate the fitting relationship between the spectral amplitude and average velocity at different x-axis (lateral) offset distances under the 960 rpm condition. The spectral data beyond a lateral offset of 4 cm tended to converge, so these data were excluded. The remaining valid data were fitted based on Equation (15), yielding $k = 2.49$ and $b = -73.99$, as shown in Figure 16. Similarly, by intersecting the line fitted to the excluded data with the linear fitting line, the intersection point $(0.39, -73.02326)$ was obtained, indicating that the critical velocity value is also 0.39 m/s.

From Figures 15 and 16, it can be seen that whether along the axial or lateral direction of the propeller, when the flow velocity is less than 0.39 m/s, the CIWS can still detect wake information, but the spectral amplitude does not change with distance. Therefore, the range within which the wake velocity information can be inferred from the CIWS data is smaller than the range in which the sensor can detect propeller noise.

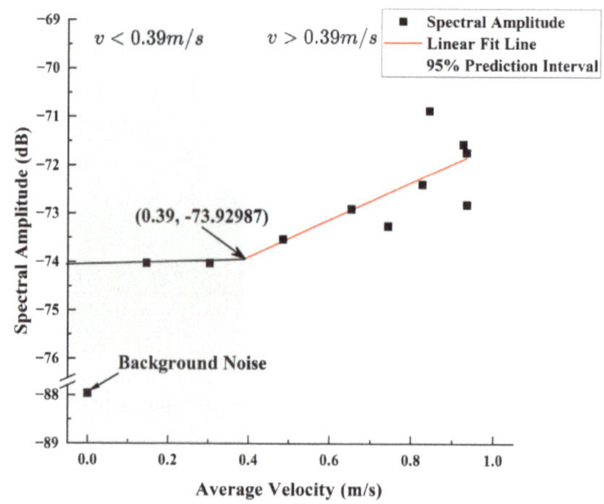

Figure 15. Fitting Performance Between Axial Spectral Amplitude at 485 Hz and Flow Velocity.

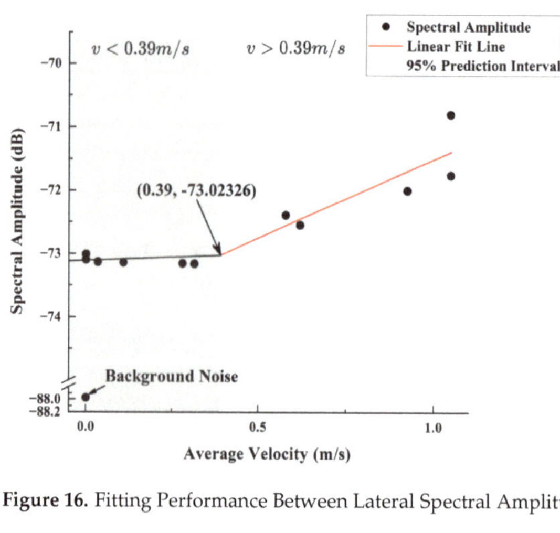

Figure 16. Fitting Performance Between Lateral Spectral Amplitude at 485 Hz and Flow Velocity.

Substituting the fitting result of the lateral spectral amplitude at 485 Hz with respect to the flow velocity into the axial fitting result yields the relationship shown in Figure 17. From Figure 17, it can be observed that the overlap of the 95% prediction interval is relatively high, suggesting that the spectral amplitude detected by the sensor is primarily influenced by the flow velocity at that position and shows low correlation to the relative flow direction.

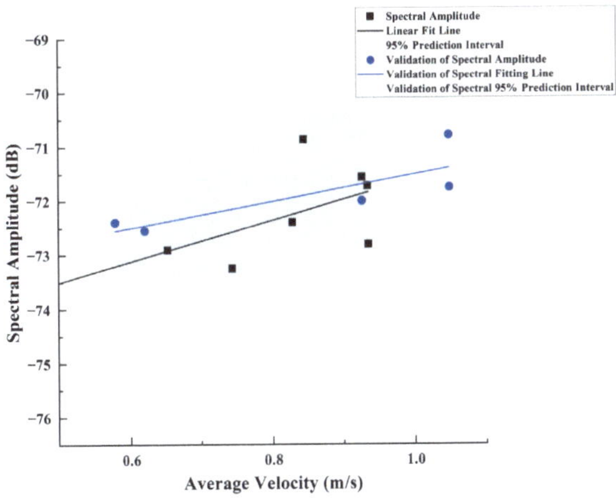

Figure 17. Explanatory Power of Axial Fitting Results for Lateral Group Data.

5.4. Wake Detection Range

By combining the data from Figures 15 and 16, we can obtain Figure 18. From the figure, it can be seen that the minimum flow velocity detection threshold for the sensor is 0.39 m/s, which is consistent with the detection range conclusions from Figures 15 and 16. For the detection data greater than 0.39 m/s, fitting using Equation (15) yields $k = 3.23$ and $b = -74.82$.

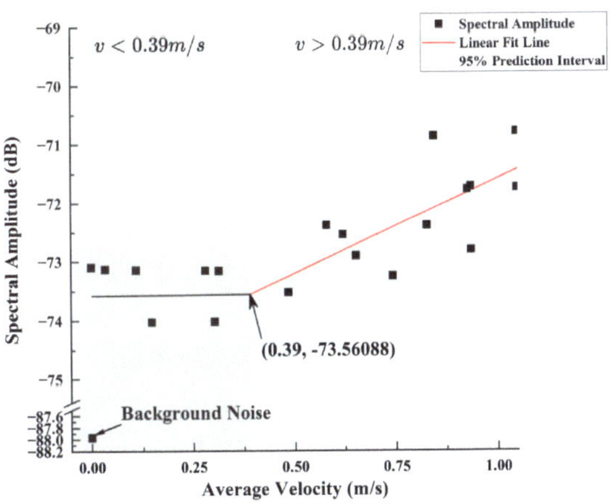

Figure 18. Fitting Results Between Mean Velocity and Spectral Amplitude at 485 Hz

By substituting the threshold value of 0.39 m/s, which can be used to infer the wake velocity from the spectral amplitude of the CIWS, into the wake velocity decay model, the curve shown in Figure 19 is obtained. The area within this curve represents the range within where the CIWS can detect wake velocity information. From the figure, it can be seen that the velocity detection range of the sensor is ±5 cm in the x-axis direction and 85 cm in the z-axis direction.

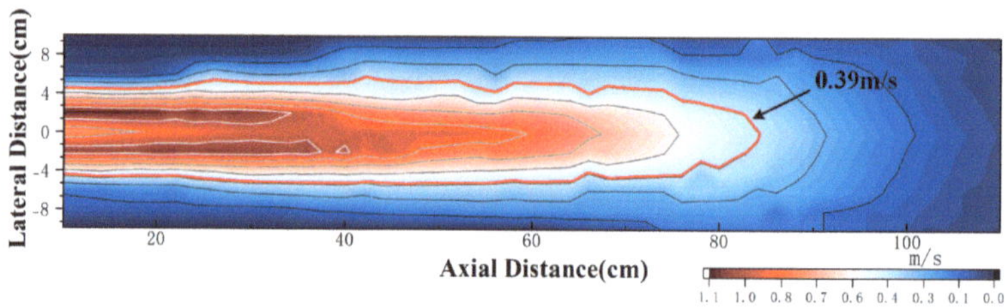

Figure 19. Effective Detection Range of Average Wake Velocity for AUV.

Further overlaying the relationship between the spectral amplitude of the CIWS and the wake velocity into Figure 20 yields the corresponding model for the sensor spectral amplitude and position, as shown in Figure 20. Using this model, underwater vehicles such as AUVs equipped with CIWSs can estimate their possible position relative to the PJP based on the sensor's spectral data. With the method above, by matching the detected velocity and the trend of position change within the wake field, the specific position of the sensor within the wake model can be established.

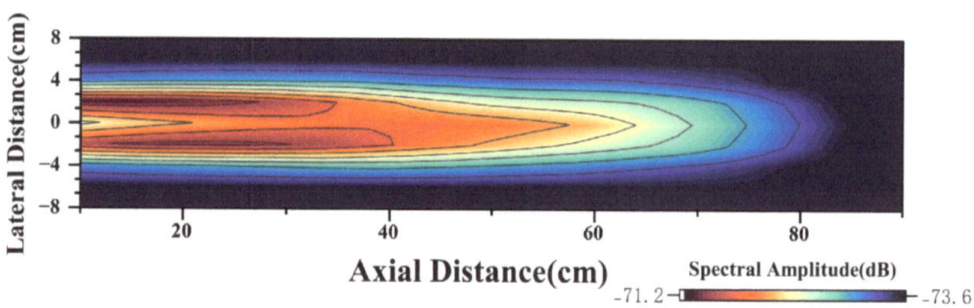

Figure 20. Contour Plot of Signal Amplitude Variation with Position.

The specific workflow for AUV wake detection and positioning is illustrated in Figure 21. Once the wake enters the CIWS, it undergoes analog-to-digital conversion (ADC) to obtain time-domain signal data. Subsequently, the time-domain data are transformed into spectral data through Fourier transform (FT). Using the linear relationship between the spectral amplitude and the mean wake velocity, the mean velocity at the current position can be determined. By performing multiple measurements, the motion curve and the corresponding velocities can be matched within the wake field model to estimate the current relative position in the wake field. This process requires further integration with the AUV navigation and control system for practical applications.

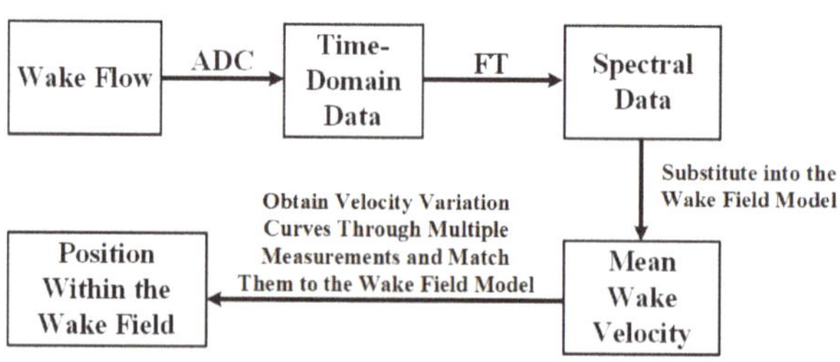

Figure 21. Workflow for AUV Wake Detection and Positioning.

6. Conclusions

This paper focuses on the feasibility and effectiveness of using CIWS for detecting and tracking AUV wakes. By analyzing the principles of CIWS, conducting experiments and analyzing the experimental data, the following findings and conclusions have been achieved:

First, the feasibility of AUV wake detection using CIWS was investigated based on the working principles of cilium. By analyzing the biomechanical model of the cilium, it was found that four forces are involved during its motion: F_m, F_k, F_u, and F_d. Spectral analysis of the mechanical model revealed that the ratio of hemispherical displacement amplitude $Y_0(f)$ to the external flow velocity amplitude $V_0(f)$ exhibits a linear relationship in the low-frequency range, providing theoretical support for subsequent experiments.

Second, using a flow velocity sensor, the flow velocities at different positions behind the PJP in a moored state were measured. Then, an average velocity model of the AUV wake flow field was established.

Third, the CIWS was used to measure different positions within the PJP wake range, obtaining time-domain and frequency-domain data of the CIWS at various positions. Combined with the previously established flow field model, the time-domain and frequency-domain data corresponding to different average velocities were obtained.

Fourth, spectral analysis of the CIWS data revealed the presence of characteristic frequencies associated with the lateral pulsation force of the PJP, specifically at 1455 Hz and its subharmonic frequency at 485 Hz. The flow velocity data and the spectral amplitude at 485 Hz for the corresponding CIWS position were linearly fitted, yielding a threshold velocity of 0.39 m/s, which could be utilized for position estimation. Further analysis presented a flow field range for estimating the relative position: ± 5 cm along the x-axis and 85 cm along the z-axis. Additionally, a linear relationship was established between the spectral amplitude A and the average velocity v within this flow field range. Based on this relationship and the propeller flow field model, it is possible to estimate the relative position of the sensor with respect to the propeller using the spectral amplitude detected by the CIWS.

In summary, with experimental and data analysis, this paper demonstrates the effectiveness of CIWS in detecting wakes of underwater vehicles, providing a novel method for underwater target detection and positioning. This research establishes a theoretical and technical foundation for underwater vehicle localization and tracking based on wake detection. The proposed method can be applied to underwater missions such as swarm formation of AUVs or detection and tracking of non-cooperative targets.

For future research to meet the demands of underwater target detection and wake tracking, the following work can be conducted based on this study: (1) Integrating CIWS onto dynamic platforms such as AUVs to assess the impact of the platform's own navigation and vibrations; (2) Conducting dual-AUV wake detection experiments to evaluate the effectiveness of detecting the wake of another sailing AUV by a navigating AUV with CIWS; (3) Conducting dual-AUV navigation experiments to explore AUV navigation and tracking control methods based on underwater target wake detection and positioning with CIWS.

Author Contributions: Conceptualization, R.W. and Y.Y.; methodology, Y.Y., P.Z. and R.W.; software, X.H. and Z.L.; validation, X.H., Y.Y. and P.Z.; formal analysis, X.H. and Z.L.; investigation, X.H. and P.Z.; resources, Y.Y. and R.W.; data curation, X.H. and Z.L.; writing—original draft preparation, X.H.; writing—review and editing, Y.Y. and X.Z.; visualization, X.H.; supervision, Y.Y., X.Z. and Z.H.; project administration, Y.Y. and Z.H.; funding acquisition, Y.Y. All authors have read and agreed to the published version of the manuscript.

Funding: This study was funded by the Strategic Priority Research Program of the Chinese Academy of Sciences (XDC03060201).

Data Availability Statement: Access to the data will be considered upon request by the authors.

Conflicts of Interest: The authors declare no conflicts of interest.

Abbreviations

The following abbreviations are used in this manuscript:

AUV	Autonomous underwater vehicle
CIWS	Cilium-inspired wake sensor
CN	Canal neuromasts
PJP	Pump-jet propeller
ADC	Analog-to-digital conversion
RMS	Root mean square
FT	Fourier transform

References

1. Zhang, W.; Wang, N.X.; Wei, S.; Du, X.; Yan, Z. Overview of unmanned underwater vehicle swarm development status and key technologies. *J. Harbin Eng. Univ.* **2020**, *41*, 289–297.
2. Zhao, Z.; Hu, Q.; Feng, H.; Feng, X.; Su, W. A cooperative hunting method for multi-AUV swarm in underwater weak information environment with obstacles. *J. Mar. Sci. Eng.* **2022**, *10*, 1266. [CrossRef]
3. Jiang, B.; Du, J.; Jiang, C.; Han, Z.; Debbah, M. Underwater searching and multi-round data collection via AUV swarms: An energy-efficient AoI-aware MAPPO approach. *IEEE Internet Things J.* **2023**, *11*, 12768–12782. [CrossRef]
4. Ghafoor, H.; Noh, Y. An overview of next-generation underwater target detection and tracking: An integrated underwater architecture. *Ieee Access* **2019**, *7*, 98841–98853. [CrossRef]
5. Wei, Q.; Yang, Y.; Zhou, X.; Hu, Z.; Li, Y.; Fan, C.; Zheng, Q.; Wang, Z. Enhancing Inter-AUV Perception: Adaptive 6-DOF Pose Estimation with Synthetic Images for AUV Swarm Sensing. *Drones* **2024**, *8*, 486. [CrossRef]
6. Wei, Q.; Yang, Y.; Zhou, X.; Fan, C.; Zheng, Q.; Hu, Z. Localization method for underwater robot swarms based on enhanced visual markers. *Electronics* **2023**, *12*, 4882. [CrossRef]
7. Wang, Q.; He, B.; Zhang, Y.; Yu, F.; Huang, X.; Yang, R. An autonomous cooperative system of multi-AUV for underwater targets detection and localization. *Eng. Appl. Artif. Intell.* **2023**, *121*, 105907. [CrossRef]
8. Lodovisi, C.; Loreti, P.; Bracciale, L.; Betti, S. Performance analysis of hybrid optical–acoustic AUV swarms for marine monitoring. *Future Internet* **2018**, *10*, 65. [CrossRef]
9. Zhou, Q.; Ji, B.; Wei, Y.; Hu, B.; Gao, Y.; Xu, Q.; Zhou, J.; Zhou, B. A bio-inspired cilia array as the dielectric layer for flexible capacitive pressure sensors with high sensitivity and a broad detection range. *J. Mater. Chem. A* **2019**, *7*, 27334–27346. [CrossRef]
10. Zhou, Z.G.; Liu, Z.W. Biomimetic cilia based on MEMS technology. *J. Bionic Eng.* **2008**, *5*, 358–365. [CrossRef]
11. Astreinidi Blandin, A.; Bernardeschi, I.; Beccai, L. Biomechanics in soft mechanical sensing: From natural case studies to the artificial world. *Biomimetics* **2018**, *3*, 32. [CrossRef]
12. van Netten, S.M. Hydrodynamics of the excitation of the cupula in the fish canal lateral line. *J. Acoust. Soc. Am.* **1991**, *89*, 310–319. [CrossRef]
13. Van Netten, S.M. Hydrodynamic detection by cupulae in a lateral line canal: Functional relations between physics and physiology. *Biol. Cybern.* **2006**, *94*, 67–85. [CrossRef] [PubMed]
14. Sengupta, D.; Trap, D.; Kottapalli, A.G. Piezoresistive carbon nanofiber-based cilia-inspired flow sensor. *Nanomaterials* **2020**, *10*, 211. [CrossRef] [PubMed]
15. Qiao, Q.; Kong, X.; Wu, S.; Liu, G.; Zhang, G.; Yang, H.; Zhang, W.; Yang, Y.; Jia, L.; He, C.; Cui, J. A bio-inspired MEMS wake detector for AUV tracking and coordinated formation. *Remote Sens.* **2023**, *15*, 2949. [CrossRef]
16. Kim, J. Wake-Responsive AUV Guidance Assisted by Passive Sonar Measurements. *J. Mar. Sci. Eng.* **2024**, *12*, 645. [CrossRef]
17. Kim, D.H.; Kim, N.; Cho, H.; Kim, S.Y. A guidance logic development for wake homing guidance system (ICCAS 2014). In Proceedings of the 2014 14th International Conference on Control, Automation and Systems (ICCAS 2014), Goyang-si, Republic of Korea, 22–25 October 2014; pp. 190–194.
18. Liu, L.; Su, S.; Huang, Z. Design of Torpedo Wake Homing System for Higher Trajectory Accuracy. *J. Unmanned Undersea Syst.* **2010**, *18*, 272–276.

19. Basohbat Novinzadeh, A.R.; Asadi Matak, M. Design of stable nonlinear guidance of an underwater vehicle in the ship wake via estimated path by particle filter. *Modares Mech. Eng.* **2017**, *17*, 260–266.
20. Shizhe, T. Underwater artificial lateral line flow sensors. *Microsyst. Technol.* **2014**, *20*, 2123–2136. [CrossRef]
21. Qiao, Q. Design and Implementation of a Bio-Inspired MEMS Wake Sensor for UUV. Master's Thesis, North University of China, Taiyuan, China, 2023.
22. Yang, Y.; Zhou, X. Research on High-precision Unmanned Underwater Vehicles Team Formation without Communication Based on Visual Positioning Technology. *Digit. Ocean. Underw. Warf.* **2022**, *5*, 50–58.
23. Rao, Z.Q. Numerical Simulation of Hydrodynamical Performance of Pump Jet Propulsor. Master's Thesis, Shanghai Jiao Tong University, Shanghai, China, 2012.

sensors

MDPI

Article

BGLE-YOLO: A Lightweight Model for Underwater Bio-Detection

Hua Zhao [1,2], Chao Xu [2,*], Jiaxing Chen [1,*], Zhexian Zhang [2] and Xiang Wang [2]

1 School of Mathematical Sciences, Hebei Normal University, Shijiazhuang 050024, China; zhaohua@hebtu.edu.cn

2 School of Engineering, Hebei Normal University, Shijiazhuang 050024, China; 17333921516@163.com (Z.Z.); wangxiang@hebtu.edu.cn (X.W.)

* Correspondence: 18790070929@163.com (C.X.); chenjx@hebtu.edu.cn (J.C.)

Abstract: Due to low contrast, chromatic aberration, and generally small objects in underwater environments, a new underwater fish detection model, BGLE-YOLO, is proposed to investigate automated methods dedicated to accurately detecting underwater objects in images. The model has small parameters and low computational effort and is suitable for edge devices. First, an efficient multi-scale convolutional EMC module is introduced to enhance the backbone network and capture the dynamic changes in targets in the underwater environment. Secondly, a global and local feature fusion module for small targets (BIG) is integrated into the neck network to preserve more feature information, reduce error information in higher-level features, and increase the model's effectiveness in detecting small targets. Finally, to prevent the detection accuracy impact due to excessive lightweighting, the lightweight shared head (LSH) is constructed. The reparameterization technique further improves detection accuracy without additional parameters and computational cost. Experimental results of BGLE-YOLO on the underwater datasets DUO (Detection Underwater Objects) and RUOD (Real-World Underwater Object Detection) show that the model achieves the same accuracy as the benchmark model with an ultra-low computational cost of 6.2 GFLOPs and an ultra-low model parameter of 1.6 MB.

Keywords: underwater fish detection; BGLE-YOLO; YOLOv8; multi-scale feature fusion; lightweight model

Academic Editors: Jingchun Zhou, Wenqi Ren, Qiuping Jiang and Yan-Tsung Peng

Received: 11 January 2025
Revised: 2 March 2025
Accepted: 3 March 2025
Published: 5 March 2025

Citation: Zhao, H.; Xu, C.; Chen, J.; Zhang, Z.; Wang, X. BGLE-YOLO: A Lightweight Model for Underwater Bio-Detection. *Sensors* **2025**, *25*, 1595. https://doi.org/10.3390/s25051595

1. Introduction

With the maturity of target detection technology on the ground, the development of underwater resource exploitation, marine ecological protection, and underwater robots has become a trend, and the vigorous growth of the marine economy is a major guarantee of national security [1]. Target detection is crucial for the protection and exploitation of seabed organisms as well as resource systems, and underwater image processing has been widely used in a variety of underwater scenarios, playing an important role in exploring underwater scenarios. Nevertheless, dynamic underwater environments make damaged underwater areas more complex and unpredictable, and the development of underwater robots requires underwater target detection algorithms with superior computational and storage capacity, which is exacerbated by the limited algorithmic storage and computational capacity at this stage. Secondly, underwater environments suffer from several problems such as low light, dense distribution of organisms, low contrast, and small object size (see Figure 1). Because of these challenges, underwater images suffer from blurred image boundaries and loss of texture information, making underwater target detection more difficult [2].

(a) (b) (c) (d)

Figure 1. Images (**a**,**b**) describe underwater image features marked by low contrast and small targets, respectively, and (**c**,**d**) describe underwater image features marked by underwater blurring and color deviations due to various attenuations, respectively.

In target detection techniques, there are two categories of algorithms: two-stage algorithms and single-stage algorithms. Two-stage algorithms first extract the candidate frame based on the image and then do a quadratic correction based on the candidate region to obtain the detection point result. Common two-stage target detection algorithms: R-CNN [3], Fast R-CNN [4], and Faster R-CNN [5]. Single-stage target detection algorithms omit the extraction of candidate frames and directly classify and localize targets on the feature map. Typical single-stage target detection algorithms: SSD [6] and the YOLO (You Only Look Once) [7,8] series. Compared to the two-stage target detection algorithms, the single-stage target detection algorithms have lower detection accuracy, but their detection speed is fast, with relatively low computational overhead and good real-time performance. The YOLO series of target detectors are widely used in academic and industrial scenarios due to their high performance and efficiency, and they are proven to be a classical approach for first-level detection networks in practical applications. However, despite the YOLO algorithm's strong performance in real-time target detection, its effectiveness is confined to particular application scenarios, such as dynamic environments underwater.

Underwater target detection differs from the ground environment in that the underwater environment is more complex, and the difficulty of creating and labeling datasets increases by orders of magnitude. Underwater targets are generally small, making them hard to capture and recognize, which inevitably results in decreased effectiveness of certain target detection algorithms. In addition to accuracy, computation, and parameterization are two indispensable components for porting target detection algorithms to underwater mobile devices. The development of detection algorithms suitable for underwater scenarios should be a combination of detection accuracy and practical applications. Recent research has been conducted to develop models specialized for underwater detection. Liu et al. [9] studied YWnet to resolve the problem related to small and blurred target sizes in underwater environments. Yeh et al. [10] introduced a lightweight algorithm for detecting underwater targets, which integrates a color conversion technique with a neural network to address the issue of color absorption. Nonetheless, these techniques often depend significantly on the natural quality of underwater images, and excessive enhancement may result in the loss of important image details, which can adversely affect detection accuracy. Existing methods mostly ignore significant computational overheads when addressing underwater environmental challenges, which hinders their practical deployment.

To address the above problems, Xu et al. [11] proposed the use of inverted residual blocks and group convolution [12] to extract deep features, which enables the feature extraction network to give priority to channels that contain a lot of information and discard insignificant ones, which simplifies the differentiation between perceptual targets and background information, further improves the accuracy of the model, and significantly reduces the memory footprint required for inference. Although it greatly decreases the memory needed for inference and improves accuracy, it occupies more computational consumption and parameter storage, limiting the storage and computational requirements for underwater image processing. Tang [13] explored the localization capabilities of small target segmentation and fuzzy target boundaries in medical image processing and found that the ability of the Global-to-Local Spatial Aggregation (GLSA) module to aggregate and represent both global and local spatial features provides significantly improved localization results for both large and small underwater targets, but its huge number of parameters potentially limits its use in resource-constrained scenarios. Chen [14] developed a streamlined backbone network using the Deformable Convolutional Network (DCN) v3 [15] to fuse feature maps from different scales and achieved a mAP@0.5 of 86.1% on the DUO dataset. Their research, however, added to the computational complexity and curtailed its application in scenarios with real-time and resource constraints. Detail-enhanced convolution (DEConv) [16] promotes feature learning and can integrate prior information to supplement the original information and enhance representation capabilities, but it is often not advisable to significantly reduce model parameters and computation at the expense of accuracy.

In order to optimize the above problems, the paper presents a BGLE-YOLOv8 model that is lightweight, building upon structural improvements in YOLOv8. The main points of the work are as follows:

1. To achieve a lighter YOLOv8 backbone network, the parameter count and computational load are designed to be lower than the original 3×3 convolution kernel for EMC convolution. Inheriting the grouping idea of Group Convolution, multi-scale feature information is extracted more efficiently by the backbone network during the feature extraction process.
2. Introducing the BIG module. The BIG module can reduce the error information generated in the high-level features as the detection depth increases. In the neck network, its local spatial detail information and global spatial semantic information extracted from the backbone part are able to perform fast and efficient multi-scale feature fusion.
3. The LSH module is introduced into the architecture because it references the fact that shared convolution can drastically lower the parameter count and enables the use of a Scale layer to scale the features when dealing with the problem of inconsistent underwater target scales detected by each detection head. Detail-enhanced convolution and group normalization are also designed to improve its detail-capturing ability and minimize the accuracy loss while keeping the number of detection head parameters and computational effort smaller.

The remainder of the paper is arranged as listed below. Section 2 presents the overall network structure as well as its individual components, fully exploring the role played by each group block in the overall network structure and the correlation between each module. Section 3 provides the experimental results, which fully confirm the validity of the proposed model through ablation and comparison experiments. Section 4 presents a discussion, summarizes the proposed model and its limitations, and suggests an outlook for the improvement of the subsequent benchmark model. Finally, Section 5 provides the research conclusion.

2. Materials and Methods

In this part, we plan to introduce the different modules of the model. Figure 2 displays the overall architecture of the baseline model and the model in this paper. The BGLE-YOLO model consists of the following parts: efficient multi-scale convolution EMC, BIG module, and lightweight detection head LSH.

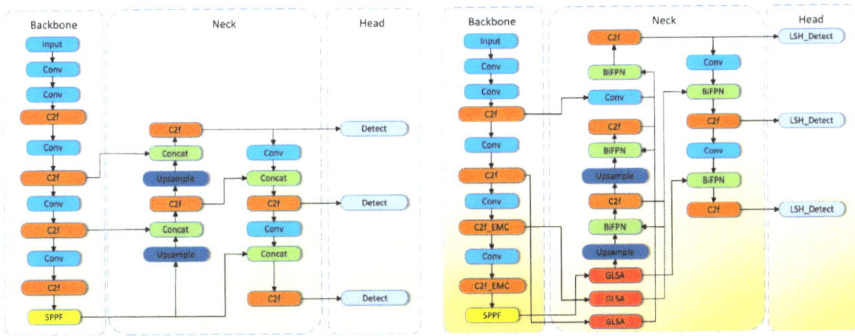

(**a**) (**b**)

Figure 2. (**a**) The diagram illustrates the architecture of YOLOv8. (**b**) The diagram depicts the architecture of BGLE-YOLO. Compared to (**a**), (**b**) adds BiFPN network, GLSA attention block, EMC convolution, and LSH detection header to (**a**).

2.1. *Efficient Multi-Scale Convolution EMC*

In the scope of underwater target detection, limited hardware resources and computing power make it tough to deploy convolutional neural networks on embedded systems or edge devices. This can usually be achieved through model compression or lightweight design. Deep convolutional neural networks [17,18] are usually composed of a large number of convolutions, which results in substantial computation, parameters, and model complexity, resulting in slow model inference speed.

Han [19] proposed the Ghost module to decompose a convolutional layer into two smaller convolutional layers. One of the convolutional layers is called the ghost convolutional layer, which only uses a small part of the channels of the original convolutional layer to calculate the output, while the other convolutional layer is called the residual convolutional layer, which uses the remaining channels to calculate the output. This decomposition technique can significantly decrease the computational load and number of parameters while preserving the network's accuracy. Although Ghostnet has achieved good performance, it does not fully consider the redundancy between feature maps, assuming that these redundant feature maps need to be fully removed to provide a comprehensive insight into the input data. MobileNet [20] uses deep convolution to perform convolutional feature extraction operations on the layer-wise channel count, but the 1×1 convolutional layer of the remaining fusion channel still takes up a considerable amount of memory and GFLOPs.

Building on previous research, this paper suggests enhancements to the network architecture, specifically targeting the underwater environment. The improved model is capable of reducing the parameter count and calculations based on previous work and maintaining detection accuracy and adaptability. These feature maps are generated on a single feature channel, with each channel's information being independent from one another. Specifically, each channel of the feature map possesses its own convolution kernel, which operates exclusively on that channel. Half of the feature maps input into the channel are not convolved, and the other half are convolved with a kernel size of 3 and a kernel size of 5. Finally, the features of each channel after the convolution operation can be fused through a point-by-point convolution. Figure 3 illustrates the EMC network structure. Based on this principle, the correlation and redundancy between redundant feature maps can be fully explained, and the problem of significantly reducing model parameters and calculations while retaining redundant feature maps and effectively improving the detection accuracy of underwater targets can be solved.

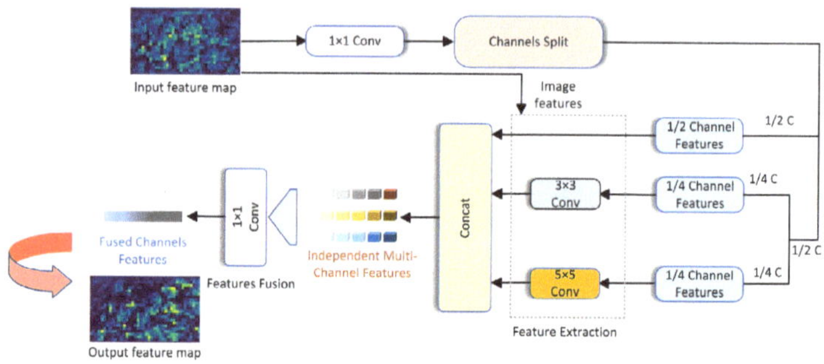

Figure 3. The structures of EMC are presented. The input feature map is channelized and then fused into an output feature map by independent multi-channel features.

When EMC replaces the original convolution and integrates it into the YOLO framework, it has several advantages, making it particularly suitable for underwater object detection. This module enables the model to pay more attention to the essential visual features for object detection by fully maintaining the redundancy and correlation among feature maps.

2.2. BIG

A major challenge in underwater fish detection is to be able to highlight key information related to the target while removing irrelevant features. Given that underwater targets are generally small and occlude each other, existing target detection algorithms struggle to effectively detect them. Traditional feature pyramid networks (FPNs) [21] are limited by unidirectional information flow, thus the Path Aggregation Network (PANet) [22] incorporates an extra bottom-up path aggregation network. To explore a more effective cross-scale feature network topology within the PANet, work [23] revealed that the search process consumes thousands of GPU hours, and the resulting network is irregular and challenging to interpret or modify. Inspired by the above works, the bi-directional feature pyramid network (BiFPN) [24] achieves better accuracy and fewer parameters and calculations than the PANet, FPN, and neural architecture search (NAS-FPN). The optimization methods of BiFPNs for cross-scale connections are as follows: deleting nodes with only one input because there is no feature fusion process for one input node. Secondly, the original input and input nodes are positioned at an identical level, allowing for more feature fusion without significantly increasing computational cost. Lastly, each bidirectional path is regarded as a feature network layer and repeated several times for more advanced feature fusion. For the feature fusion network, the BiFPN can highlight the key information of underwater targets and remove irrelevant features, truly achieving a lightweight model and better accuracy under resource constraints. The structures of the FPN, PANet, NAS-FPN, and BiFPN are shown in Figure 4.

Detecting small-scale targets in medical imaging and identifying defects in aircraft and underwater fish images are specific detection tasks. The specific target distribution is denser and more blurred, and it is hard to apply the BiFPN framework directly to achieve better detection results in complex underwater environments. To address this problem, a method BIG based on BIFPN-weighted bidirectional feature fusion is proposed, replacing the three convolution blocks that adjust the channel count using the GLSA attention module (as depicted in Figure 5).

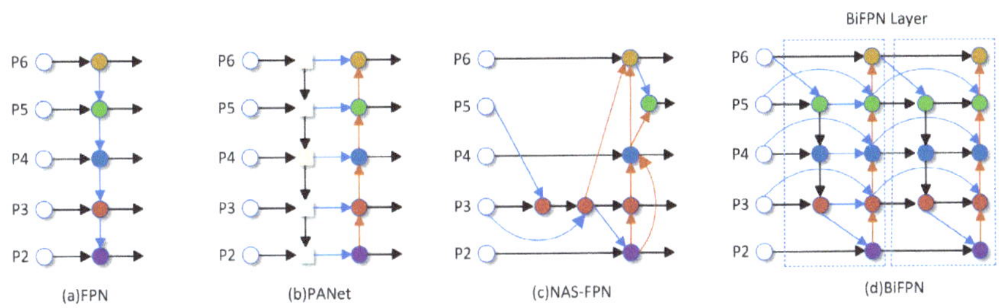

Figure 4. The structures of FPN, PANet, NAS-FPN, and BiFPN.

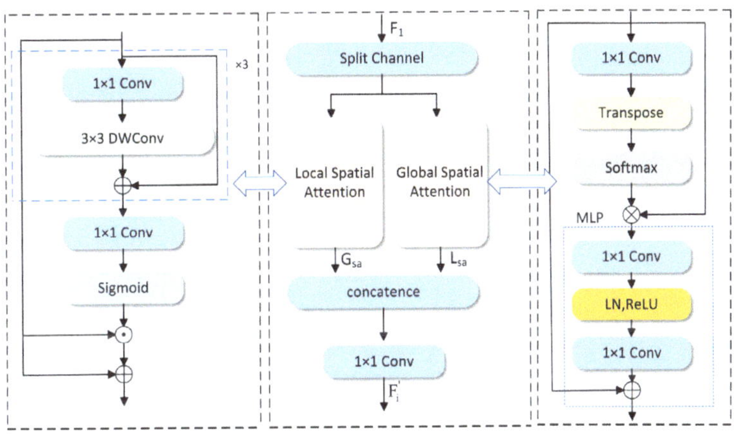

Figure 5. Introduction to the Global-to-Local Spatial Aggregation (GLSA) module.

The GLSA module is composed of two parts: the GSA module and the LSA module. GLSA enhances the attention mechanism to refine target-related information and diminish irrelevant details. To simultaneously capture global and local spatial features, it combines two independent local and global attention units. The global attention module highlights the long-range spatial relationships between pixels, complementing the local spatial attention. Meanwhile, the local attention module efficiently extracts the local features of interest areas in underwater fish images, such as small target objects, within the spatial dimension of a given feature map. Under the common strategy of weighted feature fusion and global–local spatial attention, the ability to quickly and efficiently fuse multi-scale features, covering local spatial details and global spatial semantic information extracted from the backbone, has been significantly enhanced. This dual-stream design effectively maintains local and non-local modeling, using separate channels to balance accuracy and computational resources. This design increases the mAP@0.5:0.95 of the model by 1.1%, reduces the number of parameters by 32%, and reduces the number of calculations by 6%, which strengthens the model's detection accuracy and robustness. The input feature map is represented by $\{F_i | i \in 2,3,4\}$; it uses separation channels to evenly divide the 64 channels of F_i into two sets of feature maps, as follows: $F_i^1, F_i^2 (i \in 2,3,4)$. The two sets of feature maps are, respectively, fed into the Global Spatial Attention (GSA) module and the Local Spatial Attention (LSA) module. The two attention units are finally cascaded together and then output through a 1×1 convolution layer F_i'. The whole process is as follows:

$$F_i^1, F_i^2 = Split(F_i) \tag{1}$$

$$F_i' = C_{1\times1}(Concat(G_{sa}(F_i^1), L_{sa}(F_i^2))) \tag{2}$$

Here, G_{sa} represents the global spatial attention mechanism and L_{sa} represents the local spatial attention mechanism. $F_i' \in \mathbb{R}^{\frac{H}{8} \times \frac{W}{8} \times 32}$ indicates the output of the GLSA module. The global spatial attention GSA and local spatial attention LSA are introduced below.

2.2.1. GSA Module

Underwater images are often partially blurred, color-shifted, and low-contrast, making it difficult to detect fish based on partially missing image information. Therefore, the long-range interactions between each pixel in a single image are particularly important. The work [25] proposed that the use of a self-attention mechanism and query-independent global context modeling can model the long-distance dependencies in machine translation well. Ref. [26] used the self-attention mechanism to simulate pixel-level pairwise relationships. When performing underwater image detection, the global attention module can perform global long-distance modeling based on the relationship between objects and pixels in object detection. Based on the findings from [27] that long-distance interactions can make object detection more powerful, a global spatial attention map can be generated. The process is as follows:

$$Att_G(F_i^1) = softmax(Transpose(C_{1\times 1}(F_i^1))) \tag{3}$$

$$G_{sa}(F_i^1) = MLP(Att_G(F_i^1) \otimes F_i^1) + F_i^1 \tag{4}$$

$Att_G(\cdot)$ indicates attention operation, while $C_{1\times 1}$ indicates a 1×1 convolution. $\otimes$ indicates matrix multiplication. $MLP(\cdot)$ is composed of two fully connected layers, a ReLU activation function and a normalization layer. The global spatial attention mechanism emphasizes the long-range relationship between objects and pixels in a single underwater image throughout the process.

2.2.2. LSA Module

Detecting underwater targets is a crucial technology for the advancement of intelligent underwater robots. However, small and dense targets still face severe challenges in target detection. The work [28] integrates the transformer self-attention mechanism and the coordinate attention mechanism with the adaptive histogram equalization algorithm's image enhancement technique to greatly improve underwater target feature extraction and reduce the number of blurred bounding boxes. Although it effectively reduces the accuracy loss caused by smaller targets, it increases the computational cost and parameter amount compared to the baseline model, which is very difficult to deploy on edge or embedded devices. The LSA module can effectively extract local features of the region of interest, such as small objects, on a given feature map. The response calculation of LSA is given below:

$$Att_L(F_i^2) = \sigma(C_{1\times 1}(F_c(F_i^2)) + F_i^2)) \tag{5}$$

$$L_{sa} = Att_L(F_i^2) \odot F_i^2 + F_i^2 \tag{6}$$

Among them, $F_c(\cdot)$ represents a sequence of three 1×1 convolutional layers followed by a 3×3 depth-wise separable convolutional layer, $Att_L(\cdot)$ is the local attention operation, $\sigma(\cdot)$ is the Sigmoid function, and $\odot$ is the point-by-point multiplication. The design of LSA enables this module to reduce the computational load and the number of parameters compared to standard convolution, and it can more effectively aggregate local spatial information through cascading and residual connections.

2.3. LSH

The detection head network is generally responsible for localization and classification detection. In [29,30], using shared convolutions to share heads across different feature levels not only enhances the efficiency of detector parameters but also effectively reduces the computational burden of the head network, ultimately giving the target detection head better representation capabilities. In complex underwater environments, shooting equipment often needs to simulate objects of different distances and sizes for shooting. The captured images need to be rescaled, using the scale layer and scaling the features of different sizes and distances. Inspired by detail enhancement convolution (DEConv) and group normalization (GN) [31], a lightweight detection head LSH is proposed. Figure 6 illustrates the LSH structure. The following introduces the two main components of LSH to illustrate the irreplaceable role of group normalization (GN) and detail enhancement convolution (DEConv) in the detection head.

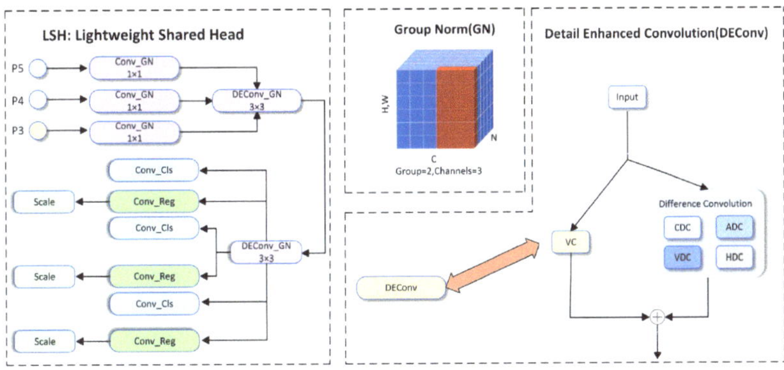

Figure 6. Convolution in LSH consists of the group normalized GN convolution and the group normalized detail-enhanced convolution DEConv. The red pixels are normalized using the same mean and variance, which are calculated by combining the values of these pixels.

2.3.1. Group Normalization

Batch normalization (BN) is a pivotal technology in deep learning development, facilitating the training of various detection networks. However, as normalization introduces problems along the batch size, the error of BN becomes uncontrollable. For underwater target detection tasks and training some larger models, deployment issues are limited. Group normalization (GN), serving as an alternative to batch normalization, achieves a better balance between accuracy and parameters. For different batch sizes, GN's error rate is 10.6% lower than BN. GN partitions the input channels into groups and computes the normalized mean and variance for each group individually. The specific calculation is as follows:

$$\hat{x}_i = \frac{1}{\sigma_i}(x_i - \mu_i) \tag{7}$$

The x above is the feature calculated by the layer. In the case of 2D images, $i = (i_N, i_C, i_H, i_W)$ is a 4D vector indexing features in the order (N, C, H, W), where N is the batch axis, C is the channel axis, and H and W are the spatial height and width axes. Among them, μ_i and σ_i can be obtained by the following formula:

$$\mu_i = \frac{1}{m}\sum_{k \in S_i} x_k \tag{8}$$

$$\sigma_i = \sqrt{\frac{1}{m}\sum_{k \in S_i} (x_k - \mu_i)^2 + \varepsilon} \tag{9}$$

where ε is a small constant, S_i is the set of pixels for calculating the average and standard value, and m is the size of the set. Batch normalization (BN) and Group normalization (GN) also differ greatly in how the set S_i is defined. Here, we mainly introduce the definition of group normalization. The set S_i definition of GN is as follows:

$$S_i = \left\{ k \middle| k_N = i_N, \left\lfloor \frac{k_C}{C/G} \right\rfloor = \left\lfloor \frac{i_C}{C/G} \right\rfloor \right\} \quad (10)$$

Here, G represents the number of groups, which defaults to 32. C/G denotes the number of channels per group. $\lfloor \cdot \rfloor$ is the rounding operation, while $\left\lfloor \frac{k_C}{C/G} \right\rfloor = \left\lfloor \frac{i_C}{C/G} \right\rfloor$ shows that index i and k belong to the same group of channels. Here, it is assumed that each group of channels is arranged sequentially along the C axis, and GN calculates the σ and μ along the (H, W) axis and a set of C/G channels. When G = 2, that is, there are 2 groups, each with three channels. The calculation method of GN is shown in Figure 6.

2.3.2. Detail Enhancement Convolution

Some previous works [32] proposed that images taken in blurry conditions often experience visual quality degradation in contrast or color distortion, which leads to performance degradation of some convolution neural network (CNN)-based methods. Specifically, the model's robustness and generalization ability are enhanced by detail enhancement convolution through the integration of prior information into standard convolution layers. Then, DEConv is converted into a vanilla convolution equivalent through the re-parameterization technique. Through such a process, the parameters and computational cost of the model are not increased. In the detail enhancement convolution, five convolution layers are used: vanilla convolution (VC), center difference convolution (CDC), angle difference convolution (ADC), vertical difference convolution (VDC), and horizontal difference convolution (HDC). They are integrated into the convolutional layers with traditional local descriptors such as Sobel [33]. Figure 6 displays the DEConv structure. To mitigate the increase in parameters and inference time resulting from deploying five convolutional layers, given the input feature F_{in}, DEConv uses re-parameterization technology to output F_{out} to the ordinary convolutional layer with the same parameters and inference time. The calculation of DEConv is expressed as (11).

$$F_{out} = DEConv(F_{in}) = \sum_{i=1}^{5} F_{in} \times K_i = F_{in} \times (\sum_{i=1}^{5} K_i) = F_{in} \times K_{cvt} \quad (11)$$

Among them, $DEConv(\cdot)$ denotes the DEConv operation, while $K_{i=1:5}$ signifies the cores of VC, CDC, ADC, HDC, and VDC, respectively. K_i indicates the convolution operation, and K_{cvt} stands for the transformed kernel that concatenates parallel convolutions.

3. Experiments and Discussion

3.1. Experimental Environment and Configuration

In this paper, the DUO dataset and the RUOD dataset are used for model implementation. The DUO dataset serves as a resource for underwater object detection in robotic harvesting [34]. This dataset collects a variety of underwater images and is equipped with more accurate annotations and a variety of challenging underwater environment images. The dataset covers four categories: holothurian, echinus, scallops, and starfish, with a total of 7782 images. In this dataset, the training set comprises 6671 images, while the test set consists of 1111 images.

The RUOD dataset [35] includes 14,000 high-resolution images and 74,903 labeled instances. Moreover, the dataset includes various environmental challenges, including haze-like effects, color bias, and light interference. It is the first generalized dataset for underwater object detection, taking into account marine objects and environmental challenges. The dataset covers ten categories: holothurian, echinus, scallop, starfish, fish, corals, diver, cuttlefish, turtle, and jellyfish. The dataset consists of 9800 training images and 4200 testing and evaluation images.

The experiments were carried out on a Linux system equipped with an NVIDIA GeForce RTX 4090D GPU and an Intel i9-14900KF CPU. The BGLE-YOLO model was developed using the PyTorch 2.4.1 deep learning framework. The software environment included CUDA 12.1 and Python 3.9. The model was trained for 300 epochs with a learning rate of 0.01. Multiple experiments were conducted through iterative parameter tuning, and finally, some key hyperparameters were standardized, and all experiments were performed with the same configuration displayed in Table 1. In order to speed up the training, the batch size was set to 32. In addition, a cache was activated for this experiment and 8 work processes were configured to improve the training efficiency. Table 1 presents the detailed parameters of the experimental setup.

Table 1. Experimental environment parameters.

Training Parameters	Values
Image size	640 × 640
Epochs	300
Batch	32
Workers	8
Learning rate	0.01
Optimizer	SGD
Cache	False
Weight decay factor	0.0005

3.2. Evaluation Metrics

In order to evaluate the performance of the BGLE-YOLO model, this paper utilizes the following evaluation metrics: Precision, AP, mAP@0.5, and mAP@0.5:0.95. True positive (TP) denotes the count of samples accurately predicted as positive, while false positive (FP) indicates the number of samples predicted as positive but incorrectly so; true negative (TN) represents the count of samples accurately predicted as negative, and false negative (FN) indicates the number of samples incorrectly predicted as negative.

Precision: *Precision* is the ratio of the positive class predicted by the model to the positive class predicted. The calculation formula is as follows:

$$Precision = \frac{TP}{TP + FP} \tag{12}$$

Average Precision (AP): The AP value is equivalent to the area beneath the precision-recall curve and the coordinate axis. The calculation formula is as follows:

$$AP = \int_0^1 P(R)dR \tag{13}$$

Mean Average Precision (mAP): The mAP value is calculated by dividing the sum of the average precision (AP) across all classes in the dataset by the total number of classes. The formula for this calculation is as follows:

$$mAP = \frac{1}{N}\sum_{i=1}^{N} AP_i \tag{14}$$

In addition to the above evaluation indicators, this study also examines the complexity of the model, namely the number of model parameters and the amount of computation.

Therefore, the parameters and GFLOP metrics are introduced to comprehensively evaluate the model's adaptability to edge devices and hardware platforms.

3.3. Ablation Experiments

3.3.1. Prediction Problem of Group Normalization in LSH

As mentioned in the previous section, the experiment replaced batch normalization (BN) in the LSH detection head with group normalization (GN). It can be seen from the experiment that the introduction of group normalization (GN) is very necessary. Table 2 presents the outcomes of the ablation experiment on the DUO dataset. When the detection head does not introduce detail enhancement convolution (DEConv), the mAP@0.5 of BGLE-YOLO with group normalization (GN) is 0.2% higher than that without GN. When detail enhancement convolution (DEConv) is introduced, the mAP@0.5 and mAP@0.5:0.95 of BGLE-YOLO with group normalization (GN) are 0.3% and 0.4% higher than those without GN, respectively. This shows that using GN alone can slightly enhance the detection performance of BGLE-YOLO without increasing the complexity of BGLE-YOLO while combining GN with DEConv can significantly enhance the classification and positioning capabilities of the LSH. The overall experiment proves that group normalization, as a substitute for batch normalization, does achieve better detection results in terms of accuracy.

Table 2. Experiments with group normalization/no group normalization are presented on the dataset DUO.

Methods	mAP@0.5 (%)	mAP@0.5:0.95 (%)
YOLOv8n	84.2	65.0
BGLE (w/o GN and DEConv)	83.5	64.9
BGLE (w/GN w/o DEConv)	83.7	64.9
BGLE (w/o GN w/DEConv)	83.9	64.6
BGLE (w/GN and DEConv)	84.2	65.0

Table 3 presents the ablation experiment results on the RUOD dataset. When the detection head does not introduce detail enhancement convolution (DEConv), the mAP@0.5 and mAP@0.5:0.95 of BGLE-YOLO after the introduction of group normalization (GN) are 1.4% and 2.4% higher than the mAP@0.5 and mAP@0.5:0.95 without GN. When LSH introduces detail enhancement convolution (DEConv), the mAP@0.5 of BGLE-YOLO after the introduction of GN is 0.1% higher than the mAP@0.5 without GN. This shows that regardless of whether DEConv is introduced or not, the introduction of GN can effectively enhance the accuracy of BGLE-YOLO.

Table 3. Experiments with group normalization/non-group normalization are presented on the dataset RUOD.

Methods	mAP@0.5 (%)	mAP@0.5:0.95 (%)
YOLOv8n	84.4	60.8
BGLE (w/o GN and DEConv)	82.0	56.2
BGLE (w/GN w/o DEConv)	83.4	58.6
BGLE (w/o GN w/DEConv)	84.0	59.6
BGLE (w/GN and DEConv)	84.1	59.6

3.3.2. Performance Comparison of DEConv at Different Positions in LSH

In the LSH detection head, the classification convolution and regression convolution learned by the shared convolution output have the same target, which often needs to consider the scale of different targets. However, the classification convolution's output parameters are shared regardless of target size, and the scale layer is unnecessary for feature scaling. To mitigate the problem of inconsistent scale in the detection head's detection target, the parameters of the regression convolution need to scale the features. From the previous section, we know that using group normalization achieves better detection results than batch normalization. Here, the shared convolution parameters are displayed by changing the replacement position of the detail enhancement convolution in the LSH detection head. For convenience, all cases in this paper use the group normalization (GN) with better performance by default. At the same time, the convolution layer using the shared convolution parameters of DEConv (two groups of normalized convolutions with a convolution kernel size of 3 × 3, as shown in Figure 5) is denoted as RPC, and the convolution layer using the non-shared convolution parameters of DEConv is denoted as LPC (three groups of normalized convolutions with a convolution kernel size of 1 × 1, as shown in Figure 6). Then, the performance comparison before and after using detail enhancement convolution under different convolution layer types is presented, and Table 4 is formed.

Table 4. Ablation experiments with DEConv added at different locations on the DUO dataset.

GN	LPC	RPC	mAP@0.5 (%)	mAP@0.5:0.95 (%)	Params (MB)	GFLOPs
			84.2	65.0	3.0	8.1
√			82.7	64.3	1.63	6.2
√	√		83.9	65.1	1.72	6.7
√		√	84.2	65.0	1.63	6.2
√	√	√	83.4	64.7	1.72	6.7

Table 4 shows the ablation experiments with DEConv considering its position on the DUO dataset. "√" means add this module. Compared with not introducing DEConv anywhere, introducing DEConv into three 1 × 1 groups of normalized convolutions alone increases mAP@0.5 and mAP@0.5:0.95 by 1.2% and 0.8%, respectively, and the number of parameters and the calculation amount increase by 6% and 8%, respectively. Compared with introducing DEConv into three 1 × 1 groups of normalized convolutions alone, introducing DEConv into two 3 × 3 groups of normalized convolutions alone increases mAP@0.5 by 0.3%, and its number of parameters and calculation amount decrease by 6% and 8%, respectively. When DEConv is introduced into three 1 × 1 groups of normalized convolutions and two 3 × 3 groups of normalized convolutions at the same time, the accuracy, number of parameters, and level of calculation are all worse than when introducing DEConv into the two types of convolutions separately. It can be seen that when all convolutions are introduced with group normalization, introducing DEConv into two 3 × 3 convolutions alone can achieve optimal accuracy while minimizing the number of parameters and computations.

Table 5 shows the ablation experiments on the position where DEConv is added on the RUOD dataset. Compared with DEConv not introduced at any position, the introduction of DEConv in three groups of 1 × 1 normalized group convolutions alone reduces mAP@0.5 and mAP@0.5:0.95 by 0.1%. The introduction of DEConv in two groups of 3 × 3 normalized convolutions alone increases mAP@0.5 by 0.1% compared to not introducing DEConv at any position. When DEConv is added to two positions at the same time, the accuracy, parameters, and computational complexity are worse than adding DEConv alone or not introducing DEConv at any position. This shows that the combination of RPC and GN can better optimize the detection accuracy of BGLE-YOLO and effectively reduce parameters and computational complexity.

Table 5. Ablation experiments with DEConv added at different locations on the RUOD dataset.

GN	LPC	RPC	mAP@0.5 (%)	mAP@0.5:0.95 (%)	Params (MB)	GFLOPs
			84.4	60.8	3.0	8.1
√			84.0	59.6	1.63	6.2
√	√		83.9	59.5	1.72	6.7
√		√	84.1	59.6	1.63	6.2
√	√	√	83.8	59.3	1.72	6.7

3.3.3. Performance Comparison of BGLE-YOLO Components on the DUO and RUOD Datasets

As indicated in Table 6, the performance of each improved component of the BGLE-YOLO model is assessed. These improved components include (1) the EMC module, which fully retains the redundancy and correlation between feature maps to make the model more lightweight, (2) the BIG feature fusion module, which integrates the two attention mechanisms of the BiFPN structure and the GLSA module, and (3) the LSH detection head. To maintain the reliability and transparency of the experimental results, the experiment uses mAP@0.5 and mAP@0.5:0.95 as well as the model parameters and the model calculation GFLOPs as the main indicators of performance evaluation.

Table 6. Comparison of BGLE-YOLO components' performance on the DUO dataset.

	Module						
EMC	BIG	LSH	Precision (%)	mAP@0.5 (%)	mAP@0.5:0.95 (%)	GFLOPs	Params (MB)
			82.6	84.2	65.0	8.1	3.0
√			83.0	84.4	65.5	7.6	2.72
	√		86.2	84.8	66.1	7.6	2.14
		√	83.4	84.2	64.9	6.5	2.36
√	√		83.5	84.3	65.7	7.3	2.0
	√	√	85.3	83.9	65.1	6.4	1.77
√	√	√	86.0	84.2	65.0	6.2	1.63

Relative to the baseline model, incorporating the EMC structure enhances model accuracy, with mAP@0.5:0.95 rising to 65.5%, which demonstrates the EMC module's crucial role in multi-scale feature extraction. When the BIG module is introduced alone, all indicators are significantly improved, especially the accuracy and mAP@0.5:0.95. This shows that the BIG module plays an indispensable role in enhancing the performance of neck network feature fusion and also enables the model to achieve better lightweight effects while maintaining accuracy. When the LSH detection head is introduced, the lowest parameter effect is achieved while the model accuracy is consistent with the baseline model.

In addition, when the EMC and BIG modules are combined, the model performance is significantly better, the overall mAP@0.5:0.95 increases by 0.7%, and the number of parameters of the model is reduced by 33.3% compared to the baseline model. When the EMC, BIG, and LSH modules are incorporated simultaneously, the model's overall performance is optimized. While the accuracy is the same as the benchmark model, the calculation amount and parameter amount are reduced by 24% and 46%, respectively. The BGLE-YOLO model is lightweight and has robust feature extraction and fusion capabilities, as indicated by experimental results, which meet the goals of detection tasks in complex underwater environments.

As indicated in Table 7, the EMC module slightly lowers the model's computational load and parameter count while boosting accuracy by 0.2%, relative to the baseline model.

When the BIG module is introduced alone, the model reduces the number of parameters by 29% and the amount of calculation by 6% while maintaining accuracy, indicating that the BIG module plays an indispensable role in achieving the lightweight effect of the model. After the LSH detection head is introduced alone, the model is superior to the baseline model in terms of accuracy, number of parameters, and amount of calculation, indicating that DEConv and GN can effectively achieve the lightweight effect of the model under the design of shared parameters.

Table 7. Performance comparison of BGLE-YOLO components on the RUOD dataset.

	Module		Precision (%)	mAP@0.5 (%)	mAP@0.5:0.95 (%)	GFLOPs	Params (MB)
EMC	BIG	LSH					
			85.2	84.4	60.8	8.1	3.0
√			85.4	84.4	60.8	7.6	2.72
	√		85.2	84.3	60.4	7.6	2.14
		√	85.4	84.5	60.3	6.5	2.36
√	√		85.3	84.2	60.1	7.3	2.0
	√	√	84.6	84.0	59.5	6.4	1.77
√	√	√	85.1	84.1	59.6	6.2	1.63

In addition, when the EMC and BIG modules are used in combination, the model accuracy is slightly worse than that of the baseline model. In the combination of BIG and LSH, the model achieves a relatively ideal parameter amount and calculation level. When the EMC, BIG, and LSH modules are introduced together, the model's overall performance is optimized. With similar accuracy, the model's parameter and calculation amounts are reduced by 46% and 24%, respectively. This fully demonstrates that the proposed model can significantly reduce the parameter level and calculation burden while taking into account the accuracy.

3.4. Comparative Experiment

3.4.1. Compared with the Traditional Lightweight YOLO Series

To emphasize the superior performance of BGLE-YOLO introduced in this paper, we first compare it with the traditional lightweight YOLO series. Table 8 displays the detailed data.

Table 8. Comparison of various YOLO network models for underwater detection on the DUO dataset.

Models	Precision (%)	mAP@0.5 (%)	mAP@0.5:0.95 (%)	Params (MB)	GFLOPs
YOLOv5n [36]	84.4	82.4	59.8	1.7	4.1
YOLOv7tiny [37]	86.3	85.1	63.2	6.0	13
YOLOv8n	82.6	84.2	65.0	3.0	8.1
YOLOv10n [38]	83.7	83.0	63.7	2.7	8.2
YOLOv11n [39]	83.7	83.6	64.9	2.6	6.3
BGLE-YOLO	86.0	84.2	65.0	1.6	6.2

Based on the data in Table 8, it can be concluded that BGLE-YOLO highlights its superior performance under lightweight requirements. Although its accuracy and mAP@0.5 are slightly lower than those of YOLOv7-tiny, its mAP@0.5:0.95 is much higher than that of YOLOv7-tiny. In terms of computational efficiency, BGLE-YOLO has only 1.63 million parameters and 6.2 GFLOPs, much lower than YOLOv7-tiny (6.01 million, 13 GFLOPs).

As indicated in Table 9, BGLE-YOLO achieves comparable accuracy to other YOLO series models with fewer parameters and computational complexity. Although YOLOv8 and

YOLOv11 are slightly higher than BGLE-YOLO in terms of mAP@0.5 and mAP@0.5:0.95, their parameters and computational complexity are higher than BGLE-YOLO, which does not meet the lightweight requirements. This indicates that the model proposed in this article is more suitable for subsequent deployment for edge devices.

Table 9. Comparative results of various YOLO family network models for underwater detection on the RUOD dataset.

Models	Precision (%)	mAP@0.5 (%)	mAP@0.5:0.95 (%)	Params (MB)	GFLOPs
YOLOv5n	85.8	83.2	53.9	1.7	4.2
YOLOv7-tiny	85.0	85.2	57.9	6.0	13.1
YOLOv8n	85.2	84.4	60.8	3.0	8.1
YOLOv10n	85.0	83.9	59.9	2.7	8.2
YOLOv11n	85.4	84.7	61.4	2.6	6.3
BGLE-YOLO	85.1	84.1	59.6	1.6	6.2

In addition to the YOLOv7-tiny model, the comparison results with other models show that BGLE-YOLO has obvious advantages in the above parameter indicators (as shown in Figures 7 and 8). BGLE-YOLO's low computational complexity and simple design make it ideal for running on devices with limited computing power, like embedded systems, edge devices, etc.

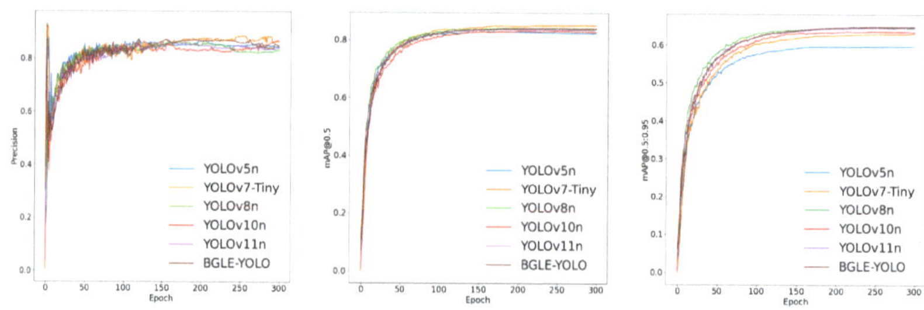

(a) (b) (c)

Figure 7. Comparison plots of the YOLO family of algorithms on the DUO dataset. (**a**) Accuracy comparison plot; (**b**) mAP@0.5 comparison plot; (**c**) mAP@0.5:0.95 comparison plot.

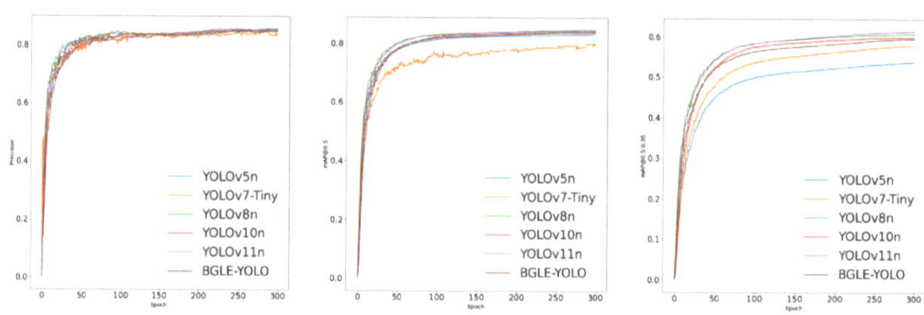

(a) (b) (c)

Figure 8. Comparison plots of the YOLO family of algorithms on the RUOD dataset. (**a**) Accuracy comparison plot; (**b**) mAP@0.5 comparison plot; (**c**) mAP@0.5:0.95 comparison plot.

3.4.2. A Brief Comparison to Other Family Models

To further emphasize the lightweight advantages of the BGLE-YOLO introduced in this paper, this section compares the YOLO family as well as other models with the BGLE-YOLO (see Figure 9). Since the number of parameters and computation amount of BGLE-YOLO tested on the two datasets are almost the same, Figure 9 is based on the indicators of the proposed model tested on the DUO dataset. In order to better explore the relationship between the model parameters, computational complexity, and accuracy, this paper selects RTMD-Tiny as another model whose parameters and computational complexity are almost the same as those of the YOLO series models, and the experiment adds another model with huge parameters and computational complexity to compare the parameters and computational complexity with the remaining models. The detailed data are presented in Tables 10 and 11.

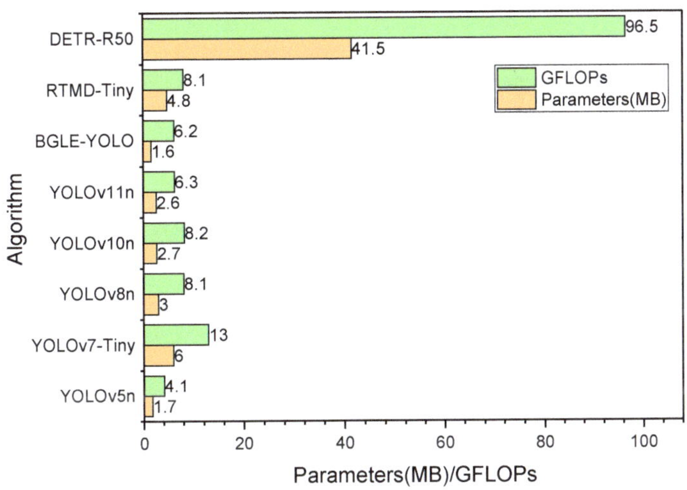

Figure 9. Comparison of parameters as well as computational effort of different models.

Table 10. Comparative results of different series of network models in underwater exploration under the DUO dataset.

Models	mAP@0.5 (%)	mAP@0.5:0.95 (%)	Params (MB)	GFLOPs
RTMD-Tiny [40]	85.6	66.5	4.8	8.1
DETR-R50 [41]	84.1	62.8	41.5	96.5
YOLOv8	84.2	65.0	3.0	8.1
BGLE-YOLO	84.2	65.0	1.6	6.2

Table 11. Comparative results of different series of network models in underwater exploration on the RUOD dataset.

Models	mAP@0.5 (%)	mAP@0.5:0.95 (%)	Params (MB)	GFLOPs
RTMD-Tiny	85.8	62.4	4.88	8
DETR-R50	85.5	59.4	41.55	91.7
YOLOv8	84.4	60.8	3.0	8.1
BGLE-YOLO	84.1	59.6	1.63	6.2

Compared with other models outside the YOLO series, BGLE-YOLO achieves higher accuracy levels with fewer parameters and computational costs on both the DUO and RUOD datasets. On the DUO dataset, RTMD-Tiny requires 200% more parameters and 23% higher computational costs than the proposed model yet only achieves marginal improvements of 1.4% in mAP@0.5 and 1.5% in mAP@0.5:0.95 metrics. This outcome contradicts the lightweight design objectives emphasized in the paper. On the RUOD dataset, DETR-R50 requires 2400% more parameters than BGLE-YOLO, and the computational cost is 1300% higher. With a high computational complexity and parameter count, mAP@0.5 is only improved by 1.4%, and mAP@0.5:0.95 is 0.2% lower than BGLE-YOLO. Obviously, the model proposed in this paper is far superior to DETR-R50 in overall performance.

3.5. Visualization of Model Detection Effects on the DUO Dataset

To highlight the detection performance of the BGLE-YOLO model in underwater target recognition and modeling, we chose three images from different scenes in the DUO dataset to qualitatively analyze the various models. In Figure 10c, except for the BGLE-YOLO model proposed in this paper, all the other models have missed detection, which indicates that the other models perform poorly in feature extraction. Although the accuracy of this paper's model is the same as that of YOLOv8n, the EMC module in BGLE-YOLO can fully account for the redundancy and correlation between feature maps, and the BIG module can fully integrate multi-scale features to mitigate leakage and false alarms.

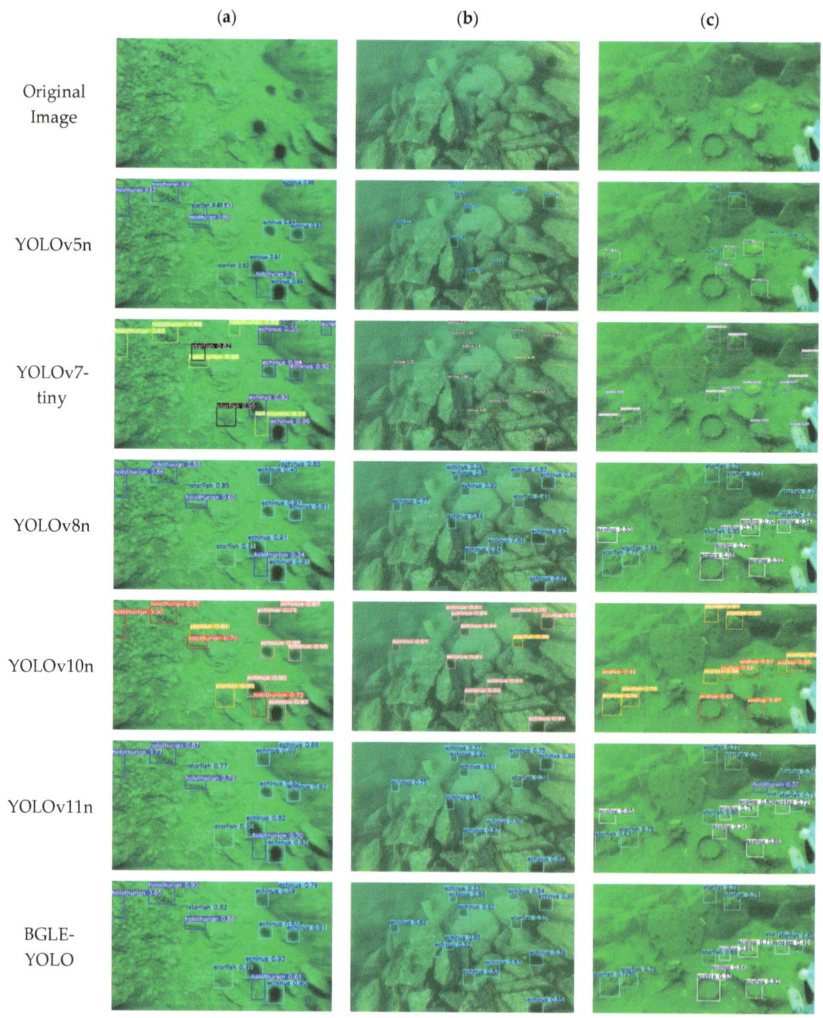

Figure 10. Qualitative comparison of the detection performance of the YOLO series of models, (**a**–**c**) showing the detection results for four categories in the DUO dataset.

3.6. Visualization of Model Detection Effects on the RUOD Dataset

To emphasize the detection performance of the BGLE-YOLO model in underwater target recognition and modeling, we selected three images of different scenes in the RUOD dataset to conduct a qualitative analysis of each model. Also, in Figure 11c, except for the BGLE-YOLO model and YOLOv11 proposed in this paper, other models missed the detection of corals, which shows that other models are prone to miss key details when extracting small target features. In Figure 11a, except for YOLOv5 and YOLOv8, other models have different degrees of missed detection when detecting scallops. This shows that factors such as multi-target mutual occlusion and small objects have formed certain obstacles to the detection of marine life. Future work aims to overcome these problems based on lightweight design.

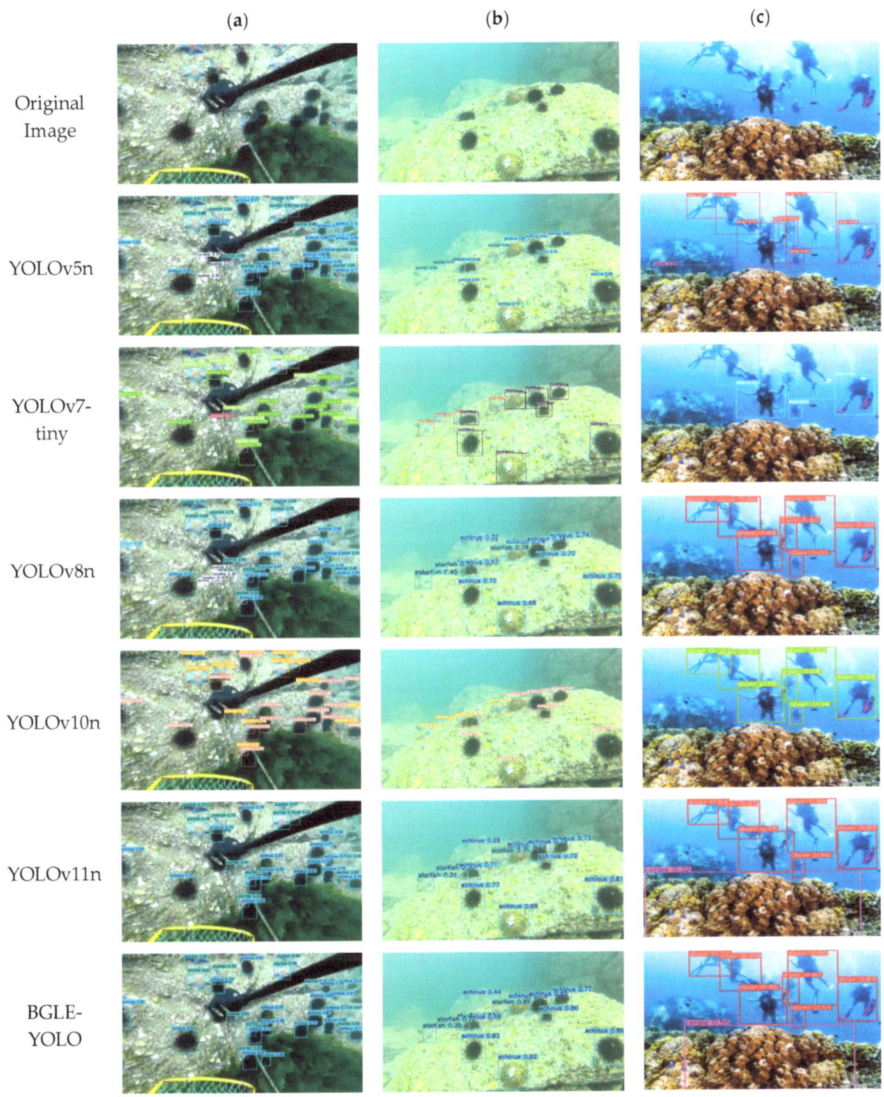

Figure 11. Qualitative comparison of the detection performance of the YOLO series of models, (**a**–**c**) showing the detection results for four categories in the RUOD dataset.

4. Discussion

4.1. Findings

This paper proposes a novel underwater fish detection method called BGLE-YOLO. It retains redundant feature maps while strengthening the correlation between feature maps by introducing EMC. Incorporating the EMC module alone can greatly decrease the parameters and computations of BGLE-YOLO. The BIG module is designed within the feature fusion network to enhance the long-range spatial relationships between pixels and effectively extract local features of interest in small underwater fish images. GN (group normalization) and DEConv (detail enhancement convolution) in the LSH module are crucial for the training of underwater target detection tasks, the balance between accuracy and parameters, and the problem of visual quality degradation in capturing images in terms of contrast or color distortion.

Ablation experiments conducted systematically verify the effectiveness of each innovative module. According to the DUO dataset ablation experiment, after the introduction of the EMC module, the mAP@0.5:0.95 of the model reached 65.5%, and the number of parameters and computational complexity were reduced by 9% and 6%, respectively. After incorporating BIG, mAP@0.5:0.95 rose to 65.7%, computational complexity dropped by 0.3GFLOPs, and the number of parameters was reduced by 21%, indicating that BIG played a key role in capturing global and local spatial features and optimizing convolution kernel parameters. Finally, the group normalization (GN) and detail enhancement convolution (DEConv) submodules in the LSH module significantly improved the performance of BGLE-YOLO. Activating the RPC position embedding DEConv and combining it with GN achieved the best accuracy, with mAP@0.5 and mAP@0.5:0.95 reaching 84.2% and 65%, respectively, and maintained the lowest level of computational complexity and parameters, which were reduced by 47% and 23%, respectively. In the ablation experiment of the RUOD dataset, BGLE-YOLO also showed a strong lightweight advantage. After adding EMC, the accuracy of the model increased to 85.4%, and the parameter level and calculation amount were reduced by 10% and 6%, respectively. With the introduction of the BIG and LSH modules, the mAP@0.5 of the model reached 84.1, and the number of parameters and calculation amount were lowered by 47% and 23%, respectively. The experiments above fully confirmed the effectiveness of these modules in enhancing model performance and reducing parameters and calculations.

4.2. Limitations and Future Works

Despite significant performance improvements on the RUOD and DUO datasets, BGLE-YOLO still faces some challenges. First, the accuracy of the model is equal to or slightly lower than the baseline model on both the RUOD and DUO datasets and higher accuracy may be required in some practical application scenarios. In addition, the generalization ability and robustness of BGLE-YOLO need to be further verified, and the model should be made more applicable to other datasets. Finally, with the development of underwater vision technology, more complex underwater environments come one after another, such as turbidity, fog effects, and color deviation. The subsequent series of work should focus on improving accuracy as much as possible with lower model parameters and computational burden. In addition, sufficient experiments should be combined with embedded or edge devices to verify effectiveness in different environments.

5. Conclusions

This research presents a novel lightweight network architecture, substituting the efficient multi-scale convolution (EMC) module to strengthen the backbone network. The neck network integrates BIG to conduct multi-scale processing, focusing on extracting local spatial detail information and global spatial semantic information. Feature fusion is conducted, and ultimately, the LSH detection head is designed to achieve the lightweight BGLE-YOLO model. The results indicate that the BGLE-YOLO model achieves the same detection accuracy as the benchmark model while significantly reducing the number of parameters and computational demands, successfully balancing accuracy and computational efficiency. The experimental part visually verifies the possibility of optimization of the proposed model. The model's performance still has room for improvement. Future work will enhance the model's detection performance and effectively reduce its parameter count and computational efficiency to ensure successful deployment on edge devices and embedded systems for underwater target detection. Additionally, to enhance the robustness of the improved model to better handle more complex marine targets and environmental challenges (such as light interference and fog effects), the detection model will add additional datasets for training.

Author Contributions: Conceptualization, H.Z., C.X., J.C. and Z.Z.; methodology, H.Z. and C.X.; software, C.X. and Z.Z.; validation, C.X.; formal analysis, Z.Z. and X.W.; investigation, C.X.; resources, C.X. and H.Z.; data curation, C.X.; writing—original draft preparation, C.X.; writing—review and editing, C.X.; visualization, C.X.; supervision, H.Z. and X.W.; project administration, H.Z. and C.X.; funding acquisition, H.Z. and J.C. All authors have read and agreed to the published version of the manuscript.

Funding: This research was funded by the National Natural Science Foundation of China, grant number 62171179, and the Hebei Normal University Horizontal Fund Project, grant number H23-035.

Institutional Review Board Statement: Not applicable.

Informed Consent Statement: Not applicable.

Data Availability Statement: The data presented in this study are available upon request from the corresponding author. The code cannot be shared due to specific reasons.

Acknowledgments: We thank the editors and the anonymous reviewers for their valuable comments and suggestions.

Conflicts of Interest: The authors declare no conflicts of interest.

References

1. Zhang, R.; Gao, Q.; Gao, K. Impact of marine industrial agglomeration on the high-quality development of the marine economy—A case study of China's coastal areas. *Ecol. Indic.* **2024**, *158*, 111410. [CrossRef]
2. Chen, X.; Fan, C.; Shi, J.; Wang, H.; Yao, H. Underwater target detection and embedded deployment based on lightweight YOLO_GN. *J. Supercomput.* **2024**, *80*, 14057–14084. [CrossRef]
3. Xie, X.; Cheng, G.; Wang, J.; Yao, X.; Han, J. Oriented R-CNN for object detection. In Proceedings of the IEEE/CVF International Conference on Computer Vision, Montreal, QC, Canada, 10–17 October 2021; pp. 3520–3529.
4. Girshick, R. Fast R-CNN. In Proceedings of the IEEE International Conference on Computer Vision (ICCV), Santiago, Chile, 7–13 December 2015; pp. 1440–1448.
5. Ren, S.; He, K.; Girshick, R.; Sun, J. Faster R-CNN: Towards real-time object detection with region proposal networks. *IEEE Trans. Pattern Anal. Mach. Intell.* **2017**, *39*, 1137–1149. [CrossRef] [PubMed]
6. Liu, W.; Anguelov, D.; Erhan, D.; Szegedy, C.; Reed, S.; Fu, C.-Y.; Berg, A.C. SSD: Single Shot MultiBox Detector. In *Lecture Notes in Computer Science*; Springer: Berlin/Heidelberg, Germany, 2016; pp. 21–37, ISBN 978-3-319-46448-0.
7. Wang, G.; Chen, Y.; An, P.; Hong, H.; Hu, J.; Huang, T. UAV-YOLOv8: A small-object-detection model based on improved YOLOv8 for UAV aerial photography scenarios. *Sensors* **2023**, *23*, 7190. [CrossRef]
8. Zhang, C.; Zhang, G.; Li, H.; Liu, H.; Tan, J.; Xue, X. Underwater target detection algorithm based on improved YOLOv4 with SemiDSConv and FIoU loss function. *Front. Mar. Sci.* **2023**, *10*, 1153416. [CrossRef]
9. Liu, P.; Qian, W.; Wang, Y. Ywnet: A convolutional block attention-based fusion deep learning method for complex underwater small target detection. *Eco. Inform.* **2024**, *79*, 102401. [CrossRef]

10. Yeh, C.H.; Lin, C.H.; Kang, L.W.; Huang, C.H.; Lin, M.H.; Chang, C.Y.; Wang, C.C. Lightweight deep neural network for joint learning of underwater object detection and color conversion. *IEEE Trans. Neural Networks Learn. Syst.* **2021**, *33*, 6129–6143. [CrossRef]
11. Xu, G.; Zhou, D.; Yuan, L.; Guo, W.; Huang, Z.; Zhang, Y. Vision-based underwater target real-time detection for autonomous underwater vehicle subsea exploration. *Front. Mar. Sci.* **2023**, *10*, 1112310. [CrossRef]
12. Krizhevsky, A.; Sutskever, I.; Hinton, G.E. ImageNet classification with deep convolutional neural networks. *Commun. ACM* **2017**, *60*, 84–90. [CrossRef]
13. Tang, F.; Xu, Z.; Huang, Q.; Wang, J.; Hou, X.; Su, J.; Liu, J. DuAT: Dual-aggregation transformer network for medical image segmentation. In Proceedings of the Chinese Conference on Pattern Recognition and Computer Vision (PRCV), Xiamen, China, 13–15 October 2023; Springer Nature: Singapore, 2023; pp. 343–356.
14. Chen, J.; Er, M.J. Dynamic YOLO for small underwater object detection. *Artif. Intell. Rev.* **2024**, *57*, 1–23. [CrossRef]
15. Wang, W.; Dai, J.; Chen, Z.; Huang, Z.; Li, Z.; Zhu, X.; Hu, X.; Lu, T.; Li, H.; Wang, X.; et al. Internimage: Exploring large-scale vision foundation models with deformable convolutions. In Proceedings of the IEEE/CVF Conference on Computer Vision and Pattern Recognition, Vancouver, BC, Canada, 17–24 June 2023; pp. 14408–14419.
16. Chen, Z.; He, Z.; Lu, Z.M. DEA-Net: Single image dehazing based on detail-enhanced convolution and content-guided attention. *IEEE Trans. Image Process.* **2024**, *33*, 1002–1015. [CrossRef] [PubMed]
17. He, K.; Zhang, X.; Ren, S.; Sun, J. Deep residual learning for image recognition. In Proceedings of the IEEE Conference on Computer Vision and Pattern Recognition, Las Vegas, NV, USA, 27–30 June 2016; pp. 770–778.
18. Chen, F.; Li, S.; Han, J.; Ren, F.; Yang, Z. Review of lightweight deep convolutional neural networks. *Arch. Comput. Methods Eng.* **2024**, *31*, 1915–1937. [CrossRef]
19. Han, K.; Wang, Y.; Tian, Q.; Guo, J.; Xu, C.; Xu, C. Ghostnet: More features from cheap operations. In Proceedings of the IEEE/CVF Conference on Computer Vision and Pattern Recognition, Seattle, WA, USA, 13–19 June 2020; pp. 1580–1589.
20. Howard, A.G. Mobilenets: Efficient convolutional neural networks for mobile vision applications. *arXiv* **2017**, arXiv:1704.04861.
21. Kong, T.; Sun, F.; Huang, W.; Liu, H.; Huang, W. Deep feature pyramid reconfiguration for object detection. *arXiv* **2018**, arXiv:1808.07993.
22. Lin, T.-Y.; Doll'ar, P.; Girshick, R.; He, K.; Hariharan, B.; Belongie, S. Feature pyramid networks for object detection. In Proceedings of the 2017 IEEE Conference on Computer Vision and Pattern Recognition (CVPR), Honolulu, HI, USA, 21–26 July 2017.
23. Elfwing, S.; Uchibe, E.; Doya, K. Sigmoid-weighted linear units for neural network function approximation in reinforcement learning. *Neural Netw.* **2018**, *107*, 3–11. [CrossRef]
24. Tan, M.; Pang, R.; Le, Q.V. Efficientdet: Scalable and efficient object detection. In Proceedings of the IEEE/CVF Conference on Computer Vision and Pattern Recognition, Seattle, WA, USA, 13–19 June 2020; pp. 10781–10790.
25. Cao, Y.; Xu, J.; Lin, S.; Wei, F.; Hu, H. Gcnet: Non-local networks meet squeeze-excitation networks and beyond. In Proceedings of the IEEE/CVF International Conference on Computer Vision Workshops, Seoul, Republic of Korea, 27–28 October 2019.
26. Zhou, Y.; Wang, F.; Zhao, J.; Yao, R.; Chen, S.; Ma, H. Spatial-temporal based multihead self-attention for remote sensing image change detection. *IEEE Trans. Circuits Syst. Video Technol.* **2022**, *32*, 6615–6626. [CrossRef]
27. Bello, I.; Zoph, B.; Vaswani, A.; Shlens, J.; Le, Q.V. Attention augmented convolutional networks. In Proceedings of the IEEE/CVF International Conference on Computer Vision, Seoul, Republic of Korea, 27 October–2 November 2019; pp. 3286–3295.
28. Liu, K.; Peng, L.; Tang, S. Underwater object detection using TC-YOLO with attention mechanisms. *Sensors* **2023**, *23*, 2567. [CrossRef]
29. Li, G.; Lin, Y.; Ouyang, D.; Li, S.; Luo, X.; Qu, X. A RGB-thermal image segmentation method based on parameter sharing and attention fusion for safe autonomous driving. *IEEE Trans. Intell. Transp. Syst.* **2023**, *25*, 5122–5137. [CrossRef]
30. Lin, T.-Y.; Goyal, P.; Girshick, R.; He, K.; Doll'ar, P. Focal loss for dense object detection. *IEEE Trans. Pattern Anal. Mach. Intell.* **2017**, *42*, 2980–2988.
31. Ioffe, S. Batch normalization: Accelerating deep network training by reducing internal covariate shift. *arXiv* **2015**, arXiv:1502.03167.
32. Tan, R.T. Visibility in bad weather from a single image. In Proceedings of the 2008 IEEE Conference on Computer Vision and Pattern Recognition, Anchorage, AK, USA, 23–28 June 2008; pp. 1–8.
33. Sobel, I.; Feldman, G. A 3×3 Isotropic Gradient Operator for Image Processing. Available online: https://www.researchgate.net/publication/285159837_A_33_isotropic_gradient_operator_for_image_processing (accessed on 2 March 2025).
34. Liu, C.; Li, H.; Wang, S.; Zhu, M.; Wang, D.; Fan, X. A dataset and benchmark of underwater object detection for robot picking. In Proceedings of the 2021 IEEE International Conference on Multimedia & Expo Workshops (ICMEW), Shenzhen, China, 5–9 July 2021; pp. 1–6.
35. Fu, C.; Liu, R.; Fan, X.; Chen, P.; Fu, H.; Yuan, W.; Zhu, M.; Luo, Z. Rethinking general underwater object detection: Datasets, challenges, and solutions. *Neurocomputing* **2023**, *517*, 243–256. [CrossRef]
36. Ultralytics. Yolov5. Available online: https://github.com/ultralytics/yolov5 (accessed on 1 November 2021).

37. Wang, C.; Bochkovskiy, A.; Liao, H.M. yolov7: Trainable Bag-of-Freebies Sets New State-of-the-Art for Real-Time Object Detectors. In Proceedings of the 2023 IEEE/CVF Conference on Computer Vision and Pattern Recognition (CVPR), Vancouver, BC, Canada, 17–24 June 2023; pp. 7464–7475.
38. Wang, A.; Chen, H.; Liu, L.; Chen, K.; Lin, Z.; Han, J.; Ding, G. YOLOv10: Real-Time End-to-End Object Detection. *arXiv* **2024**, arXiv:2405.14458.
39. Jocher, G.; Qiu, J.; Chaurasia, A. Ultralytics YOLO (Version 8.0.0) [Computer Software]. 2023. Available online: https://github.com/ultralytics/ultralytics (accessed on 2 March 2025).
40. Lyu, C.; Zhang, W.; Huang, H.; Zhou, Y.; Wang, Y.; Liu, Y.; Zhang, S.; Chen, K. Rtmdet: An empirical study of designing real-time object detectors. *arXiv* **2022**, arXiv:2212.07784.
41. Zhao, Y.; Lv, W.; Xu, S.; Wei, J.; Wang, G.; Dang, Q. Detrs beat yolos on real-time object detection. In Proceedings of the IEEE/CVF Conference on Computer Vision and Pattern Recognition, Seattle, WA, USA, 16–22 June 2024.

MDPI AG
Grosspeteranlage 5
4052 Basel
Switzerland
Tel.: +41 61 683 77 34

MDPI Books Editorial Office
E-mail: books@mdpi.com
www.mdpi.com/books

www.ingramcontent.com/pod-product-compliance
Lightning Source LLC
Chambersburg PA
CBHW041427210926
51850CB00013B/3373
* 9 7 8 3 7 2 5 8 4 1 2 1 9 *